TRUE FRIENDS Bacon

BOSWELL'S
LIFE OF JOHNSON
Vol. II

DR. SAMUEL JOHNSON

SAMUEL JOHNSON

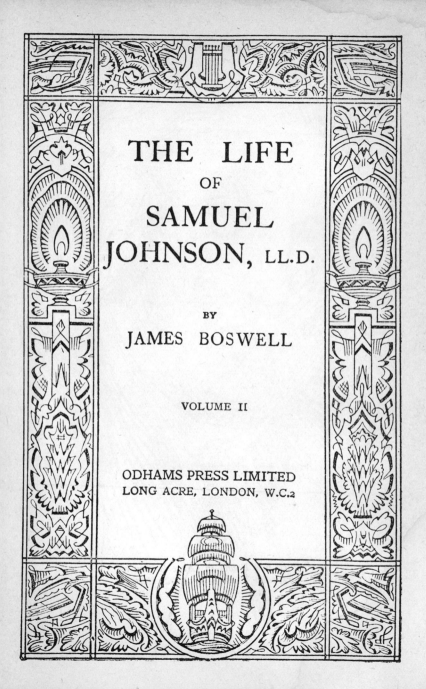

THE LIFE

OF

SAMUEL JOHNSON, LL.D.

BY

JAMES BOSWELL

VOLUME II

ODHAMS PRESS LIMITED
LONG ACRE, LONDON, W.C.2

Printed and Bound in Great Britain by
Greycaine Limited, Watford, Herts

CONTENTS OF VOLUME II.

CHAPTER X.—1778

CHAPTER XI.—1778

CHAPTER XII.—1778

CHAPTER XIII.—1778

CHAPTER XXVIII.—1784.

CHAPTER XXIX.—1784.

CHAPTER XXX.—1784

CHAPTER XXXI.—1784

THE LIFE

OF

SAMUEL JOHNSON, LL.D.

CHAPTER I.—1776

*Johnson returns to London—Dr. Butter—Mr. Wedderburne
—Mr. Macklin—Johnson's Opinions on Marriage—
Death of Dr. James—Johnson's Remedy for Melancholy
—Baretti—Lobo's "Abyssinia"—Captain Cook—Omai
—The Mitre Tavern—Lord Charles Hay—Public Schools
and Universities—Mr. Maclaurin—Law of Libel—The
Roman Catholic Religion—"The all-knowing" Mr.
Jackson—Anecdote of Mr. Fowke—Jack Ellis, the
Money Scrivener—Johnson's Ideas of Gaming—On
Conjugal Infidelity—Mr. Macbean—The Usury Laws—
Dr. Cheyne—Cibber's "Lives of the Poets"—Literary
Reviewers—Smollett—"The Spectator"—Dr. Barry—
Garrick—Genius of Thomson—Dispute between Gold-
smith and Dodsley—Mr. Cradock—Dr. Harwood—
Supper at the Crown and Anchor—Wine-drinking—
Johnson visits Bath.*

HAVING left Ashbourne in the evening, we stopped to change
horses at Derby, and availed ourselves of a moment to enjoy
the conversation of my countryman, Dr. Butter, then
physician there. He was in great indignation because
Lord Mountstuart's bill for a Scotch militia had been lost.
Dr. Johnson was as violent against it. "I am glad," said
he, "that Parliament has had the spirit to throw it out.
You wanted to take advantage of the timidity of our
scoundrels" (meaning, I suppose, the ministry). It may
be observed that he used the epithet scoundrel very commonly—not quite in the sense in which it is generally
understood, but as a strong term of disapprobation; as,
when he abruptly answered Mrs. Thrale, who had asked
him how he did, "Ready to become a scoundrel, Madam;

21

with a little more spoiling you will, I think, make me a
complete rascal." He meant, easy to become a capricious
and self-indulgent valetudinarian—a character for which I
have heard him express great disgust.

Johnson had with him upon this jaunt "Il Palmerino
d'Inghilterra," a romance praised by Cervantes; but did
not like it much. He said he read it for the language,
by way of preparation for his Italian expedition. We lay
this night at Loughborough.

On Thursday, March 28th, we pursued our journey. I
mentioned that old Mr. Sheridan complained of the ingratitude of Mr. Wedderburne and General Fraser, who had been
much obliged to him when they were young Scotchmen
entering upon life in England. JOHNSON: "Why, Sir, a
man is very apt to complain of the ingratitude of those who
have risen far above him. A man, when he gets into a
higher sphere, into other habits of life, cannot keep up all
his former connections. Then, Sir, those who knew him
formerly upon a level with themselves, may think that they
ought still to be treated as on a level, which cannot be; and
an acquaintance in a former situation may bring out things
which it would be very disagreeable to have mentioned
before higher company, though perhaps every body knows
of them." He placed this subject in a new light to me,
and showed that a man who has risen in the world must not
be condemned too harshly for being distant to former
acquaintance, even though he may have been much
obliged to them. It is, no doubt, to be wished that a
proper degree of attention should be shown by great men
to their early friends. But if, either from obtuse insensibility to difference of situation, or presumptuous forward-
ness, which will not submit even to an exterior observance
of it, the dignity of high place cannot be preserved when
they are admitted into the company of those raised above
the state in which they once were, encroachment must be
repelled, and the kinder feelings sacrificed. To one of the
very fortunate persons whom I have mentioned—namely,
Mr. Wedderburne, now Lord Loughborough—I must do
the justice to relate, that I have been assured by another
early acquaintance of his, old Mr. Macklin,[1] who assisted in
improving his pronunciation, that he found him very grateful. Macklin, I suppose, had not pressed upon his elevation
with so much eagerness as the gentleman who complained of

[1] Charles Macklin, whose real name was Mac Laughlin, was an
actor, and the author of the comedy entitled "The Man of the World,"
also of the farce called "Love-à-la-Mode." He was born in Westmeath
in 1690, and lived to the patriarchal age of 107.—ED.

him. Dr. Johnson's remark as to the jealousy entertained
of our friends who rise far above us, is certainly very just.
By this was withered the early friendship between Charles
Townshend and Akenside; and many similar instances
might be adduced.

He said, "It is commonly a weak man who marries for
love." We then talked of marrying women of fortune;
and I mentioned a common remark, that a man may be,
upon the whole, richer by marrying a woman with a very
small portion, because a woman of fortune will be propor-
tionally expensive; whereas a woman who brings none will
be very moderate in expenses. JOHNSON: "Depend upon
it, Sir, this is not true. A woman of fortune, being used to
the handling of money, spends it judiciously; but a woman
who gets the command of money for the first time upon her
marriage, has such a gust in spending it, that she throws it
away with great profusion."

He praised the ladies of the present age, insisting that
they were more faithful to their husbands, and more
virtuous in every respect, than in former times, because
their understandings were better cultivated. It was an
undoubted proof of his good sense and good disposition,
that he was never querulous, never prone to inveigh against
the present times, as is so common when superficial minds
are on the fret. On the contrary, he was willing to speak
favourably of his own age; and, indeed, maintained its
superiority in every respect, except in its reverence for
government; the relaxation of which he imputed as its
grand cause, to the shock which our monarchy received at
the Revolution, though necessary; and secondly, to the
timid concessions made to faction by successive administra-
tions in the reign of his present Majesty. I am happy to think
that he lived to see the crown at last recover its just influence.

At Leicester we read in the newspaper that Dr. James
was dead. I thought that the death of an old schoolfellow, and one with whom he had lived a good deal in
London, would have affected my fellow traveller much; but
he only said, "Ah! poor Jamy." Afterwards, however,
when we were in the chaise, he said, with more tenderness,
"Since I set out on this jaunt, I have lost an old friend and
a young one—Dr. James and poor Harry" (meaning Mr.
Thrale's son).[1]

[1] Dr. Robert James was born at Kinverstone, in Staffordshire, in
1703. His "Medical Dictionary," to which Dr. Johnson materially
contributed, was published in 1743, in 3 vols. fol. He is best known,
however, by his valuable antimonial preparation, under the name of
"James's Powder."—ED.

Having lain at St. Alban's, on Thursday, March 28th, we breakfasted the next morning at Barnet. I expressed to him a weakness of mind which I could not help; an uneasy apprehension that my wife and children, who were at a great distance from me, might perhaps be ill. "Sir," said he, "consider how foolish you would think it in *them* to be apprehensive that *you* are ill." This sudden turn relieved me for the moment; but I afterwards perceived it to be an ingenious fallacy.[1] I might, to be sure, be satisfied that they had no reason to be apprehensive about me, because I *knew* that I myself was well; but we might have mutual anxiety without the charge of folly, because each was, in some degree, uncertain as to the condition of the other.

I enjoyed the luxury of our approach to London, that metropolis which we both loved so much, for the high and varied intellectual pleasure which it furnishes. I experienced immediate happiness while whirled along with such a companion, and said to him, "Sir, you observed one day at General Oglethorpe's, that a man is never happy for the present but when he is drunk. Will you not add,—or when driving in a post-chaise?" JOHNSON: "No, Sir; you are driving rapidly *from* something, or *to* something."

Talking of melancholy, he said, "Some men, and very thinking men too, have not those vexing thoughts.[2] Sir Joshua Reynolds is the same all the year round. Beauclerk, except when ill and in pain, is the same. But I believe most men have them in the degree in which they

---

[1] Surely it is no fallacy, but a sound and rational argument. He who is perfectly well, and apprehensive concerning the state of another at a distance from him, *knows* to a certainty that the fears of that person concerning *his* health are imaginary and delusive; and hence has a rational ground for supposing that his own apprehensions concerning his absent wife or friend are equally unfounded.—MALONE.

[2] The phrase "vexing thoughts," is, I think, very expressive. It has been familiar to me from my childhood; for it is to be found in the "Psalms in Metre," used in the churches (I believe I should say *kirks*) of Scotland, Psal. xliii. v. 5.

> "Why art thou then cast down, my soul?
> What should discourage thee?
> And why with *vexing thoughts* art thou
> Disquieted in me?"

Some allowance must, no doubt, be made for early prepossession. But at a maturer period of life, after looking at various metrical versions of the Psalms, I am well satisfied that the version used in Scotland is, upon the whole, the best; and that it is vain to think of having a better. It has in general a simplicity and *unction* of sacred poesy; and in many parts its transfusion is admirable.—BOSWELL.

are capable of having them. If I were in the country, and were distressed by that malady, I would force myself to take a book; and every time I did it I should find it the easier. Melancholy, indeed, should be diverted by every means but drinking."

We stopped at Messrs. Dilly's, booksellers in the Poultry; from whence he hurried away, in a hackney-coach, to Mr. Thrale's, in the Borough. I called at his house in the evening, having promised to acquaint Mrs. Williams of his safe return; when, to my surprise, I found him sitting with her at tea, and, as I thought, not in a very good humour: for, it seems, when he had got to Mr. Thrale's, he found the coach was at the door waiting to carry Mrs. and Miss Thrale, and Signor Baretti,[1] their Italian master, to Bath. This was not showing the attention which might have been expected to the "guide, philosopher, and friend"—the *Imlac* who had hastened from the country to console a distressed mother, who, he understood, was very anxious for his return. They had, I found, without ceremony, proceeded on their intended journey. I was glad to understand from him that it was still resolved that his tour to Italy with Mr. and Mrs. Thrale should take place, of which he had entertained some doubt, on account of the loss they had suffered; and his doubts afterwards appeared to be well founded. He observed, indeed very justly, that "their loss was an additional reason for their going abroad; and if it had not been fixed that he should have been one of the party, he would force them out; but he would not advise them, unless his advice was asked, lest they might suspect that he recommended what he wished on his own account." I was not pleased that his intimacy with Mr. Thrale's family, though it no doubt contributed much to his comfort and enjoyment, was not without some degree of restraint: not, as has been grossly suggested, that it was required of him as a task to talk for the entertainment of them and their company, but that he was not quite at his ease; which, however, might partly be owing to his own honest pride—that dignity of mind which is always jealous of appearing too compliant.

On Sunday, March 31, I called on him, and showed him, as a curiosity which I had discovered, his "Translation of

---

[1] Joseph Baretti was a native of Turin; but, having resided many years in this country, he wrote the English language with great purity, as evidenced by his controversy with Mr. Sharpe, the Italian tourist. Dr. Johnson procured him the situation of Italian master in Mr. Thrale's family. He was born in 1716 and died in 1784.—Ed.

Lobo's Account of Abyssinia,"[1] which Sir John Pringle[2] had lent me, it being then little known as one of his works. He said, "Take no notice of it," or "don't talk of it." He seemed to think it beneath him, though done at six-and-twenty. I said to him, "Your style, Sir, is much improved since you translated this." He answered, with a sort of triumphant smile, "Sir, I hope it is."

On Wednesday, April 3, in the morning I found him very busy putting his books in order, and as they were generally very old ones, clouds of dust were flying around him. He had on a pair of large gloves, such as hedgers use. His present appearance put me in mind of my uncle Dr. Boswell's description of him, "A robust genius, born to grapple with whole libraries."

I gave him an account of a conversation which had passed between me and Captain Cook, the day before, at dinner, at Sir John Pringle's; and he was much pleased with the conscientious accuracy of that celebrated circumnavigator, who set me right as to many of the exaggerated accounts given by Dr. Hawkesworth of his voyages. I told him that while I was with the Captain I caught the enthusiasm of curiosity and adventure, and felt a strong inclination to go with him on his next voyage. JOHNSON: "Why, Sir, a man *does* feel so, till he considers how very little he can learn from such voyages." BOSWELL: "But one is carried away with the general grand and indistinct notion of A VOYAGE ROUND THE WORLD." JOHNSON: "Yes, Sir; but a man is to guard himself against taking a thing in general." I said I was certain that a great part of what we are told by the travellers to the South Sea must be conjecture, because they had not enough of the language of those countries to understand so much as they have related. Objects falling under the observation of the senses might be clearly known; but everything intellectual, everything abstract—politics, morals, and religion—must be darkly guessed. Dr. Johnson was of the same opinion. He, upon another occasion, when a friend mentioned to him several extraordinary facts, as communicated to him by the circumnavigators, slily observed, "Sir, I never before knew

---

[1] Jerome Lobo was a Portuguese Jesuit, who went as a missionary to Abyssinia, and wrote an account of that country, of which Dr. Johnson published an abridged translation. He was born at Lisbon in 1593, and died at Coimbra in 1678.—ED.

[2] Sir John Pringle was one of the most eminent physicians and natural philosophers of his time. He was born in Roxburghshire in 1707, and was, at this period, the President of the Royal Society, to which office he had been elected in 1772. He died in 1782.—ED.

how much I was respected by these gentlemen; they told *me* none of these things."

He had been in company with Omai, a native of one of the South Sea islands, after he had been some time in this country. He was struck with the elegance of his behaviour, and accounted for it thus: "Sir, he had passed his time, while in England, only in the best company: so that all that he had acquired of our manners was genteel. As a proof of this, Sir, Lord Mulgrave and he dined one day at Streatham; they sat with their backs to the light fronting me, so that I could not see distinctly: and there was so little of the savage in Omai, that I was afraid to speak to either, lest I should mistake one for the other."

We agreed to dine to-day at the Mitre tavern, after the rising of the House of Lords, where a branch of the litigation concerning the Douglas Estate, in which I was one of the counsel, was to come on. I brought with me Mr. Murray, Solicitor-General of Scotland, now one of the Judges of the Court of Session, with the title of Lord Henderland. I mentioned Mr. Solicitor's relation, Lord Charles Hay, with whom I knew Dr. Johnson had been acquainted. JOHNSON: " I wrote some thing for Lord Charles; and I thought he had nothing to fear from a court-martial. I suffered a great loss when he died; he was a mighty pleasing man in conversation, and a reading man. The character of a soldier is high. They who stand forth the foremost in danger for the community have the respect of mankind. An officer is much more respected than any other man who has as little money. In a commercial country money will always purchase respect. But you find an officer, who has, properly speaking, no money, is everywhere well received, and treated with attention. The character of a soldier always stands him instead." BOSWELL: " Yet, Sir, I think that common soldiers are worse thought of than other men in the same rank of life—such as labourers." JOHNSON: "Why, Sir, a common soldier is usually a very gross man, and any quality which procures respect may be overwhelmed by grossness. A man of learning may be so vicious or so ridiculous that you cannot respect him. A common soldier, too, generally eats more than he can pay for. But when a common soldier is civil in his quarters, his red coat procures him a degree of respect." The peculiar respect paid to the military character in France was mentioned. BOSWELL: " I should think that where military men are so numerous, they would be less valued as not being rare." JOHNSON: "Nay, Sir, wherever a particular character or profession is high in the estimation of a people, those who are of it will be valued above other men. We value an Englishman high in this country, and yet Englishmen are not rare in it."

Mr. Murray praised the ancient philosophers for the candour and good humour with which those of different sects disputed with each other. JOHNSON: "Sir, they disputed with good humour, because they were not in earnest as to religion. Had the ancients been serious in their belief, we should not have had their gods exhibited in the manner we find them represented in the poets. The people would not have suffered it. They disputed with good humour upon the fanciful theories, because they were not interested in the truth of them: when a man has nothing to lose he may be in good humour with his opponent. Accordingly you see, in Lucian, that the Epicurean, who argues only negatively, keeps his temper; the Stoic, who has something positive to preserve, grows angry. Being angry with one who controverts an opinion which you value, is a necessary consequence of the uneasiness which you feel. Every man who attacks my belief diminishes, in some degree, my confidence in it, and therefore makes me uneasy; and I am angry with him who makes me uneasy. Those only who believed in revelation have been angry at having their faith called in question; because they only had something upon which they could rest as matter of fact." MURRAY: "It seems to me that we are not angry at a man for controverting an opinion which we believe and value; we rather pity him." JOHNSON: "Why, Sir, to be sure when you wish a man to have that belief which you think is of infinite advantage, you wish well to him; but your primary consideration is your own quiet. If a madman were to come into this room with a stick in his hand, no doubt we should pity the state of his mind; but our primary consideration would be to take care of ourselves. We should knock him down first, and pity him afterwards. No, Sir; every man will dispute with great good humour upon a subject in which he is not interested. I will dispute very calmly upon the probability of another man's son being hanged; but if a man zealously enforces the probability that my own son will be hanged, I shall certainly not be in a very good humour with him." I added this illustration, "If a man endeavours to convince me that my wife, whom I love very much, and in whom I place great confidence, is a disagreeable woman, and is even unfaithful to me, I shall be very angry; for he is putting me in fear of being unhappy." MURRAY: "But, Sir, truth will always bear an examination." JOHNSON: "Yes, Sir; but it is painful to be forced to defend it. Consider, Sir, how should you like, though conscious of your innocence, to be tried before a jury for a capital crime once a week."

We talked of education at great schools; the advantages and disadvantages of which Johnson displayed in a luminous manner; but his arguments preponderated so much in favour of the benefit which a boy of good parts might receive at one of them, that I have reason to believe Mr. Murray was very much influenced by what he had heard to-day, in his determination to send his own son to Westminster school.—I have acted in the same manner with regard to my own two sons: having placed the eldest at Eton, and the second at Westminster. I cannot say which is best. But in justice to both those noble seminaries, I, with high satisfaction, declare, that my boys have derived from them a great deal of good, and no evil: and I trust they will, like Horace, be grateful to their father for giving them so valuable an education.

I introduced the topic, which is often ignorantly urged, that the universities of England are too rich;[1] so that learning does not flourish in them as it would do if those who teach had smaller salaries, and depended on their assiduity for a great part of their income. Johnson: "Sir, the very reverse of this is the truth; the English universities are not rich enough. Our fellowships are only sufficient to support a man during his studies to fit him for the world, and accordingly in general they are held no longer than till an opportunity offers of getting away. Now and then, perhaps, there is a fellow who grows old in his college; but this is against his will, unless he be a man very indolent indeed. A hundred a-year is reckoned a good fellowship, and that is no more than is necessary to keep a man decently as a scholar. We do not allow our fellows to marry, because we consider academical institutions as preparatory to a settlement in the world. It is only by being employed as a tutor, that a fellow can obtain anything more than a livelihood. To be sure a man, who has enough without teaching, will probably not teach; for we would all be idle if we could. In the same manner, a man who is to get nothing by teaching will not exert himself. Gresham college was intended as a place of instruction for London; able professors were to read lectures gratis; they contrived to have no scholars; whereas if they

---

[1] Dr. Adam Smith, who was for some time a professor in the University of Glasgow, has uttered, in his "Wealth of Nations," some reflections upon this subject, which are certainly not well founded, and seem to be invidious.—Boswell.

had been allowed to receive but sixpence a lecture from each scholar, they would have been emulous to have had many scholars. Every body will agree that it should be the interest of those who teach to have scholars; and this is the case in our universities. That they are too rich is certainly not true; for they have nothing good enough to keep a man of eminent learning with them for his life. In the foreign universities a professorship is a high thing. It is as much almost as a man can make by his learning; and therefore we find the most learned men abroad are in the universities. It is not so with us. Our universities are impoverished of learning, by the penury of their provisions. I wish there were many places of a thousand a-year at Oxford, to keep first-rate men of learning from quitting the University." Undoubtedly if this were the case, literature would have a still greater dignity and splendour at Oxford, and there would be grander living sources of instruction.

I mentioned Mr. Maclaurin's [1] uneasiness on account of a degree of ridicule carelessly thrown on his deceased father, in Goldsmith's "History of Animated Nature," in which that celebrated mathematician is represented as being subject to fits of yawning so violent as to render him incapable of proceeding in his lecture; a story altogether unfounded, but for the publication of which the law would give no reparation. [2] This led us to agitate the question, whether legal redress could be obtained, even when a man's deceased relation was calumniated in a publication. Mr. Murray maintained there should be reparation, unless the author could justify himself by proving the fact. JOHNSON: "Sir, it is of so much more consequence that truth should be told, than that individuals should not be made uneasy, that it is much better that the law does not restrain writing freely concerning the characters of the dead. Damages will be given to a man who is calumniated in his lifetime, because he may be hurt in his worldly interest, or at least hurt in his mind; but the law does not regard that uneasiness which a man feels on having his ancestor calumniated.

[1] John Maclaurin was the son of the celebrated Colin Maclaurin, professor of mathematics at Edinburgh. He was a member of the Faculty of Advocates, and in 1787 was raised to the judicial bench by the title of Lord Dreghorn. Maclaurin was the author of "An Essay on Literary Property." He was born at Edinburgh in 1734, and died in 1796.—ED.

[2] Dr. Goldsmith was dead before Mr. Maclaurin discovered the ludicrous error. But Mr. Nourse, the bookseller, who was the proprietor of the work, upon being applied to by Sir John Pringle, agreed very handsomely to have the leaf on which it was contained cancelled and reprinted without it, at his own expense.—BOSWELL.

That is too nice. Let him deny what is said, and let the matter have a fair chance by discussion. But if a man could say nothing against a character but what he can prove, history could not be written; for a great deal is known of men of which proof cannot be brought. A minister may be notoriously known to take bribes, and yet you may not be able to prove it." Mr. Murray suggested that the author should be obliged to show some sort of evidence, though he would not require a strict legal proof; but Johnson firmly and resolutely opposed any restraint whatever, as adverse to a free investigation of the characters of mankind.[1]

On Thursday, April 4, having called on Dr. Johnson, I said, it was a pity that truth was not so firm as to bid defiance to all attacks, so that it might be shot at as much as people chose to attempt, and yet remain unhurt. JOHNSON: "Then, Sir, it would not be shot at. Nobody attempts to dispute that two and two make four: but with contests concerning moral truth, human passions are generally mixed, and therefore it must ever be liable to assault and misrepresentation."

[1] What Dr. Johnson has here said is undoubtedly good sense: yet I am afraid that law, though defined by *Lord Coke* "the perfection of reason," is not altogether with him; for it is held in the books, that an attack on the reputation even of a dead man may be punished as a libel, because tending to a breach of the peace. There is, however, I believe, no modern decided case to that effect. In the King's Bench, Trinity Term, 1790, the question occurred on occasion of an indictment, *The King* v. *Topham,* who, as a *proprietor* of a newspaper entitled "The World," was found guilty of a libel against Earl Cowper, deceased, because certain injurious charges against his lordship were published in that paper. An arrest of judgment having been moved for, the case was afterwards solemnly argued. My friend, Mr. Const, whom I delight in having an opportunity to praise, not only for his abilities but his manners—a gentleman whose ancient German blood has been mellowed in England, and who may be truly said to unite the *baron* and the *barrister*—was one of the counsel for Mr. Topham. He displayed much learning and ingenuity upon the general question; which, however, was not decided, as the court granted an arrest chiefly on the informality of the indictment, No man has a higher reverence for the law of England than I have; but, with all deference, I cannot help thinking that prosecution by indictment, if a defendant is never to be allowed to justify, must often be very oppressive, unless juries, whom I am more and more confirmed in holding to be judges of law as well as of fact, resolutely interpose. Of late, an Act of Parliament has passed declaratory of their full right to one as well as the other, in matter of libel; and the bill having been brought in by a popular gentleman, many of his party have, in most extravagant terms, declaimed on the wonderful acquisition to the liberty of the press. For my own part, I ever was clearly of opinion that this right was inherent in the very constitution of a jury, and indeed, in sense and reason, inseparable from their important function. To establish it, therefore, by statute, is, I think, narrowing its foundation, which is the broad and deep basis of common law. Would it not rather weaken the right of

On Friday, April 5, being Good Friday, after having attended the morning service at St. Clement's church, I walked home with Johnson. We talked of the Roman Catholic religion. JOHNSON: "In the barbarous ages, Sir, priests and people were equally deceived; but afterwards there were gross corruptions introduced by the clergy, such as indulgences to priests to have concubines, and the worship of images, not, indeed, inculcated, but knowingly permitted." He strongly censured the licensed stews at Rome. BOSWELL: "So then, Sir, you would allow no irregular intercourse whatever between the sexes?" JOHNSON: "To be sure I would not, Sir. I would punish it much more than it is done, and so restrain it. In all countries there has been fornication, as in all countries there has been theft; but there may be more or less of the one, as well as of the other, in proportion to the force of law. All men will naturally commit fornication, as all men will naturally steal. And, Sir, it is very absurd to argue, as has been often done, that prostitutes are necessary to prevent the violent effects of appetite from violating the decent order of life; nay, should be permitted, in order to preserve the chastity of our wives and daughters. Depend upon it, Sir, severe laws, steadily enforced, would be sufficient against those evils, and would promote marriage."

I stated to him this case:—"Suppose a man has a daughter, who he knows has been seduced, but her misfortune is concealed from the world; should he keep her in his house? Would he not, by doing so, be accessary to imposition? And, perhaps, a worthy, unsuspecting man might come and marry this woman, unless the father inform him of the truth." JOHNSON: "Sir, he is accessary to no imposition. His daughter is in his house; and if a man courts her, he takes his chance. If a friend, or, indeed, if any

primogeniture, or any other old and universally acknowledged right, should the legislature pass an act in favour of it? In my "Letter to the People of Scotland, against diminishing the number of the Lords of Session," published in 1785, there is the following passage, which, as a concise, and, I hope, a fair and rational state of the matter, I presume to quote:— "The juries of England are judges of *law* as well as of *fact* in *many civil* and in *all criminal* trials. That my principles of *resistance* may not be misapprehended any more than my principles of *submission*, I protest that I should be the last man in the world to encourage juries to contradict rashly, wantonly, or perversely, the opinion of the judges. On the contrary, I would have them listen respectfully to the advice they receive from the bench, by which they may often be well directed in forming *their own opinion*; which, 'and not another's,' is the opinion they are to return *upon their oaths*. But where, after due attention to all that the judge has said, they are decidedly of a different opinion from him, they have not only a *power* and a *right*, but they are *bound in conscience* to bring in a verdict accordingly."—BOSWELL.

man, asks his opinion whether he should marry her, he ought to advise him against it, without telling why, because his real opinion is then required. Or, if he has other daughters who know of her frailty, he ought not to keep her in his house. You are to consider the state of life is this: we are to judge of one another's characters as well as we can; and a man is not bound in honesty or honour to tell us the faults of his daughter or of himself. A man who has debauched his friend's daughter is not obliged to say to every body—'Take care of me; don't let me enter your house without suspicion. I once debauched a friend's daughter; I may debauch yours.'"

Mr. Thrale called upon him, and appeared to bear the loss of his son with a manly composure. There was no affectation about him; and he talked, as usual, upon indifferent subjects. He seemed to me to hesitate as to the intended Italian tour, on which, I flattered myself, he and Mrs. Thrale and Dr. Johnson were soon to set out; and therefore I pressed it as much as I could. I mentioned that Mr. Beauclerk had said, that Baretti, whom they were to carry with them, would keep them so long in the little towns of his own district, that they would not have time to see Rome. I mentioned this to put them on their guard. JOHNSON: "Sir, we do not thank Mr. Beauclerk for supposing that we are to be directed by Baretti. No, Sir; Mr. Thrale is to go by my advice, to Mr. Jackson[1] (the all-knowing), and get from him a plan for seeing the most that can be seen in the time that we have to travel. We must, to be sure, see Rome, Naples, Florence, and Venice, and as much more as we can." (Speaking with a tone of animation.)

When I expressed an earnest wish for his remarks on Italy, he said, "I do not see that I could make a book upon Italy; yet I should be glad to get 200*l*. or 500*l*. by such a work." This showed both that a journal of his Tour upon the Continent was not wholly out of his contemplation, and that he uniformly adhered to that strange opinion which his indolent disposition made him utter: "No man but a blockhead ever wrote except for money." Numerous instances to refute this will occur to all who are versed in the history of literature.

He gave us one of the many sketches of character which were treasured in his mind, and which he was wont to

---

[1] A gentleman who, from his extraordinary stores of knowledge, has been styled *omniscient*. Johnson, I think very properly, altered it to *all-knowing*, as it is a *verbum solenne*, appropriated to the Supreme Being.— BOSWELL.

produce quite unexpectedly in a very entertaining manner. " I lately," said he, "received a letter from the East Indies, from a gentleman whom I formerly knew very well; he had returned from that country with a handsome fortune, as it was reckoned, before means were found to acquire those immense sums which have been brought from thence of late: he was a scholar, and an agreeable man, and lived very prettily in London, till his wife died. After her death, he took to dissipation and gaming, and lost all he had. One evening he lost 1000*l.* to a gentleman whose name I am sorry I have forgotten. Next morning he sent the gentleman 500*l.*, with an apology that it was all he had in the world. The gentleman sent the money back to him, declaring he would not accept of it; and adding, that if Mr. —— had occasion for 500*l.* more, he would lend it to him. He resolved to go out again to the East Indies, and make his fortune anew. He got a considerable appointment, and I had some intention of accompanying him. Had I thought then as I do now, I should have gone: but at that time I had objections to quitting England."

It was a very remarkable circumstance about Johnson, whom shallow observers have supposed to have been ignorant of the world, that very few men had seen greater variety of characters; and none could observe them better, as was evident from the strong yet nice portraits which he often drew. I have frequently thought that if he had made out what the French call *une catalogue raisonnée* of all the people who had passed under his observation, it would have afforded a very rich fund of instruction and entertainment. The suddenness with which his accounts of some of them started out in conversation, was not less pleasing than surprising. I remember he once observed to me, " It is wonderful, Sir, what is to be found in London. The most literary conversation that I ever enjoyed was at the table of Jack Ellis, a money-scrivener behind the Royal Exchange, with whom I at one period used to dine generally once a week."[1]

---

[1] This Mr. Ellis was, I believe, the last of that profession called *Scriveners*, which is one of the London companies, but of which the business is no longer carried on separately, but is transacted by attorneys and others. He was a man of literature and talents. He was the author of a Hudibrastic version of Maphæus's Canto, in addition to the Æneid; of some poems in Dodsley's Collections: and various other small pieces; but being a very modest man, never put his name to anything. He showed me a translation which he had made of Ovid's Epistles, very prettily done. There is a good engraved portrait of him by Pether, from a picture by Fry, which hangs in the hall of the Scriveners' Company. I visited him October 4, 1790, in his ninety-third year, and found his

Volumes would be required to contain a list of his numerous and various acquaintance, none of whom he ever forgot; and could describe and discriminate them all with precision and vivacity. He associated with persons the most widely different in manners, abilities, rank, and accomplishments. He was at once the companion of the brilliant Colonel Forrester of the Guards, who wrote "The Polite Philosopher," and of the awkward and uncouth Robert Levett; of Lord Thurlow; and Mr. Sastres, the Italian master; and has dined one day with the beautiful, gay, and fascinating Lady Craven,[1] and the next with good Mrs. Gardiner, the tallow-chandler, on Snow-hill.

On my expressing my wonder at his discovering so much of the knowledge peculiar to different professions, he told me, "I learnt what I know of law chiefly from Mr. Ballow,[2] a very able man. I learnt some too from Chambers; but was not so teachable then. One is not willing to be taught by a young man." When I expressed a wish to know more about Mr. Ballow, Johnson said, "Sir, I have seen him but once these twenty years. The tide of life has driven us different ways." I was sorry at the time to hear this; but whoever quits the creeks of private connections, and fairly gets into the great ocean of London, will by imperceptible degrees, unavoidably experience such cessations of acquaintance.

"My knowledge of physic," he added, "I learnt from Dr. James, whom I helped in writing the proposals for his Dictionary, and also a little in the Dictionary itself.[3] I

judgment distinct and clear, and his memory, though faded so as to fail him occasionally, yet, as he assured me, and I indeed perceived, able to serve him very well, after a little recollection. It was agreeable to observe that he was free from the discontent and fretfulness which too often molest old age. He, in the summer of that year, walked to Rotherhithe, where he dined and walked home in the evening. He died on the 31st of December, 1791.—BOSWELL.

[1] Lord Macartney, who, with other distinguished qualities, is remarkable also for an elegant pleasantry, told me that he met Johnson at Lady Craven's, and that he seemed jealous of any interference. "So," said his lordship, smiling, "*I kept back.*"—BOSWELL.

[2] There is an account of him in Sir John Hawkins's Life of Johnson, p. 244. Mr. Thomas Ballow was author of an excellent "Treatise of Equity," printed anonymously in 1742, and lately republished with very valuable additions, by John Fonblanque, Esq. Mr. Ballow died suddenly in London, July 26, 1782, aged seventy-five, and is mentioned in "The Gentleman's Magazine" for that year as "a great Greek scholar, and famous for his knowledge of the old philosophy."—MALONE.

[3] I have in vain endeavoured to find out what parts Johnson wrote for Dr. James. Perhaps medical men may.—BOSWELL.

also learnt from Dr. Lawrence,[1] but was then grown more stubborn."

A curious incident happened to-day, while Mr. Thrale and I sat with him. Francis announced that a large packet was brought to him from the post-office, said to have come from Lisbon, and it was charged 7l. 10s. He would not receive it, supposing it to be some trick, nor did he even look at it. But, upon inquiry afterwards, he found it was a real packet for him, from that very friend in the East Indies of whom he had been speaking; and the ship which carried it having come from Portugal, this packet, with others, had been put into the post-office at Lisbon.

I mentioned a new gaming club, of which Mr. Beauclerk had given me an account, where the members played to a desperate extent. JOHNSON: "Depend upon it, Sir, this is mere talk. Who is ruined by gaming? You will not find six instances in an age. There is a strange rout made about deep play: whereas you have many more people ruined by adventurous trade, and yet we do not hear such an outcry against it." THRALE: "There may be few people absolutely ruined by deep play; but very many are much hurt in their circumstances by it." JOHNSON: "Yes, Sir, and so are very many by other kinds of expense." I had heard him talk once before in the same manner; and at Oxford he said, "he wished he had learned to play at cards." The truth, however, is, that he loved to display his ingenuity in argument; and, therefore, would sometimes in conversation maintain opinions which he was sensible were wrong, but in supporting which, his reasoning and wit would be most conspicuous. He would begin thus: "Why, Sir, as to the good or evil of card-playing—" "Now," said Garrick, "he is thinking which side he shall take." He appeared to have a pleasure in contradiction, especially when any opinion whatever was delivered with an air of confidence; so that there was hardly any topic, if not one of the great truths of Religion and Morality, that he might not have been incited to argue, either for or against. Lord Elibank[2] had the highest admiration of his powers. He once observed to me, "Whatever opinions Johnson maintains, I will not say that he convinces me; but he never fails to show me that he has good reasons for it." I have heard Johnson pay his Lordship this high compliment: "I never

---

[1] Dr. Thomas Lawrence was a physician of considerable eminence in his profession, and in 1767 he became President of the College of Physicians, to which office he was re-elected during the ensuing seven years. He was born in 1711 and died in 1783.—ED.

[2] Patrick Lord Elibank, who died in 1778.—BOSWELL.

was in Lord Elibank's company without learning something."

We sat together till it was too late for the afternoon
service. Thrale said he had come with intention to go to
church with us. We went at seven to evening prayers at
St. Clement's church, after having drunk coffee; an indulgence, which I understood Johnson yielded to on this
occasion, in compliment to Thrale.

On Sunday, April 7, Easter-day, after having been at
St. Paul's cathedral, I came to Dr. Johnson, according
to my usual custom. It seemed to me that there was
always something peculiarly mild and placid in his manner
upon this holy festival, the commemoration of the most
joyful event in the history of our world, the resurrection
of our LORD and SAVIOUR, who, having triumphed over
death and the grave, proclaimed immortality to mankind.

I repeated to him an argument of a lady of my acquaintance, who maintained that her husband's having been
guilty of numberless infidelities, released her from conjugal
obligations, because they were reciprocal. JOHNSON:
"This is miserable stuff, Sir. To the contract of marriage,
besides the man and wife, there is a third party—Society;
and, if it be considered as a vow,—GOD: and therefore it
cannot be dissolved by their consent alone. Laws are not
made for particular cases, but for men in general. A
woman may be unhappy with her husband; but she
cannot be freed from him without the approbation of the
civil and ecclesiastical power. A man may be unhappy,
because he is not so rich as another; but he is not to seize
upon another's property with his own hand." BOSWELL:
"But, Sir, this lady does not want that the contract should
be dissolved; she only argues that she may indulge herself
in gallantries with equal freedom as her husband does,
provided she takes care not to introduce a spurious issue
into his family. You know, Sir, what Macrobius has told
of Julia." [1] JOHNSON: "This lady of yours, Sir, I think, is
very fit for a brothel '

Mr. Macbean, author of the "Dictionary of Ancient
Geography," came in. He mentioned that he had been
forty years absent from Scotland; "Ah, Boswell!" said
Johnson, smiling, "what would you give to be forty years
from Scotland?" I said, "I should not like to be so long
absent from the seat of my ancestors." This gentleman,
Mrs. Williams, and Mr. Levett dined with us.

Dr. Johnson made a remark, which both Mr. Macbean

---

[1] "Nunquam enim nisi navi plena tollo vectorem."   Lib. ii. c. v.

and I thought new. It was this: that "the law against usury is for the protection of creditors as well as debtors; for, if there were no such check, people would be apt, from the temptation of great interest, to lend to desperate persons, by whom they would lose their money. Accordingly there are instances of ladies being ruined, by having injudiciously sunk their fortunes for high annuities, which, after a few years, ceased to be paid, in consequence of the ruined circumstances of the borrower."

Mrs. Williams was very peevish; and I wondered at Johnson's patience with her now, as I had often done on similar occasions. The truth is, that his humane consideration of the forlorn and indigent state in which this lady was left by her father, induced him to treat her with the utmost tenderness, and even to be desirous of procuring her amusement, so as sometimes to incommode many of his friends, by carrying her with him to their houses, where, from her manner of eating, in consequence of her blindness, she could not but offend the delicacy of persons of nice sensations.

After coffee, we went to afternoon service in St. Clement's church. Observing some beggars in the street as we walked along, I said to him I supposed there was no civilised country in the world where the misery of want in the lowest classes of the people was prevented. JOHNSON: "I believe, Sir, there is not; but it is better that some should be unhappy, than that none should be happy, which would be the case in a general state of equality."

When the service was ended I went home with him, and we sat quietly by ourselves. He recommended Dr. Cheyne's books.[1] I said, I thought Cheyne had been reckoned whimsical.—"So he was," said he, "in some things; but there is no end of objections. There are few books to which some objection or other may not be made." He added, "I would not have you read anything else of Cheyne, but his book on Health, and his 'English Malady.'"

Upon the question whether a man who had been guilty of vicious actions would do well to force himself into solitude and sadness? JOHNSON: "No, Sir, unless it prevent him from being vicious again. With some people, gloomy penitence is only madness turned upside down. A man may

---

[1] Dr. George Cheyne was an eminent physician and writer; he was born in Scotland, but ultimately settled in London. Besides several medical works, he was the author of a mathematical treatise, entitled, "Fluxionum Methodus Inversa," which procured him admission to the Royal Society. He died in 1743, aged 82.—ED.

be gloomy, till, in order to be relieved from gloom, he has recourse again to criminal indulgences."

On Wednesday, April 10, I dined with him at Mr. Thrale's, where were Mr. Murphy and some other company. Before dinner, Dr. Johnson and I passed some time by ourselves. I was sorry to find it was now resolved that the proposed journey to Italy should not take place this year. He said, "I am disappointed, to be sure; but it is not a great disappointment." I wondered to see him bear, with a philosophical calmness, what would have made most people peevish and fretful. I perceived, however, that he had so warmly cherished the hope of enjoying classical scenes, that he could not easily part with the scheme; for he said, "I shall probably contrive to get to Italy some other way. But I won't mention it to Mr. and Mrs. Thrale, as it might vex them." I suggested that going to Italy might have done Mr. and Mrs. Thrale good. JOHNSON: "I rather believe not, Sir. While grief is fresh, every attempt to divert only irritates. You must wait till grief be *digested*, and then amusement will dissipate the remains of it."

At dinner, Mr. Murphy entertained us with the history of Mr. Joseph Simpson, a schoolfellow of Dr. Johnson's, a barrister-at-law, of good parts, but who fell into a dissipated course of life, incompatible with that success in his profession which he once had, and would otherwise have deservedly maintained; yet he still preserved a dignity in his deportment. He wrote a tragedy on the story of Leonidas, entitled, "The Patriot." He read it to a company of lawyers, who found so many faults that he wrote it over again: so then there were two tragedies on the same subject and with the same title. Dr. Johnson told us, that one of them was still in his possession. This very piece was, after his death, published by some person who had been about him, and, for the sake of a little hasty profit, was fallaciously advertised, so as to make it be believed to have been written by Johnson himself.

I said, I disliked the custom which some people had of bringing their children into company, because it in a manner forced us to pay foolish compliments to please their parents. JOHNSON: "You are right, Sir. We may be excused for not caring much about other people's children, for there are many who care very little about their own children. It may be observed, that men who, from being engaged in business, or from their course of life in whatever way, seldom see their children, do not care much about them. I myself should not have had much fondness for a child of my own."

MRS. THRALE: "Nay, Sir, how can you talk so?" JOHNSON: "At least, I never wished to have a child."

Mr. Murphy mentioned Dr. Johnson's having a design to publish an edition of Cowley. Johnson said, he did not know but he should; and he expressed his disapprobation of Dr. Hurd, for having published a mutilated edition under the title of "Select Works of Abraham Cowley." Mr. Murphy thought it a bad precedent, observing, that any author might be used in the same manner, and that it was pleasing to see the variety of an author's compositions at different periods.

We talked of Flatman's Poems; and Mrs. Thrale observed, that Pope had partly borrowed from him "The Dying Christian to his Soul." Johnson repeated Rochester's verses upon Flatman, which I think by much too severe:—

> "Nor that slow drudge in swift Pindaric strains,
> Flatman, who Cowley imitates with pains,
> And rides a jaded muse, whipt with loose reins."

I like to recollect all the passages that I heard Johnson repeat—it stamps a value on them.

He told us that the book entitled "The Lives of the Poets, by Mr. Cibber," was entirely supplied by Mr. Shiels,[1] a Scotchman, one of his amanuenses. "The booksellers,"

---

[1] In "The Monthly Review" for May, 1792, there is such a correction of the above passage as I should think myself very culpable not to subjoin:—"This account is very inaccurate. The following statement of facts we know to be true in every material circumstance:—Shiels was the principal collector and digester of the materials for the work; but as he was very raw in authorship, an indifferent writer in prose, and his language full of Scotticisms, Cibber, who was a clever, lively fellow, and then soliciting employment among the booksellers, was engaged to correct the style and diction of the whole work, then intended to make only four volumes, with power to alter, expunge, or add, as he liked. He was also to supply *notes* occasionally, especially concerning those dramatic poets with whom he had been chiefly conversant. He also engaged to write several of the lives, which, as we are told, he accordingly performed. He was further useful in striking out the Jacobitical and Tory sentiments which Shiels had industriously interspersed wherever he could bring them in; and as the success of the work appeared, after all, very doubtful, he was content with 21*l.* for his labour, besides a few sets of the books, to disperse among his friends. Shiels had nearly 70*l.*, besides the advantage of many of the best lives in the work being communicated by friends to the undertaking, and for which Mr. Shiels had the same consideration as for the rest, being paid by the sheet, for the whole. He was, however, so angry with his Whiggish supervisor (THE., like his father, being a violent stickler for the political principles which prevailed in the reign of George the Second), for so unmercifully mutilating his copy, and scouting his politics, that he wrote Cibber a challenge; but was prevented from sending it by the publisher, who fairly laughed him out of his fury. The proprietors, too, were discontented, in the end, on account of Mr. Cibber's unexpected industry; for

said he, "gave Theophilus Cibber, who was then in prison, ten guineas to allow *Mr. Cibber* to be put upon the title-page, as the author. By this, a double imposition was intended; in the first place, that it was the work of a Cibber at all; and in the second place, that it was the work of old Cibber."

Mr. Murphy said, that "the Memoirs of Gray's Life set him much higher in his estimation than his poems did; for you there saw a man constantly at work in literature." Johnson acquiesced in this; but depreciated the book I thought very unreasonably. For he said, " I forced myself to read it, only because it was a common topic of conversation. I found it mighty dull; and, as to the style, it is fit for the second table." Why he thought so I was at a loss to conceive. He now gave it as his opinion, that "Akenside was a superior poet both to Gray and Mason."

his corrections and alterations in the proof-sheets were so numerous and considerable, that the printer made for them a grievous addition to his bill; and, in fine, all parties were dissatisfied. On the whole, the work was productive of no profit to the undertakers, who had agreed, in case of success, to make Cibber a present of some addition to the twenty guineas which he had received, and for which his receipt is now in the bookseller's hands. We are farther assured that he actually obtained an additional sum; when he, soon after (in the year 1758), unfortunately embarked for Dublin, on an engagement for one of the theatres there, but the ship was cast away, and every person on board perished. There were about sixty passengers, among whom was the Earl of Drogheda, with many other persons of consequence and property.

"As to the alleged design of making the compilement pass for the work of old Mr. Cibber, the charges seem to have been founded on a somewhat uncharitable construction. We are assured that the thought was not harboured by some of the proprietors, who are still living, and we hope that it did not occur to the first designer of the work, who was also the printer of it, and who bore a respectable character.

"We have been induced to enter thus circumstantially into the foregoing detail of facts relating to the 'Lives of the Poets,' compiled by Messrs. Cibber and Shiels, from a sincere regard to that sacred principle of truth to which Dr. Johnson so rigidly adhered, according to the best of his knowledge, and which, we believe, *no consideration* would have prevailed on him to violate. In regard to the matter, which we now dismiss, he had, no doubt, been misled by partial and wrong information. Shiels was the Doctor's amanuensis; he had quarrelled with Cibber: it is natural to suppose that he told his story in his own way, and it is certain that he was not 'a very sturdy moralist.' "

This explanation appears to me very satisfactory. It is, however, to be observed that the story told by Johnson does not rest solely upon my record of his conversation, for he himself has published it in his life of Hammond, where he says, "the manuscript of Shiels is now in my possession." Very probably he had trusted to Sheils' word, and never looked at it so as to compare it with the "Lives of the Poets," as published under Mr. Cibber's name. What became of that manuscript I know not. I should have liked much to examine it. I suppose it was thrown into the fire in that impetuous combustion of papers which Johnson, I think, rashly executed when *moribundus*.—BOSWELL.

Talking of the Reviews, Johnson said, "I think them very impartial: I do not know an instance of partiality." He mentioned what had passed upon the subject of the Monthly and Critical Reviews, in the conversation with which his Majesty had honoured him. He expatiated a little more on them this evening. "The Monthly Reviewers," said he, "are not Deists; but they are Christians with as little Christianity as may be; and are for pulling down all establishments. The Critical Reviewers are for supporting the constitution, both in church and state. The Critical Reviewers, I believe, often review without reading the books through; but lay hold of a topic, and write chiefly from their own minds. The Monthly Reviewers are duller men, and are glad to read the books through."

He talked of Lord Lyttelton's extreme anxiety as an author; observing, that "he was thirty years in preparing his history, and that he employed a man to point it for him; as if (laughing) another man could point his sense better than himself." Mr. Murphy said, he understood his history was kept back several years for fear of Smollett. JOHNSON: "This seems strange to Murphy and me, who never felt that anxiety, but sent what we wrote to the press, and let it take its chance." MRS. THRALE: "The time has been, Sir, when you felt it." JOHNSON: "Why really, madam, I do not recollect a time when that was the case."

Talking of "The Spectator," he said, "It is wonderful that there is such a proportion of bad papers in the half of the work which was not written by Addison; for there was all the world to write that half, yet not a half of that half is good. One of the finest pieces in the English language is the paper on Novelty, yet we do not hear it talked of. It was written by Grove, a dissenting teacher." He would not, I perceived, call him a *clergyman*, though he was candid enough to allow very great merit to his composition. Mr. Murphy said, he remembered when there were several people alive in London, who enjoyed a considerable reputation merely from having written a paper in "The Spectator." He mentioned particularly Mr. Ince, who used to frequent Tom's coffee-house. "But," said Johnson, "you must consider how highly Steele speaks of Mr. Ince." He would not allow that the paper on carrying a boy to travel, signed *Philip Homebred*, which was reported to be written by the Lord Chancellor Hardwicke, had merit. He said, "It was quite vulgar, and had nothing luminous."

Johnson mentioned Dr. Barry's[1] System of Physic. "He

---

[1] Sir Edward Barry, Bart.—BOSWELL.

was a man," said he, "who had acquired a high reputation in Dublin, came over to England, and brought his reputation with him, but had not great success. His notion was, that pulsation occasions death by attrition; and that, therefore, the way to preserve life is to retard pulsation. But we know that pulsation is strongest in infants, and that we increase in growth while it operates in its regular course; so it cannot be the cause of destruction." Soon after this, he said something very flattering to Mrs. Thrale, which I do not recollect; but it concluded with wishing her long life. "Sir," said I, "if Dr. Barry's system be true, you have now shortened Mrs. Thrale's life, perhaps some minutes, by accelerating her pulsation."

On Thursday, April 11, I dined with him at General Paoli's, in whose house I now resided, and where I had ever afterwards the honour of being entertained with the kindest attention as his constant guest, while I was in London, till I had a house of my own there. I mentioned my having that morning introduced to Mr. Garrick, Count Neni, a Flemish nobleman of great rank and fortune, to whom Garrick talked of Abel Drugger as *a small part;* and related, with pleasant vanity, that a Frenchman who had seen him in one of his low characters, exclaimed, "*Comment! je ne le crois pas. Ce n'est pas Monsieur Garrick, ce grand homme!*" Garrick added, with an appearance of grave recollection, "If I were to begin life again, I think I should not play these low characters." Upon which I observed, "Sir, you would be in the wrong; for your great excellence is your variety of playing, your representing so well characters so very different." JOHNSON: "Garrick, Sir, was not in earnest in what he said; for, to be sure, his peculiar excellence is his variety; and, perhaps, there is not any one character which has not been as well acted by somebody else, as he could do it." BOSWELL: "Why then, Sir, did he talk so?" JOHNSON: "Why, Sir, to make you answer as you did." BOSWELL: "I don't know, Sir; he seemed to dip deep into his mind for the reflection." JOHNSON: "He had not far to dip, Sir; he had said the same thing, probably, twenty times before."

Of a nobleman raised at a very early period to high office, he said, "His parts, Sir, are pretty well for a lord, but would not be distinguished in a man who had nothing else but his parts."

A journey to Italy was still in his thoughts. He said, "A man who had not been in Italy is always conscious of an inferiority, from his not having seen what it is expected a man should see. The grand object of travelling is to see

the shores of the Mediterranean.   On those shores were the
four great Empires of the world—the Assyrian, the Persian,
the Grecian, and the Roman.   All our religion, almost all
our law, almost all our arts, almost all that sets us above
savages, has come to us from the shores of the Mediterranean."   The General observed, that "THE MEDI-
TERRANEAN would be a noble subject for a poem."

We talked of translation.   I said, I could not define it,
nor could I think of a similitude to illustrate it; but that it
appeared to me the translation of poetry could be only
imitation.   JOHNSON: "You may translate books of science
exactly.   You may also translate history, in so far as it
is not embellished with oratory, which is poetical.   Poetry,
indeed, cannot be translated; and therefore it is the poets
that preserve the languages; for we would not be at the
trouble to learn a language if we could have all that is
written in it just as well in a translation.   But as the
beauties of poetry cannot be preserved in any language
except that in which it was originally written, we learn
the language."

A gentleman maintained that the art of printing had
hurt real language, by disseminating idle writings.   JOHNSON:
"Sir, if it had not been for the art of printing, we should
now have no learning at all; for books would have perished
faster than they could have been transcribed."   This
observation seems not just, considering for how many ages
books were preserved by writing alone.[1]

The same gentleman maintained that a general diffusion
of knowledge among a people was a disadvantage, for it
made the vulgar rise above their humble sphere.   JOHNSON:
"Sir, while knowledge is a distinction, those who are
possessed of it will naturally rise above those who are not.
Merely to read and write was a distinction at first; but we
see, when reading and writing have become general, the
common people keep their stations.   And so, were higher
attainments to become general, the effect would be the
same."

"Goldsmith," he said, "referred every thing to vanity;
his virtues and his vices too were from that motive.   He was
not a social man: he never exchanged mind with you."

We spent the evening at Mr. Hoole's.   Mr. Mickle,[2] the

[1] The author did not recollect that of the books preserved (and an
infinite number was lost) all were confined to two languages.   In modern
times, and modern languages, France and Italy alone produce more
books in a given time than Greece and Rome; put England, Spain,
Germany, and the Northern kingdoms out of the question.—BURNEY.
[2] Wm. Julius Mickle, the translator of Camoens' "Lusiad," was
born in 1734, at Langholm in Dumfriesshire.   He died in 1788.—ED.

excellent translator of "The Lusiad," was there.   I have
preserved little of the conversation of this evening.   Dr.
Johnson said, "Thomson had a true poetical genius, the
power of viewing everything in a poetical light.   His
fault is such a cloud of words sometimes, that the sense
can hardly peep through.   Shiels, who compiled ' Cibber's
Lives of the Poets,' was one day sitting with me.   I took
down Thomson, and read aloud a large portion of him,
and then asked, ' Is not this fine?'   Shiels having expressed
the highest admiration, 'Well, Sir,' said I, ' I have omitted
every other line.'"

I related a dispute between Goldsmith and Mr. Robert
Dodsley, one day when they and I were dining at Tom
Davies's, in 1762.   Goldsmith asserted that there was no
poetry produced in this age.   Dodsley appealed to his own
collection, and maintained that though you could not find
a palace like Dryden's " Ode on St. Cecilia's Day," you had
villages composed of very pretty houses; and he mentioned
particularly "The Spleen."   JOHNSON: "I think Dodsley
gave up the question.   He and Goldsmith said the same
thing; only he said it in a softer manner than Goldsmith did;
for he acknowledged that there was no poetry, nothing that
towered above the common mark.   You may find wit and
humour in verse, and yet no poetry.   'Hudibras' has a
profusion of these; yet it is not to be reckoned a poem.
'The Spleen,' in Dodsley's collection, on which you say he
chiefly rested, is not poetry."   BOSWELL: "Does not Gray's
poetry, Sir, tower above the common mark?"   JOHNSON:
"Yes, Sir; but we must attend to the difference between
what men in general cannot do if they would, and what
every man may do if he would.   Sixteen-string Jack [1]
towered above the common mark."   BOSWELL: "Then, Sir,
what is poetry?"   JOHNSON: "Why, Sir, it is much easier
to say what it is not.   We all *know* what light is, but it is
not easy to *tell* what it is."

On Friday, April 12, I dined with him at our friend
Tom Davies's, where we met Mr. Cradock,[2] of Leicestershire,

[1] A noted highwayman, who, after having been several times tried
and acquitted, was at last hanged.   He was remarkable for foppery in his
dress, and particularly for wearing a bunch of sixteen strings at the knees
of his breeches.—BOSWELL.

[2] The hospitable proprietor of Gumley Hall, where he was accustomed
to entertain a large circle of literary friends.   Mr. Cradock was admitted
to the first literary circles of his day, and was in habits of intimacy with
Dr. Johnson, Boswell, Burke, Goldsmith, Doctors Parr, Farmer, and
Askew, Geo. Steevens, Lords Thurlow and Sandwich, Bishops Hurd,
Percy, and Hinchliff, &c.   "Of Dr. Johnson's manners," says Mr. Cradock,
in his Literary Memoirs, "Garrick was a great mimic, and by his

author of "Zobeide," a tragedy; a very pleasing gentleman, to whom my friend Dr. Farmer's very excellent "Essay on the Learning of Shakespeare" is addressed; and also Dr. Harwood, who has written and published various works, particularly a fantastical translation of the New Testament in modern phrase, and with a Socinian twist.

I introduced Aristotle's doctrine in his "Art of Poetry," of "the κάθαρσις τῶν παθημάτων, the purging of the passions," as the purpose of tragedy.[1] "But how are the passions to be purged by terror and pity?" said I, with an assumed air of ignorance, to incite him to talk, for which it was often necessary to employ some address. JOHNSON: "Why, Sir, you are to consider what is the meaning of purging in the original sense. It is to expel impurities from the human body. The mind is subject to the same imperfection. The passions are the greatest movers of human actions; but they are mixed with such impurities, that it is necessary they should be purged or refined by means of terror and pity. For instance, ambition is a noble passion; but by seeing upon the stage, that a man who is so excessively ambitious as to raise himself by injustice is punished, we are terrified at the fatal consequences of such a passion. In the same manner a certain degree of resentment is necessary; but if we see that a man carries it too far, we pity the object of it, and are taught to moderate that passion." My record upon this occasion does great injustice to Johnson's expression, which was so forcible and brilliant, that Mr. Cradock whispered me, "O that his words were written in a book!"

I observed the great defect of the tragedy of "Othello" was, that it had not a moral; for that no man could resist the circumstances of suspicion which were artfully suggested to Othello's mind. JOHNSON: "In the first place, Sir, we learn from Othello this very useful moral, not to make an unequal match; in the second place, we learn not to yield too readily to suspicion. The handkerchief is merely a trick, though a very pretty trick; but there are no other circumstances of reasonable suspicion, except what is related by Iago of Cassio's warm expressions concerning Desdemona in his sleep, and that depended entirely upon the assertion

imitations at times rendered Johnson abundantly ridiculous. Tom Davies monopolised his laugh, and his laugh was that of a rhinoceros!" He was the author of several works; and in 1826, just previous to his death, he published his "Literary and Miscellaneous Memoirs." Mr. Cradock was senior fellow of the Society of Antiquaries. He was born 1741-2, and died December 15, 1826.—ED.

[1] See an ingenious Essay on this subject by the late Dr. Moor, Greek professor of Glasgow.—BOSWELL.

of one man.   No, Sir, I think Othello has more moral than almost any play."

Talking of a penurious gentleman of our acquaintance, Johnson said, "Sir, he is narrow, not so much from avarice, as from impotence to spend his money.   He cannot find in his heart to pour out a bottle of wine: but he would not much care if it should sour."

He said he wished to see John Dennis's critical works collected.   Davies said they would not sell.   Dr. Johnson seemed to think otherwise.

Davies said of a well-known dramatic author, that "he lived upon *potted stories*, and that he made his way as Hannibal did, by vinegar; having begun by attacking people; particularly the players."

He reminded Dr. Johnson of Mr. Murphy's having paid him the highest compliment that ever was paid to a layman, by asking his pardon for repeating some oaths in the course of telling a story.

Johnson and I supped this evening at the Crown and Anchor tavern, in company with Sir Joshua Reynolds, Mr. Langton, Mr. Nairne, now one of the Scotch judges, with the title of Lord Dunsinan, and my very worthy friend, Sir William Forbes,[1] of Pitsligo.

We discussed the question whether drinking improved conversation and benevolence.   Sir Joshua maintained it did.   JOHNSON : "No, Sir, before dinner men meet with great inequality of understanding; and those who are conscious of their inferiority have the modesty not to talk.   When they have drunk wine, every man feels himself happy, and loses that modesty, and grows impudent and vociferous: but he is not improved: he is only not sensible of his defects."   Sir Joshua said the Doctor was talking of the effects of excess in wine; but that a moderate glass enlivened the mind, by giving a proper circulation to the blood. "I am," said he, "in very good spirits, when I get up in the morning.   By dinner-time I am exhausted; wine puts me in the same state as when I got up; and I am sure that moderate drinking makes people talk better."   JOHNSON : "No, Sir, wine gives not light, gay, ideal hilarity; but tumultuous, noisy, clamorous merriment.   I have heard none of those drunken—nay, drunken is a coarse word— none of those *vinous* flights."   SIR JOSHUA : "Because you

[1] Sir W. Forbes was the founder, in conjunction with Sir J. H. Blair, of the first banking establishment in Edinburgh.   He was an early member of the celebrated Literary Club, of which Dr. Johnson, Sir Joshua Reynolds, Garrick, and Burke, were distinguished associates. He was born at Pitsligo in 1739, and died in 1806.—ED.

have sat by, quite sober, and felt an envy of the happiness of those who were drinking." JOHNSON: "Perhaps contempt. And, Sir, it is not necessary to be drunk one's self to relish the wit of drunkenness. Do we not judge of the drunken wit, and of the dialogue between Iago and Cassio, the most excellent in its kind, when we are quite sober? Wit is wit, by whatever means it is produced; and, if good, will appear so at all times. I admit that the spirits are raised by drinking, as by the common participation of any pleasure: cock-fighting or bear-baiting will raise the spirits of a company as drinking does, though surely they will not improve conversation. I also admit, that there are some sluggish men who are improved by drinking; as there are fruits which are not good till they are rotten. There are such men, but they are medlars. I indeed allow that there have been a very few men of talents who were improved by drinking; but I maintain that I am right as to the effects of drinking in general: and let it be considered, that there is no position, however false in its universality, which is not true of some particular man." Sir William Forbes said, "Might not a man warmed with wine be like a bottle of beer, which is made brisker by being set before the fire?" "Nay," said Johnson laughing, "I cannot answer that: that is too much for me."

I observed that wine did some people harm, by inflaming, confusing, and irritating their minds; but that the experience of mankind had declared in favour of moderate drinking. JOHNSON: "Sir, I do not say it is wrong to produce self-complacency by drinking; I only deny that it improves the mind. When I drank wine I scorned to drink it when in company. I have drunk many a bottle by myself; in the first place, because I had need of it to raise my spirits; in the second place, because I would have nobody to witness its effects upon me."

He told us, "almost all his Ramblers were written just as they were wanted for the press; that he sent a certain portion of the copy of an essay, and wrote the remainder, while the former part of it was printing. When it was wanted, and he had fairly sat down to it, he was sure it would be done."

He said, that for general improvement a man should read whatever his immediate inclination prompts him to; though, to be sure, if a man has a science to learn, he must regularly and resolutely advance. He added, "What we read with inclination makes a much stronger impression. If we read without inclination, half the mind is employed in fixing the attention; so there is but one half to be em·

ployed on what we read." He told us he read Fielding's "Amelia" through without stopping.[1] He said, "If a man begins to read in the middle of a book, and feels an inclination to go on, let him not quit it, to go to the beginning. He may perhaps not feel again the inclination."

Sir Joshua mentioned Mr. Cumberland's Odes, which were just published. JOHNSON: "Why, Sir, they would have been thought as good as odes commonly are, if Cumberland had not put his name to them; but a name immediately draws censure, unless it be a name that bears down everything before it. Nay, Cumberland has made his odes subsidiary to the fame of another man.[2] They might have run well enough by themselves; but he has not only loaded them with a name, but has made them carry double."

We talked of the Reviews, and Dr. Johnson spoke of them as he did at Thrale's. Sir Joshua said, what I have often thought, that he wondered to find so much good writing employed in them, when the authors were to remain unknown, and so could not have the motive of fame. JOHNSON: "Nay, Sir, those who write in them write well in order to be paid well."

Soon after this day he went to Bath with Mr. and Mrs. Thrale. I had never seen that beautiful city, and wished to take the opportunity of visiting it, while Johnson was there. Having written to him, I received the following answer:—

"TO JAMES BOSWELL, ESQ.

"DEAR SIR,

"Why do you talk of neglect? When did I neglect you? If you will come to Bath we shall all be glad to see you. Come, therefore, as soon as you can.

"But I have a little business for you at London. Bid Francis look in the paper drawer of the chest of drawers in my bed-chamber, for two cases; one for the Attorney-General, and one for the Solicitor-General. They lie, I think, at the top of my papers; otherwise they are somewhere else, and will give me more trouble.

"Please to write to me immediately, if they can be found. Make my compliments to all our friends round the world, and to Mrs. Williams at home.

"I am, Sir, yours, &c.,
"SAM. JOHNSON."

"Search for the papers as soon as you can, that, if it is necessary, I may write to you again before you come down."

[1] We have here an involuntary testimony to the excellence of this admirable writer, to whom we have seen that Dr. Johnson *directly* allowed so little merit.—BOSWELL.
[2] Mr. Romney, the painter, who has now deservedly established a high reputation.—BOSWELL.

CHAPTER II.—1776

ON the 26th of April I went to Bath; and, on my arrival
at the Pelican inn, found lying for me an obliging invitation
from Mr. and Mrs. Thrale, by whom I was agreeably entertained almost constantly during my stay. They were gone
to the rooms; but there was a kind note from Dr. Johnson,
that he should sit at home all the evening. I went to him
directly, and before Mr. and Mrs. Thrale returned, we had
by ourselves some hours of tea-drinking and talk.

I shall group together such of his sayings as I preserved
during the few days that I was at Bath.

Of a person who differed from him in politics, he said,
" In private life he is a very honest gentleman; but I will not
allow him to be so in public life. People *may* be honest,
though they are doing wrong: that is between their Maker
and them. But *we*, who are suffering by their pernicious
conduct, are to destroy them. We are sure that [——] acts
from interest. We know what his genuine principles were.
They who allow their passions to confound the distinctions
between right and wrong, are criminal. They may be
convinced: but they have not come honestly by their
conviction."

It having been mentioned, I know not with what truth,

that a certain female political writer, whose doctrines he disliked, had of late become very fond of dress, sat hours together at her toilet, and even put on rouge:—JOHNSON: "She is better employed at her toilet than using her pen. It is better she should be reddening her own cheeks, than blackening other people's characters."

He told us that "Addison wrote Budgell's[1] papers in 'The Spectator,' at least mended them so much, that he made them almost his own; and that Draper, Tonson's partner, assured Mrs. Johnson, that the much admired Epilogue to 'The Distressed Mother,' which came out in Budgell's name, was in reality written by Addison."

"The mode of government by one may be ill adapted to a small society, but is best for a great nation. The characteristic of our own government at present is imbecility. The magistrates dare not call the guards for fear of being hanged. The guards will not come for fear of being given up to the blind rage of popular juries."

Of the father of one of our friends, he observed, "He never clarified his notions, by filtrating them through other minds. He had a canal upon his estate, where at one place the bank was too low.—'I dug the canal deeper,' said he."

He told me that "so long ago as 1748 he had read 'The Grave, a Poem,'[2] but did not like it much." I differed from him; for though it is not equal throughout, and is seldom elegantly correct, it abounds in solemn thought and poetical imagery beyond the common reach. The world has differed from him; for the poem has passed through many editions, and is still much read by people of a serious cast of mind.

A literary lady of large fortune was mentioned, as one

---

[1] Eustace Budgell was born at Exeter in 1685, and was honoured with the friendship of Addison and other literary characters of his day. He wrote numerous papers in "The Guardian," and other periodicals. One of his principal works was his "Memoirs of the Boyles." He committed suicide in 1737.—ED.

[2] I am sorry that there are no memoirs of the Reverend Robert Blair, the author of this poem. He was the representative of the ancient family of Blair, of Blair, in Ayrshire, but the estate had descended to a female, and afterwards passed to the son of her husband by another marriage. He was minister of the parish of Athelstaneford, where Mr. John Home was his successor; so that it may truly be called classic ground. His son, who is of the same name, and a man eminent for talents and learning, is now, with universal approbation, Solicitor-General of Scotland.—BOSWELL.

Since Boswell wrote, several memoirs of Mr. Blair have appeared. One will be found in the Popular Scottish Biography, by William Anderson, 1842.

who did good to many, but by no means "by stealth;" and instead of "blushing to find it fame," acted evidently from vanity. JOHNSON: "I have seen no beings who do as much good from benevolence, as she does from whatever motive. If there are such under the earth, or in the clouds, I wish they would come up or come down. What Soame Jenyns says upon this subject is not to be minded; he is a wit. No, Sir; to act from pure benevolence is not possible for finite beings. Human benevolence is mingled with vanity, interest, or some other motive."

He would not allow me to praise a lady then at Bath; observing, "She does not gain upon me, Sir; I think her empty-headed." He was, indeed, a stern critic upon characters and manners. Even Mrs. Thrale did not escape his friendly animadversion at times. When he and I were one day endeavouring to ascertain, article by article, how one of our friends could possibly spend as much money in his family as he told us he did, she interrupted us by a lively extravagant sally, on the expense of clothing his children, describing it in a very ludicrous and fanciful manner. Johnson looked a little angry, and said, "Nay, madam, when you are declaiming, declaim; and when you are calculating, calculate." At another time, when she said, perhaps affectedly, " I don't like to fly."—JOHNSON: "With *your* wings, madam, you *must* fly: but have a care, there are *clippers* abroad." How very well was this said, and how fully has experience proved the truth of it; but have they not *clipped* rather *rudely*, and gone a great deal *closer* than was necessary?

A gentleman expressed a wish to go and live three years at Otaheité, or New Zealand, in order to obtain a full acquaintance with people so totally different from all that we have ever known, and be satisfied what pure nature can do for man. JOHNSON: "What could you learn, Sir? What can savages tell, but what they themselves have seen? Of the past, or the invisible, they can tell nothing. The inhabitants of Otaheité and New Zealand are not in a state of pure nature; for it is plain they broke off from some other people. Had they grown out of the ground you might have judged of a state of pure nature. Fanciful people may talk of a mythology being amongst them; but it must be invention. They have once had religion, which has been gradually debased. And what account of their religion can you suppose to be learnt from savages? Only consider, Sir, our own state. Our religion is in a book; we have an order of men whose duty it is to teach it; we have one day in the week set apart for it, and this is in general pretty

well observed; yet ask the first ten gross men you meet, and
hear what they can tell of their religion."

On Monday, April 29, he and I made an excursion to
Bristol, where I was entertained with seeing him inquire
upon the spot into the authenticity of *"Rowley's* poetry,"[1]
as I had seen him inquire upon the spot into the authenticity
of *"Ossian's* poetry." George Catcot, the pewterer, who
was as zealous for Rowley as Hugh Blair was for *Ossian*
(I trust my reverend friend will excuse the comparison),
attended us at our inn, and with a triumphant air of lively
simplicity, called out, "I'll make Dr. Johnson a convert."
Dr. Johnson, at his desire, read aloud some of Chatterton's
fabricated verses, while Catcot stood at the back of his
chair, moving himself like a pendulum, and beating time
with his feet, and now and then looking into Dr. Johnson's
face, wondering that he was not yet convinced. We called
on Mr. Barret, the surgeon, and saw some of the *originals*, as
they were called, which were executed very artificially;
but from a careful inspection of them, and a consideration
of the circumstances with which they were attended, we
were quite satisfied of the imposture, which, indeed, has
been clearly demonstrated, from internal evidence, by
several able critics.[2]

Honest Catcot seemed to pay no attention whatever to
any objections, but insisted, as an end of all controversy,
that we should go with him to the tower of the church of
St. Mary Redcliff, and *view with our own eyes* the ancient
chest in which the manuscripts were found. To this, Dr.
Johnson good-naturedly agreed; and though troubled with
a shortness of breathing, laboured up a long flight of steps
till we came to the place where the wondrous chest stood.
"*There,*" said Catcot, with a bouncing confident credulity,
"*there* is the very chest itself." After this *ocular demonstration*, there was no more to be said. He brought to my
recollection a Scotch Highlander, a man of learning too, and
who had seen the world, attesting, and at the same time
giving his reasons for the authenticity of Fingal:—"I have
heard all that poem when I was young."—"Have you, Sir?
Pray what have you heard?"—"I have heard Ossian, Oscar,
and *every one of them.*"

Johnson said of Chatterton, "This is the most extraordinary young man that has encountered my knowledge.
It is wonderful how the whelp has written such things."

---

[1] The production of the poet Chatterton, who palmed it upon the
world as written by Rowley, a priest of Bristol in the fifteenth century.
—ED.

[2] Mr. Tyrwhitt, Mr. Warton, Mr. Malone.—BOSWELL.

We were by no means pleased with our inn at Bristol. "Let us see now," said I, "how we should describe it." Johnson was ready with his raillery. "Describe it, Sir? Why, it was so bad that Boswell wished to be in Scotland!"

After Dr. Johnson's return to London, I was several times with him at his house, where I occasionally slept in the room that had been assigned for me. I dined with him at Dr. Taylor's, at General Oglethorpe's, and at General Paoli's. To avoid a tedious minuteness, I shall group together what I have preserved of his conversation during this period also, without specifying each scene where it passed, except one, which will be found so remarkable as certainly to deserve a very particular relation. Where the place or the persons do not contribute to the zest of the conversation, it is unnecessary to encumber my page with mentioning them. To know of what vintage our wine is, enables us to judge of its value, and to drink it with more relish; but to have the produce of each vine of one vineyard, in the same year, kept separate, would serve no purpose. To know that our wine (to use an advertising phrase) is "of the stock of an Ambassador lately deceased," heightens its flavour; but it signifies nothing to know the bin where each bottle was once deposited.

"Garrick," he observed, "does not play the part of *Archer* in 'The Beaux Stratagem' well. The gentleman should break out through the footman, which is not the case as he does it."

"Where there is no education, as in savage countries, men will have the upper hand of women. Bodily strength, no doubt, contributes to this; but it would be so, exclusive of that; for it is mind that always governs. When it comes to dry understanding, man has the better."

"The little volumes entitled '*Respublicæ*,' which are very well done, were a bookseller's work."

"There is much talk of the misery which we cause to the brute creation; but they are recompensed by existence. If they were not useful to man, and therefore protected by him, they would not be nearly so numerous." This argument is to be found in the able and benignant Hutchinson's "Moral Philosophy." But the question is, whether the animals who endure such sufferings of various kinds for the service and entertainment of man, would accept of existence upon the terms on which they have it. Madame Sevigné, who, though she had many enjoyments, felt with delicate sensibility the prevalence of misery, complains of the task of existence having been imposed upon her without her consent.

"That man is never happy for the present is so true, that all his relief from unhappiness is only forgetting himself for a little while.   Life is a progress from want to want, not from enjoyment to enjoyment."

"Though many men are nominally entrusted with the administration of hospitals and other public institutions, almost all the good is done by one man, by whom the rest are driven on; owing to confidence in him and indolence in them."

"Lord Chesterfield's Letters to his Son, I think, might be made a very pretty book.   Take out the immorality, and it should be put in the hands of every young gentleman. An elegant manner and easiness of behaviour are acquired gradually and imperceptibly.   No man can say 'I'll be genteel.'   There are ten genteel women for one genteel man, because they are more restrained.   A man without some degree of restraint is insufferable; but we are all less restrained than women.   Were a woman sitting in company to put out her legs before her as most men do, we should be tempted to kick them in."   No man was a more attentive and nice observer of behaviour in those in whose company he happened to be, than Johnson; or, however strange it may seem to many, had a higher estimation of its refinements.   Lord Eliot informs me, that one day when Johnson and he were at dinner in a gentleman's house in London, upon Lord Chesterfield's letters being mentioned, Johnson surprised the company by this sentence: "Every man of any education would rather be called a rascal than accused of deficiency in *the graces.*"   Mr. Gibbon, who was present, turned to a lady who knew Johnson well, and lived much with him, and in his quaint manner tapping his box, addressed her thus: "Don't you think, Madam (looking towards Johnson), that among *all* your acquaintance you could find *one* exception?"   The lady smiled, and seemed to acquiesce.

"I read," said he, "Sharpe's Letters on Italy over again, when I was at Bath.   There is a great deal of matter in them."

"Mrs. Williams was angry that Thrale's family did not send regularly to her every time they heard from me while I was in the Hebrides.   Little people are apt to be jealous; but they should not be jealous; for they ought to consider, that superior attention will necessarily be paid to superior fortune or rank.   Two persons may have equal merit, and on that account may have an equal claim to attention; but one of them may have also fortune and rank, and so may have a double claim."

Talking of his notes on Shakespeare, he said, "I despise those who do not see that I am right in the passage where *as* is repeated, and 'asses of great charge' introduced. That on 'To be, or not to be,' is disputable." [1]

A gentleman, whom I found sitting with him one morning, said, that in his opinion the character of an infidel was more detestable than that of a man notoriously guilty of an atrocious crime. I differed from him, because we are surer of the odiousness of the one than of the error of the other. JOHNSON: "Sir, I agree with him; for the infidel would be guilty of any crime if he were inclined to it."

"Many things which are false are transmitted from book to book, and gain credit in the world. One of these is the cry against the evil of luxury. Now the truth is, that luxury produces much good. Take the luxury of buildings in London. Does it not produce real advantage in the conveniency and elegance of accommodation, and this all from the exertion of industry? People will tell you, with a melancholy face, how many builders are in gaol. It is plain they are in gaol, not for building; for rents are not fallen.—A man gives half a guinea for a dish of green peas. How much gardening does this occasion? how many labourers must the competition to have such things early in the market keep in employment? You will hear it said very gravely, 'Why was not the half-guinea, thus spent in luxury, given to the poor? To how many might it have afforded a good meal.' Alas! has it not gone to the *industrious* poor, whom it is better to support than the *idle* poor? You are much surer that you are doing good when you *pay* money to those who work, as the recompense of their labour, than when you *give* money merely in charity. Suppose the ancient luxury of a dish of peacock's brains were to be revived, how many carcases would be left to the poor at a cheap rate; and as to the rout that is made about people who are ruined by extravagance, it is no matter to the nation that some individuals suffer. When so much general productive exertion is the consequence of luxury, the nation does not care though there are debtors in gaol; nay, they would not care though their creditors were there too!"

The uncommon vivacity of General Oglethorpe's mind,

[1] It may be observed, that Mr. Malone, in his very valuable edition of Shakespeare, has fully vindicated Dr. Johnson from the idle censures which the first of these notes has given rise to. The interpretation of the other passage, which Dr. Johnson allows to be *disputable*, he has clearly shown to be erroneous.—BOSWELL.

and variety of knowledge, having sometimes made his conversation seem too desultory, Johnson observed, "Oglethorpe, Sir, never *completes* what he has to say."

He on the same account made a similar remark on Patrick Lord Elibank: "Sir, there is nothing *conclusive* in his talk."

When I complained of having dined at a splendid table without hearing one sentence of conversation worthy of being remembered, he said, "Sir, there seldom is any such conversation." Boswell: "Why then meet at table?" Johnson: "Why to eat and drink together, and to promote kindness; and, Sir, this is better done where there is no solid conversation; for when there is, people differ in opinion, and get into bad humour, or some of the company, who are not capable of such conversation, are left out, and feel themselves uneasy. It was for this reason, Sir Robert Walpole said, he always talked bawdy at his table, because in that all could join."

Being irritated by hearing a gentleman ask Mr. Levett a variety of questions concerning him when he was sitting by, he broke out, "Sir, you have but two topics, yourself and me. I am sick of both. A man," said he, "should not talk of himself, nor much of any particular person. He should take care not to be made a proverb; and therefore should avoid having any one topic of which people can say, 'We shall hear him upon it.' There was a Dr. Oldfield, who was always talking of the Duke of Marlborough. He came into a coffee-house one day, and told that his Grace had spoken in the House of Lords for half an hour. 'Did he indeed speak for half an hour?' said Belchier, the surgeon.—'Yes,'—'And what did he say of Dr. Oldfield?' —'Nothing'—'Why, then, Sir, he was very ungrateful; for Dr. Oldfield could not have spoken for a quarter of an hour, without saying something of him.'"

"Every man is to take existence on the terms on which it is given to him. To some men it is given on condition of not taking liberties, which other men may take without much harm. One may drink wine, and be nothing the worse for it; on another, wine may have effects so inflammatory as to injure him both in body and mind, and perhaps make him commit something for which he may deserve to be hanged."

"Lord Hailes's 'Annals of Scotland' have not that painted form which is the taste of this age; but it is a book which will always sell, it has such a stability of dates, such a certainty of facts, and such a punctuality of citation. I never before read Scotch history with certainty."

I asked him whether he would advise me to read the Bible with a commentary, and what commentaries he would recommend. JOHNSON: "To be sure, Sir, I would have you read the Bible with a commentary; and I would recommend Lowth and Patrick on the Old Testament, and Hammond on the New."

During my stay in London this spring, I solicited his attention to another law case, in which I was engaged. In the course of a contested election for the borough of Dunfermline, which I attended as one of my friend Colonel (afterwards Sir Archibald) Campbell's counsel, one of his political agents, who was charged with having been unfaithful to his employer, and having deserted to the opposite party for a pecuniary reward, attacked very rudely, in a newspaper, the Rev. Mr. James Thomson, one of the ministers of that place, on account of a supposed allusion to him in one of his sermons. Upon this the minister, on a subsequent Sunday, arraigned him by name from the pulpit with some severity; and the agent, after the sermon was over, rose up and asked the minister aloud, "What bribe he had received for telling so many lies from the chair of verity." I was present at this very extraordinary scene. The person arraigned, and his father and brother, who also had a share both of the reproof from the pulpit, and in the retaliation, brought an action against Mr. Thomson, in the Court of Session, for defamation and damages, and I was one of the counsel for the reverend defendant. The *liberty of the pulpit* was our great ground of defence; but we argued also on the provocation of the previous attack, and on the instant retaliation. The Court of Session, however —the fifteen judges, who are at the same time the jury— decided against the minister contrary to my humble opinion; and several of them expressed themselves with indignation against him. He was an aged gentleman, formerly a military chaplain, and a man of high spirit and honour. Johnson was satisfied that the judgment was wrong, and dictated to me the following argument in confutation of it:—

"Of the censure pronounced from the pulpit, our determination must be formed, as in other cases, by a consideration of the act itself, and the particular circumstances with which it is invested.

"The right of censure and rebuke seems necessarily appendant to the pastoral office. He, to whom the care of a congregation is intrusted, is considered as the shepherd of a flock, as the teacher of a school, as the father of a family. As a shepherd tending not his own sheep, but those of his master, he is answerable for those that stray, and those that lose themselves by straying. But no man can be answerable for losses which he has not power to prevent, or for vagrancy which he has not authority to restrain.

"As a teacher giving instruction for wages, and liable to reproach, if those whom he undertakes to inform make no proficiency, he must have the power of enforcing attendance, of awakening negligence, and repressing contradiction.

"As a father, he possesses the paternal authority of admonition, rebuke, and punishment. He cannot, without reducing his office to an empty name, be hindered from the exercise of any practice necessary to stimulate the idle, to reform the vicious, to check the petulant, and correct the stubborn.

"If we inquire into the practice of the primitive church, we shall, I believe, find the ministers of the word exercising the whole authority of this complicated character. We shall find them not only encouraging the good by exhortation, but terrifying the wicked by reproof and denunciation. In the earliest ages of the church, while religion was yet pure from secular advantages, the punishment of sinners was public censure, and open penance; penalties inflicted merely by ecclesiastical authority, at a time while the church had yet no help from the civil power; while the hand of the magistrate lifted only the rod of persecution; and when governors were ready to afford a refuge to all those who fled from clerical authority.

"That the church, therefore, had once a power of public censure is evident, because that power was frequently exercised. That it borrowed not its power from the civil authority, is likewise certain, because civil authority was at that time its enemy.

"The hour came at length, when, after three hundred years of struggle and distress, truth took possession of imperial power, and the civil laws lent their aid to the ecclesiastical constitutions. The magistrate from that time co-operated with the priest, and clerical sentences were made efficacious by secular force. But the State, when it came to the assistance of the church, had no intention to diminish its authority. Those rebukes and those censures which were lawful before were lawful still. But they had hitherto operated only upon voluntary submission. The refractory and contemptuous were at first in no danger of temporal severities, except what they might suffer from the reproaches of conscience, or the detestation of their fellow Christians. When religion obtained the support of

law, if admonitions and censures had no effect, they
were seconded by the magistrates with coercion and
punishment.

"It therefore appears, from ecclesiastical history, that
the right of inflicting shame by public censure has been
always considered as inherent in the church; and that this
right was not conferred by the civil power; for it was
exercised when the civil power operated against it. By
the civil power it was never taken away; for the Christian
magistrate interposed his office, not to rescue sinners from
censure, but to supply more powerful means of reformation;
to add pain where shame was insufficient; and when men
were proclaimed unworthy of the society of the faithful,
to restrain them by imprisonment, from spreading abroad
the contagion of wickedness.

"It is not improbable that from this acknowledged
power of public censure, grew in time the practice of
auricular confession. Those who dreaded the blast of
public reprehension, were willing to submit themselves to
the priest, by a private accusation of themselves; and to
obtain a reconciliation with the church by a kind of clan-
destine absolution and invisible penance; conditions with
which the priest would, in times of ignorance and corruption, easily comply, as they increased his influence, by
adding the knowledge of secret sins to that of notorious
offences, and enlarged his authority, by making him the
sole arbiter of the terms of reconcilement.

"From this bondage the Reformation set us free. The
minister has no longer power to press into the retirements
of conscience, to torture us by interrogatories, or put
himself in possession of our secrets and our lives. But
though we have thus controlled his usurpations, his just
and original power remains unimpaired. He may still
see, though he may not pry: he may yet hear, though he
may not question. And that knowledge which his eyes
and ears force upon him it is still his duty to use, for the
benefit of his flock. A father who lives near a wicked
neighbour may forbid his son to frequent his company.
A minister who has in his congregation a man of open and
scandalous wickedness may warn his parishioners to shun
his conversation. To warn them is not only lawful, but
not to warn them would be criminal. He may warn
them one by one in friendly converse, or by a parochial
visitation. But if he may warn each man singly, what
shall forbid him to warn them all together? Of that
which is to be made known to all, how is there any difference whether it be communicated to each singly, or to all

together? What is known to all, must necessarily be public. Whether it shall be public at once, or public by degrees, is the only question. And of a sudden and solemn publication the impression is deeper, and the warning more effectual.

"It may easily be urged, if a minister be thus left at liberty to delate sinners from the pulpit, and to publish at will the crimes of a parishioner, he may often blast the innocent and distress the timorous. He may be suspicious, and condemn without evidence; he may be rash, and judge without examination; he may be severe, and treat slight offences with too much harshness; he may be malignant and partial, and gratify his private interest or resentment under the shelter of his pastoral character.

"Of all this, there is possibility, and of all this there is danger. But if possibility of evil be to exclude good, no good ever can be done. If nothing is to be attempted in which there is danger, we must all sink into hopeless inactivity. The evils that may be feared from this practice arise not from any defect in the institution, but from the infirmities of human nature. Power, in whatever hands it is placed, will be sometimes improperly exerted; yet courts of law must judge, though they will sometimes judge amiss. A father must instruct his children, though he himself may often want instruction. A minister must censure sinners, though his censure may be sometimes erroneous by want of judgment, and sometimes unjust by want of honesty.

"If we examine the circumstances of the present case, we shall find the sentence neither erroneous nor unjust; we shall find no breach of private confidence, no intrusion into secret transactions. The fact was notorious and indubitable; so easy to be proved, that no proof was desired. The act was base and treacherous, the perpetration insolent and open, and the example naturally mischievous. The minister, however, being retired and recluse, had not yet heard what was publicly known throughout the parish; and on occasion of a public election, warned his people, according to his duty, against the crimes which public elections frequently produce. His warning was felt by one of his parishioners, as pointed particularly at himself. But instead of producing, as might be wished, private compunction and immediate reformation, it kindled only rage and resentment. He charged his minister, in a public paper, with scandal, defamation, and falsehood. The minister, thus reproached, had his own character to vindicate, upon which his pastoral authority must necessarily depend. To be charged with a defamatory lie is an injury which no man patiently endures in common life. To be charged with polluting the pastoral office with scandal and falsehood, was a violation of character still more atrocious, as it affected not only his personal but his clerical veracity. His indignation naturally rose in proportion to his honesty, and with all the fortitude of injured honesty, he dared his calumniator in the church, and at once exonerated himself from censure, and rescued his flock from deception and from danger. The man whom he accuses pretends not to be innocent; or at least only pretends; for he declines a trial. The crime of which he is accused has frequent opportunities and strong temptations. It has already spread far, with much depravation of private morals, and much injury to public happiness. To warn the people, therefore, against it was not wanton and officious, but necessary and pastoral.

"What then is the fault with which this worthy minister is charged? He has usurped no dominion over conscience. He has exerted no authority in support of doubtful and controverted opinions. He has not dragged into light a bashful and corrigible sinner. His censure was directed against a breach of morality, against an act which no man justifies. The man who appropriated this censure to himself, is evidently and notoriously guilty. His consciousness of his own wickedness incited him to attack his faithful reprover with open insolence and printed accusations. Such an attack made defence necessary; and we hope it will be at last decided that the means of defence were just and lawful."

When I read this to Mr. Burke, he was highly pleased, and exclaimed, "Well; he does his work in a workman-like manner." [1]

Mr. Thomson wished to bring the cause by appeal before the House of Lords, but was dissuaded by the advice of the noble person who lately presided so ably in that Most Honourable House, and who was then Attorney-General. As my readers will no doubt be glad also to read the opinion of this eminent man upon the same subject, I shall here insert it.

[1] As a proof of Dr. Johnson's extraordinary powers of composition, it appears from the original manuscript of this excellent dissertation, of which he dictated the first eight paragraphs on the 10th of May, and the remainder on the 13th, that there are in the whole only seven corrections, or rather variations, and those not considerable. Such were at once the vigorous and accurate emanations of his mind.— BOSWELL.

Case.

"There is herewith laid before you,
  "1.   Petition for the Reverend Mr. James Thomson, minister
         of Dunfermline.
  "2.   Answers thereto.
  "3.   Copy of the judgment of the Court of Session upon both.
  "4.   Notes of the opinions of the Judges, being the reasons
         upon which their decree is grounded.
"These papers you will please to peruse, and give your opinion,
  "Whether there is a probability of the above decree of the
         Court of Session's being reversed, if Mr. Thomson should
         appeal from the same?"

"I don't think the appeal advisable: not only because the
value of the judgment is in no degree adequate to the expense;
but because there are many chances, that upon the general complexion of the case, the impression will be taken to the disadvantage
of the appellant.

"It is impossible to approve the style of that sermon. But
the *complaint* was not less ungracious from that man, who had
behaved so ill by his original libel, and, at the time, when he
received the reproach he complains of. In the last article all the
plaintiffs are equally concerned. It struck me also with some
wonder, that the Judges should think so much fervour apposite to
the occasion of reproving the defendant for a little excess.

"Upon the matter, however, I agree with them in condemning
the behaviour of the minister; and in thinking it a subject fit for
ecclesiastical censure; and even for an action, if any individual
could qualify [1] a wrong, and a damage arising from it. But this I
doubt. The circumstance of publishing the reproach in a pulpit,
though extremely indecent, and culpable in another view, does
not constitute a different sort of wrong, or any other rule of law,
than would have obtained, if the same words had been pronounced
elsewhere. I don't know whether there be any difference in the
law of Scotland, in the definition of slander, before the Commissaries,
or the Court of Session. The common law of England does not
give way to actions for every reproachful word. An action cannot
be brought for general damages, upon any words which import
less than an offence cognizable by law; consequently, no action
could have been brought here, for the words in question. Both
laws admit the truth to be a justification in action *for words ;* and
the law of England does the same in actions for libels. The judgment, therefore, seems to me to have been wrong, in that the
Court repelled that defence.

                                          "E. Thurlow."

I am now to record a very curious incident in Dr.
Johnson's life, which fell under my observation; of which

---

[1] It is curious to observe that Lord Thurlow has here, perhaps in
compliment to North Britain, made use of a term of the Scotch Law,
which to an English reader may require explanation. To *qualify* a
wrong is to point out and establish it.—Boswell.

pars magna fui, and which I am persuaded will, with the liberal-minded, be much to his credit.

My desire of being acquainted with celebrated men of every description, had made me, much about the same time, obtain an introduction to Dr. Samuel Johnson, and to John Wilkes, Esq.[1] Two men more different could perhaps not be selected out of mankind. They had even attacked one another with some asperity in their writings; yet I lived in habits of friendship with both. I could fully relish the excellence of each; for I have ever delighted in that intellectual chemistry which can separate good qualities from evil in the same person.

Sir John Pringle, "mine own friend and my father's friend," between whom and Dr. Johnson I in vain wished to establish an acquaintance, as I respected and lived in intimacy with both of them, observed to me once, very ingeniously, "It is not in friendship as in mathematics, where two things, each equal to a third, are equal between themselves. You agree with Johnson as a middle quality, and you agree with me as a middle quality; but Johnson and I should not agree." Sir John was not sufficiently flexible—so I desisted; knowing, indeed, that the repulsion was equally strong on the part of Johnson; who, I know not from what cause, unless his being a Scotchman, had formed a very erroneous opinion of Sir John. But I conceived an irresistible wish, if possible, to bring Dr. Johnson and Mr. Wilkes together. How to manage it was a nice and difficult matter.

My worthy booksellers and friends, Messieurs Dilly in the Poultry, at whose hospitable and well-covered table I have seen a greater number of literary men, than at any other, except that of Sir Joshua Reynolds, had invited me to meet Mr. Wilkes and some other gentlemen, on Wednesday, May 15. "Pray," said I, "let us have Dr. Johnson."—"What, with Mr. Wilkes? Not for the world," said Mr. Edward Dilly; "Dr. Johnson would never forgive me."—"Come," said I, "if you'll let me negociate for you, I will be answerable that all shall go well." DILLY: "Nay, if you will take it upon you, I am sure I shall be very happy to see them both here."

Notwithstanding the high veneration which I entertained for Dr. Johnson, I was sensible that he was sometimes a little actuated by the spirit of contradiction, and

[1] Alderman and Lord Mayor of London, M.P. for Middlesex, and the proprietor of "The North Briton." His violent opposition to the government led to the abolition of general warrants. He was born in 1727, and died in 1797—ED.

by means of that I hoped I should gain my point.   I was persuaded, that if I had come upon him with a direct proposal, "Sir, will you dine in company with Jack Wilkes?" he would have flown into a passion, and would probably have answered, "Dine with Jack Wilkes, Sir, I'd as soon dine with Jack Ketch."[1]   I therefore, while we were sitting quietly by ourselves at his house in an evening, took occasion to open my plan thus:—"Mr. Dilly, Sir, sends his respectful compliments to you, and would be happy if you would do him the honour to dine with him on Wednesday next along with me, as I must soon go to Scotland."   Johnson: "Sir, I am obliged to Mr. Dilly. I will wait upon him.—"   Boswell: "Provided, Sir, I suppose, that the company which he is to have is agreeable to you."   Johnson: "What do you mean, Sir?   What do you take me for?   Do you think that I am so ignorant of the world, as to imagine that I am to prescribe to a gentleman what company he is to have at his table?"   Boswell: "I beg your pardon, Sir, for wishing to prevent you from meeting people whom you might not like. Perhaps he may have some of what he calls his patriotic friends with him."   Johnson: "Well, Sir, and what then? What care *I* for his *patriotic friends?*   Poh!"   Boswell: "I should not be surprised to find Jack Wilkes there." Johnson: "And if Jack Wilkes *should* be there, what is that to *me*, Sir?   My dear friend, let us have no more of this.   I am sorry to be angry with you; but really it is treating me strangely to talk to me as if I could not meet any company whatever, occasionally."   Boswell: "Pray forgive me, Sir: I meant well.   But you shall meet whoever comes, for me."   Thus I secured him, and told Dilly that he would find him very well pleased to be one of his guests on the day appointed.

Upon the much-expected Wednesday, I called on him about half an hour before dinner, as I often did when we were to dine out together, to see that he was ready in time, and to accompany him.   I found him buffeting his books as upon a former occasion, covered with dust, and making no preparation for going abroad.   "How is this, Sir?" said I.   "Don't you recollect that you are to dine at Mr. Dilly's?"   Johnson: "Sir, I did not think of going to Dilly's: it went out of my head.   I have ordered dinner at home with Mrs. Williams."   Boswell: "But, my dear Sir, you know you were engaged to Mr. Dilly, and I told

---

[1] This has been circulated as if actually said by Johnson: when the truth is, it was only *supposed* by me.—Boswell.

him so. He will expect you, and will be much disappointed if you don't come." JOHNSON: "You must talk to Mrs. Williams about this."

Here was a sad dilemma. I feared that what I was so confident I had secured would yet be frustrated. He had accustomed himself to show Mrs. Williams such a degree of humane attention, as frequently imposed some restraint upon him; and I knew that if she should be obstinate, he would not stir. I hastened down stairs to the blind lady's room, and told her I was in great uneasiness, for Dr. Johnson had engaged to me to dine this day at Mr. Dilly's, but that he had told me he had forgotten his engagement, and had ordered dinner at home. "Yes, Sir," said she, pretty peevishly, "Dr. Johnson is to dine at home."—"Madam," said I, "his respect for you is such, that I know he will not leave you, unless you absolutely desire it. But as you have so much of his company, I hope you will be good enough to forego it for a day; as Mr. Dilly is a very worthy man, has frequently had agreeable parties at his house for Dr. Johnson, and will be vexed if the Doctor neglects him to-day. And then, Madam, be pleased to consider my situation; I carried the message, and I assured Mr. Dilly that Dr. Johnson was to come; and no doubt he has made a dinner, and invited a company, and boasted of the honour he expected to have. I shall be quite disgraced if the Doctor is not there." She gradually softened to my solicitations, which were certainly as earnest as most entreaties to ladies upon any occasion, and was graciously pleased to empower me to tell Dr. Johnson, "That all things considered, she thought he should certainly go." I flew back to him, still in dust, and careless of what should be the event, "indifferent in his choice to go or stay;" but as soon as I had announced to him Mrs. Williams's consent, he roared, "Frank! a clean shirt"—and was very soon drest. When I had him fairly seated in a hackney-coach with me, I exulted as much as a fortune-hunter, who has got an heiress into a post-chaise with him, to set out for Gretna Green.

When we entered Mr. Dilly's drawing-room, he found himself in the midst of a company he did not know. I kept myself snug and silent, watching how he would conduct himself. I observed him whispering to Mr. Dilly, "Who is that gentleman, Sir?"—"Mr. Arthur Lee."—JOHNSON: "Too, too, too," (under his breath,) which was one of his habitual mutterings. Mr. Arthur Lee could not but be very obnoxious to Johnson, for he was not only a *patriot* but an *American*. He was afterwards minister from the United States at the Court of Madrid. "And who is the gentleman in lace?"—"Mr. Wilkes, Sir." This information confounded him still more; he had some difficulty to restrain himself, and taking up a book sat down upon a window-seat and read, or at least kept his eye intently upon it for some time, till he composed himself. His feelings, I dare say, were awkward enough. But he no doubt recollected having rated me, for supposing that he could be at all disconcerted by any company, and he, therefore, resolutely set himself to behave quite as an easy man of the world, who could adapt himself at once to the disposition and manners of those whom he might chance to meet.

The cheering sound of "Dinner is upon the table," dissolved his reverie, and we *all* sat down without any symptom of ill-humour. There were present—beside Mr. Wilkes, and Mr. Arthur Lee, who was an old companion of mine when he studied physic at Edinburgh—Mr. (now Sir John) Muller, Dr. Lettsom, and Mr. Slater the druggist. Mr. Wilkes placed himself next to Dr. Johnson, and behaved to him with so much attention and politeness, that he gained upon him insensibly. No man eat more heartily than Johnson, or loved better what was nice and delicate. Mr. Wilkes was very assiduous in helping him to some fine veal. "Pray give me leave, Sir;—It is better here—A little of the brown—Some fat, Sir—A little of the stuffing—Some gravy—Let me have the pleasure of giving you some butter—Allow me to recommend a squeeze of this orange; or the lemon, perhaps, may have more zest." —"Sir, Sir, I am obliged to you, Sir," cried Johnson, bowing, and turning his head to him with a look for some time of "surly virtue,"[1] but, in a short while, of complacency.

Foote being mentioned, Johnson said, "He is not a good mimic." One of the company added, "A merry Andrew, a buffoon!" JOHNSON: "But he has wit, too, and is not deficient in ideas, or in fertility and variety of imagery, and not empty of reading; he has knowledge enough to fill up his part. One species of wit he has in an eminent degree, that of escape. You drive him into a corner with both hands; but he's gone, Sir, when you think you have got him—like an animal that jumps over your head. Then he has a great range for wit; he never lets truth stand between him and a jest, and he is sometimes mighty coarse. Garrick is under many restraints from

[1] Johnson's "London, a Poem," v. 145.—BOSWELL.

which Foote is free." WILKES: "Garrick's wit is more like Lord Chesterfield's." JOHNSON: "The first time I was in company with Foote, was at Fitzherbert's. Having no good opinion of the fellow, I was resolved not to be pleased; and it is very difficult to please a man against his will. I went on eating my dinner pretty sullenly, affecting not to mind him; but the dog was so very comical, that I was obliged to lay down my knife and fork, throw myself back upon my chair, and fairly laugh it out. No, Sir, he was irresistible.[1] He upon one occasion experienced, in an extraordinary degree, the efficacy of his powers of entertaining. Amongst the many and various modes which he tried of getting money, he became a partner with a small-beer brewer, and he was to have a share of the profits for procuring customers amongst his numerous acquaintance. Fitzherbert was one who took his small-beer; but it was so bad that the servants resolved not to drink it. They were at some loss how to notify their resolution, being afraid of offending their master, who they knew liked Foote much as a companion. At last they fixed upon a little black boy, who was rather a favourite, to be their deputy, and deliver their remonstrance; and having invested him with the whole authority of the kitchen, he was to inform Mr. Fitzherbert, in all their names, upon a certain day, that they would drink Foote's small-beer no longer. On that day Foote happened to dine at Fitzherbert's, and this boy served at table; he was so delighted with Foote's stories, and merriment, and grimace, that when he went down stairs he told them, 'This is the finest man I have ever seen. I will not deliver your message. I will drink his small-beer.'"

Somebody observed, that Garrick could not have done this. WILKES: "Garrick would have made the small-beer still smaller. He is now leaving the stage; but he will play *Scrub* all his life." I knew that Johnson would let nobody attack Garrick but himself, as Garrick said to me, and I had heard him praise his liberality; so, to bring out his commendation of his celebrated pupil, I said, loudly, "I have heard Garrick is liberal." JOHNSON: "Yes, Sir, I know that Garrick has given away more money than any man in England that I am acquainted with, and that not from ostentatious views. Garrick was very poor when he began life; so when he came to have money, he probably was very unskilful in giving away, and saved when he

---

[1] Foote told me, that Johnson said to him, "For loud obstreperous broad-faced mirth, I know not his equal."—BOSWELL.

should not. But Garrick began to be liberal as soon as he could; and I am of opinion, the reputation of avarice, which he has had, has been very lucky for him, and prevented his having many enemies. You despise a man for avarice, but do not hate him. Garrick might have been much better attacked for living with more splendour than is suitable to a player: if they had had the wit to have assaulted him in that quarter, they might have galled him more. But they have kept clamouring about his avarice, which has rescued him from much obloquy and envy."

Talking of the great difficulty of obtaining authentic information for biography, Johnson told us, "When I was a young fellow I wanted to write the 'Life of Dryden,' and in order to get materials I applied to the only two persons then alive who had seen him; these were old Swinney,[1] and old Cibber. Swinney's information was no more than this, 'That at Will's coffee-house Dryden had a particular chair for himself, which was set by the fire in winter, and was then called his winter-chair; and it was carried out for him to the balcony in summer, and was then called his summer-chair.' Cibber could tell no more but 'That he remembered him a decent old man, arbiter of critical disputes at Will's.' You are to consider that Cibber was then at a great distance from Dryden, had, perhaps, one leg only in the room, and durst not draw in the other." BOSWELL: "But Cibber was a man of observation?" JOHNSON: "I think not." BOSWELL: "You will allow his 'Apology' to be well done." JOHNSON: "Very well done, to be sure. Sir. That book is a striking proof of the justice of Pope's remark:

'Each might his several province well command,
Would all but stoop to what they understand.'"

BOSWELL: "And his plays are good." JOHNSON: "Yes; but that was his trade; *l'esprit du corps ;* he had been all his life among players and play-writers. I wondered that he had so little to say in conversation, for he had kept the best company, and learnt all that can be got by the ear. He abused Pindar to me, and then showed me an ode of his own, with an absurd couplet making a linnet soar on an eagle's wing. I told him, that when the ancients made a simile, they always made it like something real."

[1] Owen McSwinney, who died in 1754, and bequeathed his fortune to Mrs. Woffington, the actress. He had been a manager of Drury-lane Theatre, and afterwards of the Queen's Theatre in the Haymarket. He was also a dramatic writer, having produced a comedy, entitled "The Quacks, or Love's the Physician," 1705, and two operas.—MALONE.

Mr. Wilkes remarked, that "among all the bold flights of Shakespeare's imagination, the boldest was making Birnam-wood march to Dunsinane, creating a wood where there never was a shrub; a wood in Scotland! ha! ha! ha!" And he also observed, that "the clannish slavery of the Highlands of Scotland was the single exception to Milton's remark of 'The Mountain Nymph, sweet Liberty,' being worshipped in all hilly countries. When I was at Inverary," said he, "on a visit to my old friend, Archibald Duke of Argyle, his dependants congratulated me on being such a favourite of his Grace. I said, 'It is, then, gentlemen, truly lucky for me; for if I had displeased the Duke, and he had wished it, there is not a Campbell among you but would have been ready to bring John Wilkes's head to him in a charger. It would have been only

'Off with his head! So much for *Aylesbury*.'

I was then member for Aylesbury."

Dr. Johnson and Mr. Wilkes talked of the contested passage in Horace's Art of Poetry, "*Difficile est propriè communia dicere.*" Mr. Wilkes, according to my note, gave the interpretation thus: "It is difficult to speak with propriety of common things; as, if a poet had to speak of Queen Caroline drinking tea, he must endeavour to avoid the vulgarity of cups and saucers." But upon reading my note, he tells me that he meant to say, that "the word *communia*, being a Roman law-term, signifies here things *communis juris*, that is to say, what have never yet been treated by any body; and this appears clearly from what followed,

"'————tuque
Rectius Iliacum carmen deducis in actus,
Quàm si proferres ignota indictaque primus.

You will easier make a tragedy out of the Iliad than on any subject not handled before." [1] JOHNSON: "He means

---

[1] My very pleasant friend himself, as well as others *who remember old stories*, will no doubt be surprised, when I observe that *John Wilkes* here shows himself to be of the WARBURTONIAN SCHOOL. It is nevertheless true, as appears from Dr. Hurd the Bishop of Worcester's very elegant commentary and notes on the "Epistola ad Pisones."

It is necessary to a fair consideration of the question, that the whole passage in which the words occur should be kept in view:—

"Si quid inexpertum scenæ committis, et audes
Personam formare novam; servetur ad imum
Qualis ab incœpto processerit, et sibi constet.
Difficile est propriè communia dicere: tuque
Rectius Iliacum carmen deducis in actus,

ROUND ROBIN,

SAMUEL JOHNSON, LL.D.,

WITH FAC-SIMILES OF THE SIGNATURES.

We the Circumscribers,

having read with great pleasure an intended Epitaph for the Monument of Dr. Goldsmith, which considered abstractedly appears to be, for elegant composition and masterly style, in every respect worthy of the pen of its learned Author, are yet of opinion, that the character of the Deceased as a Writer, particularly as a Poet, is perhaps not delineated with all the exactness which Dr. Johnson is capable of giving it. We therefore wish, with deference to his superior

Dr. Goldsmith · *Jos Warton* · *Edm Burke* · *Tho. Franklin* · *Wm. Chamb...* · *Joshua Reynolds* · *Samuel...*

judgment, humbly request that he would at least take the trouble of revising it; and of making such additions and alterations as he shall think proper upon a farther perusal. But if we might venture to express our wishes, they would lead us to request that he would write the Epitaph in English rather than in Latin: as we think that the memory of so eminent an English Writer ought to be perpetuated in the language to which his Works are likely to be so lasting an ornament, which we also know to have been the opinion of the late

Doctor himself.

that it is difficult to appropriate to particular persons
qualities which are common to all mankind, as Homer has
done."

WILKES: "We have no City Poet now: that is an
office which has gone into disuse. The last was Elkanah
Settle. There is something in *names* which one cannot
help feeling. Now *Elkanah Settle* sounds so *queer*, who can
expect much from that name? We should have no
hesitation to give it for John Dryden, in preference to
Elkanah Settle, from the names only, without knowing
their different merits." JOHNSON: "I suppose, Sir, Settle
did as well for Aldermen in his time, as John Home could

> Quàm si proferres ignota indictaque primus.
> Publica materies privati juris erit, si
> Non circa vilem patulumque moraberis orbem;
> Nec verbum verbo curabis reddere fidus
> Interpres; nec desilies imitator in arctum,
> Unde pedem proferre pudor vetat, aut operis lex."—v. 125.

The "Commentary" thus illustrates it: "But the formation of quite
new characters is a work of great difficulty and hazard; for here there is
no generally received and fixed *archetype* to work after, but every one
judges of common right according to the extent and comprehension of
his own idea; therefore he advises to labour and refit *old characters and
subjects*, particularly those made known and authorised by the practice
of Homer and the Epic writers."

The "Note" is, "Difficile EST PROPRIE COMMUNIA DICERE." Lambin's
Comments is, "Communia hoc loco appellat Horatius argumenta
fabularum à nullo adhuc tractata: et ita, quæ cuivis exposita sunt et in
medio quodammodo posita, quasi vacua et à nemine occupata." And
that this is the true meaning of *communia* is evidently fixed by the words
ignota indictaque, which are explanatory of it; so that the sense given it
in the commentary is unquestionably the right one. Yet, notwithstanding the clearness of the case, a late critic has this strange passage:—
"Difficile quidem esse proprià communia dicere, hoc est, materiam
vulgarem, notam et è medio petitam, ita immutare atque exornare, ut
nova et scriptori propria videatur, ultro concedimus; et maximi procul
dubio ponderis ista est observatio. Sed omnibus utrinque collatis, et
tum difficilis tum venusti, tam judicii quam ingenii ratione habita,
major videtur esse gloria fabulam formare penitus novam quàm veterem,
utcunque mutatam, de novo exhibere." (Poet. Præl., v. ii. p. 164.)
Where, having first put a wrong construction on the word *communia*,
he employs it to introduce an impertinent criticism. For where does
the poet prefer the glory of refitting *old* subjects to that of inventing new
ones? The contrary is implied in what he urges about the superior
difficulty of the latter, from which he dissuades his countrymen, only
in respect of their abilities and inexperience in these matters; and in
order to cultivate in them, which is the main view of the Epistle, a
spirit of correctness, by sending them to the old subjects, treated by
the Greek writers.

For my own part, with all deference for Dr. Hurd, who thinks the
case clear, I consider the passage, "Difficile est proprià communia dicere,"
to be a *crux* for the critics on Horace.

The explication which my Lord of Worcester treats with so much
contempt, is nevertheless countenanced by authority, which I find quoted

do now. Where did Beckford and Trecothick learn English?"

Mr. Arthur Lee mentioned some Scotch who had taken possession of a barren part of America, and wondered why they should choose it. JOHNSON: "Why, Sir, all barrenness is comparative. The *Scotch* would not know it to be barren." BOSWELL: "Come, come, he is flattering the English. You have now been in Scotland, Sir, and say if you did not see meat and drink enough there." JOHNSON: "Why yes, Sir; meat and drink enough to give the inhabitants sufficient strength to run away from home." All these quick and lively sallies were said sportively, quite in jest, and with a smile, which showed that he meant only wit. Upon this topic, he and Mr. Wilkes could perfectly

by the learned Baxter, in his edition of Horace, "*Difficile est proprié communia dicere,* h. e. res vulgares disertis verbis enarrare, vel humilè thema cum dignitate tractare. *Difficile est communes res propriis explicare verbis.* Vet. Schol." I was much disappointed to find that the great critic, Dr. Bentley, has no note on this very difficult passage, as from his vigorous and illuminate mind I should have expected to receive more satisfaction than I have yet had.

Sanadon thus treats of it: "*Propriè communia dicere ;* c'est à dire, qu'il n'est pas aisé de former à ces personnages d'imagination, des caractères particuliers et cependant vraisemblables. Comme l'on a été le maitre de les former tels qu'on a voulu, les fautes que l'on fait en cela sont moins pardonnables. C'est pourquoi Horace conseille de prendre toujours des sujets connus, tels que sont, par exemple, ceux que l'on peut tirer des poëmes d'Homère."

And Dacier observes upon it: "Après avoir marqué les deux qualité qu'il faut donner aux personnages qu'on invente, il conseille aux Poëtes tragiques, de n'user pas trop facilement de cette liberté qu'ils ont d'en inventer, car il est très difficile de reussir dans ces nouveaux caractères. Il est mal aisé, dit Horace, *de traiter proprement,* c'est à dire *convenablement,* des *sujets communs ;* c'est à dire, des sujets inventés, et qui n'ont aucun fondement ni dans l'Histoire ni dans la Fable; et il les appelle *communs,* parce qu'ils sont en disposition à tout le monde, et que tout le monde a le droit de les inventer, et qu'ils sont, comme on dit, au premier occupant." See his observations at large on this expression and the following.

After all, I cannot help entertaining some doubt whether the words, "Difficile est proprie communia dicere," may not have been thrown in by Horace to form a *separate* article in "choice of difficulties" which a poet has to encounter, who chooses a new subject; in which case, it must be uncertain which of the various explanations is the true one, and every reader has a right to decide as it may strike his own fancy. And even should the words be understood, as they generally are, to be connected both with what goes before and what comes after, the exact sense cannot be absolutely ascertained; for instance, whether *propriè* is meant to signify *in an appropriated manner,* as Dr. Johnson here understands it, or, as it is often used by Cicero, *with propriety,* or *elegantly.* In short, it is a rare instance of a defect in perspicuity in an admirable writer, who, with almost every species of excellence, is peculiarly remarkable for that quality. The length of this note, perhaps, requires an apology. Many of my readers, I doubt not, will admit that a critical discussion of a passage in a favourite classic, is very engaging.—BOSWELL.

assimilate; here was a bond of union between them, and I was conscious that as both of them had visited Caledonia, both were fully satisfied of the strange narrow ignorance of those who imagine that it is a land of famine. But they amused themselves with persevering in the old jokes. When I claimed a superiority for Scotland over England in one respect, that no man can be arrested there for a debt, merely because another swears it against him; but there must first be the judgment of a court of law ascertaining its justice; and that a seizure of the person, before judgment is obtained, can take place only if his creditor should swear that he is about to fly from the country, or, as it is technically expressed, is *in meditatione fugæ* : WILKES : "That, I should think, may be safely sworn of all the Scotch nation." JOHNSON (to Mr. Wilkes): "You must know, Sir, I lately took my friend Boswell, and showed him genuine civilised life in an English provincial town. I turned him loose at Lichfield, my native city, that he might see for once real civility : for you know he lives among savages in Scotland, and among rakes in London." WILKES : "Except when he is with grave, sober, decent people, like you and me." JOHNSON (smiling): "And we ashamed of him."

They were quite frank and easy. Johnson told the story of his asking Mrs. Macaulay to allow her footman to sit down with them, to prove the ridiculousness of the argument for the equality of mankind; and he said to me afterwards, with a nod of satisfaction, "You saw Mr. Wilkes acquiesced." Wilkes talked with all imaginable freedom of the ludicrous title given to the Attorney-General, *Diabolus Regis* ; adding, "I have reason to know something about that officer; for I was prosecuted for a libel." Johnson, who many people would have supposed must have been furiously angry at hearing this talked of so lightly, said not a word. He was now, *indeed*, "a good humoured fellow."

After dinner we had an accession of Mrs. Knowles, the Quaker lady, well known for her various talents, and of Mr. Alderman Lee. Amidst some patriotic groans, somebody, I think the Alderman, said, "Poor old England is lost." JOHNSON : "Sir, it is not so much to be lamented that old England is lost, as that the Scotch have found it."[1] WILKES : "Had Lord Bute governed Scotland only, I should not have taken the trouble to write his eulogy, and dedicate 'MORTIMER' to him."

[1] It would not become me to expatiate on this strong and pointed remark, in which a very great deal of meaning is condensed.—BOSWELL.

Mr. Wilkes held a candle to show a fine print of a beautiful female figure which hung in the room, and pointed out the elegant contour of the bosom, with the finger of an arch connoisseur. He afterwards, in a conversation with me, waggishly insisted, that all the time Johnson showed visible signs of a fervent admiration of the corresponding charms of the fair Quaker.

This record, though by no means so perfect as I could wish, will serve to give a notion of a very curious interview, which was not only pleasing at the time, but had the agreeable and benignant effect of reconciling any animosity, and sweetening any acidity, which in the various bustle of political contest, had been produced in the minds of two men, who though widely different had so many things in common—classical learning, modern literature, wit and humour, and ready repartee—that it would have been much to be regretted, if they had been for ever at a distance from each other.

Mr. Burke gave me much credit for this successful *negociation*; and pleasantly said, "that there was nothing equal to it in the whole history of the *Corps Diplomatique*."

I attended Dr. Johnson home, and had the satisfaction to hear him tell Mrs. Williams how much he had been pleased with Mr. Wilkes's company, and what an agreeable day he had passed.

I talked a good deal to him of the celebrated Margaret Caroline Rudd, whom I had visited, induced by the fame of her talents, address, and irresistible power of fascination. To a lady who disapproved of my visiting her, he said, on a former occasion, "Nay, Madam, Boswell is in the right; I should have visited her myself, were it not that they have now a trick of putting every thing into the newspapers." This evening, he exclaimed, "I envy him his acquaintance with Mrs. Rudd."

I mentioned a scheme which I had of making a tour to the Isle of Man, and giving a full account of it; and that Mr. Burke had playfully suggested as a motto,

"The proper study of mankind is MAN."

JOHNSON: "Sir, you will get more by the book than the jaunt will cost you; so you will have your diversion for nothing, and add to your reputation."

CHAPTER III.—1776-1777

Boswell's Departure for Scotland—Correspondence respecting Dr. Goldsmith's Epitaph—A literary Round Robin—General Correspondence between Johnson, Boswell, Sir Joshua Reynolds, Levett, Steevens, and Sir A. Dick—Count Manucci—Mr. Paterson—Johnson's Suasorium—Granger's Biographical Dictionary—Mr. Langton—Discordances of the Boswell Family—Dr. Blair's Sermons — Prayer for Easter-day — Steevens — Dr. Memis's Law-suit—Sir Allan Maclean's Suit—Sir A. Dick's Rural Pursuits—Shaw's Erse Grammar — Johnson's Remarks on the Erse Dialect—Johnson's Engagement to write the "Lives of the English Poets"

ON the evening of the next day, May 16, I took leave of Johnson, being to set out for Scotland. I thanked him with great warmth for all his kindness. "Sir," said he, "you are very welcome. Nobody repays it with more."

How very false is the notion that has gone round the world, of the rough, and passionate, and harsh manners of this great and good man. That he had occasional sallies of heat of temper, and that he was sometimes, perhaps, too "easily provoked" by absurdity and folly, and sometimes too desirous of triumph in colloquial contest, must be allowed. The quickness both of his perception and sensibility disposed him to sudden explosions of satire; to which his extraordinary readiness of wit was a strong and almost irresistible incitement. To adopt one of the finest images in Mr. Home's "Douglas,"

> "On each glance of thought
> Decision followed, as the thunderbolt
> Pursues the flash!"

I admit that the beadle within him was often so eager to apply the lash, that the judge had not time to consider the case with sufficient deliberation.

That he was occasionally remarkable for violence of temper may be granted; but let us ascertain the degree, and not let it be supposed that he was in a perpetual rage, and never without a club in his hand to knock down every one who approached him. On the contrary, the truth is, that by much the greatest part of his time he was civil, obliging, nay, polite in the true sense of the word; so much so, that many gentlemen who were long acquainted with him never received, or even heard a strong expression from him.

The following letters concerning an Epitaph which he wrote for the monument of Dr. Goldsmith, in Westminster Abbey, afford at once a proof of his unaffected modesty, his carelessness as to his own writings, and of the great respect which he entertained for the taste and judgment of the excellent and eminent person to whom they are addressed:—

"TO SIR JOSHUA REYNOLDS.

"DEAR SIR,   *May* 16, 1776.

"I have been kept away from you, I know not well how, and of those vexatious hinderances I know not when there will be an end. I therefore send you the poor dear Doctor's epitaph. Read it first yourself; and if you then think it right, show it to the Club. I am, you know, willing to be corrected. If you think anything much amiss, keep it to yourself till we come together. I have sent two copies, but prefer the card. The dates must be settled by Dr. Percy.

"I am, Sir, your most humble servant,
"SAM. JOHNSON."

TO THE SAME.

"SIR,   *June* 22, 1776.

"Miss Reynolds has a mind to send the Epitaph to Dr. Beattie; I am very willing, but having no copy cannot immediately recollect it. She tells me you have lost it. Try to recollect, and put down as much as you retain; you perhaps may have kept what I have dropt. The lines for which I am at a loss are something of *rerum civilium sive naturalium*.[1] It was a sorry trick to lose it; help me if you can. I am, Sir,

"Your most humble servant,
"The gout grows better but slowly."   "SAM. JOHNSON."

It was, I think, after I had left London in this year, that this epitaph gave occasion to a *Remonstrance* to the MONARCH OF LITERATURE, for an account of which I am indebted to Sir William Forbes of Pitsligo.

---

[1] These words must have been in the other copy. They are not in that which was preferred.—BOSWELL.

That my readers may have the subject more fully and clearly before them, I shall first insert the epitaph:—

OLIVARII GOLDSMITH,—
Poetæ, Physici, Historici,
Qui nullum fere scribendi genus
Non tetigit,
Nullum quod tetigit non ornavit:
Sive risus essent movendi,
Sive lacrymæ,
Affectuum potens at lenis dominator:
Ingenio sublimis, vividus, versatilis;
Oratione grandis, nitidus, venustus:—
Hoc monumento memoriam coluit
Sodalium amor,
Amicorum fides,
Lectorum veneratio.
Natus in Hiberniâ Forniæ Longfordiensis,
In loco cui nomen Pallas,
Nov. XXIX. MDCCXXXI; [1]
Eblanæ literis institutus;
Obiit Londini,
April IV, MDCCLXXIV. [2]

Sir William Forbes writes to me thus:—

"I enclose the *Round Robin*. This *jeu d' esprit* took its rise one day at dinner, at our friend Sir Joshua Reynolds's. All the company present, except myself, were friends and acquaintance of Dr. Goldsmith. The epitaph, written for him by Dr. Johnson, became the subject of conversation, and various emendations were suggested, which it was agreed should be submitted to the Doctor's consideration. But the question was, who should have the courage to propose them to him? At last it was hinted that there could be no way so good as that of a *Round Robin*, as the sailors call it, which they make use of when they enter into a conspiracy, so as not to let it be known who puts his name first or last to the paper. This proposition was instantly assented to; and Dr. Barnard, Dean of Derry, now Bishop of Killaloe, [3] drew up an address to Dr. Johnson on the occasion, replete with wit and humour, but which it was feared the Doctor might think treated the subject with too much

[1] This was a mistake, which was not discovered till after Goldsmith's monument was put in Westminster Abbey. He was born November 29, 1728; and therefore, when he died, he was in his 47th year.—MALONE.

[2] Besides this Latin Epitaph, Johnson honoured the memory of his friend Goldsmith with one short one in Greek. See chap. xxii., vol. i.—BOSWELL.

[3] This prelate, who was afterwards translated to the See of Limerick, died at Wimbledon, in Surrey, June 7, 1806, in his eightieth year. The original *Round Robin* remained in his possession; the paper, which Sir William Forbes transmitted to Mr. Boswell, being only a copy.—MALONE.

levity. Mr. Burke then proposed the address as it stands in the paper in writing, to which I had the honour to officiate as clerk.

"Sir Joshua agreed to carry it to Dr. Johnson, who received it with much good humour,[1] and desired Sir Joshua to tell the gentlemen, that he would alter the Epitaph in any manner they pleased, as to the sense of it; but *he would never consent to disgrace the walls of Westminster Abbey with an English inscription.*

"I consider this *Round Robin* as a species of literary curiosity worth preserving, as it marks, in a certain degree, Dr. Johnson's character."

My readers are presented with a faithful transcript of a paper, which I doubt not of their being desirous to see.

Sir William Forbes's observation is very just. The anecdote now related, proves, in the strongest manner, the reverence and awe with which Johnson was regarded by some of the most eminent men of his time, in various departments, and even by such of them as lived most with him; while it also confirms what I have again and again inculcated, that he was by no means of that ferocious and irascible character which has been ignorantly imagined.

This hasty composition is also to be remarked as one of the thousand instances which evince the extraordinary

[1] He, however, upon seeing Dr. Warton's name to the suggestion that the Epitaph should be in English, observed to Sir Joshua, "I wonder that Joe Warton, a scholar by profession, should be such a fool." He said, too, "I should have thought Mund Burke would have had more sense." Mr. Langton, who was one of the company at Sir Joshua's, like a sturdy scholar, refused resolutely to sign the *Round Robin.* The Epitaph is engraved upon Dr. Goldsmith's monument without any alteration. At another time, when somebody endeavoured to argue in favour of its being in English, Johnson said, "The language of the country of which a learned man was a native, is not the language fit for his epitaph, which should be in ancient and permanent language. Consider, Sir, how you should feel, were you to find, at Rotterdam, an epitaph upon Erasmus in *Dutch !*" For my own part, I think it would be best to have epitaphs written both in a learned language, and in the language of the country; so that they might have the advantage of being more universally understood, and at the same time be secured of classical stability. I cannot, however, but be of opinion that it is not sufficiently discriminative. Applying to Goldsmith equally the epithets of "Poetæ, Historici, Physici," is surely not right; for as to his claim to the last of those epithets, I have heard Johnson himself say, "Goldsmith, Sir, will give us a very fine book upon the subject; but if he can distinguish a cow from a horse, that, I believe, may be the extent of his knowledge of natural history." His book is, indeed, an excellent performance, though in some instances he appears to have trusted too much to Buffon, who, with all his theoretical ingenuity and extraordinary eloquence, I suspect had little actual information in the science on which he wrote so admirably. For instance, he tells us that the *cow* sheds her horns every two years ; a most palpable error, which Goldsmith has faithfully transferred into his book. It is wonderful that Buffon, who lived so much in the country, at his noble seat, should have fallen into such a blunder. I suppose he has confounded the *cow* with the *deer.*—BOSWELL.

promptitude of Mr. Burke; who, while he is equal to the greatest things, can adorn the least; can, with equal facility, embrace the vast and complicated speculations of politics, or the ingenious topics of literary investigation.

"DR. JOHNSON TO MRS. BOSWELL.

"Madam,   *May* 16, 1776.

"You must not think me uncivil in omitting to answer the letter with which you favoured me some time ago. I imagined it to have been written without Mr. Boswell's knowledge, and therefore supposed the answer to require, what I could not find, a private conveyance.

"The difference with Lord Auchinleck is now over; and, since young Alexander has appeared, I hope no more difficulties will arise among you; for I sincerely wish you all happy. Do not teach the young ones to dislike me, as you dislike me yourself; but let me at least have Veronica's kindness because she is my acquaintance.

"You will now have Mr. Boswell home: it is well that you have him; he has led a wild life. I have taken him to Lichfield, and he has followed Mr. Thrale to Bath. Pray take care of him and tame him. The only thing in which I have the honour to agree with you is, in loving him; and while we are so much of a mind in a matter of so much importance, our other quarrels will, I hope, produce no great bitterness.

"I am, Madam, your most humble servant,

"Sam. Johnson."

"MR. BOSWELL TO DR. JOHNSON.

"*Edinburgh, June* 25, 1776.

"You have formerly complained that my letters were too long. There is no danger of that complaint being made at present; for I find it difficult for me to write to you at all. [Here an account of having been afflicted with a return of melancholy or bad spirits.]

"The boxes of books [1] which you sent to me are arrived; but I have not yet examined the contents.   *   *   *   *

"I send you Mr. Maclaurin's paper for the negro, who claims his freedom in the Court of Session."

"DR. JOHNSON TO MR. BOSWELL.

"Dear Sir,   *July* 2, 1776.

"These black fits of which you complain perhaps hurt your memory as well as your imagination. When did I complain that your letters were too long? [2] Your last letter, after a very long

---

[1] Upon a settlement of our account of expenses, on a tour to the Hebrides, there was a balance due to me, which Dr. Johnson chose to discharge by sending books.—Boswell.

[2] Baretti told me that Johnson complained of my writing very long letters to him when I was upon the continent; which was most certainly true; but it seems my friend did not remember it.—Boswell.

delay, brought very bad news. [Here a series of reflections upon melancholy, and—what I could not help thinking strangely unreasonable in him who had suffered so much from it himself,—a good deal of severity and reproof, as if it were owing to my own fault, or that I was perhaps affecting it from a desire of distinction.]

"Read Cheyne's 'English Malady:' but do not let him teach you a foolish notion that melancholy is a proof of acuteness.   *

"To hear that you have not opened your boxes of books is very offensive. The examination and arrangement of so many volumes might have afforded you an amusement very seasonable at present, and useful for the whole of life. I am, I confess, very angry that you manage yourself so ill.   *   *   *   *   *

"I do not now say any more than that I am, with great kindness and sincerity, dear Sir,   "Your humble servant,
                                        "SAM. JOHNSON.

"It was last year determined by Lord Mansfield, in the Court of King's Bench, that a negro cannot be taken out of the kingdom without his own consent."

"DR. JOHNSON TO MR. BOSWELL.

"DEAR SIR,   *July* 16, 1776.

"I make haste to write again, lest my last letter should give you too much pain. If you really are oppressed with overpowering and involuntary melancholy, you are to be pitied rather than reproached.

        *   *   *   *   *

"Now, my dear Bozzy, let us have done with quarrels and with censure. Let me know whether I have not sent you a pretty library. There are, perhaps, many books among them which you never need read through; but there are none which it is not proper for you to know, and sometimes to consult. Of these books, of which the use is only occasional, it is often sufficient to know the contents, that, when any question arises, you may know where to look for information.

"Since I wrote, I have looked over Mr. Maclaurin's plea, and think it excellent. How is the suit carried on? If by subscription I commission you to contribute in my name what is proper. Let nothing be wanting in such a case. Dr. Drummond,[1] I see, is superseded. His father would have grieved; but he lived to obtain the pleasure of his son's election, and died before that pleasure was abated.

"Langton's lady has brought him a girl, and both are well; I dined with him the other day.

        *   *   *   *   *

[1] The son of Johnson's old friend, Mr. William Drummond (see vol. i. chap. xv.). He was a young man of such distinguished merit, that he was nominated to one of the medical professorships in the College of Edinburgh, without solicitation, while he was at Naples. Having other views, he did not accept of the honour, and soon afterwards died.—BOSWELL.

"It vexes me to tell you, that on the evening of the 29th of May I was seized by the gout, and am not quite well. The pain has not been violent, but the weakness and tenderness were very troublesome, and, what is said to be very uncommon, it has not alleviated my other disorders. Make use of youth and health while you have them; make my compliments to Mrs. Boswell.

"I am, my dear Sir, your most affectionate,
                                        "SAM. JOHNSON."

"MR. BOSWELL TO DR. JOHNSON.

"MY DEAR SIR,   *Edinburgh, July* 18, 1776.

"Your letter of the second of this month was rather a harsh medicine; but I was delighted with that spontaneous tenderness which, a few days afterwards, sent forth such balsam as your next brought me. I found myself for some time so ill, that all I could do was to preserve a decent appearance, while all within was weakness and distress. Like a reduced garrison that has some spirit left, I hung out flags, and planted all the force I could muster upon the walls. I am now much better, and I sincerely thank you for your kind attention and friendly counsel.

*   *   *   *   *

"Count Manucci [1] came here last week from travelling in Ireland. I have shown him what civilities I could on his account, on yours, and on that of Mr. and Mrs. Thrale. He has had a fall from his horse, and been much hurt. I regret this unlucky accident, for he seems to be a very amiable man."

As the evidence of what I have mentioned at the beginning of this year, I select from his private register the following passage:—

"July 25, 1776. O GOD, who hast ordained that whatever is to be desired should be sought by labour, and who, by thy blessing, bringest honest labour to good effect, look with mercy upon my studies and endeavours. Grant me, O LORD, to design only what is lawful and right; and afford me calmness of mind and steadiness of purpose, that I may so do thy will in this short life as to obtain happiness in the world to come, for the sake of Jesus Christ our Lord. Amen." [2]

It appears, from a note subjoined, that this was composed when he "purposed to apply vigorously to study, particularly of the Greek and Italian tongues."

Such a purpose, so expressed, at the age of sixty-seven, is admirable and encouraging; and it must impress all

---

[1] A Florentine nobleman, mentioned by Johnson in his "Notes of his Tour in France." I had the pleasure of becoming acquainted with him in London, in the spring of this year.—BOSWELL.

[2] "Prayers and Meditations," p. 151.—BOSWELL.

the thinking part of my readers with a consolatory confidence in habitual devotion, when they see a man of such enlarged intellectual powers as Johnson, thus, in the genuine earnestness of secrecy, imploring the aid of that Supreme Being "from whom cometh down every good and every perfect gift."

"TO SIR JOSHUA REYNOLDS.

"SIR,   *August* 3, 1776.

"A young man, whose name is Paterson, offers himself this evening to the Academy. He is the son of a man [1] for whom I have long had a kindness, and who is now abroad in distress. I shall be glad that you will be pleased to show him any little countenance, or pay him any small distinction. How much it is in your power to favour or to forward a young man I do not know; nor do I know how much this candidate deserves favour by his personal merit, or what hopes his proficiency may now give of future eminence. I recommend him as the son of my friend. Your character and station enable you to give a young man great encouragement by very easy means. You have heard of a man who asked no other favour of Sir Robert Walpole than that he would bow to him at his levee.

"I am, Sir, your most humble servant,
"SAM. JOHNSON."

"MR. BOSWELL TO DR. JOHNSON.

"*August* 30, 1776.

After giving him an account of my having examined the chest of books which he had sent to me, and which contained what may be truly called a numerous and miscellaneous *Stall Library*, thrown together at random:—

"Lord Hailes was against the decree in the case of my client, the minister; not that he justified the minister, but because the parishioner both provoked and retorted. I sent his Lordship your able argument upon the case for his perusal. His observation upon it in a letter to me was, Dr. Johnson's 'Suasorium' is pleasantly[2] and artfully composed. I suspect, however, that he has not convinced himself; for I believe that he is better read in ecclesiastical

---

[1] Samuel Paterson, formerly a bookseller, lately an auctioneer, and well known for his skill in forming catalogues of books. He died in London, Oct. 29, 1802.—MALONE.

[2] Why his Lordship uses the epithet *pleasantly*, when speaking of a grave piece of reasoning, I cannot conceive. But different men have different notions of pleasantry. I happened to sit by a gentleman one evening at the opera house in London, who, at the moment when "Medea" appeared to be in great agony at the thought of killing her children, turned to me with a smile, and said, "*funny* enough."—BOSWELL.

history, than to imagine that a Bishop or Presbyter has a right to begin censure or discipline *è cathedrâ*.[1]

"For the honour of Count Manucci, as well as to observe that exactness of truth which you have taught me, I must correct what I said in a former letter. He did not fall from his horse, which might have been an imputation on his skill as an officer of cavalry; his horse fell with him.

"I have, since I saw you, read every word of 'Granger's Biographical History.'[2] It has entertained me exceedingly, and I do not think him the *Whig* that you supposed. Horace Walpole's being his patron is, indeed, no good sign of his political principles. But he denied to Lord Mountstuart that he was a Whig, and said he had been accused by both parties of partiality. It seems he was like Pope,

'While Tories call me Whig, and Whigs a Tory.'

I wish you would look more into his book; and as Lord Mountstuart wishes much to find a proper person to continue the work upon Granger's plan, and has desired I would mention it to you, if such a man occurs, please to let me know. His Lordship will give him generous encouragement."

"TO MR. ROBERT LEVETT.

"Dear Sir,   *Brighthelmstone, Oct.* 21, 1776.

"Having spent about six weeks at this place, we have at length resolved upon returning. I expect to see you all in Fleet-street on the 30th of this month.

"I did not go into the sea till last Friday, but think to go most of this week, though I know not that it does me any good. My nights are very restless and tiresome, but I am otherwise well.

"I have written word of my coming to Mrs. Williams. Remember me kindly to Francis and Betsey.[3]

"I am, Sir, your most humble servant,
"Sam. Johnson."[4]

---

[1] Dr. Johnson afterwards told me that he was of opinion that a clergyman had this right.—Boswell.

[2] The Rev. James Granger was a native of Berkshire, and the Vicar of Shiplake, in Oxfordshire. His "Biographical History of England" was published in 4 vols. 8vo. It is a valuable and highly interesting work, which has formed the chief materials for our later biographical dictionaries. The author died of a fit of apoplexy, while administering the sacrament, in 1776.—Ed.

[3] His female servant.—Malone.

[4] For this and Dr. Johnson's other letters to Mr. Levett, I am indebted to my old acquaintance, Mr. Nathaniel Thomas, whose worth and ingenuity have been long known to a respectable though not a wide circle; and whose collection of medals would do credit to persons of greater opulence.—Boswell.

Mr. Nathaniel Thomas, who was many years editor of *The St. James's Chronicle*, died March 1, 1795.—Malone.

I again wrote to Dr. Johnson on the 21st of October, informing him that my father had, in the most liberal manner, paid a large debt for me, and that I had now the happiness of being upon very good terms with him; to which he returned the following answer:—

"TO JAMES BOSWELL, ESQ.

"DEAR SIR,   *Bolt Court, Nov.* 16, 1776.

"I had great pleasure in hearing that you are at last on good terms with your father. Cultivate his kindness by all honest and manly means. Life is but short; no time can be afforded but for the indulgence of real sorrow, or contests upon questions seriously momentous. Let us not throw away any of our days upon useless resentment, or contend who shall hold out longest in stubborn malignity. It is best not to be angry; and best, in the next place, to be quickly reconciled. May you and your father pass the remainder of your time in reciprocal benevolence!

       *   *   *   *   *

"Do you ever hear from Mr. Langton? I visit him sometimes, but he does not talk. I do not like his scheme of life; but as I am not permitted to understand it, I cannot set anything right that is wrong. His children are sweet babies.

"I hope my irreconcileable enemy, Mrs. Boswell, is well. Desire her not to transmit her malevolence to the young people. Let me have Alexander, and Veronica, and Euphemia for my friends.

"Mrs. Williams, whom you may reckon as one of your well-wishers, is in a feeble and languishing state, with little hopes of growing better. She went for some part of the autumn into the country, but is little benefited; and Dr. Lawrence confesses that his art is at an end. Death is, however, at a distance: and what more than that can we say of ourselves? I am sorry for her pain, and more sorry for her decay. Mr. Levett sound wind and limb.

"I was some weeks this autumn at Brighthelmstone. The place was very dull, and I was not well; the expedition to the Hebrides was the most pleasant journey that I ever made. Such an effort annually would give the world a little diversification.

"Every year, however, we cannot wander, and must therefore endeavour to spend our time at home as well as we can. I believe it is best to throw life into a method, that every hour may bring its employment, and every employment have its hour. Xenophon observes, in his 'Treatise of Economy,' that if everything be kept in a certain place, when anything is worn out or consumed, the vacuity which it leaves will show what is wanting; so if every part of time has its duty, the hour will call into remembrance its proper engagement.

"I have not practised all this prudence myself, but I have suffered much for want of it; and I would have you, by timely recollection and steady resolution, escape from those evils which have lain heavy upon me. I am, my dearest Boswell, your most humble servant,
                                                      "SAM. JOHNSON."

On the 16th of November I informed him that Mr. Strahan had sent me *twelve* copies of the "Journey to the Western Islands," handsomely bound, instead of the *twenty* copies which were stipulated, but which, I supposed, were to be only in sheets; requested to know how they should be distributed; and mentioned that I had another son born to me, who was named David, and was a sickly infant.

"TO JAMES BOSWELL, ESQ.

"Dear Sir,   *Dec.* 21, 1776.

"I have been for some time ill of a cold, which, perhaps, I made an excuse to myself for not writing, when in reality I knew not what to say.

"The books you must at last distribute as you think best, in my name, or your own, as you are inclined, or as you judge most proper. Every body cannot be obliged; but I wish that nobody may be offended. Do the best you can.

"I congratulate you on the increase of your family, and hope that little David is by this time well, and his mamma perfectly recovered. I am much pleased to hear of the re-establishment of kindness between you and your father. Cultivate his paternal tenderness as much as you can. To live at variance at all is uncomfortable; and variance with a father is still more uncomfortable. Besides that, in the whole dispute you have the wrong side; at least you gave the first provocations, and some of them very offensive. Let it now be all over. As you have no reason to think that your new mother has shown you any foul play, treat her with respect, and with some degree of confidence; this will secure your father. When once a discordant family has felt the pleasure of peace they will not willingly lose it. If Mrs. Boswell would but be friends with me, we might now shut the temple of Janus.

"What came of Dr. Memis's cause? Is the question about the negro determined? Has Sir Allan any reasonable hopes? What has become of poor Macquarry? Let me know the event of all these litigations. I wish particularly well to the negro and Sir Allan.

"Mrs. Williams has been much out of order; and though she is something better, is likely, in her physician's opinion, to endure her malady for life, though she may, perhaps, die of some other. Mrs. Thrale is big, and fancies that she carries a boy; if it were very reasonable to wish much about it, I should wish her not to be disappointed. The desire of male heirs is appended only to feudal tenures. A son is almost necessary to the continuance of Thrale's fortune; for what can misses do with a brew-house? Lands are fitter for daughters than trades.

"Baretti went away from Thrale's in some whimsical fit of disgust, or ill-nature, without taking any leave. It is well if he finds in another place as good an habitation, and as many conveniences. He has got five-and-twenty guineas by translating Sir

Joshua's Discourses into Italian, and Mr. Thrale gave him a hundred in the spring; so that he is yet in no difficulties.

"Colman has bought Foote's patent, and is to allow Foote for life 1600*l.* a year, as Reynolds told me, and to allow him to play so often on such terms that he may gain 400*l.* more. What Colman can get by his bargain,[1] but trouble and hazard, I do not see. I am, dear Sir, your humble servant,

"SAM. JOHNSON."

The Rev. Dr. Hugh Blair, who had long been admired as a preacher at Edinburgh, thought now of diffusing his excellent sermons more extensively, and increasing his reputation by publishing a collection of them. He transmitted the manuscript to Mr. Strahan, the printer, who, after keeping it for some time, wrote a letter to him, discouraging the publication. Such, at first, was the unpropitious state of one of the most successful theological books that has ever appeared. Mr. Strahan, however, had sent one of the sermons to Dr. Johnson for his opinion; and, after his unfavourable letter to Dr. Blair had been sent off, he received from Johnson, on Christmas-eve, a note in which was the following paragraph:—

"I have read over Dr. Blair's first sermon with more than approbation; to say it is good, is to say too little."

I believe Mr. Strahan had, very soon after this time, a conversation with Dr. Johnson concerning them, and then he very candidly wrote again to Dr. Blair, enclosing Johnson's note, and agreeing to purchase the volume, for which he and Mr. Cadell gave 100*l.* The sale was so rapid and extensive, and the approbation of the public so high, that, to their honour be it recorded, the proprietors made Dr. Blair a present, first of one sum and afterwards of another of 50*l.*, thus voluntarily doubling the stipulated price; and when he prepared another volume they gave him at once 300*l.*, being in all 500*l.*, by an agreement to which I am a subscribing witness; and now for a third octavo volume he has received no less than 600*l.*[2]

In 1777, it appears, from his "Prayers and Meditations," that Johnson suffered much from a state of mind "unsettled and perplexed," and from that constitutional

---

[1] It turned out, however, a very fortunate bargain; for Foote, though not then fifty-six, died at an inn in Dover, in less than a year, Oct. 21, 1777.—MALONE.

[2] Two more volumes were subsequently published. The fifth appeared after the death of the author, in 1801, and contained an account of his life, by the Rev. Dr. Finlayson.—ED.

gloom which, together with his extreme humility and anxiety with regard to his religious state, made him contemplate himself through too dark and unfavourable a medium. It may be said of him, that he "saw GOD in clouds." Certain we may be of his injustice to himself in the following lamentable paragraph, which it is painful to think came from the contrite heart of this great man, to whose labours the world is so much indebted:—"When I survey my past life, I discover nothing but a barren waste of time, with some disorders of body, and disturbances of the mind, very near to madness, which I hope He that made me will suffer to extenuate many faults, and excuse many deficiencies."[1] But we find his devotions in this year eminently fervent; and we are comforted by observing intervals of quiet, composure, and gladness.

On Easter-day we find the following emphatic prayer:— "Almighty and most merciful Father, who seest all our miseries, and knowest all our necessities, look down upon me, and pity me. Defend me from the violent incursion of evil thoughts, and enable me to form and keep such resolutions as may conduce to the discharge of the duties which thy providence shall appoint me; and so help me, by thy Holy Spirit, that my heart may surely there be fixed, where true joys are to be found, and that I may serve thee with a pure affection and a cheerful mind. Have mercy upon me; O God, have mercy upon me; years and infirmities oppress me, terror and anxiety beset me. Have mercy upon me, my Creator and my Judge. In all perplexities relieve and free me; and so help me by thy Holy Spirit, that I may now so commemorate the death of thy Son our Saviour JESUS CHRIST, as that when this short and painful life shall have an end, I may for his sake, be received to everlasting happiness. Amen."[2]

While he was at church, the agreeable impressions upon his mind are thus commemorated:—"I was for some time distressed, but at last obtained, I hope from the GOD of Peace, more quiet than I have enjoyed for a long time. I had made no resolution, but as my heart grew lighter, my hopes revived, and my courage increased; and I wrote with my pencil in my Common Prayer Book,

> 'Vita ordinanda.
> Biblia legenda.
> Theologiæ opera danda.
> Serviendum et lætandum.'"

---

[1] "Prayers and Meditations," p. 155.—BOSWELL.   [2] Ibid., p. 158.

Mr. Steevens,[1] whose generosity is well known, joined Dr. Johnson in kind assistance to a female relation of Dr. Goldsmith, and desired that on her return to Ireland she would procure authentic particulars of the life of her celebrated relation. Concerning her is the following letter:—

"TO GEORGE STEEVENS, ESQ.

"DEAR SIR,   *February* 25, 1777.

"You will be glad to hear that from Mrs. Goldsmith, whom we lamented as drowned, I have received a letter full of gratitude to us all, with promises to make the inquiries which we recommended to her.

"I would have had the honour of conveying this intelligence to Miss Caulfield, but that her letter is not at hand, and I know not the direction. You will tell the good news.

"I am Sir, your most, &c.,
                              "SAM. JOHNSON."

"MR. BOSWELL TO DR. JOHNSON.

"MY DEAR SIR,   *Edinburgh*, *Feb.* 14, 1777.

"My state of epistolary accounts with you at present is extraordinary. The balance, as to number, is on your side. I am indebted to you for two letters; one dated the 16th of November, upon which very day I wrote to you, so that our letters were exactly exchanged, and one dated the 21st of December last.

"My heart was warmed with gratitude by the truly kind contents of both of them; and it is amazing and vexing that I have allowed so much time to elapse without writing to you. But delay is inherent in me, by nature or by bad habit. I waited till I should have an opportunity of paying you my compliments on a new year. I have procrastinated till the new year is no longer new.

*   *   *   *   *

"Dr. Memis's cause was determined against him with 40*l.* costs. The Lord President, and two other of the Judges, dissented from the majority, upon this ground: that, although there may have been no intention to injure him by calling him *Doctor of Medicine*, instead of *Physician*, yet, as he remonstrated against the designation before the charter was printed off, and represented that it was disagreeable, and even hurtful to him, it was ill-natured to refuse to alter it, and let him have the designation to which he was certainly entitled. My own opinion is, that our court has judged wrong. The defendants were *in mala fide*, to persist in naming him in a way that he disliked. You remember poor

---

[1] The celebrated dramatic commentator. He was an elegant scholar, well versed in old English literature, and was the principal contributor to the "Biographia Dramatica." He was born at Stepney in 1736, and died in 1800.—ED.

Goldsmith, when he grew important, and wished to appear *Doctor Major*, could not bear your calling him *Goldy*. Would it not have been wrong to have named him so in your 'Preface to Shakespeare,' or in any serious permanent writing of any sort? The difficulty is, whether an action should be allowed on such petty grounds. *De minimis non curat lex.*

"The negro cause is not yet decided. A memorial is preparing on the side of slavery. I shall send you a copy as soon as it is printed. Maclaurin is made happy by your approbation of his memorial for the black.

"Macquarry was here in the winter, and we passed an evening together. The sale of his estate cannot be prevented.

"Sir Allan Maclean's suit against the Duke of Argyle, for recovering the ancient inheritance of his family, is now fairly before all our judges. I spoke for him yesterday, and Maclaurin to-day; Crosbie spoke to-day against him. Three more counsel are to be heard, and next week the cause will be determined. I send you the *Informations* or *Cases*, on each side, which I hope you will read. You said to me, when we were under Sir Allan's hospitable roof, 'I will help him with my pen.' You said it with a generous glow; and though his Grace of Argyle did afterwards mount you upon an excellent horse, upon which 'you looked like a Bishop,' you must not swerve from your purpose at Inchkenneth. I wish you may understand the points at issue, amidst our Scotch law principles and phrases.

[Here followed a full state of the case, in which I endeavoured to make it as clear as I could to an Englishman who had no knowledge of the formularies and technical language of the law of Scotland.]

"I shall inform you how the cause is decided here. But as it may be brought under the review of our Judges, and is certainly to be carried by appeal to the House of Lords, the assistance of such a mind as yours will be of consequence. Your paper on *Vicious Intromission* is a noble proof of what you can do even in Scotch law.

*   *   *   *   *

"I have not yet distributed all your books. Lord Hailes and Lord Monboddo have each received one and return you thanks. Monboddo dined with me lately, and, having drank tea, we were a good while by ourselves, and as I knew that he had read the 'Journey,' superficially, as he did not talk of it as I wished, I brought it to him, and read aloud several passages; and then he talked so, that I told him he was to have a copy *from the author*. He begged *that* might be marked on it.

*   *   *   *   *

"I ever am, my dear Sir, your most faithful
"And affectionate humble servant,
"JAMES BOSWELL."

"SIR ALEXANDER DICK[1] TO DR. SAMUEL JOHNSON.

"SIR,   *Prestonfield, Feb.* 17, 1777.

"I had yesterday the honour of receiving your book of your 'Journey to the Western Islands of Scotland,' which you were so good as to send me, by the hands of our mutual friend, Mr. Boswell, of Auchinleck; for which I return you my most hearty thanks: and, after carefully reading it over again, shall deposit it in my little collection of choice books, next our worthy friend's 'Journey to Corsica.' As there are many things to admire in both performances, I have often wished that no Travels or Journey should be published but those undertaken by persons of integrity and capacity to judge well, and describe faithfully, and in good language, the situation, condition, and manners of the countries passed through. Indeed our country of Scotland, in spite of the union of the crowns, is still in most places so devoid of clothing, or cover from hedges and plantations, that it was well you gave your readers a sound *Monitoire*, with respect to that circumstance. The truths you have told, and the purity of the language in which they are expressed, as your 'Journey' is universally read, may, and already appear to have a very good effect. For a man of my acquaintance, who has the largest nursery for trees and hedges in the country, tells me, that of late the demand upon him for these articles is doubled, and sometimes tripled. I have, therefore, listed Dr. Samuel Johnson in some of my memorandums of the principal planters and favourers of the enclosures, under a name which I took the liberty to invent from the Greek, *Papadendrion*. Lord Auchinleck and some few more are of the list. I am told that one gentleman in the shire of Aberdeen, viz., Sir Archibald Grant, has planted above fifty millions of trees on a piece of very wild ground at Monimusk. I must inquire if he has fenced them well, before he enters my list; for that is the soul of enclosing. I began myself to plant a little, our ground being too valuable for much, and that is now fifty years ago; and the trees, now in my seventy-fourth year, I look up to with reverence, and show them to my eldest son, now in his fifteenth year, and they are full the height of my country-house here, where I had the pleasure of receiving you, and hope again to have that satisfaction with our mutual friend, Mr. Boswell.

I shall always continue, with the truest esteem, dear Doctor, your most obliged

"And obedient humble servant,
                              "ALEXANDER DICK."

[1] Sir Alexander Dick was a physician of some eminence, who studied at Leyden, under Boerhaave, and was afterwards elected President of the College of Physicians at Edinburgh. In 1774, he received the gold medal from the London Society for Promoting Arts and Commerce, for his success in cultivating the true rhubarb in Britain. He was born in 1703, and died in 1785.—ED.

For a character of this very amiable man, see "Journal of a Tour to the Hebrides," 3rd. edit. p. 36.—BOSWELL.

"TO JAMES BOSWELL, ESQ.

"DEAR SIR,   *February* 18, 1777.

"It is so long since I heard any thing from you,[1] that I am not easy about it; write something to me next post. When you sent your last letter everything seemed to be mending; I hope nothing has lately grown worse. I suppose young Alexander continues to thrive, and Veronica is now very pretty company. I do not suppose the lady is yet reconciled to me, yet let her know that I love her very well, and value her very much.

"Dr. Blair is printing some sermons. If they are all like the first, which I have read, they are *sermones aurei, ac auro magis aurei*. It is excellently written both as to doctrine and language. Mr. Watson's book[2] seems to be much esteemed.

*   *   *   *   *

"Poor Beauclerk still continues very ill. Langton lives on as he used to do. His children are very pretty, and, I think, his lady loses her Scotch. Paoli I never see.

"I have been so distressed by difficulty of breathing, that I lost, as was computed, six-and-thirty ounces of blood in a few days. I am better but not well.

"I wish you would be vigilant, and get me Graham's 'Telemachus,' that was printed at Glasgow, a very little book; and '*Jonstoni Poemata*,' another little book, printed at Middleburgh.

"Mrs. Williams sends her compliments, and promises that when you come hither she will accommodate you as well as ever she can in the old room. She wishes to know whether you sent her book to Sir Alexander Gordon.

"My dear Boswell, do not neglect to write to me: for your kindness is one of the pleasures of my life, which I should be sorry to lose.

"I am, Sir, your humble servant,
"SAM. JOHNSON."

"TO DR. SAMUEL JOHNSON.

"DEAR SIR,   *Edinburgh, Feb.* 24, 1777.

"Your letter, dated the 18th instant, I had the pleasure to receive last post. Although my late long neglect, or rather delay, was truly culpable, I am tempted not to regret it, since it has produced me so valuable a proof of your regard. I did, indeed, during that inexcusable silence, sometimes divert the reproaches of my own mind, by fancying that I should hear again from you, inquiring with some anxiety about me, because for aught you knew, I might have been ill.

"You are pleased to show me that my kindness is of some consequence to you. My heart is elated at the thought. Be assured,

---

[1] By the then course of the post, my long letter of the 14th had not yet reached him.—BOSWELL.

[2] History of Philip the Second.—BOSWELL.

my dear Sir, that my affection and reverence for you are exalted and steady. I do not believe that a more perfect attachment ever existed in the history of mankind. And it is a noble attachment; for the attractions are Genius, Learning, and Piety.

"Your difficulty of breathing alarms me, and brings into my imagination an event which, although in the natural course of things I must expect at some period, I cannot view with composure.

*   *   *   *   *

"My wife is much honoured by what you say of her. She begs you may accept of her best compliments. She is to send you some marmalade of oranges of her own making.

*   *   *   *   *

"I ever am, my dear Sir, your most obliged
"And faithful humble servant,
"JAMES BOSWELL."

"TO JAMES BOSWELL, ESQ.

"DEAR SIR,   March 14, 1777.

"I have been much pleased with your late letter, and am glad that my old enemy, Mrs. Boswell, begins to feel some remorse. As to Miss Veronica's Scotch, I think it cannot be helped. An English maid you might easily have; but she would still imitate the greater number, as they would be likewise those whom she must most respect. Her dialect will not be gross. Her mamma has not much Scotch, and you have yourself very little. I hope she knows my name, and does not call me *Johnston*.[1]

"The immediate cause of my writing is this:—One Shaw, who seems a modest and a decent man, has written an Erse Grammar, which a very learned Highlander, Macbean, has, at my request, examined and approved.

"The book is very little, but Mr. Shaw has been persuaded by his friends to set it at half a guinea, though I advised only a crown, and thought myself liberal. You, whom the author considers as a great encourager of ingenious men, will receive a parcel of his proposals and receipts. I have undertaken to give you notice of them, and to solicit your countenance. You must ask no poor man, because the price is really too high. Yet such a work deserves patronage.

"It is proposed to augment our club from twenty to thirty, of which I am glad; for as we have several in it whom I do not much like to consort with,[2] I am for reducing it to a mere miscellaneous collection of conspicuous men, without any determinate character.

*   *   *   *   *

"I am, dear Sir, Most affectionately yours,
"SAM. JOHNSON.

"My respects to Madam, to Veronica, to Alexander, to Euphemia, to David."

---

[1] John*son* is the most common English formation of the surname from *John* ; John*ston* the Scotch. My illustrious friend observed, that many North Britons pronounced his name in their own way.—BOSWELL.

[2] On account of their differing from him as to religion and politics.—BOSWELL.

"MR. BOSWELL TO DR. JOHNSON.

"Edinburgh, April 4, 1777.

After informing him of the death of my little son David, and that I could not come to London this spring—

"I think it hard that I should be a whole year without seeing you. May I presume to petition for a meeting with you in the autumn? You have, I believe, seen all the cathedrals in England, except that of Carlisle. If you are to be with Dr. Taylor, at Ashbourne, it would not be a great journey to come thither. We may pass a few most agreeable days there by ourselves, and I will accompany you a good part of the way to the southward again. Pray think of this.

"You forget that Mr. Shaw's Erse Grammer was put into your hands by myself last year. Lord Eglintoune put it into mine. I am glad that Mr. Macbean approves of it. I have received Mr. Shaw's proposals for its publication, which I can perceive are written *by the hand of a* MASTER.

*   *   *   *   *

"Pray get me all the editions of 'Walton's Lives.' I have a notion that the republication of them with Notes will fall upon me, between Dr. Horne and Lord Hailes."[1]

Mr. Shaw's proposals for "An Analysis of the Scotch Celtic Language," were thus illuminated by the pen of Johnson:—

"Though the Erse Dialect of the Celtic Language has, from the earliest times, been spoken in Britain, and still subsists in the northern parts and adjacent islands, yet, by the negligence of people rather warlike than lettered, it has hitherto been left to the caprice and judgment of every speaker, and has floated in the living voice, without the steadiness of analogy, or direction of rules. An Erse Grammar is an addition to the stores of literature; and its author hopes for the indulgence always shown to those that attempt to do what was never done before. If his work shall be found defective, it is at least all his own; he is not, like other grammarians, a compiler or transcriber; what he delivers, he has learned by attentive observation among his countrymen, who perhaps will be themselves surprised to see that speech reduced to principles, which they have used only by imitation.

"The use of this book will, however, not be confined to

---

[1] None of the persons here mentioned executed the work which they had in contemplation. Walton's valuable book, however, has been correctly republished in quarto, with notes and illustrations, by the Rev. Mr. Zouch.—MALONE.

the mountains and islands; it will afford a pleasing and important subject of speculation to those whose studies lead them to trace the affinity of languages, and the migrations of the ancient races of mankind."

"TO DR. SAMUEL JOHNSON.

"MY DEAR SIR,   *Glasgow, April* 24, 1777.

"Our worthy friend Thrale's death having appeared in the newspapers, and been afterwards contradicted, I have been placed in a state of very uneasy uncertainty, from which I hoped to be relieved by you: but my hopes have as yet been vain. How could you omit to write to me on such an occasion. I shall wait with anxiety.

"I am going to Auchinleck to stay a fortnight with my father. It is better not to be there very long at one time. But frequent renewals of attention are agreeable to him.

"Pray tell me about this edition of 'The English Poets, with a preface, biographical and critical, to each author, by Samuel Johnson, LL.D.' which I see advertised. I am delighted with the prospect of it. Indeed I am happy to feel that I am capable of being so much delighted with literature. But is not the charm of this publication owing to the *magnum nomen* in the front of it?

"What do you say of Lord Chesterfield's Memoirs and Last Letters?

"My wife has made marmalade of oranges for you. I left her and my daughters and Alexander all well yesterday. I have taught Veronica to speak of you thus:—Dr. John*son*, not John*ston*.

"I remain, my dear Sir,
"Your most affectionate and obliged humble servant,
"JAMES BOSWELL."

"TO JAMES BOSWELL, ESQ.

"DEAR SIR,   *May* 3, 1777.

"The story of Mr. Thrale's death, as he had neither been sick nor in any other danger, made so little impression upon me, that I never thought about obviating its effects on anybody else. It is supposed to have been produced by the English custom of making April fools; that is, of sending one another on some foolish errand on the 1st of April.

"Tell Mrs. Boswell that I shall taste her marmalade cautiously at first. *Timeo Danaos et dona ferentes.* 'Beware,' says the Italian proverb, 'of a reconciled enemy.' But when I find it does me no harm, I shall then receive it, and be thankful for it, as a pledge of firm, and, I hope, of unalterable kindness. She is, after all, a dear, dear lady.

"Please to return Dr. Blair thanks for his sermons. The Scotch write English wonderfully well.

*   *   *   *   *

"Your frequent visits to Auchinleck, and your short stays

there, are very laudable and very judicious. Your present concord with your father gives me great pleasure; it was all that you seemed to want.

"My health is very bad, and my nights are very unquiet. What can I do to mend them? I have for this summer nothing better in prospect than a journey into Staffordshire and Derbyshire, perhaps with Oxford and Birmingham in my way.

"Make my compliments to Miss Veronica; I must leave it to *her* philosophy to comfort you for the loss of little David. You must remember, that to keep three out of four is more than your share. Mrs. Thrale has but four out of eleven.

"I am engaged to write little Lives, and little Prefaces, to a little edition of 'The English Poets.' I think I have persuaded the booksellers to insert something of Thomson; and if you could give me some information about him, for the life which we have is very scanty, I should be glad.

"I am, dear Sir,
"Your most affectionate humble servant,
"Sam. Johnson."

CHAPTER IV.—1777

To those who delight in tracing the progress of works of literature, it will be an entertainment to compare the limited design with the ample execution of that admirable performance, "The Lives of the English Poets," which is the richest, most beautiful, and indeed most perfect, production of Johnson's pen. His notion of it at this time appears in the preceding letter. He has a memorandum in this year—"29 May, Easter-eve, I treated with booksellers on a bargain, but the time was not long." [1] The bargain was concerning that undertaking; but his tender conscience seems alarmed, lest it should have intruded too much on his devout preparation for the solemnity of the ensuing day. But, indeed, very little time was necessary for Johnson's concluding a treaty with the booksellers; as he had, I believe, less attention to profit from his labours than any man to whom literature has been a profession. I shall here insert (from a letter to me from my late worthy friend, Mr. Edward Dilly, though of a later date), an account of this plan so happily conceived; since it was the occasion of procuring for us an elegant collection of the best biography and criticism of which our language can boast.

"MR. E. DILLY TO JAMES BOSWELL, ESQ.

"DEAR SIR,   *Southill, Sept. 26th,* 1777.
"You will find, by this letter, that I am still in the same calm retreat, from the noise and bustle of London, as when I wrote to

[1] "Prayers and Meditations," p. 155.—BOSWELL.

100

you last. I am happy to find you had such an agreeable meeting with your old friend, Dr. Johnson; I have no doubt your stock is much increased by the interview; few men, nay, I may say, scarcely any man, has got that fund of knowledge and entertainment as Dr. Johnson in conversation. When he opens freely, every one is attentive to what he says, and cannot fail of improvement as well as pleasure.

"The Edition of the Poets, now printing, will do honour to the English press; and a concise account of the life of each author, by Dr. Johnson, will be a very valuable addition, and stamp the reputation of this edition superior to any thing that is gone before. The first cause that gave rise to this undertaking, I believe, was owing to the little trifling edition of the Poets, printing by the Martins at Edinburgh, and to be sold by Bell in London. Upon examining the volumes which were printed, the type was found so extremely small, that many persons could not read them. Not only this inconvenience attended it, but the inaccuracy of the press was very conspicuous. These reasons, as well as the idea of an invasion of what we call our Literary Property, induced the London booksellers to print an elegant and accurate edition of all the English poets of reputation, from Chaucer to the present time.

"Accordingly, a select number of the most respectable booksellers met on the occasion; and, on consulting together, agreed, that all the proprietors of copyright in the various poets should be summoned together; and, when their opinions were given, to proceed immediately on the business. Accordingly a meeting was held, consisting of about forty of the most respectable booksellers of London, when it was agreed that an elegant and uniform edition of 'The English Poets' should be immediately printed, with a concise account of the life of each author, by Dr. Samuel Johnson; and that three persons should be deputed to wait upon Dr. Johnson, to solicit him to undertake the Lives, viz., T. Davies, Strahan, and Cadell. The Doctor very politely undertook it, and seemed exceedingly pleased with the proposal. As to the terms, it was left entirely to the Doctor to name his own; he mentioned two hundred guineas;[1] it was immediately agreed to; and a farther compliment, I believe, will be made him. A committee was likewise appointed to engage the best engravers, viz., Bartolozzi,[2] Sherwin, Hall, &c. Likewise another committee for giving directions about the paper, printing, &c., so that the whole will be conducted with spirit, and in the best manner, with respect to authorship, editorship, engravings, &c. My brother will give you a list of the Poets

[1] Johnson's moderation in demanding so small a sum is extraordinary. Had he asked one thousand, or even fifteen hundred, guineas, the booksellers, who knew the value of his name, would, doubtless, have readily given it. They have, probably, got five thousand guineas by this work in the course of twenty-five years.—MALONE.

[2] Francis Bartolozzi was born in Florence, in 1728, and came to England in 1764, when he was admitted a Member of the Royal Academy, and received extensive patronage as an engraver and artist. He was the father of the distinguished actress, Madame Vestris. He went to Lisbon in 1802, and there died in 1815.—ED.

we mean to give, many of which are within the time of the Act of Queen Anne, which Martin and Bell cannot give, as they have no property in them; the proprietors are almost all the booksellers in London, of consequence.

                    "I am, dear Sir, ever yours,
                                        "EDWARD DILLY."

I shall afterwards have occasion to consider the extensive and varied range which Johnson took, when he was once led upon ground which he trod with a peculiar delight, having long been intimately acquainted with all the circumstances of it that could interest and please.

"DR. JOHNSON TO CHARLES O'CONNOR, ESQ.[1]

"SIR,   May 19th, 1777.

"Having had the pleasure of conversing with Dr. Campbell about your character and your literary undertaking, I am resolved to gratify myself by renewing a correspondence which began and ended a great while ago, and ended, I am afraid, by my fault; a fault which, if you have not forgotten it, you must now forgive.

"If I have ever disappointed you, give me leave to tell you, that you have likewise disappointed me. I expected great discoveries in Irish antiquity, and large publications in the Irish language; but the world still remains as it was, doubtful and ignorant. What the Irish language is in itself, and to what languages it has affinity, are very interesting questions, which every man wishes to see resolved that has any philological or historical curiosity. Dr. Leland[2] begins his history too late: the ages which deserve an exact inquiry are those times (for such they were) when Ireland was the school of the west, the quiet habitation of sanctity and literature. If you could give a history, though imperfect, of the Irish nation, from its conversion to Christianity to the invasion from England, you would amplify knowledge with new views and new objects. Set about it, therefore, if you can: do what you can

[1] Mr. Joseph Cooper Walker, of the Treasury, Dublin, who obligingly communicated to me this and a former letter from Dr. Johnson to the same gentleman (for which see vol. i. chap. ix.), writes to me as follows:— "Perhaps it would gratify you to have some account of Mr. O'Connor. He is an amiable, learned, venerable old gentleman, of an independent fortune, who lives at Belanagar, in the county of Roscommon; he is an admired writer, and Member of the Irish Academy."—The above letter is alluded to in the Preface of the 2d edit. of his "Dissert." p. 3. Mr. O'Connor afterwards died at the age of eighty-two, July 1, 1791. See a well-drawn character of him in "The Gentleman's Magazine" for August, 1791.—BOSWELL.

[2] Dr. Thomas Leland was a divine and miscellaneous writer, and the author of a "History of Ireland," in 3 vols. 8vo. He was born and educated in Dublin in 1722, and appointed to the vicarage of Bray in 1768. He died in 1785.—ED.

easily do without anxious exactness. Lay the foundation, and leave the superstructure to posterity.

"I am, Sir, your humble servant,

"SAM. JOHNSON."

Early in this year came out, in two volumes quarto, the posthumous works of the learned Dr. Zachary Pearce, Bishop of Rochester:[1] being, "A Commentary, with Notes, on the Four Evangelists and the Acts of the Apostles," with other theological pieces. Johnson had now an opportunity of making a grateful return to that excellent prelate, who, we have seen, was the only person who gave him any assistance in the compilation of his Dictionary. The Bishop had left some account of his life and character, written by himself. To this Johnson made some valuable additions, and furnished to the editor, the Reverend Mr. Derby,[2] a Dedication, which I shall here insert, both because it will appear at this time with peculiar propriety, and because it will tend to propagate and increase that "fervour of *loyalty*," which in me, who boast of the name of TORY, is not only a principle but a passion.

"TO THE KING.

"SIR,

"I presume to lay before your Majesty the last labours of a learned Bishop who died in the toils and duties of his calling. He is now beyond the reach of all earthly honours and rewards; and only the hope of inciting others to imitate him, makes it now fit to be remembered that he enjoyed in his life the favour of your Majesty.

"The tumultuary life of Princes seldom permits them to survey the wide extent of national interest without losing sight of private merit; to exhibit qualities which may be imitated by the highest and the humblest of mankind; and to be at once amiable and great.

"Such characters, if now and then they appear in history, are contemplated with admiration. May it be the ambition of all your subjects to make haste with their tribute of reverence; and as posterity may learn from your Majesty how kings should live,

[1] Bishop Pearce was the son of a distiller in High Holborn, and educated at Westminster School. He became successively the Vicar of St. Martin's-in-the-Fields, Dean of Winchester, Bishop of Bangor, and, in 1756, the Bishop of Rochester. His principal works were critical and erudite editions of Longinus and Cicero. He left, among numerous charitable bequests, 5000*l.* to the College for Clergymen's Widows, at Brompton. He was born in 1690, and died in 1774.—ED.

[2] Mr. Derby was Rector of Southfleet and Longfield, in Kent. He died in 1778.—GENTLEMAN'S MAGAZINE.

may they learn likewise from your people how they should be honoured.   I am, may it please your Majesty,
"With the most profound respect,
"Your Majesty's most dutiful and devoted
"Subject and servant."

In the summer he wrote a Prologue, which was spoken before "A Word to the Wise," a comedy by Mr. Hugh Kelly,[1] which had been brought upon the stage in 1770; but he being a writer for the ministry in one of the newspapers, it fell a sacrifice to popular fury, and, in the playhouse phrase, was *damned*. By the generosity of Mr. Harris, the proprietor of Covent-garden Theatre, it was now exhibited for one night, for the benefit of the author's widow and children.   To conciliate the favour of the audience, was the intention of Johnson's Prologue, which, as it is not long, I shall here insert, as a proof that his poetical talents were in no degree impaired.

"This night presents a play, which public rage,
  Or right or wrong, once hooted from the stage:
  From zeal or malice, now no more we dread,
  For English vengeance *wars not with the dead.*
  A generous foe regards with pitying eye
  The man whom Fate has laid where all must lie.
  To wit, reviving from its author's dust,
  Be kind, ye judges, or at least be just:
  Let no renewed hostilities invade
  Th' oblivious grave's inviolable shade.
  Let one great payment every claim appease,
  And him who cannot hurt, allow to please;
  To please by scenes, unconscious of offence,
  By harmless merriment, or useful sense.
  Where aught of bright or fair the piece displays,
  Approve it only;—'tis too late to praise.
  If want of skill or want of care appear,
  Forbear to hiss;—the poet cannot hear.
  By all, like him, must praise and blame be found,
  At last, a fleeting gleam, or empty sound;
  Yet then shall calm reflection bless the night,
  When liberal pity dignified delight;
  When pleasure fired her torch at virtue's flame,
  And mirth was bounty with an humbler name."

[1] Mr. Hugh Kelly was not only the author of various dramatic pieces, but he was also a poet, a novelist, and an essayist. His "Thespis," a poem in the manner of Churchill's "Rosciad," and his "Louisa Mildmay," a novel, are familiar to most readers. He was born in 1739, near the Lakes of Killarney, and originally apprenticed to a staymaker. He died in 1777.—ED.

A circumstance which could not fail to be very pleasing to Johnson, occurred this year. The tragedy of "Sir Thomas Overbury," written by his early companion in London, Richard Savage,[1] was brought up with alterations, at Drury-lane Theatre. The Prologue to it was written by Mr. Richard Brinsley Sheridan; in which, after describing very pathetically the wretchedness of

> "Ill fated Savage, at whose birth was giv'n
> No parent but the Muse, no friend but Heav'n:"

he introduced an elegant compliment to Johnson on his Dictionary, that wonderful performance which cannot be too often or too highly praised; of which Mr. Harris, in his "Philological Inquiries,"[2] justly and liberally observes, "Such is its merit, that our language does not possess a more copious, learned, and valuable work." The concluding lines of this Prologue were these:—

> "So pleads the tale that gives to future times
> The son's misfortunes and the parent's crimes;
> There shall his fame (if own'd to-night) survive,
> Fix'd by THE HAND THAT BIDS OUR LANGUAGE LIVE."

Mr. Sheridan here at once did honour to his taste and to his liberality of sentiment, by showing that he was not prejudiced from the unlucky difference which had taken place between his worthy father and Dr. Johnson. I have already mentioned, that Johnson was very desirous of reconciliation with old Mr. Sheridan. It will, therefore, not seem at all surprising that he was zealous in acknowledging the brilliant merit of his son. While it had as yet been displayed only in the drama, Johnson proposed him as a member of THE LITERARY CLUB, observing, that "he who has written the two best comedies of his age is surely a considerable man." And he had, accordingly, the honour to be elected; for an honour it undoubtedly must be allowed to be, when it is considered of whom that society consists, and that a single black-ball excludes a candidate.

---

[1] This tragedy first appeared in 1723, and the profits thence arising amounted to 200*l*. It was the means of bringing Savage into public notice.—ED.

[1] Part i. chap. iv.—Mr. James Harris was born at Salisbury, in 1709; in 1774 he was made Secretary and Comptroller to the Queen. His writings display considerable ingenuity and philological erudition. He died in 1780.—ED.

"MR. BOSWELL TO DR. JOHNSON.

"MY DEAR SIR,   *July* 9, 1777.

"For the health of my wife and children, I have taken the little country-house at which you visited my uncle, Dr. Boswell, who, having lost his wife, is gone to live with his son. We took possession of our villa about a week ago; we have a garden of three quarters of an acre, well stocked with fruit-trees and flowers, and gooseberries and currants, and peas and beans, and cabbages, &c. &c., and my children are quite happy. I now write to you in a little study, from the window of which I see around me a verdant grove, and beyond it the lofty mountain called Arthur's Seat.

"Your last letter, in which you desire me to send you some additional information concerning Thomson, reached me very fortunately just as I was going to Lanark, to put my wife's two nephews, the young Campbells, to school there, under the care of Mr. Thomson, the master of it, whose wife is sister to the author of 'The Seasons.' She is an old woman; but her memory is very good; and she will with pleasure give me for you every particular that you wish to know, and she can tell. Pray then take the trouble to send me such questions as may lead to biographical materials. You say that the Life which we have of Thomson is scanty. Since I received your Letter I have read his Life, published under the name of Cibber; but, as you told me, really written by a Mr. Shiels; that written by Dr. Murdoch; one prefixed to an edition of 'The Seasons,' published at Edinburgh, which is compounded of both, with the addition of an anecdote of Quin's relieving Thomson from prison; the abridgment of Murdoch's account of him, in 'The Biographia Britannica,' and another abridgment of it in 'The Biographical Dictionary,' enriched with Dr. Joseph Warton's critical panegyric on 'The Seasons' in his 'Essay on the Genius and Writings of Pope:' from all these it appears to me that we have a pretty full account of this poet. However, you will, I doubt not, show me many blanks, and I shall do what can be done to have them filled up. As Thomson never returned to Scotland (which *you* will think very wise), his sister can speak from her own knowledge only, as to the early part of his life. She has some letters from him, which may probably give light as to his more advanced progress, if she will let us see them, which I suppose she will. I believe George Lewis Scott[1] and Dr. Armstrong[2] are now his only surviving companions, while he lived in and about London: and they, I dare say, can tell more of him than is yet known. My own notion is, that Thomson was a much coarser man than his friends are willing to acknowledge. His 'Seasons' are

[1] George Lewis Scott, Esq., F.R.S., an amiable and learned man, formerly Sub-Preceptor to his present Majesty, and afterwards appointed a Commissioner of Excise. He died in 1780.—MALONE.

[2] Dr. John Armstrong, the celebrated poet and physician, who has produced one of the best didactic poems in our language, entitled, "The Art of Preserving Health." He was born at Castleton, co. Roxburg, in 1709, and died in 1779.—ED.

indeed full of elegant and pious sentiments: but a rank soil, nay a dunghill, will produce beautiful flowers.

"Your edition[1] of 'The English Poets,' will be very valuable, on account of the Prefaces and Lives. But I have seen a specimen of an edition of the Poets at the Apollo press, at Edinburgh, which, for excellence in printing and engraving, highly deserves a liberal encouragement.

"Most sincerely do I regret the bad health and bad rest with which you have been afflicted; and I hope you are better. I cannot believe that the prologue, which you generously gave to Mr. Kelly's widow and children the other day, is the effusion of one in sickness and in disquietude: but external circumstances are never sure indications of the state of man. I send you a letter which I wrote to you two years ago at Wilton; and did not send it at the time, for fear of being reproved as indulging too much tenderness; and one written to you at the tomb of Melancthon, which I kept back, lest I should appear at once too superstitious and too enthusiastic. I now imagine that perhaps they may please you.

"You do not take the least notice of my proposal for our meeting at Carlisle.[2] Though I have meritoriously refrained from visiting London this year, I ask you if it would not be wrong that I should be two years without having the benefit of your conversation, when if you come down as far as Derbyshire, we may meet at the expense of a few days' journeying, and not many pounds. I wish you to see Carlisle, which made me mention that place. But if you have not a desire to complete your tour of the English cathedrals, I will take a larger share of the road between this place and Ashbourne. So tell me *where* you will fix for our passing a few days by ourselves. Now don't cry 'foolish fellow,' or 'idle dog.' Chain your humour and let your kindness play.

"You will rejoice to hear that Miss Macleod, of Rasay, is married

---

[1] Dr. Johnson was not the *editor* of this Collection of the English Poets; he merely furnished the biographical prefaces with which it is enriched; as is rightly stated in a subsequent page. He, indeed, from a virtuous motive, recommended the works of four or five poets (whom he has named) to be added to the collection; but he is no otherwise answerable for any which are found there, or any which are omitted. The poems of Goldsmith (whose life I know he intended to write, for I collected some materials for it by his desire) were omitted, in consequence of a petty exclusive interest in some of them, vested in Mr. Carnan, a bookseller.—Malone.

[2] Dr. Johnson had himself talked of our seeing Carlisle together. *High* was a favourite word of his to denote a person of rank. He said to me, "Sir, I believe we may meet at the house of a Roman Catholic lady in Cumberland; a high lady, Sir." I afterwards discovered that he meant Mrs. Strickland, sister of Charles Townley, Esq., whose very noble collection of statues and pictures is not more to be admired than his extraordinary and polite readiness in showing it, which I and several of my friends have agreeably experienced. They who are possessed of valuable stores of gratification to persons of taste, should exercise their benevolence in imparting the pleasure. Grateful acknowledgments are due to Welbore Ellis Agar, Esq., for the liberal access which he is pleased to allow to his exquisite collection of pictures.—Boswell.

to Colonel Mure Campbell, an excellent man, with a pretty good estate of his own, and the prospect of having the Earl of Loudon's fortune and honours. Is not this a noble lot for our fair Hebridean? How happy am I that she is to be in Ayrshire. We shall have the Laird of Rasay, and old Malcolm, and I know not how many gallant Macleods, and bagpipes, &c. &c., at Auchinleck. Perhaps you may meet them all there.

"Without doubt you have read what is called 'The *Life* of David Hume,' written by himself, with the letter from Dr. Adam Smith subjoined to it. Is not this an age of daring effrontery? My friend Mr. Anderson,[1] Professor of Natural Philosophy at Glasgow, at whose house you and I supped, and to whose care Mr. Windham, of Norfolk, was intrusted at that University, paid me a visit lately; and after we had talked with indignation and contempt of the poisonous productions with which this age is infested, he said there was now an excellent opportunity for Dr. Johnson to step forth. I agreed with him that you might knock Hume's and Smith's heads together, and make vain and ostentatious infidelity exceedingly ridiculous. Would it not be worth your while to crush such noxious weeds in the moral garden?

"You have said nothing to me of Dr. Dodd. I know not how you think on that subject; though the newspapers give us a saying of yours in favour of mercy to him. But I own I am very desirous that the royal prerogative of remission of punishment should be employed to exhibit an illustrious instance of the regard which God's Vicegerent will ever show to piety and virtue. If for ten righteous men the Almighty would have spared Sodom, shall not a thousand acts of goodness done by Dr. Dodd counterbalance one crime? Such an instance would do more to encourage goodness than his execution would do to deter from vice. I am not afraid of any bad consequence to society; for who will persevere for a long course of years in a distinguished discharge of religious duties, with a view to commit a forgery with impunity?

"Pray make my best compliments acceptable to Mr. and Mrs. Thrale, by assuring them of my hearty joy that the *Master*, as you call him, is alive. I hope I shall often taste his champagne—*soberly*.

"I have not heard from Langton for a long time; I suppose he is as usual,

> 'Studious the busy moments to deceive.'

*   *   *   *   *

"I remain, my dear Sir, your most affectionate
"And faithful humble servant,
"James Boswell."

On the 23rd of June I again wrote to Dr. Johnson, enclosing a shipmaster's receipt for a jar of orange mar-

---

[1] Mr. John Anderson was the founder of an educational institution in Glasgow, denominated "The Andersonian University," established for the use of unacademical classes. He was born at Roseneath, co. Dumbarton, in 1726, and died in 1796.—Ed.

malade, and a large packet of Lord Hailes's "Annals of Scotland."

"TO JAMES BOSWELL, ESQ.

"Dear Sir,   *June* 28, 1777.

"I have just received your packet from Mr. Thrale's, but have not daylight enough to look much into it. I am glad that I have credit enough with Lord Hailes to be trusted with more copy. I hope to take more care of it than of the last. I return Mrs. Boswell my affectionate thanks for her present, which I value as a token of reconciliation.

"Poor Dodd was put to death yesterday, in opposition to the recommendation of the jury—the petition of the city of London— and a subsequent petition signed by three-and-twenty thousand hands. Surely the voice of the public, when it calls so loudly, and only for mercy, ought to be heard.

"The saying that was given me in the papers I never spoke; but I wrote many of his petitions, and some of his letters. He applied to me very often. He was, I am afraid, long flattered with hopes of life; but I had no part in the dreadful delusion; for as soon as the king had signed his sentence, I obtained from Mr. Chamier an account of the disposition of the court towards him, with a declaration that there *was no hope even of a respite*. This letter immediately was laid before Dodd; but he believed those whom he wished to be right, as it is thought, till within three days of his end. He died with pious composure and resolution. I have just seen the ordinary that attended him. His address to his fellow-convicts offended the Methodists; but he had a Moravian with him much of his time. His moral character is very bad: I hope all is not true that is charged upon him. Of his behaviour in prison an account will be published.

"I give you joy of your country-house and your pretty garden: and hope some time to see you in your felicity. I was much pleased with your two letters that had been kept so long in store; [1] and rejoice at Miss Rasay's advancement, and wish Sir Allan success.

"I hope to meet you somewhere towards the north, but am loth

---

[1] Since they have been so much honoured by Johnson, I shall here insert them:—

"TO MR. SAMUEL JOHNSON.

"*Sunday*, Sept. 30, 1764.

"My ever dear and much respected Sir,—

"You know my solemn enthusiasm of mind. You love me for it, and I respect myself for it, because in so far as I resemble Mr. Johnson. You will be agreeably surprised when you learn the reason of my writing this letter. I am at Wittemberg, in Saxony. I am in the old church where the Reformation was first preached, and where some of the Reformers lie interred. I cannot resist the serious pleasure of writing to Mr. Johnson from the tomb of Melancthon. My paper rests upon the gravestone of that great and good man, who was undoubtedly the worthiest of all the Reformers. He wished to reform abuses which had been introduced into the Church; but had no private resentment to gratify. So mild was he, that when his aged mother consulted him with anxiety on the perplexing disputes of the times, he advised her 'to keep to the old religion.' At this tomb, then, my ever dear and respected friend,

to come quite to Carlisle. Can we not meet at Manchester? But we will settle it in some other letters.

"Mr. Seward,[1] a great favourite at Streatham, has been, I think, enkindled by our travels with a curiosity to see the Highlands. I have given him letters to you and Beattie. He desires that a lodging may be taken for him at Edinburgh, against his arrival. He is just setting out.

"Langton has been exercising the militia. Mrs. Williams is, I fear, declining. Dr. Lawrence says he can do no more. She is gone to summer in the country, with as many conveniences about her as she can expect; but I have no great hope. We must all die: may we all be prepared!

"I suppose Miss Boswell reads her book, and young Alexander takes to his learning. Let me hear about them; for everything that belongs to you, belongs in a more remote degree, and not, I hope, very remote, to, dear Sir,

"Yours affectionately,
"SAM. JOHNSON."

TO THE SAME.

"DEAR SIR,   *June 24, 1777.*

"This gentleman is a great favourite at Streatham, and therefore you will easily believe that he has very valuable qualities. Our

I vow to thee an eternal attachment. It shall be my study to do what I can to render your life happy; and if you die before me, I shall endeavour to do honour to your memory; and, elevated by the remembrance of you, persist in noble piety. May God, the father of all beings, ever bless you, and may you continue to love

"Your most affectionate friend and devoted servant,
"JAMES BOSWELL."

TO DR. SAMUEL JOHNSON
"MY DEAR SIR,   *Wilton-house,* April 22, 1775.

"Every scene of my life confirms the truth of what you have told me, 'there is no certain happiness in this state of being.' I am here, amidst all that you know is at Lord Pembroke's, and yet I am weary and gloomy. I am just setting out for the house of an old friend in Devonshire, and shall not get back to London for a week yet. You said to me last Good Friday, with a cordiality that warmed my heart, that if I came to settle in London, we should have a day fixed every week to meet by ourselves and talk freely. To be thought worthy of such a privilege cannot but exalt me. During my present absence from you, while, notwithstanding the gaiety which you allow me to possess, I am darkened by temporary clouds, I beg to have a few lines from you—a few lines merely of kindness, as a *viaticum* till I see you again. In your 'Vanity of Human Wishes,' and in Parnell's 'Contentment,' I find the only sure means of enjoying happiness; or, at least, the hopes of happiness. I ever am, with reverence and affection, most faithfully yours,

"JAMES BOSWELL."

[1] William Seward, Esq., F.R.S., editor of "Anecdotes of some Distinguished Persons," &c., in four volumes 8vo., well known to a numerous and valuable acquaintance for his literature, love of the fine arts, and social virtues. I am indebted to him for several communications concerning Johnson.—BOSWELL.

This gentleman, who was born in 1747, and was educated at the Charter-house, and at Oxford, died in London. April 24, 1799.—MALONE.

narrative has kindled him with a desire of visiting the Highlands after having already seen a great part of Europe. You must receive him as a friend, and, when you have directed him to the curiosities of Edinburgh, give him instructions and recommendations for the rest of his journey.   I am, dear Sir,

"Your most humble servant,

"SAM. JOHNSON."

Johnson's benevolence to the unfortunate was, I am confident, as steady and active as that of any of those who have been most eminently distinguished for that virtue.   Innumerable proofs of it I have no doubt will be for ever concealed from mortal eyes.   We may, however, form some judgment of it from the many and very various instances which have been discovered.   One, which happened in the course of this summer, is remarkable from the name and connection of the person who was the object of it.   The circumstance to which I allude is ascertained by two letters, one to Mr. Langton, and another to the Reverend Dr. Vyse, rector of Lambeth, son of the respectable clergyman at Lichfield, who was contemporary with Johnson, and in whose father's family Johnson had the happiness of being kindly received in his early years.

"DR. JOHNSON TO BENNET LANGTON, ESQ.

"DEAR SIR,   June 29, 1777.

"I have lately been much disordered by a difficulty of breathing, but am now better.   I hope your house is well.

"You know we have been talking lately of St. Cross, at Winchester; I have an old acquaintance whose distress makes him very desirous of an hospital, and I am afraid I have not strength enough to get him into the Chartreux.   He is a painter, who never rose higher than to get his immediate living, and from that, at eighty-three, he is disabled by a slight stroke of the palsy, such as does not make him at all helpless on common occasions, though his hand is not steady enough for his art.

"My request is, that you will try to obtain a promise of the next vacancy from the Bishop of Chester.   It is not a great thing to ask, and I hope we shall obtain it.   Dr. Warton has promised to favour him with his notice, and I hope he may end his days in peace.

"I am, Sir, your most humble servant,

"SAM. JOHNSON."

"TO THE REVEREND DR. VYSE, AT LAMBETH.

"SIR,   July 9, 1777.

"I doubt not but you will readily forgive me for taking the liberty of requesting your assistance in recommending an old friend to his Grace the Archbishop as Governor of the Charter-house.

"His name is De Groot; he was born at Gloucester. I have known him many years. He has all the common claims to charity, being old, poor, and infirm in a great degree. He has likewise another claim, to which no scholar can refuse attention; he is by several descents the nephew of Hugo Grotius; of him, from whom perhaps every man of learning has learnt something. Let it not be said that in any lettered country a nephew of Grotius asked a charity and was refused. I am, Reverend Sir, your most humble servant,

"SAM. JOHNSON."

"TO THE REVEREND DR. VYSE, AT LAMBETH.

"*July* 22, 1777.

"IF any notice should be taken of the recommendation which I took the liberty of sending you, it will be necessary to know that Mr. De Groot is to be found at No. 8, in Pye-street, Westminster. This information, when I wrote, I could not give you; and being going soon to Lichfield, think it necessary to be left behind me. More I will not say. You will want no persuasion to succour the nephew of Grotius. I am, Sir,

"Your most humble servant,
"SAM. JOHNSON."

"THE REVEREND DR. VYSE TO MR. BOSWELL.

"SIR,   Lambeth, June 9, 1777.

"I have searched in vain for the letter which I spoke of, and which I wished, at your desire, to communicate to you. It was from Dr. Johnson, to return me thanks for my application to Archbishop Cornwallis in favour of poor De Groot.[1] He rejoices at the success it met with, and is lavish in the praise he bestows upon his favourite, Hugo Grotius. I am really sorry that I cannot find this letter, as it is worthy of the writer. That which I send you enclosed,[2] is at your service. It is very short, and will not perhaps be thought of any consequence, unless you should judge proper to consider it as a proof of the very humane part which Dr. Johnson took in behalf of a distressed and deserving person. I am, Sir,

"Your most obedient humble servant,
"W. VYSE."[3]

[1] Through the benevolent intercession of Dr. Johnson, aided by Dr. Vyse, poor De Groot was admitted as a gentleman pensioner into the Charter-house, where he died in 1779.—ED.

[2] The preceding letter.—BOSWELL.

[3] Dr. Vyse, at my request, was so obliging as once more to endeavour to recover the letter of Johnson, to which he alludes, but without success; for April 23, 1800, he wrote to me thus:—"I have again searched, but in vain, for one of his letters, in which he speaks, in his own nervous style, of Hugo Grotius.—De Groot was clearly a descendant of the family of Grotius, and Archbishop Cornwallis willingly complied with Dr. Johnson's request."—MALONE.

"DR. JOHNSON TO MR. EDWARD DILLY.

"Sir,   *Bolt-court, Fleet-street, July* 7, 1777.

"To the collection of English Poets I have recommended the volume of Dr. Watts to be added; his name has long been held by me in veneration, and I would not willingly be reduced to tell of him only that he was born and died.   Yet of his life I know very little, and therefore must pass him in a manner very unworthy of his character, unless some of his friends will favour me with the necessary information.   Many of them must be known to you: and by your influence perhaps I may obtain some instruction.   My plan does not exact much; but I wish to distinguish Watts, a man who never wrote but for a good purpose.   Be pleased to do for me what you can.   I am, sir,

"Your humble servant,
"Sam. Johnson."

"TO DR. SAMUEL JOHNSON.

"My dear Sir,   *Edinburgh, July* 15, 1777.

"The fate of poor Dr. Dodd made a dismal impression upon my mind.

        *   *   *   *   *

"I had sagacity enough to divine that you wrote his speech to the Recorder, before sentence was pronounced.   I am glad you have written so much for him; and I hope to be favoured with an exact list of the several pieces when we meet.

"I received Mr. Seward, as the friend of Mr. and Mrs. Thrale, and as a gentleman recommended by Dr. Johnson to my attention. I have introduced him to Lord Kames, Lord Monboddo, and Mr. Nairne.   He is gone to the Highlands with Dr. Gregory; when he returns I shall do more for him.

"Sir Allan Maclean has carried that branch of his cause, of which we had good hopes: the President and one other Judge only were against him.   I wish the House of Lords may do as well as the Court of Session has done.   But Sir Allan has not the lands of *Brolos* quite cleared by this judgment, till a long account is made up of debts and interest on the one side, and rents on the other. I am, however, not much afraid of the balance.

"Macquarry's estates, Staffa and all, were sold yesterday, and bought by a Campbell.   I fear he will have little or nothing left out of the purchase-money.

"I send you the case against the negro, by Mr. Cullen, son to Dr. Cullen, in opposition to Maclaurin's for liberty, of which you have approved.   Pray read this, and tell me what you think as a *Politician*, as well as a *Poet*, upon this subject.

"Be so kind as to let me know how your time is to be distributed next autumn.   I will meet you at Manchester, or where you please; but I wish you would complete your tour of the cathedrals, and come to Carlisle, and I will accompany you a part of the way homewards.

"I am ever most faithfully yours,
"James Boswell."

"TO JAMES BOSWELL, ESQ.

"DEAR SIR,   *July* 22, 1777.

"Your notion of the necessity of an early interview is very pleasing to both my vanity and tenderness.   I shall, perhaps, come to Carlisle another year; but my money has not held out so well as it used to do.   I shall go to Ashbourne, and I purpose to make Dr. Taylor invite you.   If you live awhile with me at his house, we shall have much time to ourselves, and our stay will be no expense to us or him.   I shall leave London the 28th; and, after some stay at Oxford and Lichfield, shall probably come to Ashbourne about the end of your Session; but of all this you shall have notice.   Be satisfied we will meet somewhere.

"What passed between me and poor Dr. Dodd, you shall know more fully when we meet.

"Of law-suits there is no end; poor Sir Allan must have another trial, for which, however, his antagonist cannot be much blamed, having two judges on his side.   I am more afraid of the debts than of the House of Lords.   It is scarcely to be imagined to what debts will swell, that are daily increasing by small additions, and how carelessly in a state of desperation debts are contracted. Poor Macquarry was far from thinking that when he sold his islands he should receive nothing.   For what were they sold?   And what was their yearly value?   The admission of money into the Highlands will soon put an end to the feudal modes of life, by making those men landlords who were not chiefs.   I do not know that the people will suffer by the change; but there was in the patriarchal authority something venerable and pleasing.   Every eye must look with pain on a *Campbell* turning the *Macquarrys* at will out of their *sedes avidæ*, their hereditary island.

"Sir Alexander Dick is the only Scotsman liberal enough not to be angry that I could not find trees where trees were not.   I was much delighted by his kind letter.

"I remember Rasay with too much pleasure not to partake of the happiness of any part of that amiable family.   Our ramble in the islands hangs upon my imagination; I can hardly help imagining that we shall go again.   Pennant seems to have seen a great deal which we did not see: when we travel again, let us look better about us.

"You have done right in taking your uncle's house.   Some change in the form of life gives from time to time a new epocha of existence. In a new place there is something new to be done, and a different system of thought arises in the mind.   I wish I could gather currants in your garden.   Now fit up a little study, and have your books ready at hand; do not spare a little money, to make your habitation pleasing to yourself.

"I have dined lately with poor dear ——.   I do not think he goes on well.   His table is rather coarse, and he has his children too much about him.[1]   But he is a very good man.

---

[1] This very just remark, I hope, will be constantly held in remembrance by parents, who are in general too apt to indulge their own fond feelings for their children at the expense of their friends.   The common custom of introducing them after dinner is highly injudicious.   It is agreeable

"Mrs. Williams is in the country, to try if she can improve her health; she is very ill. Matters have come so about, that she is in the country with very good accommodation; but age, and sickness, and pride, have made her so peevish, that I was forced to bribe the maid to stay with her, by a secret stipulation of half-a-crown a week over her wages.

"Our CLUB ended its session about six weeks ago. We now only meet to dine once a fortnight. Mr. Dunning, the great lawyer, is one of our members. The Thrales are well.

"I long to know how the negro's cause will be decided. What is the opinion of Lord Auchinleck, or Lord Hailes, or Lord Monboddo? I am, dear Sir,

"Your most affectionate, &c.
"SAM. JOHNSON."

"DR. JOHNSON TO MRS. BOSWELL.

"MADAM,   *July* 22, 1777.

"Though I am well enough pleased with the taste of sweetmeats, very little of the pleasure which I received at the arrival of your jar of marmalade arose from eating it. I received it as a token of friendship, as a proof of reconciliation, things much sweeter than sweetmeats, and upon this consideration I return you, dear Madam, my sincerest thanks. By having your kindness I think I have a double security for the continuance of Mr. Boswell's, which it is not to be expected that any man can long keep, when the influence of a lady so highly and so justly valued operates against him. Mr. Boswell will tell you that I was always faithful to your interest, and always endeavoured to exalt you in his estimation. You must now do the same for me. We must all help one another, and you must now consider me as, dear Madam,

"Your most obliged and most humble servant,
"SAM. JOHNSON."

"MR. BOSWELL TO DR. JOHNSON.

"MY DEAR SIR,   *Edinburgh, July* 28, 1777.

"This is the day on which you were to leave London, and I have been amusing myself, in the intervals of my law-drudgery, with figuring you in the Oxford post-coach. I doubt, however, if you have had so merry a journey as you and I had in that vehicle last year, when you made so much sport with Gwyn, the architect. Incidents upon a journey are recollected with peculiar pleasure; they are preserved in brisk spirits, and come up again in our minds, tinctured with that gaiety, or at least that animation with which we first perceived them."

*   *   *   *   *

enough that they should appear at any other time; but they should not be suffered to poison the moments of festivity by attracting the attention of the company, and in a manner compelling them, from politeness, to say what they do not think.—BOSWELL.

I added that something had occurred which I was afraid might prevent me from meeting him; and that my wife had been affected with complaints which threatened a consumption, but was now better.

"TO JAMES BOSWELL, ESQ.

"Dear Sir,   *Oxford, Aug. 4, 1777.*

"Do not disturb yourself about our interviews; I hope we shall have many; nor think it anything hard or unusual, that your design of meeting me is interrupted.   We have both endured greater evils, and have greater evils to expect.

"Mrs. Boswell's illness makes a more serious distress. Does the blood rise from her lungs or from her stomach? From little vessels broken in the stomach there is no danger. Blood from the lungs is, I believe, always frothy, as mixed with wind. Your physicians know very well what is to be done. The loss of such a lady would, indeed, be very afflictive, and I hope she is in no danger. Take care to keep her mind as easy as is possible.

"I have left Langton in London. He has been down with the militia, and is again quiet at home, talking to his little people, as, I suppose, you do sometimes. Make my compliments to Miss Veronica.[1] The rest are too young for ceremony.

"I cannot but hope that you have taken your country house at a very seasonable time, and that it may conduce to restore or establish Mrs. Boswell's health, as well as provide room and exercise for the young ones. That you and your lady may both be happy, and long enjoy your happiness, is the sincere and earnest wish of
"Dear Sir, your most, &c.,
"Sam. Johnson."

"MR. BOSWELL TO DR. JOHNSON.

[Informing him that my wife had continued to grow better, so that my alarming apprehensions were relieved; and that I had hoped to disengage myself from the other embarrassment which had occurred, and therefore requesting to know particularly when he intended to be at Ashbourne.]

"TO JAMES BOSWELL, ESQ.

"Dear Sir,   *Aug. 30, 1777.*

"I am this day come to Ashbourne, and have only to tell you, that Dr. Taylor says you shall be welcome to him, and you know how welcome you will be to me. Make haste to let me know when you may be expected.

[1] This young lady, the author's eldest daughter, and at this time about five years old, died in London, of a consumption, four months after her father, Sept. 26, 1795.—Malone.

"Make my compliments to Mrs. Boswell, and tell her I hope we shall be at variance no more.   I am, dear Sir, your most humble servant,

"SAM. JOHNSON."

"TO JAMES BOSWELL, ESQ.

"DEAR SIR,   *Ashbourne, Sept.* 1, 1777.

"On Saturday I wrote a very short letter, immediately upon my arrival hither, to show you that I am not less desirous of the interview than yourself.   Life admits not of delays; when pleasure can be had, it is fit to catch it: every hour takes away part of the things that please us, and perhaps part of our disposition to be pleased.   When I came to Lichfield, I found my old friend Harry Jackson dead.   It was a loss, and a loss not to be repaired, as he was one of the companions of my childhood.   I hope we may long continue to gain friends; but the friends which merit or usefulness can procure us are not able to supply the place of old acquaintance, with whom the days of youth may be retraced, and those images revived which gave the earliest delight.   If you and I live to be much older, we shall take great delight in talking over the Hebridean Journey.

"In the mean time it may not be amiss to contrive some other little adventure, but what it can be I know not; leave it, as Sidney says,

'To virtue, fortune, time, and woman's breast;[1]

for I believe Mrs. Boswell must have some part in the consultation.

"One thing you will like.   The Doctor, so far as I can judge, is likely to leave us enough to ourselves.   He was out to-day before

---

[1] By an odd mistake, in the first three editions we find a reading in this line to which Dr. Johnson would by no means have subscribed; *wine* having been substituted for *time*.   That error, probably, was a mistake in the transcript of Johnson's original letter, his handwriting being often very difficult to read.   The other deviation in the beginning of the line (*virtue* instead of *nature*) must be attributed to his memory having deceived him; and therefore, has not been disturbed.

The verse quoted is the concluding line of a sonnet of Sidney's, of which the earliest copy, I believe, is found in Harrington's translation of Ariosto, 1591, in the notes on the eleventh book:—"And therefore," says he, "that excellent verse of Sir Philip Sidney, in his first ARCADIA (which, I know not by what mishap, is left out in the printed booke, 4to, 1590), is, in mine opinion, worthie to be praised and followed, to make a good and virtuous wife:—

'Who doth desire that chaste his wife should bee,
    First be he true, for truth doth truth deserve;
Then be he such, as she his worth may see,
    And, alwaies one, credit with her preserve;
Not toying kynd, nor causelessly unkynd,
    Not stirring thoughts, nor yet denying right,
Not spying faults, nor in plaine errors blind,
    Never hard hand, nor ever rayns [reins] too light;
As far from want, as far from vain expence,
    Th' one doth enforce, the t'other doth entice;

I came down, and, I fancy, will stay out to dinner.   I have brought the papers about poor Dodd, to show you, but you will soon have dispatched them.

"Before I came away, I sent poor Mrs. Williams into the country, very ill of a pituitous defluxion, which wastes her gradually away, and which her physician declares himself unable to stop.   I supplied her, as far as could be desired, with all conveniences to make her excursion and abode pleasant and useful.   But I am afraid she can only linger a short time in a morbid state of weakness and pain.

"The Thrales, little and great, are all well, and purpose to go to Brighthelmstone at Michaelmas.   They will invite me to go with them, and perhaps I may go, but I hardly think I shall like to stay the whole time; but of futurity we know but little.

"Mrs. Porter is well; but Mrs. Aston, one of the ladies at Stowhill, has been struck with a palsy, from which she is not likely ever to recover.   How soon may such a stroke fall upon us!

"Write to me, and let us know when we may expect you.   I am, dear Sir,

> "Your most humble servant,
> "SAM. JOHNSON."

"MR. BOSWELL TO DR. JOHNSON.

"Edinburgh, Sept. 9, 1777.

[After informing him that I was to set out next day, in order to meet him at Ashbourne.]

"I have a present for you from Lord Hailes—the fifth book of 'Lactantius,' which he has published with Latin notes.   He is also to give you a few anecdotes for your 'Life of Thomson,' who I find was private tutor to the present Earl of Haddington, Lord Hailes's cousin, a circumstance not mentioned by Dr. Murdoch.   I have keen expectations of delight from your edition of the English Poets.

"I am sorry for poor Mrs. Williams's situation.   You will, however, have the comfort of reflecting on your kindness to her.

> Allow good companie, but drive from thence
> All filthie mouths that glorie in their vice:
> This done, thou hast no more but leave the rest
> To *nature,* fortune, *time,* and woman's breast.' "

I take this opportunity to add, that in England's "Parnassus," a collection of poetry printed in 1600, the second couplet of this sonnet is thus corruptly exhibited:—

> "Then *he be* such as *he* his *words* may see,
> And alwaies one credit *which* her preserve:"

a variation which I the rather mention, because the readings of that book have been triumphantly quoted when they happened to coincide with the sophistications of the SECOND folio edition of Shakespeare's plays in 1632, as adding I know not what degree of authority and authenticity to the latter; as if the corruptions of one book (and that abounding with the grossest falsifications of the authors from whose works its extracts are made) could give any kind of support to another, which, in every page, is still more adulterated and unfaithful.—MALONE.

Mr. Jackson's death, and Mrs. Aston's palsy, are gloomy circumstances. Yet surely we should be habituated to the uncertainty of life and health. When my mind is unclouded by melancholy, I consider the temporary distresses of this state of being as 'light afflictions,' by stretching my mental view into that glorious after-existence, when they will appear to be as nothing. But present pleasures and present pains must be felt. I lately read 'Rasselas' over again with great satisfaction.

"Since you are desirous to hear about Macquarry's sale, I shall inform you particularly. The gentleman who purchased Ulva is Mr. Campbell of Auchnaba; our friend Macquarry was proprietor of two-thirds of it, of which the rent was 156l. 5s. 1½d. This parcel was set up at 4,069l. 5s. 1d., but it sold for no less than 5,540l. The other third of Ulva, with the island of Staffa, belonged to Macquarry of Ormaig. Its rent, including that of Staffa, 83l. 12s. 2½d. —set up at 2,178l. 16s. 4d.—sold for no less than 3,540l. The Laird of Col wished to purchase Ulva, but he thought the price too high. There may, indeed, be great improvements made there, both in fishing and agriculture; but the interest of the purchase-money exceeds the rent so very much, that I doubt if the bargain will be profitable. There is an island called Little Colonsay, of 10l. yearly rent, which I am informed has belonged to the Macquarrys of Ulva for many ages, but which was lately claimed by the Presbyterian Synod of Argyle, in consequence of a grant made to them by Queen Anne. It is believed that their claim will be dismissed, and that Little Colonsay will also be sold for the advantage of Macquarry's creditors. What think you of purchasing this island, and endowing a school or college there, the master to be a clergyman of the Church of England? How venerable would such an institution make the name of Dr. Samuel Johnson in the Hebrides! I have, like yourself, wonderful pleasure in recollecting our travels in those islands. The pleasure is, I think, greater than it reasonably should be, considering that we had not much either of beauty or elegance to charm our imaginations, or of rude novelty to astonish. Let us, by all means, have another expedition. I shrink a little from our scheme of going up the Baltic[1] I am sorry you have already been

---

[1] It appears that Johnson, now in his sixty-eighth year, was seriously inclined to realise the project of our going up the Baltic, which I had started when we were in the Isle of Sky, for he thus writes to Mrs. Thrale; Letters, vol. i., p. 366:—

"*Ashbourne*, Sept. 13, 1777.

"Boswell, I believe, is coming. He talks of being here to-day: I shall be glad to see him; but he shrinks from the Baltic expedition, which, I think, is the best scheme in our power. What we shall substitute, I know not. He wants to see Wales; but, except the woods of *Bachycraigh*, what is there in Wales that can fill the hunger of ignorance, or quench the thirst of curiosity? We may, perhaps, form some scheme or other; but, in the phrase of *Hockley in the Hole*, it is pity he has not a *better bottom*."

Such an ardour of mind, and vigour of enterprise, is admirable at any age; but more particularly so at the advanced period at which Johnson was then arrived. I am sorry now that I did not insist on our executing that scheme. Besides the other objects of curiosity and

in Wales; for I wish to see it. Shall we go to Ireland, of which I have seen but little? We shall try to strike out a plan when we are at Ashbourne.

"I am ever,
"Your most faithful humble servant,
"JAMES BOSWELL."

"TO JAMES BOSWELL, ESQ."

"DEAR SIR,   Ashbourne, Sept. 11, 1777.

"I write to be left at Carlisle, as you direct me; but you cannot have it. Your letter, dated Sept. 6, was not at this place till this day, Thursday, Sept. 11; and I hope you will be here before this is at Carlisle.[1] However, what you have not going, you may have returning; and as I believe I shall not love you less after our interview, it will then be as true as it is now, that I set a very high value upon your friendship, and count your kindness as one of the chief felicities of my life. Do not fancy that an intermission of writing is a decay of kindness. No man is always in a disposition to write; nor has any man at all times something to say.

"That distrust which intrudes so often on your mind is a mode of melancholy which, if it be the business of a wise man to be happy, it is foolish to indulge; and, if it be a duty to preserve our faculties entire for their proper use, it is criminal. Suspicion is very often an useless pain. From that, and all other pains, I wish you free and safe; for I am, dear Sir,

"Most affectionately yours,
"SAM. JOHNSON."

observation, to have seen my illustrious friend received, as he probably would have been, by a prince so eminently distinguished for his variety of talents and acquisitions as the late King of Sweden; and by the Empress of Russia, whose extraordinary abilities, information, and magnanimity, astonish the world, would have afforded a noble subject for contemplation and record. This reflection may, possibly, be thought too visionary by the more sedate and cold-blooded part of my readers; yet I own I frequently indulge it with an earnest, unavailing regret.—BOSWELL.

[1] It so happened, the letter was forwarded to my house at Edinburgh.—BOSWELL.

CHAPTER V.—1777

*Boswell's Arrival at Ashbourne—Grief for the Loss of Friends
—"Journey to the Western Islands"—Ashbourne School
—Poor Curates—Johnson's zealous Interference and
Correspondence on behalf of Dr. Dodd—Petition of the
City of London in his Favour—Dodd's Petition to the
King—Mr. Jenkinson—Mr. Fitzherbert—Dr. Taylor—
Hamilton's Poems—The Rev. Mr. Seward—Johnson's
Opinions of Hume—Gen. Paoli's Sentiments of the Fear
of Death—Dr. Butter—Duties of a Biographer—The
Stuart Family—Coxeter's Collections of the Poets—
Johnson's Criticisms on Lyric Poetry.*

On Sunday evening, Sept. 14, I arrived at Ashbourne, and
drove directly up to Dr. Taylor's door, Dr. Johnson and he
appeared before I had got out of the post-chaise, and
welcomed me cordially.

I told them that I had travelled all the preceding night,
and gone to bed at Leek in Staffordshire; and that when I
rose to go to church in the afternoon I was informed there
had been an earthquake, of which, it seems, the shock had
been felt in some degree at Ashbourne. JOHNSON: "Sir,
it will be much exaggerated in popular talk: for, in the
first place, the common people do not accurately adapt
their thoughts to the objects; nor, secondly, do they
accurately adapt their words to their thoughts: they do
not mean to lie; but, taking no pains to be exact, they
give you very false accounts. A great part of their
language is proverbial. If any thing rocks at all, they say
it rocks like a cradle; and in this way they go on."

The subject of grief for the loss of relations and friends
being introduced, I observed that it was strange to consider
how soon it in general wears away. Dr. Taylor mentioned
a gentleman of the neighbourhood as the only instance he
had ever known of a person who had endeavoured to
retain grief. He told Dr. Taylor, that after his lady's
death, which affected him deeply, he resolved that the
grief, which he cherished with a kind of sacred fondness,
should be lasting; but that he found he could not keep it

long. JOHNSON: "All grief for what cannot in the course
of nature be helped soon wears away; in some sooner
indeed, in some later; but it never continues very long,
unless where there is madness, such as will make a man have
pride so fixed in his mind, as to imagine himself a king;
or any other passion in an unreasonable way: for all
unnecessary grief is unwise, and therefore will not long be
retained by a sound mind. If, indeed, the cause of our
grief is occasioned by our own misconduct, if grief is
mingled with remorse of conscience, it should be lasting."
BOSWELL: "But, Sir, we do not approve of a man who
very soon forgets the loss of a wife or a friend." JOHNSON:
"Sir, we disapprove of him, not because he soon forgets
his grief; for the sooner it is forgotten the better, but
because we suppose, that if he forgets his wife or his friend
soon, he has not had much affection for them. '

I was somewhat disappointed in finding that the
edition of the English Poets, for which he was to write
Prefaces and Lives, was not an undertaking directed by
him: but that he was to furnish a Preface and Life to any
poet the booksellers pleased. I asked him if he would do
this to any dunce's works, if they asked him. JOHNSON:
"Yes, Sir; and *say* he was a dunce." My friend seemed
now not much to relish talking of this edition.

On Monday, September 15, Dr. Johnson observed that
everybody commended such parts of his "Journey to the
Western Islands," as were in their own way. "For
instance," said he, "Mr. Jackson (the all-knowing) told me
there was more good sense upon trade in it, than he should
hear in the House of Commons in a year, except from
Burke. Jones commended the part which treats of
language; Burke that which describes the inhabitants of
mountainous countries."

After breakfast, Johnson carried me to see the garden
belonging to the school of Ashbourne, which is very prettily
formed upon a bank, rising gradually behind the house.
The Reverend Mr. Langley, the head-master, accompanied
us.

While we sat basking in the sun upon a seat here, I
introduced a common subject of complaint, the very small
salaries which many curates have, and I maintained that
no man should be invested with the character of a clergyman, unless he has a security for such an income as will
enable him to appear respectable; that, therefore, a
clergyman should not be allowed to have a curate, unless
he gives him a hundred pounds a year; if he cannot do that,
let him perform the duty himself. JOHNSON: "To be

sure, Sir, it is wrong that any clergyman should be without a reasonable income; but as the church revenues were sadly diminished at the Reformation, the clergy who have livings cannot afford, in many instances, to give good salaries to curates, without leaving themselves too little; and if no curate were to be permitted unless he had a hundred pounds a-year, their number would be very small, which would be a disadvantage, as then there would not be such choice in the nursery for the church, curates being candidates for the higher ecclesiastical offices, according to their merit and good behaviour." He explained the system of the English hierarchy exceedingly well. "It is not thought fit," said he, "to trust a man with the care of a parish till he has given proof as a curate that he shall deserve such a trust." This is an excellent *theory:* and if the *practice* were according to it, the church of England would be admirable indeed. However, as I have heard Dr. Johnson observe as to the universities, bad practice does not infer that the *constitution* is bad.

We had with us at dinner several of Dr. Taylor's neighbours, good civil gentlemen, who seemed to understand Dr. Johnson very well, and not to consider him in the light that a certain person did, who being struck, or rather stunned by his voice and manner, when he was afterwards asked what he thought of him, answered, "He's a tremendous companion."

Johnson told me, that "Taylor was a very sensible acute man, and had a strong mind; that he had great activity in some respects, and yet such a sort of indolence, that if you should put a pebble upon his chimney-piece you would find it there, in the same state, a year afterwards."

And here is a proper place to give an account of Johnson's humane and zealous interference in behalf of the Rev. Dr. William Dodd, formerly Prebendary of Brecon, and Chaplain in Ordinary to his Majesty; celebrated as a very popular preacher, an encourager of charitable institutions, and author of a variety of works, chiefly theological. Having unhappily contracted expensive habits of living, partly occasioned by licentiousness of manners, he in an evil hour, when pressed by want of money, and dreading an exposure of his circumstances, forged a bond, of which he attempted to avail himself to support his credit, flattering himself with hopes that he might be able to repay its amount without being detected. The person, whose name he thus rashly and criminally presumed to falsify, was the Earl of Chesterfield, to whom he had been tutor, and who he perhaps, in the warmth of his feelings, flattered himself would have generously paid the money in case of an alarm being taken, rather than suffer him to fall a victim to the dreadful consequences of violating the law against forgery, the most dangerous crime in a commercial country; but the unfortunate divine had the mortification to find that he was mistaken. His noble pupil appeared against him, and he was capitally convicted.[1]

Johnson told me that Dr. Dodd was very little acquainted with him, having been but once in his company, many years previous to this period (which was precisely the state of my own acquaintance with Dodd); but in his distress he bethought himself of Johnson's persuasive power of writing, if haply it might avail to obtain for him the royal mercy. He did not apply to him directly, but, extraordinary as it may seem, through the late Countess of Harrington,[2] who wrote a letter to Johnson, asking him to employ his pen in favour of Dodd. Mr. Allen, the printer, who was Johnson's landlord and next neighbour in Bolt-court, and for whom he had much kindness, was one of Dodd's friends, of whom, to the credit of humanity be it recorded, that he had many who did not desert him, even after his infringement of the law had reduced him to the state of a man under sentence of death. Mr. Allen told me that he carried Lady Harrington's letter to Johnson, that Johnson read it walking up and down his chamber, and seemed much agitated; after which he said, "I will do what I can"; and certainly he did make extraordinary exertions.

He, this evening, as he had obligingly promised in one of his letters, put into my hands the whole series of his writings upon this melancholy occasion, and I shall present my readers with the abstract which I made from the collection; in doing which I studied to avoid copying what had appeared in print, and now make part of the edition of "Johnson's Works," published by the Booksellers of London, but taking care to mark Johnson's variations in some of the pieces there exhibited.

Dr. Johnson wrote, in the first place, Dr. Dodd's " Speech

---

[1] There are many acts of Dr. Dodd's life, which appear not only indiscreet but scandalous. He had been one of the King's chaplains, but was dismissed for an attempt at simony. He married a woman of very inferior station, and of equivocal character, Mary Perkins, who died mad in 1784. At the time when Johnson took so deep an interest in obtaining his pardon, Dodd was in his 49th year.—ED.

[2] Caroline, eldest daughter of Charles Fitzroy, Duke of Grafton, and wife of William, the second Earl of Harrington.—MALONE.

to the Recorder of London," at the Old Bailey, when
sentence of death was about to be pronounced upon him.

He wrote, also, "The Convict's Address to his unhappy
Brethren," a sermon delivered by Dr. Dodd, in the chapel
of Newgate. According to Johnson's manuscript it began
thus after the text, *What shall I do to be saved?*—"These
were the words with which the keeper, to whose custody
Paul and Silas were committed by their prosecutors,
addressed his prisoners, when he saw them freed from their
bonds by the perceptible agency of divine favour, and was
therefore irresistibly convinced that they were not offenders
against the laws, but martyrs to the truth."

Dr. Johnson was so good as to mark for me with his
own hand, on a copy of this sermon, which is now in my
possession, such passages as were added by Dr. Dodd.
They are not many. Whoever will take the trouble to
look at the printed copy, and attend to what I mention,
will be satisfied of this.

There is a short introduction by Dr. Dodd, and he also
inserted this sentence, "You see with what confusion and
dishonour I now stand before you;—no more in the pulpit
of instruction, but on this humble seat with yourselves."
The *notes* are entirely Dodd's own, and Johnson's writing
ends at the words, "the thief whom he pardoned on the
cross." What follows was supplied by Dr. Dodd himself.

The other pieces mentioned by Johnson in the above-
mentioned collection, are two letters, one to the Lord
Chancellor Bathurst, (not Lord North, as is erroneously
supposed), and one to Lord Mansfield;—A Petition from
Dr. Dodd to the King;—A Petition from Mrs. Dodd to
the Queen;—Observations of some length inserted in the
newspapers, on occasion of Earl Percy's having presented
to his Majesty a petition for mercy to Dodd, signed by
twenty thousand people, but all in vain. He told me that
he had also written a petition from the City of London;
"but," said he, with a significant smile, "they *mended* it."[1]

---

[1] Having unexpectedly, by the favour of Mr. Stone, of London-field,
Hackney, seen the original in Johnson's handwriting, of "The Petition
of the City of London to his Majesty in favour of Dr. Dodd," I now
present it to my readers, with such passages as were omitted, enclosed
in crotchets, and the additions or variations marked in italics:—

"That William Dodd, Doctor of Laws, now lying under sentence of
death *in your Majesty's Jail of Newgate*, for the crime of forgery, has, for
a great part of his life, set a useful and laudable example of diligence
in his calling [and, as we have reason to believe, has exercised his
ministry with great fidelity and efficacy], *which, in many instances, has
produced the most happy effect*. That he has been the first institutor,
[or] *and* a very earnest and active promoter of several modes of useful

The last of these articles which Johnson wrote is "Dr. Dodd's last solemn Declaration," which he left with the sheriff at the place of execution. Here, also, my friend marked the variations on a copy of that piece now in my possession. Dodd inserted, "I never knew or attended to the calls of frugality, or the needful minuteness of painful economy"; and in the next sentence he introduced the words which I distinguish by *italics*: "My life for some *few unhappy* years past has been *dreadfully erroneous.*" Johnson's expression was *hypocritical*; but his remark on the margin is, "With this he said he could not charge himself."

Having thus authentically settled what part of the "Occasional Papers," concerning Dr. Dodd's miserable situation, came from the pen of Johnson, I shall proceed to present my readers with my record of the unpublished writings relating to that extraordinary and interesting matter.

I found a letter to Dr. Johnson from Dr. Dodd, May 23, 1777, in which "The Convict's Address" seems clearly to be meant:—

"I am so penetrated, my ever dear Sir, with a sense of your extreme benevolence towards me, that I cannot find words equal to the sentiments of my heart.

*   *   *   *   *

"You are too conversant in the world to need the slightest hint from me, of what infinite utility the Speech[1] on the awful day has been to me. I experience every hour some good effect from it. I am sure that effects still more salutary and important must follow from *your kind and intended favour.* I will labour—God being my helper—to do justice to it from the pulpit. I am sure, had I your sentiments constantly to deliver from thence, in all their mighty force and power, not a soul could be left unconvinced and unpersuaded."

*   *   *   *   *

He added,

"May GOD ALMIGHTY bless and reward, with his choicest comforts, your philanthropic actions, and enable me at all times

charity, and [that] therefore [he] may be considered as having been on many occasions a benefactor to the public. [That when they consider his past life, they are willing to suppose his late crime to have been not the consequence of habitual depravity, but the suggestion of some sudden and violent temptation.] [That] *Your Petitioners,* therefore, considering his case as, in some of its circumstances, unprecedented and peculiar, *and encouraged by your Majesty's known clemency,* [they] most humbly recommend the said William Dodd to [his] *your* Majesty's most gracious consideration, in hopes that he will be found not altogether [unfit] *unworthy* to stand an example of Royal Mercy."—BOSWELL.

[1] His speech at the Old Bailey, when found guilty.—BOSWELL.

to express what I feel of the high and uncommon obligation which I owe to the *first man* in our times."

On Sunday, June 22, he writes, begging Dr. Johnson's assistance in framing a supplicatory letter to his Majesty:—

"If his Majesty would be pleased of his royal clemency to spare me and my family the horrors and ignominy of a *public death*, which the *public* itself is solicitous to wave, and to grant me in some silent distant corner of the globe to pass the remainder of my days in penitence and prayer, I would bless his clemency and be humbled."

This letter was brought to Dr. Johnson when in church. He stooped down and read it, and wrote, when he went home, the following letter for Dr. Dodd to the King:—

"Sir,
"May it not offend your Majesty, that the most miserable of men applies himself to your clemency, as his last hope and his last refuge; that your mercy is most earnestly and humbly implored by a clergyman, whom your laws and judges have condemned to the horror and ignominy of a public execution.

"I confess the crime, and own the enormity of its consequences, and the danger of its example. Nor have I the confidence to petition for impunity; but humbly hope that public security may be established, without the spectacle of a clergyman dragged through the streets, to a death of infamy, amidst the derision of the profligate and profane; and that justice may be satisfied with irrevocable exile, perpetual disgrace, and hopeless penury.

"My life, Sir, has not been useless to mankind. I have benefited many. But my offences against God are numberless, and I have had little time for repentance. Preserve me, Sir, by your prerogative of mercy, from the necessity of appearing unprepared at that tribunal, before which kings and subjects must stand at last together. Permit me to hide my guilt in some obscure corner of a foreign country, where, if I can ever attain confidence to hope that my prayers will be heard, they shall be poured with all the fervour of gratitude for the life and happiness of your Majesty.
"I am, Sir,
"Your Majesty's, &c."

Subjoined to it was written as follows:—

"TO DR. DODD.
"Sir,
"I most seriously enjoin you not to let it be at all known that I have written this letter, and to return the copy to Mr Allen in a cover to me. I hope I need not tell you that I wish it success.—But do not indulge hope.—Tell nobody."

It happened luckily that Mr. Allen was pitched on to assist in this melancholy office, for he was a great friend of Mr. Akerman, the keeper of Newgate. Dr. Johnson never went to see Dr. Dodd. He said to me, "It would have done *him* more harm, than good to Dodd, who once expressed a desire to see him, but not earnestly."

Dr. Johnson, on the 20th of June, wrote the following letter:—

"TO THE RIGHT HONOURABLE CHARLES JENKINSON.

"SIR,

"Since the conviction and condemnation of Dr. Dodd, I have had, by the intervention of a friend, some intercourse with him, and I am sure I shall lose nothing in your opinion by tenderness and commiseration. Whatever be the crime, it is not easy to have any knowledge of the delinquent, without a wish that his life may be spared; at least when no life has been taken away by him. I will, therefore, take the liberty of suggesting some reasons for which I wish this unhappy being to escape the utmost rigour of his sentence.

"He is, so far as I can recollect, the first clergyman of our church who has suffered public execution for immorality; and I know not whether it would not be more for the interests of religion to bury such an offender in the obscurity of perpetual exile, than to expose him in a cart, and on the gallows, to all who for any reason are enemies to the clergy.

"The supreme power has, in all ages, paid some attention to the voice of the people; and that voice does not least deserve to be heard, when it calls out for mercy. There is now a very general desire that Dodd's life should be spared. More is not wished; and, perhaps, this is not too much to be granted.

"If you, Sir, have an opportunity of enforcing these reasons, you may, perhaps, think them worthy of consideration; but whatever you determine I most respectfully entreat that you will be pleased to pardon, for this intrusion,

"Sir, your most obedient and most humble servant,

"SAM. JOHNSON."

It has been confidently circulated with invidious remarks, that to this letter no attention whatever was paid by Mr. Jenkinson (afterwards Earl of Liverpool), and that he did not even deign to show the common civility of owning the receipt of it. I could not but wonder at such conduct in the noble Lord, whose own character and just elevation in life, I thought must have impressed him with all due regard for great abilities and attainments. As the story had been much talked of, and apparently from good authority, I could not but have animadverted upon it in this work, had it been as was alleged; but from my earnest love of truth, and having found reason to think that there might be a mistake, I presumed to write to his Lordship, requesting an explanation; and it is with the sincerest pleasure that I am enabled to assure the world that there is no foundation for it, the fact being, that owing to some neglect or accident, Johnson's letter never came to Lord Hawkesbury's hands. I should have thought it strange indeed, if that noble Lord had undervalued my illustrious friend; but instead of this being the case, his Lordship, in the very polite answer with which he was pleased immediately to honour me, thus expresses himself:—" I have always respected the memory of Dr. Johnson, and admire his writings; and I frequently read many parts of them with pleasure and great improvement."

All applications for the Royal Mercy having failed, Dr. Dodd prepared himself for death; and with a warmth of gratitude wrote to Dr. Johnson as follows:—

June 25, Midnight.

"Accept, thou *great* and *good* heart, my earnest and fervent thanks and prayers for all thy benevolent and kind efforts in my behalf.—Oh, Dr. Johnson! as I sought your knowledge at an early hour in life, would to heaven I had cultivated the love and acquaintance of so excellent a man!—I pray God most sincerely to bless you with the highest transports—the infelt satisfaction of *humane* and benevolent exertions!—And admitted, as I trust I shall be, to the realms of bliss before you, I shall hail *your* arrival there with transports, and rejoice to acknowledge that you were my Comforter, my Advocate, and my *Friend !* God *be ever* with *you !*"

Dr. Johnson lastly wrote to Dr. Dodd this solemn and soothing letter:—

"TO THE REVEREND DR. DODD.

"Dear Sir,   *June 26, 1777.*

"That which is appointed to all men is now coming upon you. Outward circumstances, the eyes and the thoughts of men, are below the notice of an immortal being about to stand the trial for eternity, before the Supreme Judge of heaven and earth. Be comforted: your crime, morally or religiously considered, has no very deep dye of turpitude. It corrupted no man's principles; it attacked no man's life. It involved only a temporary and repairable injury. Of this, and of all other sins, you are earnestly to repent; and may God, who knoweth our frailty, and desireth not our death, accept your repentance, for the sake of his Son Jesus Christ our Lord.

"In requital of those well intended offices which you are pleased

B.L.J.: II—E*

so emphatically to acknowledge, let me beg that you make in your devotions one petition for my eternal welfare."

"I am, dear Sir,

"Your most affectionate servant,

"SAM. JOHNSON."

Under the copy of this letter I found written, in Johnson's own hand, "Next day, June 27, he was executed."

To conclude this interesting episode with an useful application, let us now attend to the reflections of Johnson at the end of the "Occasional Papers," concerning the unfortunate Dr. Dodd.—"Such were the last thoughts of a man whom we have seen exulting in popularity, and sunk in shame. For his reputation, which no man can give to himself, those who conferred it are to answer. Of his public ministry the means of judging were sufficiently attainable. He must be allowed to preach well, whose sermons strike his audience with forcible conviction. Of his life, those who thought it consistent with his doctrine did not originally form false notions. He was at first what he endeavoured to make others; but the world broke down his resolution, and he in time ceased to exemplify his own instructions. Let those who are tempted to his faults tremble at his punishment; and those whom he impressed from the pulpit with religious sentiments endeavour to confirm them, by considering the regret and self-abhorrence with which he reviewed in prison his deviations from rectitude."

Johnson gave us this evening, in his happy discriminative manner, a portrait of the late Mr. Fitzherbert of Derbyshire. "There was," said he, "no sparkle, no brilliancy in Fitzherbert; but I never knew a man who was so generally acceptable. He made every body quite easy, overpowered nobody by the superiority of his talents, made no man think worse of himself by being his rival, seemed always to listen, did not oblige you to hear much from him, and did not oppose what you said. Every body liked him, but he had no friend, as I understand the word, nobody with whom he exchanged intimate thoughts. People were willing to think well of everything about him. A gentleman was making an affected rant, as many people do, of great feelings about 'his dear son,' who was at school near London; how anxious he was lest he might be ill, and what he would give to see him. 'Can't you,' said Fitzherbert, 'take a post-chaise and go to him.' This, to be sure, *finished* the affected man, but there was not much

in it.[1]   However, this was circulated as wit for a whole
winter, and I believe part of a summer too: a proof that
he was no very witty man.   He was an instance of the truth
of the observation, that a man will please more upon the
whole by negative qualities than by positive; by never
offending, than by giving a great deal of delight.   In the
first place, men hate more steadily than they love; and if
I have said something to hurt a man once, I shall not get
the better of this, by saying many things to please
him."

Tuesday, September 16, Dr. Johnson having mentioned
to me the extraordinary size and price of some cattle
reared by Dr. Taylor, I rode out with our host, surveyed
his farm, and was shown one cow which he had sold for
a hundred and twenty guineas, and another for which he
had been offered a hundred and thirty.   Taylor thus
described to me his old schoolfellow and friend, Johnson:—
"He is a man of a very clear head, great power of words,
and a very gay imagination; but there is no disputing with
him.   He will not hear you, and, having a louder voice
than you, must roar you down."

In the afternoon I tried to get Dr. Johnson to like the
Poems of Mr. Hamilton, of Bangour, which I had brought
with me: I had been much pleased with them at a very
early age: the impression still remained on my mind; it
was confirmed by the opinion of my friend the Honourable
Andrew Erskine, himself both a good poet and a critic,
who thought Hamilton as true a poet as ever wrote, and
that his not having fame was unaccountable.   Johnson,
upon repeated occasions, while I was at Ashbourne, talked
slightingly of Hamilton.   He said there was no power of
thinking in his verses, nothing that strikes one, nothing
better than what you generally find in magazines; and that
the highest praise they deserved was, that they were very
well for a gentleman to hand about among his friends.   He
said the imitation of *Ne sit ancillæ tibi amor*, &c., was too
solemn; he read part of it at the beginning.   He read the

---

[1] Dr. Gisborne, Physician to his Majesty's Household, has obligingly
communicated to me a fuller account of this story than had reached
Dr. Johnson.   The affected gentleman was the late John Gilbert Cooper,
Esq., author of a Life of Socrates, and of some poems in Dodsley's
collection.   Mr. Fitzherbert found him one morning apparently in such
violent agitation, on account of the indisposition of his son, as to seem
beyond the power of comfort.   At length, however, he exclaimed,
"I'll write an Elegy."   Mr. Fitzherbert, being satisfied by this of the
sincerity of his emotions, slily said, "Had not you better take a post-
chaise, and go and see him?"   It was the shrewdness of the insinuation
which made the story be circulated.—BOSWELL.

beautiful pathetic song, "Ah! the poor Shepherd's mournful fate!" and did not seem to give attention to what I had been used to think tender elegant strains, but laughed at the rhyme, in Scotch pronunciation, *wishes* and *blushes*, reading *wushes*—and there he stopped. He owned that the epitaph on Lord Newhall was pretty well done. He read the "Inscription in a Summer-house," and a little of the imitations of Horace's Epistles; but said he found nothing to make him desire to read on. When I urged that there were some good poetical passages in the book— "Where," said he, "will you find so large a collection without some?" I thought the description of Winter might obtain his approbation:—

> "See Winter, from the frozen north,
>   Drives his iron chariot forth!
>   His grisly hand in icy chains
>   Fair Tweeda's silver flood constrains," &c.

He asked why an "*iron* chariot?" and said "icy chains" was an old image. I was struck with the uncertainty of taste, and somewhat sorry that a poet whom I had long read with fondness was not approved by Dr. Johnson. I comforted myself with thinking that the beauties were too delicate for his robust perceptions. Garrick maintained that he had not a taste for the finest productions of genius; but I was sensible, that when he took the trouble to analyse critically, he generally convinced us that he was right.

In the evening the Reverend Mr. Seward, of Lichfield, who was passing through Ashbourne, in his way home, drank tea with us. Johnson described him thus:—"Sir, his ambition is to be a fine talker; so he goes to Buxton, and such places, where he may find companies to listen to him. And, Sir, he is a valetudinarian,—one of those who are always mending themselves. I do not know a more disagreeable character than a valetudinarian, who thinks he may do any thing that is for his ease, and indulges himself in the grossest freedoms. Sir, he brings himself to the state of a hog in a sty."

Dr. Taylor's nose happening to bleed, he said it was because he had omitted to have himself blooded four days after a quarter of a year's interval. Dr. Johnson, who was a great dabbler in physic, disapproved much of periodical bleeding. "For," said he, "you accustom yourself to an evacuation which Nature cannot perform of herself, and therefore she cannot help you, should you, from forgetfulness or any other cause, omit it; so you may be suddenly suffocated. You may accustom yourself to other periodical evacuations, because, should you omit them, Nature can supply the omission; but Nature cannot open a vein to blood you."[1] "I do not like to take an emetic," said Taylor, "for fear of breaking some small vessels." "Poh!" said Johnson, "if you have so many things that will break, you had better break your neck at once, and there's an end on't. You will break no small vessels" (blowing with high derision).

I mentioned to Dr. Johnson, that David Hume's persisting in his infidelity, when he was dying, shocked me much. JOHNSON: "Why should it shock you, Sir? Hume owned he had never read the Testament with attention. Here then was a man who had been at no pains to inquire into the truth of religion, and had continually turned his mind the other way. It was not to be expected that the prospect of death would alter his way of thinking, unless GOD should send an angel to set him right." I said I had reason to believe that the thought of annihilation gave Hume no pain. JOHNSON: "It was not so, Sir. He had a vanity in being thought easy. It is more probable that he should assume an appearance of ease, than so very improbable a thing should be, as a man not afraid of going (as, in spite of his delusive theory, he cannot be sure but he may go) into an unknown state, and not being uneasy at leaving all he knew. And you are to consider that, upon his own principle of annihilation, he had a motive to speak the truth." The horror of death, which I had always observed in Dr. Johnson, appeared strong to-night. I ventured to tell him that I had been for moments in my life not afraid of death; therefore I could suppose another man in that state of mind for a considerable space of time. He said, "He never had a moment in which death was not terrible to him." He added, that it had been observed, that scarce any man dies in public but with apparent resolution; from that desire of praise which never quits us. I said, Dr. Dodd seemed willing to die, and full of hopes of happiness. "Sir," said he, "Dr. Dodd would have given both his hands and both his legs to have lived. The better a man is, the more he is afraid of death, having a clearer view of infinite purity." He owned that our being in an unhappy uncertainty as to our salvation was mysterious; and said, "Ah! we must wait till we are in another state of being to have many

---

[1] Nature, however, may supply the evacuation by an hæmorrhage.— KEARNEY.

things explained to us." Even the powerful mind of
Johnson seemed foiled by futurity. But I thought that the
gloom of uncertainty in solemn religious speculation, being
mingled with hope, was yet more consolatory than the
emptiness of infidelity. A man can live in thick air, but
perishes in an exhausted receiver.

Dr. Johnson was much pleased with a remark which
I told him was made to me by General Paoli:—"That
it is impossible not to be afraid of death; and that those
who at the time of dying are not afraid, are not thinking
of death, but of applause, or something else, which keeps
death out of their sight: so that all men are equally
afraid of death when they see it; only some have a power
of turning their sight away from it better than others."

On Wednesday, September 17, Dr. Butter, physician
at Derby, drank tea with us; and it was settled that Dr.
Johnson and I should go on Friday and dine with him.
Johnson said, "I'm glad of this." He seemed weary of
the uniformity of life at Dr. Taylor's.

Talking of biography, I said, in writing a life, a man's
peculiarities should be mentioned, because they mark his
character. JOHNSON: "Sir, there is no doubt as to
peculiarities; the question is, whether a man's vices should
be mentioned; for instance, whether it should be mentioned that Addison and Parnell drank too freely; for
people will probably more easily indulge in drinking from
knowing this; so that more ill may be done by the example,
than good by telling the whole truth." Here was an
instance of his varying from himself in talk; for when
Lord Hailes and he sat one morning calmly conversing
in my house at Edinburgh, I well remember that Dr.
Johnson maintained that "if a man is to write *A Panegyric*,
he may keep vices out of sight: but if he professes to write
A Life, he must represent it really as it was"; and when
I objected to the danger of telling that Parnell drank to
excess, he said, that "it would produce an instructive
caution to avoid drinking, when it was seen that even the
learning and genius of Parnell could be debased by it."
And in the Hebrides he maintained, as appears from my
"Journal,"[1] that a man's intimate friend should mention
his faults, if he writes his life.

He had this evening (partly, I suppose, from the spirit
of contradiction to his Whig friend) a violent argument
with Dr. Taylor, as to the inclinations of the people of
England at this time towards the royal family of Stuart.

[1] "Journal of a Tour to the Hebrides," 3d edit., p. 240.—BOSWELL.

He grew so outrageous as to say, "that if England were fairly polled the present king would be sent away to-night, and his adherents hanged to-morrow." Taylor, who was as violent a Whig as Johnson was a Tory, was roused by this to a pitch of bellowing. He denied loudly what Johnson said, and maintained that there was an abhorrence against the Stuart family, though he admitted that the people were not much attached to the present king.[1] Johnson: "Sir, the state of the country is this: the people knowing it to be agreed on all hands that this king has not the hereditary right to the crown, and there being no hope that he who has it can be restored, have grown cold and indifferent upon the subject of loyalty, and have no warm attachment to any king. They would not, therefore, risk anything to restore the exiled family. They would not give 20s. a piece to bring it about. But if a mere vote could do it, there would be twenty to one; at least, there would be a very great majority of voices for it. For, Sir, you are to consider that all those who think a king has a right to his crown, as a man has to his estate, which is the just opinion, would be for restoring the king who certainly has the hereditary right, could he be trusted with it; in which there would be no danger now, when laws and every thing else are so much advanced; and every king will govern by the laws. And you must also consider, Sir, that there is nothing on the other side to oppose this; for it is not alleged by any one that the present family has any inherent right: so that the Whigs could not have a contest between two rights."

Dr. Taylor admitted, that if the question as to hereditary right were to be tried by a poll of the people of England, to be sure the abstract doctrine would be given in favour of the family of Stuart; but he said the conduct of that family, which occasioned their expulsion, was so fresh in the minds of the people, that they would not vote for a restoration. Dr. Johnson, I think, was contented with the admission as to the hereditary right, leaving the original point in dispute, viz. what the people upon the whole would do, taking in right and affection; for he said, people were afraid of a change, even though they think it right. Dr. Taylor said something of the slight foundation of the hereditary right of the house of Stuart. "Sir,"

---

[1] Dr. Taylor was very ready to make this admission, because the party with which he was connected was not in power. There was then some truth in it, owing to the pertinacity of factious clamour. Had he lived till now, it would have been impossible for him to deny that his Majesty possesses the warmest affection of his people.—Boswell.

said Johnson, "the house of Stuart succeeded to the full right of both the houses of York and Lancaster, whose common source had the undisputed right. A right to a throne is like a right to anything else. Possession is sufficient, where no better right can be shown. This was the case with the royal family of England, as it is now with the king of France: for as to the first beginning of the right we are in the dark."

Thursday, September 18. Last night Dr. Johnson had proposed that the crystal lustre, or chandelier, in Dr. Taylor's large room should be lighted up some time or other. Taylor said it should be lighted up next night. "That will do very well," said I, "for it is Dr. Johnson's birthday." When we were in the Isle of Sky, Johnson had desired me not to mention his birthday. He did not seem pleased at this time that I mentioned it, and said somewhat sternly, "he would *not* have the lustre lighted the next day."

Some ladies, who had been present yesterday when I mentioned his birthday, came to dinner to-day, and plagued him unintentionally by wishing him joy. I know not why he disliked having his birthday mentioned, unless it were that it reminded him of his approaching nearer to death, of which he had a constant dread.

I mentioned to him a friend of mine who was formerly gloomy from low spirits, and much distressed by the fear of death, but was now uniformly placid, and contemplated his dissolution without any perturbation. "Sir," said Johnson, "this is only a disordered imagination taking a different turn."

We talked of a collection being made of all the English Poets who had published a volume of poems. Johnson told me "that a Mr. Coxeter,"[1] whom he knew, had gone the greatest length towards this, having collected, I think, about five hundred volumes of poets whose works were little known; but that upon his death Tom Osborne bought them, and they were dispersed, which he thought a pity, as it was curious to see any series complete; and in every volume of poems something good may be found."

He observed, that a gentleman of eminence in literature

---

[1] Thomas Coxeter, Esq., who had also made a large collection of old plays, and from whose manuscript notes "The Lives of the English Poets," by Shiels and Cibber, were principally compiled, as should have been mentioned in a former page. See pp. 40—41 of this volume. [Mr. Coxeter was bred at Trinity College, Oxford, and died in London, April 17, 1747, in his fifty-ninth year. A particular account of him may be found in "The Gentleman's Magazine" for 1781, p. 173.—MALONE.

had got into a bad style of Poetry of late. "He puts,"
said he, "a very common thing in a strange dress till he
does not know it himself, and thinks other people do not
know it." BOSWELL: "That is owing to his being so much
versant in old English poetry." JOHNSON: "What is that
to the purpose, Sir? If I say a man is drunk, and you
tell me it is owing to his taking much drink, the matter is
not mended. No, Sir, —— has taken to an odd mode.
For example, he'd write thus.—

> 'Hermit hoar, in solemn cell,
>   Wearing out life's evening gray.'

Gray evening is common enough; but *evening gray* he'd
think fine. Stay—we'll make out the stanza:—

> 'Hermit hoar, in solemn cell,
>   Wearing out life's evening gray,
>   Smite thy bosom, sage, and tell,
>   What is bliss, and which the way?'"

BOSWELL: "But why smite his bosom, Sir?" JOHNSON:
"Why to show he was in earnest" (smiling).—He, at an
after period, added the following stanza:—

> "Thus I spoke; and speaking sigh'd,
>   Scarce repressed the starting tear;
>   When the smiling sage replied—
>   Come, my lad, and drink some beer." [1]

I cannot help thinking the first stanza very good solemn
poetry, as also the first three lines of the second. Its last
line is an excellent burlesque surprise on gloomy sentimental inquirers. And, perhaps, the advice as good as
can be given to a low-spirited, dissatisfied being:—"Don't
trouble your head with sickly thinking: take a cup and be
merry."

---

[1] As some of my readers may be gratified by reading the progress of
this little composition, I shall insert it from my notes.—"When Dr.
Johnson and I were sitting *tête-à-tête* at the Mitre Tavern, May 9, 1778,
he said, '*Where* is bliss' would be better. He then added a ludicrous
stanza, but would not repeat it, lest I should take it down. It was
somewhat as follows; the last line I am sure I remember:—

> 'While I thus   cried,
>   seer,
>   The hoary   replied,
>   Come, my lad, and drink some beer.'

In spring, 1779, when in better humour, he made the second stanza,
as in the text. There was only one variation afterwards made on my
suggestion, which was changing *hoary*, in the third line, to *smiling*, both
to avoid a sameness with the epithet in the first line, and to describe the
hermit in his pleasantry. He was then very well pleased that I should
preserve it."—BOSWELL.

CHAPTER VI.—1777

FRIDAY. September 19, after breakfast, Dr. Johnson and
I set out in Dr. Taylor's chaise to go to Derby. The day
was fine, and we resolved to go by Keddlestone, the seat
of Lord Scarsdale, that I might see his Lordship's fine
house. I was struck with the magnificence of the building;
and the extensive park, with the finest verdure, covered
with deer, and cattle, and sheep, delighted me. The
number of old oaks, of an immense size, filled me with a
sort of respectful admiration. For one of them, 60*l.* was
offered. The excellent smooth gravel roads; the large
piece of water formed by his Lordship from some small
brooks, with a handsome barge upon it: the venerable
Gothic church, now the family chapel, just by the house;
in short, the grand group of objects agitated and distended
my mind in a most agreeable manner. "One should
think," said I, "that the proprietor of all this *must* be
happy."—"Nay, Sir," said Johnson, "all this excludes
but one evil—poverty."[1]

---

[1] When I mentioned Dr. Johnson's remark to a lady of admirable good
sense and quickness of understanding, she observed, "It is true, all this
excludes only one evil; but how much good does it let in?"—To this
observation much praise has been justly given. Let me then now do

Our names were sent up, and a well-dressed elderly housekeeper, a most distinct articulator, showed us the house; which I need not describe, as there is an account of it published in "Adams' Works in Architecture." Dr. Johnson thought better of it to-day than when he saw it before; for he had lately attacked it violently, saying, "It would do excellently for a town-hall. The large room with the pillars," said he, "would do for the judges to sit in at the assizes; the circular room for a jury-chamber; and the room above for prisoners." Still he thought the large room ill-lighted, and of no use but for dancing in; and the bed-chambers but indifferent rooms: and that the immense sum which it cost was injudiciously laid out. Dr. Taylor had put him in mind of his *appearing* pleased with the house. "But," said he, "that was when Lord Scarsdale was present. Politeness obliges us to appear pleased with a man's works when he is present. No man will be so ill-bred as to question you. You may therefore pay compliments without saying what is not true. I should say to Lord Scarsdale of his large room, 'My Lord, this is the most *costly* room that I ever saw,' which is true."

Dr. Manningham, physician in London, who was visiting at Lord Scarsdale's, accompanied us through many of the rooms; and soon afterwards my Lord himself, to whom Dr. Johnson was known, appeared, and did the honours of the house. We talked of Mr. Langton. Johnson, with a warm vehemence of affectionate regard, exclaimed, "The earth does not bear a worthier man than Bennet Langton." We saw a good many fine pictures, which I think are described in one of "Young's Tours." There is a printed catalogue of them, which the housekeeper put into my hand; I should like to view them at leisure. I was much struck with Daniel interpreting Nebuchadnezzar's dream, by Rembrandt.—We were shown a pretty large library. In his Lordship's dressing-room lay Johnson's small Dictionary: he showed it to me with some eagerness, saying, "Look'ye! *Quæ regio in terris nostri non plena laboris!*" He observed, also, Goldsmith's "Animated Nature;" and said, "Here's our friend! The poor Doctor would have been happy to hear of this."

In our way Johnson strongly expressed his love of driving fast in a post-chaise. "If," said he, "I had no

myself the honour to mention that the lady who made it was the late Margaret Montgomerie, my very valuable wife, and the very affectionate mother of my children, who, if they inherit her good qualities, will have no reason to complain of their lot. *Dos magna parentum virtus*.—Boswell.

duties, and no reference to futurity, I would spend my life in driving briskly in a post-chaise with a pretty woman; but she should be one who could understand me, and would add something to the conversation." I observed, that we were this day to stop just where the Highland army did in 1745. JOHNSON: "It was a noble attempt." BOSWELL: "I wish we could have an authentic history of it." JOHNSON: "If you were not an idle dog you might write it, by collecting from everybody what they can tell, and putting down your authorities." BOSWELL: "But I could not have the advantage of it in my lifetime." JOHNSON: "You might have the satisfaction of its fame, by printing it in Holland; and as to profit, consider how long it was before writing came to be considered in a pecuniary view. Baretti says, he is the first man that ever received copy-money in Italy." I said that I would endeavour to do what Dr. Johnson suggested; and I thought that I might write so as to venture to publish my "History of the Civil War in Great Britain in 1745 and 1746," without being obliged to go to a foreign press.[1]

When we arrived at Derby, Dr. Butter accompanied us to see the manufactory of China there. I admired the ingenuity and delicate art with which a man fashioned clay into a cup, a saucer, or a tea-pot, while a boy turned round a wheel to give the mass rotundity. I thought this as excellent in its species of power, as making good verses in its species. Yet I had no respect for this potter. Neither, indeed, has a man of any extent of thinking for a mere verse-maker, in whose numbers, however perfect, there is no poetry, no mind. The china was beautiful; but Dr. Johnson justly observed it was too dear; for that he could have vessels of silver, of the same size, as cheap as what were made of porcelain.

I felt a pleasure in walking about Derby, such as I always have in walking about any town to which I am not accustomed. There is an immediate sensation of novelty; and one speculates on the way in which life is passed in it, which, although there is a sameness everywhere upon the whole, is yet minutely diversified. The minute diversities in everything are wonderful. Talking of shaving the other night at Dr. Taylor's, Dr. Johnson said, "Sir, of a thousand shavers, two do not shave so much alike as not to be distinguished." I thought this not possible, till he specified

[1] I am now happy to understand that Mr. John Home (who was himself gallantly in the field for the reigning family in that interesting warfare, but is generous enough to do justice to the other side), is preparing an account of it for the press.—BOSWELL.

so many of the varieties in shaving:—holding the razor more
or less perpendicular;—drawing long or short strokes;—
beginning at the upper part of the face, or the under—at
the right side or the left side. Indeed, when one considers what variety of sounds can be uttered by the wind-
pipe, in the compass of a very small aperture, we may be
convinced how many degrees of difference there may be in
the application of a razor.

We dined with Dr. Butter,[1] whose lady is daughter of
my cousin, Sir John Douglas, whose grandson is now pre-
sumptive heir of the noble family of Queensberry. Johnson
and he had a good deal of medical conversation. Johnson
said, he had somewhere or other given an account of Dr.
Nichols's discourse "*De Animâ Medicâ.*" He told us,
"that whatever a man's distemper was, Dr. Nichols would
not attend him as a physician, if his mind was not at ease;
for he believed that no medicines would have any influence.
He once attended a man in trade, upon whom he found
none of the medicines he prescribed had any effect; he
asked the man's wife privately whether his affairs were
not in a bad way? She said no. He continued his attendance some time, still without success. At length the mans'
wife told him, she had discovered that her husband's
affairs *were* in a bad way. When Goldsmith was dying,
Dr. Turton said to him, 'Your pulse is in greater disorder
than it should be, from the degree of fever which you have:
is your mind at ease?' Goldsmith answered it was not."

After dinner, Mrs. Butter went with me to see the silk-
mill which Mr. John Lombe had had a patent for,[2] having
brought away the contrivance from Italy. I am not very
conversant with mechanics; but the simplicity of this
machine, and its multiplied operations, struck me with
an agreeable surprise. I had learnt from Dr. Johnson,
during this interview, not to think with a dejected indifference of the works of art and the pleasures of life, because
life is uncertain and short; but to consider such indifference
as a failure of reason, a morbidness of mind; for happiness
should be cultivated as much as we can, and the objects
which are instrumental to it should be steadily considered
as of importance, with a reference not only to ourselves,

[1] Dr. Butter was at this time a practising physician at Derby. He
afterwards removed to London, where he died in his 79th year, March
22, 1805. He is author of several medical tracts.—MALONE.

[2] See Hutton's "History of Derby," a book which is deservedly
esteemed for its information, accuracy, and good narrative. Indeed
the age in which we live is eminently distinguished by topographical
excellence.—BOSWELL.

but to multitudes in successive ages. Though it is proper
to value small parts, as

"Sands make the mountain, moments make the year;"

yet we must contemplate, collectively, to have a just estimation of objects. One moment's being uneasy or not,
seems of no consequence; yet this may be thought of the
next, and the next, and so on, till there is a large portion
of misery. In the same way one must think of happiness,
of learning, of friendship. We cannot tell the precise
moment when friendship is formed. As in filling a vessel
drop by drop, there is at last a drop which makes it run
over; so in a series of kindnesses there is at last one which
makes the heart run over. We must not divide objects
of our attention into minute parts, and think separately of
each part. It is by contemplating a large mass of human
existence, that a man, while he sets a just value on his own
life, does not think of his death as annihilating all that is
great and pleasing in the world, as if actually *contained
in his mind*, according to Berkeley's reverie. If his
imagination be not sickly and feeble, it "wings its distant
way" far beyond himself, and views the world in unceasing
activity of every sort. It must be acknowledged, however,
that Pope's plaintive reflection, that all things would be as
gay as ever, on the day of his death, is natural and common.
We are apt to transfer to all around us our own gloom,
without considering that at any given point of time there
is, perhaps, as much youth and gaiety in the world as at
another. Before I came into this life, in which I have had
so many pleasant scenes, have not thousands and tens of
thousands of deaths and funerals happened, and have not
families been in grief for their nearest relations? But have
those dismal circumstances at all affected *me*? Why then
should the gloomy scenes which I experience or which I
know, affect others? Let us guard against imagining that
there is an end of felicity upon earth, when we ourselves
grow old, or are unhappy.

Dr. Johnson told us at tea, that when some of Dr. Dodd's
pious friends were trying to console him by saying that he
was going to leave "a wretched world," he had honesty
enough not to join in the cant:—"No, no," said he, "it
has been a very agreeable world to me." Johnson added,
"I respect Dodd for thus speaking the truth; for, to be
sure, he had for several years enjoyed a life of great
voluptuousness."

He told us that Dodd's city friends stood by him so,

that a thousand pounds were ready to be given to the gaoler, if he would let him escape. He added, that he knew a friend of Dodd's who walked about Newgate for some time on the evening before the day of his execution, with five hundred pounds in his pocket, ready to be paid to any of the turnkeys who could get him out; but it was too late, for he was watched with much circumspection. He said, Dodd's friends had an image of him made of wax, which was to have been left in his place; and he believed it was carried into the prison.

Johnson disapproved of Dr. Dodd's leaving the world persuaded that "The Convict's Address to his unhappy Brethren" was of his own writing. "But, Sir," said I, "you contributed to the deception; for when Mr. Seward expressed a doubt to you that it was not Dodd's own, because it had a great deal more force of mind in it than anything known to be his, you answered, 'Why should you think so? Depend upon it, Sir, when a man knows he is to be hanged in a fortnight, it concentrates his mind wonderfully.'" JOHNSON: "Sir, as Dodd got it from me to pass as his own, while that could do him any good, that was an *implied promise* that I should not own it. To own it, therefore, would have been telling a lie, with the addition of breach of promise, which was worse than simply telling a lie to make it be believed it was Dodd's. Besides, Sir, I did not *directly* tell a lie: I left the matter uncertain. Perhaps I thought that Seward would not believe it the less to be mine for what I said; but I would not put it in his power to say I had owned it."

He praised Blair's Sermons: "Yet," said he, (willing to let us see he was aware that fashionable fame, however deserved, is not always the most lasting,) "perhaps they may not be reprinted after seven years; at least not after Blair's death."

He said, "Goldsmith was a plant that flowered late. There appeared nothing remarkable about him when he was young; though when he got high in fame, one of his friends began to recollect something of his being distinguished at College.[1] Goldsmith in the same manner recollected more of that friend's early years, as he grew a greater man."

I mentioned that Lord Monboddo told me he awaked every morning at four, and then for his health got up and walked in his room naked, with the window open, which

---

[1] He *was* distinguished in college, as appears from a circumstance mentioned by Dr. Kearney. See vol. i., chap. xiii.—MALONE.

he called taking *an air bath;* after which he went to bed again, and slept two hours more. Johnson, who was always ready to beat down anything that seemed to be exhibited with disproportionate importance, thus observed: "I suppose, Sir, there is no more in it than this, he wakes at four, and cannot sleep till he chills himself, and makes the warmth of the bed a grateful sensation."

I talked of the difficulty of rising in the morning. Dr. Johnson told me, "that the learned Mrs. Carter,[1] at that period when she was eager in study, did not awake as early as she wished, and she therefore had a contrivance, that, at a certain hour, her chamber-light should burn a string to which a heavy weight was suspended, which then fell with a strong sudden noise: this roused her from her sleep, and then she had no difficulty in getting up." But I said *that* was my difficulty; and wished there could be some medicine invented which would make one rise without pain, which I never did, unless after lying in bed a very long time. Perhaps there may be something in the stores of nature which could do this. I have thought of a pulley to raise me gradually; but that would give me pain, as it would counteract my internal inclination. I would have something that can dissipate the *vis inertiœ,* and give elasticity to the muscles. As I imagine that the human body may be put, by the operation of other substances, into any state in which it has ever been; and as I have experienced a state in which rising from bed was not disagreeable, but easy, nay, sometimes agreeable; I suppose that this state may be produced, if we knew by what. We can heat the body, we can cool it; we can give it tension or relaxation; and surely it is possible to bring it into a state in which rising from bed will not be a pain.

Johnson observed, that "a man should take a sufficient quantity of sleep, which Dr. Mead says is between seven and nine hours." I told him, that Dr. Cullen said to me, that a man should not take more sleep than he can take at once.

---

[1] This was the learned and accomplished Elizabeth Carter, whose name is frequently mentioned in these Memoirs. She was born at Deal in 1717, and was the daughter of the Rev. Dr. Nicholas Carter, through whose instructions she became acquainted with the Latin and Greek languages. She was also well skilled in French, Spanish, German, Italian, Portuguese, Arabic, and Hebrew. She was known as the translator of Crousay's "Critique on Pope's Essay on Man," Algarotti's "Explanation of Newton's Philosophy," and of "Epictetus." After her decease, six volumes of her Correspondence were published, which display great intellectual powers. Mr. Cave was the means of first introducing her to many authors and scholars of note, and among those was Dr. Johnson, with whom she continued on terms of intimacy as long as he lived. She died in Clarges-street, in 1806.—ED.

JOHNSON: "This rule, Sir, cannot hold in all cases; for many people have their sleep broken by sickness; and surely Cullen would not have a man to get up, after having slept but an hour. Such a regimen would soon end in a *long sleep*."[1] Dr. Taylor remarked, I think very justly, that "a man who does not feel an inclination to sleep at the ordinary times, instead of being stronger than other people, must not be well; for a man in health has all the natural inclinations to eat, drink, and sleep in a strong degree."

Johnson advised me to-night not to *refine* in the education of my children. "Life," said he, "will not bear refinement; you must do as other people do."

As we drove back to Ashbourne, Dr. Johnson recommended to me, as he had often done, to drink water only: "For," said he, "you are then sure not to get drunk; whereas, if you drink wine, you are never sure." I said, drinking wine was a pleasure which I was unwilling to give up. "Why, Sir," said he, "there is no doubt that not to drink wine is a great deduction from life: but it may be necessary." He, however, owned that, in his opinion, a free use of wine did not shorten life; and said, he would not give less for the life of a certain Scotch Lord (whom he named) celebrated for hard drinking, than for that of a sober man. "But stay," said he, with his usual intelligence and accuracy of inquiry, "does it take much wine to make him drunk?" I answered, "a great deal either of wine or strong punch." "Then," said he, "that is the worse." I presume to illustrate my friend's observation thus:—"A fortress which soon surrenders has its walls less shattered, than when a long and obstinate resistance is made."

I ventured to mention a person who was as violent a Scotsman as he was an Englishman; and literally had the same contempt for an Englishman compared with a Scotsman, that he had for a Scotsman compared with an English-

---

[1] This regimen was, however, practised by Bishop Ken, of whom Hawkins (*not Sir John*) in his life of that venerable prelate, p. 4, tells us, "And that neither his study might be the aggressor on his hours of instruction, or what he judged his duty, prevent his improvements; or both, his closet addresses to his GOD; he strictly accustomed himself to but one sleep, which often obliged him to rise at one or two of the clock in the morning, and sometimes sooner; and grew so habitual, that it continued with him almost till his last illness. And so lively and cheerful was his temper, that he would be very facetious and entertaining to his friends in the evening, even when it was perceived that with difficulty he kept his eyes open, and then seemed to go to rest with no other purpose than the refreshing and enabling him with more vigour and cheerfulness to sing his morning hymn, as he then used to do to his lute before he put on his clothes."—BOSWELL.

man; and that he would say of Dr. Johnson, "Damned rascal! to talk as he does of the Scotch." This seemed, for a moment, "to give him pause." It perhaps presented his extreme prejudice against the Scotch in a point of view somewhat new to him, by the effect of *contrast*.

By the time when we returned to Ashbourne, Dr. Taylor was gone to bed. Johnson and I sat up a long time by ourselves.

He was much diverted with an article which I showed him in "The Critical Review" of this year, giving an account of a curious publication, entitled, "A Spiritual Diary and Soliloquies, by John Rutty, M.D." Dr. Rutty was one of the people called Quakers, a physician of some eminence in Dublin, and author of several works. This Diary, which was kept from 1753 to 1775, the year in which he died, and was now published in two volumes octavo, exhibited, in the simplicity of his heart, a minute and honest register of the state of his mind; which, though frequently laughable enough, was not more so than the history of many men would be, if recorded with equal fairness.

The following specimens were extracted by the Reviewers:—

"Tenth month, 1753.
"23.   Indulgence in bed an hour too long.
"Twelfth month, 17.   An hypochondriac obnubilation from
    wind and indigestion.
"Ninth month, 28.   An over dose of whisky.
"29.   A dull, cross, choleric day.
"First month, 1757—22.   A little swinish at dinner and repast.
"31.   Dogged on provocation.
"Second month, 5.   Very dogged or snappish.
"14.   Snappish on fasting.
"26.   Cursed snappishness to those under me, on a bodily
    indisposition.
"Third month, 11.   On a provocation, exercised a dull resent-
    ment for two days instead of scolding.
"22.   Scolded too vehemently.
"23.   Dogged again.
"Fourth month, 29.   Mechanically and sinfully dogged."

Johnson laughed heartily at this good quietist's self-condemning minutes; particularly at his mentioning, with such a serious regret, occasional instances of "*swinishness* in eating, and *doggedness of temper*." He thought the observations of the Critical Reviewers upon the importance of a man to himself so ingenious and so well expressed, that I shall here introduce them.

After observing, that "there are few writers who have gained any reputation by recording their own actions," they say,—

"We may reduce the egotists to four classes. In the *first* we have Julius Cæsar: he relates his own transactions; but he relates them with peculiar grace and dignity, and his narrative is supported by the greatness of his character and achievements. In the *second* class we have Marcus Antoninus: this writer has given us a series of reflections on his own life; but his sentiments are so noble, his morality so sublime, that his meditations are universally admired. In the *third* class we have some others of tolerable credit, who have given importance to their own private history by an intermixture of literary anecdotes, and the occurrences of their own times: the celebrated *Huetius* has published an entertaining volume upon this plan '*De rebus ad eum pertinentibus.*' In the *fourth* class we have the journalists, temporal and spiritual: Elias Ashmole,[1] William Lilly,[2] George Whitefield,[3] John Wesley,[4] and a thousand other old women and fanatic writers of memoirs and meditations."

I mentioned to him that Dr. Hugh Blair, in his lectures on Rhetoric and Belles Lettres, which I heard him deliver at Edinburgh, had animadverted on the Johnsonian style as too pompous; and attempted to imitate it, by giving a sentence of Addison in "The Spectator," No. 411, in the manner of Johnson. When treating of the utility of the pleasures of imagination in preserving us from vice, it is observed of those "who know not how to be idle and innocent," that "their very first step out of business is into vice or folly," which Dr. Blair supposed would have been expressed in "The Rambler" thus: "Their very first step

---

[1] Elias Ashmole was the founder of the Ashmolean Museum at Oxford. In the early part of his life he ardently devoted himself to alchemy. He was born in 1617, and died in 1692.—ED.

[2] The well-known astrologer, who was employed during the civil wars, both by Charles I. and the Parliamentary forces, in astrological predictions; and those contained in his almanacs are represented to have produced a great effect upon the soldiers and the populace. He was born in Leicestershire in 1602, and died at Horsham in 1681.—ED.

[3] Whitefield was the founder of the Calvinistic Methodists, and one of the most popular and zealous preachers of his time. He was born at Gloucester in 1714, and died at Newburyport, in New England, in 1770.—ED.

[4] Wesley was a contemporary and the fellow-labourer of Whitefield, and the great founder of Methodism; but a disagreement arising on the subject of Calvinistic and Arminian doctrines, a separation soon took place; and hence two distinct sects arose. Wesley was born in 1703, and died in 1791.—ED.

out of the regions of business is into the perturbation of vice, or the vacuity of folly." [1] JOHNSON: "Sir, these are not the words I should have used. No, Sir; the imitators of my style have not hit it. Miss Aikin has done it the best; for she has imitated the sentiment as well as the diction."

I intend, before this work is concluded, to exhibit specimens of imitation of my friend's style in various modes; some caricaturing or mimicking it, and some formed upon it, whether intentionally or with a degree of similarity to it, of which, perhaps, the writers were not conscious.

In Baretti's Review, which he published in Italy under the title of "FRUSTA LETTERARIA," it is observed, that Dr. Robertson, the historian, had formed his style upon that of "*Il célèbre Samuele Johnson*." My friend himself was of that opinion; for he once said to me, in a pleasant humour, "Sir, if Robertson's style be faulty, he owes it to me; that is, having too many words, and those too big ones."

I read to him a letter which Lord Monboddo had written to me, containing some critical remarks upon the style of his "Journey to the Western Islands of Scotland." His Lordship praised the very fine passage upon landing at Icolmkill; [2] but his own style being exceedingly dry and hard, he disapproved of the richness of Johnson's language, and of his frequent use of metaphorical expressions.

---

[1] When Dr. Blair published his "Lectures," he was invidiously attacked for having omitted his censure on Johnson's style, and, on the contrary, praising it highly. But before that time Johnson's "Lives of the Poets" had appeared, in which his style was considerably easier than when he wrote "The Rambler." It would, therefore, have been uncandid in Blair, even supposing his criticism to have been just, to have preserved it.—BOSWELL.

[2] "We were now treading that illustrious island, which was once the luminary of the Caledonian regions, whence savage clans and roving barbarians derived the benefits of knowledge, and the blessings of religion. To abstract the mind from all local emotion would be impossible if it were endeavoured, and would be foolish if it were possible. Whatever withdraws us from the power of our senses, whatever makes the past, the distant, or the future predominate over the present, advances us in the dignity of thinking beings. Far from me, and from my friends, be such frigid philosophy, as may conduct us, indifferent and unmoved, over any ground which has been dignified by wisdom, bravery, or virtue. The man is little to be envied, whose patriotism would not gain force upon the plain of Marathon, or whose piety would not grow warmer among the ruins of Iona."

Had our tour produced nothing else but this sublime passage, the world must have acknowledged that it was not made in vain. Sir Joseph Banks, the present respectable President of the Royal Society, told me he was so much struck on reading it, that he clasped his hands together, and remained for some time in an attitude of silent admiration.—BOSWELL.

Johnson: "Why, Sir, this criticism would be just, if, in my style, superfluous words, or words too big for the thoughts, could be pointed out; but this I do not believe can be done. For instance, in the passage which Lord Monboddo admires, 'We were now treading that illustrious region,' the word *illustrious* contributes nothing to the mere narration; for the fact might be told without it: but it is not therefore superfluous; for it awakes the mind to peculiar attention, where something of more than usual importance is to be presented. 'Illustrious!'—for what? and then the sentence proceeds to expand the circumstances connected with Iona. And, Sir, as to metaphorical expression, that is a great excellence in style, when it is used with propriety, for it gives you two ideas for one; conveys the meaning more luminously, and generally with a perception of delight."

He told me that he had been asked to undertake the new edition of "The Biographia Britannica," but had declined it; which he afterwards said to me he regretted. In this regret many will join, because it would have procured us more of Johnson's most delightful species of writing; and, although my friend Dr. Kippis[1] has hitherto discharged the task judiciously, distinctly, and with more impartiality than might have been expected from a Separatist, it were to have been wished that the superintendence of this literary Temple of Fame had been assigned to "a friend to the constitution in Church and State." We should not then have had it too much crowded with obscure dissenting teachers, doubtless men of merit and worth, but not quite to be numbered amongst "the most eminent persons who have flourished in Great Britain and Ireland."[2]

[1] After having given to the public the first five volumes of a new edition of the "Biographia Britannica," between the years 1788 and 1793, Dr. Kippis died, October 8, 1795; and the work is not likely to be soon completed.—Malone.

[2] In this censure, which has been carelessly uttered, I carelessly joined. But in justice to Dr. Kippis, who, with that manly, candid good temper which marks his character, set me right, I now with pleasure retract it; and I desire it may be particularly observed, as pointed out by him to me, that "The new lives of dissenting divines, in the first four volumes of the second edition of 'The Biographia Britannica,' are those of John Abernethy, Thomas Amory, George Benson, Hugh Broughton (the learned Puritan), Simon Browne, Joseph Boyse (of Dublin), Thomas Cartwright (the learned Puritan), and Samuel Chandler. The only doubt I have ever heard suggested is, whether there should have been an article of Dr. Amory. But I was convinced, and am still convinced, that he was entitled to one, from the reality of his learning, and the excellent and candid nature of his practical writings.

"The new lives of clergymen of the Church of England, in the same four volumes, are as follow:—John Balguy, Edward Bentham, George

On Saturday, September 20, after breakfast, when Taylor was gone out to his farm, Dr. Johnson and I had a serious conversation by ourselves on melancholy and madness; which he was, I always thought, erroneously inclined to confound together. Melancholy, like "great wit," may be "near allied to madness;" but there is, in my opinion, a distinct separation between them. When he talked of madness, he was to be understood as speaking of those who were in any great degree disturbed, or, as it is commonly expressed, "troubled in mind." Some of the ancient philosophers held, that all deviations from right reason were madness; and whoever wishes to see the opinions both of ancients and moderns upon this subject, collected and illustrated with a variety of curious facts, may read Dr. Arnold's very entertaining work.[1]

Johnson said, "A madman loves to be with people whom he fears; not as a dog fears the lash, but of whom he stands in awe." I was struck with the justness of this observation. To be with those of whom a person, whose mind is wavering and dejected, stands in awe, represses and composes an uneasy tumult of spirits,[2] and consoles him with the contemplation of something steady, and at least comparatively great.

Berkeley (Bishop of Cloyne), William Berriman, Thomas Birch, William Borlase, Thomas Bott, James Bradley, Thomas Broughton, John Brown, John Burton, Joseph Butler (Bishop of Durham), Thomas Carte, Edmund Castell, Edmund Chishull, Charles Churchill, William Clarke, Robert Clayton (Bishop of Clogher), John Conybeare (Bishop of Bristol), George Costard, and Samuel Croxall.—I am not conscious," says Kippis, "of any partiality in conducting the work. I would not willingly insert a dissenting minister that does not justly deserve to be noticed, or omit an established clergyman that does. At the same time I shall not be deterred from introducing dissenters into 'The Biographia,' when I am satisfied that they are entitled to that distinction, from their writings, learning, and merit."

Let me add, that the expression "A friend to the constitution in Church and State," was not meant by me as any reflection upon this reverend gentleman, as if he were an enemy to the political constitution of his country, as established at the Revolution, but, from my steady and avowed predilection for a *Tory*, was quoted from Johnson's Dictionary, where that distinction is so defined.—BOSWELL.

[1] "Observations on Insanity," by Thomas Arnold, M.D., London, 1782. —BOSWELL.

[2] Carden composed his mind, tending to madness (or rather actually mad, for such he seems in his writings, learned as they are), by exciting voluntary pain. V. Card. Op. et Vit.—KEARNEY.

This was Jerome Carden, an Italian physician of considerable note in his time, but of great eccentricity of character. With all his talents he appears to have been a consummate empiric, and strongly addicted to astrology. Having predicted the time of his death, he is said to have starved himself in order to verify the prediction. He wrote on a great variety of subjects, and in 1663 his works were printed at Lyons in 10 vols. fol. He was born in 1501, and died in 1576.

He added, "Madmen are all sensual in the lower stages
of the distemper. They are eager for gratifications to
soothe their minds, and divert their attention from the
misery which they suffer; but when they grow very ill,
pleasure is too weak for them, and they seek for pain.[1]
Employment, Sir, and hardships prevent melancholy. I
suppose in all our army in America there was not one man
who went mad."

We entered seriously upon a question of much importance to me, which Johnson was pleased to consider with
friendly attention. I had long complained to him that I
felt discontented in Scotland, as too narrow a sphere, and
that I wished to make my chief residence in London, the
great scene of ambition, instruction, and amusement: a
scene, which was to me, comparatively speaking, a heaven
upon earth. JOHNSON: "Why, Sir, I never knew any one
who had such a *gust* for London as you have, and I cannot
blame you for your wish to live there; yet, Sir, were I in
your father's place, I should not consent to your settling
there; for I have the old feudal notions, and I should be
afraid that Auchinleck would be deserted, as you would
soon find it more desirable to have a country-seat in a
better climate. I own, however, that to consider it as a
duty to reside on a family estate is a prejudice; for we must
consider that working-people get employment equally,
and the produce of the land is sold equally, whether a great
family resides at home or not; and if the rents of an estate
be carried to London, they return again in the circulation
of commerce; nay, Sir, we must perhaps allow, that carrying
the rents to a distance is a good, because it contributes to
that circulation. We must, however, allow that a well-
regulated great family may improve a neighbourhood in
civility and elegance, and give an example of good order,
virtue, and piety; and so its residence at home may be of
much advantage. But if a great family be disorderly and

---

[1] We read in the Gospels, that those unfortunate persons who were
possessed with evil spirits (which, after all, I think is the most probable
cause of madness, as was first suggested to me by my respectable friend
Sir John Pringle), had recourse to pain, tearing themselves, and jumping
sometimes into the fire, sometimes into the water. Mr. Seward has
furnished me with a remarkable anecdote in confirmation of Dr. Johnson's
observation. A tradesman who had acquired a large fortune in London,
retired from business, and went to live at Worcester. His mind, being
without its usual occupation, and having nothing else to supply its
place, preyed upon itself, so that existence was a torment to him. At
last he was seized with the stone; and a friend who found him in one of
its severest fits, having expressed his concern, "No, no, Sir," said he,
"don't pity me; what I now feel is ease, compared with that torture
of mind from which it relieves me."—BOSWELL.

vicious, its residence at home is very pernicious to a neighbourhood. There is not now the same inducement to
live in the country as formerly; the pleasures of social life
are much better enjoyed in town; and there is no longer in
the country that power and influence in proprietors of land
which they had in old times, and which made the country
so agreeable to them. The Laird of Auchinleck now is
not near so great a man as the Laird of Auchinleck was a
hundred years ago."

I told him, that one of my ancestors never went from
home without being attended by thirty men on horseback.
Johnson's shrewdness and spirit of inquiry were exerted
upon every occasion. "Pray," said he, "how did your
ancestor support his thirty men and thirty horses when
he went at a distance from home, in an age when there was
hardly any money in circulation?" I suggested the same
difficulty to a friend who mentioned Douglas's going to the
Holy Land with a numerous train of followers. Douglas
could, no doubt, maintain followers enough while living
upon his own lands, the produce of which supplied them
with food; but he could not carry that food to the Holy
Land; and as there was no commerce by which he could be
supplied with money, how could he maintain them in foreign
countries?

I suggested a doubt, that if I were to reside in London,
the exquisite zest with which I relished it in occasional
visits might go off, and I might grow tired of it. JOHNSON:
"Why, Sir, you find no man, at all intellectual, who is
willing to leave London. No, Sir, when a man is tired of
London, he is tired of life; for there is in London all that
life can afford."

To obviate his apprehension, that by settling in London
I might desert the seat of my ancestors, I assured him that
I had old feudal principles to a degree of enthusiasm;
and that I felt all the *dulcedo* of the *natale solum*. I
reminded him, that the Laird of Auchinleck had an elegant
house, in front of which he could ride ten miles forward
upon his own territories, upon which he had upwards of
six hundred people attached to him; that the family-seat
was rich in natural romantic beauties of rock, wood, and
water; and that in my "morn of life" I had appropriated
the finest descriptions in the ancient classics to certain
scenes there, which were thus associated in my mind.
That when all this was considered, I should certainly
pass a part of the year at home, and enjoy it the
more from variety, and from bringing with me a share
of the intellectual stores of the metropolis. He listened

to all this, and kindly "hoped it might be as I now supposed."

He said, a country gentleman should bring his lady to visit London as soon as he can, that they may have agreeable topics for conversation when they are by themselves.

As I meditated trying my fortune in Westminster Hall, our conversation turned upon the profession of the law in England. JOHNSON: "You must not indulge too sanguine hopes, should you be called to our bar. I was told, by a very sensible lawyer, that there are a great many chances against any man's success in the profession of the law; the candidates are so numerous, and those who get large practice so few. He said it was by no means true that a man of good parts and application is sure of having business, though he indeed allowed that if such a man could but appear in a few causes, his merit would be known, and he would get forward; but that the great risk was, that a man might pass half a lifetime in the Courts and never have an opportunity of showing his abilities."[1]

We talked of employment being absolutely necessary to preserve the mind from wearying and growing fretful, especially in those who have a tendency to melancholy; and I mentioned to him a saying which somebody had related of an American savage, who, when a European was expatiating on all the advantages of money, put this question: "Will it purchase *occupation?*" JOHNSON: "Depend upon it, Sir, this saying is too refined for a savage. And, Sir, money *will* purchase occupation; it will purchase all the conveniences of life; it will purchase variety of company; it will purchase all sorts of entertainment."

I talked to him of "Forster's Voyage to the South Seas," which pleased me; but I found he did not like it. "Sir," said he, "there is a great affectation of fine writing in it." BOSWELL: "But he carries you along with him." JOHNSON: "No, Sir; he does not carry *me* along with him; he leaves me behind him; or, rather, indeed, he sets me before him, for he makes me turn over many leaves at a time!"

[1] Now, at the distance of fifteen years since this conversation passed, the observation which I have had an opportunity of making in Westminster Hall has convinced me that, however true the opinion of Dr. Johnson's legal friend may have been some time ago, the same certainty of success cannot now be promised to the same display of merit. The reasons, however, of the rapid rise of some, and the disappointment of others equally respectable, are such as it might seem invidious to mention, and would require a longer detail than would be proper for this work.—BOSWELL.

B.L.J.: II—F

On Sunday, September 21, we went to the church of Ashbourne, which is one of the largest and most luminous that I have seen in any town of the same size. I felt great satisfaction in considering that I was supported in my fondness for solemn public worship by the general concurrence and munificence of mankind.

Johnson and Taylor were so different from each other, that I wondered at their preserving an intimacy. Their having been at school and college together, might, in some degree, account for this; but Sir Joshua Reynolds has furnished me with a stronger reason; for Johnson mentioned to him that he had been told by Taylor he was to be his heir. I shall not take upon me to animadvert upon this; but certain it is that Johnson paid great attention to Taylor. He now, however, said to me, "Sir, I love him; but I do not love him more; my regard for him does not increase. As it is said in the Apocrypha, 'his talk is of bullocks.'[1] I do not suppose he is very fond of my company. His habits are by no means sufficiently clerical; this he knows that I see; and no man likes to live under the eye of perpetual disapprobation."

I have no doubt that a good many sermons were composed for Taylor by Johnson. At this time I found, upon his table, a part of one which he had newly begun to write; and *Concio pro Tayloro* appears in one of his diaries. When to these circumstances we add the internal evidence from the power of thinking and style in the collection which the Reverend Mr. Hayes had published, with the *significant* title of "Sermons *left for publication* by the Reverend John Taylor, LL.D." our conviction will be complete.

I, however, would not have it thought that Dr. Taylor, though he could not write like Johnson (as, indeed, who could?) did not sometimes compose sermons as good as those which we generally have from very respectable divines. He showed me one with notes on the margin in Johnson's handwriting; and I was present when he read another to Johnson, that he might have his opinion of it, and Johnson said it was "very well." These, we may be sure, were not Johnson's; for he was above little arts or tricks of deception.

Johnson was by no means of opinion, that every man of a learned profession should consider it as incumbent upon him, or as necessary to his credit, to appear as an

---

[1] Ecclesiasticus, chap. xxxviii. v. 25. The whole chapter may be read as an admirable illustration of the superiority of cultivated minds over the gross and illiterate.—BOSWELL.

author. When, in the ardour of ambition for literary fame, I regretted to him one day that an eminent judge had nothing of it, and therefore would leave no perpetual monument of himself to posterity: "Alas, Sir," said Johnson, "what a mass of confusion should we have, if every bishop, and every judge, every lawyer, physician, and divine, were to write books."

I mentioned to Johnson a respectable person of a very strong mind, who had little of that tenderness which is common to human nature; as an instance of which, when I suggested to him that he should invite his son, who had been settled ten years in foreign parts, to come home and pay him a visit, his answer was, "No, no; let him mind his business." JOHNSON: " I do not agree with him, Sir, in this.   Getting money is not all a man's business: to cultivate kindness is a valuable part of the business of life."

In the evening, Johnson, being in very good spirits, entertained us with several characteristical portraits; I regret that any of them escaped my retention and diligence. I found from experience, that to collect my friend's conversation so as to exhibit it with any degree of its original flavour, it was necessary to write it down without delay. To record his sayings, after some distance of time, was like preserving or pickling long-kept and faded fruits, or other vegetables, which, when in that state, have little or nothing of their taste when fresh.

I shall present my readers with a series of what I gathered this evening from the Johnsonian garden.

"My friend, the late Earl of Cork, had a great desire to maintain the literary character of his family; he was a genteel man, but did not keep up the dignity of his rank.   He was so generally civil, that nobody thanked him for it."

"Did we not hear so much said of Jack Wilkes, we should think more highly of his conversation.   Jack has a great variety of talk; Jack is a scholar, and Jack has the manners of a gentleman.   But after hearing his name sounded from pole to pole, as the phœnix of convivial felicity, we are disappointed in his company.   He has always been *at me:* but I would do Jack a kindness, rather than not.   The contest is now over."

"Garrick's gaiety of conversation has delicacy and elegance: Foote makes you laugh more; but Foote has the air of a buffoon paid for entertaining the company.   He, indeed, well deserves his hire."

"Colley Cibber once consulted me as to one of his birth-day Odes, a long time before it was wanted.   I objected very freely to several passages. Cibber lost patience, and would not read his ode to an end. When we had done with criticism, we walked over to Richardson's,[1] the author of 'Clarissa,' and I wondered to find Richardson displeased that I 'did not treat Cibber with more *respect.*' Now, Sir, to talk of *respect* for a *player!*" (smiling disdainfully.) BOSWELL: "There, Sir, you are always heretical; you never will allow merit to a player." JOHNSON: "Merit, Sir; what merit? Do you respect a rope-dancer, or a ballad-singer?" BOSWELL: "No, Sir; but we respect a great player, as a man who can conceive lofty sentiments, and can express them gracefully." JOHNSON: "What, Sir, a fellow who claps a hump on his back, and a lump on his leg, and cries, '*I am Richard the Third?*' Nay, Sir, a ballad-singer is a higher man, for he does two things: he repeats and he sings. There is both recitation and music in his performance; the player only recites." BOSWELL: "My dear Sir, you may turn anything into ridicule. I allow that a player of farce is not entitled to respect; he does a little thing: but he who can represent exalted characters, and touch the noblest passions, has very respectable powers; and mankind have agreed in admiring great talents for the stage. We must consider, too, that a great player does what very few people are capable to do: his art is a very rare faculty. *Who* can repeat Hamlet's soliloquy, 'To be, or not to be,' as Garrick does it?" JOHNSON: "Anybody may. Jemmy there (a boy about eight years old, who was in the room) will do it as well in a week." BOSWELL: "No, no, Sir; and as a proof of the merit of great acting, and of the value which mankind set upon it, Garrick has got 100,000*l.*" JOHNSON: "Is getting 100,000*l.* a proof of excellence? That has been done by a scoundrel commissary."

This was most fallacious reasoning. I was *sure*, for

[1] This was Samuel Richardson, the celebrated novelist; and, as he died in 1761, the incident above related must have taken place some years previously. Richardson was an extraordinary man. He was by trade a printer, and received his education at a common day-school in Derbyshire, where he was born, in 1689. He followed his business in a court in Fleet-street, and resided in Salisbury-square, adjoining. In 1740, he published his "Pamela," the popularity of which was so great, that it passed through five editions in one year. His "Clarissa," his "History of Sir Charles Grandison," and other productions, were also eminently successful. By the interest of Mr. Speaker Onslow, he was appointed printer of "The Journal of the House of Commons;" and in 1754 he was chosen Master of the Stationers' Company. He was an intimate friend of Johnson's; and at his house the latter was a frequent visitor. His "Correspondence" with persons of eminence (with his Life, by Mrs. Barbauld), was published in 1804.—ED.

once, that I had the best side of the argument. I boldly maintained the just distinction between a tragedian and a mere theatrical droll; between those who rouse our terror and pity, and those who only make us laugh. "If," said I, "Betterton and Foote were to walk into this room, you would respect Betterton much more than Foote." JOHNSON: "If Betterton were to walk into this room with Foote, Foote would soon drive him out of it. Foote, Sir, *quatenus* Foote, has powers superior to them all."

On Monday, September 22, when at breakfast, I unguardedly said to Dr. Johnson, "I wish I saw you and Mrs. Macaulay together." He grew very angry; and, after a pause, while a cloud gathered on his brow, he burst out, "No, Sir, you would not see us quarrel, to make you sport. Don't you know that it is very uncivil to *pit* two people against one another?"—Then, checking himself, and wishing to be more gentle, he added, " I do not say you should be hanged or drowned for this: but it *is* very uncivil." Dr. Taylor thought him in the wrong, and spoke to him privately of it; but I afterwards acknowledged to Johnson that I was to blame, for I candidly owned, that I meant to express a desire to see a contest between Mrs. Macaulay and him; but then I knew how the contest would end; so that I was to see him in triumph. JOHNSON: "Sir, you cannot be sure how a contest will end; and no man has a right to engage two people in a dispute by which their passions may be inflamed, and they may part with bitter resentment against each other. I would sooner keep company with a man from whom I must guard my pockets, than with a man who contrives to bring me into a dispute with somebody that he may hear it. This is the great fault of ——— (naming one of our friends,) endeavouring to introduce a subject upon which he knows two people in the company differ." BOSWELL: "But he told me, Sir, he does it for instruction." JOHNSON: "Whatever the motive be, Sir, the man who does so, does very wrong. He has no more right to instruct himself at such risk, than he has to make two people fight a duel, that he may learn how to defend himself."

He found great fault with a gentleman of our acquaintance for keeping a bad table. "Sir," said he, "when a man is invited to dinner he is disappointed if he does not get something good. I advised Mrs. Thrale, who has no card-parties at her house, to give sweetmeats, and such good things, in an evening, as are not commonly given, and she would find company enough come to her: for everybody loves to have things which please the palate put in their way, without trouble or preparation." Such was his attention to the *minutiæ* of life and manners.

He thus characterised the Duke of Devonshire, grandfather of the present representative of that very respectable family: "He was not a man of superior abilities, but he was a man strictly faithful to his word. If, for instance, he had promised you an acorn, and none had grown that year in his woods, he would not have contented himself with that excuse: he would have sent to Denmark for it. So unconditional was he in keeping his word—so high as to the point of honour." This was a liberal testimony from the Tory Johnson to the virtue of a great Whig nobleman.

Mr. Burke's "Letter to the Sheriffs of Bristol, on the affairs of America," being mentioned, Johnson censured the composition much, and he ridiculed the definition of a free government, viz.—"For any practical purpose, it is what the people think so." [1]—"I will let the King of France govern me on those conditions," said he, "for it is to be governed just as I please." And when Dr. Taylor talked of a girl being sent to a parish workhouse, and asked how much she could be obliged to work, "Why," said Johnson, "as much as is reasonable: and what is that? as much as *she thinks* reasonable."

Dr. Johnson obligingly proposed to carry me to see Ilam, a romantic scene, now belonging to a family of the name of Port, but formerly the seat of the Congreves. I suppose it is well described in some of the tours. Johnson described it distinctly and vividly, at which I could not but express to him my wonder; because, though my eyes, as he observed, were better than his, I could not by any means equal him in representing visible objects. I said, the difference between us in this respect was as that between a man who has a bad instrument, but plays well on it, and a man who has a good instrument, on which he can play very imperfectly.

I recollect a very fine amphitheatre, surrounded with hills covered with woods, and walks neatly formed along the side of a rocky steep, on the quarter next the house, with recesses under projections of rock, overshadowed with trees; in one of which recesses, we are told, Congreve wrote his "Old Bachelor." We viewed a remarkable natural curiosity at Ilam; two rivers bursting near each other from the rock, not from immediate springs, but after having run for many miles under ground. Plott, in his "History of Staffordshire" (p. 69), gives an account of

[1] Edit. 2, p. 53.—BOSWELL.

this curiosity; but Johnson would not believe it, though we had the attestation of the gardener, who said, he had put in corks, where the river *Manyfold* sinks into the ground, and had caught them in a net, placed before one of the openings where the water bursts out. Indeed such subterraneous courses of water are found in various parts of our globe.[1]

Talking of Dr. Johnson's unwillingness to believe extraordinary things, I ventured to say, "Sir, you come near Hume's argument against miracles, 'That it is more probable witnesses should lie, or be mistaken, than that they should happen.'" JOHNSON: "Why, Sir, Hume, taking the proposition simply, is right. But the Christian revelation is not proved by the miracles alone, but as connected with prophecies, and with the doctrines in confirmation of which the miracles were wrought."

He repeated his observation, that the differences among Christians are really of no consequence. "For instance," said he, "if a Protestant objects to a Papist, 'You worship images'; the Papist can answer, 'I do not insist on your doing it; you may be a very good Papist without it: I do it only as a help to my devotion.'" I said, the great article of Christianity is the revelation of immortality. Johnson admitted it was so.

In the evening, a gentleman-farmer who was on a visit at Dr. Taylor's, attempted to dispute with Johnson in favour of Mungo Campbell, who shot Alexander, Earl of Eglintoune, upon his having fallen when retreating from his Lordship, who he believed was about to seize his gun, as he had threatened to do. He said he should have done just as Campbell did. JOHNSON: "Whoever would do as Campbell did deserves to be hanged; not that I could, as a juryman, have found him legally guilty of murder; but I am glad they found means to convict him." The gentleman-farmer said, "A poor man has as much honour as a rich man, and Campbell had *that* to defend." Johnson exclaimed, "A poor man has no honour." The English yeoman, not dismayed, proceeded: "Lord Eglintoune was a damned fool to run on upon Campbell, after being warned that Campbell would shoot him if he did." Johnson, who could not bear anything like swearing, angrily replied, "He was *not a damned* fool: he only thought too well of Campbell. He did not believe Campbell would be such a *damned* scoundrel, as to do so *damned* a thing." His

[1] See Plott's "History of Staffordshire," p. 88, and the authorities referred to by him.—BOSWELL.

emphasis on *damned*, accompanied with frowning looks, reproved his opponent's want of decorum in *his* presence.

Talking of the danger of being mortified by rejection, when making approaches to the acquaintance of the great, I observed, "I am, however, generally for trying, 'Nothing venture, nothing have.'" JOHNSON: "Very true, Sir; but I have always been more afraid of failing, than hopeful of success." And, indeed, though he had all just respect for rank, no man ever less courted the favour of the great.

During this interview at Ashbourne, Johnson seemed to be more uniformly social, cheerful, and alert, than I had almost ever seen him. He was prompt on great occasions and on small. Taylor, who praised everything of his own to excess; in short, "whose geese were all swans," as the proverb says, expatiated on the excellence of his bull-dog, which he told us was "perfectly well-shaped." Johnson, after examining the animal attentively, thus repressed the vain-glory of our host:—"No, Sir, he is *not* well-shaped; for there is not the quick transition from the thickness of the forepart to the *tenuity*—the thin part—behind, which a bull-dog ought to have." This *tenuity* was the only *hard word* that I heard him use during this interview, and, it will be observed, he instantly put another expression in its place. Taylor said, a small bull-dog was as good as a large one. JOHNSON: "No, Sir; for in proportion to his size he has strength; and your argument would prove that a good bull-dog may be as small as a mouse." It was amazing how he entered with perspicuity and keenness upon everything that occurred in conversation. Most men, whom I know, would no more think of discussing a question about a bull-dog, than of attacking a bull.

I cannot allow any fragment whatever that floats in my memory concerning the great subject of this work to be lost. Though a small particular may appear trifling to some, it will be relished by others; while every little spark adds something to the general blaze; and to please the true, candid, warm admirers of Johnson, and in any degree increase the splendour of his reputation, I bid defiance to the shafts of ridicule, or even malignity. Showers of them have been discharged at my "Journal of a Tour to the Hebrides;" yet it still sails unhurt along the stream of time, and, as an attendant upon Johnson,

"Pursues the triumph, and partakes the gale."

One morning after breakfast, when the sun shone bright, we walked out together, and "pored" for some time with

placid indolence upon an artificial water-fall, which Dr.
Taylor had made by building a strong dyke of stone across
the river behind the garden.   It was now somewhat
obstructed by branches of trees and other rubbish, which
had come down the river, and settled close to it.   Johnson,
partly from a desire to see it play more freely, and partly
from the inclination to activity which will animate, at
times, the most inert and sluggish mortal, took a long pole
which was lying on the bank, and pushed down several
parcels of this wreck with painful assiduity, while I stood
quietly by, wondering to behold the sage thus curiously
employed, and smiling with a humourous satisfaction each
time when he carried his point.   He worked till he was
quite out of breath; and having found a large dead cat, so
heavy that he could not move it after several efforts,
"Come," said he, throwing down the pole, "*you* shall take
it now;" which I accordingly did, and being a fresh man,
soon made the cat tumble over the cascade.   This may be
laughed at as too trifling to record; but it is a small characteristic trait in the Flemish picture which I give of my
friend, and in which, therefore, I mark the most minute
particulars.   And let it be remembered, that "Æsop at
play" is one of the instructive apologues of antiquity.

I mentioned an old gentleman of our acquaintance
whose memory was beginning to fail.   Johnson: "There
must be a diseased mind, where there is a failure of memory
at seventy.   A man's head, Sir, must be morbid, if he
fails so soon."   My friend, being now himself sixty-eight,
might think thus: but I imagine, that *threescore and ten*,
the Psalmist's period of sound human life in later ages, may
have a failure, though there be no disease in the constitution.

Talking of Rochester's Poems, he said, he had given
them to Mr. Steevens to castrate[1] for the edition of the
Poets, to which he was to write prefaces.   Dr. Taylor (the
only time I ever heard him say any thing witty[2]) observed,
that "if Rochester had been castrated himself his ex-
ceptional poems would not have been written."   I asked
if Burnet had not given a good Life of Rochester.   Johnson:
"We have a good *Death:* there is not much *Life.*"   I asked
whether Prior's poems were to be printed entire; Johnson
said they were.   I mentioned Lord Hailes's censure of

---

[1] This was unnecessary, for it had been done in the early part of the
present century by Jacob Tonson.—Malone.

[2] I am told, that Horace Earl of Oxford has a collection of *Bon-mots*
by persons who never said but one.—Boswell.

Prior, in his preface to a collection of "Sacred Poems," by various hands, published by him at Edinburgh a great many years ago, where he mentions, "those impure tales which will be the eternal opprobrium of their ingenious author." JOHNSON: "Sir, Lord Hailes has forgot. There is nothing in Prior that will excite to lewdness. If Lord Hailes thinks there is, he must be more combustible than other people." I instanced the tale of "Paulo Purganti and his Wife." JOHNSON: "Sir, there is nothing there, but that his wife wanted to be kissed, when poor Paulo was out of pocket. No, Sir, Prior is a lady's book. No lady is ashamed to have it standing in her library."

The hypochondriac disorder being mentioned, Dr. Johnson did not think it so common as I supposed. "Dr. Taylor," said he, "is the same one day as another. Burke and Reynolds are the same. Beauclerk, except when in pain, is the same. I am not so myself; but this I do not mention commonly."

I complained of a wretched changefulness, so that I could not preserve, for any long continuance, the same views of anything. It was most comfortable to me to experience, in Dr. Johnson's company, a relief from this uneasiness. His steady, vigorous mind held firm before me those objects which my own feeble and tremulous imagination frequently presented, in such a wavering state, that my reason could not judge well of them.

Dr. Johnson advised me to-day to have as many books about me as I could; that I might read upon any subject upon which I had a desire for instruction at the time. "What you read *then*," said he, "you will remember; but if you have not a book immediately ready, and the subject moulds in your mind, it is a chance if you have again a desire to study it." He added, "If a man never has an eager desire for instruction, he shall prescribe a task for himself. But it is better when a man reads from immediate inclination."

He repeated a good many lines of Horace's Odes, while we were in the chaise; I remember particularly the Ode "*Eheu, fugaces,*" [l. ii. Od. xiv.]

He said, the dispute as to the comparative excellence of Homer or Virgil [1] was inaccurate. "We must consider,"

---

[1] I am informed by Mr. Langton, that a great many years ago he was present when this question was agitated between Dr. Johnson and Mr. Burke; and, to use Johnson's phrase, they "talked their best;" Johnson for Homer, Burke for Virgil. It may well be supposed to have been one of the ablest and most brilliant contests that ever was exhibited. How much must we regret that it has not been preserved.—BOSWELL.

said he, "whether Homer was not the greatest poet, though
Virgil may have produced the finest poem.[1] Virgil was
indebted to Homer for the whole invention of the structure
of an epic poem, and for many of his beauties."

He told me, that Bacon was a favourite author with
him; but he had never read his works till he was compiling
his English Dictionary, in which, he said, I might see
Bacon very often quoted. Mr. Seward recollects his
having mentioned, that a Dictionary of the English
Language might be compiled from Bacon's works alone,
and that he had once an intention of giving an edition of
Bacon, at least of his English works, and writing the Life
of that great man. Had he executed this intention, there
can be no doubt that he would have done it in a most
masterly manner. Mallet's Life of Bacon has no inconsiderable merit as an acute and elegant dissertation relative
to its subject; but Mallet's mind was not comprehensive
enough to embrace the vast extent of Lord Verulam's
genius and research. Dr. Warburton therefore observed,
with witty justness, "that Mallet,[2] in his Life of Bacon, had
forgotten that he was a philosopher; and if he should write
the Life of the Duke of Marlborough, which he had undertaken to do, he would probably forget that he was a
General."

Wishing to be satisfied what degree of truth there was
in a story which a friend of Johnson's and mine had told me
to his disadvantage, I mentioned it to him in direct terms;
and it was to this effect: that a gentleman who had lived
in great intimacy with him, shown him much kindness,
and even relieved him from a spunging-house, having
afterwards fallen into bad circumstances, was one day,
when Johnson was at dinner with him, seized for debt,
and carried to prison; that Johnson sat still, undisturbed,
and went on eating and drinking; upon which the gentleman's sister, who was present, could not suppress her
indignation: "What, Sir," said she, "are you so unfeeling
as not even to offer to go to my brother in his distress;
you who have been so much obliged to him?" And that

---

[1] But where is the *inaccuracy*, if the admirers of Homer contend that
he was not only prior to Virgil in point of time, but superior in excellence?
—J. Boswell, Jun.

[2] David Mallet, whose real name was Malloch, was a poet, dramatist,
and miscellaneous writer of some repute in his day. Pope and Bolingbroke were among his intimate friends, through whose influence he was
appointed Under Secretary to the Prince of Wales. His writings are
occasionally tinged with the scepticism of the Bolingbroke school. He
was born about 1700, at Crief, in Perthshire, and died in 1765.—Ed.

Johnson answered, "Madam, I owe him no obligation; what he did for me, he would have done for a dog."

Johnson assured me, that the story was absolutely false; but like a man conscious of being in the right, and desirous of completely vindicating himself from such a charge, he did not arrogantly rest on a mere denial, and on his general character, but proceeded thus:—"Sir, I was very intimate with that gentleman, and was once relieved by him from an arrest; but I never was present when he was arrested, never knew that he was arrested, and I believe he never was in difficulties after the time when he relieved me. I loved him much; yet, in talking of his general character, I may have said, though I do not remember that I ever did say so, that as his generosity proceeded from no principle, but was a part of his profusion, he would do for a dog, what he would do for a friend; but I never applied this remark to any particular instance, and certainly not to his kindness to me. If a profuse man, who does not value his money, and gives a large sum to a whore, gives half as much, or an equally large sum, to relieve a friend, it cannot be esteemed as virtue. This was all that I could say of that gentleman; and, if said at all, it must have been said after his death. Sir, I would have gone to the world's end to relieve him. The remark about the dog, if made by me, was such a sally as might escape one when painting a man highly."

CHAPTER VII.—1777

*Johnson's Remarks on Philology—Grainger's "Ode on Soli-
tude"—Effects of Music—Johnson's Opinions on Happi-
ness—Conference in Dr. Taylor's Garden—Slave Trade
—American Independence—Corruption of the British
Parliament—Boswell's Departure for Scotland—Edensor
Inn, and ludicrous Character given of Johnson—
Correspondence between Boswell and Johnson—The
Negro Cause decided—Mr. Florence Wilson—Mr.
Saunders Welch—Advice to Travellers—Parnell the
Poet—"Taxation no Tyranny"—Rumoured Death of
Johnson*

On Tuesday, September 23, Johnson was remarkably
cordial to me. It being necessary for me to return to
Scotland soon, I had fixed on the next day for my setting
out, and I felt a tender concern at the thought of parting
with him. He had, at this time, frankly communicated
to me many particulars, which are inserted in this work
in their proper places; and once, when I happened to
mention that the expense of my jaunt would come to
much more than I had computed, he said, "Why, Sir, if
the expense were to be an inconvenience, you would have
reason to regret it; but, if you have had the money to spend,
I know not that you could have purchased as much pleasure
with it in any other way."

During this interview at Ashbourne, Johnson and I
frequently talked with wonderful pleasure of mere trifles
which had occurred in our tour to the Hebrides; for it had
left a most agreeable and lasting impression upon his mind.

He found fault with me for using the phrase to *make*
money. "Don't you see," said he, "the impropriety of it?
To *make* money is to *coin* it: you should say *get* money."
The phrase, however, is, I think, pretty current. But
Johnson was at all times jealous of infractions upon the
genuine English Language, and prompt to repress colloquial barbarisms; such as *pledging myself*, for *undertaking;
line*, for *department*, or *branch*, as the *civil line*, the *banking
line*. He was particularly indignant against the almost

165

universal use of the word *idea* in the sense of *notion* or *opinion*, when it is clear that *idea* can only signify something of which an image can be formed in the mind.   We may have an *idea* or *image* of a mountain, a tree, a building; but we cannot surely have an *idea* or *image* of an *argument* or *proposition*.   Yet we hear the sages of the law " delivering their *ideas* upon the question under consideration"; and the first speakers in Parliament "entirely coincided in the *idea* which has been ably stated by an honourable member"; —or "reprobating an *idea* unconstitutional, and fraught with the most dangerous consequences to a great and free country."   Johnson called this "modern cant."

I perceived that he pronounced the word *heard*, as if spelt with a double *e*, *heerd*, instead of sounding it *herd*, as is most usually done.[1]   He said, his reason was, that if it were pronounced *herd*, there would be a single exception from the English pronunciation of the syllable *ear*, and he thought it better not to have that exception.

He praised Grainger's "Ode on Solitude,"[2] in Dodsley's collection, and repeated, with great energy, the exordium:—

"O Solitude, romantic maid,
    Whether by nodding towers you tread;
Or haunt the desert's trackless gloom,
    Or hover o'er the yawning tomb;
Or climb the Andes' clifted side,
    Or by the Nile's coy source abide;
Or, starting from your half-year's sleep,
    From Hecla view the thawing deep;
Or, at the purple dawn of day,
    Tadmor's marble waste survey—"

observing, "This, Sir, is very noble."

In the evening our gentleman-farmer, and two others, entertained themselves and the company with a great number of tunes on the fiddle.   Johnson desired to have "Let ambition fire thy mind," played over again, and appeared to give a patient attention to it; though he owned to me that he was very insensible to the power of music.   I told him that it affected me to such a degree, as

---

[1] In the age of Queen Elizabeth this word was frequently written, as doubtless it was pronounced, *hard*.—MALONE.

[2] Grainger was a physician as well as a poet, who, after taking his medical degree, settled in London; but having little practice, he chiefly supported himself by writing for the press.   He afterwards went to St. Christopher's, in the West Indies, where he married, and successfully established himself, but did not entirely lay aside his pen.   He was born at Dunse, in Scotland, in 1723, and died in 1767.

often to agitate my nerves painfully, producing in my mind
alternate sensations of pathetic dejection, so that I was
ready to shed tears; and of daring resolution, so that I was
inclined to rush into the thickest part of the battle. "Sir,"
said he, "I should never hear it, if it made me such a fool."

Much of the effect of music, I am satisfied, is owing to
the association of ideas. That air, which instantly and
irresistibly excites in the Swiss,[1] when in a foreign land, the
maladie du pays, has, I am told, no intrinsic power of
sound. And I know, from my own experience, that
Scotch reels, though brisk, make me melancholy, because
I used to hear them in my early years, at a time when
Mr. Pitt called for soldiers "from the mountains of the
north," and numbers of brave Highlanders were going
abroad, never to return. Whereas the airs in "The
Beggar's Opera," many of which are very soft, never fail
to render me gay, because they are associated with the
warm sensations and high spirits of London.—This evening,
while some of the tunes of ordinary composition were
played with no great skill, my frame was agitated, and I
was conscious of a generous attachment to Dr. Johnson,
as my preceptor and friend, mixed with an affectionate
regret that he was an old man, whom I should probably
lose in a short time. I thought I could defend him at
the point of my sword. My reverence and affection for
him were in full glow. I said to him, "My dear Sir, we
must meet every year if you don't quarrel with me."
JOHNSON: "Nay, Sir, you are more likely to quarrel with
me, than I with you. My regard for you is greater almost
than I have words to express; but I do not choose to be
always repeating it; write it down in the first leaf of your
pocket-book, and never doubt of it again."

I talked to him of misery being the "doom of man,"
in this life, as displayed in his "Vanity of Human Wishes."
Yet I observed that things were done upon the supposition
of happiness; grand houses were built, fine gardens were
made, splendid places of public amusement were contrived,
and crowded with company. JOHNSON: "Alas, Sir, these
are all only struggles for happiness. When I first entered
Ranelagh, it gave an expansion and gay sensation to my
mind, such as I never experienced anywhere else. But,
as Xerxes wept when he viewed his immense army, and
considered that not one of that great multitude would be

---

[1] The "Ranz des Vaches," which so strongly affected the Swiss soldiers,
when on foreign service, as to cause them to desert. Rousseau informs
us that the air was forbidden under pain of death.

alive a hundred years afterwards, so it went to my heart to consider that there was not one in all that brilliant circle that was not afraid to go home and think; but that the thoughts of each individual there would be distressing when alone." This reflection was experimentally just. The feeling of languor,[1] which succeeds the animation of gaiety, is itself a very severe pain; and when the mind is then vacant, a thousand disappointments and vexations rush in and excruciate. Will not many even of my fairest readers allow this to be true?

I suggested, that being in love, and flattered with hopes of success, or having some favourite scheme in view for the next day, might prevent that wretchedness of which we have been talking. JOHNSON: "Why, Sir, it may sometimes be as you suppose; but my conclusion is in general but too true."

While Johnson and I stood in calm conference by ourselves in Dr. Taylor's garden, at a pretty late hour in a serene autumn night, looking up to the heavens, I directed the discourse to the subject of a future state. My friend was in a placid and most benignant frame of mind. "Sir," said he, "I do not imagine that all things will be made clear to us immediately after death, but that the ways of Providence will be explained to us very gradually." I ventured to ask him whether, although the words of some texts of Scripture seemed strong in support of the dreadful doctrine of an eternity of punishment, we might not hope that the denunciation was figurative, and would not literally be executed. JOHNSON: "Sir, you are to consider the intention of punishment in a future state. We have no reason to be sure that we shall then be no longer liable to offend against GOD. We do not know that even the angels are quite in a state of security; nay, we know that some of them have fallen. It may, therefore, perhaps, be necessary, in order to preserve both men and angels in rectitude, that they should have continually before them the punishment of those who have deviated from it; but we may hope that by some other means a fall from rectitude may be prevented. Some of the texts of Scripture upon

---

[1] Pope mentions,

"Stretch'd on the rack of a too easy chair."

But I recollect a couplet quite apposite to my subject in "Virtue, an Ethic Epistle," a beautiful and instructive poem, by an anonymous writer, in 1758; who, treating of pleasure in excess, says,

"Till langour, suffering on the rack of bliss,
    Confess that man was never made for this.—BOSWELL.

this subject are, as you observe, indeed strong; but they may admit of a mitigated interpretation." He talked to me upon this awful and delicate question in a gentle tone, and as if afraid to be decisive.

After supper I accompanied him to his apartment, and at my request he dictated to me an argument in favour of the negro who was then claiming his liberty, in an action in the Court of Session in Scotland. He had always been very zealous against slavery in every form, in which I with all deference thought that he discovered "a zeal without knowledge." Upon one occasion, when in company with some very grave men at Oxford, his toast was, "Here's to the next insurrection of the negroes in the West Indies." His violent prejudice against our West Indian and American settlers appeared whenever there was an opportunity. Towards the conclusion of his "Taxation no Tyranny," he says, "How is it that we hear the loudest *yelps* for liberty among the drivers of negroes?" and in his conversation with Mr. Wilkes he asked, "Where did Beckford and Trecothick learn English?" That Trecothick could both speak and write good English is well known. I myself was favoured with his correspondence concerning the brave Corsicans. And that Beckford could speak it with a spirit of honest resolution even to his Majesty, as his "faithful Lord Mayor of London," is commemorated by the noble monument erected to him in Guildhall.

The argument dictated by Dr. Johnson was as follows:—

"It must be agreed that in most ages many countries have had part of their inhabitants in a state of slavery; yet it may be doubted whether slavery can ever be supposed the natural condition of man. It is impossible not to conceive that men in their original state were equal; and very difficult to imagine how one would be subjected to another but by violent compulsion. An individual may, indeed, forfeit his liberty by a crime; but he cannot, by that crime, forfeit the liberty of his children. What is true of a criminal seems true likewise of a captive. A man may accept life from a conquering enemy on condition of perpetual servitude; but it is very doubtful whether he can entail that servitude on his descendants; for no man can stipulate without commission for another. The condition which he himself accepts, his son or grandson perhaps would have rejected. If we should admit, what perhaps may with more reason be denied, that there are certain relations between man and man which may make slavery necessary and just, yet it can never be proved that he who is now suing for his freedom ever stood in any of those relations. He is certainly subject by no law, but that of violence, to his present master, who pretends no claim to his obedience, but that he bought him from a merchant of slaves, whose right to sell him never was examined. It is said that according to the constitutions of Jamaica he was legally enslaved; these constitutions are merely positive, and apparently injurious to the rights of mankind, because whoever is exposed to sale is condemned to slavery without appeal, by whatever fraud or violence he might have been originally brought into the merchant's power. In our own times princes have been sold by wretches to whose care they were entrusted, that they might have a European education; but when once they were brought to a market in the plantations, little would avail either their dignity or their wrongs. The laws of Jamaica afford a negro no redress. His colour is considered as a sufficient testimony against him. It is to be lamented that moral right should ever give way to political convenience. But if temptations of interest are sometimes too strong for human virtue, let us at least retain a virtue where there is no temptation to quit it. In the present case there is apparent right on one side, and no convenience on the other. Inhabitants of this island can neither gain riches nor power by taking away the liberty of any part of the human species. The sum of the argument is this.—No man is by nature the property of another— The defendant is, therefore, by nature free—The rights of nature must be some way forfeited before they can be justly taken away—That the defendant has by any act forfeited the rights of nature we require to be proved, and if no proof of such forfeiture can be given, we doubt not the justice of the court will declare him free."

I record Dr. Johnson's argument fairly upon this particular case; where, perhaps, he was in the right. But I beg leave to enter my most solemn protest against his general doctrine with respect to the *slave trade*. For I will resolutely say, that his unfavourable notion of it was owing to prejudice, and imperfect or false information. The wild and dangerous attempt which has for some time been persisted in to obtain an act of our Legislature, to abolish so very important and necessary a branch of commercial interest, must have been crushed at once, had not the insignificance of the zealots who vainly took the lead in it, made the vast body of planters, merchants, and others, whose immense properties are involved in the trade, reasonably enough suppose that there could be no danger.

The encouragement which the attempt has received excites my wonder and indignation; and though some men of superior abilities have supported it—whether from a love of temporary popularity, when prosperous, or a love of general mischief, when desperate—my opinion is unshaken. To abolish a *status*, which in all ages GOD has sanctioned, and man has continued, would not only be *robbery* to an innumerable class of our fellow-subjects, but it would be extreme cruelty to the African savages, a portion of whom it saves from massacre, or intolerable bondage in their own country, and introduces into a much happier state of life; especially now when their passage to the West Indies, and their treatment there, is humanely regulated.[1]   To abolish this trade would be to

"—— shut the gates of mercy on mankind."

Whatever may have passed elsewhere concerning it, the House of Lords is wise and independent:—

Intaminatis fulgit honoribus;
Nec sumit aut ponit secures
Arbitrio popularis auræ.[2]

I have read, conversed, and thought much upon the subject, and would recommend to all who are capable of conviction an excellent tract by my learned and ingenious friend John Ranby, Esq., entitled, "Doubts on the Abolition of the Slave Trade." To Mr. Ranby's "Doubts," I will apply Lord Chancellor Hardwicke's expression in praise of a Scotch law book, called "Dirleton's Doubts." "His *Doubts*," said his Lordship, "are better than most people's *Certainties*."

When I said now to Johnson, that I was afraid I kept him too late up, "No, Sir," said he, "I don't care though I sit all night with you." This was an animated speech from a man in his sixty-ninth year.

Had I been as attentive not to displease him as I ought to have been, I know not but this vigil might have been fulfilled; but I unluckily entered upon the controversy concerning the right of Great Britain to tax America, and attempted to argue in favour of our fellow-subjects on the other side of the Atlantic. I insisted that America might be very well governed, and made to yield sufficient revenue

[1] Fox energetically observed in the House of Commons, "There can be no regulations for robbery and murder!"—ED.
[2] Horat. Carm. 1. iii. Od. ii. 18.

by the means of *influence*, as exemplified in Ireland, while the people might be pleased with the imagination of their participating of the British constitution, by having a body of representatives, without whose consent money could not be exacted from them.   Johnson could not bear my thus opposing his avowed opinion, which he had exerted himself with an extreme degree of heat to enforce; and the violent agitation into which he was thrown, while answering, or rather reprimanding me, alarmed me so, that I heartily repented of my having unthinkingly introduced the subject.   I myself, however, grew warm, and the change was great, from the calm state of philosophical discussion in which we had a little before been pleasingly employed.

I talked of the corruption of the British Parliament, in which I alleged that any question, however unreasonable or unjust, might be carried by a venal majority; and I spoke with high admiration of the Roman Senate, as if composed of men sincerely desirous to resolve what they should think best for their country.   My friend would allow no such character to the Roman Senate; and he maintained that the British Parliament was not corrupt, and that there was no occasion to corrupt its members; asserting, that there was hardly ever any question of great importance before Parliament, any question in which a man might not very well vote either upon one side or the other.   He said, there had been none in his time except that respecting America.

We were fatigued by the contest, which was produced by my want of caution; and he was not then in the humour to slide into easy and cheerful talk.   It therefore so happened, that we were, after an hour or two, very willing to separate and go to bed.

On Wednesday, September 24, I went into Dr. Johnson's room before he got up, and finding that the storm of the preceding night was quite laid, I sat down upon his bed-side, and he talked with as much readiness and good humour as ever.   He recommended to me to plant a considerable part of a large moorish farm which I had purchased, and he made several calculations of the expense and profit; for he delighted in exercising his mind on the science of numbers.   He pressed upon me the importance of planting at the first in a very sufficient manner, quoting the saying "*In bello non licet bis errare*": and adding, "This is equally true in planting."

I spoke with gratitude of Dr. Taylor's hospitality; and as evidence that it was not on account of his good table alone that Johnson visited him often. I mentioned a little anecdote which had escaped my friend's recollection, and at hearing which repeated, he smiled. One evening, when I was sitting with him, Frank delivered this message: "Sir, Dr. Taylor sends his compliments to you, and begs you will dine with him to-morrow. He has got a hare." "My compliments," said Johnson, "and I'll dine with him—hare or rabbit."

After breakfast I departed, and pursued my journey northwards. I took my post-chaise from the Green Man, a very good inn at Ashbourne, the mistress of which, a mighty civil gentlewoman, courtesying very low, presented me with an engraving of the sign of her house; to which she had subjoined, in her own handwriting, an address in such singular simplicity of style, that I have preserved it pasted upon one of the boards of my original Journal at this time, and shall here insert it for the amusement of my readers:—

"M. Killingley's duty waits upon Mr. Boswell, is exceedingly obliged to him for this favour; whenever he comes this way, hopes for the continuance of the same. Would Mr. Boswell name the house to his extensive acquaintance, it would be a singular favour conferr'd on one who has it not in her power to make any other return but her most grateful thanks, and sincerest prayers for his happiness in time, and in a blessed eternity.

"Tuesday morn."

From this meeting at Ashbourne I derived a considerable accession to my Johnsonian store. I communicated my original Journal to Sir William Forbes, in whom I have always placed deserved confidence; and what he wrote to me concerning it is so much to my credit as the biographer of Johnson, that my readers will, I hope, grant me their indulgence for here inserting it: "It is not once or twice going over it," says Sir William, "that will satisfy me; for I find in it a high degree of instruction as well as entertainment; and I derive more benefit from Dr. Johnson's admirable discussions than I should be able to draw from his personal conversation; for, I suppose there is not a man in the world to whom he discloses his sentiments so freely as to yourself."

I cannot omit a curious circumstance which occurred at Edensor inn, close to Chatsworth, to survey the magnificence of which I had gone a considerable way out of my road to Scotland. The inn was then kept by a very jolly landlord, whose name, I think, was Malton. He happened to mention that "the celebrated Dr. Johnson had been in his house." I inquired *who* this Dr. Johnson was, that I might hear my host's notion of him. "Sir," said he, "Johnson, the great writer; *Oddity*, as they call him. He's the greatest writer in England; he writes for the ministry; he has a correspondence abroad, and lets them know what's going on."

My friend, who had a thorough dependence upon the authenticity of my relation, without any *embellishment*, as *falsehood* or *fiction* is too gently called, laughed a good deal at this representation of himself.

"MR. BOSWELL TO DR. JOHNSON.

"MY DEAR SIR,   *Edinburgh, Sept.* 29, 1777.

"By the first post I inform you of my safe arrival at my own house, and that I had the comfort of finding my wife and children all in good health.

"When I look back upon our late interview, it appears to me to have answered expectation better than almost any scheme of happiness that I ever put in execution. My journal is stored with wisdom and wit; and my memory is filled with the recollection of lively and affectionate feelings, which now, I think, yield me more satisfaction than at the time when they were first excited. I have experienced this upon other occasions. I shall be obliged to you if you will explain it to me; for it seems wonderful that pleasure should be more vivid at a distance than when near. I wish you may find yourself in a humour to do me this favour; but I flatter myself with no strong hope of it; for I have observed that, unless upon very serious occasions, your letters to me are not *answers* to those which I write."

[I then expressed much uneasiness that I had mentioned to him the name of the gentleman who had told me the story so much to his disadvantage, the truth of which he had completely refuted; for that my having done so might be interpreted as a breach of confidence, and offend one whose society I valued—therefore earnestly requesting that no notice might be taken of it to anybody, till I should be in London, and have an opportunity to talk it over with the gentleman.]

"TO JAMES BOSWELL, ESQ.

"DEAR SIR,   *London, Nov.* 29, 1777.

"You will wonder, or you have wondered, why no letter has come from me. What you wrote at your return, had in it such a strain of cowardly caution as gave me no pleasure. I could not well do what you wished: I had no need to vex you with a refusal. I have seen Mr. Beauclerk, and as to him have set all right, without any inconvenience, so far as I know, to you. Mrs. Thrale had forgot the story. You may now be at ease.

"And at ease I certainly wish you for the kindness that you showed in coming so long a journey to see me. It was pity to keep you so long in pain, but, upon reviewing the matter, I do not see what I could have done better than I did.

"I hope you found at your return my dear enemy and all her little people quite well, and had no reason to repent of your journey. I think on it with great gratitude.

"I was not well when you left me at the Doctor's, and I grew worse; yet I stayed on, and at Lichfield was very ill. Travelling, however, did not make me worse; and when I came to London, I complied with a summons to go to Brighthelmstone, where I saw Beauclerk, and stayed three days.

"Our Club has recommenced last Friday, but I was not there. Langton has another wench.[1] Mrs. Thrale is in hopes of a young brewer. They got by their trade last year a very large sum, and their expenses are proportionate.

"Mrs. Williams's health is very bad. And I have had for some time a very difficult and laborious respiration; but I am better by purges, abstinence, and other methods. I am yet, however, much behind hand in my health and rest.

"Dr. Blair's sermons are now universally commended; but let him think that I had the honour of first finding and first praising his excellences. I did not stay to add my voice to that of the public.

"My dear Friend, let me thank you once more for your visit; you did me great honour, and I hope met with nothing that displeased you. I stayed long at Ashbourne, not much pleased, yet awkward at departing. I then went to Lichfield, where I found my friend at Stowhill very dangerously diseased. Such is life. Let us try to pass it well, whatever it be, for there is surely something beyond it.

Well, now, I hope all is well. Write as soon as you can to, dear Sir,

"Your affectionate servant,
"Sam. Johnson."

"TO DR. SAMUEL JOHNSON.

"My dear Sir, *Edinburgh, Nov. 29, 1777.*

"This day's post has at length relieved me from much uneasiness, by bringing me a letter from you. I was, indeed, doubly uneasy—on my own account and yours. I was very anxious to be secured against any bad consequences from my imprudence in mentioning the gentleman's name who had told me a story to your disadvantage; and as I could hardly suppose it possible that you would delay so long to make me easy, unless you were ill, I was not a little apprehensive about you. You must not be offended, when I venture to tell you that you appear to me to have been too rigid

---

[1] A daughter born to him.—Boswell.

upon this occasion. The 'cowardly caution which gave you no pleasure,' was suggested to me by a friend here, to whom I mentioned the strange story and the detection of its falsity, as an instance how one may be deceived by what is apparently very good authority. But, as I am still persuaded that as I might have obtained the truth, without mentioning the gentleman's name, it was wrong in me to do it, I cannot see that you are just in blaming my caution; but if you were ever so just in your disapprobation, might you not have dealt more tenderly with me?

"I went to Auchinleck about the middle of October, and passed some time with my father very comfortably.

*   *   *   *

"I am engaged in a criminal prosecution against a country schoolmaster, for indecent behaviour to his female scholars. There is no statute against such abominable conduct; but it is punishable at common law. I shall be obliged to you for your assistance in this extraordinary trial. I ever am, my dear Sir,

"Your faithful humble servant,
"JAMES BOSWELL."

About this time I wrote to Johnson giving him an account of the decision of the *Negro cause*, by the Court of Session, which by those who hold even the mildest and best regulated slavery in abomination (of which number I do not hesitate to declare that I am none), should be remembered with high respect, and to the credit of Scotland; for it went upon a much broader ground than the case of *Somerset*, which was decided in England;[1] being truly the general question, whether a perpetual obligation of service to one master in any mode should be sanctified by the law of a free country. A negro, then, called *Joseph Knight*, a native of Africa, who having been brought to Jamaica in the usual course of the slave-trade, and purchased by a Scotch gentleman in that island, had attended his master to Scotland; where it was officiously suggested to him that he would be found entitled to his liberty without any limitation. He accordingly brought his action, in the course of which the advocates on both sides did themselves great honour. Mr. Maclaurin has had the praise of Johnson, for his argument[2] in favour of the negro, and Mr. Macconochie distinguished himself on the same

[1] See State Trials, vol. xi. p. 339, and Mr. Hargrave's argument.—BOSWELL.

[2] The motto to it was happily chosen:

"Quamvis ille niger, quamvis tu candidus esses."

I cannot avoid mentioning a circumstance no less strange than true, that a brother Advocate in considerable practice, but of whom it certainly cannot be said, *Ingenuas didicit fideliter artes*, asked Mr. Maclaurin, with a face of flippant assurance, "Are these words your own?"—BOSWELL.

side, by his ingenuity and extraordinary research. Mr. Cullen, on the part of the master, discovered good information and sound reasoning; in which he was well supported by Mr. James Ferguson, remarkable for a manly understanding, and a knowledge both of books and the world. But I cannot too highly praise the speech which Mr. Henry Dundas generously contributed to the cause of the sooty stranger. Mr. Dundas's Scottish accent, which has been so often in vain obtruded as an objection to his powerful abilities in Parliament, was no disadvantage to him in his own country. And I do declare, that upon this memorable question he impressed me, and I believe all his audience, with such feelings as were produced by some of the most eminent orations of antiquity. This testimony I liberally give to the excellence of an old friend, with whom it has been my lot to differ very widely upon many political topics; yet I persuade myself without malice. A great majority of the Lords of Session decided for the negro. But four of their number, the Lord President, Lord Elliott, Lord Monboddo, and Lord Covington, resolutely maintained the lawfulness of a *status*, which has been acknowledged in all ages and countries, and that when freedom flourished, as in old Greece and Rome.

"TO JAMES BOSWELL, ESQ.

"Dear Sir,   *December* 27, 1777.

"This is the time of the year in which all express their good wishes to their friends, and I send mine to you and your family. May your lives be long, happy, and good. I have been much out of order, but, I hope, do not grow worse.

"The crime of the schoolmaster whom you are engaged to prosecute is very great, and may be suspected to be too common. In our law it would be a breach of the peace and a misdemeanour; that is, a kind of indefinite crime, not capital, but punishable at the discretion of the Court. You cannot want matter; all that needs to be said will easily occur.

"Mr. Shaw, the author of the Gaelic Grammar, desires me to make a request for him to Lord Eglintoune, that he may be appointed Chaplain to one of the new-raised regiments.

"All our friends are as they were; little has happened to them of either good or bad. Mrs. Thrale ran a great black hair-dressing pin into her eye; but by great evacuation she kept it from inflaming, and it is almost well. Miss Reynolds has been out of order, but is better. Mrs. Williams is in a very poor state of health.

"If I should write on, I should, perhaps, write only complaints, and therefore I will content myself with telling you, that I love to think on you, and to hear from you; and that I am, dear Sir,

"Yours faithfully,

"Sam. Johnson."

"TO DR. SAMUEL JOHNSON.

"DEAR SIR,   *Edinburgh, Jan. 8, 1778.*

"Your congratulations upon a new year are mixed with complaint: mine must be so too. My wife has for some time been very ill, having been confined to the house these three months by a severe cold, attended with alarming symptoms.

[Here I gave a particular account of the distress which the person, upon every account most dear to me, suffered; and of the dismal state of apprehension in which I now was: adding, that I never stood more in need of his consoling philosophy.]

"Did you ever look at a book written by Wilson, a Scotchman, under the Latin name of *Volusenus*, according to the custom of literary men at a certain period. It is entitled '*De Animi Tranquillitate.*' I earnestly desire tranquillity. *Bona res quies ;* but I fear I shall never attain it: for, when unoccupied, I grow gloomy, and occupation agitates me to feverishness.

          *   *   *   *   *

"I am, dear Sir,
"Your most affectionate humble servant,
"JAMES BOSWELL."

"TO JAMES BOSWELL, ESQ.

"DEAR SIR,   *Jan. 24, 1778.*

"To a letter so interesting as your last, it is proper to return some answer, however little I may be disposed to write.

"Your alarm at your lady's illness was reasonable, and not disproportionate to the appearance of the disorder. I hope your physical friend's conjecture is now verified, and all fear of a consumption at an end: a little care and exercise will then restore her. London is a good air for ladies; and if you bring her hither I will do for her what she did for me—I will retire from my apartments for her accommodation. Behave kindly to her, and keep her cheerful.

"You always seem to call for tenderness. Know then, that in the first month of the present year I very highly esteem and very cordially love you. I hope to tell you this at the beginning of every year as long as we live; and why should we trouble ourselves to tell or hear it oftener?

"Tell Veronica, Euphemia, and Alexander, that I wish them, as well as their parents, many happy years.

"You have ended the negro's cause much to my mind. Lord Auchinleck and dear Lord Hailes were on the side of liberty. Lord Hailes's name reproaches me; but if he saw my languid neglect of my own affairs, he would rather pity than resent my neglect of his. I hope to mend, *ut et mihi vivam et amicis.*

"I am, dear Sir, yours affectionately,
"SAM. JOHNSON."

"My service to my fellow-traveller, Joseph."

Johnson maintained a long and intimate friendship with Mr. Welch, who succeeded the celebrated Henry Fielding as one of his Majesty's Justices of the Peace for Westminster; kept a regular office for the police of that great district; and discharged his important trust, for many years, faithfully and ably. Johnson, who had an eager and unceasing curiosity to know human life in all its variety, told me that he attended Mr. Welch in his office for a whole winter, to hear the examinations of the culprits; but that he found an almost uniform tenor of misfortune, wretchedness, and profligacy. Mr. Welch's health being impaired, he was advised to try the effect of a warm climate; and Johnson, by his interest with Mr. Chamier, procured him leave of absence to go to Italy, and a promise that the pension or salary of two hundred pounds a year, which Government allowed him, should not be discontinued. Mr. Welch accordingly went abroad, accompanied by his daughter Anne, a young lady of uncommon talents and literature.

"TO SAUNDERS WELCH, ESQ., AT THE ENGLISH COFFEE-HOUSE, ROME

"Dear Sir,   Feb. 3, 1778.

"To have suffered one of my best and dearest friends to pass almost two years in foreign countries without a letter, has a very shameful appearance of inattention. But the truth is, there was no particular time in which I had any thing particular to say; and general expressions of good will, I hope, our long friendship is grown too solid to want.

"Of public affairs you have information from the newspapers wherever you go, for the English keep no secret; and of other things, Mrs. Nollekens informs you. My intelligence could therefore be of no use; and Miss Nancy's letters made it unnecessary to write to you for information: I was likewise for some time out of humour, to find that motion and nearer approaches to the sun, did not restore your health so fast as I expected. Of your health, the accounts have lately been more pleasing; and I have the gratification of imagining to myself a length of years which I hope you have gained, and of which the enjoyment will be improved by a vast accession of images and observations which your journeys and various residence have enabled you to make and accumulate. You have travelled with this felicity, almost peculiar to yourself, that your companion is not to part from you at your journey's end; but you are to live on together, to help each other's recollection, and to supply each other's omissions. The world has few greater pleasures than that which two friends enjoy, in tracing back, at some distant time, those transactions and events through which they have passed together. One of the old man's miseries is, that he cannot easily find a companion able to partake with him of the past. You and your fellow-traveller have this comfort in store, that your conversation will be not easily exhausted; one will always be glad to say what the other will always be willing to hear.

"That you may enjoy this pleasure long, your health must have your constant attention. I suppose you propose to return this year. There is no need of haste: do not come hither before the height of summer, that you may fall gradually into the inconveniences of your native clime. July seems to be the proper month. August and September will prepare you for the winter. After having travelled so far to find health, you must take care not to lose it at home; and I hope a little care will effectually preserve it.

"Miss Nancy has doubtless kept a constant and copious journal. She must not expect to be welcome when she returns, without a great mass of information. Let her review her journal often, and set down what she finds herself to have omitted, that she may trust to memory as little as possible, for memory is soon confused by a quick succession of things; and she will grow every day less confident of the truth of her own narratives, unless she can recur to some written memorials. If she has satisfied herself with hints, instead of full representations, let her supply the deficiency now, while her memory is yet fresh, and while her father's memory may help her. If she observes this direction, she will not have travelled in vain; for she will bring home a book with which she may entertain herself to the end of life. If it were not now too late, I would advise her to note the impression which the first sight of anything new and wonderful made upon her mind. Let her now set her thoughts down as she can recollect them; for, faint as they may already be, they will grow every day fainter.

"Perhaps I do not flatter myself unreasonably when I imagine that you may wish to know something of me. I can gratify your benevolence with no account of health. The hand of time, or of disease, is very heavy upon me. I pass restless and uneasy nights, harassed with convulsions of my breast, and flatulencies at my stomach; and restless nights make heavy days. But nothing will be mended by complaints, and therefore I will make an end. When we meet, we will try to forget our cares and our maladies, and contribute, as we can, to the cheerfulness of each other. If I had gone with you, I believe I should have been better; but I do not know that it was in my power.

"I am, dear Sir, your most humble Servant,
"SAM. JOHNSON."

This letter, while it gives admirable advice how to travel to the best advantage, and will therefore be of very general use, is another eminent proof of Johnson's warm and affectionate heart.[1]

[1] The friendship between Mr. Welch and him was unbroken. Mr. Welch died not many months before him, and bequeathed him five guineas for a ring, which Johnson received with tenderness, as a kind memorial. His regard was constant for his friend Mr. Welch's daughters; of whom, Jane is married to Mr. Nollekens the statuary, whose merit is too well known to require any praise from me.—BOSWELL.

"TO DR. SAMUEL JOHNSON.

"My dear Sir,   *Edinburgh, Feb.* 26, 1778.

"Why I have delayed, for near a month, to thank you for your last affectionate letter, I cannot say; for my mind has been in better health these three weeks than for some years past. I believe I have evaded till I could send you a copy of Lord Hailes's opinion on the negro's cause, which he wishes you to read, and correct any errors that there may be in the language; for, says he, 'we live in a critical, though not in a learned age; and I seek to screen myself under the shield of Ajax.' I communicated to him your apology for keeping the sheets of his 'Annals' so long. He says, 'I am sorry to see that Dr. Johnson is in a state of languor. Why should a sober Christian, neither an enthusiast nor a fanatic, be very merry or very sad?' I envy his Lordship's comfortable constitution; but well do I know that languor and dejection will afflict the best, however excellent their principles. I am in possession of Lord Hailes's opinion in his own handwriting, and have had it for some time. My excuse, then, for procrastination must be, that I wanted to have it copied; and I have now put that off so long, that it will be better to bring it with me than send it, as I shall probably get you to look at it sooner, when I solicit you in person.

"My wife, who is, thank God, a good deal better, is much obliged to you for your very polite and courteous offer of your apartment: but if she goes to London, it will be best for her to have lodgings in the more airy vicinity of Hyde Park. I however, doubt much if I shall be able to prevail with her to accompany me to the metropolis; for she is so different from you and me, that she dislikes travelling; and she is so anxious about her children, that she thinks she should be unhappy if at a distance from them. She therefore wishes rather to go to some country place in Scotland, where she can have them with her.

"I purpose being in London about the 20th of next month, as I think it creditable to appear in the House of Lords as one of Douglas's counsel, in the great and last competition between Duke Hamilton and him.

*   *   *   *   *

"I am sorry poor Mrs. Williams is so ill: though her temper is unpleasant, she has always been polite and obliging to me. I wish many happy years to good Mr. Levett, who, I suppose holds his usual place at your breakfast-table.[1]

"I ever am, my dear Sir,
"Your affectionate humble servant,
"James Boswell."

---

[1] Dr. Percy, the Bishop of Dromore, humorously observed, that Levett used to breakfast on the crust of a roll, which Johnson, after tearing out the crumb for himself, threw to his humble friend.—Boswell.

Perhaps the word *threw* is here too strong. Dr. Johnson never treated Levett with contempt; it is clear indeed, from various circumstances, that he had great kindness for him. I have often seen Johnson at breakfast, accompanied, or rather attended, by Levett, who had always the management of the tea-kettle.—Malone.

TO THE SAME.

"My dear Sir,   *Edinburgh, Feb.* 28, 1778.

"You are at present busy amongst the English poets, preparing, for the public instruction and entertainment, Prefaces, biographical and critical. It will not, therefore, be out of season to appeal to you for the decision of a controversy which has arisen between a lady and me concerning a passage in Parnell. That Poet tells us, that his Hermit quitted his cell

> '———— to know the world by sight,
> To find if *books* or *swains* report it right;
> (For yet by *swains alone* the world he knew,
> Whose feet came wand'ring o'er the nightly dew.)'

I maintain, that there is an inconsistency here: for as the hermit's notions of the world were formed from the reports both of *books* and *swains*, he could not justly be said to know by *swains alone.* Be pleased to judge between us, and let us have your reasons.[1]

"What do you say to '*Taxation no Tyranny,*' now, after Lord North's declaration, or confession, or whatever else his conciliatory speech should be called? I never differed from you in politics but upon two points,—the Middlesex Election, and the Taxation of the Americans by the British *Houses of Representatives.* There is a *charm* in the word *Parliament,* so I avoid it. As I am a steady and a warm Tory, I regret that the King does not see it to be better for him to receive constitutional supplies from his American subjects by the voice of their own assemblies, where his Royal person is represented, than through the medium of his British subjects. I am persuaded that the power of the Crown, which I wish to increase, would be greater when in contact with all its dominions, than if 'the rays of regal bounty'[2] were 'to shine' upon America, through that dense troubled body, a modern British Parliament. But enough of this subject; for your angry voice at Ashbourne upon it still sounds awful 'in my mind's *ears.*'

"I ever am, my dear Sir,
"Your most affectionate humble servant,
"James Boswell."

TO THE SAME.

"My dear Sir,   *Edinburgh, March* 12, 1778.

"The alarm of your late illness distressed me but a few hours, for on the evening of the day that it reached me I found it contradicted in 'The London Chronicle,' which I could depend upon as authentic concerning you, Mr. Strahan being the printer of

[1] See the subject discussed in a subsequent page, under May 3, 1779.—Malone.
[2] Alluding to a line in his "Vanity of Human Wishes," describing Cardinal Wolsey in his state of elevation:—

"Through him the rays of regal bounty shine."—Boswell.

it.   I did not see the paper in which 'the approaching extinction of a bright luminary' was announced.   Sir William Forbes told me of it; and he says he saw me so uneasy that he did not give me the report in such strong terms as he read it.   He afterwards sent me a letter from Mr. Langton to him, which relieved me much. I am, however, not quite easy, as I have not heard from you; and now I shall not have that comfort before I see you, for I set out for London to-morrow before the post comes in.   I hope to be with you on Wednesday morning; and I ever am, with the highest veneration, my dear Sir, your most obliged, faithful, and affectionate humble servant,

                                        "James Boswell."

CHAPTER VIII.—1778

*Boswell's Arrival in London—Mrs. Desmoulins—Johnson's
Benevolent Liberality—Mr. Howard of Lichfield—Tom
Davies—Johnson's Advice on Law Pleading—Charac-
teristic Trait of Johnson—Thomas à Kempis—Lord
Trimlestown—Sir Robert Sibbald—Johnson's Advice on
Strict Adherence to Truth—His Opinion on Ghosts—
John Wesley—Jennings and Alcibiades' Dog—Floren-
tine Boar—Emigration—The House of Commons—
Place-hunters—Irish Language—Thicknesse's Travels—
Anecdote of Sir Godfrey Kneller—Dr. Kennedy's Tragedy
—On Shooting a Highwayman—Mr. Dunning—Dr.
Campbell and his Wine-drinking—Mrs. Montagu—Mr.
Harris—Johnson's Opinion of Wine-drinking—Gold-
smith—Charles V.—Sermons—Scotland—Davies—On
Absenteeism*

On Wednesday, March 18, I arrived in London, and was
informed by good Mr. Francis, that his master was better,
and was gone to Mr. Thrale's at Streatham, to which place
I wrote to him, begging to know when he would be in town.
He was not expected for some time; but next day having
called on Dr. Taylor, in Dean's-yard, Westminster, I found
him there, and was told he had come to town for a few hours.
He met me with his usual kindness, but instantly returned
to the writing of something on which he was employed when
I came in, and on which he seemed much intent. Finding
him thus engaged, I made my visit very short, and had no
more of his conversation, except his expressing a serious
regret that a friend of ours was living at too much expense,
considering how poor an appearance he made: "If," said he,
"a man has splendour from his expense, if he spends his
money in pride or in pleasure, he has value; but if he lets
others spend it for him, which is most commonly the case,
he has no advantage from it."

On Friday, March 20, I found him at his own house,
sitting with Mrs. Williams, and was informed that the
room formerly allotted to me was now appropriated to a

charitable purpose; Mrs. Desmoulins,[1] and I think her daughter, and a Miss Carmichael, being all lodged in it. Such was his humanity, and such his generosity, that Mrs. Desmoulins herself told me he allowed her half-a-guinea a week. Let it be remembered, that this was above a twelfth part of his pension.

His liberality, indeed, was at all periods of his life very remarkable.   Mr. Howard, of Lichfield, at whose father's house Johnson had in his early years been kindly received, told me that when he was a boy at the Charter-house, his father wrote to him to go and pay a visit to Mr. Samuel Johnson, which he accordingly did, and found him in an upper room of poor appearance.   Johnson received him with much courteousness, and talked a great deal to him as to a schoolboy, of the course of his education, and other particulars.   When he afterwards came to know and understand the high character of this great man, he recollected his condescension with wonder.   He added, that when he was going away, Mr. Johnson presented him with half-a-guinea; and this, said Mr. Howard, was at a time when he probably had not another.

We retired from Mrs. Williams to another room.   Tom Davies soon after joined us.   He had now unfortunately failed in his circumstances and was much indebted to Dr. Johnson's kindness in obtaining for him many alleviations of his distress.   After he went away, Johnson blamed his folly in quitting the stage, by which he and his wife got 500*l.* a year.   I said, I believed it was owing to Churchill's attack upon him,

> "He mouths a sentence, as curs mouth a bone."

JOHNSON: "I believe so too, Sir.   But what a man is he, who is to be driven from the stage by a line?   Another line would have driven him from his shop."

I told him that I was engaged as counsel at the bar of the House of Commons to oppose a road bill in the county of Stirling, and asked him what mode he would advise me to follow in addressing such an audience.   JOHNSON: "Why, Sir, you must provide yourself with a good deal of extraneous matter, which you are to produce occasionally, so as to fill up the time; for you must consider, that they do not listen much.   If you begin with the strength of your cause, it may be lost before they begin to listen.   When you catch a moment of attention, press the merits of the

---

[1] Daughter of Dr. Swinfen, Johnson's godfather, and widow): Mr. Desmoulins a writing-master.—BOSWELL.

question upon them." He said, as to one point of the merits, that he thought "it would be a wrong thing to deprive the small landholders of the privilege of assessing themselves for making and repairing the high roads; *it was destroying a certain portion of liberty, without a good reason, which was always a bad thing.*" When I mentioned this observation next day to Mr. Wilkes, he pleasantly said, "What! does *he* talk of liberty? *Liberty* is as ridiculous in *his* mouth as *Religion* in *mine.*" Mr. Wilkes's advice, as to the best mode of speaking at the bar of the House of Commons, was not more respectful towards the senate, than that of Dr. Johnson: "Be as impudent as you can, as merry as you can, and say whatever comes uppermost. Jack Lee[1] is the best heard there of any counsel; and he is the most impudent dog, and always abusing us."

In my interview with Dr. Johnson this evening, I was quite easy, quite as his companion; upon which I find in my Journal the following reflection: "So ready is my mind to suggest matter for dissatisfaction, that I felt a sort of regret that I was so easy. I missed that awful reverence with which I used to contemplate Mr. Samuel Johnson, in the complex magnitude of his literary, moral, and religious character. I have a wonderful superstitious love of *mystery ;* when, perhaps, the truth is, that it is owing to the cloudy darkness of my own mind. I should be glad that I am more advanced in my progress of being, so that I can view Dr. Johnson with a steadier and clearer eye. My dissatisfaction to-night was foolish. Would it not be foolish to regret that we shall have less mystery in a future state? That 'we now see in a glass darkly,' but shall 'then see face to face?'"—This reflection, which I thus freely communicate, will be valued by the thinking part of my readers, who may have themselves experienced a similar state of mind.

He returned next day to Streatham, to Mr. Thrale's; where, as Mr. Strahan once complained to me, "he was in a great measure absorbed from the society of his old friends." I was kept in London by business, and wrote to him on the 27th, that a separation from him for a week, when we were so near, was equal to a separation for a year, when we were at four hundred miles distance." I went to Streatham, on Monday, March 30. Before he appeared, Mrs. Thrale made a very characteristical remark:—"I do not know for certain what will please Dr. Johnson: but I know for certain that it will displease him to praise anything, even, what he likes, extravagantly."

[1] Afterwards Solicitor-general under the Rockingham administration.

At dinner he laughed at querulous declamations against the age, on account of luxury,—increase of London,—scarcity of provisions,—and other such topics. "Houses," said he, "will be built till rents fall; and corn is more plentiful now than ever it was."

I had before dinner repeated a ridiculous story told me by an old man, who had been a passenger with me in the stage-coach to-day. Mrs. Thrale having taken occasion to allude to it, in talking to me, called it "The story told you by the old *woman*."—"Now, Madam," said I, "give me leave to catch you in the fact: it was not an old *woman*, but an old *man*, whom I mentioned as having told me this." I presumed to take an opportunity, in presence of Johnson, of showing this lively lady how ready she was, unintentionally, to deviate from exact authenticity of narration.

Thomas à Kempis, he observed, must be a good book,[1] as the world has opened its arms to receive it. It is said to have been printed, in one language or other, as many times as there have been months since it first came out.[2] I always was struck with this sentence in it: "Be not angry that you cannot make others as you wish them to be, since you cannot make yourself as you wish to be."[3]

He said, "I was angry with Hurd about Cowley, for having published a selection of his works: but, upon better consideration, I think there is no impropriety in a man's publishing as much as he chooses of any author, if he does not put the rest out of the way. A man, for instance, may print the Odes of Horace alone." He seemed to be in a more indulgent humour than when this subject was discussed between him and Mr. Murphy.

When we were at tea and coffee, there came in Lord Trimlestown, in whose family was an ancient Irish peerage; but it suffered by taking the generous sides in the troubles of the last century.[4] He was a man of pleasing conversation, and was accompanied by a young gentleman, his son.

---

[1] His treatise "De Imitatione Christi," which some have attributed to Gerson. He was born at a village of the same name in the diocese of Cologne, in 1380, and died in 1471.—ED.

[2] The first edition was in 1492. Between that period and 1792, according to this account, there were three thousand six hundred editions. But this is very improbable.—MALONE.

[3] The original passage is:—Si non potes te talem facere, qualem vis, quomodo poteris alium ad tuum habere beneplacitum? De Imit. Christ. lib. i. cap. xvi.—J. BOSWELL, JUN.

[4] Since this was written, the attainder has been reversed; and Nicholas Barnewall is now a peer of Ireland with this title. The person mentioned in the text had studied physic, and prescribed *gratis* to the poor. Hence arose the subsequent conversation.—MALONE.

I mentioned that I had in my possession the Life of Sir Robert Sibbald, the celebrated Scottish antiquary, and founder of the Royal College of Physicians at Edinburgh, in the original manuscript in his own handwriting; and that it was, I believed, the most natural and candid account of himself that ever was given by any man.[1] As an instance, he tells that the Duke of Perth, then Chancellor of Scotland, pressed him very much to come over to the Roman Catholic faith: that he resisted all his Grace's arguments for a considerable time, till one day he felt himself, as it were, instantaneously convinced, and with tears in his eyes ran into the Duke's arms, and embraced the ancient religion; that he continued very steady in it for some time, and accompanied his Grace to London one winter, and lived in his household; that there he found the rigid fasting prescribed by the church very severe upon him; that this disposed him to reconsider the controversy, and having then seen that he was in the wrong, he returned to Protestantism. I talked of some time or other publishing this curious life. MRS. THRALE: "I think you had as well let alone that publication. To discover such weakness exposes a man when he is gone." JOHNSON: "Nay, it is an honest picture of human nature. How often are the primary motives of our greatest actions as small as Sibbald's, for his re-conversion?" MRS. THRALE: "But may they not as well be forgotten?" JOHNSON: "No, Madam, a man loves to review his own mind. That is the use of a diary, or journal." LORD TRIMLESTOWN: "True, Sir. As the ladies love to see themselves in a glass: so a man likes to see himself in his journal." BOSWELL: "A very pretty allusion." JOHNSON: "Yes, indeed." BOSWELL: "And as a lady adjusts her dress before a mirror, a man adjusts his character by looking at his journal." I next year found the very same thought in Atterbury's "Funeral Sermon on Lady Cutts;" where, having mentioned her diary, he says, "In this glass she every day dressed her mind." This is a proof of coincidence, and not of plagiarism; for I had never read that sermon before.

Next morning, while we were at breakfast, Johnson gave a very earnest recommendation of what he himself practised with the utmost conscientiousness: I mean a strict attention to truth, even in the most minute particulars. "Accustom

[1] Sir Robert Sibbald was physician and geographer to Charles II. Among his works are "Scotia Illustrata," and "The Liberty and Independency of the Kingdom and Church of Scotland." He was born near Leslie, in Fifeshire, in 1643, and died in 1712.—ED.

your children," said he, "constantly to this; if a thing
happened at one window, and they, when relating it, say
that it happened at another, do not let it pass, but instantly
check them; you do not know where deviation from truth
will end." BOSWELL: "It may come to the door; and when
once an account is at all varied in one circumstance, it may
by degrees be varied so as to be totally different from what
really happened." Our lively hostess, whose fancy was
impatient of the rein, fidgeted at this, and ventured to say,
"Nay, this is too much. If Mr. Johnson should forbid
me to drink tea, I would comply, as I should feel the restraint only twice a day; but little variations in narrative
must happen a thousand times a-day, if one is not perpetually watching." JOHNSON: "Well, Madam, and you
ought to be perpetually watching. It is more from carelessness about truth than from intentional lying, that there
is so much falsehood in the world."

In his review of Dr. Warton's "Essay on the Writings
and Genius of Pope," Johnson has given the following
salutary caution upon this subject:—"Nothing but experience could evince the frequency of false information,
or enable any man to conceive that so many groundless
reports should be propagated, as every man of eminence
may hear of himself. Some men relate what they think,
as what they know; some men of confused memories and
habitual inaccuracy, ascribe to one man what belongs to
another; and some talk on, without thought or care. A
few men are sufficient to broach falsehoods, which are
afterwards innocently diffused by successive relaters."[1]
Had he lived to read what Sir John Hawkins and Mrs.
Piozzi have related concerning himself, how much would
he have found his observation illustrated. He was indeed
so much impressed with the prevalence of falsehood,
voluntary or unintentional, that I never knew any person
who, upon hearing an extraordinary circumstance told,
discovered more of the *incredulus odi*. He would say,
with a significant look and decisive tone, "It is not so.
Do not tell this again."[2] He inculcated upon all his friends
the importance of perpetual vigilance against the slightest
degrees of falsehood; the effect of which, as Sir Joshua

[1] Literary Magazine, 1756, p. 37.—BOSWELL.

[2] The following plausible but over-prudent counsel on this subject
is given by an Italian writer [Dante], quoted by *Redi*, "*De Generatione
Insectorum*," with the epithet of "*divini poetæ*."

"Sempre à quel ver che a faccia di menzogna
Dei l'uom chiuder le labbra quanto ei puote
Però ché senza colpa fa vergogna."—BOSWELL.

Reynolds observed to me, has been, that all who were of his *school* are distinguished for a love of truth and accuracy, which they would not have possessed in the same degree, if they had not been acquainted with Johnson.

Talking of ghosts, he said, "It is wonderful that five thousand years have now elapsed since the creation of the world, and still it is undecided whether or not there has ever been an instance of the spirit of any person appearing after death. All argument is against it; but all belief is for it."

He said, "John Wesley's conversation is good, but he is never at leisure. He is always obliged to go at a certain hour. This is very disagreeable to a man who loves to fold his legs and have out his talk, as I do."

On Friday, April 3, I dined with him in London, in a company where were present several eminent men,[1] whom I shall not name, but distinguish their parts in the conversation by different letters.

F. "I have been looking at this famous antique marble dog of Mr. Jennings,[2] valued at a thousand guineas, said to be Alcibiades' dog." JOHNSON: "His tail then must be docked. That was the mark of Alcibiades' dog." E. "A thousand guineas! The representation of no animal whatever is worth so much. At this rate a dead dog would indeed be better than a living lion." JOHNSON: "Sir, it is not the worth of the thing, but of the skill in forming it, which is so highly estimated. Every thing that enlarges the sphere of human powers, that shows man he can do what he thought he could not do, is valuable. The first man who balanced a straw upon his nose; Johnson, who rode upon three horses at a time; in short, all such men deserved the applause of mankind, not on account of the use of what they did, but of the dexterity which they exhibited." BOSWELL: "Yet a misapplication of time and assiduity is not to be encouraged. Addison, in one of his 'Spectators' commends the judgment of a King, who, as a suitable reward to a man that by long perseverance had attained to the art of throwing a barley-corn through the eye of a needle, gave him a bushel of barley." JOHNSON: "He must have been a King of Scotland, where barley is

[1] Presumed to be members of the Literary Club, whose names Boswell here conceals.—ED.

[2] Mr. Henry Constantine Jennings was a distinguished antiquary and virtuoso, who spent a large fortune in the collecting of statues and antiques, with which he decorated his magnificent residence at Shiplake, in Oxfordshire. After experiencing many vicissitudes he died in 1819, as a prisoner in the rules of the King's Bench, aged 88.—ED.

scarce." F.: "One of the most remarkable antique figures of an animal is the boar at Florence." Johnson: "The first boar that is well made in marble should be preserved as a wonder. When men arrive at a facility of making boars well, then the workmanship is not of such value, but they should however be preserved as examples, and as a greater security for the restoration of the art, should it be lost."

E.: "We hear prodigious complaints at present of emigration. I am convinced that emigration makes a country more populous." J.: "That sounds very much like a paradox." E.: "Exportation of men, like exportation of all other commodities, makes more be produced." Johnson: "But there would be more people were there not emigration, provided there were food for more." E.: "No; leave a few breeders, and you'll have more people than if there were no emigration." Johnson: "Nay, Sir, it is plain there will be more people, if there are more breeders. Thirty cows in good pasture will produce more calves than ten cows, provided they have good bulls." E.: "There are bulls enough in Ireland." Johnson (smiling): "So, Sir, I should think from your argument." Boswell: "You said, exportation of men, like exportation of other commodities, makes more be produced. But a bounty is given to encourage the exportation of corn, and no bounty is given for the exportation of men; though, indeed, those who go, gain by it." R.: "But the bounty on the exportation of corn is paid at home." E.: "That's the same thing." Johnson: "No, Sir." R.: "A man who stays at home, gains nothing by his neighbour's emigrating." Boswell: "I can understand that emigration may be the cause that more people may be produced in a country; but the country will not therefore be the more populous; for the people issue from it. It can only be said that there is a flow of people. It is an encouragement to have children, to know that they can get a living by emigration." R.: "Yes, if there were an emigration of children under six years of age. But they don't emigrate till they could earn their livelihood in some way at home." C.: "It is remarkable that the most unhealthy countries, where there are the most destructive diseases, such as Egypt and Bengal, are the most populous." Johnson: "Countries which are the most populous have the most destructive diseases. *That* is the true state of the proposition." C.: "Holland is very unhealthy, yet it is exceedingly populous." Johnson: "I know not that Holland is unhealthy. But its populousness is owing to an influx of people from all other countries.   Disease cannot be the cause of populousness, for it not only carries off a great proportion of the people; but those who are left are weakened, and unfit for the purposes of increase."

R.: "Mr. E. I don't mean to flatter, but when posterity reads one of your speeches in Parliament, it will be difficult to believe that you took so much pains, knowing with certainty that it could produce no effect, that not one vote would be gained by it."   E.: "Waving your compliment to me, I shall say in general, that it is very well worth while for a man to take pains to speak well in Parliament.   A man, who has vanity, speaks to display his talents; and if a man speaks well, he gradually establishes a certain reputation and consequence in the general opinion, which sooner or later will have its political reward.   Besides, though not one vote is gained, a good speech has its effect.   Though an act which has been ably opposed passes into a law, yet in its progress it is modelled, and it is softened in such a manner, that we see plainly the minister has been told that the members attached to him are so sensible of its injustice or absurdity from what they have heard, that it must be altered."   JOHNSON: "And, Sir, there is a gratification of pride.   Though we cannot out-vote them we will out-argue them.   They shall not do wrong without its being shown both to themselves and to the world. '   E.: "The House of Commons is a mixed body (I except the minority, which I hold to be pure [smiling], but I take the whole house).   It is a mass by no means pure; but neither is it wholly corrupt, though there is a large proportion of corruption in it.   There are many members who generally go with the minister, who will not go all lengths.   There are many honest well-meaning country gentlemen who are in Parliament only to keep up the consequence of their families.   Upon most of these a good speech will have influence."   JOHNSON: "We are all more or less governed by interest.   But interest will not make us do everything. In a case which admits of doubt, we try to think on the side which is for our interest, and generally bring ourselves to act accordingly.   But the subject must admit of diversity of colouring; it must receive a colour on that side.   In the House of Commons there are members enough who will not vote what is grossly unjust or absurd.   No, Sir, there must always be right enough, or appearance of right, to keep wrong in countenance."   BOSWELL: "There is surely always a majority in Parliament who have places, or who want to have them, and who therefore will be generally ready to support government without requiring any pretext." E: "True, Sir; that majority will always follow.

> 'Quò clamor vocat et turba faventium.'"

Boswell: "Well now, let us take the common phrase, Place-hunters. I thought they had hunted without regard to anything, just as their huntsman, the minister, leads, looking only to the prey."[1] J.: "But taking your metaphor, you know that in hunting there are few so desperately keen as to follow without reserve. Some do not choose to leap ditches and hedges, and risk their necks, or gallop over steeps, or even to dirty themselves in bogs and mire." Boswell: "I am glad there are some good, quiet, moderate political hunters." E.: "I believe in any body of men in England I should have been in the minority: I have always been in the minority." P.: "The House of Commons resembles a private company. How seldom is any man convinced by another's argument; passion and pride rise against it." R.: "What would be the consequence, if a minister, sure of a majority in the House of Commons, should resolve that there should be no speaking at all upon his side." E.: "He must soon go out. That has been tried; but it was found it would not do."———

E.: "The Irish language is not primitive; it is Teutonic, a mixture of the northern tongues; it has much English in it." Johnson: "It may have been radically Teutonic; but the English and High Dutch have no similarity to the eye, though radically the same. Once, when looking into Low Dutch, I found, in a whole page, only one word similar to English; *stroem*, like *stream*, and it signified *tide*." E.: "I remember having seen a Dutch Sonnet, in which I found this word, *roesnopies*. Nobody would at first think that this could be English; but, when we inquire, we find *roes*, rose, and *nopie*, knob; so we have *rosebuds*."

Johnson: "I have been reading Thicknesse's Travels, which I think are entertaining." Boswell: "What, Sir, a good book?" Johnson: "Yes, Sir, to read once; I do not say you are to make a study of it, and digest it; and I

---

[1] Lord Bolingbroke, who, however detestable as a metaphysician, must be allowed to have had admirable talents as a political writer, thus describes the House of Commons, in his Letter to Sir William Wyndham:—"You know the nature of that assembly; they grow, like hounds, fond of the man who shows them game, and by whose halloo they are used to be encouraged."—Boswell.

believe it to be a true book in his intention. All travellers generally mean to tell truth; though Thicknesse observes, upon Smollett's account of his alarming a whole town in France by firing a blunderbuss, and frightening a French nobleman till he made him tie on his portmanteau, that he would be loth to say Smollett had told two lies in one page; but he had found the only town in France where these things could have happened. Travellers must often be mistaken. In everything, except where mensuration can be applied, they may honestly differ. There has been, of late, a strange turn in travellers to be displeased."

E.: "From the experience which I have had—and I have had a great deal—I have learnt to think *better* of mankind." JOHNSON: "From my experience I have found them worse in commercial dealings, more disposed to cheat, than I had any notion of; but more disposed to do one another good than I had conceived." J.: "Less just and more beneficent." JOHNSON: "And really it is wonderful, considering how much attention is necessary for men to take care of themselves, and ward off immediate evils which press upon them, it is wonderful how much they do for others. As it is said of the greatest liar, that he tells more truth than falsehood; so it may be said of the worst man, that he does more good than evil." BOSWELL: "Perhaps from experience men may be found *happier* than we suppose." JOHNSON: "No, Sir; the more we inquire we shall find men less happy." P.: "as to thinking better or worse of mankind from experience, some cunning people will not be satisfied unless they have put men to the test, as they think. There is a very good story told of Sir Godfrey Kneller,[1] in his character of a justice of the peace. A gentleman brought his servant before him, upon an accusation of having stolen some money from him: but it having come out that he had laid it purposely in the servant's way, in order to try his honesty, Sir Godfrey sent the master to prison."[2] JOHNSON: "To resist temptation once is not a

[1] Sir Godfrey Kneller was an eminent portrait painter, who was munificently patronised by Charles II., James II., and William III.; for the latter of whom he painted the "Beauties at Hampton-court." He was born at Lubeck about 1648, and continued to practise his art till after he was 70 years of age. He died in 1723, after amassing a large fortune.—ED.

[2] Pope thus introduces this story:—

> 'Faith! in such case if you should prosecute,
> I think Sir Godfrey should decide the suit,
> Who sent the thief who stole the cash away,
> And punish'd him that put it in his way."

Imit. of Horace, book ii. epist. 2.—BOSWELL.

sufficient proof of honesty. If a servant, indeed, were to resist the continued temptation of silver lying in a window, as some people let it lie, when he is sure his master does not know how much there is of it, he would give a strong proof of honesty. But this is a proof to which you have no right to put a man. You know, humanly speaking, there is a certain degree of temptation, which will overcome any virtue. Now, in so far as you approach temptation to a man, you do him an injury; and, if he is overcome, you share his guilt." P.: "And, when once overcome, it is easier for him to be got the better of again." BOSWELL: "Yes, you are his seducer; you have debauched him. I have known a man resolved to put friendship to the test, by asking a friend to lend him money, merely with that view, when he did not want it." JOHNSON: "That is very wrong, Sir. Your friend may be a narrow man, and yet have many good qualities; narrowness may be his only fault. Now you are trying his general character as a friend, by one particular singly, in which he happens to be defective, when in truth, his character is composed of many particulars."

E.: "I understand the hogshead of claret, which this society was favoured with by our friend the Dean, is nearly out; I think he should be written to, to send another of the same kind. Let the request be made with a happy ambiguity of expression, so that we may have the chance of his sending *it* also as a present." JOHNSON: "I am willing to offer my services as secretary on this occasion." P.: As many as are for Dr. Johnson being secretary hold up your hands.—Carried unanimously." BOSWELL: "He will be our Dictator." JOHNSON: "No, the company is to dictate to me. I am only to write for wine; and I am quite disinterested, as I drink none; I shall not be suspected of having forged the application. I am no more than humble *scribe*." E.: "Then you shall *prescribe*." BOSWELL: "Very well. The first play of words to-day." J.: "No, no; the *bulls* in Ireland." JOHNSON: "Were I your Dictator, you should have no wine. It would be my business *cavere ne quid detrimenti Respublica caperet*, and wine is dangerous. Rome was ruined by luxury" (smiling). E.: "If you allow no wine as Dictator, you shall not have me for your master of horse."

On Saturday, April 4, I drank tea with Johnson at Dr. Taylor's, where he had dined. He entertained us with an account of a tragedy written by a Dr. Kennedy (not the Lisbon physician). "The catastrophe of it," said he, "was, that a King, who was jealous of his Queen with his prime minister, mutilated himself.[1] This tragedy was actually shown about in manuscript to several people, and, amongst others, to Mr. Fitzherbert, who repeated to me two lines of the prologue:—

> 'Our hero's fate we have but gently touch'd;
> The fair might blame us, if it were less couch'd.'

It is hardly to be believed what absurd and indecent images men will introduce into their writings, without being sensible of the absurdity and indecency. I remember Lord Orrery told me, that there was a pamphlet written against Sir Robert Walpole, the whole of which was an allegory on the PHALLIC OBSCENITY. The Duchess of Buckingham asked Lord Orrery *who* this person was? He answered he did not know. She said she would send to Mr. Pulteney, who, she supposed, would inform her. So, then, to prevent her from making herself ridiculous, Lord Orrery sent her Grace a note, in which he gave her to understand what was meant."

He was very silent this evening: and read in a variety of books: suddenly throwing down one and taking up another.

He talked of going to Streatham that night. TAYLOR: "You'll be robbed, if you do: or you must shoot a highwayman. Now, I would rather be robbed than do that; I would not shoot a highwayman." JOHNSON: "But I would rather shoot him in the instant when he is attempting to rob me, than afterwards swear against him at the Old Bailey, to take away his life, after he has robbed me. I am surer I am right in the one case than in the other. I may be mistaken as to the man when I swear: I cannot be mistaken if I shoot him in the act. Besides, we feel less reluctance to take away a man's life, when we are heated by the injury, than to do it at a distance of time by an oath, after we have cooled." BOSWELL: "So, Sir, you would rather act from the motive of private passion, than that of public advantage." JOHNSON: "Nay, Sir, when I shoot the highwayman I act from both." BOSWELL: "Very well, very well. There is no catching him."

---

[1] The reverse of the story of *Combabus*, on which Mr. David Hume told Lord Macartney, that a friend of his had written a tragedy. It is, however, possible that I may have been inaccurate in my perception of what Dr. Johnson related, and that he may have been talking of the same ludicrous tragical subject that Mr. Hume had mentioned.—BOSWELL.

The story of Combabus, which was originally told by Lucian, may be found in Bayle's Dictionary.—MALONE.

JOHNSON: "At the same time, one does not know what to say. For, perhaps, one may, a year after, hang himself from uneasiness for having shot a highwayman![1] Few minds are fit to be trusted with so great a thing." BOSWELL: "Then, Sir, you would not shoot him?" JOHNSON: "But I might be vexed afterwards for that, too."

Thrale's carriage not having come for him, as he expected, I accompanied him some part of the way home to his own house. I told him that I had talked of him to Mr. Dunning a few days before, and had said, that in his company we did not so much interchange conversation, as listen to him; and that Dunning observed upon this, "One is always willing to listen to Dr. Johnson:" to which I answered, "That is a great deal from you, Sir." "Yes, Sir," said Johnson, "a great deal indeed. Here is a man willing to listen, to whom the world is listening all the rest of the year." BOSWELL: "I think, Sir, it is right to tell one man of such a handsome thing, which has been said of him by another. It tends to increase benevolence." JOHNSON: "Undoubtedly, it is right, Sir."

On Tuesday, April 7, I breakfasted with him at his house. He said, "nobody was content." I mentioned to him a respectable person in Scotland whom he knew; and I asserted, that I really believed he was always content. JOHNSON: "No, Sir, he is not content with the present; he has always some new scheme, some new plantation, something which is future. You know he was not content as a widower; for he married again." BOSWELL: "But he is not restless." JOHNSON: "Sir, he is only locally at rest. A chemist is locally at rest; but his mind is hard at work. This gentleman has done with external exertions. It is too late for him to engage in distant projects." BOSWELL: "He seems to amuse himself quite well: to have his attention fixed, and his tranquillity preserved by very small matters. I have tried this; but it would not do with me." JOHNSON (laughing): "No, Sir; it must be born

[1] The late Duke of Montrose was generally said to have been uneasy on that account; but I can contradict the report from his Grace's own authority. As he used to admit me to very easy conversation with him, I took the liberty to introduce the subject. His Grace told me that when riding one night near London, he was attacked by two highwaymen on horseback, and that he instantly shot one of them, upon which the other galloped off; that his servant who was very well mounted, proposed to pursue him and take him, but that his Grace said, 'No, we have had blood enough: I hope the man may live to repent." His Grace, upon my presuming to put the question, assured me, that his mind was not at all clouded by what he had thus done in self-defence.—BOSWELL.

with a man to be contented to take up with little things. Women have a great advantage that they may take up with little things, without disgracing themselves; a man cannot, except with fiddling. Had I learnt to fiddle, I should have done nothing else." Boswell: "Pray, Sir, did you ever play on any musical instrument?" Johnson: "No, Sir, I once bought me a flageolet; but I never made out a tune." Boswell: "A flageolet, Sir?—so small an instrument?[1] I should liked to hear you play on the violoncello. *That* should have been *your* instrument." Johnson: "Sir, I might as well have played on the violoncello as another; but I should have done nothing else. No, Sir; a man would never undertake great things could he be amused with small. I once tried knotting. Dempter's sister undertook to teach me; but I could not learn it." Boswell: "So, Sir, it will be related in pompous narrative, 'Once for his amusement he tried knotting; nor did this Hercules disdain the distaff.'" Johnson: "Knitting of stockings is a good amusement. As a freeman of Aberdeen, I should be a knitter of stockings." He asked me to go down with him and dine at Mr. Thrale's at Streatham, to which I agreed. I had lent him "An Account of Scotland, in 1702," written by a man of various inquiry, an English Chaplain to a regiment stationed there. Johnson: "It is sad stuff, Sir, miserably written, as books in general then were. There is now an elegance of style universally diffused. No man now writes so ill as 'Martin's Account of the Hebrides' is written. A man could not write so ill, if he should try. Set a merchant's clerk now to write, and he'll do better."

He talked to me with serious concern of a certain female friend's "laxity of narration, and inattention to truth."—"I am as much vexed," said he, "at the ease with which she hears it mentioned to her, as at the thing itself. I told her, 'Madam, you are contented to hear every day said to you, what the highest of mankind have died for, rather than bear.'—You know, Sir, the highest of mankind have died rather than bear to be told they have uttered a falsehood. Do talk to her of it: I am weary."

Boswell: "Was not Dr. John Campbell a very inaccurate man in his narrative, Sir? He once told me, that he drank

---

[1] When I told this to Miss Seward, she smiled, and repeated, with admirable readiness from "Acis and Galatea,"

"Bring me a hundred reeds of ample growth,
To make a pipe for my CAPACIOUS MOUTH."—Boswell.

thirteen bottles of port at a sitting."[1] JOHNSON: "Why, Sir, I do not know that Campbell ever lied with pen and ink; but you could not entirely depend on anything that he told you in conversation, if there was fact mixed with it. However, I loved Campbell; he was a solid orthodox man; he had a reverence for religion. Though defective in practice, he was religious in principle; and he did nothing grossly wrong that I have heard."[2]

I told him, that I had been present the day before when Mrs. Montagu, the literary lady, sat to Miss Reynolds for her picture; and that she said, "she had bound up Mr. Gibbon's History without the last two offensive chapters; for that she thought the book so far good, as it gave, in an elegant manner, the substance of the bad writers *medii ævi*, which the late Lord Lyttleton advised her to read." JOHNSON: "Sir, she has not read them: she shows none of this impetuosity to me: she does not know Greek, and, I fancy, knows little Latin. She is willing you should think she knows them; but she does not say she does." BOSWELL: "Mr. Harris, who was present, agreed with her." JOHNSON: "Harris was laughing at her, Sir. Harris is a sound solid scholar; he does not like interlopers. Harris, however, is a prig, and a bad prig.[3] I looked into his book, and thought he did not understand his own system." BOSWELL: "He says plain things in a formal and abstract

---

[1] Lord Macartney observes upon this passage, "I have heard him tell many things, which, though embellished by their mode of narrative, had their foundation in truth; but I never remember anything approaching to this. If he had written it, I should have supposed some wag had put the figure of one before the three."—I am, however, absolutely certain that Dr. Campbell told me it, and I gave particular attention to it, being myself a lover of wine, and therefore curious to hear whatever is remarkable concerning drinking. There can be no doubt that some men can drink, without suffering any injury, such a quantity as to others appears incredible. It is but fair to add, that Dr. Campbell told me, he took a very long time to this great potation; and I have heard Dr. Johnson say, "Sir, if a man drinks very slowly, and lets one glass evaporate before he takes another, I know not how long he may drink." Dr. Campbell mentioned a Colonel of Militia who sat with him all the time and drank equally.—BOSWELL.

[2] Dr. John Campbell died about two years before this conversation took place; Dec. 10, 1776.—MALONE.

[3] What my friend meant by these words concerning the amiable philosopher of Salisbury, I am at a loss to understand. A friend suggests, that Johnson thought his *manner* as a writer affected, while at the same time the *matter* did not compensate for that fault. In short, that he meant to make a remark quite different from that which a *celebrated gentleman* made on a very eminent physician: "He is a coxcomb, but a satisfactory coxcomb."—BOSWELL.

The *celebrated gentleman* here alluded to, was the late Right Honourable William Gerard Hamilton.—MALONE.

way, to be sure; but his method is good: for to have clear notions upon any subject, we must have recourse to analytic arrangement." JOHNSON: "Sir, it is what everybody does, whether they will or no. But sometimes things may be made darker by definition. I see a *cow*. I define her, *Animal quadrupes ruminans cornutum*. But a goat ruminates, and a cow may have no horns. *Cow* is plainer." BOSWELL: "I think Dr. Franklin's definition of *Man* a good one—'A tool-making animal.'" JOHNSON: "But many a man never made a tool: and suppose a man without arms, he could not make a tool."

Talking of drinking wine, he said, "I did not leave off wine because I could not bear it! I have drunk three bottles of port without being the worse for it. University College has witnessed this." BOSWELL: "Why, then, Sir, did you leave it off?" JOHNSON: "Why, Sir, because it is much better for a man to be sure that he is never to be intoxicated, never to lose the power over himself. I shall not begin to drink wine till I grow old, and want it." BOSWELL: "I think, Sir, you once said to me, that not to drink wine was a great deduction from life." JOHNSON: "It is a diminution of pleasure, to be sure; but I do not say a diminution of happiness. There is more happiness in being rational." BOSWELL: "But if we could have pleasure always, should not we be happy? The greatest part of men would compound for pleasure." JOHNSON: "Supposing we could have pleasure always, an intellectual man would not compound for it. The greatest part of men would compound, because the greatest part of men are gross." BOSWELL: "I allow there may be greater pleasure than from wine. I have had more pleasure from your conversation. I have indeed; I assure you I have." JOHNSON: "When we talk of pleasure, we mean sensual pleasure. When a man says, he had pleasure with a woman, he does not mean conversation, but something of a very different nature. Philosophers tell you, that pleasure is *contrary* to happiness. Gross men prefer animal pleasure. So there are men who have preferred living among savages. Now what a wretch must he be, who is content with such a conversation as can be had among savages! You may remember an officer at Fort Augustus, who had served in America, told us of a woman whom they were obliged to *bind*, in order to get her back from savage life." BOSWELL: "She must have been an animal, a beast." JOHNSON: "Sir, she was a speaking cat."

I mentioned to him that I had become very weary in

a company where I heard not a single intellectual sentence, except that "a man who had been settled ten years in Minorca was become a much inferior man to what he was in London, because a man's mind grows narrow in a narrow place." Johnson: "A man's mind grows narrow in a narrow place, whose mind is enlarged only because he has lived in a large place: but what is got by books and thinking, is preserved in a narrow place as well as in a large place. A man cannot know modes of life as well in Minorca as in London; but he may study mathematics as well in Minorca." Boswell: "I don't know, Sir, if you had remained ten years in the Isle of Col, you would not have been the man you now are." Johnson: "Yes, Sir, if I had been there from fifteen to twenty-five; but not if from twenty-five to thirty-five." Boswell: "I own, Sir, the spirits which I have in London make me do everything with more readiness and vigour. I can talk twice as much in London as anywhere else."

Of Goldsmith, he said, "He was not an agreeable companion, for he talked always for fame. A man who does so never can be pleasing. The man who talks to unburden his mind is the man to delight you. An eminent friend of ours is not so agreeable as the variety of his knowledge would otherwise make him, because he talks partly from ostentation."

Soon after our arrival at Thrale's, I heard one of the maids calling eagerly on another, to go to Dr. Johnson. I wondered what this could mean. I afterwards learnt, that it was to give her a Bible, which he had brought from London as a present to her.

He was for a considerable time occupied in reading "*Mémoires de Fontenelle,*" leaning and swinging upon the low gate into the court, without his hat.

I looked into Lord Kaimes's "Sketches of the History of Man;" and mentioned to Dr. Johnson his censure of Charles the Fifth, for celebrating his funeral obsequies in his lifetime, which I told him, I had been used to think a solemn and affecting act. Johnson: "Why, Sir, a man may dispose his mind to think so of that act of Charles; but it is so liable to ridicule, that if one man out of ten thousand laughs at it, he'll make the other nine thousand nine hundred and ninety-nine laugh too." I could not agree with him in this.

Sir John Pringle had expressed a wish that I would ask Dr. Johnson's opinion what were the best English sermons for style. I took an opportunity to-day of mentioning several to him. Atterbury? Johnson: "Yes, Sir, one of the best." BOSWELL: "Tillotson?" JOHNSON: "Why, not now. I should not advise a preacher at this day to imitate Tillotson's style; though I don't know; I should be cautious of objecting to what has been applauded by so many suffrages.—South is one of the best, if you except his peculiarities, and his violence, and sometimes coarseness of language.—Seed has a very fine style; but he is not very theological.—Jortin's sermons are very elegant.—Sherlock's style too is very elegant, though he has not made it his principal study.—And you may add Smallridge. All the latter preachers have a good style. Indeed, nobody now talks much of style: everybody composes pretty well. There are no such inharmonious periods as there were a hundred years ago. I should recommend Dr. Clarke's sermons, were he orthodox. However, it is very well known *where* he is not orthodox, which was upon the doctrine of the Trinity, as to which he is a condemned heretic: so one is aware of it." BOSWELL: "I like Ogden's Sermons on Prayer very much, both for neatness of style and subtilty of reasoning." JOHNSON: "I should like to read all that Ogden has written." BOSWELL: "What I wish to know is, what sermons afford the best specimen of English pulpit eloquence." JOHNSON: "We have no sermons addressed to the passions, that are good for anything; if you mean that kind of eloquence." A CLERGYMAN (whose name I do not recollect): "Were not Dodd's sermons addressed to the passions?" JOHNSON: "They were nothing, Sir, be they addressed to what they may."

At dinner Mrs. Thrale expressed a wish to go and see Scotland. JOHNSON: "Seeing Scotland, Madam, is only seeing a worse England. It is seeing the flower gradually fade away to the naked stalk. Seeing the Hebrides, indeed, is seeing quite a different scene."

Our poor friend, Mr. Thomas Davies, was soon to have a benefit at Drury-lane theatre, as some relief to his unfortunate circumstances. We were all warmly interested for his success, and had contributed to it. However, we thought there was no harm in having our joke, when he could not be hurt by it. I proposed that he should be brought on to speak a Prologue upon the occasion; and I began to mutter fragments of what it might be; as, that when now grown *old*, he was obliged to cry, "Poor Tom's *a-cold ;*"—that he owned he had been driven from the stage by a Churchill, but that was no disgrace, for a Churchill had beat the French;—that he had been satirised as "mouthing a sentence as curs mouth a bone," but he was now glad of a bone to pick. "Nay," said Johnson, "I would have him to say,

> 'Mad Tom is come to see the world again.'"

He and I returned to town in the evening. Upon the road, I endeavoured to maintain, in argument, that a landed gentleman is not under any obligation to reside upon his estate; and that by living in London he does no injury to his country. JOHNSON: "Why, Sir, he does no injury to his country in general, because the money which he draws from it gets back again into circulation; but to his particular district, his particular parish, he does an injury. All that he has to give away is not given to those who have the first claim to it. And though I have said that the money circulates back, it is a long time before that happens. Then, Sir, a man of family and estate ought to consider himself as having the charge of a district, over which he is to diffuse civility and happiness." [1]

[1] See however, the conversation under Sept. 20, 1777, where his decision on this subject is more favourable to the absentee.—MALONE.

CHAPTER IX.—1778

NEXT day I found him at home in the morning. He
praised Delany's "Observations on Swift;" said that his
book and Lord Orrery's might both be true, though one
viewed Swift more, and the other less favourably; and
that, between both, we might have a complete notion
of Swift.

Talking of a man's resolving to deny himself the use
of wine, from moral and religious considerations, he said,
"He must not doubt about it. When one doubts as to
pleasure, we know what will be the conclusion. I now
no more think of drinking wine than a horse does. The
wine upon the table is no more for me than for the dog
that is under the table."

On Thursday, April 9, I dined with him at Sir Joshua
Reynolds's, with the Bishop of St. Asaph (Dr. Shipley),
Mr. Allan Ramsay,[1] Mr. Gibbon, Mr. Cambridge, and Mr.
Langton. Mr. Ramsay had lately returned from Italy,
and entertained us with his observations upon Horace's
villa, which he had examined with great care. I relished
this much, as it brought fresh into my mind what I had
viewed with great pleasure thirteen years before. The

---

[1] Allan Ramsay, painter to his Majesty, who died 10th of August,
1784, in the seventy-first year of his age, much regretted by his friends.
—BOSWELL.

Bishop, Dr. Johnson, and Mr. Cambridge joined with Mr. Ramsay in recollecting the various lines in Horace relating to the subject.

Horace's journey to Brundusium being mentioned, Sat. l. i. 5, Johnson observed, that the brook which he describes is to be seen now, exactly as at that time: and that he had often wondered how it happened, that small brooks, such as this, kept the same situation for ages, notwithstanding earthquakes, by which even mountains have been changed, and agriculture, which produces such a variation upon the surface of the earth. CAMBRIDGE: "A Spanish writer has this thought in a poetical conceit. After observing that most of the solid structures of Rome are totally perished, while the Tiber remains the same, he adds,

> 'Lo que erà firme huió, solamente
> Lo Fugitivo permanece y dura.'"

JOHNSON: "Sir, that is taken from Janus Vitalis:—

> ' ——————— immota labescunt;
> Et quæ perpetuò sunt agitata manent.'"

The Bishop said, it appeared from Horace's writings that he was a cheerful contented man. JOHNSON: "We have no reason to believe that, my Lord. Are we to think Pope was happy, because he says so in his writings? We see in his writings what he wished the state of his mind to appear. Dr. Young, who pined for preferment, talks with contempt of it in his writings, and affects to despise everything that he did not despise." BISHOP OF ST. ASAPH: "He was like other chaplains, looking for vacancies: but that is not peculiar to the clergy. I remember when I was with the army, after the battle of Lafeldt, the officers seriously grumbled that no general was killed." CAMBRIDGE: "We may believe Horace more, when he says,—

> 'Romæ Tibur amem ventosus, Tibure Romam;'

than when he boasts of his consistency:—

> 'Me constare mihi scis, et discedere tristem,
> Quandocunque trahunt invisa negotia Romam.'"

BOSWELL: "How hard is it that man can never be at rest."
RAMSAY: "It is not in his nature to be at rest. When he is at rest, he is in the worst state that he can be in; for

he has nothing to agitate him.   He is then like the man in
the Irish song—

> 'There lived a young man in Ballinacrazy,
>   Who wanted a wife for to make him un*a*isy.'"

Goldsmith being mentioned, Johnson observed that it
was long before his merit came to be acknowledged: that
he once complained to him, in ludicrous terms of distress,
"Whenever I write anything, the public *make a point* to
know nothing about it:" but that his "Traveller," [1] brought
him into high reputation.   LANGTON: "There is not one
bad line in that poem—no one of Dryden's careless verses."
SIR JOSHUA: "I was glad to hear Charles Fox say, it was
one of the finest poems in the English language."   LANGTON:
"Why were you glad?   You surely had no doubt of this
before."   JOHNSON: "No; the merit of 'The Traveller'
is so well established, that Mr. Fox's praise cannot augment
it, nor his censure diminish it."   SIR JOSHUA: "But his
friends may suspect they had too great a partiality for
him."   JOHNSON: "Nay, Sir, the partiality of his friends
was always against him.   It was with difficulty we could
give him a hearing.   Goldsmith had no settled notions
upon any subject; so he talked always at random.   It
seemed to be his intention to blurt out whatever was in
his mind, and see what would become of it.   He was angry
too, when caught in an absurdity; but it did not prevent
him from falling into another the next minute.   I remember
Chamier,[2] after talking with him some time, said, 'Well, I
do believe he wrote this poem himself: and, let me tell
you, that is believing a great deal.'   Chamier once asked
him, what he meant by *slow*, the last word in the first
line of 'The Traveller,'

> 'Remote, unfriended, melancholy, slow.'

Did he mean tardiness of locomotion?   Goldsmith, who
would say something without consideration, answered,
'Yes.'   I was sitting by, and said, 'No, Sir; you do not
mean tardiness of locomotion; you mean that sluggishness
of mind which comes upon a man in solitude.'   Chamier
believed then that I had written the line, as much as if
he had seen me write it.   Goldsmith, however, was a man,
who, whatever he wrote, did it better than any other man

---

[1] First published in 1765.—MALONE.

[2] Anthony Chamier, Esq., a member of the LITERARY CLUB, and
Under-Secretary of State.   He died Oct. 12, 1780.—MALONE.

could do. He deserved a place in Westminster Abbey;
and every year he lived, would have deserved it better.
He had indeed been at no pains to fill his mind with
knowledge. He transplanted it from one place to another;
and it did not settle in his mind; so he could not tell what
was in his own books."

We talked of living in the country. JOHNSON: "No
wise man will go to live in the country, unless he has some
thing to do which can be better done in the country.
For instance: if he is to shut himself up for a year to study
a science, it is better to look out to the fields, than to an
opposite wall. Then if a man walks out in the country,
there is nobody to keep him from walking in again; but
if a man walks out in London, he is not sure when he shall
walk in again. A great city is, to be sure, the school for
studying life; and 'the proper study of mankind is man,'
as Pope observes."   BOSWELL: "I fancy London is the best
place for society: though I have heard that the very first
society of Paris is still beyond anything that we have here."
JOHNSON: "Sir, I question if in Paris such a company as
is sitting round this table could be got together in less than
half a-year. They talk in France of the felicity of men and
women living together: the truth is, that there the men
are not higher than the women, they know no more than
the women do, and they are not held down in their conversation by the presence of women." RAMSAY: "Literature
is upon the growth; it is in its spring in France; here it is
rather *passée*."   JOHNSON: "Literature was in France long
before we had it. Paris was the second city for the revival
of letters: Italy had it first, to be sure. What have we
done for literature, equal to what was done by the Stephani
and others in France? Our literature came to us through
France. Caxton printed only two books, Chaucer and
Gower, that were not translations from the French; and
Chaucer, we know, took much from the Italians. No,
Sir, if literature be in its spring in France, it is a second
spring; it is after a winter. We are now before the French
in literature; but we had it long after them in England;
any man who wears a sword and a powdered wig, is ashamed
to be illiterate. I believe it is not so in France. Yet there
is, probably, a great deal of learning in France, because
they have such a number of religious establishments; so
many men who have nothing else to do but to study.
I do not know this, but I take it upon the common principles
of chance. Where there are many shooters, some will
hit."

We talked of old age. Johnson (now in his seventieth

year), said "It is a man's own fault, it is from want of use, if his mind grows torpid in old age." The bishop asked, if an old man does not lose faster than he gets. JOHNSON: "I think not, my Lord, if he exerts himself." One of the company rashly observed, that he thought it was happy for an old man that insensibility comes upon him. JOHNSON (with a noble elevation and disdain): "No, Sir, I should never be happy by being less rational." BISHOP OF ST. ASAPH: "Your wish then, Sir, is γηράσκειν διδασκόμενος." [1] JOHNSON: "Yes, my Lord." His Lordship mentioned a charitable establishment in Wales, where people were maintained, and supplied with everything, upon the condition of their contributing the weekly produce of their labour; and he said they grew quite torpid for the want of property. JOHNSON: "They have no object for hope. Their condition cannot be better. It is rowing without a port."

One of the company asked him the meaning of the expression in Juvenal, *unius lacertæ*. JOHNSON: "I think it clear enough; as much ground as one may have a chance to find a lizard upon."

Commentators have differed as to the exact meaning of the expression by which the poet intended to enforce the sentiment contained in the passage where these words occur. It is enough that they mean to denote even a very small possession, provided it be a man's own.—

> "Est aliquid, quocunque loco, quocunque recessu,
> Unius sese dominum fecisse *lacertæ*." [2]

This season there was a whimsical fashion in the newspapers of applying Shakespeare's words to describe living persons well known in the world; which was done under the title of "Modern Characters from Shakespeare;" many of which were admirably adapted. The fancy took so much, that they were afterwards collected into a pamphlet. Somebody said to Johnson, across the table, that he had not been in those characters. "Yes," said he, "I have. I should have been sorry to be left out." He then repeated what had been applied to him,

> "You must borrow me GARAGANTUA's mouth."

---

[1] To grow old in learning.
[2] Juvenal, Sat. iii. 230.—Thus translated by Gifford:—
   "And sure—in any corner we can get—
   To call *one lizard* ours, is something yet."

Miss Reynolds not perceiving at once the meaning of this, he was obliged to explain it to her, which had something of an awkward and ludicrous effect. "Why, Madam, it has a reference to me, as using big words, which require the mouth of a giant to pronounce them. Garagantua is the name of a giant in Rabelais." Boswell: "But, Sir, there is another amongst them for you:—

> He would not flatter Neptune for his trident,
> Or Jove for his power to thunder.'"

Johnson: "There is nothing marked in that. No, Sir, Garagantua is the best." Notwithstanding this ease and good humour, when I, a little while afterwards, repeated his sarcasm on Kenrick, which was received with applause, he asked, " *Who* said that?" and on my suddenly answering *Garagantua*, he looked serious, which was a sufficient indication that he did not wish it to be kept up.

When we went to the drawing-room, there was a rich assemblage. Besides the company who had been at dinner, there were Mr. Garrick, Mr. Harris of Salisbury, Dr. Percy, Dr. Burney,[1] the Honourable Mrs. Cholmondeley, Miss Hannah More, &c. &c.

After wandering about in a kind of pleasing distraction for some time, I got into a corner with Johnson, Garrick, and Harris. Garrick (to Harris): "Pray, Sir, have you read Potter's Æschylus?" Harris: "Yes: and think it pretty." Garrick (to Johnson): "And what think you, Sir, of it?" Johnson: "I thought what I read of it *verbiage;* but upon Mr. Harris's recommendation I will read a play. (To Mr. Harris.) Don't prescribe two." Mr. Harris suggested one, I do not remember which. Johnson: "We must try its effect as an English poem; that is the way to judge of the merit of a translation. Translations are, in general, for people who cannot read the original." I mentioned the vulgar saying, that Pope's Homer was not a good representation of the original. Johnson: "Sir, it is the greatest work of the kind that has ever been produced." Boswell: "The truth is, it is impossible perfectly to translate poetry. In a different language it may be the same tune, but it has not the same tone. Homer plays it on a bassoon; Pope on a flageolet." Harris: "I think heroic poetry is best in blank verse;

---

[1] This was Dr. Charles Burney, the musical composer, who was father of the great critic and scholar, and author of a "General History of Music." He was born at Shrewsbury in 1726, and died in 1814.—Ed.

yet it appears that rhyme is essential to English poetry, from our deficiency in metrical quantities. In my opinion, the chief excellence of our language is numerous prose." JOHNSON: "Sir William Temple[1] was the first writer who gave cadence to English prose.[2] Before this time they were careless of arrangement, and did not mind whether a sentence ended with an important word, or an insignificant word, or with what part of speech it was concluded." Mr. Langton, who now had joined us, commended Clarendon. JOHNSON: "He is objected to for his parentheses, his involved clauses, and his want of harmony. But he is supported by his matter. It is, indeed, owing to a plethory of matter that his style is so faulty: every *substance* (smiling to Mr. Harris), has so many *accidents*. To be distinct, we must talk *analytically*. If we analyse language, we must speak of it grammatically; if we analyse argument, we must speak of it logically." GARRICK: "Of all the translations that ever were attempted, I think Elphinston's Martial the most extraordinary. He consulted me upon it, who am a little of an epigrammatist myself, you know. I told him freely, 'You don't seem to have that turn.' I asked him if he was serious; and finding he was, I advised

---

[1] This eminent statesman and scholar was born in 1628. In 1674 he was appointed Ambassador to the States-general, and in 1679 became Secretary of State. When he resigned that position he was often visited in his retirement by Charles II., James II., and William III. He has published "Observations on the United Provinces," and other miscellaneous writings. He died in 1700.—ED.

[2] The author, in vol. i., p. 162, says that Johnson once told him, "that he had formed his style upon that of Sir William Temple, and upon Chambers's Proposal for his Dictionary. He certainly was mistaken; or, if he imagined at first that he was imitating Temple, he was very unsuccessful, for nothing can be more unlike than the simplicity of Temple and the richness of Johnson."

This observation, on the first view, seems perfectly just; but on a closer examination it will, I think, appear to have been founded on a misapprehension. Mr. Boswell understood Johnson too literally. He did not, I conceive, mean that he endeavoured to imitate Temple's style in all its parts; but that he formed his style on him and Chambers (perhaps the paper published in 1737, relative to his second edition, entitled "Considerations," &c.) taking from each what was most worthy of imitation. The passage before us, I think, shows, that he learned from Temple to modulate his periods, and, *in that respect only*, made him his pattern. In this view of the subject, there is no difficulty. He might learn from Chambers, compactness, strength, and precision (in opposition to the laxity of style which had long prevailed); from Sir Thomas Browne (who was also certainly one of his archetypes), *pondera verborum*, vigour and energy of expression; and from Temple, harmonious arrangement, the due collocation of words, and the other arts and graces of composition here enumerated: and yet, after all, his style might bear no striking resemblance to that of any of these writers, though it had profited by each.—MALONE.

him against publishing. Why, his translation is more difficult to understand than the original. I thought him a man of some talents; but he seems crazy in this." JOHNSON: "Sir, you have done what I had not courage to do. But he did not ask my advice, and I did not force it upon him to make him angry with me." GARRICK: "But as a friend, Sir—." JOHNSON: "Why, such a friend as I am with him—no." GARRICK: "But if you see a friend going to tumble over a precipice?" JOHNSON: "That is an extravagant case, Sir. You are sure a friend will thank you for hindering him from tumbling over a precipice; but, in the other case, I should hurt his vanity, and do him no good. He would not take my advice. His brother-in-law, Strahan, sent him a subscription of 50*l*., and said he would send him 50*l*. more, if he would not publish." GARRICK: "What! eh! is Strahan a good judge of an epigram? Is not he rather an *obtuse* man, eh?" JOHNSON: "Why, Sir, he may not be a judge of an epigram; but you see he is a judge of what is *not* an epigram." BOSWELL: "It is easy for you, Mr. Garrick, to talk to an author as you talked to Elphinston; you, who have been so long the manager of a theatre, rejecting the plays of poor authors. You are an old judge, who have often pronounced sentence of death. You are a practised surgeon, who have often amputated limbs: and though this may have been for the good of your patients, they cannot like you. Those who have undergone a dreadful operation are not very fond of seeing the operator again." GARRICK: "Yes, I know enough of that. There was a reverend gentleman (Mr. Hawkins), who wrote a tragedy, the SIEGE of something,[1] which I refused." HARRIS: "So the siege was raised." JOHNSON: "Ay, he came to me and complained; and told me that Garrick said his play was wrong in the *concoction*. Now, what is the concoction of a play?" (Here Garrick started, and twisted himself, and seemed sorely vexed; for Johnson told me he believed the story was true.) GARRICK: "I—I—I—said, *first* concoction."[2] JOHNSON (smiling): "Well, he left out *first*. And Rich, he said, refused him *in false English*: he could show it under his hand." GARRICK: "He wrote to me in violent wrath, for having refused his play: 'Sir, this is growing a very serious and terrible affair. I am resolved to publish

[1] It was called "The Siege of Aleppo." Mr. Hawkins, the author of it, was formerly Professor of Poetry at Oxford. It is printed in his "Miscellanies," 3 vols. octavo.—BOSWELL.

[2] Garrick had high authority for this expression. Dryden uses it in one of his critical essays.—MALONE.

my play. I will appeal to the world; and how will your judgment appear!' I answered, 'Sir, notwithstanding all the seriousness, and all the terrors, I have no objection to your publishing your play; and as you live at a great distance (Devonshire, I believe), if you will send it to me, I will convey it to the press.' I never heard more of it, —ha! ha! ha!"

On Friday, April 10, I found Johnson at home in the morning. We resumed the conversation of yesterday. He put me in mind of some of it which escaped my memory, and enabled me to record it more perfectly than I otherwise could have done. He was much pleased with my paying so great attention to his recommendation in 1763, the period when our acquaintance began, that I should keep a journal; and I could perceive he was secretly pleased to find so much of the fruit of his mind preserved; and as he had been used to imagine and say that he always laboured when he said a good thing, it delighted him, on a review, to find that his conversation teemed with point and imagery.

I said to him, "You were yesterday, Sir, in remarkably good humour; but there was nothing to offend you, nothing to produce irritation or violence. There was no bold offender. There was not one capital conviction. It was a maiden assize. You had on your white gloves."

He found fault with our friend Langton for having been too silent. "Sir," said I, "you will recollect that he very properly took up Sir Joshua for being glad that Charles Fox had praised Goldsmith's 'Traveller,' and you joined him." JOHNSON: "Yes, Sir, I knocked Fox on the head, without ceremony. Reynolds is too much under Fox and Burke at present. He is under the *Fox star*, and the *Irish constellation*. He is always under some planet." BOSWELL: "There is no Fox Star." JOHNSON: "But there is a Dog star." BOSWELL: "They say, indeed, a fox and a dog are the same animal."

I reminded him of a gentleman, who, Mrs. Cholmondeley said, was first talkative from affectation, and then silent from the same cause; that he first thought, "I shall be celebrated as the liveliest man in every company;" and then, all at once, "Oh! it is much more respectable to be grave, and look wise." "He has reversed the Pythagorean discipline, by being first talkative, and then silent. He reverses the course of nature too; he was first the gay butterfly, and then the creeping worm." Johnson laughed loud and long at this expansion and illustration of what he himself had told me.

We dined together with Mr. Scott (now Sir William

Scott, his Majesty's Advocate-General),[1] at his chambers in the Temple; nobody else there. The company being small, Johnson was not in such spirits as he had been the preceding day, and for a considerable time little was said. At last he burst forth: "Subordination is sadly broken down in this age. No man, now, has the same authority which his father had,—except a gaoler. No master has it over his servants; it is diminished in our colleges; nay, in our grammar schools." BOSWELL: "What is the cause of this, Sir?" JOHNSON: "Why the coming in of the Scotch" (laughing sarcastically). BOSWELL: "That is to say, things have been turned topsy-turvy. But your serious cause." JOHNSON: "Why, Sir, there are many causes, the chief of which is, I think, the great increase of money. No man now depends upon the Lord of a Manor, when he can send to another country, and fetch provisions. The shoe-black at the entry of my court does not depend on me. I can deprive him but of a penny a day, which he hopes somebody else will bring him; and that penny I must carry to another shoe-black; so the trade suffers nothing. I have explained, in my 'Journey to the Hebrides,' how gold and silver destroy feudal subordination. But, besides, there is a general relaxation of reverence. No son now depends upon his father, as in former times. Paternity used to be considered as of itself a great thing, which had a right to many claims. That is, in general, reduced to very small bounds. My hope is, that as anarchy produces tyranny, this extreme relaxation will produce *freni strictio*."

Talking of fame, for which there is so great a desire, I observed how little there is of it in reality, compared with the other objects of human attention. "Let every man recollect, and he will be sensible how small a part of his time is employed in talking or thinking of Shakespeare, Voltaire, or any of the most celebrated men that have ever lived, or are now supposed to occupy the attention and admiration of the world. Let this be extracted and compressed; into what a narrow space will it go!" I then slily introduced Mr. Garrick's fame, and his assuming the airs of a great man. JOHNSON: "Sir, it is wonderful how *little* Garrick assumes. No, Sir, Garrick *fortunam reverenter habet*. Consider, Sir,—celebrated men, such as you have mentioned, have had their applause at a distance; but Garrick had it dashed in his face, sounded in his ears, and went home every night with the plaudits of a thousand

---

[1] Now (1804) Judge of the Court of Admiralty, and Master of the Faculties.—MALONE.

in his *cranium*. Then, Sir, Garrick did not *find*, but *made* his way to the tables, the levees, and almost the bed-chambers of the great. Then, Sir, Garrick had under him a numerous body of people; who, from fear of his power and hopes of his favour, and admiration of his talents, were constantly submissive to him. And here is a man who has advanced the dignity of his profession. Garrick has made a player a higher character." Scott: "And he is a very sprightly writer too." Johnson: "Yes, Sir; and all this supported by great wealth of his own acquisition. If all this had happened to me, I should have had a couple of fellows with long poles walking before me, to knock down everybody that stood in the way. Consider, if all this had happened to Cibber or Quin, they'd have jumped over the moon. Yet Garrick speaks to *us*" (smiling). Boswell: "And Garrick is a very good man, a charitable man." Johnson: "Sir, a liberal man. He has given away more money than any man in England. There may be a little vanity mixed; but he has shown that money is not his first object." Boswell: "Yet Foote used to say of him, that he walked out with an intention to do a generous action; but turning the corner of a street, he met with the ghost of a halfpenny, which frightened him." Johnson: "Why, Sir, that is very true, too; for I never knew a man of whom it could be said with less certainty to-day, what he will do to-morrow, than Garrick; it depends so much on his humour at the time." Scott: "I am glad to hear of his liberality. He has been represented as very saving." Johnson: "With his domestic saving we have nothing to do. I remember drinking tea with him long ago, when Peg Woffington[1] made it, and he grumbled at her for making it too strong.[2] He had then begun to feel money in his purse, and did not know when he should have enough of it."

On the subject of wealth, the proper use of it, and the effects of that art which is called economy, he observed, "It is wonderful to think how men of very large estates not only spend their yearly incomes, but are often actually in want of money. It is clear they have not value for what

---

[1] Margaret Woffington was the elder sister of Mrs. Cholmondeley, wife of the Hon. and Rev. George Cholmondeley, and an actress of some celebrity. She was born in Dublin in 1718, and her first appearance in London was at Covent-garden Theatre, in 1738, in the character of "Sir Harry Wildair," in which she was eminently successful. Her society was extensively sought by persons of rank and talent. She died in 1760.

[2] When Johnson told this little anecdote to Sir Joshua Reynolds, he mentioned a circumstance which he omitted to-day:—"Why," said Garrick, "it is as red as blood."—Boswell.

they spend.   Lord Shelburne told me, that a man of high rank, who looks into his own affairs, may have all that he ought to have, all that can be of any use, or appear with any advantage, for 5,000*l.* a-year.   Therefore a great proportion must go in waste; and, indeed, this is the case with most people, whatever their fortune is."   BOSWELL: "I have no doubt, Sir, of this.   But how is it?   What is waste?"   JOHNSON: "Why, Sir, breaking bottles, and a thousand other things.   Waste cannot be accurately told, though we are sensible how destructive it is.   Economy on the one hand, by which a certain income is made to maintain a man genteelly, and waste on the other, by which, on the same income another man lives shabbily, cannot be defined.   It is a very nice thing; as one man wears his coat out much sooner than another, we cannot tell how."

We talked of war.   JOHNSON: "Every man thinks meanly of himself for not having been a soldier, or not having been at sea."   BOSWELL: "Lord Mansfield does not."   JOHNSON: "Sir, if Lord Mansfield were in a company of General Officers and Admirals who have been in service, he would shrink; he'd wish to creep under the table."   BOSWELL: "No; he'd think he could *try* them all."   JOHNSON: "Yes, if he could catch them; but they'd try him much sooner.   No, Sir; were Socrates and Charles the Twelfth of Sweden both present in any company, and Socrates to say, 'Follow me, and hear a lecture in philosophy;' and Charles, laying his hand on his sword, to say, 'Follow me, and dethrone the Czar;' a man would be ashamed to follow Socrates.   Sir, the impression is universal: yet it is strange.   As to the sailor, when you look down from the quarter-deck to the space below, you see the utmost extremity of human misery: such crowding, such filth, such stench!"   BOSWELL: "Yet sailors are happy."   JOHNSON: "They are happy as brutes are happy, with a piece of fresh meat,—with the grossest sensuality.   But, Sir, the profession of soldiers and sailors has the dignity of danger.   Mankind reverence those who have got over fear, which is so general a weakness."   SCOTT: "But is not courage mechanical, and to be acquired?"   JOHNSON: "Why, yes, Sir, in a collective sense.   Soldiers consider themselves only as a part of a great machine."   SCOTT: "We find people fond of being sailors."   JOHNSON: "I cannot account for that, any more than I can account for other strange perversions of imagination."

His abhorrence of the profession of a sailor was uniformly violent; but in conversation he always exalted the profession of a soldier. And yet I have, in my large and various collection of his writings, a letter to an eminent friend, in which he expresses himself thus: "My godson called on me lately. He is weary, and rationally weary, of a military life. If you can place him in some other state, I think you may increase his happiness, and secure his virtue. A soldier's time is passed in distress and danger, or in idleness and corruption." Such was his cool reflection in his study; but whenever he was warmed and animated by the presence of company, he, like other philosophers, whose minds are impregnated with poetical fancy, caught the common enthusiasm for splendid renown.

He talked of Mr. Charles Fox, of whose abilities he thought highly, but observed, that he did not talk much at our CLUB. I have heard Mr. Gibbon remark, "that Mr. Fox could not be afraid of Dr. Johnson; yet he certainly was very shy of saying anything in Dr. Johnson's presence." Mr. Scott now quoted what was said of Alcibiades by a Greek poet, to which Johnson assented.[1]

He told us, that he had given Mrs. Montagu a catalogue of all Daniel De Foe's works of imagination; most, if not all, of which, as well as of his other works, he now enumerated, allowing a considerable share of merit to a man who, bred a tradesman, had written so variously and so well. Indeed his "Robinson Crusoe" is enough of itself to establish his reputation.

He expressed great indignation at the imposture of the Cock-lane ghost, and related with much satisfaction, how he had assisted in detecting the cheat, and had published an account of it in the newspapers. Upon this subject, I incautiously offended him, by pressing him with too many questions, and he showed his displeasure. I apologised, saying that "I asked questions in order to

---

[1] Wishing to discover the ancient observation here referred to, I applied to Sir William Scott on the subject, but he had no recollection of it. My old and very learned friend, Dr. Michael Kearney, formerly senior fellow of Trinity College, Dublin, and now Archdeacon of Raphoe in Ireland, has, however, most happily elucidated this passage. He remarks to me, that "Mr. Boswell's memory must here have deceived him, and that Mr. Scott's observation must have been, that Mr. Fox, in the instance mentioned, might be considered as the *reverse* of *Phœax*, of whom, as Plutarch relates in the Life of Alcibiades, Eupolis the tragedian said, '*It is true he can talk, and yet he is no* speaker.'"

If this discovery had been made by a scholiast on an ancient author, with what ardour and exuberant praise would Bentley or Taylor have spoken of it. Sir William Scott, to whom I communicated Dr. Kearney's remark, is perfectly satisfied that it is correct. For the other observations, we are indebted to the same gentleman. Every classical reader will lament that they are not more numerous.—MALONE.

be instructed and entertained; I repaired eagerly to the fountain; but that the moment he gave me a hint, the moment he put a lock upon the well, I desisted." "But, Sir," said he, "that is forcing one to do a disagreeable thing:" and he continued to rate me. "Nay, Sir," said I, "when you have put a lock upon the well, so that I can no longer drink, do not make the fountain of your wit play upon me and wet me."

He sometimes could not bear being teased with questions. I was once present when a gentleman asked so many, as, "What did you do, Sir?"—"What did you say, Sir?" that he at last grew enraged, and said, "I will not be put to the *question*. Don't you consider, Sir, that these are not the manners of a gentleman? I will not be baited with *what* and *why*; what is this? what is that? why is a cow's tail long? why is a fox's tail bushy?" The gentleman, who was a good deal out of countenance, said, "Why, Sir, you are so good, that I venture to trouble you." JOHNSON: "Sir, my being so *good* is no reason why you should be so *ill*."

Talking of the Justitia hulk at Woolwich, in which criminals were punished, by being confined to labour, he said, "I do not see that they are punished by this: they must have worked equally, had they never been guilty of stealing. They now only work; so, after all, they have gained; what they stole is clear gain to them; the confinement is nothing. Every man who works is confined: the smith to his shop, the tailor to his garret." BOSWELL: "And Lord Mansfield to his Court." JOHNSON: "Yes, Sir. You know the notion of confinement may be extended, as in the song, 'Every island is a prison.' There is, in Dodsley's collection, a copy of verses to the author of that song."

Smith's Latin verses on Pococke, the great traveller,[1] were mentioned. He repeated some of them, and said, they were Smith's best verses.

He talked with an uncommon animation of travelling into distant countries; that the mind was enlarged by it, and that an acquisition of dignity of character was derived from it. He expressed a particular enthusiasm with respect to visiting the wall of China. I caught it for the moment, and said I really believed I should go and see the wall of

[1] Smith's verses are on Edward Pococke, the great Oriental linguist. He travelled, it is true; but Dr. Richard Pococke, late Bishop of Ossory, who published Travels through the East, is usually called *the great traveller*.—KEARNEY.

China, had I not children, of whom it was my duty to take care. "Sir," said he, "by doing so, you would do what would be of importance in raising your children to eminence. There would be a lustre reflected upon them from your spirit and curiosity. They would be at all times regarded as the children of a man who had gone to view the wall of China—I am serious, Sir."

When we had left Mr. Scott's, he said, "Will you go home with me?"—"Sir," said I, "it is late; but I'll go with you for three minutes." JOHNSON: "Or *four*." We went to Mrs. Williams's room, where we found Mr. Allen, the printer, who was the landlord of his house in Bolt-court, a worthy, obliging man, and his very old acquaintance; and what was exceedingly amusing, though he was of a very diminutive size, he used, even in Johnson's presence, to imitate the stately periods and slow and solemn utterance of the great man. I, this evening, boasted, that although I did not write what is called stenography, or short-hand, in appropriated characters devised for the purpose, I had a method of my own of writing half words, and leaving out some altogether, so as yet to keep the substance and language of any discourse which I had heard so much in view, that I could give it very completely soon after I had taken it down. He defied me, as he had once defied an actual short-hand writer; and he made the experiment by reading slowly and distinctly a part of Robertson's "History of America," while I endeavoured to write it in my way of taking notes. It was found that I had it very imperfectly; the conclusion from which was, that its excellence was principally owing to a studied arrangement of words, which could not be varied or abridged without an essential injury.

On Sunday, April 12, I found him at home before dinner; Dr. Dodd's poem, entitled "Thoughts in Prison," was lying upon his table. This appearing to me an extraordinary effort by a man who was in Newgate for a capital crime, I was desirous to hear Johnson's opinion of it; to my surprise he told me he had not read a line of it. I took up the book, and read a passage to him. JOHNSON: "Pretty well, if you are previously disposed to like them." I read another passage, with which he was better pleased. He then took the book into his own hands, and having looked at the prayer at the end of it, he said, "What *evidence* is there that this was composed the night before he suffered? *I* do not believe it." He then read aloud where he prays for the king, &c., and observed, "Sir, do you think that a man, the night before he is to be

hanged, cares for the succession of a royal family?—
Though he *may* have composed this prayer then. A man,
who has been canting all his life, may cant to the last.—
And yet a man, who has been refused a pardon, after so
much petitioning, would hardly be praying thus fervently
for the king."

He and I, and Mrs. Williams, went to dine with the
Reverend Dr. Percy. Talking of Goldsmith, Johnson said,
he was very envious. I defended him, by observing, that
he owned it frankly upon all occasions. JOHNSON: "Sir,
you are enforcing the charge. He had so much envy,
that he could not conceal it. He was so full of it, that he
overflowed. He talked of it, to be sure, often enough.
Now, Sir, what a man avows he is not ashamed to think;
though many a man thinks what he is ashamed to avow.
We are all envious naturally; but by checking envy we
get the better of it. So we are all thieves naturally;
a child always tries to get at what it wants the nearest
way. By good instruction and good habits this is cured,
till a man has not even an inclination to seize what is
another's; has no struggle with himself about it."

And here I shall record a scene of too much heat
between Dr. Johnson and Dr. Percy, which I should have
suppressed, were it not that it gave occasion to display
the truly tender and benevolent heart of Johnson, who,
as soon as he found a friend was at all hurt by anything
which he had "said in his wrath," was not only prompt
and desirous to be reconciled, but exerted himself to make
ample reparation.

Books of Travels having been mentioned, Johnson
praised Pennant[1] very highly, as he did at Dunvegan, in
the Isle of Sky.[2] Dr. Percy knowing himself to be the
heir male of the ancient Percys[3] and having the warmest

---

[1] Thomas Pennant, the celebrated naturalist, and tourist. The principal works which emanated from his pen were his "British Zoology," a
"Tour in Scotland," his "Account of London," and "Literary Memoirs;"
all works of considerable repute. He was born in Downing, co. Flint.,
and died in 1718.

[2] "Journal of a Tour to the Hebrides," edit. 3, p. 221.—BOSWELL.

[3] See this accurately stated, and the descent of his family from the
Earls of Northumberland clearly deduced, in the Reverend Dr. Nash's
excellent "History of Worcestershire, vol. ii. p. 318. The Doctor has
subjoined a note, in which he says, "The Editor hath seen and carefully
examined the proofs of all the particulars above-mentioned, now in the
possession of the Reverend Thomas Percy."

The same proofs I have also myself carefully examined, and have
seen some additional proofs which have occurred since the Doctor's
book was published; and both as a Lawyer accustomed to the consideration of evidence, and as a Genealogist versed in the study of pedigrees.

and most dutiful attachment to the noble House of Northumberland, could not sit quietly and hear a man praised, who had spoken disrespectfully of Alnwick-castle, and the Duke's pleasure-grounds, especially as he thought meanly of his travels. He therefore opposed Johnson eagerly. JOHNSON: "Pennant, in what he has said of Alnwick, has done what he intended; he has made you very angry." PERCY: "He has said, the garden is trim, which is representing it, like a citizen's parterre, when the truth is, there is a very large extent of fine turf and gravel walks." JOHNSON: "According to your own account, Sir, Pennant is right. It *is* trim. Here is grass cut close, and gravel rolled smooth. Is not that trim? The extent is nothing against that; a mile may be as trim as a square yard. Your extent puts me in mind of the citizen's enlarged dinner, two pieces of roast beef and two puddings. There is no variety, no mind exerted in laying out the ground, no trees." PERCY: "He pretends to give the natural history of Northumberland, and yet takes no notice of the immense number of trees planted there of late." JOHNSON: "That, Sir, has nothing to do with the *natural* history; that is, *civil* history. A man who gives the natural history of the oak, is not to tell how many oaks have been planted in this place or that. A man who gives the natural history of the cow, is not to tell how many cows are milked at Islington. The animal is the same, whether milked in the Park or at Islington." PERCY: "Pennant does not describe well; a carrier who goes along the side of Lochlomond would describe it better." JOHNSON: "I think he describes very well." PERCY: "I travelled after him." JOHNSON: "And *I* travelled after him." PERCY: "But, my good friend, you are short-sighted, and do not see so well as I do." I wondered at Dr. Percy's venturing thus. Dr. Johnson said nothing at the time; but inflammable particles were collecting for a cloud to burst. In a little while Dr. Percy said something more in disparagement of Pennant. JOHNSON (pointedly): "This is the resentment of a narrow mind, because he did not find everything in Northumberland." PERCY (feeling

I am fully satisfied. I cannot help observing, as a circumstance of no small moment, that in tracing the Bishop of Dromore's genealogy, essential aid was given by the late Elizabeth Duchess of Northumberland, heiress of that illustrious house; a lady not only of high dignity of spirit, such as became her noble blood, but of excellent understanding and lively talents. With a fair pride I can boast of the honour of her Grace's correspondence, specimens of which adorn my archives.—BOSWELL.

the stroke): "Sir, you may be as rude as you please." JOHNSON: "Hold, Sir! Don't talk of rudeness; remember, Sir, you told me (puffing hard with passion struggling for a vent) I was short-sighted. We have done with civility. We are to be as rude as we please." PERCY: "Upon my honour, Sir, I did not mean to be uncivil." JOHNSON: "I cannot say so, Sir; for I *did* mean to be uncivil, thinking *you* had been uncivil." Dr. Percy rose, ran up to him, and taking him by the hand, assured him affectionately that his meaning had been misunderstood; upon which a reconciliation instantly took place. JOHNSON: "My dear Sir, I am willing you shall *hang* Pennant." PERCY (resuming the former subject): "Pennant complains that the helmet is not hung out to invite to the hall of hospitality.[1] Now, I never heard that it was a custom to hang out a *helmet*." JOHNSON: "Hang him up, hang him up." BOSWELL (humouring the joke): "Hang out his skull instead of a helmet, and you may drink ale out of it in your hall of Odin, as he is your enemy; that will be truly ancient. *There* will be 'Northern Antiquities.'"[2] JOHNSON: "He's a *Whig*, Sir; a *sad dog*, (smiling at his own violent expressions, merely for *political* difference of opinion). But he's the best traveller I ever read; he observes more things than any one else does."

I could not help thinking that this was too high praise of a writer who traversed a wide extent of country in such haste, that he could put together only curt frittered fragments of his own, and afterwards procured supplemental intelligence from parochial ministers, and others not the best qualified or most impartial narrators, whose ungenerous prejudice against the house of Stuart glares in misrepresentation: a writer, who at best treats merely of superficial objects, and shows no philosophical investigation of character and manners, such as Johnson has exhibited in his masterly "Journey" over part of the same ground; and who, it should seem from a desire of ingratiating himself with the Scotch, has flattered the people of North Britain so inordinately and with so little discrimination, that the

---

[1] It certainly was a custom, as appears from the following passage in Perce-forest, vol. iii. p. 108:—"Fasoient mettre au plus hault de leur hostel un *heaulme, en signe* que tous les gentils hommes et gentilles femmes entrassent hardiment en leur hostel comme en leur propre," &c.—KEARNEY.

The author's second son, Mr. James Boswell, late of Brazen-nose College, in Oxford, and now of the Inner Temple, had noticed this passage in Perce-forest, and suggested to me the same remark.—MALONE.

[2] The title of a book translated by Dr. Percy.—BOSWELL.

judicious and candid amongst them must be disgusted, while they value more the plain, just, yet kindly report of Johnson.

Having impartially censured Mr. Pennant as a traveller in Scotland, let me allow him, from authorities much better than mine, his deserved praise as an able zoologist: and let me also, from my own understanding and feelings, acknowledge the merits of his "London," which, though said to be not quite accurate in some particulars, is one of the most pleasing topographical performances that ever appeared in any language. Mr. Pennant, like his country-men in general, has the true spirit of a *gentleman*. As a proof of it, I shall quote from his "London" the passage in which he speaks of my illustrious friend:—" I must by no means omit *Bolt-court*, the long residence of Dr. Samuel Johnson, a man of the strongest natural abilities, great learning, a most retentive memory, of the deepest and most unaffected piety and morality, mingled with those numerous weaknesses and prejudices which his friends have kindly taken care to draw from their dread abode.[1]   I brought on myself his transient anger, by observing that 'in his tour in *Scotland* he once had long and woeful experience of oats being the food of men in *Scotland*, as they were of horses in *England*.' It was a national reflection unworthy of him, and I shot my bolt. In return he gave me a tender hug.[2] *Con amore* he also said of me, '*The dog is a Whig*.'[3]   I admired the virtues of Lord *Russell*,[4] and pitied his fall. I should have been a Whig at the Revolution. There have been periods since, in which I should have been, what I now am, a moderate Tory, a supporter, as far as my little influence extends, of a well-poised balance between the crown and people: but should the scale preponderate against the *Salus populi*, that moment may it be said '*The* dog's a *Whig* !'"

We had a calm after the storm, staid the evening and

---

[1] This is the common cant against faithful Biography. Does the worthy gentleman mean that I, who was taught discrimination of character by Johnson, should have omitted his frailties, and, in short, have *bedaubed* him as the worthy gentleman has bedaubed Scotland?—BOSWELL.

[2] See Dr. Johnson's "Journey to the Western Islands," p. 296:—see his Dictionary, article *Oats:*—and my "Voyage to the Hebrides," first edit.—PENNANT.

[3] Mr. Boswell's Journal, p. 386.—PENNANT.

[4] The illustrious but unfortunate Lord William Russell,—third son of the first Duke of Bedford, who was accused, by the partisans of the Court, in the reign of Charles II., of being engaged in the "Rye House Plot."

supped, and were pleasant and gay.   But Dr. Percy told
me he was very uneasy at what had passed: for there was
a gentleman there who was acquainted with the Northumberland family, to whom he hoped to have appeared
more respectable, by showing how intimate he was with
Dr. Johnson, and who might now, on the contrary, go
away with an opinion to his disadvantage.   He begged I
would mention this to Dr. Johnson, which I afterwards
did.   His observation upon it was, "This comes of *stratagem ;* had he told me that he wished to appear to advantage before that gentleman, he should have been at the
top of the house all the time."   He spoke of Dr. Percy in
the handsomest manner.   "Then, Sir," said I, "may I be
allowed to suggest a mode by which you may effectually
counteract any unfavourable report of what passed.   I
will write a letter to you upon the subject of the unlucky
contest of that day, and you will be kind enough to put in
writing, as an answer to that letter, what you have now
said; and as Lord Percy is to dine with us at General
Paoli's soon, I will take an opportunity to read the correspondence in his Lordship's presence."   This friendly scheme
was accordingly carried into execution without Dr. Percy's
knowledge.   Johnson's letter placed Dr. Percy's unquestionable merit in the fairest point of view: and I contrived
that Lord Percy should hear the correspondence, by introducing it at General Paoli's, as an instance of Dr. Johnson's
kind disposition towards one in whom his Lordship was
interested.   Thus every unfavourable impression was
obviated, that could have possibly been made on those by
whom he wished most to be regarded.   I breakfasted the
day after with him, and informed him of my scheme, and
its happy completion, for which he thanked me in the
warmest terms, and was highly delighted with Dr. Johnson's
letter in his praise, of which I gave him a copy.   He said,
"I would rather have this than degrees from all the
universities in Europe.   It will be for me, and my children,
and grand-children."   Dr. Johnson having afterwards
asked me if I had given him a copy of it, and being told
I had, was offended, and insisted that I should get it back,
which I did.   As, however, he did not desire me to destroy
either the original or the copy, or forbid me to let it be
seen, I think myself at liberty to apply to it his general
declaration to me concerning his own letters,—"That he
did not choose they should be published in his lifetime;
but had no objection to their appearing after his death."
I shall therefore insert this kindly correspondence, having
faithfully narrated the circumstances accompanying it.

"TO DR. SAMUEL JOHNSON.

"My dear Sir,

"I beg leave to address you in behalf of our friend Dr. Percy, who was much hurt by what you said to him that day we dined at his house;[1] when, in the course of the dispute as to Pennant's merit as a traveller, you told Percy that 'he had the resentment of a narrow mind against Pennant, because he did not find everything in Northumberland.' Percy is sensible that you did not mean to injure him; but he is vexed to think that your behaviour to him on that occasion may be interpreted as a proof that he is despised by you, which I know is not the case. I have told him that the charge of being narrow-minded was only as to the particular point in question; and that he had the merit of being a martyr to his noble family.

"Earl Percy is to dine with General Paoli next Friday; and I should be sincerely glad to have it in my power to satisfy his Lordship how well you think of Dr. Percy, who, I find, apprehends that your good opinion of him may be of very essential consequence; and who assures me, that he has the highest respect and the warmest affection for you.

"I have only to add, that my suggesting this occasion for the exercise of your candour and generosity, is altogether unknown to Dr. Percy, and proceeds from my good-will towards him, and my persuasion that you will be happy to do him an essential kindness. I am, more and more, my dear Sir, your most faithful

"And affectionate humble servant,

"James Boswell.."

"TO JAMES BOSWELL, ESQ.

"Sir,   *April* 23, 1778.

"The debate between Dr. Percy and me is one of those foolish controversies which begin upon a question of which neither party cares how it is decided, and which is, nevertheless, continued to acrimony, by the vanity with which every man resists confutation. Dr. Percy's warmth proceeded from a cause, which perhaps does him more honour than he could have derived from juster criticism. His abhorrence of Pennant proceeded from his opinion that Pennant had wantonly and indecently censured his patron. His anger made him resolve that, for having been once wrong, he never should be right. Pennant has much in his notions that I do not like; but still I think him a very intelligent traveller. If Percy is really offended, I am sorry; for he is a man whom I never knew to offend any one. He is a man very willing to learn, and very able to teach; a man out of whose company I never go without having learned something. It is sure that he vexes me sometimes, but I am afraid it is by making me feel my own ignorance. So much extension of mind, and so much minute accuracy of inquiry, if you survey your whole circle of acquaintance, you will find so scarce, if you find it

---

[1] Sunday, April 12, 1778.—Boswell.

at all, that you will value Percy by comparison.   Lord Hailes is
somewhat like him: but Lord Hailes does not, perhaps, go beyond
him in research; and I do not know that he equals him in elegance.
Percy's attention to poetry has given grace and splendour to his
studies of antiquity.   A mere antiquarian is a rugged being.

"Upon the whole, you see that what I might say in sport or
petulance to him, is very consistent with full conviction of his
merit.   I am, dear Sir,

"Your most, &c.,
"SAM. JOHNSON."

"TO THE REVEREND DR. PERCY, NORTHUMBERLAND HOUSE.

"DEAR SIR,   *South Audley-street, April* 25.

"I wrote to Dr. Johnson on the subject of the *Pennantian* controversy; and have received from him an answer which will delight
you.   I read it yesterday to Dr. Robertson at the exhibition; and
at dinner to Lord Percy, General Oglethorpe, &c., who dined with
us at General Paoli's; who was also a witness to the high *testimony*
to your honour.

General Paoli desires the favour of your company next Tuesday
to dinner, to meet Dr. Johnson.   If I can, I will call on you to-day.
I am, with sincere regard,

"Your most obedient humble servant,
"JAMES BOSWELL." [1]

[1] Though the Bishop of Dromore kindly answered the letters which I
wrote to him relative to Dr. Johnson's early history: yet, in justice to
him, I think it proper to add that the account of the foregoing conversation, and the subsequent transaction, as well as of some other conversations in which he is mentioned, has been given to the public without
previous communication with his Lordship.—BOSWELL.

CHAPTER X.—1778

ON Monday, April 13, I dined with Johnson at Mr. Langton's, where were Dr. Porteus, then bishop of Chester, now of London, and Dr. Stinton. He was at first in a very silent mood. Before dinner he said nothing but "Pretty baby," to one of the children. Langton said very well to me afterwards, that he could repeat Johnson's conversation before dinner, as Johnson had said that he could repeat a complete chapter of "The Natural History of Iceland," from the Danish of *Horrebow*, the whole of which was exactly thus:—

"CHAP. LXXII. *Concerning Snakes.*

"There are no snakes to be met with throughout the whole island."

At dinner we talked of another mode in the newspapers of giving modern characters in sentences from the classics, and of the passage—

"Parcus deorum cultor et infrequens,
Insanientis dum sapientiæ
Consultus erro, nunc retrorsum
Vela dare, atque iterare cursus
Cogor relictos—"[1]

[1] Horat. Carm. l. i. Od. 34.

being well applied to Soame Jenyns;[1] who, after having wandered in the wilds of infidelity, had returned to the Christian faith. Mr. Langton asked Johnson as to the propriety of *sapientiæ consultus*. JOHNSON: "Though *consultus* was primarily an adjective, like *amicus* it came to be used as a substantive. So we have *juris consultus*, a consult in law."

We talked of the styles of different painters, and how certainly a connoisseur could distinguish them. I asked if there was as clear a difference of styles in language as in painting, or even as in hand-writing, so that the composition of every individual may be distinguished? JOHNSON: "Yes. Those who have a style of eminent excellence, such as Dryden and Milton, can always be distinguished." I had no doubt of this; but what I wanted to know was, whether there was really a peculiar style to every man whatever, as there is certainly a peculiar hand-writing, a peculiar countenance, not widely different in many, yet always enough to be distinctive:—

"———————— facies non omnibus una,
Nec diversa tamen."[2]

The Bishop thought not; and said, he supposed that many pieces in Dodsley's collection of poems, though all very pretty, had nothing appropriated in their style, and in that particular could not be at all distinguished. JOHNSON: "Why, Sir, I think every man whatever has a peculiar style, which may be discovered by nice examination and comparison with others: but a man must write a great deal to make his style obviously discernible. As logicians say, this appropriation of style is infinite *in potestate*, limited *in actu*."

Mr. Topham Beauclerk came in the evening, and he and Dr. Johnson and I stayed to supper. It was mentioned that Dr. Dodd had once wished to be a member of the LITERARY CLUB. JOHNSON: "I should be sorry if any of our club were hanged. I will not say but some of them deserve it." BEAUCLERK (supposing this to be aimed at persons for whom he had at that time a wonderful fancy, which, however, did not last long) was irritated, and eagerly said: "You, Sir, have a friend (naming him) who

[1] Soame Jenyns was the only son of Sir Roger Jenyns, and M.P. for Cambridgeshire. His principal works are, "A Free Inquiry into the Origin of Evil," and a "View of the Internal Evidence of the Christian Religion." He was born in 1704, and died in 1787.

[2] Ovid. Met. ii. 13.

deserves to be hanged; for he speaks behind their backs against those with whom he lives on the best terms, and attacks them in the newspapers. *He* certainly ought to be *kicked*." JOHNSON: "Sir, we all do this in some degree: '*Veniam petimus damusque vicissim.*' To be sure it may be done so much, that a man may deserve to be kicked." BEAUCLERK: "He is very malignant." JOHNSON: "No, Sir; he is not malignant. He is mischievous, if you will. He would do no man an essential injury; he may, indeed, love to make sport of people by vexing their vanity. I, however, once knew an old gentleman who was absolutely malignant. He really wished evil to others, and rejoiced at it." BOSWELL: "The gentleman, Mr. Beauclerk, against whom you are so violent, is, I know, a man of good principles." BEAUCLERK: "Then he does not wear them out in practice."

Dr. Johnson (who, as I have observed before, delighted in discrimination of character, and having a masterly knowledge of human nature was willing to take men as they are, imperfect, and with a mixture of good and bad qualities,) I suppose thought he had said enough in defence of his friend, of whose merits, notwithstanding his exceptionable points, he had a just value; and added no more on the subject.

On Tuesday, April 14, I dined with him at General Oglethorpe's, with General Paoli and Mr. Langton. General Oglethorpe declaimed against luxury. JOHNSON: "Depend upon it, Sir, every state of society is as luxurious as it can be. Men always take the best they can get." OGLETHORPE: "But the best depends much upon ourselves; and if we can be as well satisfied with plain things, we are in the wrong to accustom our palates to what is high-seasoned and expensive. What says Addison in his 'Cato,' speaking of the Numidian?

> 'Coarse are his meals, the fortune of the chace;
> Amid the running stream he slakes his thirst,
> Toils all the day, and at the approach of night,
> On the first friendly bank he throws him down;
> Or rests his head upon a rock till morn;
> And if the following day he chance to find
> A new repast, or an untasted spring,
> Blesses his stars, and thinks it luxury.'

Let us have *that* kind of luxury, Sir, if you will." JOHNSON: "But hold, Sir; to be merely satisfied is not enough. It is in refinement and elegance that the civilised man differs from the savage. A great part of our industry and all our ingenuity is exercised in procuring pleasure; and, Sir, a hungry man has not the same pleasure in eating a plain dinner that a hungry man has in eating a luxurious dinner. You see I put the case fairly. A hungry man may have as much, nay, more pleasure in eating a plain dinner, than a man grown fastidious has in eating a luxurious dinner. But I suppose the man who decides between the two dinners to be equally a hungry man."

Talking of different governments,—JOHNSON: "The more contracted power is, the more easily it is destroyed. A country governed by a despot is an inverted cone. Government there cannot be so firm, as when it rests upon a broad basis gradually contracted, as the government of Great Britain, which is founded on the Parliament, then is in the privy-council, then in the king." BOSWELL: "Power, when contracted into the person of the despot, may be easily destroyed, as the prince may be cut off. So Caligula wished that the people of Rome had but one neck, that he might cut them off at a blow." OGLE-THORPE: "It was of the Senate he wished that. The Senate, by its usurpation, controlled both the emperor and the people. And don't you think that we see too much of that in our own Parliament?"

Dr. Johnson endeavoured to trace the etymology of Maccaronic verses, which he thought were of Italian invention from *maccaroni;* but on being informed that this would infer that they were the most common and easy verses, maccaroni being the most ordinary and simple food, he was at a loss: for he said, "He rather should have supposed it to import, in its primitive signification, a composition of several things;[1] for maccaronic verses are verses made out of a mixture of different languages; that is, of one language with the termination of another." I suppose we scarcely know of a language in any country where there is any learning, in which that motley ludicrous species of composition may not be found. It is particularly droll in Low Dutch. The "*Polemo-middinia*" of Drummond of Hawthornden, in which there is a jumble of many

---

[1] Dr. Johnson was right in supposing that this kind of poetry derived its name from *maccherone.* "Ars ista poetica" (says Merlin Coccaio, whose true name was Theophilo Folengo) "nuncupatur ARS MACARONICA, a *macaronibus* derivata; qui *macarones* sunt quoddam pulmentum, farinâ, caseo, butyro compaginatum, grossum, rude, et rusticanum. Ideo MACARONICA nil nisi grossedinem, ruditatem, et VOCABULAZZOS debet in se continere." (*Warton's Hist. of Eng. Poet.* ii. 357.) Folengo's true name was taken up in consequence of his having been instructed in his youth by Virago Coccaio. He died in 1544.—MALONE.

languages moulded, as if it were all in Latin, is well known. Mr. Langton made us laugh heartily at one in the Grecian mould, by Joshua Barnes, in which are to be found such comical *Anglo-hellenisms* as Κλύββοισιν ἔβανχθεν: "They were banged with clubs."

On Wednesday, April 15, I dined with Dr. Johnson at Mr. Dilly's, and was in high spirits, for I had been a good part of the morning with Mr. Orme, the able and eloquent historian of Hindostan, who expressed a great admiration of Johnson. "I do not care," said he, "on what subject Johnson talks: but I love better to hear him talk than anybody. He either gives you new thoughts or a new colouring. It is a shame to the nation that he has not been more liberally rewarded. Had I been George the Third, and thought as he did about America, I would have given Johnson three hundred a-year for his 'Taxation no Tyranny' alone." I repeated this, and Johnson was much pleased with such praise from such a man as Orme.

At Mr. Dilly's to-day were Mrs. Knowles, the ingenious Quaker lady,[1] Miss Seward, the poetess of Lichfield, the Reverend Dr. Mayo, and the Rev. Mr. Beresford, tutor to the Duke of Bedford. Before dinner Dr. Johnson seized upon Mr. Charles Sheridan's[2] "Account of the late Revolution in Sweden," and seemed to read it ravenously, as if he devoured it, which was to all appearance his method of studying. "He knows how to read better than any one," said Mrs. Knowles; "he gets at the substance of a book directly; he tears out the heart of it." He kept it wrapped up in the table-cloth in his lap during the time of dinner, from an avidity to have one entertainment in readiness, when he should have finished another; resembling (if I may use so coarse a simile) a dog who holds a bone in his paws in reserve, while he eats something else which has been thrown to him.

The subject of cookery having been very naturally introduced at a table where Johnson, who boasted of the niceness of his palate, owned that "he always found a good dinner," he said, "I could write a better book of cookery than has ever yet been written; it should be a book upon philosophical principles. Pharmacy is now made much more simple. Cookery may be made so too. A prescription, which is now compounded of five ingredients,

---

[1] Dr. Johnson, describing her needle-work in one of his letters to Mr. Thrale, uses the learned word *sutile;* which Mrs. Thrale has mistaken, and made the phrase injurious by writing "*futile* pictures."—BOSWELL.
[2] The elder brother of R. B. Sheridan, Esq. He died in 1806.—MALONE.

had formerly fifty in it. So in cookery, if the nature of the ingredients be well known, much fewer will do. Then, as you cannot make bad meat good, I would tell what is the best butcher's meat, the best beef, the best pieces: how to choose young fowls; the proper seasons of different vegetables; and then how to roast and boil, and compound." DILLY: "Mrs. Glasse's 'Cookery,' which is the best, was written by Dr. Hill. Half the *trade*[1] know this." JOHNSON: "Well, Sir, this shows how much better the subject of cookery may be treated by a philosopher. I doubt if the book be written by Dr. Hill; for, in Mrs. Glasse's 'Cookery,' which I have looked into, saltpetre and sal-prunella are spoken of as different substances, whereas sal-prunella is only saltpetre burnt on charcoal; and Hill could not be ignorant of this. However, as the greatest part of such a book is made by transcription, this mistake may have been carelessly adopted. But you shall see what a book of cookery I shall make? I shall agree with Mr. Dilly for the copyright." MISS SEWARD: "That would be Hercules with the distaff indeed." JOHNSON: "No, Madam. Women can spin very well; but they cannot make a good book of cookery."

JOHNSON: "Oh! Mr. Dilly—you must know that an English Benedictine Monk at Paris has translated 'The Duke of Berwick's Memoirs,' from the original French, and has sent them to me to sell. I offered them to Strahan, who sent them back with this answer:—'That the first book he had published was the Duke of Berwick's Life, by which he had lost: and he hated the name.'—Now I honestly tell you that Strahan has refused them; but I also honestly tell you, that he did it upon no principle, for he never looked into them." DILLY: "Are they well translated, Sir?" JOHNSON: "Why, Sir, very well—in a style very current and very clear. I have written to the Benedictine to give me an answer upon two points:—What evidence is there that the letters are authentic? (for if they are not authentic they are nothing);—And how long will it be before the original French is published? For if the French edition is not to appear for a considerable time, the translation will be almost as valuable as an original book. They will make two volumes in octavo; and I have undertaken to correct every sheet as it comes from the press." Mr. Dilly desired to see them, and said he would send for them.

---

[1] As Physicians are called *the Faculty*, the Counsellors at Law *the Profession*, the Booksellers of London are denominated *the Trade*. Johnson disapproved of these denominations.—BOSWELL.

He asked Dr. Johnson if he would write a preface for them. JOHNSON: "No, Sir. The Benedictines were very kind to me, and I'll do what I undertook to do; but I will not mingle my name with them. I am to gain nothing by them. I'll turn them loose upon the world, and let them take their chance." DR. MAYO: "Pray, Sir, are Ganganelli's letters authentic?" JOHNSON: "No, Sir. Voltaire put the same question to the editor of them that I did to Macpherson—Where are the originals?"

Mrs. Knowles affected to complain that men had much more liberty allowed them than women. JOHNSON: "Why, Madam, women have all the liberty they should wish to have. We have all the labour and the danger, and the women all the advantage. We go to sea, we build houses, we do everything, in short, to pay our court to the women." MRS. KNOWLES: "The Doctor reasons very wittily, but not convincingly. Now, take the instance of building; the mason's wife, if she is ever seen in liquor, is ruined; the mason may get himself drunk as often as he pleases, with little loss of character; nay, may let his wife and children starve." JOHNSON: "Madam, you must consider, if the mason does get himself drunk, and let his wife and children starve, the parish will oblige him to find security for their maintenance. We have different modes of restraining evil. Stocks for the men, a ducking-stool for women, and a pound for beasts. If we require more perfection from women than from ourselves, it is doing them honour. And women have not the same temptations that we have; they may always live in virtuous company; men must mix in the world indiscriminately. If a woman has no inclination to do what is wrong, being secured from it is no restraint to her. I am at liberty to walk into the Thames; but if I were to try it, my friends would restrain me in Bedlam, and I should be obliged to them." MRS. KNOWLES: "Still, Doctor, I cannot help thinking it a hardship that more indulgence is allowed to men than to women. It gives a superiority to men, to which I do not see how they are entitled." JOHNSON: "It is plain, Madam, one or other must have the superiority. As Shakespeare says, 'If two men ride on a horse, one must ride behind.'" DILLY: "I suppose, Sir, Mrs. Knowles would have them ride in panniers, one on each side." JOHNSON: "Then, Sir, the horse would throw them both." MRS. KNOWLES: "Well, I hope that in another world the sexes will be equal." BOSWELL: "That is being too ambitious, Madam. We might as well desire to be equal with the angels. We shall all, I hope, be happy in a future state, but we must not expect to be all happy in the same degree. It is enough, if we be happy according to our several capacities. A worthy carman will get to heaven as well as Sir Isaac Newton. Yet, though equally good, they will not have the same degree of happiness." JOHNSON: "Probably not."[1]

Upon this subject I had once before sounded him, by mentioning the late Rev. Mr. Brown of Utrecht's image; that a great and small glass, though equally full, did not hold an equal quantity; which he threw out to refute David Hume's saying, that a little Miss, going to dance at a ball, in a fine dress, was as happy as a great orator, after having made an eloquent and applauded speech. After some thought, Johnson said, "I come over to the parson."[2] As an instance of coincidence of thinking, Mr. Dilly told me, that Dr. King, a late dissenting minister in London, said to him, upon the happiness in a future state of good men of different capacities, "A pail does not hold so much as a tub; but if it be equally full, it has no reason to complain. Every saint in heaven will have as much happiness as he can hold." Mr. Dilly thought this a clear though a familiar illustration of the phrase, "One star differeth from another in brightness."

Dr. Mayo having asked Johnson's opinion of Soame Jenyns' "View of the Internal Evidence of the Christian Religion;"—JOHNSON: "I think it a pretty book; not very theological indeed; and there seems to be an affectation of ease and carelessness, as if it were not suitable to his character to be very serious about the matter." BOSWELL: "He may have intended this to introduce his book the better among genteel people, who might be unwilling to read too grave a treatise. There is a general levity in the age. We have physicians now with bag-wigs, may we not have airy divines, at least somewhat less solemn in their appearance than they used to be?" JOHNSON: "Jenyns might mean as you say." BOSWELL: "*You* should like his book, Mrs. Knowles, as it maintains, as your *friends* do, that courage is not a Christian virtue." MRS. KNOWLES: "Yes, indeed, I like him there; but I cannot agree with him, that friendship is not a Christian virtue." JOHNSON: "Why, Madam, strictly speaking, he is right. All friendship is preferring the interest of a friend,

---

[1] See on this question Bishop Hall's Epistles, Dec. iii. Epist. 6, "Of the different degrees of heavenly glory, and of our mutual knowledge of each other above."—MALONE.

[2] See vol. i. p. 348, where also this subject is discussed.—MALONE.

to the neglect, or, perhaps, against the interest of others;
so that an old Greek said, 'He that has *friends* has *no friend.*'
Now Christianity recommends universal benevolence,—
to consider all men as our brethren; which is contrary to
the virtue of friendship, as described by the ancient
philosophers.   Surely, Madam, your sect must approve of
this; for you call all men *friends.*"   MRS. KNOWLES: "We
are commanded to do good to all men, 'but especially to
them who are of the household of Faith.'"   JOHNSON:
"Well, Madam, the household of Faith is wide enough."
MRS. KNOWLES: "But, Doctor, our Saviour had twelve
Apostles, yet there was *one* whom he *loved.* John was
called 'the disciple whom Jesus loved.'"   JOHNSON (with
eyes sparkling benignantly): "Very well, indeed, Madam.
You have said very well."   BOSWELL: "A fine application.
Pray, Sir, had you ever thought of it?"   JOHNSON: "I
had not, Sir."

From this pleasing subject, he, I know not how or why,
made a sudden transition to one upon which he was a
violent aggressor; for he said, "I am willing to love all
mankind, *except an American;*" and his inflammable
corruption bursting into horrid fire, he, "breathed out
threatenings and slaughter;" calling them, "Rascals—
robbers—pirates;" and exclaiming, he'd "burn and destroy
them."   Miss Seward, looking to him with mild but steady
astonishment, said, "Sir, this is an instance that we are
always most violent against those whom we have injured."
—He was irritated still more by this delicate and keen
reproach; and roared out another tremendous volley,
which one might fancy could be heard across the Atlantic.
During this tempest I sat in great uneasiness, lamenting
his heat of temper, till, by degrees, I diverted his attention
to other topics.

DR. MAYO (to Dr. Johnson): "Pray, Sir, have you read
Edwards, of New England, on Grace?"   JOHNSON: "No,
Sir."   BOSWELL: "It puzzled me so much as to the freedom
of the human will, by stating, with wonderful acute
ingenuity, our being actuated by a series of motives which
we cannot resist, that the only relief I had was to, forget
it."   MAYO: "But he makes the proper distinction between
moral and physical necessity."   BOSWELL: "Alas, Sir,
they come both to the same thing. You may be bound
as hard by chains when covered by leather as when the
iron appears.   The argument for the moral necessity of
human actions is always, I observe, fortified by supposing
universal prescience to be one of the attributes of the
Deity."   JOHNSON: "You are surer that you are free, than

you are of prescience; you are surer that you can lift up your finger or not as you please, than you are of any conclusion from a deduction of reasoning. But let us consider a little the objection from prescience. It is certain I am either to go home to-night or not; that does not prevent my freedom." BOSWELL: "That it is certain you are *either* to go home or not, does not prevent your freedom: because the liberty of choice between the two is compatible with that certainty. But if *one* of these events be certain *now*, you have no *future* power of volition. If it be certain you are to go home to-night, you *must* go home." JOHNSON: "If I am well acquainted with a man, I can judge with great probability how he will act in any case, without his being restrained by my judging. GOD may have this probability increased to certainty." BOSWELL: "When it is increased to *certainty*, freedom ceases, because that cannot be certainly foreknown, which is not certain at the time; but if it be certain at the time, it is a contradiction in terms to maintain that there can be afterwards any *contingency* dependant upon the exercise of will or anything else." JOHNSON: "All theory is against the freedom of the will: all experience for it."—I did not push the subject any farther. I was glad to find him so mild in discussing a question of the most abstract nature, involved with theological tenets, which he generally would not suffer to be in any degree opposed.[1]

He, as usual, defended luxury: "You cannot spend money in luxury without doing good to the poor. Nay, you do more good to them by spending it in luxury—you make them exert industry; whereas, by giving it, you keep them idle. I own, indeed, there may be more virtue in giving it immediately in charity, than in spending it in luxury; though there may be pride in that too." Miss Seward asked, if this was not Mandeville's doctrine of "private vices public benefits."[2] JOHNSON: "The fallacy of that book is, that Mandeville defines neither vices nor benefits. He reckons among vices everything that gives pleasure. He takes the narrowest system of morality, monastic morality, which holds pleasure itself to be a

---

[1] If any of my readers are disturbed by this thorny question, I beg leave to recommend to them Letter 69, of Montesquieu's *Lettres Persanes*; and the late Mr. John Palmer of Islington's Answer to Dr. Priestley's mechanical arguments for what he absurdly calls "Philosophical necessity."—BOSWELL.

[2] Bernard Mandeville was a Dutch physician, born at Dort, about 1670; but he eventually settled in London, and published a variety of works, the principal of which is "The Fable of the Bees, or Private Vices made Public Benefits." He died in 1733.—ED.

vice, such as eating salt with our fish, because it makes it eat better; and he reckons wealth as a public benefit, which is by no means always true. Pleasure of itself is not a vice. Having a garden, which we all know to be perfectly innocent, is a great pleasure. At the same time, in this state of being there are many pleasures vices, which, however, are so immediately agreeable that we can hardly abstain from them. The happiness of heaven will be, that pleasure and virtue will be perfectly consistent. Mandeville puts the case of a man who gets drunk at an ale-house; and says it is a public benefit, because so much money is got by it to the public. But it must be considered, that all the good gained by this, through the gradation of alehouse-keeper, brewer, maltster, and farmer, is over-balanced by the evil caused to the man and his family by his getting drunk. This is the way to try what is vicious, by ascertaining whether more evil than good is produced by it upon the whole, which is the case in all vice. It may happen that good is produced by vice, but not as vice; for instance, a robber may take money from its owner, and give it to one who will make a better use of it. Here is good produced; but not by the robbery as robbery, but as translation of property. I read Mandeville forty, or, I believe, fifty years ago. He did not puzzle me; he opened my views into real life very much. No; it is clear that the happiness of society depends on virtue. In Sparta, theft was allowed by general consent: theft, therefore, was *there* not a crime, but then there was no security; and what a life must they have had, when there was no security. Without truth there must be a dissolution of society. As it is, there is so little truth, that we are almost afraid to trust our ears; but how should we be, if falsehood were multiplied ten times! Society is held together by communication and information; and I remember this remark of Sir Thomas Brown's, 'Do the devils lie? No; for then hell could not subsist.'"

Talking of Miss Hannah More, a literary lady, he said, "I was obliged to speak to Miss Reynolds, to let her know that I desired she would not flatter me so much." Somebody now observed, "She flatters Garrick." JOHNSON: "She is in the right to flatter Garrick. She is in the right for two reasons; first, because she has the world with her, who have been praising Garrick these thirty years; and secondly, because she is rewarded for it by Garrick. Why should she flatter *me* ? I can do nothing for her. Let her carry her praise to a better market. (Then turning to Mrs. Knowles): "You, Madam, have been flattering me all the evening; I wish you would give Boswell a little now. If you knew his merit as well as I do, you would say a great deal; he is the best travelling companion in the world."

Somebody mentioned the Rev. Mr. Mason's prosecution of Mr. Murray, the bookseller, for having inserted in a collection of "Gray's Poems," only fifty lines, of which Mr. Mason had still the exclusive property, under the statute of Queen Anne; and that Mr. Mason had persevered, notwithstanding his being requested to name his own terms of compensation.[1] Johnson signified his displeasure at Mr. Mason's conduct very strongly; but added, by way of showing that he was not surprised at it, "Mason's a Whig." MRS. KNOWLES (not hearing distinctly): "What! a prig, Sir?" JOHNSON: "Worse, Madam; a Whig! But he is both."

I expressed a horror at the thought of death. MRS. KNOWLES: "Nay, thou shouldst not have a horror for what is the gate of life." JOHNSON (standing upon the hearth rolling about, with a serious, solemn, and somewhat gloomy air): "No rational man can die without uneasy apprehension." MRS. KNOWLES: "The Scriptures tell us, 'The righteous shall have *hope* in his death.'" JOHNSON: "Yes, Madam; that is, he shall not have despair. But, consider, his hope of salvation must be founded on the terms on which it is promised that the mediation of our SAVIOUR shall be applied to us,—namely, obedience; and where obedience has failed, then, as suppletory to it, repentance. But what man can say that his obedience has been such as he would approve of in another, or even in himself upon close examination, or that his repentance has not been such as to require being repented of? No man can be sure that his obedience and repentence will obtain salvation." MRS. KNOWLES: "But divine intimation of acceptance may be made to the soul." JOHNSON: "Madam, it may; but I should not think the better of a man who should tell me, on his death-bed, he was sure of salvation. A man cannot be sure himself that he has divine intimation of acceptance; much less can he make others sure that he has it." BOSWELL: "Then, Sir, we must be contented to acknowledge that death is a terrible thing." JOHNSON: "Yes, Sir. I have made no approaches to a state which can look on it as not terrible." MRS. KNOWLES (seeming to enjoy a pleasing serenity in the persuasion of benignant

[1] See "A Letter to W. Mason, A.M., from J. Murray, bookseller in London," 2d. edit. p. 20.—BOSWELL.

divine light): "Does not St. Paul say, 'I have fought the good fight of faith, I have finished my course; henceforth is laid up for me a crown of life?'" JOHNSON: "Yes, Madam; but here was a man inspired, a man who had been converted by supernatural interposition." BOSWELL: "In prospect death is dreadful; but in fact we find that people die easy." JOHNSON: "Why, Sir, most people have not *thought* much of the matter, so cannot *say* much, and it is supposed they die easy. Few believe it certain they are then to die; and those who do, set themselves to behave with resolution, as a man does who is going to be hanged:—he is not the less unwilling to be hanged." MISS SEWARD: "There is one mode of the fear of death, which is certainly absurd: and that is the dread of annihilation, which is only a pleasing sleep without a dream." JOHNSON: "It is neither pleasing nor sleep; it is nothing. Now mere existence is so much better than nothing, that one would rather exist even in pain, than not exist." BOSWELL: "If annihilation be nothing, then existing in pain is not a comparative state, but is a positive evil, which I cannot think we should choose. I must be allowed to differ here; and it would lessen the hope of a future state founded on the argument, that the Supreme Being, who is good as he is great, will here-after compensate for our present sufferings in this life. For if existence, such as we have it here, be com-paratively a good, we have no reason to complain, though no more of it should be given to us. But if our only state of existence were in this world, then we might with some reason complain that we are so dissatisfied with our enjoyments compared with our desires." JOHNSON: "The lady confounds annihilation, which is nothing, with the apprehension of it, which is dreadful. It is in the apprehension of it that the horror of annihilation consists."

Of John Wesley, he said, "He can talk well on any subject." BOSWELL: "Pray, Sir, what has he made of his story of the ghost?" JOHNSON: "Why, Sir, he believes it; but not on sufficient authority. He did not take time enough to examine the girl. It was at Newcastle, where the ghost was said to have appeared to a young woman several times, mentioning something about the right to an old house, advising application to be made to an attorney, which was done; and, at the same time, saying the attorney would do nothing, which proved to be the fact. 'This,' says John, 'is a proof that a ghost knows our thoughts.' Now (laughing) it is not necessary to know our thoughts, to tell that an attorney will sometimes do nothing. Charles Wesley, who is a more stationary man, does not believe the story. I am sorry that John did not take more pains to inquire into the evidence for it." Miss Seward (with an incredulous smile): "What, Sir, about a ghost?" Johnson (with solemn vehemence): "Yes, Madam; this is a question which, after five thousand years, is yet undecided: a question, whether in theology or philosophy, one of the most important that can come before the human understanding."

Mrs. Knowles mentioned, as a proselyte to Quakerism, Miss [—— ——,] a young lady well known to Dr. Johnson, for whom he had shown much affection; while she ever had, and still retained, a great respect for him. Mrs. Knowles at the same time took an opportunity of letting him know "that the amiable young creature was sorry at finding that he was offended at her leaving the Church of England and embracing a simpler faith;" and, in the gentlest and most persuasive manner, solicited his kind indulgence for what was sincerely a matter of conscience. Johnson (frowning very angrily): "Madam, she is an odious wench. She could not have any proper conviction that it was her duty to change her religion, which is the most important of all subjects, and should be studied with all care, and with all the helps we can get. She knew no more of the Church which she left, and that which she embraced, than she did of the difference between the Copernican and Ptolemaic systems." Mrs. Knowles: "She had the New Testament before her." Johnson: "Madam, she could not understand the New Testament, the most difficult book in the world, for which the study of a life is required." Mrs. Knowles: "It is clear as to essentials." Johnson: "But not as to controversial points. The heathens were easily converted, because they had nothing to give up; but we ought not, without very strong conviction indeed, to desert the religion in which we have been educated. That is the religion given you, the religion in which it may be said Providence has placed you. If you live conscientiously in that religion, you may be safe. But error is dangerous indeed, if you err when you choose a religion for yourself." Mrs. Knowles: "Must we then go by implicit faith?" Johnson: "Why, Madam, the greatest part of our knowledge is implicit faith; and as to religion, have we heard all that a disciple of Confucius, all that a Mahometan, can say for himself?" He then rose again into a passion, and attacked the young proselyte in the severest terms of reproach, so that both ladies seemed to be much shocked.[1]

We remained together till it was pretty late. Notwithstanding occasional explosions of violence, we were all delighted upon the whole with Johnson. I compared him at this time to a warm West Indian climate, where you have a bright sun, quick vegetation, luxuriant foliage, luscious fruits; but where the same heat sometimes produces thunder, lightning, earthquakes, in a terrible degree.

April 17, being Good Friday, I waited on Johnson, as usual. I observed at breakfast, that although it was a part of his abstemious discipline, on this most solemn fast, to take no milk in his tea, yet when Mrs. Desmoulins inadvertently poured it in, he did not reject it. I talked of the strange indecision of mind, and imbecility in the common occurrences of life, which we may observe in some people. JOHNSON: "Why, Sir, I am in the habit of getting others to do things for me." BOSWELL: "What, Sir! have you that weakness?" JOHNSON: "Yes, Sir. But I always think afterwards I should have done better for myself."

I told him that at a gentleman's house, where there was thought to be such extravagance or bad management that he was living much beyond his income, his lady had objected to the cutting of a pickled mango, and that I had taken an opportunity to ask the price of it, and found that it was only two shillings; so here was a very poor saving. JOHNSON: "Sir, that is the blundering economy of a narrow understanding. It is stopping one hole in a sieve."

I expressed some inclination to publish an account of my Travels upon the continent of Europe, for which I had

---

[1] Mrs. Knowles, not satisfied with the fame of her needlework, the "*sutile pictures*" mentioned by Johnson, in which she has indeed displayed much dexterity, nay, with the fame of reasoning better than women generally do, as I have fairly shown her to have done, communicated to me a Dialogue of considerable length, which, after many years had elapsed, she wrote down as having passed between Dr. Johnson and her at this interview. As I had not the least recollection of it, and did not find the smallest trace of it in my *Record* taken at the time, I could not in consistency with my firm regard to authenticity, insert it in my work. It has, however, been published in "The Gentleman's Magazine," for June, 1791. It chiefly relates to the principles of the sect called *Quakers;* and no doubt the lady appears to have greatly the advantage of Dr. Johnson in argument as well as expression. From what I have now stated, and from the internal evidence of the paper itself, any one who may have the curiosity to peruse it, will judge whether it was wrong in me to reject it, however willing to gratify Mrs. Knowles.— BOSWELL.

a variety of materials collected.   JOHNSON: "I do not say, Sir, you may not publish your travels; but I give you my opinion, that you would lessen yourself by it.   What can you tell of countries so well known as those upon the continent of Europe, which you have visited?"   BOSWELL: "But I can give an entertaining narrative, with many incidents, anecdotes, *jeux d'esprit*, and remarks, so as to make very pleasant reading."   JOHNSON: "Why, Sir, most modern travellers in Europe who have published their travels, have been laughed at: I would not have you added to the number.[1]   The world is now not contented to be merely entertained by a traveller's narrative; they want to learn something.   Now some of my friends asked me, why I did not give some account of my travels in France.   The reason is plain: intelligent readers had seen more of France than I had.   *You* might have liked my travels in France, and THE CLUB might have liked them; but, upon the whole, there would have been more ridicule than good produced by them."   BOSWELL: "I cannot agree with you, Sir.   People would like to read what you say of anything.   Suppose a face has been painted by fifty painters before; still we love to see it done by Sir Joshua."   JOHNSON: "True, Sir, but Sir Joshua cannot paint a face when he has not time to look on it."   BOSWELL: "Sir, a sketch of any sort by him is valuable.   And, Sir, to talk to you in your own style (raising my voice and shaking my head), you *should* have given us your Travels in France.   I am *sure* I am right, and *there's an end on't.*"

I said to him that it was certainly true, as my friend Dempster had observed in his letter to me upon the subject, that a great part of what was in his "Journey to the Western Islands of Scotland" had been in his mind before he left London.   JOHNSON: "Why yes, Sir, the topics were; and books of travels will be good in proportion to what a man has previously in his mind; his knowing what to observe; his power of contrasting one mode of life with another.   As the Spanish proverb says, 'He who would bring home the wealth of the Indies must carry the wealth of the Indies with him.'   So it is in travelling: a man must carry knowledge with him, if he would bring home knowledge."   BOSWELL: "The proverb, I suppose, Sir, means he must carry a large stock with him to trade with."   JOHNSON: "Yes, Sir."

---

[1] I believe, however, I shall follow my own opinion; for the world has shown a very flattering partiality to my writings on many occasions. —BOSWELL.

It was a delightful day.   As we walked to St. Clement's Church, I again remarked that Fleet-street was the most cheerful scene in the world.   "Fleet-street," said I, "is in my mind more delightful than Tempé."   JOHNSON: "Ay, Sir; but let it be compared with Mull."

There was a very numerous congregation to-day at St. Clement's Church, which Dr. Johnson said he observed with pleasure.

CHAPTER XI.—1778

AND now I am to give a pretty full account of one of the most curious incidents in Johnson's life, of which he himself has made the following minute on this day:—" In my return from church I was accosted by Edwards, an old fellow-collegian, who had not seen me since 1729. He knew me, and asked if I remembered one Edwards; I did not at first recollect the name, but gradually, as we walked along, recovered it, and told him a conversation that had passed at an alehouse between us. My purpose is to continue our acquaintance."[1]

It was in Butcher-row that this meeting happened. Mr. Edwards, who was a decent-looking elderly man in grey clothes, and a wig of many curls, accosted Johnson with familiar confidence, knowing who he was, while Johnson returned his salutation with a courteous formality, as to a stranger. But as soon as Edwards had brought to his recollection their having been at Pembroke College together nine-and-forty years ago, he seemed much pleased, asked where he lived, and said he should be glad to see him in Bolt-court. EDWARDS: "Ah, Sir! we are old men now." JOHNSON (who never liked to think of being old): "Don't let us discourage one another." EDWARDS: "Why,

---

[1] "Prayers and Meditations," p. 164.— BOSWELL.

Doctor, you look stout and hearty, I am happy to see you so; for the newspapers told us you were very ill." JOHNSON: "Ah, Sir, they are always telling lies of *us old fellows.*"

Wishing to be present at more of so singular a conversation as that between two fellow-collegians, who had lived forty years in London without ever having chanced to meet, I whispered to Mr. Edwards that Dr. Johnson was going home, and that he had better accompany him now. So Edwards walked along with us, I eagerly assisting to keep up the conversation. Mr. Edwards informed Dr. Johnson that he had practised long as a solicitor in Chancery, but that he now lived in the country upon a little farm, about sixty acres, just by Stevenage in Hertfordshire, and that he came to London, (to Barnard's Inn, No. 6) generally twice a week. Johnson appearing to me in a reverie, Mr. Edwards addressed himself to me, and expatiated on the pleasure of living in the country. BOSWELL: "I have no notion of this, Sir. What you have to entertain you, is, I think, exhausted in half an hour." EDWARDS: "What! don't you love to have hope realised? I see my grass, and my corn, and my trees growing. Now, for instance, I am curious to see if this frost has not nipped my fruit trees." JOHNSON (who we did not imagine was attending): "You find, Sir, you have fears as well as hopes." So well did he see the whole, when another saw but the half of a subject.

When we got to Dr. Johnson's house, and were seated in his library, the dialogue went on admirably. EDWARDS: "Sir, I remember you would not let us say *prodigious* at College. For even then, Sir (turning to me), he was delicate in language, and we all feared him.[1] JOHNSON (to Edwards): "From your having practised the law long, Sir, I presume you must be rich." EDWARDS: No, Sir, I got a good deal of money; but I had a number of poor relations to whom I gave great part of it." JOHNSON: "Sir, you have been rich in the most valuable sense of the word." EDWARDS: "But I shall not die rich." JOHNSON: "Nay, sure, Sir, it is better to *live* rich, than to *die* rich." EDWARDS: "I wish I had continued at College." JOHNSON: "Why do you wish that, Sir?" EDWARDS: "Because I think I should have had a much easier life than mine has been. I should have been a parson, and had a good living, like Bloxham and several others, and lived comfortably."

---

[1] Johnson said to me afterwards, "Sir, they respected me for literature; and yet it was not great but by comparison. Sir, it is amazing how little literature there is in the world."—BOSWELL.

JOHNSON: "Sir, the life of a parson, of a conscientious clergyman, is not easy. I have always considered a clergyman as the father of a larger family than he is able to maintain. I would rather have Chancery suits upon my hands than the cure of souls. No, Sir, I do not envy a clergyman's life as an easy life, nor do I envy the clergyman who makes it an easy life." Here taking himself up all of a sudden, he exclaimed, "Oh, Mr. Edwards! I'll convince you that I recollect you. Do you remember our drinking together at an alehouse near Pembroke-gate? At that time you told me of the Eton boy, who, when verses on our SAVIOUR's turning water into wine were prescribed as an exercise, brought up a single line, which was highly admired:—

'Vidit et erubuit lympha pudica DEUM.'[1]

And I told you of another fine line in 'Camden's Remains,' an eulogy upon one of our kings, who was succeeded by his son, a prince of equal merit:—

'Mira cano, Sol occubuit, nox nulla secuta est.'"

EDWARDS: "You are a philosopher, Dr. Johnson. I have tried too in my time to be a philosopher; but I don't know how, cheerfulness was always breaking in."—Mr. Burke, Sir Joshua Reynolds, Mr. Courtenay, Mr. Malone, and, indeed, all the eminent men to whom I have mentioned this, have thought it an excellent trait of character. The truth is, that philosophy, like religion, is too generally supposed to be hard and severe, at least so grave as to exclude all gaiety.

EDWARDS: "I have been twice married, Doctor. You, I suppose, have never known what it was to have a wife."

JOHNSON: "Sir, I have known what it was to have a wife,

---

[1] This line has frequently been attributed to Dryden, when a King's Scholar at Westminster. But neither Eton nor Westminster have in truth any claim to it, the line being borrowed, with a slight change (as Mr. Bindley has observed to me), from an Epigram by Crashaw, which was published in his EPIGRAMMATA SACRA, first printed at Cambridge without the author's name, in 1634, 8vo.—The original is much more elegant than the copy, the water being personified, and the word on which the point of the Epigram turns being reserved to the close of the line:—

"JOANN. 2.—*Aquæ in vinum versæ*
Unde rubor vestris et non sua purpura lymphis?
Quæ rosa mirantes tam nova mutat aquas?
Numen, convivæ, præsens agnoscite numen,
Nympha pudica DEUM vidit, et *erubuit*."—MALONE.

and (in a solemn, tender, faltering tone) I have known what it was to *lose a wife*.—I had almost broke my heart."

EDWARDS: "How do you live, Sir? For my part I must have my regular meals, and a glass of good wine. I find I require it." JOHNSON: "I now drink no wine, Sir. Early in life I drank wine: for many years I drank none. I then for some years drank a great deal." EDWARDS: "Some hogsheads, I warrant you." JOHNSON: "I then had a severe illness, and left it off, and I have never begun it again. I never felt any difference upon myself from eating one thing rather than another. There are people, I believe, who feel a difference; but I am not one of them. And as to regular meals, I have fasted from the Sunday's dinner to the Tuesday's dinner without any inconvenience. I believe it is best to eat just as one is hungry: but a man who is in business, or a man who has a family, must have stated meals. I am a straggler. I may leave this town and go to Grand Cairo, without being missed here or observed there." EDWARDS: "Don't you eat supper, Sir?" JOHNSON: "No, Sir." EDWARDS: "For my part, now, I consider supper as a turnpike through which one must pass, in order to get to bed." [1]

JOHNSON: "You are a lawyer, Mr. Edwards. Lawyers know life practically. A bookish man should always have them to converse with. They have what he wants." EDWARDS: "I am grown old: I am sixty-five." JOHNSON: "I shall be sixty-eight next birthday. Come, Sir, drink water, and put in for a hundred."

Mr. Edwards mentioned a gentleman who had left his whole fortune to Pembroke College. JOHNSON: "Whether to leave one's whole fortune to a college be right, must depend upon circumstances. I would leave the interest of a fortune I bequeathed to a college to my relations or my friends for their lives. It is the same thing to a college, which is a permanent society, whether it gets the money now or twenty years hence; and I would wish to make my relations or friends feel the benefit of it."

This interview confirmed my opinion of Johnson's most humane and benevolent heart. His cordial and placid behaviour to an old fellow-collegian, a man so different from himself, and his telling him that he would go down to his farm and visit him, showed a kindness of disposition very rare at an advanced age. He observed, "How wonderful it was that they had both been in London

---

[1] I am not absolutely sure but this was my own suggestion, though it is truly in the character of Edwards.—BOSWELL.

forty years, without having ever once met, and both walkers in the street too!" Mr. Edwards, when going away, again recurred to his consciousness of senility, and looking full in Johnson's face, said to him, "You'll find in Dr. Young,

> 'O my coevals! remnants of yourselves.'"

Johnson did not relish this at all; but shook his head with impatience. Edwards walked off seemingly highly pleased with the honour of having been thus noticed by Dr. Johnson. When he was gone I said to Johnson, I thought him but a weak man. Johnson: "Why, yes, Sir. Here is a man who has passed through life without experience: yet I would rather have him with me than a more sensible man who will not talk readily. This man is always willing to say what he has to say." Yet Dr. Johnson had himself by no means that willingness which he praised so much, and I think so justly; for who has not felt the painful effect of the dreary void, when there is a total silence in a company, for any length of time; or, which is as bad, or perhaps worse, when the conversation is with difficulty kept up by a perpetual effort?

Johnson once observed to me, "Tom Tyers described me the best: 'Sir,' said he, 'you are like a ghost: you never speak till you are spoken to.'"

The gentleman whom he thus familiarly mentioned, was Mr. Thomas Tyers, son of Mr. Jonathan Tyers, the founder of that excellent place of public amusement, Vauxhall Gardens, which must ever be an estate to its proprietor, as it is peculiarly adapted to the taste of the English nation; there being a mixture of curious show— gay exhibition—music, vocal and instrumental, not too refined for the general ear; for all which only a shilling is paid;[1] and, though last not least, good eating and drinking for those who choose to purchase that regale. Mr. Thomas Tyers was bred to the law; but having a handsome fortune, vivacity of temper, and eccentricity of mind, he could not confine himself to the regularity of practice. He therefore ran about the world with a pleasant carelessness, amusing everybody by his desultory conversation. He abounded

---

[1] In summer 1792, additional and more expensive decorations having been introduced, the price of admission was raised to 2s. I cannot approve of this. The company may be more select; but a number of the honest commonalty are, I fear, excluded from sharing in elegant and innocent entertainment. An attempt to abolish the shilling gallery at the playhouse has been very properly counteracted.—Boswell.

in anecdote, but was not sufficiently attentive to accuracy. I therefore cannot venture to avail myself much of a biographical sketch of Johnson which he published, being one among the various persons ambitious of appending their names to that illustrious friend. That sketch is, however, an entertaining little collection of fragments. Those which he published of Pope and Addison are of higher merit; but his fame must chiefly rest upon his "Political Conferences," in which he introduces several eminent persons delivering their sentiments in the way of dialogue, and discovers a considerable share of learning, various knowledge, and discernment of character. This much may I be allowed to say of a man who was exceedingly obliging to me, and who lived with Dr. Johnson in as easy a manner as almost any of his very numerous acquaintance.

Mr. Edwards had said to me aside, that Dr. Johnson should have been of a profession. I repeated the remark to Johnson, that I might have his own thoughts on the subject. JOHNSON: "Sir, it *would* have been better that I had been of a profession. I ought to have been a lawyer." BOSWELL: "I do not think, Sir, it would have been better, for we should not have had the English Dictionary." JOHNSON: "But you would have had Reports." BOSWELL: "Ay; but there would not have been another who could have written the Dictionary. There would have been many very good judges. Suppose you had been Lord Chancellor; you would have delivered opinions with more extent of mind, and in a more ornamented manner, than perhaps any Chancellor ever did, or ever will do. But, I believe, causes have been as judiciously decided as you could have done." JOHNSON: "Yes, Sir. Property has been as well settled."

Johnson, however, had a noble ambition floating in his mind, and had, undoubtedly, often speculated on the possibility of his supereminent powers being rewarded in this great and liberal country by the highest honours of the state. Sir William Scott informs me, that upon the death of the late Lord Lichfield, who was Chancellor of the University of Oxford, he said to Johnson, "What a pity it is, Sir, that you did not follow the profession of the law. You might have been Lord Chancellor of Great Britain, and attained to the dignity of the peerage; and now that the title of Lichfield, your native city, is extinct, you might have had it." Johnson, upon this, seemed much agitated; and, in an angry tone, exclaimed, "Why will you vex me by suggesting this, when it is too late?"

But he did not repine at the prosperity of others. The

late Dr. Thomas Leland told Mr. Courtenay, that when
Mr. Edmund Burke showed Johnson his fine house and
lands near Beaconsfield,[1] Johnson coolly said, "*Non
equidem invideo ; miror magis.*"[2]

Yet no man had a higher notion of the dignity of literature than Johnson, or was more determined in maintaining
the respect which he justly considered as due to it.   Of this,
besides the general tenor of his conduct in society, some
characteristical instances may be mentioned.

He told Sir Joshua Reynolds, that once when he dined
in a numerous company of booksellers, where the room
being small, the head of the table, at which he sat, was
almost close to the fire, he persevered in suffering a great
deal of inconvenience from the heat, rather than quit his
place, and let one of them sit above him.

Goldsmith, in his diverting simplicity, complained one
day, in a mixed company, of Lord Camden.   "I met him,"
said he, "at Lord Clare's house in the country, and he took
no more notice of me than if I had been an ordinary man."
The company having laughed heartily, Johnson stood forth
in defence of his friend.   "Nay, gentlemen," said he, "Dr.
Goldsmith is in the right.   A nobleman ought to have
made up to such a man as Goldsmith; and I think it is
much against Lord Camden that he neglected him."

Nor could he patiently endure to hear, that such respect
as he thought due only to higher intellectual qualities
should be bestowed on men of slighter, though perhaps more

---

[1] In the county of Bucks, about five miles from High Wycombe.   It
is considered as one of the most healthy situations in the kingdom.

[2] I am not entirely without suspicion that Johnson may have felt a
little momentary envy; for no man loved the good things of this life
better than he did; and he could not but be conscious that he deserved
a much larger share of them than he ever had.   I attempted in a newspaper to comment on the above passage in the manner of Warburton,
who must be allowed to have shown uncommon ingenuity in giving to
any author's text whatever meaning he chose it should carry.   As this
imitation may amuse my readers, I shall here introduce it:—

"No saying of Dr. Johnson's has been more misunderstood than his
applying to Mr. Burke, when he first saw him at his fine place at Beaconsfield, *Non equidem invideo; miror magis.*   These two celebrated men had
been friends for many years before Mr. Burke entered on his parliamentary career.   They were both writers, both members of the Literary
Club; when, therefore, Dr. Johnson saw Mr. Burke in a situation so much
more splendid than that to which he himself had attained, he did not
mean to express that he thought it a disproportionate prosperity; but
while he, as a philosopher, asserted an exemption from envy, *non equidem
invideo*, he went on in the words of the poet, *miror magis*; thereby signifying either that he was occupied in admiring what he was glad to see;
or, perhaps, that considering the general lot of men of superior abilities,
he wondered that Fortune, who is represented as blind, should, in this
instance, have been so just."—Boswell.

amusing, talents. I told him, that one morning, when I went
to breakfast with Garrick, who was very vain of his intimacy
with Lord Camden, he accosted me thus:—"Pray now, did
you—did you meet a little lawyer turning the corner, eh?"
—"No, Sir," said I. "Pray what do you mean by the
question?"—"Why," replied Garrick, with an affected
indifference, yet as if standing on tip-toe, "Lord Camden has
this moment left me. We have had a long walk together."
JOHNSON: "Well, Sir, Garrick talked very properly. Lord
Camden *was* a *little lawyer* to be associated so familiarly
with a player."

Sir Joshua Reynolds observed, with great truth, that
Johnson considered Garrick to be as it were his *property*.
He would allow no man either to blame or to praise Garrick
in his presence, without contradicting him.

Having fallen into a very serious frame of mind, in which
mutual expressions of kindness passed between us, such
as would be thought too vain in me to repeat, I talked with
regret of the sad inevitable certainty that one of us must
survive the other. JOHNSON: "Yes, Sir, that is an affecting
consideration. I remember Swift, in one of his letters to
Pope, says, ' I intend to come over, that we may meet once
more; and when we must part, it is what happens to all
human beings.'" BOSWELL: "The hope that we shall see
our departed friends again must support the mind."
JOHNSON: "Why yes, Sir."[1] BOSWELL: "There is a strange
unwillingness to part with life, independent of serious fears
as to futurity. A reverend friend of ours [Dr.Percy] tells
me, that he feels an uneasiness at the thoughts of leaving
his house, his study, his books." JOHNSON: "This is foolish
in [Percy]. A man need not be uneasy on these grounds;
for, as he will retain his consciousness, he may say with the
philosopher, *Omnia mea mecum porto.*" BOSWELL: "True,
Sir; we may carry our books in our heads; but still there is
something painful in the thought of leaving for ever what
has given us pleasure. I remember, many years ago, when
my imagination was warm, and I happened to be in a
melancholy mood, it distressed me to think of going into
a state of being in which Shakespeare's poetry did not exist.
A lady whom I then much admired, a very amiable woman,
humoured my fancy, and relieved me by saying, 'The first
thing you will meet in the other world will be an elegant
copy of Shakespeare's works presented to you.'" Dr.
Johnson smiled benignantly at this, and did not appear
to disapprove of the notion.

[1] See, on the same subject, vol. i. p. 451, &c.—MALONE.

We went to St. Clement's church again in the afternoon, and then returned and drank tea and coffee in Mrs. Williams's room, Mrs. Desmoulins doing the honours of the tea-table. I observed that he would not even look at a proof-sheet of his "Life of Waller" on Good Friday.

Mr. Allen, the printer, brought a book on Agriculture,[1] which was printed, and was soon to be published. It was a very strange performance, the author having mixed in it his own thoughts upon various topics, along with his remarks on ploughing, sowing, and other farming operations. He seemed to be an absurd, profane fellow, and had introduced in his book many sneers at religion, with equal ignorance and conceit. Dr. Johnson permitted me to read some passages aloud. One was, that he resolved to work on Sunday, and did work, but he owned he felt *some* weak compunction: and he had this very curious reflection:— "I was born in the wilds of Christianity, and the briars and thorns still hang about me." Dr. Johnson could not help laughing at this ridiculous image, yet was very angry at the fellow's impiety. "However," said he, "the reviewers will make him hang himself." He, however, observed, "that formerly there might have been a dispensation obtained for working on Sunday in the time of harvest." Indeed, in ritual observances, were all the ministers of religion what they should be, and what many of them are, such a power might be wisely and safely lodged with the Church.

On Saturday, April 18, I drank tea with him. He praised the late Mr. Duncombe,[2] of Canterbury, as a pleasing man. "He used to come to me; I did not seek much after *him*. Indeed, I never sought much after anybody." Boswell: "Lord Orrery, I suppose." Johnson: "No, Sir, I never went to him but when he sent for me." Boswell: "Richardson." Johnson: "Yes, Sir; but I sought after George Psalmanazar the most. I used to go and sit with him at an alehouse in the City."

I am happy to mention another instance which I discovered of his *seeking after* a man of merit. Soon after the Honourable Daines Barrington had published his excellent "Observations on the Statutes,"[3] Johnson waited on that worthy and learned gentleman: and having told

[1] Marshall's "Minutes of Agriculture."—Chalmers.
[2] William Duncombe, Esq. He married the sister of John Hughes, the poet; was the author of two tragedies, and other ingenious productions; and died Feb. 26, 1769, aged 79.—Malone.
[3] 4to, 1766. The worthy author died many years after Johnson, March 13, 1800, aged about 74.—Malone.

him his name, courteously said, "I have read your book, Sir, with great pleasure, and wish to be better known to you." Thus began an acquaintance, which was continued with mutual regard as long as Johnson lived.

Talking of a recent seditious delinquent,[1] he said, "They should set him in the pillory, that he may be punished in a way that would disgrace him." I observed, that the pillory does not always disgrace. And I mentioned an instance of a gentleman, who I thought was not dishonoured by it. JOHNSON: "Ay, but he was, Sir. He could not mouth and strut as he used to do, after having been there. People are not willing to ask a man to their tables who has stood in the pillory."

The gentleman who had dined with us at Dr. Percy's came in. Johnson attacked the Americans with intemperate vehemence of abuse. I said something in their favour; and added that I was always sorry when he talked on that subject. This, it seems, exasperated him, though he said nothing at the time. The cloud was charged with sulphureous vapour, which was afterwards to burst in thunder.——We talked of a gentleman who was running out his fortune in London; and I said, "We must get him out of it. All his friends must quarrel with him, and that will soon drive him away." JOHNSON: "Nay, Sir, we'll send *you* to him. If your company does not drive a man out of his house, nothing will." This was a horrible shock, for which there was no visible cause. I afterwards asked him, why he had said so harsh a thing. JOHNSON: "Because, Sir, you made me angry about the Americans." BOSWELL: "But why did you not take your revenge directly?" JOHNSON (smiling): "Because, Sir, I had nothing ready. A man cannot strike till he has weapons." This was a candid and pleasant confession.

He showed me to-night his drawing-room, very genteelly fitted up; and said, "Mrs. Thrale sneered, when I talked of my having asked you and your lady to live at my house. I was obliged to tell her, that you would be in as respectable a situation in my house as in hers. Sir, the insolence of wealth will creep out." BOSWELL: "She has a little both of the insolence of wealth, and the conceit of parts." JOHNSON: "The insolence of wealth is a wretched thing; but the conceit of parts has some foundation. To be sure it should not be. But who is without it?' BOSWELL: "Yourself, Sir." JOHNSON: "Why, I play no tricks. I lay

---

[1] Horne Tooke.

no traps."   BOSWELL: "No, Sir.   You are six feet high, and you only do not stoop."

We talked of the numbers of people that sometimes have composed the household of great families.   I mentioned that there were a hundred in the family of the present Earl of Eglintoune's father.   Dr. Johnson seeming to doubt it, I began to enumerate.   "Let us see: my Lord and my Lady, two."   JOHNSON: "Nay, Sir, if you are to count by twos, you may be long enough."   BOSWELL: "But now I add two sons and seven daughters, and a servant for each, that will make twenty: so we have the fifth part already."   JOHNSON: "Very true.   You get at twenty pretty readily; but you will not so readily get farther on.   We grow to five feet pretty readily; but it is not so easy to grow to seven."

On Sunday, April 19, being Easter day, after the solemnities of the festival in St. Paul's church, I visited him but could not stay to dinner.   I expressed a wish to have the arguments for Christianity always in readiness, that my religious faith might be as firm and clear as any proposition whatever, so that I need not be under the least uneasiness, when it should be attacked.   JOHNSON: "Sir, you cannot answer all objections.   You have demonstration for a First Cause: you see He must be good as well as powerful, because there is nothing to make Him otherwise, and goodness of itself is preferable.   Yet you have against this, what is very certain, the unhappiness of human life.   This, however, gives us reason to hope for a future state of compensation, that there may be a perfect system.   But of that we are not sure, till we had a positive revelation."   I told him that his "Rasselas" had often made me unhappy; for it represented the misery of human life so well, and so convincingly to a thinking mind, that if at any time the impression wore off, and I felt myself easy, I began to suspect some delusion.

On Monday, April 20, I found him at home in the morning.   We talked of a gentleman who we apprehended was gradually involving his circumstances by bad management.   JOHNSON: "Wasting a fortune is evaporation by a thousand imperceptible means.   If it were a stream, they'd stop it.   You must speak to him.   It is really miserable.   Were he a gamester, it could be said he had hopes of winning.   Were he a bankrupt in trade, he might have grown rich; but he has neither spirit to spend, nor resolution to spare.   He does not spend fast enough to have pleasure from it.   He has the crime of prodigality, and the wretchedness of parsimony. If a man is killed in a duel, he is killed as many a one has been killed; but it is a sad thing for a man to lie down and die; to bleed to death, because he has not fortitude enough to sear the wound, or even to stitch it up."—I cannot but pause a moment to admire the fecundity of fancy, and choice of language, which in this instance, and indeed on almost all occasions, he displayed. It was well observed by Dr. Percy, now Bishop of Dromore, "The conversation of Johnson is strong and clear, and may be compared to an antique statue, where every vein and muscle is distinct and bold. Ordinary conversation resembles an inferior cast."

On Saturday, April 25, I dined with him at Sir Joshua Reynolds's, with the learned Dr. Musgrave;[1] Counsellor Leland of Ireland, son to the historian; Mrs. Cholmondeley, and some more ladies. "The Project," a new poem, was read to the company by Dr. Musgrave. JOHNSON: "Sir, it has no power. Were it not for the well-known names with which it is filled, it would be nothing: the names carry the poet, not the poet the names." MUSGRAVE: "A temporary poem always entertains us." JOHNSON: "So does an account of the criminals hanged yesterday entertain us."

He proceeded:—"Demosthenes Taylor,[2] as he was called (that is, the editor of Demosthenes), was the most silent man, the merest statue of a man that I had ever seen. I once dined in company with him, and all he said during the whole time was no more than *Richard*. How a man should say only Richard, it is not easy to imagine. But it was thus: Dr. Douglas[3] was talking of Dr. Zachary Grey, and was ascribing to him something that was written by Dr. Richard Grey.[4] So, to correct him, Taylor said (imitating his affected sententious emphasis and nod), '*Richard*.'"

[1] Samuel Musgrave, M.D., editor of "Euripides," and author of "Dissertations on the Grecian Mythology," &c.; published in 1782, after his death, by Mr. Tyrwhitt.—MALONE.

[2] This was Thomas Taylor, the learned Grecian, commonly termed "The Platonist." His translations from the Greek are very numerous; but the most important are the work of Aristotle, Plato, and Pausanias. He died in 1835.—ED.

[3] Dr. Douglas had been travelling tutor to Lord Pulteney, and afterwards obtained the Deanery of Windsor. In 1787 he was raised to the see of Carlisle, and in 1792 to that of Salisbury. He was the vindicator of Milton against the charges of plagiarism, and entered the lists against David Hume, by publishing "The Criterion; or, a Discourse on Miracles." He was born at Pittenweem, Fifeshire, in 1721, and died in 1807.—ED.

[4] They were contemporaries, and both Doctors of Divinity. Dr. Zachary Grey is well known for his edition of "Hudibras," his "Notes on Shakespeare," and his "Answer to Neale's History of the Puritans." He died in 1766, aged 79.—Dr. Richard Grey was the author of "Memoria

Mrs. Cholmondeley, in a high flow of spirits, exhibited some lively sallies of hyperbolical compliment to Johnson, with whom she had been long acquainted, and was very easy. He was quick in catching the *manner* at the moment, and answered her somewhat in the style of the hero of a romance, "Madam, you crown me with unfading laurels."

I happened, I know not how, to say that a pamphlet meant a prose piece. JOHNSON: "No, Sir. A few sheets of poetry unbound are a pamphlet,[1] as much as a few sheets of prose." MUSGRAVE: "A pamphlet may be understood to mean a poetical piece in Westminster Hall, that is, in formal language; but in common language it is understood to mean prose." JOHNSON (and here was one of the many instances of his knowing clearly and telling exactly how a thing is): "A pamphlet is understood in common language to mean prose only from this, that there is so much more prose written than poetry; as when we say a *book*, prose is understood for the same reason, though a book may as well be in poetry as in prose. We understand what is most general, and we name what is less frequent."

We talked of a lady's verses on Ireland. MISS REYNOLDS: "Have you seen them, Sir?" JOHNSON: "No, Madam; I have seen a translation from Horace, by one of her daughters. She showed it me." MISS REYNOLDS: "And how was it, Sir?" JOHNSON: "Why, very well for a young Miss's verses; that is to say, compared with excellence, nothing; but very well for the person who wrote them. I am vexed at being shown verses in that manner." MISS REYNOLDS: "But if they should be good, why not give them hearty praise?" JOHNSON: "Why, Madam, because I have not then got the better of my bad humour from having been shown them. You must consider, Madam, beforehand, they may be bad, as well as good. Nobody has a right to put another under such a difficulty that he must either hurt the person by telling the truth, or hurt himself by telling what is not true." BOSWELL: "A man often shows his writings to people of eminence, to obtain from them,

---

Technica," "A System of Ecclesiastical Law," and "A New and Easy Method of Learning Hebrew without Points." He was born in 1693, and died in 1771. Thus it was easy to confound the name of the one with the other.—ED.

[1] Dr. Johnson is here perfectly correct, and is supported by the usage of preceding writers. So in MUSARUM DELICIÆ, a collection of poems, 8vo. 1656 (the writer is speaking of Suckling's play entitled AGLAURA, printed in folio):—

"This great voluminous *pamphlet* may be said,
To be like one that hath more hair than head."—MALONE.

either from their good nature, or from their not being able to tell the truth firmly, a commendation, of which he may afterwards avail himself." JOHNSON: "Very true, Sir. Therefore the man who is asked by an author what he thinks of his work is put to the torture, and is not obliged to speak the truth; so that what he says is not considered as his opinion; yet he has said it, and cannot retract it; and this author, when mankind are hunting him with a canister at his tail, can say, 'I would not have published had not Johnson, or Reynolds, or Musgrave, or some other good judge, commended the work.' Yet I consider it as a very difficult question in conscience, whether one should advise a man not to publish a work, if profit be his object; for the man may say, 'Had it not been for you, I should have had the money.' Now you cannot be sure; for you have only your own opinion, and the public may think very differently." SIR JOSHUA REYNOLDS: "You must, upon such an occasion, have two judgments; one as to the real value of the work, the other as to what may please the general taste of the time." JOHNSON: "But you can be *sure* of neither; and therefore I should scruple much to give a suppressive vote. Both Goldsmith's comedies were once refused; his first by Garrick, his second by Colman, who was prevailed on at last, by much solicitation, nay, a kind of force, to bring it on. His 'Vicar of Wakefield,' I myself did not think would have had much success. It was written and sold to a bookseller, before his 'Traveller,' but published after—so little expectation had the bookseller from it. Had it been sold after 'The Traveller,' he might have had twice as much money for it, though sixty guineas was no mean price. The bookseller had the advantage of Goldsmith's reputation from the 'Traveller' in the sale, though Goldsmith had it not in selling the copy." SIR JOSHUA REYNOLDS: "'The Beggars' Opera' affords a proof how strangely people will differ in opinion about a literary performance. Burke thinks it has no merit." JOHNSON: "It was refused by one of the houses; but I should have thought it would succeed, not from any great excellence in the writing, but from the novelty, and the general spirit and gaiety of the piece, which keeps the audience always attentive, and dismisses them in good humour."

We went to the drawing-room, where was a considerable increase of company. Several of us got round Johnson, and complained that he would not give us an exact catalogue of his works, that there might be a complete edition. He smiled, and evaded our entreaties. That he intended to do it, I have no doubt, because I have heard him say so;

and I have in my possession an imperfect list, fairly written
out, which he entitles "Historia Studiorum."   I once got
from one of his friends a list, which there was pretty good
reason to suppose was accurate, for it was written down in
his presence by this friend, who enumerated each article
aloud, and had some of them mentioned to him by Mr.
Levett, in concert with whom it was made out; and Johnson,
who heard all this, did not contradict it.   But when I
showed a copy of this list to him, and mentioned the evidence
for its exactness, he laughed, and said, " I was willing to let
them go on as they pleased, and never interfered."   Upon
which I read to him, article by article, and got him positively
to own or refuse; and then, having obtained certainty so
far, I got some other articles confirmed by him directly,
and afterwards, from time to time, made additions under
his sanction.

His friend, Edward Cave, having been mentioned,
he told us, "Cave used to sell ten thousand of 'The
Gentleman's Magazine;' yet such was then his minute
attention and anxiety that the sale should not suffer
the smallest decrease, that he would name a particular
person who he heard had talked of leaving off the
Magazine, and would say, 'Let us have something good
next month.'"

It was observed, that avarice was inherent in some
dispositions.   JOHNSON: "No man was born a miser,
because no man was born to possession.   Every man is born
cupidos—desirous of getting, but not avarus—desirous of
keeping."   BOSWELL: "I have heard old Mr. Sheridan
maintain, with much ingenuity, that a complete miser is a
happy man; a miser who gives himself wholly to the one
passion of saving."   JOHNSON: "That is flying in the face
of all the world, who have called an avaricious man a
miser, because he is miserable.   No, Sir, a man who both
spends and saves money is the happiest man, because he has
both enjoyments."

The conversation having turned on Bon-mots, he quoted,
from one of the Ana, an exquisite instance of flattery in a
maid of honour in France, who being asked by the Queen
what o'clock it was, answered, "What your Majesty
pleases."   He admitted that Mr. Burke's classical pun
upon Mr. Wilkes's being carried on the shoulders of the mob

"————————numerisque fertur
Lege solutus,"[1]

was admirable; and though he was strangely unwilling to

[1] Horat. Carm. iv. od. ii. 11.

allow to that extraordinary man the talent of wit,[1] he also laughed with approbation at another of his playful conceits; which was, that 'Horace has in one line given a description of a good desirable manor:[2]

'Est modus in rebus, sunt certi denique fines;[3]

that is to say, a *modus* as to the tithes, and certain *fines.*"

He observed, "A man cannot with propriety speak of himself, except he relates simple facts, as, ' I was at Richmond;' or what depends on mensuration, as, 'I am six feet high.' He is sure he has been at Richmond; he is sure he is six feet high; but he cannot be sure he is wise, or that he has any other excellence. Then, all censure of a man's self is oblique praise. It is in order to show how much he can spare. It has all the invidiousness of self-praise, and all the reproach of falsehood." BOSWELL: "Sometimes it may proceed from a man's strong consciousness of his faults being observed. He knows that others would throw him down, and therefore he had better lie down softly of his own accord."

---

[1] See this question fully investigated in the Notes upon my "Journal of a Tour to the Hebrides," edit. 3, p. 21, *et seq.* And here, as a lawyer mindful of the maxim *Suum cuique tribuito,* I cannot forbear to mention, that the additional Note beginning with "I find since the former edition," is not mine, but was obligingly furnished by Mr. Malone, who was so kind as to superintend the press while I was in Scotland, and the first part of the second edition was printing. He would not allow me to ascribe it to its proper author; but, as it is exquisitely acute and elegant, I take this opportunity, without his knowledge, to do him justice.—BOSWELL.

[2] 1 Sat. i. 106.

[3] This, as both Mr. Bindley and Dr. Kearney have observed to me, is the motto to "An Enquiry into Customary Estates and Tenants' Rights, &c.—with some considerations for restraining excessive fines." By Everard Fleetwood, Esq., 8vo., 1731. But it is probably a mere coincidence. Mr. Burke perhaps never saw that pamphlet.—MALONE.

CHAPTER XII.—1778

*Mauritius Lowe, the Artist—Whigs and Tories—Cowards—
Wine-drinking—Mrs. Rudd—Tasso—Thucydides and
Homer—Mrs. Boscawen—Conversation respecting John-
son—Pope—Greece and Rome—State of Ancient Britain
—Mr. Henry—Dr. Robertson—Embassy to the King
of Siam—Allan Ramsay—Johnson's Rudeness to
Boswell—Dr. Blair's Sermon—Addison—East Indians
—Lord Kaimes's Sketches—Madame Lapouchin—Molly
Aston—Dining at the Mitre—On sensual Intercourse—
Imagination—Virtue and Vice—The Bat*

ON Tuesday, April 28, Johnson was engaged to dine at
General Paoli's, where, as I have already observed, I was
still entertained in elegant hospitality, and with all the
ease and comfort of a home. I called on him and accompanied him in a hackney-coach. We stopped first at the
bottom of Hedge-lane, into which he went to leave a letter,
"with good news for a poor man in distress," as he told me.
I did not question him particularly as to this. He himself
often resembled Lady Bolingbroke's lively description of
Pope, that "he was *un politique aux choux et aux raves.*"
He would say, "I dine to-day in Grosvenor-square;" this
might be with a duke; or perhaps, "I dine to-day at the
other end of the town;" or, "A gentleman of great eminence
called on me yesterday." He loved thus to keep things
floating in conjecture: *Omne ignotum pro magnifico est.* I
believe I ventured to dissipate the cloud, to unveil the
mystery, more freely and frequently than any of his
friends. We stopped again at Wirgman's, the well-known
toy-shop, in St. James's-street, at the corner of St. James's-
place, to which he had been directed, but not clearly, for
he searched about some time, and could not find it at first,
and said, "To direct one only to a corner shop is *toying* with
one." I suppose he meant this as a play upon the word *toy ;*
it was the first time I knew him to stoop to such sport.
After he had been some time in the shop, he sent for me to
come out of the coach, and help him to choose a pair of
silver buckles, as those he had were too small. Probably.

this alteration in dress had been suggested by Mrs. Thrale, by associating with whom his external appearance was much improved. He got better clothes, and the dark colour, from which he never deviated, was enlivened by metal buttons. His wigs, too, were much better, and during their travels in France he was furnished with a Paris-made wig, of handsome construction. This choosing of silver buckles was a negotiation. "Sir," said he, "I will not have the ridiculous large ones now in fashion, and I will give no more than a guinea for a pair." Such were the *principles* of the business; and, after some examination, he was fitted. As we drove along I found him in a talking humour, of which I availed myself. BOSWELL: "I was this morning in Ridley's shop, Sir; and was told that the collection called '*Johnsoniana*' has sold very much." JOHNSON: "Yet 'The Journey to the Hebrides' has not had a great sale."[1] BOSWELL: "That is strange." JOHNSON: "Yes, Sir; for in that book I have told the world a great deal that they did not know before."

BOSWELL: "I drank chocolate, Sir, this morning with Mr. Eld; and, to my no small surprise, found him to be a *Staffordshire Whig*, a being which I did not believe had existed." JOHNSON: "Sir, there are rascals in all countries." BOSWELL: "Eld said, a Tory was a creature generated between a nonjuring parson and one's grandmother." JOHNSON: "And I have always said, the first Whig was the Devil." BOSWELL: He certainly was, Sir. The Devil was impatient of subordination; he was the first who resisted power:—

'Better to reign in Hell, than serve in Heaven.'"

At General Paoli's were Sir Joshua Reynolds, Mr. Langton, Marchese Gherardi of Lombardy, and Mr. John Spottiswoode the younger, of Spottiswoode,[2] the solicitor.

---

[1] Here he either was mistaken, or had a different notion of an extensive sale from what is generally entertained: for the fact is, that four thousand copies of that excellent work were sold very quickly. A new edition has been printed since his death, besides that in the collection of his works.—BOSWELL.

Another edition has been printed since Mr. Boswell wrote the above, besides repeated editions in the general collection of his works during the last ten years.—MALONE.

[2] In the phraseology of Scotland, I should have said, "Mr. John Spottiswoode the younger, *of that ilk*." Johnson knew that sense of the word very well, and has thus explained it in his Dictionary, *voce* ILK—"It also signifies 'the same;' as *Mackintosh of that ilk* denotes a gentleman whose surname and the title of his estate are the same."—BOSWELL.

At this time fears of an invasion were circulated; to obviate which, Mr. Spottiswoode observed, that Mr. Fraser, the engineer, who had lately come from Dunkirk, said that the French had the same fears of us.   JOHNSON: "It is thus that mutual cowardice keeps us in peace.   Were one-half of mankind brave, and one-half cowards, the brave would be always beating the cowards.   Were all brave, they would lead a very uneasy life; all would be continually fighting; but being all cowards, we go on very well."

We talked of drinking wine.   JOHNSON: "I require wine only when I am alone.   I have then often wished for it, and often taken it."   SPOTTISWOODE: "What, by way of a companion, Sir?"   JOHNSON: "To get rid of myself—to send myself away.   Wine gives great pleasure, and every pleasure is of itself a good.   It is a good, unless counter-balanced by evil.   A man may have a strong reason not to drink wine: and that may be greater than the pleasure. Wine makes a man better pleased with himself.   I do not say that it makes him more pleasing to others.   Sometimes it does.   But the danger is, that while a man grows better pleased with himself, he may be growing less pleasing to others.[1]   Wine gives a man nothing.   It neither gives him knowledge nor wit; it only animates a man, and enables him to bring out what a dread of the company has repressed. It only puts in motion what has been locked up in frost. But this may be good or it may be bad."   SPOTTISWOODE: "So, Sir, wine is a key which opens a box; but this box may be either full or empty?"   JOHNSON: "Nay, Sir, conversation is the key; wine is a pick-lock, which forces open the box, and injures it.   A man should cultivate his mind so as to have that confidence and readiness, without wine, which wine gives."   BOSWELL: "The great difficulty of resisting wine is from benevolence.   For instance, a good worthy man asks you to taste his wine, which he has had twenty years in his cellar."   JOHNSON: "Sir, all this notion about benevolence arises from a man's imagining himself to be of more importance to others than he really is.   They don't care a farthing whether he drinks wine or not."   SIR JOSHUA REYNOLDS · "Yes, they do for the time."   JOHNSON: "For the time!—if they care this minute, they forget it the next.   And as for the good worthy man—how do you know

---

[1] It is observed in Waller's Life, in "The Biographia Britannica," that he drank only water; and that while he sat in a company who were drinking wine "he had the dexterity to accommodate his discourse to the pitch of theirs as it *sunk*."   If excess in drinking be meant, the re-mark is acutely just.   But surely a moderate use of wine gives a gaiety of spirits which water drinkers know not.—BOSWELL.

he is good and worthy?   No good and worthy man will insist upon another man's drinking wine.   As to the wine twenty years in the cellar—of ten men, three say this, merely because they must say something; three are telling a lie, when they say they have had the wine twenty years; three would rather save the wine; one, perhaps, cares.   I allow it is something to please one's company; and people are always pleased with those who partake pleasure with them.   But after a man has brought himself to relinquish the great personal pleasure which arises from drinking wine, any other consideration is a trifle.   To please others by drinking wine, is something only, if there be nothing against it.   I should, however, be sorry to offend worthy men:

> 'Curst be the verse, how well soe'er it flow,
>   That tends to make one worthy man my foe.'"

BOSWELL: "Curst be the *spring*, the *water*."   JOHNSON: "But let us consider what a sad thing it would be, if we were obliged to drink or do anything else that may happen to be agreeable to the company where we are."   LANGTON: "By the same rule you must join with a gang of cut-purses."   JOHNSON: "Yes, Sir; but yet we must do justice to wine; we must allow it the power it possesses.   To make a man pleased with himself, let me tell you, is doing a very great thing:—

> '*Si patriæ volumus, si* Nobis *vivere cari.*'"

I was at this time myself a water-drinker, upon trial, by Johnson's recommendation.   JOHNSON: "Boswell is a bolder combatant that Sir Joshua : he argues for wine without the help of wine; but Sir Joshua with it."   SIR JOSHUA REYNOLDS: "But to please one's company is a strong motive."   JOHNSON (who from drinking only water supposed every body who drank wine to be elevated): "I won't argue any more with you, Sir.   You are too far gone."   SIR JOSHUA: "I should have thought so, indeed, Sir, had I made such a speech as you have now done."   JOHNSON (drawing himself in, and I really thought blushing): "Nay, don't be angry.   I did not mean to offend you."   SIR JOSHUA: "At first the taste of wine was disagreeable to me; but I brought myself to drink it, that I might be like other people.   The pleasure of drinking wine is so connected with pleasing your company, that altogether there is something of social goodness in it."   JOHNSON: "Sir, this is only saying the same thing over again."   SIR JOSHUA: "No, this is new."   JOHNSON: "You put it in new words, but it is an old thought. This is one of the disadvantages of wine, it makes a man mistake words for thoughts." Boswell: "I think it is a new thought; at least it is in a new *attitude*." Johnson: "Nay, Sir, it is only in a new coat; or an old coat with a new facing. (Then laughing heartily)—It is the old dog in a new doublet. An extraordinary instance, however, may occur where a man's patron will do nothing for him, unless he will drink: *there* may be a good reason for drinking."

I mentioned a nobleman, who I believed was really uneasy, if his company would not drink hard. Johnson: "That is from having had people about him whom he has been accustomed to command." Boswell: "Supposing I should be *tête-à-tête* with him at table." Johnson: "Sir, there is no more reason for your drinking with *him*, than his being sober with *you*." Boswell: "Why, that is true; for it would do him less hurt to be sober, that it would do me to get drunk." Johnson: "Yes, Sir: and from what I have heard of him, one would not wish to sacrifice himself to such a man. If he must always have somebody to drink with him, he should buy a slave, and then he would be sure to have it. They who submit to drink as another pleases, make themselves his slaves." Boswell: "But, Sir, you will surely make allowance for the duty of hospitality. A gentleman who loves drinking, comes to visit me." Johnson: "Sir, a man knows whom he visits; he comes to the table of a sober man." Boswell: "But, Sir, you and I should not have been so well received in the Highlands and Hebrides, if I had not drunk with our worthy friends. If I drunk water only as you did, they would not have been so cordial." Johnson: "Sir William Temple mentions, that in his travels through the Netherlands he had two or three gentlemen with him; and when a bumper was necessary he put it on *them*. Were I to travel again through the islands, I would take Sir Joshua with me to take the bumpers." Boswell: "But, Sir, let me put a case. Suppose Sir Joshua should take a jaunt into Scotland; he does me the honour to pay me a visit at my house in the country; I am overjoyed at seeing him; we are quite by ourselves: shall I unsociably and churlishly let him sit drinking by himself? No, no, my dear Sir Joshua, you shall not be treated so, I *will* take a bottle with you."

The celebrated Mrs. Rudd being mentioned,—Johnson: "Fifteen years ago I should have gone to see her." Spottiswoode: "Because she was fifteen years younger?" Johnson: "No, Sir; but now they have a trick of putting everything into the newspapers."

He begged of General Paoli to repeat one of the introductory stanzas of the first book of Tasso's "Jerusalem," which he did, and then Johnson found fault with the simile of sweetening the edges of a cup for a child being transferred from Lucretius into an epic poem. The General said he did not imagine Homer's poetry was so ancient as is supposed, because he ascribes to a Greek colony circumstances of refinement not found in Greece itself at a later period, when Thucydides wrote. JOHNSON: "I recollect but one passage quoted by Thucydides from Homer, which is not to be found in our copies of Homer's works; I am for the antiquity of Homer, and think that a Grecian colony by being nearer Persia might be more refined than the mother country."

On Wednesday, April 29, I dined with him at Mr. Allan Ramsay's, where were Lord Binning, Dr. Robertson the historian, Sir Joshua Reynolds, and the Honourable Mrs. Boscawen, widow of the Admiral, and mother of the present Viscount Falmouth;[1] of whom, if it be not presumptuous in me to praise her, I would say, that her manners are the most agreeable, and her conversation the best, of any lady with whom I ever had the happiness to be acquainted. Before Johnson came, we talked a good deal of him; Ramsay said, he had always found him a very polite man, and that he treated him with great respect, which he did very sincerely. I said, I worshipped him. ROBERTSON: "But some of you spoil him: you should not worship him; you should worship no man." BOSWELL: "I cannot help worshipping him,—he is so much superior to other men." ROBERTSON: "In criticism, and in wit and conversation, he is no doubt very excellent; but in other respects he is not above other men; he will believe anything, and will strenuously defend the most minute circumstances connected with the Church of England." BOSWELL: "Believe me, Doctor, you are much mistaken as to this; for when you talk with him calmly in private, he is very liberal in his way of thinking." ROBERTSON: "He and I have been always very gracious; the first time I met him was one evening at Strahan's, when he had just had an unlucky altercation with Adam Smith; to

[1] Mrs. Frances Boscawen was the daughter of William Evelyn Granville, Esq., of St. Clair, Kent, and was married, in 1742, to Admiral Boscawen, brother of the second Viscount Falmouth, on whose death, in 1782, the son of the Admiral and of Mrs. Boscawen succeeded to the peerage. Thus, if the above was penned in 1778, Boswell would be wrong in calling Mrs. Boscawen the "mother of the *present* Viscount Falmouth;" she was only his sister-in-law. We must therefore infer that the above was written subsequently to 1782.—ED.

whom he had been so rough, that Strahan, after Smith was gone, had remonstrated with him, and told him that I was coming soon, and that he was uneasy to think that he might behave in the same manner to me. 'No, no, Sir,' said Johnson, 'I warrant you Robertson and I shall do very well.' Accordingly he was gentle and good-humoured and courteous with me the whole evening; and he has been so upon every occasion that we have met since. I have often said (laughing) that I have been in a great measure indebted to Smith for my good reception." Boswell: "His power of reasoning is very strong, and he has a peculiar art of drawing characters, which is as rare as good portrait painting." Sir Joshua Reynolds: "He is undoubtedly admirable in this; but, in order to mark the characters which he draws, he overcharges them, and gives people more than they really have, whether good or bad."

No sooner did he, of whom we had been thus talking so easily, arrive, than we were all as quiet as a school upon the entrance of the head-master; and were very soon sat down to a table covered with such variety of good things, as contributed not a little to dispose him to be pleased.

Ramsay: "I am old enough to have been a contemporary of Pope. His poetry was highly admired in his lifetime,—more a great deal than after his death." Johnson: "Sir, it has not been less admired since his death; no authors ever had so much fame in their own lifetime as Pope and Voltaire; and Pope's poetry has been as much admired since his death as during his life; it has only not been as much talked of; but that is owing to its being now more distant, and people having other writings to talk of. Virgil is less talked of than Pope, and Homer is less talked of than Virgil; but they are not less admired. We must read what the world reads at the moment. It has been maintained that this superfetation, this teeming of the press in modern times, is prejudicial to good literature, because it obliges us to read so much of what is of inferior value, in order to be in the fashion; so that better works are neglected for want of time, because a man will have more gratification of his vanity in conversation, from having read modern books, than from having read the best works of antiquity. But it must be considered, that we have now more knowledge generally diffused; all our ladies read now, which is a great extension. Modern writers are the moons of literature; they shine with reflected light, with light borrowed from the ancients. Greece appears to me to be the fountain of knowledge; Rome of elegance." RAMSAY: "I suppose Homer's 'Iliad' to be a collection of pieces which had been written before his time. I should like to see a translation of it in poetical prose, like the book of Ruth or Job." ROBERTSON: "Would you, Dr. Johnson, who are master of the English language, but try your hand upon a part of it." JOHNSON: "Sir, you could not read it without the pleasure of verse."[1]

We talked of antiquarian researches. JOHNSON: "All that is really *known* of the ancient state of Britain is contained in a few pages. We *can* know no more than what the old writers have told us; yet what large books have we upon it, the whole of which, excepting such parts as are taken from those old writers, is all a dream, such as Whittaker's 'Manchester.' I have heard Henry's[2] 'History of Britain' well spoken of. I am told it is carried on in separate divisions, as the civil, the military, the religious history. I wish much to have one branch well done, and that is the history of manners of common life." ROBERTSON: "Henry should have applied his attention to that alone, which is enough for any man; and he might have found a great deal scattered in various books, had he read solely with that view. Henry erred in not selling his first volume at a moderate price to the booksellers, that they might have pushed him on till he had got reputation. I sold my 'History of Scotland' at a moderate price, as a work by which the booksellers might either gain or not; and Cadell has told me that Millar and he have got six thousand pounds by it. I afterwards received a much higher price for my writings. An author should sell his first work for what the booksellers will give, till it shall appear whether he is an author of merit, or, which is the same thing as to purchase-money, an author who pleases the public."

Dr. Robertson expatiated on the character of a certain nobleman [Lord Clive]; that he was one of the strongest-minded men that ever lived; that he would sit in company quite sluggish, while there was nothing to call forth his intellectual vigour; but the moment that any important subject was started—for instance, how this country is to be

[1] This experiment, which Madame Dacier made in vain, has since been tried in our own language by the editor of "Ossian," and we must either think very meanly of his abilities, or allow that Dr. Johnson was in the right. And Mr. Cowper, a man of real genius, has miserably failed in his blank verse translation.—BOSWELL.

[2] Dr. Robert Henry was minister of one of the churches in Edinburgh, and his "History of Great Britain" was published in 6 vols. 4to. He was born at St. Ninians, near Stirling, in 1718, and died in 1790.—ED.

defended against a French invasion—he would rouse himself, and show his extraordinary talents with the most powerful ability and animation. JOHNSON: "Yet this man cut his own throat. The true strong and sound mind is the mind that can embrace equally great things and small. Now, I am told the King of Prussia will say to a servant, 'Bring me a bottle of such a wine, which came in such a year; it lies in such a corner of the cellars.' I would have a man great in great things, and elegant in little things." He said to me afterwards, when we were by ourselves, "Robertson was in a mighty romantic humour; he talked of one whom he did not know; but I *downed* him with the King of Prussia." "Yes, Sir," said I, "you threw a *bottle* at his head."

An ingenious gentleman was mentioned, concerning whom both Robertson and Ramsay agreed that he had a constant firmness of mind; for after a laborious day, and amidst a multiplicity of cares and anxieties, he would sit down with his sisters, and be quite cheerful and good-humoured. Such a disposition, it was observed, was a happy gift of nature. JOHNSON: "I do not think so; a man has from nature a certain portion of mind; the use he makes of it depends upon his own free will. That a man has always the same firmness of mind I do not say; because every man feels his mind less firm at one time than another; but I think a man's being in good or bad humour depends upon his will." I, however, could not help thinking that a man's humour is often uncontrollable by his will.

Johnson harangued against drinking wine. "A man," said he, "may choose whether he will have abstemiousness and knowledge, or claret and ignorance." Dr. Robertson (who is very companionable) was beginning to dissent as to the prescription of claret. JOHNSON (with a placid smile): "Nay, Sir, you shall not differ with me; as I have said that the man is most perfect who takes in the most things, I am for knowledge and claret." ROBERTSON (holding a glass of generous claret in his hand): "Sir, I can only drink your health." JOHNSON: "Sir, I should be sorry if *you* should be ever in such a state as to be able to do nothing more." ROBERTSON: "Dr. Johnson, allow me to say, that in one respect I have the advantage of you; when you were in Scotland you would not come to hear any of our preachers, whereas, when I am here, I attend your public worship without scruple, and, indeed, with great satisfaction." JOHNSON: "Why, Sir, that is not so extraordinary; the King of Siam sent ambassadors to

Louis the Fourteenth; but Louis the Fourteenth sent none to the King of Siam."[1]

Here my friend for once discovered a want of knowledge or forgetfulness, for Louis the Fourteenth did send an embassy to the King of Siam,[2] and the Abbé Choisi, who was employed in it, published an account of it in two volumes.

Next day, Thursday, April 30, I found him at home by himself. JOHNSON: "Well, Sir, Ramsay gave us a splendid dinner. I love Ramsay. You will not find a man in whose conversation there is more instruction, more information, and more elegance, than in Ramsay's." BOSWELL: "What I admire in Ramsay, is his continuing to be so young." JOHNSON: "Why, yes, Sir, it is to be admired. I value myself upon this, that there is nothing of the old man in my conversation. I am now sixty-eight, and I have no more of it than at twenty-eight." BOSWELL: "But, Sir, would you not wish to know old age? He who is never an old man, does not know the whole of human life; for old age is one of the divisions of it." JOHNSON: "Nay, Sir, what talk is this?" BOSWELL: "I mean, Sir, the Sphinx's description of it—morning, noon, and night. I would know night, as well as morning and noon." JOHNSON: "What, Sir, would you know what it is to feel the evils of old age? Would you have the gout? Would you have decrepitude?" Seeing him heated, I would not argue farther; but I was confident that I was in the right. I would, in due time, be a Nestor, an elder of the people; and there *should* be some difference between the conversation of twenty-eight and sixty-eight.[3] A grave picture should not be gay. There is a serene, solemn, placid old age. JOHNSON: "Mrs. Thrale's mother said of me what flattered me much. A clergyman was complaining of want of society in the country where he lived, and said, 'They talk of *runts ;*' that

---

[1] Mrs. Piozzi confidently mentions this as having passed in Scotland. "Anecdotes," p. 92.—BOSWELL.

[2] The Abbé de Choisi was sent by Louis XIV. on an embassy to the King of Siam in 1683 with a view, it has been said, to convert the King of that country to Christianity.—MALONE.

[3] Johnson clearly meant (what the author has often elsewhere mentioned), that he had none of the listlessness of old age, that he had the same *activity and energy of mind* as formerly; not that a man of sixty-eight might dance in a public assembly with as much propriety as he could at twenty-eight. His conversation, being the product of much various knowledge, great acuteness and extraordinary wit, was equally well suited to every period of life; and as in his youth it probably did not exhibit any unbecoming levity, so certainly in his later years it was totally free from the garrulity and querulousness of old age.—MALONE.

is, young cows.[1] 'Sir,' said Mrs. Salusbury, 'Mr. Johnson
would learn to talk of runts,' meaning that I was a man who
would make the most of my situation, whatever it was."
He added, " I think myself a very polite man."

On Saturday, May 2, I dined with him at Sir Joshua
Reynolds's, where there was a very large company, and a
great deal of conversation; but owing to some circumstances
which I cannot now recollect, I have no record of any part
of it, except that there were several people there by no
means of the Johnsonian school; so that less attention was
paid to him than usual, which put him out of humour; and
upon some imaginary offence from me, he attacked me with
such rudeness that I was vexed and angry, because it gave
those persons an opportunity of enlarging upon his supposed
ferocity and ill-treatment of his best friends. I was so
much hurt, and had my pride so much roused, that I kept
away from him for a week; and, perhaps, might have kept
away much longer, nay, gone to Scotland without seeing
him again, had not we fortunately met and been reconciled.
To such unhappy chances are human friendships liable!

On Friday, May 8, I dined with him at Mr. Langton's.
I was reserved and silent, which I supposed he perceived,
and might recollect the cause. After dinner, when Mr.
Langton was called out of the room, and we were by ourselves, he drew his chair near to mine, and said, in a tone
of conciliating courtesy, "Well, how have you done?"
BOSWELL: "Sir, you have made me very uneasy by your
behaviour to me when we were last at Sir Joshua Reynolds's.
You know, my dear Sir, no man has a greater respect and
affection for you, or would sooner go to the end of the world
to serve you. Now, to treat me so—." He insisted that
I had interrupted him, which I assured him was not the
case, and proceeded, "But why treat me so before people
who neither love you nor me?" JOHNSON: "Well, I am
sorry for it. I'll make it up to you twenty different ways,
as you please." BOSWELL: "I said to-day to Sir Joshua,
when he observed that you *tossed* me sometimes, I don't
care how often, or how high he tosses me, when only friends
are present, for then I fall upon soft ground; but I do not
like falling on stones, which is the case when enemies are

---

[1] Such is the signification of this word in Scotland, and it should
seem in Wales. (See Skinner in *v.*) But the heifers of Scotland and
Wales, when brought to England, being always smaller than those of
this country, the word *runt* has acquired a secondary sense, and generally
signifies a heifer diminutive in size, small beyond the ordinary growth
of that animal; and in this sense alone the word is acknowledged by Dr.
Johnson in his Dictionary.—MALONE.

present. I think this is a pretty good image, Sir." JOHNSON: "Sir, it is one of the happiest I ever have heard."

The truth is, there was no venom in the wounds which he inflicted at any time, unless they were irritated by some malignant infusion by other hands. We were instantly as cordial again as ever, and joined in hearty laugh at some ludicrous but innocent peculiarities of one of our friends. BOSWELL: "Do you think, Sir, it is always culpable to laugh at a man to his face?" JOHNSON: "Why, Sir, that depends upon the man and the thing. If it is a slight man, and a slight thing, you may; for you take nothing valuable from him."

He said, " I read yesterday Dr. Blair's sermon on Devotion, from the text 'Cornelius, a devout man.' His doctrine is the best limited, the best expressed; there is the most warmth without fanaticism, the most rational transport. There is one part of it which I disapprove, and I'd have him correct it; which is, that, 'he who does not feel joy in religion is far from the kingdom of heaven!' There are many good men whose fear of GOD predominates over their love. It may discourage. It was rashly said. A noble sermon it is, indeed. I wish Blair would come over to the Church of England."

When Mr. Langton returned to us, the "flow of talk" went on. An eminent author being mentioned:—JOHNSON: "He is not a pleasant man. His conversation is neither instructive nor brilliant. He does not talk as if impelled by any fulness of knowledge or vivacity of imagination. His conversation is like that of any other sensible man. He talks with no wish either to inform or to hear, but only because he thinks it does not become [Dr. Robertson] to sit in a company and say nothing."

Mr. Langton having repeated the anecdote of Addison having distinguished between his powers in conversation and in writing, by saying, " I have only ninepence in my pocket; but I can draw for a thousand pounds:"—JOHNSON: "He had not that retort ready, Sir; he had prepared it beforehand." LANGTON (turning to me): "A fine surmise. Set a thief to catch a thief."

Johnson called the East Indians barbarians. BOSWELL: " You will except the Chinese, Sir?" JOHNSON: "No, Sir." BOSWELL: "Have they not arts?" JOHNSON: "They have pottery." BOSWELL: "What do you say to the written characters of their language?" JOHNSON: "Sir, they have not an alphabet. They have not been able to form what all other nations have formed." BOSWELL: "There is more

learning in their language than in any other, from the
immense number of their characters." JOHNSON: "It is
only more difficult from its rudeness; as there is more
labour in hewing down a tree with a stone than with an
axe."

He said, " I have been reading Lord Kaimes's 'Sketches
of the History of Man.' In treating of severity of punishment, he mentions that of Madame Lapouchin, in Russia;
but he does not give it fairly; for I have looked at *Chappe
d'Auteroche*,[1] from whom he has taken it.   He stops where
it is said that the spectators thought her innocent, and leaves
out what follows,—that she nevertheless was guilty.   Now
this is being as culpable as one can conceive, to misrepresent
fact in a book;[2] and for what motive?   It is like one of those
lies which people tell, one cannot see why.   The woman's
life was spared and no punishment was too great for the
favourite of an Empress who had conspired to dethrone
her mistress."   BOSWELL: "He was only giving a picture

---

[1] "Voyage en Sibérie," par M. l'Abbé Chappe d'Auteroche, 3 vols.
fol., 1761.—ED.

[2] On consulting the two authorities above mentioned, we find that
Lord Kaimes (b. i., sketch v.) has given the details of this barbarous
punishment almost in the very words of the Abbé Chappe, with the
exception of one slight omission, which Johnson considers the height of
culpability, but which appears quite unnecessary to the story.   As the
narrative, however, is short, and illustrative of early Russian barbarism,
it is worth extracting.   The omitted passage, of which Johnson so bitterly
complains, is supplied within brackets:—

"No traveller who visited St. Petersburgh during the reign of the
Empress Elizabeth can be ignorant of Madame Lapouchin, the great
ornament of that Court.   Her intimacy with a foreign Ambassador
having brought her under suspicion of plotting against the government,
she was condemned to undergo the punishment of the knout.   At the
place of execution she appeared in a genteel undress, which heightened
her beauty.   Of whatever indiscretion she might have been guilty, the
sweetness of her countenance and her composure left not the spectators
the slightest suspicion of guilt.   [Abbé Chappe here remarks (to quote
his own words):—'*Tous ceux que j'ai consultés par la suite m'ont cependant
assuré qu'elle étoit coupable.*']   Her youth also, her beauty, her life and
spirit pleaded for her, but all in vain; she was deserted by all, and
abandoned to surly executioners, whom she beheld with astonishment,
seeming to doubt whether such preparations were intended for her.   The
cloak that covered her bosom being pulled off, modesty took the alarm,
and made her start back; she turned pale, and burst into tears.   One
of the executioners stripped her naked to the waist, seized her with
both hands, and threw her on his back, raising her some inches from
the ground.   The other executioner, laying hold of her delicate limbs
with his rough fists, put her in a posture for receiving the punishment.
Then, laying hold of the knout, a sort of whip made of a leathern strap,
he, with a single stroke, tore off a slip of skin from the neck downward,
repeating his strokes till all the skin of her back was cut off in small
slips.   The executioner *finished his task with cutting out her tongue!* after
which she was banished to Siberia."—ED.

of the lady in her sufferings." JOHNSON: "Nay, don't endeavour to palliate this. Guilt is a principal feature in the picture.——Kaimes is puzzled with a question that puzzled me when I was a very young man. Why is it that the interest of money is lower when money is plentiful; for five pounds has the same proportion of value to a hundred pounds when money is plentiful, as when it is scarce? A lady explained it to me. ' It is,' said she, 'because when money is plentiful there are so many more who have money to lend, that they bid down one another. Many have then a hundred pounds; and one says, Take mine rather than another's, and you shall have it at four per cent.'" BOSWELL: "Does Lord Kaimes decide the question?" JOHNSON: " I think he leaves it as he found it." BOSWELL: " This must have been an extraordinary lady who instructed you, Sir. May I ask who she was?" JOHNSON: "Molly Aston,[1] Sir, the sister of those ladies with whom you dined at Lichfield.——I shall be at home to-morrow." BOSWELL: "Then let us dine by ourselves at the Mitre, to keep up the old custom 'the custom of the manor,' custom of the Mitre." JOHNSON: "Sir, so it shall be."

On Saturday, May 9, we fulfilled our purpose of dining by ourselves at the Mitre, according to old custom. There was, on these occasions, a little circumstance of kind attention to Mrs. Williams, which must not be omitted. Before coming out, and leaving her to dine alone, he gave her her choice of a chicken, a sweetbread, or any other little nice thing, which was carefully sent to her from the tavern, ready-drest.

---

[1] Johnson had an extraordinary admiration of this lady, notwithstanding she was a violent Whig. In answer to her high-flown speeches for *Liberty*, he addressed to her the following Epigram, of which I presume to offer a translation:—

> "Liber ut esse velim, suasisti, pulcra Maria,
> Ut maneam liber, pulcra Maria, vale."
> (Adieu, Maria! since you'd have me free;
> For who beholds thy charms a slave must be.)

A correspondent of "The Gentleman's Magazine," who subscribes himself SCIOLUS, to whom I am indebted for several excellent remarks, observes, "The turn of Dr. Johnson's lines to Miss Aston, whose Whig principles he had been combating, appears to me to be taken from an ingenious epigram in 'The Menagiana' (vol. iii. p. 367, edit. 1716), on a young lady who appeared at a masquerade, *habillé en Jesuite*, during the fierce contentions of the followers of Molinos and Jansenius concerning free-will:—

> "On s'étonne ici que Caliste
> Ait pris l'habit de Moliniste,
> Puisque cette jeune beauté
> Ote a chacun sa liberté,
> N'est ce pas une Janseniste?"—BOSWELL.

Our conversation to-day, I know not how, turned, I think for the only time at any length during our long acquaintance, upon the sensual intercourse between the sexes, the delight of which he ascribed chiefly to imagination. "Were it not for imagination, Sir," said he, "a man would be as happy in the arms of a chambermaid as of a duchess. But such is the adventitious charm of fancy, that we find men who have violated the best principles of society, and ruined their fame and their fortune, that they might possess a woman of rank." It would not be proper to record the particulars of such a conversation in moments of unreserved frankness, when nobody was present on whom it could have any hurtful effect. That subject, when philosophically treated, may surely employ the mind in a curious discussion, and as innocently as anatomy; provided that those who do treat it keep clear of inflammatory incentives.

"From grave to gay, from lively to severe," we were soon engaged in very different speculation, humbly and reverently considering and wondering at the universal mystery of all things, as our imperfect faculties can now judge of them. "There are," said he, "innumerable questions to which the inquisitive mind can in this state receive no answer: Why do you and I exist? Why was this world created? Since it was to be created, why was it not created sooner?"

On Sunday, May 10, I supped with him at Mr. Hoole's, with Sir Joshua Reynolds. I have neglected the memorial of this evening, so as to remember no more of it than two particulars; one, that he strenuously opposed an argument by Sir Joshua, that virtue was preferable to vice, considering this life only; and that a man would be virtuous were it only to preserve his character; and that he expressed much wonder at the curious formation of the bat, a mouse with wings, saying, that it was almost as strange a thing in physiology, as if the fabulous dragon could be seen.

CHAPTER XIII.—1778

ON Tuesday, May 12, I waited on the Earl of Marchmont,
to know if his lordship would favour Dr. Johnson with
information concerning Pope, whose Life he was about to
write. Johnson had not flattered himself with the hopes
of receiving any civility from this nobleman: for he said to
me, when I mentioned Lord Marchmont as one who could
tell him a good deal about Pope, "Sir, he will tell *me*
nothing" I had the honour of being known to his lordship,
and applied to him of myself, without being commissioned
by Johnson. His lordship behaved in the most polite and
obliging manner, promised to tell all he recollected about
Pope, and was so very courteous as to say, "Tell Dr.
Johnson I have a great respect for him, and am ready to
show it in any way I can. I am to be in the City to-morrow,
and will call at his house as I return." His lordship, however, asked, "Will he write 'the Lives of the Poets' impartially? He was the first that brought Whig and Tory
into a dictionary. And what do you think of his definition
of *Excise!* Do you know the history of his aversion to the
word *transpire?*" Then taking down the folio dictionary,
he showed it with this censure on its secondary sense: "To
escape from secresy to notice; a sense lately innovated
from France, without necessity." The truth was, Lord

274

Bolingbroke, who left the Jacobites, first used it; therefore it was to be condemned. He should have shown what word would do for it, if it was unnecessary. I afterwards put the question to Johnson. "Why, Sir," said he, "*get abroad.*" BOSWELL: "That, Sir, is using two words." JOHNSON: "Sir, there is no end of this. You may as well insist to have a word for old age." BOSWELL: "Well, Sir, *Senectus.*" JOHNSON: "Nay, Sir, to insist always that there should be one word to express a thing in English, because there is one in another language, is to change the language."

I availed myself of this opportunity to hear from his lordship many particulars both of Pope and Lord Bolingbroke, which I have in writing.

I proposed to Lord Marchmont that he should revise Johnson's "Life of Pope." "So," said his lordship, "you would put me in a dangerous situation. You know he knocked down Osborne, the bookseller."

Elated with the success of my spontaneous exertion to procure material and respectable aid to Johnson for his very favourite work, "The Lives of the Poets," I hastened down to Mr. Thrale's, at Streatham, where he now was, that I might ensure his being at home next day; and after dinner, when I thought he would receive the good news in the best humour, I announced it eagerly: "I have been at work for you to-day, Sir. I have been with Lord Marchmont. He bade me tell you he has a great respect for you, and will call on you to-morrow at one o'clock, and communicate all he knows about Pope." Here I paused, in full expectation that he would be pleased with this intelligence, would praise my active merit, and would be alert to embrace such an offer from a nobleman. But whether I had shown an over-exultation, which provoked his spleen, or whether he was seized with a suspicion that I had obtruded him on Lord Marchmont, and humbled him too much, or whether there was anything more than an unlucky fit of ill-humour, I know not; but to my surprise, the result was—JOHNSON: "I shall not be in town to-morrow. I don't care to know about Pope." Mrs. Thrale (surprised as I was, and a little angry): "I suppose, Sir, Mr. Boswell thought that as you are to write Pope's Life, you would wish to know about him." JOHNSON: "Wish! why, yes. If it rained knowledge, I'd hold out my hand; but I would not give myself the trouble to go in quest of it." There was no arguing with him at the moment. Sometime afterwards he said, "Lord Marchmont will call on me, and then I shall call on Lord Marchmont." Mrs. Thrale was uneasy at his unaccountable caprice, and told me that if I did not take care to bring about a meeting between Lord Marchmont and him, it would never take place, which would be a great pity. I sent a card to his lordship, to be left at Johnson's house, acquainting him that Dr. Johnson could not be in town next day, but would do himself the honour of waiting on him at another time. I give this account fairly, as a specimen of that unhappy temper with which this great and good man had occasionally to struggle, from something morbid in his constitution. Let the most censorious of my readers suppose himself to have a violent fit of the toothache, or to have received a severe stroke on the shinbone, and when in such a state to be asked a question, and if he has any candour he will not be surprised at the answers which Johnson sometimes gave in moments of irritation, which, let me assure them, is exquisitely painful. But it must not be erroneously supposed that he was, in the smallest degree, careless concerning any work which he undertook, or that he was generally thus peevish. It will be seen that in the following year he had a very agreeable interview with Lord Marchmont, at his lordship's house, and this very afternoon he soon forgot any fretfulness, and fell into conversation as usual.

I mentioned a reflection having been thrown out against four Peers for having presumed to rise in opposition to the opinion of the twelve judges, in a cause in the House of Lords, as if that were indecent. JOHNSON: "Sir, there is no ground for censure. The Peers are judges themselves, and supposing them really to be of a different opinion, they might from duty be in opposition to the judges, who were there only to be consulted."

In this observation I fully concurred with him; for, unquestionably, all the Peers are vested with the highest judicial powers, and when they are confident that they understand a cause, are not obliged—nay, ought not—to acquiesce in the opinion of the ordinary law judges, or even in that of those who, from their studies and experience, are called the law lords. I consider the Peers in general as I do a jury, who ought to listen with respectful attention to the sages of the law; but, if after hearing them, they have a firm opinion of their own, are bound as honest men to decide accordingly. Nor is it so difficult for them to understand even law questions, as is generally thought, provided they will bestow sufficient attention upon them. This observation was made by my honoured relation the late Lord Cathcart, who had spent his life in camps and courts: yet he assured me that he could form a clear opinion upon most of the causes that came before the House of Lords, "as they were so well enucleated in the cases."

Mrs. Thrale told us that a curious clergyman of our acquaintance had discovered a licentious stanza, which Pope had originally in his "Universal Prayer," before the stanza,

> 'What conscience dictates to be done,
> Or warns us not to do," &c.

It was this—

> "Can sins of moment claim the rod
>   Of everlasting fires?
> And that offend great Nature's God,
>   Which Nature's self inspires?"

and that Dr. Johnson observed, "It had been borrowed from Guarini."[1] There are, indeed, in Pastor Fido, many such flimsy superficial reasonings, as that in the last two lines of this stanza.

Boswell: "In that stanza of Pope's, *rod of fires* is certainly a bad metaphor." Mrs. Thrale: "And *sins of moment* is a faulty expression; for its true import is *momentous*, which cannot be intended." Johnson: "It must have been written 'of *moments*.' Of *moment* is *momentous*; of *moments*, *momentary*. I warrant you, however, Pope wrote this stanza, and some friend struck it out. Boileau[2] wrote some such thing, and Arnaud[3] struck it out, saying, '*Vous gagnerez deux ou trois impies, et perdrez je ne sais combien des honnêtes gens.*' These fellows want to say a daring thing, and don't know how to go about it. Mere poets know no more of fundamental principles than—." Here he was interrupted somehow. Mrs. Thrale mentioned Dryden. Johnson: "He puzzled himself about predestination. How foolish it was in Pope to give all his friendship to lords, who thought they honoured him by being with him; and to choose such lords as Burlington and Cobham, and Bolingbroke! Bathurst was negative, a pleasing man;

[1] Battista Guarini was an Italian poet of some celebrity, whose principal composition was a pastoral drama, entitled "Pastor Fido." He was born at Ferrara in 1537, and was secretary to Ferdinand de Medicis, Grand Duke of Tuscany, as well as to the Duke of Urbino. He died in 1612.

[2] Boileau, as a poet and a satirist, enjoyed a reputation in France very similar to that of Pope in England. He was born in 1636, and died in 1711.

[3] This was Francis Arnaud, the author of numerous poems, plays, and prose fictions, who was favourably noticed by Voltaire and Frederick of Prussia.

and I have heard no ill of Marchmont; and then always saying, 'I do not value you for being a lord,' which was a sure proof that he did.   I never say I do not value Boswell more for being born to an estate, because I do not care." Boswell: "Nor for being a Scotchman?" Johnson: "Nay, Sir, I do value you more for being a Scotchman. You are a Scotchman without the faults of Scotchmen. You would not have been so valuable as you are, had you not been a Scotchman."

Talking of divorces, I asked if Othello's doctrine was not plausible:

> "He that is robb'd, not wanting what is stolen,
> Let him not know't, and he's not robb'd at all."

Dr. Johnson and Mrs. Thrale joined against this. Johnson: "Ask any man if he'd wish not to know of such an injury." Boswell: "Would you tell your friend to make him unhappy?" Johnson: "Perhaps, Sir, I should not; but that would be from prudence on my own account.   A man would tell his father."   Boswell: "Yes; because he would not have spurious children to get any share of the family inheritance." Mrs. Thrale: "Or he would tell his brother." Boswell: "Certainly, his *elder* brother."   Johnson: "You would tell your friend of a woman's infamy, to prevent his marrying a whore; there is the same reason to tell him of his wife's infidelity, when he is married, to prevent the consequences of imposition.   It is a breach of confidence not to tell a friend." Boswell: "Would you tell Mr. ——?" (naming a gentleman who assuredly was not in the least danger of such a miserable disgrace, though married to a fine woman). Johnson: "No, Sir; because it would do no good; he is so sluggish, he'd never go to Parliament and get through a divorce."

He said of one of our friends: "He is ruining himself without pleasure.   A man who loses at play, or who runs out his fortune at court, makes his estate less, in hopes of making it bigger (I am sure of this word, which was often used by him); but it is a sad thing to pass through the quagmire of parsimony to the gulf of ruin.   To pass over the flowery path of extravagance is very well."

Amongst the numerous prints pasted on the walls of the dining-room at Streatham, was Hogarth's "Modern Midnight Conversation."   I asked him what he knew of Parson Ford, who makes a conspicuous figure in the riotous group. Johnson: "Sir, he was my acquaintance and relation, my mother's nephew.   He had purchased a living in the country, but not simoniacally. I never saw him but in the country. I have been told he was a man of great parts: very profligate, but I never heard he was impious."   BOSWELL: "Was there not a story of his ghost having appeared?"   JOHNSON: "Sir, it was believed. A waiter at the Hummums, in which house Ford died, had been absent for some time, and returned, not knowing that Ford was dead. Going down to the cellar, according to the story, he met him; going down again, he met him a second time. When he came up, he asked some of the people of the house what Ford could be doing there. They told him Ford was dead. The waiter took a fever, in which he lay for some time. When he recovered he said he had a message to deliver to some women from Ford; but he was not to tell what or to whom. He walked out; he was followed; but somewhere about St. Paul's they lost him. He came back, and said he had delivered the message, and the women exclaimed, 'Then we are all undone!' Dr. Pellet, who was not a credulous man, inquired into the truth of this story, and he said the evidence was irresistible. My wife went to the Hummums (it is a place where people get themselves cupped). I believe she went with intention to hear about this story of Ford. At first they were unwilling to tell her; but after they had talked to her, she came away satisfied that it was true. To be sure the man had a fever, and this vision may have been the beginning of it. But if the message to the women, and their behaviour upon it, were true as related, there was something supernatural. That rests upon his word, and there it remains."

After Mrs. Thrale was gone to bed, Johnson and I sat up late. We resumed Sir Joshua Reynold's argument on the preceding Sunday, that a man would be virtuous though he had no other motive than to preserve his character. JOHNSON: "Sir, it is not true; for, as to this world, vice does not hurt a man's character."   BOSWELL: "Yes, Sir, debauching a friend's wife will."   JOHNSON: "No, Sir. Who thinks the worse of —— for it?"   BOSWELL: 'Lord —— was not his friend."   JOHNSON: "That is only a circumstance, Sir, a slight distinction. He could not get into the house but by Lord ——. A man is chosen knight of the shire, not the less for having debauched ladies."   BOSWELL: "What, Sir, if he debauched the ladies of gentlemen in the county, will there not be a general resentment against him?"   JOHNSON: "No, Sir, he will lose those particular gentlemen; but the rest will not trouble their heads about it" (warmly).   BOSWELL: "Well, Sir, I cannot think so."   JOHNSON: "Nay, Sir, there is no talking with a man who will dispute what everybody knows (angrily) Don't you know this?" BOSWELL: "No, Sir; and I wish to think better of your country than you represent it. I knew in Scotland a gentleman obliged to leave it for debauching a lady, and in one of our counties an earl's brother lost his election, because he had debauched the lady of another earl in that county, and destroyed the peace of a noble family."

Still he would not yield. He proceeded: "Will you not allow, Sir, that vice does not hurt a man's character so as to obstruct his prosperity in life, when you know that [Lord Clive] was loaded with wealth and honours; a man who had acquired his fortune by such crimes, that his consciousness of them impelled him to cut his own throat." BOSWELL: "You will recollect, Sir, that Dr. Robertson said, he cut his throat because he was weary of still life, little things not being sufficient to move his great mind." JOHNSON (very angry): "Nay, Sir, what stuff is this? You had no more this opinion after Robertson said it than before. I know nothing more offensive than repeating what one knows to be foolish things, by way of continuing a dispute, to see what a man will answer—to make him your butt!" (angrier still). BOSWELL: "My dear Sir, I had no such intention as you seem to suspect. I had not indeed. Might not this nobleman have felt everything 'weary, stale, flat, and unprofitable,' as Hamlet says." JOHNSON: "Nay, if you are to bring in gabble, I'll talk no more. I will not upon my honour." My readers will decide upon this dispute.

Next morning I stated to Mrs. Thrale at breakfast, before he came down, the dispute of last night as to the influence of character upon success in life. She said he was certainly wrong, and told me that a baronet lost an election in Wales because he had debauched the sister of a gentleman in the country, whom he made one of his daughters invite as her companion at his seat in the country, when his lady and his other children were in London. But she would not encounter Johnson upon the subject.

I stayed all this day with him at Streatham. He talked a great deal in very good humour.

Looking at Messrs. Dilly's splendid edition of Lord Chesterfield's miscellaneous works, he laughed, and said: "Here are now two speeches ascribed to him, both of which were written by me; and the best of it is, they have found out that one is like Demosthenes, and the other like Cicero."

He censured Lord Kaimes's "Sketches of the History of

Man," for misrepresenting Clarendon's account of the appearance of Sir George Villier's ghost, as if Clarendon were weakly credulous, when the truth is, that Clarendon only says that the story was upon a better foundation of credit than usually such discourses are founded upon; nay, speaks thus of the person who was reported to have seen the vision, "the poor man, *if he had been at all waking*," which Lord Kaimes has omitted. He added, "in this book it is maintained that virtue is natural to a man, and that if we would but consult our own hearts we should be virtuous. Now, after consulting our own hearts all we can, and with all the helps we have, we find how few of us are virtuous. This is saying a thing which all mankind know not to be true." BOSWELL: "Is not modesty natural?" JOHNSON: "I cannot say, Sir, as we find no people quite in a state of nature; but I think the more they are taught, the more modest they are. The French are a gross, ill-bred, untaught people: a lady there will spit on the floor and rub it with her foot. What I gained by being in France was, learning to be better satisfied with my own country. Time may be employed to more advantage from nineteen to twenty-four, almost in any way than in travelling; when you set travelling against mere negation, against doing nothing, it is better to be sure; but how much more would a young man improve were he to study during those years. Indeed, if a young man is wild, and must run after women and bad company, it is better this should be done abroad, as, on his return, he can break off such connexions, and begin at home a new man, with a character to form and acquaintances to make. How little does travelling supply to the conversation of any man who has travelled; how little to Beauclerk?" BOSWELL: "What say you to Lord [Charlemont]?" JOHNSON: "I never but once heard him talk of what he had seen, and that was of a large serpent in one of the pyramids of Egypt." BOSWELL: "Well, I happened to hear him tell the same thing, which made me mention him."

I talked of a country life. JOHNSON: "Were I to live in the country, I would not devote myself to the acquisition of popularity. I would live in a much better way, much more happily. I would have my time at my own command." BOSWELL: "But, Sir, is it not a sad thing to be at a distance from all our literary friends?" JOHNSON: "Sir, you will by-and-by have enough of this conversation, which now delights you so much."

As he was a zealous friend of subordination, he was at all times watchful to repress the vulgar cant against the manners of the great. "High people, Sir," said he, "are the best; take a hundred ladies of quality, you'll find them better wives, better mothers, more willing to sacrifice their own pleasure to their children, than a hundred other women. Tradeswomen (I mean the wives of tradesmen) in the city, who are worth from 10,000*l*. to 15,000*l*., are the worst creatures upon the earth, grossly ignorant, and thinking viciousness fashionable. Farmers, I think, are often worthless fellows. Few lords will cheat; and if they do, they'll be ashamed of it; farmers cheat, and are not ashamed of it; they have all the sensual vices too of the nobility, with cheating into the bargain. There is as much fornication and adultery amongst farmers as amongst noblemen." BOSWELL: "The notion of the world, Sir, however, is, that the morals of women of quality are worse than those in lower stations." JOHNSON: "Yes, Sir, the licentiousness of one woman of quality makes more noise than that of a number of women in lower stations; then, Sir, you are to consider the malignity of women in the city against women of quality, which will make them believe anything of them—such as that they call their coachmen to bed. No, Sir; so far as I have observed, the higher in rank, the richer ladies are, they are the better instructed and the more virtuous."

This year the Reverend Mr. Horne published his "Letter to Mr. Dunning, on the English Particle." Johnson read it, and, though not treated in it with sufficient respect, he had candour enough to say to Mr. Seward, "Were I to make a new edition of my Dictionary, I would adopt several[1] of Mr. Horne's etymologies; I hope they did not put the dog in the pillory for his libel; he has too much literature for that."

On Saturday, May 16, I dined with him at Mr. Beau-clerk's with Mr. Langton, Mr. Steevens, Dr. Higgins, and some others. I regret very feelingly every instance of my remissness in recording his *memorabilia ;* I am afraid it is the condition of humanity (as Mr. Windham, of Norfolk, once observed to me, after having made an admirable speech in the House of Commons, which was highly applauded, but which he afterwards perceived might have been better): "that we are more uneasy from thinking of our wants, than happy in thinking of our acquisitions."

---

[1] In Mr. Horne Tooke's enlargement of that "Letter," which he has since published with the title of "᾽Επεα πτερόεντα; or, the Diversions of Purley," he mentions this compliment, as if Dr. Johnson, instead of *several* of his etymologies, had said *all*. His recollection having thus magnified it, shows how ambitious he was of the approbation of so great a man.—BOSWELL.

This is an unreasonable mode of disturbing our tranquillity, and should be corrected; let me then comfort myself with the large treasure of Johnson's conversation which I have preserved for my own enjoyment and that of the world, and let me exhibit what I have upon each occasion, whether more or less, whether a bulse, or only a few sparks of a diamond.

He said, "Dr. Mead lived more in the broad sunshine of life than almost any man."

The disaster of General Burgoyne's army was then the common topic of conversation. It was asked why piling their arms was insisted upon as a matter of such consequence, when it seemed to be a circumstance so inconsiderate in itself. JOHNSON: "Why, Sir, a French author says, '*Il y a beaucoup de puerilités dans la guerre.*' All distinctions are trifles, because great things can seldom occur, and those distinctions are settled by custom. A savage would as willingly have his meat sent to him in the kitchen, as eat it at the table here: as men become civilised, various modes of denoting honourable preference are invented."

He this day made the observations upon the similarity between "Rasselas" and "Candide," which I have inserted in its proper place, when considering his admirable philosophical Romance. He said, "*Candide*," he thought, had more power in it than anything that *Voltaire* had written.

He said, "The lyrical part of Horace never can be perfectly translated; so much of the excellence is in the numbers and the expression. Francis has done it the best; I'll take his, five out of six, against them all."

On Sunday, May 17, I presented to him Mr. Fullarton, of Fullarton, who has since distinguished himself so much in India, to whom he naturally talked of travels, as Mr. Brydone accompanied him in his tour to Sicily and Malta. He said, "the information which we have from modern travellers is much more authentic than what we had from ancient travellers; ancient travellers guessed; modern travellers measure. The Swiss admit that there is but one error in Stanyan. If Brydone were more attentive to his Bible, he would be a good traveller."

He said, "Lord Chatham was a Dictator; he possessed the power of putting the State in motion; now there is no power; all order is relaxed." BOSWELL: "Is there no hope of a change to the better?" JOHNSON: "Why, yes, Sir, when we are weary of this relaxation. So the City of London will appoint its Mayors again by seniority." BOSWELL: "But is not that taking a mere chance for having a good or a bad Mayor?" JOHNSON: "Yes, Sir; but the evil of competition is greater than that of the worst Mayor that can come; besides there is no more reason to suppose that the choice of a rabble will be right, than that chance will be right."

On Tuesday, May 19, I was to set out for Scotland in the evening. He was engaged to dine with me at Mr. Dilly's; I waited upon him to remind him of his appointment, and attend him thither; he gave me some salutary counsel, and recommended vigorous resolution against any deviation from moral duty. BOSWELL: "But you would not have me to bind myself by a solemn obligation?" JOHNSON (much agitated): "What! a vow. Oh, no, Sir; a vow is a horrible thing: it is a snare for sin. The man who cannot go to heaven without a vow, may go—" Here standing erect in the middle of his library, and rolling grand, his pause was truly a curious compound of the solemn and the ludicrous; he half-whistled in his usual way, when pleasant, and he paused, as if checked by religious awe. Methought he would have added—to Hell—but was restrained. I humoured the dilemma. "What, Sir," said I. "*In cœlum jusseris ibit?*" alluding to his imitation of it,—

"And bid him go to hell, to hell he goes."

I had mentioned to him a slight fault in his noble "Imitation of the Tenth Satire of Juvenal," a too near recurrence of the verb *spread*, in his description of the young Enthusiast at College:—

"Through all his veins the fever of renown
    Spreads from the strong contagion of the gown;
    O'er Bodley's dome his future labours *spread*,
    And Bacon's mansion trembles o'er his head."

He had desired me to change *spreads* to *burns*; but for perfect authenticity I now had it done with his own hand.[1] I thought this alteration not only cured the fault, but was more poetical, as it might carry an allusion to the shirt by which Hercules was inflamed.

We had a quiet, comfortable meeting at Mr. Dilly's; nobody there but ourselves. Mr. Dilly mentioned somebody having wished that Milton's "Tractate on Education" should be printed along with his Poems in the edition of

---

[1] The slip of paper on which he made the correction is deposited by me in the noble library to which it relates, and to which I have presented other pieces of his handwriting.—BOSWELL.

the English Poets then going on. Johnson: "It would be breaking in upon the plan; but would be of no great consequence. So far as it would be anything, it would be wrong: Education in England has been in danger of being hurt by two of its greatest men, Milton and Locke. Milton's plan is impracticable, and I suppose has never been tried. Locke's, I fancy, has been tried often enough, but is very imperfect; it gives too much to one side, and too little to the other; it gives too little to literature—I shall do what I can for Dr. Watts; but my materials are very scanty. His poems are by no means his best works; I cannot praise his poetry itself highly; but I can praise its design."

My illustrious friend and I parted with assurances of affectionate regard.

I wrote to him on the 25th of May, from Thorpe in Yorkshire, one of the seats of Mr. Bosville, and gave him an account of my having passed a day at Lincoln, unexpectedly, and therefore without having any letters of introduction, but that I had been honoured with civilities from the Rev. Mr. Simpson, an acquaintance of his, and Captain Broadley, of the Lincolnshire Militia; but more particularly from the Rev. Dr. Gordon, the Chancellor, who first received me with great politeness as a stranger, and, when I informed him who I was, entertained me at his house with the most flattering attention; I also expressed the pleasure with which I had found that our worthy friend, Langton, was highly esteemed in his own country town.

"TO DR. SAMUEL JOHNSON.

"My dear Sir,   *Edinburgh, June* 18, 1778.

*   *   *   *   *

"Since my return to Scotland, I have been again at Lanark, and have had more conversation with Thomson's sister. It is strange that Murdoch, who was his intimate friend, should have mistaken his mother's maiden name, which he says was Hume, whereas Hume was the name of his grandmother by the mother's side. His mother's name was Beatrix Trotter,[1] a daughter of Mr. Trotter, of Fogo, a small proprietor of land. Thomson had one brother, whom he had with him in England as his amanuensis; but he was seized with a consumption, and having returned to Scotland, to try what his native air would do for him, died young. He had three sisters, one married to Mr. Bell, minister of the parish of Strathaven; one to Mr. Craig, father of the ingenious architect,

---

[1] Dr. Johnson was by no means attentive to minute accuracy in his "Lives of the Poets," for, notwithstanding my having detected this mistake, he has continued it.—Boswell.

who gave the plan of the New Town of Edinburgh; and one to Mr. Thomson, master of the grammar-school at Lanark. He was of a humane and benevolent disposition: not only sent valuable presents to his sisters, but a yearly allowance in money, and was always wishing to have it in his power to do them more good. Lord Lyttleton's observation, 'that he loathed much to write,' was very true. His letters to his sister, Mrs. Thomson, were not frequent, and in one of them he says, 'All my friends who know me know how backward I am to write letters, and never impute the negligence of my hand to the coldness of my heart.' I send you a copy of the last letter which she had from him; she never heard that he had any intention of going into holy orders. From this late interview with his sister I think much more favourably of him, as I hope you will. I am eager to see more of your Prefaces to the Poets: I solace myself with the few proof-sheets which I have.

"I send another parcel of Lord Hailes's 'Annals,' which you will please to return to me as soon as you conveniently can. He says, 'he wishes you would cut a little deeper;' but he may be proud that there is so little occasion to use the critical knife. I ever am, my dear Sir, your faithful and affectionate humble servant,

"JAMES BOSWELL."

Mr. Langton has been pleased, at my request, to favour me with some particulars of Dr. Johnson's visit to Warley camp,[1] where this gentleman was at the time stationed as a Captain in the Lincolnshire militia. I shall give them in his own words, in a letter to me:—

"It was in the summer of the year 1778 that he complied with my invitation to come down to the camp at Warley, and he stayed with me about a week. The scene appeared, notwithstanding a great degree of ill health that he seemed to labour under, to interest and amuse him, as agreeing with the disposition that I believe you know he constantly manifested towards inquiring into subjects of the military kind. He sat, with a patient degree of attention, to observe the proceedings of a regimental court-martial, that happened to be called in the time of his stay with us; and one night, as late as eleven o'clock, he accompanied the Major of the regiment in going what are styled the *Rounds*, where he might observe the forms of visiting the guards, for seeing that they and their sentries are ready in their duty on their several posts. He took occasion to converse at times on military topics, one in particular that I see the mention of, in your 'Journal of a Tour to the Hebrides,' which lies open before me, as to gunpowder; which he spoke of to the same effect, in part, that you relate.

"On one occasion, when the regiment were going through their exercise, he went quite close to the men at one of the extremities of it, and watched all their practice attentively; and when he came away his remark was, 'The men indeed do load their muskets and fire with wonderful celerity.' He was likewise particular in inquiring

[1] Warley is a small township, near Halifax, in Yorkshire.

to know what was the weight of the musket balls in use, and within what distance they might be expected to take effect when fired off.

" In walking among the tents, and observing the difference between those of the officers and private men, he said, that the superiority of accommodation of the better conditions of life, to that of the inferior ones, was never exhibited to him in so distinct a view.   The civilities paid to him in the camp were from the gentlemen of the Lincolnshire regiment, one of the officers of which accommodated him with a tent in which he slept; and from General Hall who very courteously invited him to dine with him, where he appeared to be very well pleased with this entertainment, and the civilities he received on the part of the General;[1] the attention likewise of the General's aid-de-camp, Captain Smith, seemed to be very welcome to him, as appeared by their engaging in a great deal of discourse together.   The gentlemen of the East York regiment likewise, on being informed of his coming, solicited his company at dinner; but by that time he had fixed his departure, so that he could not comply with the invitation."

"TO JAMES BOSWELL, ESQ.

"Sir,   London, July 3, 1778.

"I have received two letters from you, of which the second complains of the neglect shown to the first.   You must not tie your friends to such punctual correspondence.   You have all possible assurances of my affection and esteem; and there ought to be no need of reiterated professions.   When it may happen that I can give you either counsel or comfort, I hope it will never happen to me that I should neglect you; but you must not think me criminal or cold, if I say nothing when I have nothing to say.

"You are now happy enough.   Mrs. Boswell is recovered; and I congratulate you upon the probability of her long life.   If general approbation will add anything to your enjoyment, I can tell you that I have heard you mentioned as *a man whom everybody likes*. I think life has little more to give.

"[Langton] has gone to his regiment.   He has laid down his coach, and talks of making more contractions of his expense; how he will succeed I know not.   It is difficult to reform a household gradually; it may be better done by a system totally new.   I am afraid he has always something to hide.   When we pressed him to go to ——, he objected the necessity of attending his navigation; yet he could talk of going to Aberdeen, a place not much nearer his navigation.   I believe he cannot bear the thought of living at [Langton] in a state of diminution; and of appearing among the gentlemen of the neighbourhood *shorn of his beams*.   This is natural, but it is cowardly.   What I told him of the increasing expense of a growing family seems to have struck him.   He certainly had gone

[1] When I one day at Court expressed to General Hall my sense of the honour he had done my friend, he politely answered, "Sir, I did *myself* honour."—Boswell.

on with very confused views, and we have, I think, shown him that he is wrong; though, with the common deficience of advisers, we have not shown him how to do right.

"I wish you would a little correct or restrain your imagination, and imagine that happiness, such as life admits, may be had at other places as well as London. Without asserting [1] Stoicism, it may be said, that it is our business to exempt ourselves as much as we can from the power of external things. There is but one solid basis of happiness, and that is, the reasonable hope of a happy futurity. This may be had everywhere.

"I do not blame your preference of London to other places, for it is really to be preferred, if the choice is free; but few have the choice of their place, or their manner of life; and mere pleasure ought not to be the prime motive of action.

"Mrs. Thrale, poor thing, has a daughter. Mr. Thrale dislikes the times, like the rest of us. Mrs. Williams is sick; Mrs. Desmoulins is poor. I have miserable nights. Nobody is well but Mr. Levett.

"I am, dear Sir, your most, &c.,
"SAM. JOHNSON."

In the course of this year there was a difference between him and his friend Mr. Strahan, the particulars of which it is unnecessary to relate. Their reconciliation was communicated to me in a letter from Mr. Strahan in the following words:—

"The notes I showed you that passed between him and me were dated in March last. The matter lay dormant till July 27, when he wrote to me as follows:—

'TO WILLIAM STRAHAN, ESQ.

'SIR,

It would be very foolish for us to continue strangers any longer. You can never by persistency make wrong right. If I resented too acrimoniously, I resented only to yourself. Nobody ever saw or heard what I wrote. You saw that my anger was over; for in a day or two I came to your house. I have given you a longer time, and I hope you have made so good use of it as to be no longer on evil terms with, Sir, your, &c.,

'SAM. JOHNSON.'

"On this I called upon him, and he has since dined with me."

After this time the same friendship as formerly continued between Dr. Johnson and Mr. Strahan. My friend mentioned to me a little circumstance of his attention,

---

[1] I suspect that this is a misprint, and that Johnson wrote "without *affecting* Stoicism;" but the original letter being burned in a mass of papers in Scotland, I have not been able to ascertain whether my conjecture is well founded or not. The expression in the text, however, may be justified.—MALONE.

which, though we may smile at it, must be allowed to have its foundation in a nice and true knowledge of human life. "When I write to Scotland," said he, "I employ Strahan to frank my letters, that he may have the consequence of appearing a Parliament man among his countrymen."

"TO CAPTAIN LANGTON,[1] WARLEY CAMP.

"Dear Sir,   *October* 31, 1778.

"When I recollect how long ago I was received with so much kindness at Warley Common, I am ashamed that I have not made some inquiries after my friends.

"Pray how many sheep-stealers did you convict? and how did you punish them?   When are you to be cantoned in better habitations?   The air grows cold, and the ground damp.   Longer stay in the camp cannot be without much danger to the health of the common men, if even the officers can escape.

"You see that Dr. Percy is now Dean of Carlisle; about five hundred a year, with a power of presenting himself to some good living. He is provided for.   •

"The session of the Club is to commence with that of the Parliament.   Mr. Banks [2] desires to be admitted; he will be a very honourable accession.

"Did the king please you?   The Coxheath men, I think, have some reason to complain: Reynolds says your camp is better than theirs.

"I hope you find yourself able to encounter this weather.   Take care of own health; and, as you can, of your men.   Be pleased to make my compliments to all the gentlemen whose notice I have had, and whose kindness I have experienced.

"I am, dear Sir,
"Your most humble servant,
"Sam. Johnson."

I wrote to him on the 18th of August, the 18th of September, and the 6th of November; informing him of my having another son born, whom I had called James; that I had passed some time at Auchinleck; that the Countess of Loudoun, now in her ninety-ninth year, was as fresh as when he saw her, and remembered him with respect; and that his mother by adoption, the Countess of Eglintoune, had said to me, "Tell Mr. Johnson I love him exceedingly; that I had again suffered much from bad

---

[1] Dr. Johnson here addresses his worthy friend, Bennet Langton, Esq., by his title as Captain of the Lincolnshire militia, in which he has since been most deservedly raised to the rank of Major.—Boswell.

[2] Afterwards Sir Joseph Banks, the distinguished President of the Royal Society.

spirits; and that, as it was very long since I heard from him, I was not a little uneasy."

The continuance of his regard for his friend Dr. Burney appears from the following letters:—

"TO THE REVEREND DR. WHEELER, OXFORD.

"DEAR SIR,   *London, November* 2, 1778.

"Dr. Burney, who brings this paper, is engaged in a History of Music; and having been told by Dr. Markham of some MSS. relating to his subject, which are in the library of your College, is desirous to examine them.   He is my friend, and therefore I take the liberty of entreating your favour and assistance in his inquiry; and can assure you, with great confidence, that if you knew him he would not want any intervenient solicitation to obtain the kindness of one who loves learning and virtue as you love them.

"I have been flattering myself all the summer with the hope of paying my annual visit to my friends, but something has obstructed me; I still hope not to be long without seeing you.   I should be glad of a little literary talk, and glad to show you, by the frequency of my visits, how eagerly I love it, when you talk it.

"I am, dear Sir, your most humble servant,
"SAM. JOHNSON."

"TO THE REVEREND DR. EDWARDS, OXFORD.

"SIR,   *London, November* 2, 1778.

"The bearer, Dr. Burney, has had some account of a Welsh manuscript in the Bodleian library, from which he hopes to gain some materials for his History of Music; but being ignorant of the language, is at a loss where to find assistance.   I make no doubt but you, Sir, can help him through his difficulties, and therefore take the liberty of recommending him to your favour, as I am sure you will find him a man worthy of every civility that can be shown, and every benefit that can be conferred.

"But we must not let Welsh drive us from Greek.   What comes of Xenophon?   If you do not like the trouble of publishing the book, do not let your commentaries be lost.   Contrive that they may be published somewhere.

"I am, Sir, your humble servant,
"SAM. JOHNSON."

These letters procured Dr. Burney great kindness and friendly offices from both of these gentlemen, not only on that occasion but in future visits to the university.   The same year Dr. Johnson not only wrote to Dr. Joseph Warton in favour of Dr. Burney's younger son, who was to be placed in the College of Winchester, but accompanied him when he went thither.

We surely cannot but admire the benevolent exertions

of this great and good man, especially when we consider how grievously he was afflicted with bad health, and how uncomfortable his home was made by the perpetual jarring of those whom he charitably accommodated under his roof.   He has sometimes suffered me to talk jocularly of his group of females, and call them his *Seraglio*.   He thus mentions them, together with honest Levett, in one of his letters to Mrs. Thrale:—"Williams hates everybody; Levett hates Desmoulins, and does not love Williams; Desmoulins hates them both; Poll[1] loves none of them."

"TO JAMES BOSWELL, ESQ.

"Dear Sir,   *November* 21, 1778.

"It is indeed a long time since I wrote, and think you must have some reason to complain; however, you must not let small things disturb you when you have such a fine addition to your happiness as a new boy, and I hope your lady's health is restored by bringing him. It seems very probable that a little care will now restore her, if any remains of her complaints are left.

"You seem, if I understand your letter, to be gaining ground at Auchinleck—an incident that would give me great delight.

*   *   *   *   *   *

"When any fit of anxiety, or gloominess, or perversion of mind, lays hold upon you, make it a rule not to publish it by complaints, but exert your whole care to hide it. By endeavouring to hide it you will drive it away. Be always busy.

"The Club is to meet with the Parliament; we talk of electing Banks, the traveller; he will be a reputable member.

"Langton has been encamped with his company of militia on Warley-common; I spent five days amongst them. He signalised himself as a diligent officer, and has very high respect in the regiment. He presided when I was there at a court-martial; he is now quartered in Hertfordshire; his lady and little ones are in Scotland. Paoli came to the camp, and commended the soldiers.

"Of myself I have no great matters to say; my health is not restored; my nights are restless and tedious. The best night that I have had these twenty years was at Fort Augustus.

"I hope soon to send you a few Lives to read.

"I am, dear sir, your most affectionate,
"Sam. Johnson."

About this time the Rev. Mr. John Hussey, who had been some time in trade, and was then a clergyman of the Church of England, being about to undertake a journey to Aleppo and other parts of the East, which he accomplished, Dr. Johnson (who had long been in habits of

---

[1] Miss Carmichael.—Boswell.

intimacy with him), honoured him with the following letter:—

"TO MR. JOHN HUSSEY.

"DEAR SIR,   *December* 29, 1778.

"I have sent you the 'Grammar,' and have left you two books more, by which I hope to be remembered. Write my name in them: we may perhaps see each other no more. You part with my good wishes, nor do I despair of seeing you return. Let no opportunities of vice corrupt you; let no bad example seduce you; let the blindness of Mahometans confirm you in Christianity. God bless you.

"I am, dear Sir,
"Your affectionate, humble servant,
"SAM. JOHNSON."

Johnson this year expressed great satisfaction at the publication of the first volume of "Discourses to the Royal Academy," by Sir Joshua Reynolds, whom he always considered as one of his literary school. Much praise indeed is due to those excellent Discourses which are so universally admired, and for which the author received from the Empress of Russia a gold snuff-box, adorned with her profile in *bas relief* set in diamonds; and containing, what is infinitely more valuable, a slip of paper, on which are written, with her Imperial Majesty's own hand, the following words:—"*Pour le Chevalier Reynolds, en temoignage du contentement que j'ai ressentie à la lecture de ses excellens discours sur la Peinture.*"

CHAPTER XIV.—1779

Publication of Johnson's "Lives of the Poets"—Death of Garrick—Rev. Mr. Falconer—Philidor—Tasker's Ode —A Man of the World—Goldsmith's "Vicar of Wakefield"—Letters of Junius—Sheridan—Advantages of London—Good Friday—Easter-Day—Skinning an Eel—Claret, Port, and Brandy—Shakespeare's Witches—Beauty of Loch-lomond—Dr. Drummond—Love of Liberty—Execution of Hackman—Altercation between Johnson and Beauclerk — Mallet — Mr. Fitzherbert — Friendship — Garrick—Chesterfield—Johnson's Ideas of Drinking—Dr. Taylor—Parental Affection—Johnson's Interview with Lord Marchmont—Pope—Parnell's "Hermit"—Boswell's Departure for Scotland—Correspondence—Boswell's Introduction to John Wesley—Death of Edward Dilly

THIS year Johnson gave the world a luminous proof that the vigour of his mind, in all its faculties, whether memory, judgment, or imagination, was not in the least abated; for this year came out the first four volumes of his "Prefaces, biographical and critical, to the most eminent of the English Poets," published by the booksellers of London. The remaining volumes came out in the year 1780. The Poets were selected by the several booksellers who had the honorary copyright, which is still preserved among them by mutual compact, notwithstanding the decision of the House of Lords against the perpetuity of Literary Property. We have his own authority,[1] that by his recommendation the poems of Blackmore, Watts, Pomfret, and Yalden, were added to the Collection. Of this work I shall speak more particularly hereafter.

On the 22nd of January I wrote to him on several topics, and mentioned, that, as he had been so good as to permit me to have the proof sheets of his "Lives of the Poets," I had written to his servant Francis to take care of them for me.

[1] Life of Watts.—BOSWELL.

"MR. BOSWELL TO DR. JOHNSON.

"MY DEAR SIR,   *Edinburgh, Feb. 2, 1779.*

"Garrick's death is a striking event; not that we should be surprised with the death of any man who has lived sixty-two years,[1] but because there was a *vivacity* in our late celebrated friend, which drove away the thoughts of *death* from any association with *him*. I am sure you will be tenderly affected with his departure; and I would wish to hear from you upon the subject. I was obliged to him in my days of effervescence in London, when poor Derrick was my governor; and since that time I received many civilities from him. Do you remember how pleasing it was, when I received a letter from him at Inverary, upon our first return to civilised living, after our Hebridean journey. I shall always remember him with affection as well as admiration.

"On Saturday last, being the 30th of January, I drank coffee and old port, and had solemn conversation with the Reverend Mr. Falconer, a nonjuring bishop, a very learned and worthy man. He gave two toasts, which you will believe I drank with cordiality —Dr. Samuel Johnson, and Flora Macdonald. I sat about four hours with him, and it was really as if I had been living in the last century. The Episcopal Church of Scotland, though faithful to the royal house of Stuart has never accepted of any *congé d'élire*, since the Revolution; it is the only true Episcopal Church in Scotland, as it has its own succession of bishops. For as to the episcopal clergy, who take the oaths to the present government, they indeed follow the rites of the Church of England; but, as Bishop Falconer observed, 'they are not *Episcopals;* for they are under no bishop, as a bishop cannot have authority beyond his diocese.' This venerable gentleman did me the honour to dine with me yesterday, and he laid his hands upon the heads of my little ones. We had a good deal of curious literary conversation, particularly about Mr. Thomas Ruddiman, with whom he lived in great friendship.

"Any fresh instance of the uncertainty of life makes one embrace more closely a valuable friend. My dear and much respected Sir, may GOD preserve you long in this world while I am in it.

"I am ever your much obliged

"And affectionate humble servant,

"JAMES BOSWELL."

[1] On Mr. Garrick's monument, in Lichfield Cathedral, he is said to have died, "aged 64 years." But it is a mistake, and Mr. Boswell is perfectly correct. Garrick was baptised at Hereford, Feb. 28, 1716–17, and died at his house in London, Jan. 20, 1779. The inaccuracy of lapidary inscriptions is well known.—MALONE.
The following is a copy of the inscription on Garrick's monument,— the figures 64, referred to by Malone, having been altered to 63.
EVA MARIA, relict of DAVID GARRICK, ESQ.,
raised this monument to the memory of her beloved husband,
who died the 20th of January, 1779, aged 63 years.
He had not only the amiable qualities of private life,
but such astonishing dramatic talents,
as to well verify the observation of his friend,
"His death eclipsed the gaiety of nations,
and impoverished the public stock of harmless pleasure."

On the 23rd of February I wrote to him again, complaining of his silence, as I had heard he was ill, and had written to Mr. Thrale for information concerning him; and I announced my intention of soon being again in London.

"TO JAMES BOSWELL, ESQ.

"Dear Sir,   *March* 13, 1779.

"Why should you take such delight to make a bustle, to write to Mr. Thrale that I am negligent, and to Francis to do what is so very unnecessary. Thrale, you may be sure, cared not about it; and I shall spare Francis the trouble, by ordering a set both of the Lives and Poets to dear Mrs. Boswell,[1] in acknowledgment of her marmalade. Persuade her to accept them, and accept them kindly. If I thought she would receive them scornfully, I would send them to Miss Boswell, who, I hope, has yet none of her mamma's ill-will to me.

"I would send sets of Lives, four volumes, to some other friends, to Lord Hailes first. His second volume lies by my bed-side; a book surely of great labour, and to every just thinker of great delight. Write me word to whom I shall send besides: would it please Lord Auchinleck? Mrs. Thrale waits in the coach.
                                        "I am, dear Sir, &c.,
                                        "Sam. Johnson."

This letter crossed me on the road to London, where I arrived on Monday, March 15; and next morning, at a late hour, found Dr. Johnson sitting over his tea, attended by Mrs. Desmoulins, Mr. Levett, and a clergyman, who had come to submit some poetical pieces to his revision. It is wonderful what a number and variety of writers, some of them even unknown to him, prevailed on his good-nature to look over their works, and suggest corrections and improvements. My arrival interrupted for a little while the important business of this true representative of Bayes. Upon its being resumed, I found that the subject under immediate consideration was a translation yet in manuscript, of the "Carmen Seculare" of Horace, which had this year been set to music, and performed as a public entertainment in London, for the joint benefit of Monsieur Philidor[2] and Signor Baretti. When Johnson had done reading, the author asked him bluntly, "If, upon the whole, it was a good translation?" Johnson, whose regard for truth was uncommonly strict, seemed to be puzzled for a

[1] He sent a set elegantly bound and gilt, which was received as a very handsome present.—Boswell.

[2] Andrew Philidor is celebrated as the most skilful chess-player of his age. His "Analysis of Chess," published in 1777, still retains its value as an authority. He was a member of the chess-club thirty years;

moment what answer to make, as he certainly could not honestly commend the performance, with exquisite address he evaded the question, thus, "Sir, I do not say that it may not be made a very good translation." Here nothing whatever in favour of the performance was affirmed, and yet the writer was not shocked. A printed "Ode to the Warlike Genius of Britain" came next in review. The bard was a lank bony figure, with short black hair; he was writhing himself in agitation while Johnson read, and showing his teeth in a grin of earnestness, exclaimed in broken sentence, and in a keen, sharp tone, "Is that poetry, Sir? Is it Pindar?" JOHNSON: "Why, Sir, there is a great deal of what is called poetry." Then turning to me, the poet cried, "My muse has not been long upon the town, and (pointing to the Ode) it trembles under the hand of the great critic." Johnson, in a tone of displeasure asked him, "Why do you praise Anson?" I did not trouble him by asking his reason for this question. He proceeded, "Here is an error, Sir; you have made Genius feminine."—"Palpable, Sir," cried the enthusiast; "I know it. But (in a lower tone) it was to pay a compliment to the Duchess of Devonshire, with which her Grace was pleased. She is walking across Coxheath, in the military uniform, and I suppose her to be the Genius of Britain." JOHNSON: "Sir, you are giving a reason for it; but that will not make it right. You may have a reason why two and two should make five; but they will still make but four."

Although I was several times with him in the course of the following days, such it seems were my occupations, or such my negligence, that I have preserved no memorial of his conversation till Friday, March 26, when I visited him. He said he expected to be attacked on account of his "Lives of the Poets." "However," said he, "I would rather be attacked than unnoticed. For the worse thing you can do to an author is to be silent as to his works. An assault upon a town is a bad thing; but starving it is still worse; an assault may be unsuccessful; you may have more men killed than you kill; but if you starve the town, you are sure of victory."

Talking of a friend of ours associating with persons of very discordant principles and characters, I said he was a very universal man, quite a man of the world. JOHNSON:

and of his skill in that game a stronger proof could not be given than that of his defeating blindfolded, at the same time, two of the best players of the Club. He was born at Dreux, in France, in 1726, and died in 1795.

"Yes, Sir; but one may be so much a man of the world, as to be nothing in the world. I remember a passage in Goldsmith's 'Vicar of Wakefield,' which he was afterwards fool enough to expunge—'I do not love a man who is zealous for nothing.'" Boswell: "That was a fine passage." Johnson : "Yes, Sir ; there was another fine passage, too, which he struck out: 'When I was a young man, being anxious to distinguish myself, I was perpetually starting new propositions. But I soon gave this over; for I found that generally what was new was false.'"[1] I said I did not like to sit with people of whom I had not a good opinion. Johnson: "But you must not indulge your delicacy too much; or you will be a *tête-à-tête* man all your life."

During my stay in London this spring, I find I was unaccountably negligent in preserving Johnson's sayings, more so than at any time when I was happy enough to have an opportunity of hearing his wisdom and wit. There is no help for it now. I must content myself with presenting such scraps as I have. But I am nevertheless ashamed and vexed to think how much has been lost. It is not that there was a bad crop this year; but that I was not sufficiently careful in gathering it in. I therefore, in some instances, can only exhibit a few detached fragments.

Talking of the wonderful concealment of the author of the celebrated letters signed *Junius ;* he said, "I should have believed Burke to be Junius, because I know no man but Burke who is capable of writing these letters; but Burke spontaneously denied it to me. The case would have been different, had I asked him if he was the author; a man so questioned, as to an anonymous publication, may think he has a right to deny it."

He observed that his old friend, Mr. Sheridan, had been honoured with extraordinary attention in his own country, by having had an exception made in his favour in an Irish act of Parliament concerning insolvent debtors. "Thus to be singled out," said he "by Legislature, as an object of public consideration and kindness, is a proof of no common merit."

[1] Dr. Burney, in a note introduced in a former page, has mentioned this circumstance concerning Goldsmith, as communicated to him by Dr. Johnson, not recollecting that it occurred here. His remark, however, is not wholly superfluous, as it ascertains that the words which Goldsmith had put into the mouth of a fictitious character in "The Vicar of Wakefield," and which, as we learn from Dr. Johnson, he afterwards expunged, related, like many other passages in his novel, to himself.—Malone.

At Streatham, on Monday, March 29, at breakfast, he maintained that a father had no right to control the inclinations of his daughters in marriage.

On Wednesday, March 31, when I visited him, and confessed an excess of which I had very seldom been guilty —that I had spent a whole night in playing at cards, and that I could not look back on it with satisfaction—instead of a harsh animadversion, he mildly said, "Alas, Sir, on how few things can we look back with satisfaction."

On Thursday, April 1, he commended one of the Dukes of Devonshire for "a dogged veracity." He said too, "London is nothing to some people; but to a man whose pleasure is intellectual, London is the place. And there is no place where economy can be so well practised as in London: more can be had here for the money, even by ladies, than any where else. You cannot play tricks with your fortune in a small place; you must make an uniform appearance. Here a lady may have well-furnished apartments, an elegant dress, without any meat in her kitchen."

I was amused by considering with how much ease and coolness he could write or talk to a friend, exhorting him not to suppose that happiness was not to be found as well in other places as in London; when he himself was at all times sensible of its being, comparatively speaking, a heaven upon earth. The truth is, that by those who from sagacity, attention, and experience, have learnt the full advantage of London, its pre-eminence over every other place, not only for variety of enjoyment, but for comfort, will be felt with a philosophical exultation. The freedom from remark and petty censure, with which life may be passed there, is a circumstance which a man who knows the teasing restraint of a narrow circle must relish highly. Mr. Burke, whose orderly and amiable domestic habits might make the eye of observation less irksome to him than to most men, said once very pleasantly in my hearing, "Though I have the honour to represent Bristol, I should not like to live there; I should be obliged to be so much *upon my good behaviour.*" In London, a man may live in splendid society at one time, and in frugal retirement at another, without animadversion. There, and there alone, a man's own house is truly his *castle*, in which he can be in perfect safety from intrusion whenever he pleases. I never shall forget how well this was expressed to me one day by Mr. Meynell: "The chief advantage of London," said he, "is, that a man is always *so near his burrow.*"

He said of one of his old acquaintances, "He is very fit for a travelling governor. He knows French very well.

He is a man of good principles; and there would be no danger that a young gentleman should catch his manner; for it is so very bad, that it must be avoided. In that respect he would be like the drunken Helot."

A gentleman has informed me, that Johnson said of the same person, "Sir, he has the most *inverted* understanding of any man whom I have ever known."

On Friday, April 2, being Good-Friday, I visited him in the morning as usual; and finding that we insensibly fell into a train of ridicule upon the foibles of one of our friends, a very worthy man, I, by way of a check, quoted some good admonition from "The Government of the Tongue"—that very pious book. It happened also remarkably enough, that the subject of the sermon preached to us to-day by Dr. Burrows, the rector of St. Clement Danes, was the certainty that at the last day we must give an account of "the deeds done in the body;" and amongst various acts of culpability he mentioned evil-speaking. As we were moving slowly along in the crowd from church, Johnson jogged my elbow, and said, "Did you attend to the sermon?"—"Yes, Sir," said I, "it was very applicable to *us.*" He, however, stood upon the defensive. "Why, Sir, the sense of ridicule is given us, and may be lawfully used. The author of 'The government of the Tongue' would have us treat all men alike."

In the interval between morning and evening service, he endeavoured to employ himself earnestly in devotional exercise; and, as he has mentioned in his "Prayers and Meditations" [p. 173], gave me "*Les Pensées de Pascal,*" that I might not interrupt him. I preserve the book with reverence. His presenting it to me is marked upon it with his own hand, and I have found in it a truly divine unction. We went to church again in the afternoon.

On Saturday, April 3, I visited him at night, and found him sitting in Mrs. Williams's room, with her, and one who he afterwards told me was a natural son[1] of the second Lord Southwell. The table had a singular appearance, being covered with a heterogeneous assemblage of oysters and porter for his company, and tea for himself. I mentioned my having heard an eminent physician, who was himself a Christian, argue in favour of universal toleration, and maintain, that no man could be hurt by another man's differing from him in opinion. JOHNSON:

[1] Mr. Mauritius Lowe, a painter.—MALONE.

"Sir, you are, to a certain degree, hurt by knowing that even one man does not believe."

On Easter-day, after solemn service at St. Paul's, I dined with him; Mr. Allen, the printer, was also his guest. He was uncommonly silent; and I have not written down anything, except a single curious fact, which, having the sanction of his inflexible veracity, may be received as a striking instance of human insensibility and inconsideration. As he was passing by a fishmonger who was skinning an eel alive, he heard him "curse it, because it would not lie still."

On Wednesday, April 7, I dined with him at Sir Joshua Reynolds's. I have not marked what company was there. Johnson harangued upon the qualities of different liquors; and spoke with great contempt of claret, as so weak, that "a man would be drowned by it before it made him drunk." He was persuaded to drink one glass of it, that he might judge, not from recollection, which might be dim, but from immediate sensation. He shook his head, and said, "Poor stuff! No, Sir, claret is the liquor for boys; port for men: but he who aspires to be a hero (smiling) must drink brandy. In the first place, the flavour of brandy is most grateful to the palate; and then brandy will do soonest for a man what drinking *can* do for him. There are, indeed, few who are able to drink brandy. That is a power rather to be wished for than attained. And yet," proceeded he, "as in all pleasure hope is a considerable part, I know not but fruition comes too quick by brandy. Florence wine I think the worst; it is wine only to the eye; it is wine neither while you are drinking it, nor after you have drunk it: it neither pleases the taste, nor exhilarates the spirits." I reminded him how heartily he and I used to drink wine together, when we were first acquainted; and how I used to have a headache after setting up with him. He did not like to have this recalled, or, perhaps, thinking that I boasted improperly, resolved to have a witty stroke at me; "Nay, Sir, it was not the *wine* that made your head ache, but the *sense* that I put into it." BOSWELL: "What, Sir, will sense make the head ache?" JOHNSON: "Yes, Sir (with a smile), when it is not used to it."—No man who has a true relish of pleasantry could be offended at this; especially if Johnson in a long intimacy had given him repeated proofs of his regard and good estimation. I used to say, that as he had given me 1000*l.* in praise, he had a good right now and then to take a guinea from me.

On Thursday, April 8, I dined with him at Mr. Allan

Ramsay's, with Lord Graham and some other company. We talked of Shakespeare's witches. JOHNSON: "They are beings of his own creation; they are a compound of malignity and meanness, without any abilities; and are quite different from the Italian magician. King James says, in his 'Dæmonology,' 'Magicians command the devils: witches are their servants.' The Italian magicians are elegant beings." RAMSAY: "Opera witches, not Drury-lane witches." Johnson observed, that abilities might be employed in a narrow sphere, as in getting money, which he said he believed no man could do, without vigorous parts, though concentrated to a point. RAMSAY: "Yes, like a strong horse in a mill, he pulls better."

Lord Graham, while he praised the beauty of Loch Lomond, on the banks of which is his family seat, complained of the climate, and said he could not bear it. JOHNSON: "Nay, my Lord, don't talk so: you may bear it well enough. Your ancestors have borne it more years than I can tell." This was a handsome compliment to the antiquity of the House of Montrose. His Lordship told me afterwards, that he had only affected to complain of the climate; lest, if he had spoken as favourably of his country as he really thought, Dr. Johnson might have attacked it. Johnson was very courteous to Lady Margaret Macdonald. "Madam," said he, "when I was in the Isle of Sky, I heard of the people running to take the stones off the road, lest Lady Margaret's horse should stumble."

Lord Graham commended Dr. Drummond at Naples as a man of extraordinary talents; and added, that he had a great love of liberty. JOHNSON: "He is *young*, my Lord (looking to his Lordship with an arch smile); all *boys* love liberty, till experience convinces them they are not so fit to govern themselves as they imagined. We are all agreed as to our own liberty: we would have as much of it as we can get; but we are not agreed as to the liberty of others; for in proportion as we take, others must lose. I believe we hardly wish that the mob should have liberty to govern us. When that was the case some time ago, no man was at liberty not to have candles in his windows." RAMSAY: "The result is, that order is better than confusion." JOHNSON: "The result is, that order cannot be had but by subordination."

On Friday, April 16, I had been present at the trial of the unfortunate Mr. Hackman, who, in a fit of frantic jealous love, had shot Miss Ray, the favourite of a nobleman. Johnson, in whose company I had dined to-day with some other friends, was much interested by my account of what passed, and particularly with his prayer for the mercy of heaven. He said, in a solemn fervid tone, "I hope he *shall* find mercy."

This day a violent altercation arose between Johnson and Beauclerk [at the club], which having made much noise at the time, I think it proper, in order to prevent any future misrepresentation, to give a minute account of it.

In talking of Hackman, Johnson argued, as Judge Blackstone had done, that his being furnished with two pistols was a proof that he meant to shoot two persons. Mr. Beauclerk said, "No; for that every wise man who intended to shoot himself took two pistols, that he might be sure of doing it at once. Lord ———'s cook shot himself with one pistol, and lived ten days in great agony. Mr. ———, who loved buttered muffins, but durst not eat them because they disagreed with his stomach, resolved to shoot himself; and then he eat three buttered muffins for breakfast, before shooting himself, knowing that he should not be troubled with indigestion: *he* had two charged pistols; one was found lying charged upon the table by him, after he had shot himself with the other."—"Well," said Johnson, with an air of triumph, "you see here one pistol was sufficient." Beauclerk replied smartly, "Because it happened to kill him." And either then or very little afterwards, being piqued at Johnson's triumphant remark, added, "This is what you don't know, and I do." There was then a cessation of the dispute; and some minutes intervened, during which, dinner and the glass went on cheerfully; when Johnson suddenly and abruptly exclaimed, "Mr. Beauclerk, how came you to talk so petulantly to me, as, 'This is what you don't know, but what I know?' One thing I know, which *you* don't seem to know, that you are very uncivil." BEAUCLERK: "Because *you* began by being uncivil (which you always are)." The words in parentheses were, I believe, not heard by Dr. Johnson. Here again there was a cessation of arms. Johnson told me that the reason why he waited at first some time without taking any notice of what Mr. Beauclerk said, was because he was thinking whether he should resent it. But when he considered that there were present a young Lord and an eminent traveller, two men of the world with whom he had never dined before, he was apprehensive that they might think they had a right to take such liberties with him as Beauclerk did, and therefore resolved he would not let it pass; adding, "that he would not appear a coward." A little while after this, the conversation turned on the violence of Hackman's temper. Johnson then said, "It was his business to *command* his temper, as my friend Mr. Beauclerk should have done some time ago." BEAUCLERK: "I should learn of *you*, Sir." JOHNSON: "Sir, you have given *me* opportunities enough of learning, when I have been in *your* company. No man loves to be treated with contempt." BEAUCLERK (with a polite inclination toward Johnson): "Sir, you have known me twenty years, and however I may have treated others, you may be sure I could never treat you with contempt." JOHNSON: "Sir, you have said more than was necessary." Thus it ended; and Beauclerk's coach not having come for him till very late, Dr. Johnson and another gentleman sat with him a long time after the rest of the company were gone; and he and I dined at Beauclerk's on the Saturday se'nnight following.

After this tempest had subsided, I recollect the following particulars of his conversation:—

"I am always for getting a boy forward in his learning, for that is a sure good. I would let him at first read *any* English book which happens to engage his attention; because you have done a great deal when you have brought him to have entertainment from a book. He'll get better books afterwards."

"Mallet, I believe, never wrote a single line of his projected Life of the Duke of Marlborough. He groped for materials, and thought of it till he had exhausted his mind. Thus it sometimes happens that men entangle themselves in their own schemes."

"To be contradicted in order to force you to talk is mighty unpleasing. You *shine*, indeed; but it is by being *ground*."

Of a gentleman who made some figure among the *Literati* of his time (Mr. Fitzherbert), he said, "What eminence he had was by a felicity of manner; he had no more learning than what he could not help."

On Saturday, April 24, I dined with him at Mr. Beauclerk's, with Sir Joshua Reynolds, Mr. Jones (afterwards Sir William), Mr. Langton, Mr. Steevens, Mr. Paradise, and Dr. Higgins. I mentioned that Mr. Wilkes had attacked Garrick to me, as a man who had no friend. JOHNSON: "I believe he is right, Sir. [Οἱ φίλοι, οὐ φίλος] —He had friends but no friend. Garrick was so diffused, he had no man to whom he wished to unbosom himself. He found people always ready to applaud him, and that always for the same thing; so he saw life with great uniformity." I took upon me, for once, to fight with

Goliath's weapons, and play the sophist.—"Garrick did not need a friend, as he got from everybody all that he wanted. What is a friend? One who supports and comforts you, while others do not. Friendship, you know, Sir, is the cordial drop, 'to make the nauseous draught of life go down;' but if the draught be not nauseous, if it be all sweet, there is no occasion for that drop." JOHNSON: "Many men would not be content to live so. I hope I should not. They would wish to have an intimate friend, with whom they might compare minds and cherish private virtues." One of the company mentioned Lord Chesterfield as a man who had no friend. JOHNSON: "There were more materials to make friendship in Garrick, had he not been so diffused." BOSWELL: "Garrick was pure gold, but beat out to thin leaf. Lord Chesterfield was tinsel." JOHNSON: "Garrick was a very good man, the most cheerful man of his age; a decent liver in a profession which is supposed to give indulgence to licentiousness; and a man who gave away, freely, money acquired by himself. He begun the word with a great hunger for money; the son of a half-pay officer, bred in a family whose study was to make fourpence do as much as others made fourpence halfpenny do. But when he had got money he was very liberal." I presumed to animadvert on his eulogy on Garrick, in his "Lives of the Poets." "You say, Sir, his death eclipsed the gaiety of nations." JOHNSON: "I could not have said more or less. It is the truth: *eclipsed*, not *extinguished*; and his death *did* eclipse: it was like a storm." BOSWELL: "But why nations? Did his gaiety extend farther than his own nation?" JOHNSON: "Why, Sir, some exaggeration must be allowed. Besides, nations may be said—if we allow the Scotch to be a nation—to have gaiety—which they have not. *You* are an exception, though. Come, gentlemen, let us candidly admit that there is one Scotchman who is cheerful." BEAUCLERK: "But he is a very unnatural Scotchman." I, however, continued to think the compliment to Garrick hyperbolically untrue. His acting had ceased some time before his death; at any rate he had acted in Ireland but a short time, at an early period of his life, and never in Scotland. I objected also to what appears an anti-climax of praise, when contrasted with the preceding panegyric, "and diminished the public stock of harmless pleasure!" "Is not *harmless pleasure* very tame?" JOHNSON: "Nay, Sir, harmless pleasure is the highest praise. Pleasure is a word of dubious import; pleasure is, in general, dangerous, and pernicious to virtue; to be able, therefore, to furnish pleasure that is harmless pleasure pure and unalloyed, is as great a power as man can possess." This was, perhaps, as ingenious a defence as could be made; still, however, I was not satisfied.

A celebrated wit being mentioned, he said, "One may say of him as was said of a French wit, *Il n'a de l'esprit que contre Dieu.* I have been several times in company with him, but never perceived any strong power of wit. He produces a general effect by various means; he has a cheerful countenance and a gay voice. Besides, his trade is wit. It would be as wild in him to come into company without merriment, as for a highwayman to take the road without his pistols."

Talking of the effects of drinking, he said, "Drinking may be practised with great prudence; a man who exposes himself when he is intoxicated, has not the art of getting drunk; a sober man who happens occasionally to get drunk, readily enough goes into a new company, which a man who has been drinking should never do. Such a man will undertake anything: he is without skill in inebriation. I used to slink home when I had drunk too much. A man accustomed to self-examination will be conscious when he is drunk, though an habitual drunkard will not be conscious of it. I knew a physician who for twenty years was not sober; yet in a pamphlet, which he wrote upon fevers, he appealed to Garrick and me for his vindication from a charge of drunkenness. A bookseller (naming him), who got a large fortune by trade, was so habitually and equally drunk, that his most intimate friends never perceived that he was more sober at one time than another."

Talking of celebrated and successful irregular practisers in physic, he said, "Taylor[1] was the most ignorant man I ever knew, but sprightly; Ward, the dullest. Taylor challenged me once to talk Latin with him (laughing). I quoted some of Horace, which he took to be part of my own speech. He said a few words well enough." Beau-clerk: "I remember, Sir, you said, that Taylor was an instance how far impudence could carry ignorance." Mr. Beauclerk was very entertaining this day, and told us a number of short stories in a lively and elegant manner, and with that air of *the world* which has I know not what impressive effect, as if there were something more than is expressed, or than, perhaps, we could perfectly understand. As Johnson and I accompanied Sir Joshua Reynolds in his coach, Johnson said, "There is in Beauclerk a pre-dominance over his company that one does not like. But

[1] The Chevalier Taylor, the celebrated Oculist.—Malone.

he is a man who has lived so much in the world, that he has a short story on every occasion; he is always ready to talk, and is never exhausted."

Johnson and I passed the evening at Miss Reynolds's, Sir Joshua's sister. I mentioned that an eminent friend of ours, talking of the common remark, that affection descends, said that "this was wisely contrived for the preservation of mankind; for which it was not so necessary that there should be affection from children to parents, as from parents to children; nay, there should be no harm in that view though children should at a certain age eat their parents." JOHNSON: "But, Sir, if this were known generally to be the case, parents would not have affection for children." BOSWELL: "True, Sir; for it is in expectation of a return that parents are so attentive to their children; and I know a very pretty instance of a little girl of whom her father was very fond, who once, when he was in a melancholy fit, and had gone to bed, persuaded him to rise in good humour by saying, 'My dear papa, please to get up, and let me help you on with your clothes, that I may learn to do it when you are an old man.'"

Soon after this time a little incident occurred which I will not suppress, because I am desirous that my work should be, as much as is consistent with the strictest truth, an antidote to the false and injurious notions of his character, which have been given by others, and therefore I infuse every drop of genuine sweetness into my biographical cup.

"TO DR. JOHNSON.

"MY DEAR SIR,   South Audley-street, Monday, April 26.

"I am in great pain with an inflamed foot, and obliged to keep my bed, so am prevented from having the pleasure to dine at Mr. Ramsay's to-day, which is very hard; and my spirits are sadly sunk. Will you be so friendly as to come and sit an hour with me in the evening. I am ever your most faithful

"And affectionate humble servant,
"JAMES BOSWELL."

"TO MR. BOSWELL.

"Harley-street.

"Mr. Johnson laments the absence of Mr. Boswell, and will come to him."

He came to me in the evening, and brought Sir Joshua Reynolds. I need scarcely say that their conversation, while they sat by my bedside, was the most pleasing opiate to pain that could have been administered.

Johnson, being now better disposed to obtain informa-tion concerning Pope than he was last year, sent by me to my Lord Marchmont a present of those volumes of his "Lives of the Poets," which were at this time published, with a request to have permission to wait on him; and his lordship, who had called on him twice, obligingly appointed Saturday, the 1st of May, for receiving us.

On that morning, Johnson came to me from Streatham, and, after drinking chocolate at General Paoli's, in South Audley-street, we proceeded to Lord Marchmont's, in Curzon-street. His lordship met us at the door of his library, and with great politeness said to Johnson, " I am not going to make an encomium upon *myself*, by telling you the high respect I have for *you*, Sir."   Johnson was exceedingly courteous, and the interview, which lasted about two hours, during which the earl communicated his anecdotes of Pope, was as agreeable as I could have wished. When we came out, I said to Johnson, that, considering his lordship's civility, I should have been vexed if he had again failed to come. " Sir," said he, " I would rather have given twenty pounds than not have come."   I accompanied him to Streatham, where we dined, and returned to town in the evening.

On Monday, May 3, I dined with him at Mr. Dilly's. I pressed him this day for his opinion on the passage on Parnell, concerning which I had in vain questioned him in several letters, and at length obtained it in *due form of law* :—

"CASE for Dr. JOHNSON's Opinion:
3rd of May, 1779.

"PARNELL, in his 'Hermit,' has the following passage:

"To clear this doubt, to know the world by sight
To find if *books* and *swains* report it right:
(For yet by *swains alone* the world he knew,
Whose feet came wandering o'er the nightly dew)."

Is there not a contradiction in its being first supposed that the Hermit knew *both* what books and swains reported of the world; yet *afterwards* said, that he knew it by swains *alone* ?"

"*I think it an inaccuracy.   He mentions two instructors in the first line, and says he had only one in the next.*" [1]

---

[1] "I do not," says Mr. Malone, "see any difficulty in this passage, and wonder that Dr. Johnson should have acknowledged it to be *inaccurate*. The Hermit, it should be observed, had no actual experience of the world whatsoever; all his knowledge concerning it had been obtained.

This evening I set out for Scotland.

"TO MRS. LUCY PORTER, IN LICHFIELD.

"DEAR MADAM,   May 4, 1779.

"Mr. Green has informed me that you are much better; I hope
I need not tell you that I am glad of it.   I cannot boast of being
much better; my old nocturnal complaint still pursues me, and my
respiration is difficult, though much easier than when I left you the
summer before last.   Mr. and Mrs. Thrale are well; Miss has been
a little indisposed; but she is got well again.   They have since the
loss of their boy had two daughters; but they seem likely to want
a son.

"I hope you had some books which I sent you.   I was sorry for
poor Mrs. Adey's death, and am afraid you will be sometimes
solitary; but endeavour, whether alone or in company, to keep
yourself cheerful.   My friends likewise die very fast; but such is
the state of man.

"I am, dear love, your most humble servant,
                                         "SAM. JOHNSON."

He had, before I left London, resumed the conversation
concerning the appearance of a ghost at Newcastle-upon-
Tyne, which Mr. John Wesley believed, but to which
Johnson did not give credit.   I was, however, desirous to
examine the question closely, and at the same time wished
to be made acquainted with Mr. John Wesley; for though
I differed from him in some points, I admired his various
talents, and loved his pious zeal.   At my request, therefore,
Dr. Johnson gave me a letter of introduction to him.

in two ways: from *books*, and from the *relations* of those country swains
who had seen a little of it.   The plain meaning, therefore, is 'To clear
his doubts concerning Providence, and to obtain some knowledge of the
world by actual experience: to see whether the accounts furnished by
books, or by the oral communications of swains, were just representations
of it; [I say, *swains*], for his oral or *vivâ voce* information had been obtained from that part of mankind *alone*,' &c.   The word *alone* here does
not relate to the whole of the preceding line as has been supposed, but,
by a common license, to the words, *of all mankind*, which are understood,
and of which it is restrictive.''—Mr. Malone, it must be owned, has shown
much critical ingenuity in his explanation of this passage.   His interpretation, however, seems to me much too recondite.   The *meaning* of
the passage may be certain enough; but surely the expression is confused,
and one part of it contradictory to the other.—BOSWELL.

But why *too recondite?*   When a meaning is given to a passage by
understanding words in an uncommon sense, the intrepretation may be
said to be *recondite*, and, however ingenious, may be suspected not to
be sound; but when words are explained in their ordinary acceptation,
and the explication, which is fairly deduced from them without any
force or constraint, is also perfectly justified by the context, it surely
may be safely accepted; and the calling such an explication *recondite*,
when *nothing else can be said against it*, will not make it the less just.—
MALONE.

"TO THE REV. MR. JOHN WESLEY.

"Sir,   *May* 3, 1779.

"Mr. Boswell, a gentleman who has been long known to me, is desirous of being known to you, and has asked this recommendation, which I give him with great willingness, because I think it very much to be wished that worthy and religious men should be acquainted with each other.   I am, Sir,

"Your most humble servant,

"Sam. Johnson."

Mr. Wesley, being in the course of his ministry at Edinburgh, I presented this letter to him, and was very politely received. I begged to have it returned to me, which was accordingly done. His state of the evidence as to the ghost did not satisfy me.

I did not write to Johnson, as usual, upon my return to my family, but tried how he would be affected by my silence. Mr. Dilly sent me a copy of a note which he received from him on the 13th of July, in these words:—

"TO MR. DILLY.

"Sir,

"Since Mr. Boswell's departure I have never heard from him; please to send word what you know of him, and whether you have sent my books to his lady.   I am, &c.

"Sam. Johnson."

My readers will not doubt that his solicitude about me was very flattering.

"TO JAMES BOSWELL, ESQ.

"Dear Sir,   *July* 13, 1779.

"What can possibly have happened, that keeps us two such strangers to each other? I expected to have heard from you when you came home; I expected afterwards. I went into the country and returned, and yet there is no letter from Mr. Boswell. No ill I hope has happened; and if ill should happen, why should it be concealed from him who loves you? Is it a fit of humour, that has disposed you to try who can hold out longest without writing? If it be, you have the victory. But I am afraid of something bad; set me free from my suspicions.

"My thoughts are at present employed in guessing the reason of your silence: you must not expect that I should tell you anything, if I had any thing to tell. Write, pray write to me, and let me know what is, or what has been the cause of this long interruption.

"I am, dear Sir,

"Your most affectionate humble servant,

"Sam. Johnson."

"TO DR. SAMUEL JOHNSON.

"MY DEAR SIR,   *Edinburgh, July* 17, 1779.

"What may be justly denominated a supine indolence of mind has been my state of existence since I last returned to Scotland. In a livelier state I had often suffered severely from long intervals of silence on your part; and I had even been chid by you for expressing my uneasiness. I was willing to take advantage of my insensibility, and, while I could bear the experiment, to try whether your affection for me would, after an unusual silence on my part, make you write first. This afternoon I have had very high satisfaction by receiving your kind letter of inquiry, for which I most gratefully thank you. I am doubtful if it was right to make the experiment; though I have gained by it. I was beginning to grow tender, and to upbraid myself, especially after having dreamt two nights ago that I was with you. I and my wife, and my four children, are all well. I would not delay one post to answer your letter; but as it is late, I have not time to do more. You shall soon hear from me, upon many and various particulars; and I shall never again put you to any test. I am, with veneration, my dear Sir,

" Your much obliged and faithful humble servant,

"JAMES BOSWELL."

On the 22nd of July I wrote to him again, and gave him an account of my last interview with my worthy friend, Mr. Edward Dilly, at his brother's house at Southill, in Bedfordshire, where he died soon after I parted from him, leaving me a very kind remembrance of his regard.

I informed him that Lord Hailes, who had promised to furnish him with some anecdotes for his "Lives of the Poets," had sent me three instances of Prior's borrowing from Gombauld, in "Recueil des Poètes," tome iii. Epigram "To John I owed great obligation," p. 25. "To the Duke of Noailles," p. 32. "Sauntering Jack and Idle Joan," p. 25.

My letter was a pretty long one, and contained a variety of particulars: but he, it should seem, had not attended to it; for his next to me was as follows:—

"TO JAMES BOSWELL, ESQ.

MY DEAR SIR,   *Streatham, Sept.* 9, 1799.

"Are you playing the same trick again, and trying who can keep silence longest? Remember that all tricks are either knavish or childish: and that it is as foolish to make experiments upon the constancy of a friend as upon the chastity of a wife.

"What can be the cause of this second fit of silence I cannot conjecture; but after one trick I will not be cheated by another, nor will I harass my thoughts with conjectures about the motives of a man who, probably, acts only by caprice. I therefore suppose you are well, and that Mrs. Boswell is well too: and that the fine summer has restored Lord Auchinleck.   I am much better than you left me; I think I am better than when I was in Scotland.

"I forgot whether I informed you that poor Thrale has been in great danger.   Mrs. Thrale likewise has miscarried, and been much indisposed.   Everybody else is well; Langton is in camp.   I intend to put Lord Hailes's description of Dryden[1] into another edition, and, as I know his accuracy, wish he would consider the dates, which I could not always settle to my own mind.

"Mr. Thrale goes to Brighthelmstone about Michaelmas to be jolly and ride a hunting.   I shall go to town, or perhaps to Oxford. Exercise and gaiety, or rather carelessness, will, I hope, dissipate all remains of his malady; and I likewise hope, by the change of place, to find some opportunities of growing yet better myself.

"I am, dear Sir, your humble servant,

"Sam. Johnson."

---

[1] Which I communicated to him from his Lordship: but it has not yet been published.   I have a copy of it.—Boswell.

The few notices concerning Dryden, which Lord Hailes had collected, the author afterwards gave me.—Malone.

CHAPTER XV.—1779—1780

MY readers will not be displeased at being told every slight circumstance of the manner in which Dr. Johnson contrived to amuse his solitary hours. He sometimes employed himself in chemistry, sometimes in watering and pruning a vine, sometimes in small experiments, at which those who may smile should recollect that there are moments which admit of being soothed only by trifles.[1]

On the 20th of September, I defended myself against his suspicion of me, which I did not deserve; and added, "Pray, let us write frequently. A whim strikes me, that we should send off a sheet once a week, like a stage-coach, whether it be full or not: nay, though it should be empty, The very sight of your handwriting would comfort me;

---

[1] In one of his manuscript Diaries, there is the following entry, which marks his curious minute attention:—"July 26, 1768. I shaved my nail by accident in whetting the knife about an eighth of an inch from the bottom, and about a fourth from the top. This I measure that I may know the growth of nails: the whole is about five-eighths of an inch." Another of the same kind appears:—" Aug. 7, 1779. *Partem brachii dextri carpo proximam et cutem pectoris circa mamillam dextram rasi, ut notum fieret quanto temporis pili renovarentur.*" And, "Aug. 15, 1783. I cut from the vine 41 leaves, which weighed five oz. and a-half and eight scruples. I lay them upon my bookcase, to see what weight they will lose by drying."—BOSWELL.

and were a sheet to be thus sent regularly, we should much oftener convey something, were it only a few kind words."

My friend, Colonel James Stuart, second son of the Earl of Bute, who had distinguished himself as a good officer of the Bedfordshire militia, had taken a public-spirited resolution to serve his country in its difficulties, by raising a regular regiment, and taking the command of it himself. This, in the heir of the immense property of Wortley, was highly honourable. Having been in Scotland recruiting, he obligingly asked me to accompany him to Leeds, then the head-quarters of his corps; from thence to London for a short time, and afterwards to other places to which the regiment might be ordered. Such an offer, at a time of the year when I had full leisure, was very pleasing; especially as I was to accompany a man of sterling good sense, information, discernment, and conviviality; and was to have a second crop in one year of London and Johnson. Of this I informed my illustrious friend, in characteristical warm terms, in a letter dated the 30th of September, from Leeds.

On Monday, October 4, I called at his house before he was up. He sent for me to his bed-side, and expressed his satisfaction at this incidental meeting, with as much vivacity as if he had been in the gaiety of youth. He called briskly, "Frank, go and get coffee, and let us breakfast *in splendour.*"

During this visit to London I had several interviews with him, which it is unnecessary to distinguish particularly. I consulted him as to the appointment of guardians to my children in case of my death. "Sir," said he, "do not appoint a number of guardians. When there are many, they trust one to another, and the business is neglected. I would advise you to choose only one; let him be a man of respectable character, who, for his own credit, will do what is right; let him be a rich man, so that he may be under no temptation to take advantage; and let him be a man of business, who is used to conduct affairs with ability and expertness, to whom, therefore, the execution of the trust would not be burdensome."

On Sunday, October 10, we dined together at Mr. Strahan's. The conversation having turned on the prevailing practice of going to the East Indies in quest of wealth;—Johnson: "A man had better have 10,000*l.* at the end of ten years passed in England, than 20,000*l.* at the end of ten years passed in India, because you must compute what you *give* for money; and a man who has lived ten years in India, has given up ten years of social comfort, and all those advantages which arise from living in England. The ingenious Mr. Brown, distinguished by the name of 'Capability Brown,' told me that he was once at the seat of Lord Clive, who had returned from India with great wealth; and that he showed him at the door of his bed-chamber a large chest, which he said he had once had full of gold; upon which Brown observed, 'I am glad you can bear it so near your bed-chamber.'"

We talked of the state of the poor in London.—JOHNSON: "Saunders Welch, the Justice, who was once high-constable of Holborn, and had the best opportunities of knowing the state of the poor, told me that I under-rated the number, when I computed that twenty a-week, that is, above a thousand a-year, died of hunger; not absolutely of immediate hunger, but of the wasting and other diseases which are the consequences of hunger. This happens only in so large a place as London, where people are not known. What we are told about the great sums got by begging is not true; the trade is overstocked. And, you may depend upon it, there are many who cannot get work. A particular kind of manufacture fails; those who have been used to work at it, can, for sometime, work at nothing else. You meet a man begging; you charge him with idleness: he says, 'I am willing to labour. Will you give me work?'—'I cannot.' 'Why then you have no right to charge me with idleness.'"

We left Mr. Strahan's at seven, as Johnson had said he intended to go to evening prayers. As we walked along he complained of a little gout in his toe, and said, "I shan't go to prayers to-night; I shall go to-morrow: whenever I miss church on a Sunday, I resolve to go another day. But I do not always do it." This was a fair exhibition of that vibration between pious resolutions and indolence, which many of us have often experienced.

I went home with him, and we had a long, quiet conversation.

I read him a letter from Dr. Hugh Blair concerning Pope (in writing whose life he was now employed), which I shall insert as a literary curiosity.[1]

[1] The Rev. Dr. Law, Bishop of Carlisle, in the Preface to his valuable edition of Archbishop King's "Essay on the Origin of Evil," mentions that the principles maintained in it had been adopted by Pope in his "Essay on Man;" and adds, "The fact, notwithstanding such denial (Bishop Warburton's), might have been strictly verified by an unexceptionable testimony, viz., that of the late Lord Bathurst, who saw the very same system of the τὸ βέλτιον (taken from the Archbishop) in Lord Bolingbroke's own hand, lying before Mr. Pope, while he was

As it is clear that the House of Commons may expel, and expel again and again, why not allow of the power to incapacitate for that Parliament, rather than have a perpetual contest kept up between Parliament and the people." Lord Newhaven took the opposite side; but respectfully said, "I speak with great deference to you, Dr. Johnson; I speak to be instructed." This had its full effect on my friend. He bowed his head almost as low as the table to a complimenting nobleman, and called out, "My Lord, my Lord, I do not desire all this ceremony; let us tell our minds to one another quietly." After the debate was over, he said "I have got lights on the subject to-day, which I had not before." This was a great deal from him, especially as he had written a pamphlet upon it.

He observed, "The House of Commons was originally not a privilege of the people, but a check for the Crown on the House of Lords. I remember Henry VIII. wanted them to do something; they hesitated in the morning, but did it in the afternoon. He told them, 'It is well you did, or half your heads should have been upon Temple-bar.' But the House of Commons is now no longer under the power of the Crown, and therefore must be bribed." He added, "I have no delight in talking of public affairs."

Of his fellow-collegian, the celebrated Mr. George Whitefield, he said, "Whitefield never drew as much attention as a mountebank does; he did not draw attention by doing better than others, but by doing what was strange. Were Astley to preach a sermon standing upon his head on a horse's back, he would collect a multitude to hear him; but no wise man would say he made a better sermon for that. I never treated Whitefield's ministry with contempt: I believe he did good. He had devoted himself to the lower classes of mankind, and among them he was of use. But when familiarity and noise claim the praise due to knowledge, art, and elegance, we must beat down such pretensions."

What I have preserved of his conversation during the remainder of my stay in London at this time, is only what follows:—I told him that when I objected to keeping company with a notorious infidel, a celebrated friend of ours said to me, "I do not think that men who live laxly in the world as you and I do, can with propriety assume such an authority: Dr. Johnson may, who is uniformly exemplary in his conduct. But it is not very consistent to shun an infidel to-day, and get drunk to-morrow." Johnson: "Nay, Sir, this is sad reasoning. Because a man cannot be right in all things, is he to be right in nothing?

Because a man sometimes gets drunk, is he therefore to steal? This doctrine would very soon bring a man to the gallows."

After all, however, it is a difficult question how far sincere Christians should associate with the avowed enemies of religion; for, in the first place, almost every man's mind may be more or less 'corrupted by evil communications;' secondly, the world may very naturally suppose that they are not really in earnest in religion, who can easily bear its opponents; and, thirdly, if the profane find themselves quite well received by the pious, one of the checks upon an open declaration of their infidelity, and one of the probable chances of obliging them seriously to reflect, which their being shunned would do, is removed.

He, I know not why, showed upon all occasions an aversion to go to Ireland, where I proposed to him that we should make a tour. JOHNSON: "It is the last place where I should wish to travel." BOSWELL: "Should you not like to see Dublin, Sir?" JOHNSON: "No, Sir; Dublin is only a worse capital." BOSWELL: "Is not the Giant's Causeway worth seeing?" JOHNSON: "Worth seeing? Yes; but not worth going to see."

Yet he had a kindness for the Irish nation, and thus generously expressed himself to a gentleman from that country, on the subject of an *union* which artful politicians have often had in view, "Do not make an union with us, Sir; we should unite with you, only to rob you. We should have robbed the Scotch, if they had had any thing of which we could have robbed them."

Of an acquaintance of ours, whose manners and everything about him, though expensive, were coarse, he said, "Sir, you see in him vulgar prosperity."

A foreign minister of no very high talents, who had been in his company for a considerable time quite overlooked, happened luckily to mention that he had read some of his "Rambler" in Italian, and admired it much. This pleased him greatly. He observed that the title had been translated, "Il Genio Errante," though I have been told it was rendered more ludicrously, "Il Vagabondo;" and finding that this minister gave such a proof of his taste, he was all attention to him, and on the first remark which he made, however simple, exclaimed, "The Ambassador says well. His Excellency observes——." And then he expanded and enriched the little that had been said, in so strong a manner, that it appeared something of consequence. This was exceedingly entertaining to the company who were present, and many a time afterwards it furnished a pleasant topic of merriment: *"The Ambassador says well,"* became a laughable term of applause, when no mighty matter had been expressed.

I left London on Monday, October 18, and accompanied Colonel Stuart to Chester, where his regiment was to lie for some time.

"MR. BOSWELL TO DR. JOHNSON.

"MY DEAR SIR, *Chester, October* 22, 1779.

"It was not till one o'clock on Monday morning that Colonel Stuart and I left London; for we chose to bid a cordial adieu to Lord Mountstuart, who was to set out on that day on his embassy to Turin. We drove on excellently, and reached Lichfield in good time enough that night. The Colonel had heard so preferable a character of the George, that he would not put up at the Three Crowns, so that I did not see our host, Wilkins. We found at the George as good accommodation as we could wish to have, and I fully enjoyed the comfortable thought that *I was in Lichfield again.* Next morning it rained very hard; and as I had much to do in a little time, I ordered a post-chaise, and between eight and nine, sallied forth to make a round of visits. I first went to Mr. Green, hoping to have had him to accompany me to all my other friends, but he was engaged to attend the Bishop of Sodor and Man, who was then lying at Lichfield very ill of the gout. Having taken a hasty glance at the additions to Green's museum, from which it was not so easy to break away, I next went to the Friary, where I at first occasioned some tumult in the ladies, who were not prepared to receive *company* so early: but my *name,* which has by wonderful felicity come to be closely associated with yours, soon made all easy; and Mrs. Cobb and Miss Adey re-assumed their seats at the breakfast table, which they had quitted with some precipitation. They received me with the kindness of an old acquaintance; and after we had joined in a cordial chorus to *your* praise, Mrs. Cobb gave *me* the high satisfaction of hearing that you said, 'Boswell is a man who, I believe, never left a house without leaving a wish for his return.' And she afterwards added, that she bid you tell me, that if ever I came to Lichfield, she hoped I would take a bed at the Friary. From thence I drove to Peter Garrick's, where I also found a very flattering welcome. He appeared to me to enjoy his usual cheerfulness; and he very kindly asked me to come when I could, and pass a week with him. From Mr. Garrick's, I went to the Palace to wait on Mr. Seward. I was first entertained by his lady and daughter, he himself being in bed with a cold, according to his valetudinary custom. But he desired to see me; and I found him dressed in his black gown, with a white flannel night-gown above it; so that he looked like a Dominican friar. He was good-humoured and polite; and under his roof too my reception was very pleasing. I then proceeded to Stowhill, and first paid my respects to Mrs. Gastrell, whose conversation I was not willing to quit. But my sand-glass was now beginning to run low, as I could not trespass too long on the Colonel's kindness, who obligingly waited for me; so I hastened to Mrs. Aston's,[1] whom I found much better than I feared I should; and there I met a brother-in-law of these ladies, who talked much of you, and very well too, as it appeared to me. It then only remained to visit Mrs. Lucy Porter, which I did, I really believe, with sincere satisfaction on both sides. I am sure I was glad to see her again; and, as I take her to be very honest, I trust she was glad to see me again; for she expressed herself so that I could not doubt of her being in earnest. What a great keystone of kindness, my dear Sir, were you that morning; for we were all held together by our common attachment to you. I cannot say that I ever passed two hours with more self-complacency than I did those two at Lichfield. Let me not entertain any suspicion that this is idle vanity. Will not you confirm me in my persuasion, that he who finds himself so regarded has just reason to be happy?

"We got to Chester about midnight on Tuesday; and here again I am in a state of much enjoyment. Colonel Stuart and his officers treat me with all the civility I could wish; and I play my part admirably. *Lætus aliis, sapiens sibi*, the classical sentence which you, I imagine, invented the other day, is exemplified in my present existence. The Bishop to whom I had the honour to be known several years ago, shows me much attention; and I am edified by his conversation. I must not omit to tell you, that his Lordship admires, very highly, your Prefaces to the Poets. I am daily obtaining an extension of agreeable acquaintance: so that I am kept in animated variety; and the study of the place itself, by the assistance of books, and of the Bishop, is sufficient occupation. Chester pleases my fancy more than any town I ever saw. But I will not enter upon it at all in this letter.

"How long I shall stay here I cannot yet say. I told a very pleasing young lady,[2] niece to one of the Prebendaries, at whose house I saw her, 'I have come to Chester, Madam, I cannot tell how; and far less can I tell how I am to get away from it. Do not think me too juvenile.' I beg it of you, my dear Sir, to favour me with a letter while I am here, and add to the happiness of a happy friend, who is ever, with affectionate veneration, most sincerely yours,

"JAMES BOSWELL."

"If you do not write directly, so as to catch me here, I shall be disappointed. Two lines from you will keep my lamp burning bright."

"TO JAMES BOSWELL, ESQ.

"DEAR SIR,   *London, October* 27, 1779.

"Why should you importune me so earnestly to write? Of what importance can it be to hear of distant friends, to a man who finds himself welcome wherever he goes, and makes new friends faster than he can want them? If, to the delight of such universal kindness of reception, anything can be added by knowing that you

---

[1] A maiden sister of Johnson's favourite, Molly Aston, who married Captain Brodie of the Navy.—MALONE.

[2] Miss Letitia Barnston.—BOSWELL.

retain my good-will, you may indulge yourself in the full enjoyment of that small addition.

"I am glad that you made the round of Lichfield with so much success: the oftener you are seen the more you are liked. It was pleasing to me to read that Mrs. Aston was so well, and that Lucy Porter was so glad to see you.

"In the place where you now are, there is much to be observed: and you will easily procure yourself skilful directors. But what will you do to keep away the *black dog* that worries you at home? If you would, in compliance with your father's advice, inquire into the old tenures and old characters of Scotland, you would certainly open to yourself many striking scenes of the manners of the middle ages. The feudal system, in a country half-barbarous, is naturally productive of great anomalies in civil life. The knowledge of past times is naturally growing less in all cases not of public record; and the past time of Scotland is so unlike the present, that it is already difficult for a Scotchman to image the economy of his grandfather. Do not be tardy nor negligent; but gather up eagerly what can yet be found.[1]

"We have, I think, once talked of another project—a History of the late insurrection in Scotland, with all its incidents. Many falsehoods are passing into uncontradicted history. Voltaire, who loved a striking story, has told what he could not find to be true.

"You may make collections for either of these projects, or for both, as opportunities occur, and digest your materials at leisure. The great direction which Burton has left to men disordered like you, is this—*Be not solitary; be not idle:* which I would thus modify; —If you are idle, be not solitary; if you are solitary be not idle.

"There is a letter for you, from

"Your humble servant,
"SAM. JOHNSON."

"TO DR. SAMUEL JOHNSON.

"My dear Sir,   *Carlisle, Nov. 7, 1779.*

"That I should importune you to write to me at Chester, is not wonderful, when you consider what an avidity I have for delight; and that the *amor* of pleasure, like the *amor nummi*, increases in proportion with the quantity which we possess of it. Your letter, so full of polite kindness and masterly counsel, came like a large treasure upon me, while already glittering with riches. I was quite enchanted at Chester; so that I could with difficulty quit it. But the enchantment was the reverse of that of Circé; for so far was there from being anything sensual in it, that I was *all mind.* I do not mean all reason only; for my fancy was kept finely in play.

---

[1] I have a valuable collection made by my father, which, with some additions and illustrations of my own, I intend to publish. I have some hereditary claim to be an antiquary, not only from my father, but as being descended, by the mother's side, from the able and learned Sir John Skene, whose merit bids defiance to all the attempts which have been made to lessen his fame.—BOSWELL.

And why not?—If you please I will send you a copy or an abridgment of my Chester journal, which is truly a log-book of felicity.

"The Bishop treated me with a kindness which was very flattering. I told him that you regretted you had seen so little of Chester. His Lordship bade me tell you, that he should be glad to show you more of it. I am proud to find the friendship with which you honour me is known in so many places.

"I arrived here late last night. Our friend the Dean has been gone from hence some months; but I am told at my inn, that he is very *populous* (popular.) However, I found Mr. Law, the Archdeacon, son to the Bishop, and with him I have breakfasted and dined very agreeably. I got acquainted with him at the assizes here about a year and a half ago; he is a man of great variety of knowledge, uncommon genius, and, I believe, sincere religion. I received the holy sacrament in the Cathedral in the morning, this being the first Sunday in the month; and was at prayers there in the morning. It is divinely cheering to me to think that there is a Cathedral so near Auchinleck; and I now leave Old England in such a state of mind as I am thankful to GOD for granting me.

"The *black dog* that worries me at home I cannot but dread; yet, as I have been for some time past in a military train, I trust I shall *repulse* him. To hear from you will animate me like the sound of a trumpet; I therefore hope, that soon after my return to the northern field, I shall receive a few lines from you.

"Colonel Stuart did me the honour to escort me in his carriage to show me Liverpool, and from thence back again to Warrington, where we parted.[1] In justice to my valuable wife, I must inform you she wrote to me, that as I was so happy, she would not be so selfish as to wish me to return sooner than business absolutely required my presence. She made my clerk write to me a post or two after to the same purpose, by commission from her; and this day a kind letter from her met me at the Post-office here, acquainting me that she and the little ones were well, and expressing all their wishes for my return home.

"I am, more and more, my dear Sir, your affectionate
                                    "And obliged humble servant,
                                              "JAMES BOSWELL."

"TO JAMES BOSWELL, ESQ.

"DEAR SIR,   *London, Nov.* 13, 1779.
"Your last letter was not only kind but fond. But I wish you to get rid of all intellectual excesses, and neither to exalt your pleasures, nor aggravate your vexations beyond their real and natural state. Why should you not be as happy at Edinburgh as at Chester? *In culpa est animus, qui se non effugit usquam.* Please yourself with your wife and children, and studies, and practice.

---

[1] His regiment was afterwards ordered to Jamaica, where he accompanied it, and almost lost his life by the climate. This impartial order, I should think a sufficient refutation of the idle rumour that "there was still something behind the throne greater than the throne itself."—BOSWELL.

" I have sent a petition,[1] from Lucy Porter, with which I leave it to your discretion whether it is proper to comply.   Return me her letter, which I have sent, that you may know the whole case, and not be seduced to anything that you may afterwards repent.   Miss Doxy perhaps you know to be Mr. Garrick's niece.

" If Dean Percy can be popular at Carlisle, he may be very happy. He has in his disposal two livings, each equal, or almost equal in value to the deanery, he may take one himself, and give the other to his son.

" How near is the Cathedral to Auchinleck, that you are so much delighted with it?   It is I suppose, at least an hundred and fifty miles off.   However, if you are pleased, it is so far well.

" Let me know what reception you have from your father, and the state of his health.   Please him as much as you can, and add no pain to his last years.

" Of our friends here I can recollect nothing to tell you.   I have neither seen nor heard of Langton.   Beauclerk is just returned from Brighthelmstone, I am told much better.   Mr. Thrale and his family are still there; and his health is said to be visibly improved; he has not bathed but hunted.

" At Bolt-court there is much malignity, but of late little open hostility.   I have had a cold, but it is gone.

" Make my compliments to Mrs. Boswell, &c.
" I am, Sir, your humble servant,
" Sam. Johnson."

On November 22, and December 21, I wrote to him from Edinburgh, giving a very favourable report of the family of Miss Doxy's lover—that after a good deal of inquiry I had discovered the sister of Mr. Francis Stewart, one of his amanuenses when writing his Dictionary; that I had, as desired by him, paid her a guinea for an old pocket-book of her brother's, which he had retained: and that the good woman, who was in very moderate circumstances, but contented and placid, wondered at his scrupulous and liberal honesty, and received the guinea as if sent her by Providence.   That I had repeatedly begged of him to keep his promise to send his letter to Lord Chesterfield, and that this memento, like *Delenda est Carthago*, must be in every letter that I should write to him, till I had obtained my object.

In 1780, the world was kept in impatience for the completion of Johnson's "Lives of the Poets," upon which he was employed so far as his indolence allowed him to labour.

I wrote to him on January 1, and March 13, sending him my notes of Lord Marchmont's information concerning

[1] Requesting me to inquire concerning the family of a gentleman who was then paying his addresses to Miss Doxy.—Boswell.

Pope, complaining that I had not heard from him for almost four months, though he was two letters in my debt; that I had suffered again from melancholy; hoping that he had been in so much better company (the Poets), that he had not time to think of his distant friends; for if that were the case, I should have some recompense for my uneasiness; that the state of my affairs did not admit of my coming to London this year, and begging he would return me Goldsmith's two poems, with his lines marked.

His friend Dr. Lawrence, having now suffered the greatest affliction to which a man is liable, and which Johnson himself had felt in the most severe manner, Johnson wrote to him in an admirable strain of sympathy and pious consolation.

"TO DR. LAWRENCE.

"DEAR SIR,   *January* 20, 1780.

"At a time when all your friends ought to show their kindness, and with a character which ought to make all that know you your friends, you may wonder that you have yet heard nothing from me.

"I have been hindered by a vexatious cough, for which within these ten days I have been bled once, fasted four or five times, taken physic five times, and opiates, I think six. This day it seems to remit.

"The loss, dear Sir, which you have lately suffered, I felt many years ago, and know, therefore, how much has been taken from you, and how little help can be had from consolation. He that outlives a wife whom he has loved, sees himself disjointed from the only mind that has the same hopes, and fears, and interest; from the only companion with whom he has shared much good or evil; and with whom he could set his mind at liberty, to retrace the past or anticipate the future. The continuity of being is lacerated; the settled course of sentiment and action is stopped: and life stands suspended and motionless, till it is driven by external causes into a new channel. But the time of suspense is dreadful.

"Our first recourse, in this distressed solitude, is, perhaps for want of habitual piety, to a gloomy acquiescence in necessity. Of two mortal beings, one must lose the other; but surely there is a higher and better comfort to be drawn from the consideration of that Providence which watches over all, and a belief that the living and the dead are equally in the hands of God, who will reunite those whom he has separated; or who sees that it is best not to reunite.

"I am, dear Sir,
"Your most affectionate and most humble servant,
"SAM. JOHNSON."

"TO JAMES BOSWELL, ESQ.

"DEAR SIR,   *April* 8, 1780.

"Well, I had resolved to send you the Chesterfield letter; but I will write once again without it. Never impose tasks upon mortals. To require two things is the way to have them both undone.

"For the difficulties which you mention in your affairs I am sorry; but difficulty is now very general: it is not therefore less grievous, for there is less hope of help. I pretend not to give you advice, not knowing the state of your affairs; and general counsels about prudence and frugality would do you little good. You are, however, in the right not to increase your own perplexity by a journey hither; and I hope that by staying at home you will please your father.

"Poor dear Beauclerk[1]—*nec, ut soles, dabis joca*. His wit and his folly, his acuteness and maliciousness, his merriment and reasoning, are now over. Such another will not often be found among mankind. He directed himself to be buried by the side of his mother—an instance of tenderness which I hardly expected. He has left his children to the care of Lady Di, and if she dies, of Mr. Langton, and of Mr. Leicester, his relation, and a man of good character. His library has been offered for sale to the Russian Ambassador.[2]

"Dr. Percy, notwithstanding all the noise of the newspapers, has had no literary loss.[3] Clothes and moveables were burnt to the value of about £100; but his papers, and I think his books, were all preserved.

"Poor Mr. Thrale has been in extreme danger from an apoplectical disorder, and recovered, beyond the expectation of his physicians; he is now at Bath, that his mind may be quiet, and Mrs. Thrale and Miss are with him.

"Having told you what has happened to your friends, let me say something to you of yourself. You are always complaining of melancholy, and I conclude from those complaints that you are fond of it. No man talks of that which he is desirous to conceal, and every man desires to conceal that of which he is ashamed. Do not pretend to deny it; *manifestum habemus furem;* make it an invariable and obligatory law to yourself, never to mention your own mental diseases; if you are never to speak of them you will think on them but little, and if you think little of them, they will molest you rarely. When you talk of them, it is plain that you want either praise or pity; for praise there is no room, and pity will do you no good; therefore, from this hour speak no more, think no more about them.

"Your transaction with Mrs. Stewart gave me great satisfaction; I am much obliged to you for your attention. Do not lose sight of her; your countenance may be of great credit, and of consequence of great advantage to her. The memory of her brother is yet fresh in my mind; he was an ingenious and worthy man.

"Please to make my compliments to your lady and to the young

---

[1] The Hon. Topham Beauclerk died March 11, 1780.—MALONE.

[2] Mr. Beauclerk's library was sold by public auction in April and May, 1781, for £5,011.—MALONE.

[3] By a fire in Northumberland House, where he had an apartment, in which I have passed many an agreeable hour.—BOSWELL.

ladies. I should like to see them, pretty loves. I am, dear Sir, yours affectionately,

"SAM. JOHNSON."

Mrs. Thrale being now at Bath with her husband, the correspondence between Johnson and her was carried on briskly. I shall present my readers with one of her original letters to him at this time, which will amuse them probably more than those well-written but studied epistles which she has inserted in her collection, because it exhibits the easy vivacity of their literary intercourse. It is also of value as a key to Johnson's answer, which she has printed by itself, and of which I shall subjoin extracts.

"MRS. THRALE TO DR. JOHNSON.

"*Bath, Friday, April* 28.

"I had a very kind letter from you yesterday, dear Sir, with a most circumstantial date. You took trouble with my circulating letter, Mr. Evans writes me word, and I thank you sincerely for so doing; one might do mischief else not being on the spot.

"Yesterday's evening was passed at Mrs. Montagu's: there was Mr. Melmoth;[1] I do not like him *though*, nor he me; it was expected we should have pleased each other; he is, however, just Tory enough to hate the Bishop of Peterborough[2] for Whiggism, and Whig enough to abhor you for Toryism.

"Mrs. Montagu flattered him finely; so he had a good afternoon on't. This evening we spend at a concert. Poor Queeney's[3] sore eyes have just released her; she had a long confinement, and could neither read nor write, so my master[4] treated her very good-naturedly with the visits of a young woman in this town, a tailor's daughter, who professes music, and teaches so as to give six lessons a day to ladies, at five and threepence a lesson. Miss Burney says, she is a great performer; and I respect the wench for getting her living so prettily; she is very modest and pretty-mannered, and not seventeen years old.

"You live in a fine whirl indeed; if I did not write regularly you would half-forget me, and that would be very wrong, for I *felt* my regard for you in my *ace* last night, when the criticisms were going on.

"This morning it was all connoisseurship; we went to see some pictures painted by a gentleman artist, Mr. Taylor, of this place; my master makes one everywhere, and has got a good dawdling companion to ride with him now. * * * * * * He looks

---

[1] Mr. Wm. Melmoth is known in literary history as the translator of the Letters of Cicero and Pliny, and as the author of "Fitzosborne's Letters." He died in 1799, aged 89.—ED.

[2] Dr. John Hinchliffe.—BOSWELL.

[3] A kind of nick-name given to Mrs. Thrale's eldest daughter, whose name being *Esther* she might be assimilated to a *Queen*.—BOSWELL.

[4] Mr. Thrale.—BOSWELL.

well enough, but I have no notion of health for a man whose mouth cannot be sewed up.   Burney and I and Queeney tease him every meal he eats, and Mrs. Montagu is quite serious with him; but what *can* one do?   He will eat, I think, and if he does eat I know he will not live; it makes me very unhappy, but I must bear it. Let me always have your friendship.

"I am, most sincerely, dear Sir,
"Your faithful servant,
"H. L. T."

"DR. JOHNSON TO MRS. THRALE.

"Dearest Madam,   *London, May* 1, 1780.
"Mr. Thrale never will live abstinently, till he can persuade himself to live by rule.[1] * * * * * *   Encourage, as you can, the musical girl.

"Nothing is more common than mutual dislike, where mutual approbation is particularly expected.   There is often on both sides a vigilance not over benevolent; and as attention is strongly excited, so that nothing drops unheeded, any difference in taste or opinion, and some difference where there is no restraint will commonly appear, immediately generates dislike.

"Never let criticism operate on your face or your mind; it is very rarely that an author is hurt by his critics.   The blaze of reputation cannot be blown out, but it often dies in the socket; a very few names may be considered as perpetual lamps that shine unconsumed.   From the author of 'Fitzosborne's Letters.' I cannot think myself in much danger.   I met him only once about thirty years ago, and in some small dispute reduced him to whistle; having not seen him since, that is the last impression.   Poor Moore, the fabulist, was one of the company.

"Mrs. Montagu's long stay, against her own inclination, is very convenient.   You would, by your own confession, want a companion; and she is *par pluribus;* conversing with her, you may *find variety in one.*"

On the 2nd of May I wrote to him, and requested that we might have another meeting somewhere in the north of England, in the autumn of this year.

From Mr. Langton I received soon after this time a letter, of which I extract a passage, relative both to Mr. Beauclerk and Dr. Johnson.

"The melancholy information you have received concerning Mr. Beauclerk's death is true.   Had his talents been directed in any sufficient degree as they ought, I have always been strongly of opinion that they were calculated to make an illustrious figure; and that opinion, as it had been in part formed upon Dr. Johnson's judgment, receives more and more confirmation by hearing what, since his death, Dr. Johnson has said concerning

[1] I have taken the liberty to leave out a few lines.—Boswell.

them: a few evenings ago, he was at Mr. Vesey's, where Lord Althorpe, who was one of a numerous company there, addressed Dr. Johnson on the subject of Mr. Beauclerk's death, saying, 'Our CLUB has had a great loss since we met last.' He replied, 'A loss, that perhaps the whole nation could not repair!' The Doctor then went on to speak of his endowments, and particularly extolled the wonderful ease with which he uttered what was highly excellent. He said, that 'no man ever was so free when he was going to say a good thing, from a *look* that expressed that it was coming; or, when he had said it, from a look that expressed that it had come.' At Mr. Thrale's, some days before, when we were talking on the same subject, he said, referring to the same idea of his wonderful facility, 'Thomas Beauclerk's talents were those which he had felt himself more disposed to envy, than those of any whom he had known.'

"On the evening I have spoken of above, at Mr. Vesey's, you would have been much gratified, as it exhibited an instance of the high importance in which Dr. Johnson's character is held, I think even beyond any I ever before was witness to. The company consisted chiefly of ladies, among whom were the Duchess Dowager of Portland, and the Duchess of Beaufort, whom I suppose, from her rank, I must name before her mother Mrs. Boscawen, and her elder sister Mrs. Lewson, who was likewise there; Lady Lucan, Lady Clermont, and others of note both for their station and understandings. Among the gentlemen were Lord Althorpe, whom I have before named, Lord Macartney, Sir Joshua Reynolds, Lord Lucan, Mr. Wraxal, whose book you have probably seen, 'The Tour to the Northern Parts of Europe;' a very agreeable ingenious man; Dr. Warren, Mr. Pepys, the Master in Chancery, whom I believe you know, and Dr. Barnard, the Provost of Eton. As soon as Dr. Johnson was come in, and had taken a chair, the company began to collect round him, till they became not less than four, if not five, deep; those behind standing, and listening over the heads of those that were sitting near him. The conversation for some time was chiefly between Dr. Johnson and the Provost of Eton, while the others contributed occasionally their remarks. Without attempting to detail the particulars of the conversation, which, perhaps, if I did, I should spin my account to a tedious length, I thought, my dear Sir, this general account of the respect with which our valued friend was attended to, might be acceptable."

"TO THE REVEREND DR. FARMER.

"SIR,   *May* 25, 1780.
"I know your disposition to second any literary attempt, and therefore venture upon the liberty of entreating you to procure from College or University registers, all the dates or other informations which they can supply relating to Ambrose Philips, Broome, and Gray, who were all at Cambridge, and of whose lives I am to give such accounts as I can gather. Be pleased to forgive this trouble from, Sir,

"Your most humble servant,
"SAM. JOHNSON."

CHAPTER XVI.—1780

Johnson's Account of the Riots of London—Lord George Gordon committed to the Tower—John Wilkes—Conduct of Mr. Akerman, Governor of Newgate—Correspondence —Boswell's Brother David—Dr. Beattie—Davies' Memoirs of Garrick—Dr. Dunbar—Advice to Divines —Johnson's Instructions on the Composition of Sermons —Civilisation of a Parish—Dr. Wheeler—Boswell's pressing Invitations to Johnson—Southwark Election— —Lady Southwell and Mauritius Lowe—Mr. Macbean— Lord Thurlow—Mr. Thrale's Election Defeat—Mrs. Desmoulins a Candidate for the Office of Matron of the Chartreux

WHILE Johnson was thus engaged in preparing a delightful literary entertainment for the world, the tranquillity of the metropolis of Great Britain was unexpectedly disturbed, by the most horrid series of outrage that ever disgraced a civilised country. A relaxation of some of the severe penal provisions against our fellow-subjects of the Catholic communion had been granted by the legislature, with an opposition so inconsiderable that the genuine mildness of Christianity, united with liberal policy, seemed to have become general in this island. But a dark and malignant spirit of persecution soon showed itself, in an unworthy petition for the repeal of the wise and humane statute. That petition was brought forward by a mob, with the evident purpose of intimidation, and was justly rejected. But the attempt was accompanied and followed by such daring violence as is unexampled in history. Of this extraordinary tumult, Dr. Johnson has given the following concise, lively, and just account in his "Letters to Mrs. Thrale:"[1]

"On Friday,[2] the good Protestants met in Saint George's-Fields, at the summons of Lord George Gordon,[3] and marching to West-

---

[1] Vol. ii. I have selected passages from several letters, without mentioning dates.—BOSWELL.

[2] June 2.—BOSWELL.

[3] The son of Cosmo George, Duke of Gordon, one of the most turbulent politicians of the time. He sat in Parliament for Luggershall, and became conspicuous by his opposition to ministers, especially on

331

minster, insulted the Lords and Commons, who all bore it with great tameness. At night the outrages began by the demolition of the mass-house by Lincoln's-inn.

"An exact journal of a week's defiance of government I cannot give you. On Monday Mr. Strahan, who had been insulted, spoke to Lord Mansfield [1] (who had, I think, been insulted too,) of the licentiousness of the populace; and his lordship treated it as a very slight irregularity. On Tuesday night they pulled down Fielding's house,[2] and burnt his goods in the street. They had gutted, on Monday, Sir George Savile's house, but the building was saved. On Tuesday evening, leaving Fielding's ruins, they went to Newgate to demand their companions, who had been seized demolishing the chapel. The keeper could not release them but by the Mayor's permission, which he went to ask; at his return he found all the prisoners released, and Newgate in a blaze. They then went to Bloomsbury, and fastened upon Lord Mansfield's house, which they pulled down; and as for his goods, they totally burnt them. They have since gone to Caen-wood, but a guard was there before them. They plundered some Papists, I think, and burnt a mass-house in Moorfields the same night.

"On Wednesday I walked with Dr. Scot to look at Newgate, and found it in ruins, with the fire yet glowing. As I went by, the Protestants were plundering the Sessions House at the Old Bailey. There were not, I believe, a hundred; but they did their work at leisure, in full security, without sentinels, without trepidation, as men lawfully employed in full day. Such is the cowardice of a commercial place. On Wednesday they broke open the Fleet, and the King's Bench, and the Marshalsea, and Wood-street Compter, and Clerkenwell Bridewell, and released all the prisoners.

"At night they set fire to the Fleet, and to the King's Bench, and I know not how many other places; and one might see the glare of conflagration fill the sky from many parts. The sight was dreadful. Some people were threatened; Mr. Strahan advised me to take care of myself. Such a time of terror you have been happy in not seeing

"The King said in council, 'That the magistrates had not done their duty, but that he would do his own:' and a proclamation was published directing us to keep our servants within doors, as the peace was now to be preserved by force. The soldiers were sent out to different parts, and the town is now (June 9) at quiet.

---

the Roman Catholic question. Being the principal cause of the No Popery riots, he was arrested and tried for high treason; but no evidence being adduced of such a design, he was acquitted. Being then convicted of having libelled the French Ambassador, the Queen of France, and the criminal justice of his country, he fled to Holland; but he was subsequently arrested, sent home, and committed to Newgate, where he died in 1793.—ED.

[1] Then Lord Chief Justice of the King's Bench. His Lordship was a high Tory; hence the hostility of the mob was strongly directed against him.

[2] This is not quite correct. Sir John Fielding was, I think, then dead. It was Justice Hyde's house in St. Martin's-street, Leicester Fields, that was gutted and his goods burnt in the street.—BOSWELL.

"The soldiers are stationed so as to be everywhere within call: there is no longer any body of rioters, and the individuals are hunted to their holes, and led to prison; Lord George was last night sent to the Tower. Mr. John Wilkes was this day in my neighbourhood, to seize the publisher of a seditious paper.

"Several chapels have been destroyed, and several inoffensive Papists have been plundered, but the high sport was to burn the gaols. This was a good rabble trick. The debtors and the criminals were all set at liberty; but of the criminals, as has always happened, many are already retaken; and two pirates have surrendered themselves, and it is expected that they will be pardoned.

"Government now acts again with its proper force; and we are all under the protection of the King and the law. I thought that it would be agreeable to you and my master to have my testimony to the public security; and that you would sleep more quietly when I told you that you were safe.

"There has, indeed, been an universal panic, from which the King was the first that recovered. Without the concurrence of his ministers, or the assistance of the civil magistrates, he put the soldiers in motion, and saved the town from calamities, such as a rabble's government must naturally produce.

"The public has escaped a very heavy calamity. The rioters attempted the Bank on Wednesday night, but in no great number; and, like other thieves, with no great resolution. Jack Wilkes headed the party that drove them away. It is agreed that if they had seized the Bank on Tuesday, at the height of the panic, when no resistance had been prepared, they might have carried irrecoverably away whatever they had found. Jack, who was always zealous for order and decency, declares that if he be trusted with power, he will not leave a rioter alive. There is, however, now no longer any need of heroism or bloodshed; no blue riband [1] is any longer worn."

Such was the end of this miserable sedition, from which London was delivered by the magnanimity of the Sovereign himself. Whatever some may maintain, I am satisfied that there was no combination or plan, either domestic or foreign; but that the mischief spread by a gradual contagion of frenzy, augmented by the quantities of fermented liquors, of which the deluded populace possessed themselves in the course of their depredations.

I should think myself very much to blame, did I here neglect to do justice to my esteemed friend Mr. Akerman, the keeper of Newgate, who long discharged a very important trust with an uniform intrepid firmness, and at the same time a tenderness and a liberal charity, which entitle him to be recorded with distinguished honour.

Upon this occasion, from the timidity and negligence of

---

[1] Lord George Gordon and his followers, during these outrages, wore blue ribands in their hats.—MALONE.

the magistracy on the one hand, and the almost incredible exertions of the mob on the other, the first prison of this great country was laid open, and the prisoners set free; but that Mr. Akerman,[1] whose house was burnt, would have prevented all this, had proper aid been sent him in due time, there can be no doubt.

Many years ago, a fire broke out in the brick part which was built as an addition to the old gaol of Newgate. The prisoners were in consternation and tumult, calling out, "We shall be burnt—we shall be burnt! Down with the gate—down with the gate!" Mr. Akerman hastened to them, showed himself at the gate, and having, after some confused vociferation of "Hear him—hear him!" obtained a silent attention, he then calmly told them, that the gates must not go down; that they were under his care, and that they should not be permitted to escape; but that he could assure them, they need not be afraid of being burnt, for that the fire was not in the prison, properly so called, which was strongly built with stone; and that if they would engage to be quiet, he himself would come to them, and conduct them to the farther end of the building, and would not go out till they gave him leave. To this proposal they agreed; upon which Mr. Akerman, having first made them fall back from the gate, went in, and with a determined resolution ordered the outer turnkey upon no account to open the gate, even though the prisoners (though he trusted they would not) should break their word, and by force bring himself to order it. "Never mind me," said he, "should that happen." The prisoners peaceably followed him, while he conducted them through passages of which he had the keys, to the extremity of the gaol, which was most distant from the fire. Having by this very judicious conduct fully satisfied them that there was no immediate risk, if any at all, he then addressed them thus: "Gentlemen, you are now convinced that I told you true. I have no doubt that the engines will soon extinguish this fire; if they should not a sufficient guard will come, and you shall be all taken out, and lodged in the Compters. I assure you, upon my word and honour, that I have not a farthing insured. I have left my house, that I might take care of you. I will keep my promise, and stay with you if you insist upon it; but if you will allow me to go out, and look after my family and property, I shall be obliged to you." Struck with his behaviour, they called out, "Master Akerman, you have done bravely; it was very kind in you: by all means go and

[1] Governor of Newgate.—Ed.

take care of your own concerns." He did so accordingly, while they remained and were all preserved.

Johnson has been heard to relate the substance of this story with high praise, in which he was joined by Mr. Burke. My illustrious friend, speaking of Mr. Akerman's kindness to his prisoners, pronounced this eulogy upon his character: —"He who has long had constantly in his view the worst of mankind, and is yet eminent for the humanity of his disposition, must have had it originally in a great degree, and continued to cultivate it very carefully."

In the course of this month my brother David waited upon Dr. Johnson with the following letter of introduction, which I had taken care should be lying ready on his arrival in London:—

"TO DR. SAMUEL JOHNSON.

"My dear Sir,   *Edinburgh, April* 29, 1780.

"This will be delivered to you by my brother David, on his return from Spain. You will be glad to see the man who vowed to 'stand by the old castle of Auchinleck, with heart, purse, and sword;' that romantic family solemnity devised by me, of which you and I talked with complacency upon the spot. I trust that twelve years of absence have not lessened his feudal attachment and that you will find him worthy of being introduced to your acquaintance. I have the honour to be, with affectionate veneration, my dear Sir,
                    "Your most faithful humble servant,
                                        "James Boswell."

Johnson received him very politely, and has thus mentioned him in a letter to Mrs. Thrale;[1] "I have had with me a brother of Boswell's, a Spanish merchant,[2] whom the war has driven from his residence at Valencia; he is gone to see his friends, and will find Scotland but a sorry place after twelve years' residence in a happier climate. He is a very agreeable man, and speaks no Scotch."

"TO DR. BEATTIE, AT ABERDEEN.

"Sir,   *Bolt-court, Fleet-street, August* 21, 1780.

"More years[3] than I have any delight to reckon have past since you and I saw one another; of this, however, there is no reason for making reprehensory complaint:—*Sic fata ferunt.* But methinks there might pass some small interchange of regard between us.

---

[1] Vol. ii. Mrs. Piozzi has omitted the name, she best knows why.—Boswell.

[2] Now settled in London.—Boswell.

[3] I had been five years absent from London.—Beattie.

If you say that I ought to have written, I now write; and I write to tell you that I have much kindness for you and Mrs. Beattie; and that I wish your health better, and your life long.   Try change of air, and come a few degrees southwards; a softer climate may do you both good; winter is coming in; and London will be warmer, and gayer, and busier, and more fertile for amusement than Aberdeen.

"My health is better; but that will be little in the balance, when I tell you that Mrs. Montagu has been very ill, and is, I doubt, now but weakly.   Mr. Thrale has been very dangerously disordered; but is much better, and I hope will totally recover.   He has withdrawn himself from business the whole summer.   Sir Joshua and his sister are well: and Mr. Davies has got great success as an author,[1] generated by the corruption of a bookseller.   More news I have not to tell you, and therefore you must be contented with hearing, what I know not whether you much wish to hear,[2] that I am, Sir,

"Your most humble servant,
"SAM. JOHNSON."

"TO JAMES BOSWELL, ESQ.

"DEAR SIR,   London, Aug. 21, 1780.

"I find you have taken one of your fits of taciturnity, and have resolved not to write till you are written to; it is but a peevish humour, but you shall have your way.

"I have sat at home in Bolt-court all the summer, thinking to write the Lives, and a great part of the time only thinking.   Several of them, however, are done, and I still think to do the rest.

"Mr. Thrale and his family have, since his illness, passed their time first at Bath, and then at Brighthelmstone; but I have been at neither place.   I would have gone to Lichfield if I could have had time, and I might have had time if I had been active; but I have missed much, and done little.

"In the late disturbances, Mr. Thrale's house and stock were in great danger; the mob was pacified at their first invasion, with about 50l. in drink and meat; and at their second, were driven away by the soldiers.   Mr. Strahan got a garrison into his house, and maintained them a fortnight; he was so frighted that he removed part of his goods.   Mrs. Williams took shelter in the country.

"I know not whether I shall get a ramble this autumn; it is

---

[1] Meaning his entertaining "Memoirs of David Garrick, Esq.," of which Johnson (as Davies informed me) wrote the first sentence; thus giving, as it were, the key-note to the performance.   It is, indeed, very characteristical of its author, beginning with a maxim, and proceeding to illustrate.   "All excellence has a right to be recorded.   I shall therefore think it superfluous to apologise for writing the life of a man, who, by an uncommon assemblage of private virtues, adorned the highest eminence in a public profession."—BOSWELL.

[2] I wish he had omitted the suspicion expressed here, though I believe he meant nothing but jocularity; for though he and I differed sometimes in opinion, he well knew how much I loved and revered him. —BEATTIE.

now about the time when we were travelling. I have, however, better health than I had then, and hope you and I may yet show ourselves on some part of Europe, Asia or Africa.[1] In the meantime let us play no trick, but keep each other's kindness by all means in our power.

"The bearer of this is Dr. Dunbar, of Aberdeen, who has written and published a very ingenious book,[2] and who I think has a kindness for me, and will, when he knows you, have a kindness for you.

"I suppose your little ladies are grown tall; and your son has become a learned young man. I love them all, and I love your naughty lady, whom I never shall persuade to love me. When the Lives are done, I shall send them to complete her collection, but must send them in paper, as, for want of a pattern, I cannot bind them to fit the rest. I am, Sir,

"Yours most affectionately,
"SAM. JOHNSON."

This year he wrote to a young clergyman in the country the following very excellent letter, which contains valuable advice to Divines in general:—

"DEAR SIR,   *Boll-court, Aug.* 30, 1780.
"Not many days ago Dr. Lawrence showed me a letter, in which you make mention of me: I hope, therefore, you will not be displeased that I endeavour to preserve your good-will by some observations which your letter suggested to me.

"You are afraid of falling into some improprieties in the daily service by reading to an audience that requires no exactness. Your fear, I hope, secures you from danger. They who contract absurd habits are such as have no fear. It is impossible to do the same thing very often, without some peculiarity of manner; but that manner may be good or bad, and a little care will at least preserve it from being bad; to make it good, there must, I think, be something of natural or casual felicity, which cannot be taught.

"Your present method of making your sermons seems very judicious. Few frequent preachers can be supposed to have sermons more their own than yours will be. Take care to register, somewhere or other, the authors from whom your several discourses are borrowed; and do not imagine that you shall always remember, even what perhaps you now think it impossible to forget.

---

[1] It will no doubt be remarked how he avoids the *rebellious* land of America. This puts me in mind of an anecdote for which I am obliged to my worthy social friend Governor Richard Penn: "At one of Miss E. Hervey's assemblies, Dr. Johnson was following her up and down the room; upon which Lord Abington observed to her, 'Your great friend is very fond of you: you can go nowhere without him.' 'Ay,' said she, 'he would follow me to any part of the world.' 'Then,' said the Earl, 'ask him to go with you to *America*.'"—BOSWELL.

[2] Dr. Dunbar was Professor of Philosophy in King's College, Aberdeen, and author of "Essays on the History of Mankind in Rude and Uncultivated Ages." He died in 1779.—ED.

"My advice, however, is, that you attempt, from time to time, an original sermon; and in the labour of composition, do not burden your mind with too much at once; do not exact from yourself at one effort of ex-cogitation, propriety of thought and elegance of expression. Invent first, and then embellish. The production of something, where nothing was before, is an act of greater energy than the expansion or decoration of the thing produced. Set down diligently your thoughts as they rise in the first words that occur; and when you have matter, you will easily give it form: nor, perhaps, will this method be always necessary; for by habit your thoughts and diction will flow together.

"The composition of sermons is not very difficult: the divisions not only help the memory of the hearer, but direct the judgment of the writer; they supply sources of invention, and keep every part in its proper place.

"What I like least in your letter is your account of the manners of your parish; from which I gather, that it has been long neglected by the parson. The Dean of Carlisle,[1] who was then a little rector in Northamptonshire, told me, that it might be discerned whether or no there was a clergyman resident in a parish, by the civil or savage manner of the people. Such a congregation as yours stands in need of much reformation; and I would not have you think it impossible to reform them. A very savage parish was civilised by a decayed gentlewoman, who came among them to teach a petty school. My learned friend Dr. Wheeler of Oxford, when he was a young man, had the care of a neighbouring parish for 15l. a year, which he was never paid; but he counted it a convenience, that it compelled him to make a sermon weekly. One woman he could not bring to the communion; and when he reproved or exhorted her, she only answered, that she was no scholar. He was advised to set some good woman or man of the parish, a little wiser than herself, to talk to her in a language level to her mind. Such honest, I may call them holy, artifices, must be practised by every clergyman; for all means must be tried by which souls may be saved. Talk to your people, however, as much as you can; and you will find, that the more frequently you converse with them upon religious subjects, the more willingly they will attend, and the more submissively they will learn. A clergyman's diligence always makes him venerable. I think I have now only to say, that in the momentous work you have undertaken, I pray GOD to bless you. I am, Sir,
"Your most humble servant,
"SAM. JOHNSON."

My next letters to him were dated August 24, September 6, and October 1, and from them I extract the following passages:—

"My brother David and I find the long-indulged fancy of our comfortable meeting again at Auchinleck, so well realised, that it

[1] Dr. Percy, now Bishop of Dromore.—BOSWELL.

in some degree confirms the pleasing hopes of *O preclarum diem!* in a future state.

"I beg that you may never again harbour a suspicion of my indulging a peevish humour, or playing tricks; you will recollect, that when I confessed to you, that I had once been intentionally silent to try your regard, I gave you my word and honour that I would not do so again.

"I rejoice to hear of your good state of health; I pray God to continue it long. I have often said, that I would willingly have ten years added to my life, to have ten from yours; I mean, that I would be ten years older to have you ten years younger. But let me be thankful for the years during which I have enjoyed your friendship, and please myself with the hopes of enjoying it many years to come in this state of being, trusting always, that in another state we shall meet never to be separated. Of this we can form no notion; but the thought, though indistinct, is delightful, when the mind is calm and clear.

"The riots in London were certainly horrible; but you gave me no account of your own situation during the barbarous anarchy. A description of it by Dr. Johnson would be a great painting;[1] you might write another 'London, a Poem.'

"I am charmed with your condescending affectionate expression, 'Let us keep each other's kindness by all the means in our power.' My revered friend! how elevating is it to my mind, that I am found worthy to be a companion to Dr. Samuel Johnson! all that you have said in grateful praise of Mr. Walmsley, I have long thought of you; but we are both Tories, which has a very general influence upon our sentiments. I hope that you will agree to meet me at York, about the end of this month; or if you will come to Carlisle, that would be better still, in case the Dean be there.   Please to consider, that to keep each other's kindness, we should every year have that free and intimate communication of mind which can be had only when we are together. We should have both our solemn and our pleasant talk."

"I write now for the third time, to tell you that my desire for our meeting this autumn is much increased.   I wrote to Squire Godfrey Bosville, my Yorkshire chief, that I should, perhaps, pay him a visit, as I was to hold a conference with Dr. Johnson, at York.   I give you my word and honour that I said not a word of his inviting you; but he wrote to me as follows:—

"'I need not tell you I shall be happy to see you here the latter end of this month, as you propose; and I shall likewise be in hopes that you will persuade Dr. Johnson to finish the conference here. It will add to the favour of your own company, if you prevail upon such an associate to assist your observations. I have often been entertained with his writings, and I once belonged to a club of which he was a member, and I never spent an evening there, but I heard something from him well worth remembering.'

"We have thus, my dear Sir, good comfortable quarters in the neighbourhood of York, where you may be assured we shall be

---

[1] I had not then seen his letters to Mrs. Thrale.—Boswell.

heartily welcome. I pray you then resolve to set out; and let not the year 1780 be a blank in our social calendar, and in that record of wisdom and wit, which I keep with so much diligence, to your honour, and the instruction and delight of others."

Mr. Thrale had now another contest for the representation in Parliament of the borough of Southwark, and Johnson kindly lent him his assistance by writing advertisements and letters for him. I shall insert one as a specimen:—

"TO THE WORTHY ELECTORS OF THE BOROUGH OF SOUTHWARK.

"GENTLEMEN,   *Southwark, Sept.* 5, 1780.

"A new Parliament being now called, I again solicit the honour of being elected for one of your representatives; and solicit it with the greater confidence, as I am not conscious of having neglected my duty, or of having acted otherwise than as becomes the independent representative of independent constituents; superior to fear, hope, and expectation, who has no private purposes to promote, and whose prosperity is involved in the prosperity of his country. As my recovery from a very severe distemper is not yet perfect, I have declined to attend the Hall, and hope an omission so necessary will not be harshly censured.

" I can only send my respectful wishes, that all your deliberations may tend to the happiness of the kingdom, and the peace of the borough.

"I am, Gentlemen, your most faithful
"And obedient servant,
"HENRY THRALE."

"TO THE RIGHT HONOURABLE LADY SOUTHWELL,[1] DUBLIN.

"MADAM,   *Bolt-court, Fleet-street, London, Sept.* 9, 1780.

"Among the numerous addresses of condolence which your great loss must have occasioned, be pleased to receive this from one

---

[1] Margaret, the second daughter and one of the co-heiresses of Arthur Cecil Hamilton, Esq. She was married in 1741 to Thomas George, the third Baron, and first Viscount Southwell, and lived with him in the most perfect connubial felicity till September, 1780, when Lord Southwell died, a loss which she never ceased to lament to the hour of her own dissolution, in her eighty-first year, August 16, 1802. The "illustrious example of piety and fortitude," to which Dr. Johnson alludes, was the submitting, when past her fiftieth year, to an extremely painful surgical operation, which she endured with extraordinary firmness and composure, not allowing herself to be tied to her chair, nor uttering a single moan. This slight tribute of affection to the memory of these two most amiable and excellent persons, who were not less distinguished by their piety, beneficence, and unbounded charity, than by a suavity of manners which endeared them to all who knew them, it is hoped, will be forgiven from one who was honoured by their kindness and friendship from his childhood.—MALONE.

whose name perhaps you have never heard, and to whom your Ladyship is known only by the reputation of your virtue, and to whom your Lord was known only by his kindness and beneficence.

"Your Ladyship is now again summoned to exert that piety of which you once gave, in a state of pain and danger, so illustrious an example; and your Lord's beneficence may be still continued by those who, with his fortune, inherit his virtues.

"I hope to be forgiven the liberty which I shall take of informing your Ladyship, that Mr. Mauritius Lowe, a son of your late Lord's father,[1] had by recommendation to your Lord, a quarterly allowance of 10*l.*, the last of which, due July 26, he has not received: he was in hourly hope of his remittance, and flattered himself that on October 26th he should have received the whole half year's bounty, when he was struck with the dreadful news of his benefactor's death.

"May I presume to hope, that his want, his relation, and his merit, which excited his Lordship's charity, will continue to have the same effect upon those whom he has left behind; and that, though he has lost one friend, he may not yet be destitute. Your Ladyship's charity cannot easily be exerted where it is wanted more; and to a mind like yours, distress is a sufficient recommendation.

"I hope to be allowed the honour of being,
        "Madam, your Ladyship's most humble servant,
                                    "SAM. JOHNSON."

On his birth-day, Johnson has this note:—

"I am now beginning the seventy-second year of my life, with more strength of body, and greater vigour of mind, than I think is common at that age."

But still he complains of sleepless nights and idle days, and forgetfulness, or neglect of resolutions. He thus pathetically expresses himself:—

"Surely I shall not spend my whole life with my own total disapprobation."—"Prayers and Meditations," p. 185.

Mr. Macbean, whom I have mentioned more than once, as one of Johnson's humble friends, a deserving but unfortunate man, being now oppressed by age and poverty, Johnson solicited the Lord Chancellor Thurlow, to have him admitted into the Charter-house. I take the liberty to insert his Lordship's answer, as I am eager to embrace every

---

[1] Thomas, the second Lord Southwell, who died in London in 1766. Johnson was well acquainted with this nobleman, and said, "he was the highest bred man, without insolence, that he was ever in company with." His younger brother, Edmund Southwell, lived in intimacy with Johnson for many years. (See an account of him in Hawkins' Life of Johnson, p. 405.) He died in London, Nov. 22, 1772.—BOSWELL.

In opposition to the Knight's unfavourable representation of this gentleman, to whom I was indebted for my first introduction to Johnson, I take this opportunity to add, that he appeared to me a pious man, and was very fond of leading the conversation to religious subjects.—MALONE.

occasion of augmenting the respectable notion which should ever be entertained of my illustrious friend:—

"TO DR. SAMUEL JOHNSON.

"SIR, *London, October* 24, 1780.

"I have this moment received your letter, dated the 19th, and returned from Bath.

"In the beginning of the summer I placed one in the Chartreux, without the sanction of a recommendation so distinct and so authorative as yours of Macbean; and I am afraid that, according to the establishment of the House, the opportunity of making the charity so good amends will not soon recur. But whenever a vacancy shall happen, if you'll favour me with notice of it, I will try to recommend him to the place, even though it should not be my turn to nominate.

"I am, Sir, with great regard,
"Your most faithful and obedient servant,
"THURLOW."

"TO JAMES BOSWELL, ESQ.

"DEAR SIR, *Oct.* 17, 1780.

"I am sorry to write you a letter that will not please you, and yet it is at last what I resolve to do. This year must pass without an interview; the summer has been foolishly lost, like many other of my summers and winters. I hardly saw a green field, but stayed in town to work, without working much.

"Mr. Thrale's loss of health has lost him the election; he is now going to Brighthelmstone, and expects me to go with him; and how long I shall stay, I cannot tell. I do not much like the place, but yet I shall go, and stay while my stay is desired. We must, therefore, content ourselves with knowing what we know as well as man can know the mind of man, that we love one another, and that we wish each other's happiness, and that the lapse of a year cannot lessen our mutual kindness.

"I was pleased to be told that I accused Mrs. Boswell unjustly, in supposing that she bears me ill-will. I love you so much, that I would be glad to love all that love you, and that you love; and I have love very ready for Mrs. Boswell, if she thinks it worthy of acceptance. I hope all the young ladies and gentlemen are well.

"I take a great liking to your brother. He tells me that his father received him kindly, but not fondly; however, you seemed to have lived well enough at Auchinleck, while you stayed. Make your father as happy as you can.

"You lately told me of your health: I can tell you in return, that my health has been, for more than a year past, better than it has been for many years before. Perhaps it may please GOD to give us some time together before we are parted.

"I am, dear Sir,
"Yours most affectionately,
"SAM. JOHNSON."

"TO THE REVEREND DR. VYSE, AT LAMBETH.

"Sir,   *December* 30, 1780.

"I hope you will forgive the liberty I take, in soliciting your interposition with his Grace the Archbishop: my first petition was successful, and I therefore venture on a second.

"The matron of the Chartreux is about to resign her place, and Mrs. Desmoulins, a daughter of the late Dr. Swinfen, who was well known to your father, is desirous of succeeding her. She has been accustomed, by keeping a boarding school, to the care of children, and I think is very likely to discharge her duty. She is in great distress, and therefore may probably receive the benefit of a charitable foundation. If you wish to see her, she will be willing to give an account of herself.

"If you shall be pleased, Sir, to mention her favourably to his Grace, you will do a great act of kindness to, Sir, your most obliged

"And most humble servant,

"Sam. Johnson."

CHAPTER XVII.—1780—1781

Langton's Johnsoniana—Anecdotes of Johnson, and his Opinions on various Subjects—Theocritus—Callimachus —Maittaire—On Employing the Poor—Lockman— Physical and Moral Truth—Huggins—Mrs. Clive— Farquhar—Garrick—Langley—Spence—Dr. Foster— Mrs. Lennox—Beauclerk—Lord Elibank—Mr. Dossie— Toleration—Johnson's Memory—Dr. Parr—Machinery of Pagan Poets—Hospitality—Rev. Dr. Farmer— Joshua Barnes—Dodsley's "Cleone"—Goldsmith's Ignorance—Adam Smith—Burke—Bishop Berkeley— Mr. Vesey — Richardson — Archbishop Secker — Dr. Blagden—Johnson's Religious Sentiments—Dr. Francklin's Demonax.

BEING disappointed in my hopes of meeting Johnson this year, so that I could hear none of his admirable sayings, I shall compensate for this want by inserting a collection of them, for which I am indebted to my worthy friend Mr. Langton, whose kind communications have been separately interwoven in many parts of this work. Very few articles of this collection were committed to writing by himself, he not having that habit; which he regrets, and which those who know the numerous opportunities he had of gathering the rich fruits of Johnsonian wit and wisdom, must ever regret. I however found, in conversation with him, that a good store of "Johnsoniana" was treasured in his mind; and I compared it to Herculaneum, or some old Roman field, which, when dug, fully rewards the labour employed. The authenticity of every article is unquestionable. For the expression, I, who wrote them down in his presence, am partly answerable.

"Theocritus is not deserving of very high respect as a writer; as to the pastoral part, Virgil is very evidently superior. He wrote, when there had been a larger influx of knowledge into the world than when Theocritus lived. Theocritus does not abound in description, though living in a beautiful country: the manners painted are coarse and gross. Virgil has much more description, more sentiment,

344

more of nature, and more of art. Some of the most excellent parts of Theocritus are, where Castor and Pollux, going with the other Argonauts, land on the Bebrycian coast, and there fall into a dispute with Amycus, the king of that country; which is as well conducted as Euripides could have done it; and the battle is well related. Afterwards they carry off a woman, whose two brothers come to recover her, and expostulate with Castor and Pollux on their injustice; but they pay no regard to the brothers, and a battle ensues, where Castor and his brother are triumphant. Theocritus seems not to have seen that the brothers have the advantage in their argument over his Argonaut heroes. 'The Sicilian Gossips' is a piece of merit."

"Callimachus is a writer of little excellence. The chief thing to be learned from him is his account of Rites and Mythology; which, though desirable to be known for the sake of understanding other parts of ancient authors, is the least pleasing or valuable part of their writings."

"Maittaire's account of the Stephani, is a heavy book. He seems to have been a puzzle-headed man, with a large share of scholarship, but with little geometry or logic in his head, without method, and possessed of little genius. He wrote Latin verses from time to time, and published a set in his old age, which he called 'Senilia;' in which he shows so little learning or taste in writing, as to make Carteret a dactyl. In matters of genealogy, it is necessary to give the bare names as they are; but in poetry, and in prose of any elegance in the writing, they require to have inflection given to them. His book of the Dialects is a sad heap of confusion. The only way to write on them is to tabulate them with notes, added at the bottom of the page, and references."[1]

It may be questioned whether there is not some mistake as to the methods of employing the poor, seemingly on a supposition that there is a certain portion of work left undone for want of persons to do it; but if that is otherwise, and all the materials we have are actually worked up, or all the manufactures we can use or dispose of are already executed, then what is given to the poor, who are to be set

[1] The name of Michael Maittaire, as a learned critic and bibliographer, has been so fully established, that these sweeping censures appear to be entirely uncalled for. His editions of the Greek and Latin classics, which are extremely numerous, are celebrated for their learning and accuracy; and his great work, "The Annales Typographici ab Artis Inventione," still maintains itself as a valuable standard authority. He was born in France and educated at Christ Church, Oxford, of which college he became second master. He was born in 1668, and died in 1747.—Ed.

at work, must be taken from some who now have it; as time must be taken for learning (according to Sir William Petty's observation), a certain part of those very materials that, as it is, are properly worked up, must be spoiled by the unskilfulness of novices. We may apply to well-meaning but misjudging persons, in particulars of this nature, what Giannone said to a monk who wanted what he called to *convert* him: '*Tu sei santo, ma tu non sei filosopho.*' It is an unhappy circumstance that one might give away five hundred pounds in a year to those that importune in the streets, and not do any good."

"There is nothing more likely to betray a man into absurdity, than *condescension ;* when he seems to suppose his understanding too powerful for his company."

"Having asked Mr. Langton if his father and mother had sat for their pictures, which he thought it right for each generation of a family to do, and being told they had opposed it, he said, 'Sir, among the anfractuosities of the human mind, I know not if it may not be one, that there is a superstitious reluctance to sit for a picture.'"

"John Gilbert Cooper related, that soon after the publication of his Dictionary, Garrick being asked by Johnson what people said of it, told him, that among other animadversions, it was objected that he cited authorities which were beneath the dignity of such a work, and mentioned Richardson. 'Nay,' said Johnson, 'I have done worse than that: I have cited *thee*, David.'"

"Talking of expense, he observed, with what munificence a great merchant will spend his money, both from his having it at command, and from his enlarged views by calculation of a good effect upon the whole. 'Whereas,' said he, 'you will hardly ever find a country gentleman, who is not a good deal disconcerted at an unexpected occasion for his being obliged to lay out ten pounds.'"

"When in good humour, he would talk of his own writings with a wonderful frankness and candour, and would even criticise them with the closest severity. One day, having read over one of his Ramblers, Mr. Langton asked him how he liked that paper; he shook his head, and answered, 'Too wordy.' At another time, when one was reading his tragedy of 'Irene,' to a company at a house in the country, he left the room; and somebody having asked him the reason of this, he replied, 'Sir, I thought it had been better.'"

"Talking of a point of delicate scrupulosity of moral conduct, he said to Mr. Langton, 'Men of harder minds than ours will do many things from which you and I would shrink; yet, Sir, they will, perhaps, do more good in life than we. But let us try to help one another. If there be a wrong twist, it may be set right. It is not probable that two people can be wrong the same way.'"

"Of the preface to Capel's Shakespeare,[1] he said, 'If the man would have come to me, I would have endeavoured to endow his purposes with words: for as it is, he doth gabble monstrously.'"

"He related, that he had once in a dream a contest of wit with some other person, and that he was very much mortified by imagining that his opponent had the better of him. 'Now,' said he, 'one may mark here the effect of sleep in weakening the power of reflection; for had not my judgment failed me, I should have seen, that the wit of this supposed antagonist, by whose superiority I felt myself depressed, was as much furnished by me, as that which I thought I had been uttering in my own character.'"

"One evening, in my company, an ingenious and learned gentleman read to him a letter of compliment which he had received from one of the professors of a foreign university. Johnson, in an irritable fit, thinking there was too much ostentation, said, 'I never receive any of these tributes of applause from abroad. One instance I recollect of a foreign publication, in which mention is made of *l'illustre Lockman.*'"[2]

"Of Sir Joshua Reynolds, he said, 'Sir, I know no man who has passed through life with more observation than Reynolds.'"

"He repeated to Mr. Langton, with great energy in the Greek, our Saviour's gracious expression concerning the forgiveness of Mary Magdalen,[3] Ἡ πίστις σοῦ σέσωκέ σε· πορεύου εἰς εἰρήνην· 'Thy faith hath saved thee; go in peace.' (Luke vii. 50.) He said, 'the manner of this dismission is exceedingly affecting.'"

"He thus defined the difference between physical and moral truth. 'Physical truth is, when you tell a thing as it actually is. Moral truth is, when you tell a thing sincerely and precisely as it appears to you. I say such a one walked

---

[1] It is said that Capel spent more than twenty years in preparing this edition of Shakespeare. He was not only a dramatic critic, but the editor of a volume of ancient poetry entitled "Prolusiones," and other works. He was born in 1713, and died in 1781.—ED.

[2] Secretary to the British Herring Fishery, remarkable for an extraordinary number of occasional verses, not of eminent merit.— BOSWELL.

[3] It does not appear that the woman forgiven was Mary Magdalen.— KEARNEY.

across the street: if he really did so, I told a physical truth. If I thought so, though I should have been mistaken, I told a moral truth.'"[1]

"Huggins, the translator of Ariosto, and Mr. Thomas Warton, in the early part of his literary life, had a dispute concerning that poet, of whom Mr. Warton, on his 'Observations on Spenser's Fairy Queen,' gave some account which Huggins attempted to answer with violence, and said, 'I will *militate* no longer against his *nescience*.' Huggins was master of the subject, but wanted expression. Mr. Warton's knowledge of it was then imperfect, but his manner lively and elegant. Johnson said, 'It appears to me, that Huggins has ball without powder, and Warton powder without ball.'"

"Talking of the farce of 'High Life below Stairs,' he said, 'Here is a farce which is really very diverting, when you see it acted; and yet one may read it, and not know that one has been reading anything at all.'"

"He used at one time to go occasionally to the green-room of Drury-lane Theatre, where he was much regarded by the players, and was very easy and facetious with them. He had a very high opinion of Mrs. Clive's[2] comic powers, and conversed more with her than with any of them. He said, 'Clive, Sir, is a good thing to sit by; she always understands what you say.' And she said of him, 'I love to sit by Dr. Johnson; he always entertains me.' One night, when 'The Recruiting Officer' was acted, he said to Mr. Holland, who had been expressing an apprehension that Dr. Johnson would disdain the works of Farquhar:[3] 'No, Sir, I think Farquhar a man whose writings have considerable merit.'"

"His friend Garrick was so busy in conducting the drama, that they could not have so much intercourse as

[1] This account of the difference between moral and physical truth is in Locke's "Essay on Human Understanding," and many other books.— KEARNEY.

[2] Mrs. Catherine Clive was the daughter of an Irish gentleman named Ruftar, and the wife of Mr. Clive the barrister; from whom she had separated before entering upon the stage. Her wit and intelligence caused her society to be courted by persons of the first rank and station. She died in 1785.—ED.

[3] George Farquhar was an Irishman, and one of the most successful dramatic writers of the time in which he flourished. His first production was, "Love in a Bottle," which was performed at Drury-lane, in 1698, with complete success. But his best and last effort was the well-known comedy of "The Beaux Stratagem." He was born at Londonderry, in 1678, and died at the premature age of 29, when he had arrived at the zenith of popularity.

Mr. Garrick used to profess an anxious wish that there should be.[1] There might, indeed, be something in the contemptuous severity as to the merit of acting, which this old preceptor nourished in himself, that would mortify Garrick after the great applause which he received from the audience. For though Johnson said of him, 'Sir, a man who has a nation to admire him every night, may well be expected to be somewhat elated;' yet he would treat theatrical matters with a ludicrous slight. He mentioned one evening, 'I met David coming off the stage, dressed in a woman's riding-hood, when he acted in *The Wonder*. I came full upon him, and I believe he was not pleased.'"

"Once he asked Tom Davies, whom he saw drest in a fine suit of clothes, 'And what art thou to-night?' Tom answered, 'The Thane of Ross;' (which it will be recollected is a very inconsiderable character.) 'O brave!' said Johnson."

"Of Mr. Longley, at Rochester, a gentleman of very considerable learning, whom Dr. Johnson met there, he said, 'My heart warms towards him. I was surprised to find in him such nice acquaintance with the metre in the learned languages: though I was somewhat mortified that I had it not so much to myself, as I should have thought.'"

"Talking of the minuteness with which people will record the sayings of eminent persons, a story was told, that when Pope was on a visit to Spence at Oxford, as they looked from the window they saw a gentleman commoner, who was just come in from riding, amusing himself with whipping at a post. Pope took occasion to say, 'That young gentleman seems to have little to do.' Mr. Beauclerk observed, 'Then, to be sure, Spence turned round and wrote that down;' and went on to say to Dr. Johnson, 'Pope, Sir, would have said the same of you, if he had seen you distilling.' JOHNSON: 'Sir, if Pope had told me of my distilling, I would have told him of his grotto.'"

"He would allow no settled indulgence of idleness upon principle, and always repelled every attempt to urge excuses for it. A friend one day suggested, that it was not wholesome to study soon after dinner. JOHNSON: "Ah, Sir, don't give way to such a fancy. At one time of my life I had taken it into my head that it was not wholesome to study between breakfast and dinner.'"

[1] In a letter written by Johnson to a friend in Jan. 1742-3, he says, "I never see Garrick."—MALONE.

"Mr. Beauclerk one day repeated to Dr. Johnson Pope's lines,

> 'Let modest Foster, if he will, excel
> Ten metropolitans in preaching well:'

Then, asked the Doctor, 'Why did Pope say this?' JOHNSON: 'Sir, he hoped it would vex somebody.'"

"Dr. Goldsmith, upon occasion of Mrs. Lennox's bringing out a play,[1] said to Dr. Johnson at the CLUB, that a person had advised him to go and hiss it, because she had attacked Shakespeare in her book called 'Shakespeare Illustrated.' JOHNSON: 'And did not you tell him that he was a rascal?' GOLDSMITH: 'No, Sir, I did not. Perhaps he did not mean what he said.' JOHNSON: 'Nay, Sir, if he lied, it is a different thing.' Colman slily said, (but it is believed Dr. Johnson did not hear him,) 'Then the proper expression should have been,—Sir, if you don't lie, you are a rascal.'"

"His affection for Topham Beauclerk was so great, that when Beauclerk was labouring under that severe illness which at last occasioned his death, Johnson said, (with a voice faltering with emotion,) 'Sir, I would walk to the extent of the diameter of the earth to save Beauclerk.'"

"One night at the CLUB he produced a translation of an epitaph which Lord Elibank had written in English, for his Lady, and requested of Johnson to turn it into Latin for him. Having read *Domina de North et Gray*, he said to Dyer,[2] 'You see, Sir, what barbarism we are compelled to make use of, when modern titles are to be specifically mentioned in Latin inscriptions.' When he had read it once aloud, and there had been a general approbation expressed by the company, he addressed himself to Mr. Dyer in particular, and said, 'Sir, I beg to have your judgment, for I know your nicety.' Dyer then very properly desired to read it over again; which having done, he pointed out an incongruity in one of the sentences. Johnson immediately assented to the observation, and said, 'Sir, this is owing to an alteration of a part of the sentence, from the form in which I had first written it; and I believe, Sir, you may have remarked, that the making a partial change,

---

[1] Probably "The Sisters," a comedy performed one night only, at Covent Garden, in 1769. Dr. Goldsmith wrote an excellent epilogue to it. Mrs. Lennox, whose maiden name was Ramsay, died in London in distressed circumstances, in her eighty-fourth year, January 4, 1804.—MALONE.

[2] See vol. i. p. 353.—MALONE.

without a due regard to the general structure of the sentence, is a very frequent cause of error in composition.'"

"Johnson was well acquainted with Mr. Dossie, author of a treatise on Agriculture; and said of him, 'Sir, of the objects which the Society of Arts have chiefly in view, the chemical effects of bodies operating upon other bodies, he knows more than almost any man.' Johnson, in order to give Mr. Dossie his vote to be a member of this Society, paid up an arrear which had run on for two years. On this occasion he mentioned a circumstance, as characteristic of the Scotch. 'One of that nation,' said he, 'who had been a candidate, against whom I had voted, came up to me with a civil salutation. Now, Sir, this is their way. An Englishman would have stomached it, and been sulky, and never have taken farther notice of you; but a Scotchman, Sir, though you vote nineteen times against him, will accost you with equal complaisance after each time, and the twentieth time, Sir, he will get your vote.'"

"Talking on the subject of toleration, one day when some friends were with him in his study, he made his usual remark, that the State has a right to regulate the religion of the people, who are the children of the State. A clergyman having readily acquiesced in this, Johnson, who loved discussion, observed, 'But, Sir, you must go round to other states than our own. You do not know what a Brahmin has to say for himself.[1] In short, Sir, I have got no farther than this: every man has a right to utter what he thinks truth, and every other man has a right to knock him down for it. Martyrdom is the test.'"

"A man, he observed, should begin to write soon: for, if he waits till his judgment is matured, his inability, through want of practice to express his conceptions, will make the disproportion so great between what he sees and what he can attain, that he will probably be discouraged from writing at all. As a proof of the justness of this remark, we may instance what is related of the great Lord Granville;[2] that after he had written his letter, giving an account of the battle of Dettingen, he said, 'Here is a letter, expressed in terms not good enough for a tallow-chandler to have used.'"

"Talking of a court-martial that was sitting upon a very momentous public occasion, he expressed much doubt of

[1] Here Lord Macartney remarks, A Brahmin or any cast of the Hindoos will neither admit you to be of their religion, nor be converted to yours:—a thing which struck the Portuguese with the greatest astonishment, when they first discovered the East Indies."—BOSWELL.

[2] John, the first Earl Granville, who died January 2, 1763.—MALONE.

an enlightened decision; and said, that perhaps there was not a member of it who, in the whole course of his life, had ever spent an hour by himself in balancing probabilities."

"Goldsmith one day brought to the CLUB a printed Ode, which he, with others, had been hearing read by its author in a public room, at the rate of five shillings each for admission. One of the company having read it aloud, Dr. Johnson said, 'Bolder words and more timorous meaning, I think never were brought together.'"

"Talking of Gray's Odes, he said, 'They are forced plants, raised in a hotbed; and they are poor plants; they are but cucumbers after all.' A gentleman present, who had been running down Ode-writing in general, as a bad species of poetry, unluckily said, 'Had they been literally cucumbers, they had been better things than Odes.'—'Yes, Sir,' said Johnson, 'for a *hog*.'"

"His distinction of the different degrees of attainment of learning was thus marked upon two occasions. Of Queen Elizabeth he said, 'She had learning enough to have given dignity to a bishop;' and of Mr. Thomas Davies he said, 'Sir, Davies has learning enough to give credit to a clergyman.'"

"He used to quote with great warmth, the saying of Aristotle recorded by Diogenes Laertius; 'that there was the same difference between one learned and unlearned, as between the living and the dead.'"

"It is very remarkable, that he retained in his memory very slight and trivial as well as important things. As an instance of this, it seems that an inferior domestic of the Duke of Leeds had attempted to celebrate his grace's marriage in such homely rhymes as he could make; and this curious composition having been sung to Dr. Johnson, he got it by heart, and used to repeat it in a very pleasant manner. Two of the stanzas were these:—

> 'When the Duke of Leeds shall married be
> To a fine young Lady of high quality,
> How happy will that gentlewoman be
> In his Grace of Leeds's good company.

> 'She shall have all that's fine and fair,
> And the best of silk and satin shall wear:
> And ride in a coach to take the air,
> And have a house in St. James's-square.'[1]

[1] The correspondent of "The Gentleman's Magazine" who subscribes himself SCIOLUS, furnishes the following supplement:—
"A lady of my acquaintance remembers to have heard her uncle

To hear a man, of the weight and dignity of Johnson, repeating such humble attempts at poetry, had a very amusing effect.   He, however, seriously observed of the last stanza repeated by him, that it nearly comprised all the advantages that wealth can give.''

"An eminent foreigner, when he was shown the British Museum, was very troublesome with many absurd inquiries. 'Now there, Sir,' said he, 'is the difference between an Englishman and a Frenchman.'   A Frenchman must be always talking, whether he knows anything of the matter or not; an Englishman is content to say nothing, when he has nothing to say.'"

"His unjust contempt for foreigners, was, indeed, extreme.   One evening, at Old Slaughter's coffee-house, when a number of them were talking loud about little matters, he said, 'Does not this confirm old Meynell's observation—*For any thing I see, foreigners are fools !*'"

"He said, that once, when he had a violent toothache, a Frenchman accosted him thus: '*Ah, Monsieur, vous étudiez trop.*'"

"Having spent an evening at Mr. Langton's with the Reverend Dr. Parr,[1] he was much pleased with the conversation of that learned gentleman; and, after he was gone, said to Mr. Langton, 'Sir, I am obliged to you for having asked me this evening.   Parr is a fair man.   I do not know when I have had an occasion of such free controversy.

sing those homely stanzas more than forty-five years ago.   He repeated the second thus:

> 'She shall breed young lords and ladies fair,
> And ride abroad in a coach and three pair,
> And the best, &c.
> And have a house,' &c.

And remembered a third which seems to have been the introductory one, and is believed to have been the only remaining one:

> 'When the Duke of Leeds shall have made his choice
> Of a charming young lady that's beautiful and wise,
> She'll be the happiest young gentlewoman under the skies,
> As long as the sun and moon shall rise,
> And how happy shall,'" &c.

It is with pleasure I add that this stanza could never be more truly applied than at this present time [1792.]—BOSWELL.

[1] Dr. Samuel Parr was one of the most learned and accomplished scholars of the age.   He was selected as the writer of the Latin Epitaph recorded on Johnson's monument in St. Paul's Cathedral.   In 1778, he was appointed master of the grammar school at Norwich, at the recommendation of Dr. Johnson; and in 1802 Sir Francis Burdett gave him the rectory of Graffham, in the county of Huntingdon.   Soon after his death, which took place in 1825, at the age of 79, his Memoirs were published in 2 vols. 8vo., and subsequently a collection of his numerous works in 8 vols.—ED.

It is remarkable how much of a man's life may pass without meeting with any instance of this kind of open discussion.'"

"We may fairly institute a criticism between Shakespeare and Corneille, as they both had, though in a different degree, the lights of a latter age.   It is not so just between the Greek dramatic writers and Shakespeare.   It may be replied to what is said by one of the remarkers on Shakespeare, that though Darius's shade had *prescience*, it does not necessarily follow that he had all *past* particulars revealed to him.'"

"Spanish plays, being wildly and improbably farcical, would please children here, as children are entertained with stories full of prodigies; their experience not being sufficient to cause them to be so readily startled at deviations from the natural course of life.   The machinery of the Pagans is uninteresting to us.   When a goddess appears in Homer or Virgil, we grow weary; still more so in the Grecian tragedies, as in that kind of composition a nearer approach to Nature is intended.   Yet there are good reasons for reading romances; as—the fertility of invention, the beauty of style and expression, the curiosity of seeing with what kind of performances the age and country in which they were written was delighted; for it is to be apprehended, that at the time when very wild improbable tales were well received, the people were in a barbarous state, and so on the footing of children, as had been explained."

" It is evident enough that no one who writes now can use the Pagan deities and mythology: the only machinery, therefore, seems that of ministering spirits, the ghosts of the departed, witches, and fairies, though these latter, as the vulgar superstition concerning them (which, while in its force, infected at least the imagination of those that had more advantage in education, though their reason set them free from it), is every day wearing out, seem likely to be of little farther assistance in the machinery of poetry.   As I recollect, Hammond introduces a hag or witch into one of his love elegies, where the effect is unmeaning and disgusting."

"The man who uses his talent of ridicule in creating or grossly exaggerating the instances he gives, who imputes absurdities that did not happen, or when a man was a little ridiculous describes him as having been very much so, abuses his talents greatly.   The great use of delineating absurdities, is, that we may know how far human folly can go; the account, therefore, ought of absolute necessity to be faithful.   A certain character (naming the person) as to the general cast of it, is well described by Garrick, but a great deal of the phraseology he uses in it, is quite his own, particularly in the proverbial comparisons, 'obstinate as a pig,' &c., but I don't know whether it might not be true of Lord ————— that from a too great eagerness of praise and popularity, and a politeness carried to a ridiculous excess, he was likely, after asserting a thing in general, to give it up again in parts. For instance, if he had said Reynolds was the first of painters, he was capable enough of giving up, as objections might happen to be severally made, first, his outline,—then the grace in form,—then the colouring,—and lastly, to have owned that he was such a mannerist, that the disposition of his pictures was all alike.''

"For hospitality, as formerly practised, there is no longer the same reason; heretofore the poorer people were more numerous, and from want of commerce, their means of getting a livelihood more difficult; therefore the supporting them was an act of great benevolence; now that the poor can find maintenance for themselves, and their labour is wanted, a general undiscerning hospitality tends to ill, by withdrawing them from their work to idleness and drunkenness. Then, formerly rents were received in kind, so that there was a great abundance of provisions in possession of the owners of the lands, which, since the plenty of money afforded by commerce, is no longer the case.''

"Hospitality to strangers and foreigners in our country is now almost at an end, since, from the increase of them that come to us, there have been a sufficient number of people that have found an interest in providing inns and proper accommodations, which is in general a more expedient method for the entertainment of travellers. Where the travellers and strangers are few, more of that hospitality subsists, as it has not been worth while to provide places of accommodation. In Ireland there is still hospitality to strangers, in some degree; in Hungary and Poland probably more.''

"Colman, in a note on his translation of Terence, talking of Shakespeare's learning, asks, 'What says Farmer to this? What says Johnson?' Upon this he observed, 'Sir, let Farmer answer for himself: I never engaged in this controversy, I always said Shakespeare had Latin enough to grammaticise his English.'''

"A clergyman, whom he characterised as one who loved to say little oddities, was affecting one day, at a bishop's table, a sort of slyness and freedom not in character, and repeated, as if part of 'The Old Man's Wish,' a song by Dr. Walter Pope, a verse bordering on licentiousness. Johnson rebuked him in the finest manner, by first showing that he did not know the passage he was aiming at, and thus humbling him: 'Sir, that is not the song: it is thus.' And he gave it right. Then looking steadfastly on him, 'Sir, there is a part of that song which I should wish to exemplify in my own life:—

'May I govern my passions with absolute sway!'"

"Being asked if Barnes[1] knew a good deal of Greek, he answered, 'I doubt, Sir, he was *unoculus inter cæcos.*'"[2]

"He used frequently to observe, that men might be very eminent in a profession, without our perceiving any particular power of mind in them in conversation. 'It seems strange,' said he, 'that a man should see so far to the right, who sees so short a way to the left. Burke is the only man whose common conversation corresponds with the general fame which he has in the world. Take up whatever topic you please, he is ready to meet you.'"

"A gentleman, by no means deficient in literature, having discovered less acquaintance with one of the Classics than Johnson expected, when the gentleman left the room, he observed, 'You see, now, how little anybody reads.' Mr. Langton happening to mention his having read a good deal in Clenardus's Greek Grammar, 'Why, Sir,' said he, 'who is there in this town who knows anything of Clenardus but you and I?' And upon Mr. Langton's mentioning that he had taken the pains to learn by heart the Epistle of St. Basil, which is given in that Grammar as a praxis, 'Sir,' said he, 'I never made such an effort to attain Greek.'"

"Of Dodsley's 'Public Virtue,' a poem, he said, 'It was fine *blank;* (meaning to express his usual contempt for blank verse:) however, this miserable poem did not sell, and my poor friend Doddy said, Public virtue was not a subject to interest the age.'"[3]

---

[1] The Rev. Joshua Barnes, the learned editor of Homer, Euripides, and Anacreon. He was author of "The Life of Edward III.," and published a poem "On the History of Esther." He was born in 1654, and died in 1712.—ED.

[2] Johnson, in his Life of Milton, after mentioning that great poet's extraordinary fancy that the world was in its decay, and that his book was to be written in an age too late for heroic poesy, thus concludes: "However inferior to the heroes who were born in better ages, he might still be great among his contemporaries, with the hope of growing every day greater in the dwindle of posterity; he might still be a giant among the pigmies, *the one-eyed monarch of the blind.*"—J. BOSWELL, JUN.

[3] The name of Dodsley, as an intimate friend of Johnson, is frequently mentioned in the course of these memoirs. As an author and a bookseller he was one of the most remarkable characters of his time. He

"Mr. Langton, when a very young man, read Dodsley's 'Cleone,' a tragedy, to him, not aware of his extreme impatience to be read to. As it went on he turned his face to the back of his chair, and put himself into various attitudes, which marked his uneasiness. At the end of an act, however, he said, 'Come, let's have some more, let's go into the slaughter-house again, Lanky. But I am afraid there is more blood than brains.' Yet he afterwards said, 'When I heard you read it I thought higher of its power of language: when I read it myself I was more sensible of its pathetic effect;' and then he paid it a compliment which many will think very extravagant. 'Sir,' said he, 'if Otway had written this play, no other of his pieces would have been remembered.' Dodsley himself, upon this being repeated to him, said, 'It was too much:' it must be remembered, that Johnson always appeared not to be sufficiently sensible of the merit of Otway.' "[1]

"'Snatches of reading,' said he, 'will not make a Bentley or a Clarke. They are, however, in a certain degree advantageous. I would put a child into a library (where no unfit books are) and let him read at his choice. A child should not be discouraged from reading anything that he takes a liking to, from a notion that it is above his reach. If that be the case, the child will soon find it out and desist; if not, he of course gains the instruction; which is so much the more likely to come, from the inclination with which he takes up the study.'"

"Though he used to censure carelessness with great vehemence, he owned, that he once, to avoid the trouble of locking up five guineas, hid them, he forgot where, so that he could not find them."

"A gentleman who introduced his brother to Dr. Johnson, was earnest to recommend him to the Doctor's notice, which he did by saying, 'When we have sat together

was born at Mansfield in 1703, and was originally apprenticed to a stocking weaver, which trade he left, and became footman to the Hon. Mrs. Lowther. While he was in this situation, he brought out a volume of poems, entitled "The Muse in Livery," and a dramatic satire, called "The Toyshop," which being patronised by Pope, and successfully brought out on the stage, enabled Dodsley to commence business as a bookseller in Pall Mall. He still continued his literary pursuits, and produced "Cleone," a tragedy, besides many light dramas and poems. He was the projector of "The Annual Register," which is still published by the trade. He died in 1764, having retired from business after a prosperous career.—ED.

[1] This assertion concerning Johnson's insensibility to the pathetic powers of Otway is too *round*. I once asked him, whether he did not think Otway frequently tender, when he answered, "Sir, he is all tenderness."—BURNEY.

some time, you'll find my brother grow very entertaining.'
—'Sir,' said Johnson, 'I can wait.'"

"When the rumour was strong that we should have
a war, because the French would assist the Americans,
he rebuked a friend with some asperity for supposing it,
saying, 'No, Sir, national faith is not yet sunk so low.'"

"In the latter part of his life, in order to satisfy himself
whether his mental faculties were impaired, he resolved
that he would try to learn a new language, and fixed upon
the Low Dutch for that purpose, and this he continued till
he had read about one half of 'Thomas à Kempis;' and
finding that there appeared no abatement of his power of
acquisition, he then desisted, as thinking the experiment
had been duly tried. Mr. Burke justly observed, that this
was not the most vigorous trial, Low Dutch being a
language so near to our own; had it been one of the
languages entirely different, he might have been very soon
satisfied."

"Mr. Langton and he having gone to see a Freemason's
funeral procession, when they were at Rochester, and some
solemn music being played on French horns, he said, 'This
is the first time that I have ever been affected by musical
sounds;' adding, 'that the impression made upon him was of
a melancholy kind.' Mr. Langton saying that this effect
was a fine one—JOHNSON: 'Yes, if it softens the mind so as
to prepare it for the reception of salutary feelings, it may be
good: but inasmuch as it is melancholy *per se*, it is bad.'" [1]

"Goldsmith had long a visionary project, that some
time or other, when his circumstances should be easier, he
would go to Aleppo, in order to acquire a knowledge, as
far as might be, of any arts peculiar to the East, and introduce them into Britain. When this was talked of in Dr.
Johnson's company, he said, 'Of all men Goldsmith is the
most unfit to go out upon such an inquiry; for he is utterly
ignorant of such arts as we already possess, and consequently
could not know what would be accessions to our present
stock of mechanical knowledge. Sir, he would bring home
a grinding-barrow, which you see in every street in London,
and think he had furnished a wonderful improvement.'"

"'Greek, Sir,' said he, 'is like lace; every man gets as
much of it as he can.'" [2]

---

[1] The French horn, however, is so far from being melancholy *per se*,
that when the strain is light, and in the field, there is nothing so cheerful!
It was the funeral occasion, and probably the solemnity of the strain,
that produced the plaintive effect here mentioned.—BURNEY.

[2] It should be remembered, that this was said twenty-five or thirty
years ago, when lace was very generally worn.—MALONE.

"When Lord Charles Hay, after his return from America, was preparing his defence to be offered to the court-martial which he had demanded, having heard Mr. Langton as high in expressions of admiration of Johnson as he usually was, he requested that Dr. Johnson might be introduced to him; and Mr. Langton having mentioned it to Johnson, he very kindly and readily agreed, and being presented by Mr. Langton to his lordship, while under arrest, he saw him several times; upon one of which occasions Lord Charles read to him what he had prepared, which Johnson signified his approbation of, saying, 'It is a very good soldierly defence.' Johnson said, that he had advised his lordship, that as it was in vain to contend with those who were in possession of power, if they would offer him the rank of lieutenant-general, and a government, it would be better judged to desist from urging his complaints. It is well known that his lordship died before the sentence was made known."

"Johnson one day gave high praise to Dr. Bentley's verses [1] in Dodsley's Collection, which he recited with his

---

[1] Dr. Johnson, in his Life of Cowley, says, that these are "the only English verses which Bentley is known to have written." I shall here insert them, and hope my readers will apply them.

> "Who strives to mount Parnassus' hill,
>   And thence poetic laurels bring,
> Must first acquire due force and skill,
>   Must fly with swan's or eagle's wing.
>
> "Who Nature's treasures would explore,
>   Her mysteries and arcana know,
> Must high as lofty Newton soar,
>   Must stoop as delving Woodward low.
>
> "Who studies ancient laws and rites,
>   Tongues, arts, and arms, and history;
> Must drudge, like Selden, days and nights,
>   And in the endless labour die.
>
> "Who travels in religious jars,
>   (Truth mixt with error, shades with rays,)
> Like Whiston, wanting pyx or stars,
>   In ocean wide or sinks or strays.
>
> "But grant our hero's hope, long toil
>   And comprehensive genius crown,
> All sciences, all arts his spoil,
>   Yet what reward, or what renown?
>
> "Envy, innate in vulgar souls,
>   Envy steps in and stops his rise;
> Envy with poison'd tarnish fouls
>   His lustre, and his worth decries.   ["He lives

usual energy.   Dr. Adam Smith, who was present, observed, in his decisive professorial manner, ' Very well—very well.' Johnson, however, added, 'Yes, they *are* very well, Sir; but you may observe in what manner they are well.   They are the forcible verses of a man of a strong mind, but not accustomed to write verse; for there is some uncouthness in the expression.'" [1]

"Drinking tea one day at Garrick's with Mr. Langton, he was questioned if he was not somewhat of a heretic as to Shakespeare; said Garrick, 'I doubt he is a little of an infidel.'   'Sir,' said Johnson, 'I will stand by the lines I have written on Shakespeare in my Prologue at the opening of your theatre.'   Mr. Langton suggested that, in the line

'And panting Time toil'd after him in vain,'

Johnson might have had in his eye the passage in 'The Tempest,' where Prospero says of Mirando,

'——— She will outstrip all praise,
     And make it halt behind her.'

Johnson said nothing.   Garrick then ventured to observe, '*I* do not think that the happiest line in the praise of Shakespeare.'   Johnson exclaimed (smiling),   'Prosaical

"He lives inglorious or in want,
     To college and old books confined;
Instead of learn'd, he's call'd pedant,
     Dunces advanced, he's left behind.
Yet left content, a genuine Stoic he,
     Great without patron, rich without South Sea."—
                                        BOSWELL.

A different and probably a more accurate copy of these spirited verses is to be found in "The Grove, or a Collection of Original Poems and Translations," &c. 1721.   In this miscellany the last stanza, which in Dodsley's copy is unquestionably uncouth, is thus exhibited:

"*Inglorious or by wants inthrall'd,*
     To college and old books confined
A pedant from his learning call'd,
     Dunces advanced, he's left behind."—J. BOSWELL, JUN.

[1] The difference between Johnson and Smith is apparent even in this slight instance.   Smith was a man of extraordinary application, and had his mind crowded with all manner of subjects; but the force, acuteness, and vivacity of Johnson were not to be found there.   He had book-making so much in his thoughts, and was so chary of what might be turned to account in that way, that he once said to Sir Joshua Reynolds that he made it a rule, when in company, never to talk of what he understood.   Beauclerk had for a short time a pretty high opinion of Smith's conversation.   Garrick, after listening to him for a while, as to one of whom his expectations had been raised, turned slily to a friend, and whispered him, "What say you to this?—eh? *flabby,* I think."—BOSWELL.

rogues! next time I write I'll make both time and space pant.'"[1]

"It is well known that there was formerly a rude custom for those who were sailing upon the Thames to accost each other as they passed in the most abusive language they could invent, generally, however, with as much satirical humour as they were capable of producing. Addison gives a specimen of this ribaldry, in number 383 of 'The Spectator,' when Sir Roger de Coverly and he are going to Spring-garden. Johnson was once eminently successful in this species of contest; a fellow having attacked him with some coarse raillery, Johnson answered him thus, 'Sir, your wife, *under pretence of keeping a bawdy-house*, is a receiver of stolen goods.' One evening when he and Mr. Burke and Mr. Langton were in company together, and the admirable scolding of Timon of Athens was mentioned, this instance of Johnson's was quoted, and thought to have at least equal excellence."

"As Johnson always allowed the extraordinary talents of Mr. Burke, so Mr. Burke was fully sensible of the wonderful powers of Johnson. Mr. Langton recollects having passed an evening with both of them, when Mr. Burke repeatedly entered upon topics which it was evident he would have illustrated with extensive knowledge and richness of expression; but Johnson always seized upon the conversation, in which, however, he acquitted himself in a most masterly manner. As Mr. Burke and Mr. Langton were walking home, Mr. Burke observed that Johnson had been very great that night. Mr. Langton joined in this, but added, he could have wished to hear more from another person, plainly intimating that he meant Mr. Burke. 'Oh, no,' said Mr. Burke, 'it is enough for me to have rung the bell to him.'"

---

[1] I am sorry to see, in "The Transactions of the Royal Society of Edinburgh," vol. ii, "An Essay on the Character of Hamlet," written, I should suppose, by a very young man, though called "Reverend;" who speaks with presumptuous petulance of the first literary character of his age. Amidst a cloudy confusion of words (which hath of late too often passed in Scotland for *Metaphysics*), he thus ventures to criticise one of the noblest lines in our language:—''Dr. Johnson has remarked, that 'time toiled after him in vain.' But I should apprehend, that this is *entirely to mistake the character*. Time toils after *every great man*, as well as after Shakespeare. The *workings* of an ordinary mind *keep pace*, indeed, with time; they move no faster; *they have their beginning, their middle, and their end*; but superior natures can *reduce these into a point*. They do not, indeed, *suppress* them; but they *suspend*, or they *lock them up in the breast*." The learned Society, under whose sanction such gabble is ushered into the world, would do well to offer a premium to any one who will discover its meaning.—BOSWELL.

"Beauclerk having observed to him of one of their friends, that he was awkward at counting money, 'Why, Sir,' said Johnson, 'I am likewise awkward at counting money. But then, Sir, the reason is plain: I have had very little money to count.'"

"He had an abhorrence of affectation. Talking of old Mr. Langton, of whom he said, 'Sir, you will seldom see such a gentleman, such are his stores of literature, such his knowledge in divinity, and such his exemplary life;' he added, 'and, Sir, he has no grimace, no gesticulation, no bursts of admiration on trivial occasions; he never embraces you with an overacted cordiality.'"

"Being in company with a gentleman who thought fit to maintain Dr. Berkeley's ingenious philosophy, that nothing exists but as perceived by some mind; when the gentleman was going away, Johnson said to him, 'Pray, Sir, don't leave us; for we may perhaps forget to think of you, and then you will cease to exist.'"[1]

"Goldsmith, upon being visited by Johnson one day in the Temple, said to him, with a little jealousy of the appearance of his accommodation, 'I shall soon be in better chambers than these.' Johnson at the same time checked him, and paid him a handsome compliment, implying that a man of his talents should be above attention to such distinctions. 'Nay, Sir, never mind that. *Nil te quæsiveris extra.*'"

"At the time when his pension was granted to him, he said, with a noble literary ambition, 'Had this happened twenty years ago, I should have gone to Constantinople to learn Arabic, as Pococke[2] did.'"

"As an instance of the niceness of his taste, though he praised West's translation of Pindar, he pointed out the following passages as faulty, by expressing a circumstance so minute as to detract from the general dignity which should prevail:—

'Down, then, from thy glittering *nail*,
Take, O muse, thy Dorian lyre.'"

[1] Dr. Berkeley was the Bishop of Cloyne, and a metaphysical writer of great celebrity. His bold hypothesis of the non-existence of material objects in Nature otherwise than in the mind, excited extraordinary attention at the time. Pope ascribed to him "every virtue under heaven!" He was born at Kilerin, in Ireland, in 1684, and died in 1753. —ED.

[2] Dr. Edward Pococke was Hebrew Professor at Oxford, and a celebrated orientalist. He was born in 1604, and died in 1691.—ED.

"When Mr. Vesey[1] was proposed as a member of the Literary Club, Mr. Burke began by saying that he was a man of gentle manners. 'Sir,' said Johnson, 'you need say no more. When you have said a man of gentle manners, you have said enough.'"

"The late Mr. Fitzherbert told Mr. Langton that Johnson said to him, 'Sir, a man has no more right to *say* an uncivil thing, than to *act* one; no more right to say a rude thing to another than to knock him down.'"

"'My dear friend Dr. Bathurst,' said he, with a warmth of approbation, 'declared, he was glad that his father, who was a West Indian planter, had left his affairs in total ruin, because having no estate he was not under the temptation of having slaves.'"

"Richardson had little conversation, except about his own works, of which Sir Joshua Reynolds said he was always willing to talk, and glad to have them introduced. Johnson, when he carried Mr. Langton to see him, professed that he could bring him out into conversation, and used this illusive expression, 'Sir, I can make him *rear*.' But he failed; for in that interview Richardson said little else than that there lay in the room a translation of his 'Clarissa' into German."[2]

"Once when somebody produced a newspaper, in which there was a letter of stupid abuse of Sir Joshua Reynolds, of which Johnson himself came in for a share, 'Pray,' said he, 'let us have it read aloud from beginning to end;' which being done, he with a ludicrous earnestness, and not directing his look to any particular person, called out, 'Are we alive after this satire?'"

"He had a strong prejudice against the political character

[1] The Right Honourable Agmondesham Vesey was elected a member of the LITERARY CLUB in 1773, and died in 1784.—MALONE.

[2] A literary lady has favoured me with a characteristic anecdote of Richardson. One day at his country house at Northend, where a large company was assembled at dinner, a gentleman who was just returned from Paris, willing to please Mr. Richardson, mentioned to him a very flattering circumstance,—that he had seen his Clarissa lying on the king's brother's table. Richardson observing that part of the company were engaged in talking to each other, affected then not to attend to it. But by and by, when there was a general silence, and he thought that the flattery might be fully heard, he addressed himself to the gentleman, "I think, Sir, you were saying something about—," pausing in a high flutter of expectation. The gentleman, provoked at his inordinate vanity, resolved not to indulge it, and with an exquisitely sly air of indifference answered, "A mere trifle, Sir, not worth repeating." The mortification of Richardson was visible, and he did not speak ten words more the whole day. Dr. Johnson was present, and appeared to enjoy it much.—BOSWELL.

of Secker,[1] one instance of which appeared at Oxford, where he expressed great dissatisfaction at his varying the old established toast, 'Church and King.' 'The Archbishop of Canterbury,' said he (with an affected smooth smiling grimace), 'drinks Constitution in Church and State.' Being asked what difference there was between the two toasts, he said, 'Why, Sir, you may be sure he meant something.' Yet when the life of that prelate, prefixed to his sermons by Dr. Porteus and Dr. Stinton, his chaplains, first came out, he read it with the utmost avidity, and said, 'It is a life well written, and that well deserves to be recorded.'"

"Of a certain noble lord, he said, 'Respect him you could not; for he had no mind of his own. Love him you could not; for that which you could do with him, every one else could.'"

"Of Dr. Goldsmith he said, 'No man was more foolish when he had not a pen in his hand, or more wise when he had.'"

"He told, in his lively manner, the following literary anecdote:—'Green and Guthrie, an Irishman and a Scotchman, undertook a translation of Duhalde's History of China. Green said of Guthrie, that he knew no English, and Guthrie of Green, that he knew no French; and these two undertook to translate Duhalde's History of China. In this translation there was found "the twenty-sixth day of the new moon." Now, as the whole age of the moon is but twenty-eight days, the moon, instead of being new, was nearly as old as it could be. The blunder arose from their mistaking the word *neuvième* (ninth) for *nouvelle* or *neuve* (new).'"

"Talking of Dr. Blagden's copiousness and precision of communication, Dr. Johnson said, 'Blagden, Sir, is a delightful fellow.'"

"On occasion of Dr. Johnson's publishing his pamphlet of 'The False Alarm,' there came out a very angry answer (by many supposed to be by Mr. Wilkes). Dr. Johnson determined on not answering it; but, in conversation with Mr. Langton, mentioned a particular or two, which, if he *had*

[1] Secker, the Archbishop of Canterbury, was originally educated with the view of becoming a dissenting minister,—his family and connexions being Dissenters; but from conscientious scruples he eventually conformed to the Church of England, took orders, and obtained rapid preferment. He was successively elevated to the Sees of Bristol in 1735, Oxford in 1737, and Canterbury in 1758, in which last situation he conducted himself with great dignity and munificence. He was born at Sibthorpe, in Nottinghamshire, in 1693, and died in 1768. His Sermons, Charges, and other works have been published in 12 vols.—ED.

replied to it, he might perhaps have inserted. In the answerer's pamphlet, it had been said with solemnity, 'Do you consider, Sir, that a House of Commons is to the people as a creature is to its Creator?' 'To this question,' said Dr. Johnson, 'I could have replied that, in the first place, the idea of a Creator must be such as that he has a power to unmake or annihilate his creature.'"

"'Then it cannot be conceived that a creature can make laws for its Creator.'"[1]

"'Depend upon it,' said he, 'that if a man *talks* of his misfortunes, there is something in them that is not disagreeable to him; for where there is nothing but pure misery, there never is any recourse to the mention of it.'"

"A man must be a poor beast, that should *read* no more in quantity than he could *utter* aloud."

"Imlac in 'Rasselas,' I spelt with a *c* at the end, because it is less like English, which should always have the Saxon *k* added to the *c*."

"Many a man is mad in certain instances, and goes through life without having it perceived; for example, a madness has seized a person of supposing himself obliged literally to pray continually; had the madness turned the opposite way, and the person thought it a crime ever to pray, it might not improbably have continued unobserved."

"He apprehended that the delineation of *characters* in the end of the first book of 'The Retreat of the Ten Thousand,' was the first instance of the kind that was known."

"'Supposing,' said he, 'a wife to be of a studious or argumentative turn, it would be very troublesome; for instance, if a woman should continually dwell upon the subject of the Arian heresy.'"

"No man speaks concerning another, even suppose it be in his praise, if he thinks he does not hear him, exactly as he would if he thought he was within hearing."

"'The applause of a single human being is of great consequence.' This he said to me with great earnestness of manner, very near the time of his decease, on occasion

---

[1] His profound adoration of the GREAT FIRST CAUSE was such as to set him above that "Philosophy and vain deceit," with which men of narrow conceptions have been infected. I have heard him strongly maintain that "what is right is not so from any natural fitness, but because GOD wills it to be right;" and it is certainly so, because he has predisposed the relations of things so as that which he wills must be right.—BOSWELL.

of having desired me to read a letter addressed to him from some person in the north of England, which, when I had done, and he asked me what the contents were, as I thought being particular upon it might fatigue him, it being of great length, I only told him in general that it was highly in his praise; and then he expressed himself as above."

"He mentioned with an air of satisfaction what Baretti had told him, that, meeting in the course of his studying English, with an excellent paper in 'The Spectator,' one of four that were written by the respectable dissenting minister, Mr. Grove, of Taunton, and observing the genius and energy of mind that it exhibits, it greatly quickened his curiosity to visit our country; as he thought, if such were the lighter periodical essays of our authors, their productions on more weighty occasions must be wonderful indeed."

"He observed once, at Sir Joshua Reynolds's, that a beggar in the street will more readily ask alms from a *man*, though there should be no marks of wealth in his appearance, than from even a well-dressed *woman*;[1] which he accounted for from the great degree of carefulness as to money that is to be found in women; saying farther upon it, that the opportunities in general that they possess of improving their condition are much fewer than men have; and adding, as he looked round the company, which consisted of men only, 'There is not one of us who does not think he might be richer, if he would use his endeavour.'"

"He thus characterised an ingenious writer of his acquaintance:—'Sir, he is an enthusiast by rule.'"

"'*He may hold up that* SHIELD *against all his enemies*,' was an observation on Homer, in reference to his description of the shield of Achilles, made by Mrs. Fitzherbert, wife to his friend Mr. Fitzherbert, of Derbyshire, and respected by Dr. Johnson as a very fine one. He had in general a very high opinion of that lady's understanding."

"An observation of Bathurst's may be mentioned, which Johnson repeated, appearing to acknowledge it to be well founded, namely, it was somewhat remarkable how seldom, on occasion of coming into the company of any new person, one felt any wish or inclination to see him again."

This year the Rev. Dr. Francklin, having published a

---

[1] Sterne is of a direct contrary opinion. See his "Sentimental Journey," Article, *The Mystery*.—BOSWELL.

translation of "Lucian," inscribed to him the *Demonax*
thus:—

"To Dr. SAMUEL JOHNSON, the Demonax of the present age,
this piece is inscribed by a sincere admirer of his respectable talents.
"THE TRANSLATOR."

Though upon a particular comparison of Demonax and
Johnson, there does not seem to be a great deal of similarity
between them, this dedication is a just compliment from
the general character given by Lucian of the ancient
sage—" ἄριστον ὧν οἶδα ἐγὼ φιλοσόφων γενόμενον," (*the best philosopher whom I have ever seen or known*).

CHAPTER XVIII.—1781

Johnson's "Lives of the Poets" completed—John Nichols—
The various Readings in "The Lives"—Cowley—Waller
—Milton—Dr. Towers' Remarks on the Writings
of Johnson—Dryden—Pope—Bishop Warburton—Dr.
Broome—Lord Somerville—Addison—Parnell—Black-
more — Ambrose Philips — Congreve — Tickell —
Akenside—Lyttelton—Miss Boothby—Herbert Croft—
Young's "Night Thoughts"—Swift—Rev. Joseph Spence
—Attacks on "The Lives of the Poets"

IN 1781, Johnson at last completed his "Lives of the Poets,"
of which he gives this account:—"Some time in March I
finished 'The Lives of the Poets,' which I wrote in my usual
way, dilatorily and hastily, unwilling to work, and working
with vigour and haste." In a memorandum previous to
this, he says of them:—"Written, I hope, in such a manner
as may tend to the promotion of piety."

This is the work which, of all Dr. Johnson's writings, will
perhaps be read most generally, and with most pleasure.
Philology and biography were his favourite pursuits, and
those who lived most in intimacy with him, heard him upon all
occasions, when there was a proper opportunity, take delight
in expatiating upon the various merits of the English Poets;
upon the niceties of their characters, and the events of
their progress through the world which they contribute
to illuminate. His mind was so full of that kind of information, and it was so well arranged in his memory, that in
performing what he had undertaken in this way, he had
little more to do than to put his thoughts upon paper,
exhibiting first each poet's life, and then subjoining a critical
examination of his genius and works. But when he began
to write, the subject swelled in such a manner, that, instead
of prefaces to each poet of no more than a few pages, as he
had originally intended,[1] he produced an ample, rich, and

---

[1] His design is thus announced in his *Advertisement*:—"The booksellers
having determined to publish a body of English Poetry, I was persuaded
to promise them a preface to the works of each author; an undertaking,
as it was then presented to my mind, not very tedious or difficult. My
purpose was only to have allotted to every poet an advertisement, like
that which we find in the French Miscellanies, containing a few dates,

most entertaining view of them in every respect.   In this
he resembled Quintilian, who tells us, that in the composition of his Institutions of Oratory, "*Latius se tamen aperiente
materiâ, plus quàm imponebatur oneris sponte suscepi.*"   The
booksellers, justly sensible of the great additional value of
the copyright, presented him with another hundred pounds,
over and above two hundred, for which his agreement was
to furnish such prefaces as he thought fit.

This was, however, but a small recompense for such a
collection of biography, and such principles and illustrations
of criticism, as, if digested and arranged in one system by
some modern Aristotle or Longinus, might form a code
upon that subject, such as no other nation can show.   As
he was so good as to make me a present of the greatest part
of the original and indeed only manuscript of this admirable
work, I have an opportunity of observing with wonder the
correctness with which he rapidly struck off such glowing
composition.   He may be assimilated to the Lady in Waller,
who could impress with "Love at first sight:"

> "Some other nymphs with colours faint,
>   And pencil slow, may Cupid paint,
>   And a weak heart in time destroy;
> She has a stamp, and prints the boy."

That he, however, had a good deal of trouble, and some
anxiety in carrying on the work, we see from a series of
letters to Mr. Nichols, the printer,[1] whose variety of literary

and a general character; but I have been led beyond my intention, I
hope by the honest desire of giving useful pleasure."—BOSWELL.

[1] Thus:—"In the Life of Waller, Mr. Nichols will find a reference
to the Parliamentary History, from which a long quotation is to be
inserted.   If Mr. Nichols cannot easily find the book, Mr. Johnson will
send it from Streatham."

"Clarendon is here returned."

"By some accident, I laid *your* note upon Duke up so safely, that I
cannot find it.   Your informations have been of great use to me.   I
must beg it again; with another list of our authors, for I have laid that
with the other.   I have sent Stepney's epitaph.   Let me have the
revises as soon as can be.   Dec. 1778."

"I have sent Philips, with his epitaphs, to be inserted.   The fragment
of a preface is hardly worth the impression, but that we may seem to
do something.   It may be added to the life of Philips.   The Latin page
is to be added to the Life of Smith.   I shall be at home to revise the
two sheets of Milton.   March 1, 1779."

"Please to get me the last edition of Hughes's letters; and try to get
Dennis upon Blackmore, and upon Cato, and anything of the same writer
against Pope.   Our materials are defective."

"As Waller professed to have imitated Fairfax, do you think a few
pages of Fairfax would enrich our edition?   Few readers have seen
it, and it may please them.   But it is not necessary."

inquiry and obliging disposition rendered him useful to Johnson. Mr. Steevens appears, from the papers in my possession, to have supplied him with some anecdotes and quotations; and I observe the fair hand of Mrs. Thrale as one of his copyists of select passages. But he was principally indebted to my steady friend, Mr. Isaac Reed, of Staple-inn, whose extensive and accurate knowledge of English literary history I do not express with exaggeration, when I say it is wonderful; indeed his labours have proved it to the world; and all who have the pleasure of his acquaintance can bear testimony to the frankness of his communications in private society.

It is not my intention to dwell upon each of Johnson's "Lives of the Poets," or attempt an analysis of their merits, which, were I able to do it, would take up too much room in this work; yet I shall make a few observations upon some of them, and insert a few various readings.

The Life of Cowley he himself considered as the best of the whole, on account of the dissertation which it contains on the Metaphysical Poets. Dryden, whose critical abilities were equal to his poetical, had mentioned them in his excellent dedication of his Juvenal, but had barely mentioned them. Johnson has exhibited them at large, with such happy illustration from their writings, and in so luminous a manner, that indeed he may be allowed the full merit of novelty, and to have discovered to us, as it were, a new planet in the poetical hemisphere.

It is remarked by Johnson, in considering the words of a poet,[1] that "amendments are seldom made without some token of a rent;" but I do not find that this is applicable to prose.[2] We shall see that though his amendments in this

"An account of the lives and works of some of the most eminent English poets. By, &c.—'The English Poets, biographically and critically considered by SAM. JOHNSON.'—Let Mr. Nichols take his choice, or make another to his mind. May, 1781."

"You somehow forgot the advertisement for the new edition. It was not enclosed. Of Gay's letters I see not that any use can be made, for they give no information of anything. That he was a member of a Philosophical Society is something; but surely he could be but a corresponding member. However, not having his life here, I know not how to put it in, and it is of little importance."

See several more in "The Gentleman's Magazine," 1785. The editor of that Miscellany, in which Johnson wrote for several years, seems justly to think that every fragment of so great a man is worthy of being preserved.—BOSWELL.

[1] Life of Sheffield.—BOSWELL.

[2] See, however, p. 350 of this volume, where the same remark is made, and Johnson is there speaking of *prose*. In his Life of Dryden, his observations in the opera of "King Arthur," furnish a striking instance of the truth of his remark.—MALONE.

work are for the better, there is nothing of the *pannus assutus ;* the texture is uniform: and indeed, what had been there at first is very seldom unfit to have remained.

Various Readings[1] *in the Life of* COWLEY.

"All [future votaries of] *that may hereafter pant for* solitude.

"To conceive and execute the [agitation or perception] *pains and the pleasures* of other minds.

"The wide effulgence of [the blazing] *a summer* noon."

In the Life of Waller,[2] Johnson gives a distinct and animated narrative of public affairs in that variegated period, with strong yet nice touches of character; and having a fair opportunity to display his political principles, does it with an unqualified manly confidence, and satisfies his readers how nobly he might have executed a Tory history of his country.

So easy in his style in these Lives, that I do not recollect more than three uncommon or learned words; one, when giving an account of the approach of Waller's mortal disease, he says, "he found his legs grow *tumid ;*" by using the expression his legs swelled, he would have avoided this; and there would have been no impropriety in its being followed by the interesting question to his physician, "What that *swelling* meant?" Another, when he mentions that Pope had *emitted* proposals; when *published*, or *issued*, would have been more readily understood; and a third, when he calls Orrery and Dr. Delany,[3] writers both undoubtedly

---

[1] The original reading is enclosed in crotchets, and the present one is printed in italics.—BOSWELL.

[2] The name of Waller has been justly celebrated by Pope, and the elegance and ease which he imparted to English versification, at an early period of our literary history, render the praise not undeserved:—

"And learn to praise the easy vigour of a line,
Where Denham's strength and Waller's sweetness join."

The life of Edward Waller was an eventful one. He was born at Coleshill, in Warwickshire, in 1605, entered Parliament in his eighteenth year, and was deeply engaged in the great political struggles of Charles I. with his Parliament. At one time he was sent to the Tower, and condemned to be hanged for conspiring to deliver the City of London to the king; but saved himself by an abject submission and a liberal distribution of money, and went into temporary exile. His prolific muse afterwards celebrated, with equal power and genius, the praises of Cromwell, of Charles II., and of James. After the Restoration he was elected to Parliament, where, by his eloquence and wit, he was the delight of the House of Commons. He died in 1687, at the age of eighty-two.—ED.

[3] This is the Rev. Patrick Delany, who was the author of a work entitled "Observations on Lord Orrery's Remarks on the Life and Writings of Swift," on which Dr. Johnson (p. 204 this vol.) bestowed his commendations. It was published in 1754, and excited considerable

veracious ; when *true, honest,* or *faithful* might have been used.   Yet it must be owned that none of these are *hard* or *too big* words: that custom would make them seem as easy as any others; and that a language is richer and capable of more beauty of expression by having a greater variety of synonymes.

His dissertation upon the unfitness of poetry for the awful subjects of our holy religion, though I do not entirely agree with him, has all the merit of originality, with uncommon force and reasoning.

Various Readings in the Life of WALLER.

"Consented to [the insertion of their names] *their own nomination.*

"[After] *paying* a fine of ten thousand pounds.

"Congratulating Charles the Second on his [coronation] *recovered right.*

"He that has flattery ready for all whom the vicissitudes of the world happen to exalt, must be [confessed to degrade his powers] *scorned as a prostituted mind.*

"The characters by which Waller intended to distinguish his writings are [elegance] *sprightliness* and dignity.

"Blossoms to be valued only as they [fetch] *foretell* fruits.

"Images such as the superficies of nature [easily] *readily* supplies.

"[His] *Some* applications [are sometimes] *may be thought* too remote and unconsequential.

"His images are [sometimes confused] *not always distinct.*"

Against his Life of Milton, the hounds of Whiggism have opened in full cry.   But of Milton's great excellence as a poet, where shall we find such a blazon as by the hand of Johnson?   I shall select only the following passage concerning "Paradise Lost:"

"Fancy can hardly forbear to conjecture with what temper Milton surveyed the silent progress of his work, and marked his reputation stealing its way in a kind of subterraneous current, through fear and silence.   I cannot but conceive him calm and confident, little disappointed, not at all dejected, relying on his own merit with steady consciousness, and waiting, without impatience, the vicissitudes of opinion, and the impartiality of a future generation."

Indeed even Dr. Towers, who may be considered as one of the warmest zealots of the Revolution Society itself,

attention at the time.   He was born in Ireland in 1686, and had the reputation of being a scholar and a versatile writer.   In 1732 he published "Revelation examined with Candour."   In 1738 appeared his "Reflections upon Polygamy," and shortly afterwards his "Life of David." From Lord Carteret he was so fortunate as to receive some valuable church preferment.   He died in 1768.—ED.

allows that "Johnson has spoken in the highest terms of the abilities of that great poet, and has bestowed on his principal poetical compositions the most honourable encomiums." [1]

That a man, who venerated the church and monarchy as Johnson did, should speak with a just abhorrence of Milton as a politician, or rather as a daring foe to good polity, was surely to be expected; and to those who censure him, I would recommend his commentary on Milton's celebrated complaint of his situation, when, by the lenity of Charles the Second—"a lenity of which," as Johnson well observes, "the world has had perhaps no other example"—he, who had written in justification of the murder of his sovereign, was safe under an *Act of Oblivion*. "No sooner is he safe than he finds himself in danger, *fallen on evil days and evil tongues, with darkness and with dangers compassed round*. This darkness, had his eyes been better employed, had undoubtedly deserved compassion; but to add the mention of danger was ungrateful and unjust. He was fallen, indeed, on *evil* days; the time was come in which regicides could no longer boast their wickedness. But of *evil tongues* for Milton to complain, required impudence at least equal to his other powers;—Milton, whose warmest advocates must allow that he never spared any asperity of reproach, or brutality of insolence."

I have, indeed, often wondered how Milton, "an acrimonious and surly Republican"—"a man who in his domestic relations was so severe and arbitrary,"[2] and whose head was filled with the hardest and most dismal tenets of Calvinism, should have been such a poet; should not only

---

[1] See "An Essay on the Life, Character, and Writings of Dr. Samuel Johnson," London, 1787; which is very well written, making a proper allowance for the democratical bigotry of its author, whom I cannot however but admire for his liberality in speaking thus of my illustrious friend:—

"He possessed extraordinary powers of understanding, which were much cultivated by study, and still more by meditation and reflection. His memory was remarkably retentive, his imagination uncommonly vigorous, and his judgment keen and penetrating. He had a strong sense of the importance of religion; his piety was sincere, and sometimes ardent; and his zeal for the interests of virtue was often manifested in his conversation and in his writings. The same energy which was displayed in his literary productions was exhibited also in his conversation, which was various, striking, and instructive; and perhaps no man ever equalled him for nervous and pointed repartees.

"His Dictionary, his moral Essays, and his productions in polite literature, will convey useful instruction, and elegant entertainment, as long as the language in which they are written shall be understood."—BOSWELL.

[2] Johnson's Life of Milton.—BOSWELL.

have written with sublimity, but with beauty, and even gaiety; should have exquisitely painted the sweetest sensations of which our nature is capable; imaged the delicate raptures of connubial love; nay, seemed to be animated with all the spirit of revelry. It is a proof that in the human mind the departments of judgment and imagination, perception and temper, may sometimes be divided by strong partitions; and that the light and shade in the same character may be kept so distinct as never to be blended.[1]

In the Life of Milton, Johnson took occasion to maintain his own and the general opinion of the excellence of rhyme over blank verse, in English poetry; and quotes this apposite illustration of it by "an ingenious critic," that *it seems to be verse only to the eye.*[2] The gentleman whom he thus characterises is (as he told Mr. Seward) Mr. Lock, of Norbury Park, in Surrey, whose knowledge and taste in the fine arts is universally celebrated; with whose elegance of manners the writer of the present work has felt himself much impressed, and to whose virtues a common friend, who has known him long, and is not much addicted to flattery, gives the highest testimony.

Various Readings in the Life of MILTON.

"I cannot find any meaning but this which [his most bigoted advocates] *even kindness and reverence* can give.

"[Perhaps no] *scarcely any* man ever wrote so much, and praised so few.

"A certain [rescue] *preservative* from oblivion.

"Let me not be censured for this digression, as [contracted] *pedantic* or paradoxical.

"Socrates rather was of opinion that what we had to learn was how to [obtain and communicate happiness] *do good and avoid evil.*

"Its elegance [who can exhibit?] *is less attainable.*"

I could, with pleasure, expatiate upon the masterly execution of the Life of Dryden, which, we have seen,[3] was one of

---

[1] Mr. Malone thinks it is rather a proof that he felt nothing of those cheerful sensations which he has described; that on these topics it is the *poet,* and not the *man,* that writes.—BOSWELL.

[2] One of the most natural instances of the effect of blank verse occurred to the late Earl of Hopeton. His Lordship observed one of his shepherds poring in the fields upon Milton's "Paradise Lost;" and having asked him what book it was, the man answered, "An't please your Lordship, this is a very odd sort of an author: he would fain rhyme, but cannot get at it."—BOSWELL.

[3] See p. 69.—BOSWELL.

Johnson's literary projects at an early period, and which it is remarkable that, after desisting from it, from a supposed scantiness of materials, he should, at an advanced age, have exhibited so amply.

His defence of that great poet against the illiberal attacks upon him, as if his embracing the Roman Catholic communion had been a time-serving measure, is a piece of reasoning at once able and candid.   Indeed, Dryden himself, in his "Hind and Panther," hath given such a picture of his mind, that they who know the anxiety for repose as to the awful subject of our state beyond the grave, though they may think his opinion ill-founded, must think charitably of his sentiment:—

"But, gracious God, how well dost thou provide
    For erring judgments an unerring guide!
    Thy throne is darkness in the abyss of light,
    A blaze of glory that forbids the sight.
    O! teach me to believe thee thus conceal'd,
    And search no farther than thyself reveal'd;
    But Her alone for my director take,
    Whom thou hast promised never to forsake.
    My thoughtless youth was wing'd with vain desires,
    My manhood long misled by wand'ring fires,
    Follow'd false lights; and when their glimpse was gone,
    My pride struck out new sparkles of her own.
    Such was I, such by nature still I am;
    Be thine the glory, and be mine the shame.
    Good life be now my task: my doubts are done,
    What more could shock my faith than Three in One?"

In drawing Dryden's character, Johnson has given, though I suppose unintentionally, some touches of his own. Thus: "The power that predominated in his intellectual operations was rather strong reason than quick sensibility. Upon all occasions that were presented, he studied rather than felt; and produced sentiments not such as nature enforces, but meditation supplies.   With the simple and elemental passions as they spring separate in the mind, he seems not much acquainted.   He is, therefore, with all his variety of excellence, not often pathetic; and had so little sensibility of the power of effusions purely natural, that he did not esteem them in others."   It may, indeed, be observed, that in all the numerous writings of Johnson, whether in prose or verse, and even in his Tragedy, of which the subject is the distress of an unfortunate princess, there is not a single passage that ever drew a tear.

Various Readings in the Life of DRYDEN.

"The reason of this general perusal, Addison has attempted to [find in] *derive from* the delight which the mind feels in the investigation of secrets.

"His best actions are but [convenient] *inability* of wickedness.

"When once he had engaged himself in disputation, [matter] *thoughts* flowed in on either side.

"The abyss of an un-ideal [emptiness] *vacancy.*

"These, like [many other harlots,] *the harlots of other men*, had his love though not his approbation.

"He [sometimes displays] *descends to display* his knowledge with pedantic ostentation.

"French words which [were then used in] *had then crept into* conversation."

The Life of Pope was written by Johnson *con amore*, both from the early possession which that writer had taken of his mind, and from the pleasure which he must have felt, in for ever silencing all attempts to lessen his poetical fame, by demonstrating his excellence, and pronouncing the following triumphant eulogium:—"After all this, it is surely superfluous to answer the question that has once been asked, Whether Pope was a poet? otherwise than by asking in return, if Pope be not a poet, where is poetry to be found? To circumscribe poetry by a definition, will only show the narrowness of the definer; though a definition which shall exclude Pope will not easily be made. Let us look round upon the present time, and back upon the past; let us inquire to whom the voice of mankind has decreed the wreath of poetry; let their productions be examined, and their claims stated, and the pretensions of Pope will be no more disputed."

I remember once to have heard Johnson say, "Sir, a thousand years may elapse before there shall appear another man with a power of versification equal to that of Pope." That power must undoubtedly be allowed its due share in enhancing the value of his captivating composition.

Johnson, who had done liberal justice to Warburton in his edition of Shakespeare, which was published during the life of that powerful writer, with still greater liberality took an opportunity, in the Life of Pope, of paying the tribute due to him when he was no longer in "high place," but numbered with the dead.[1]

---

[1] Of Johnson's conduct towards Warburton, a very honourable notice is taken by the editor of "Tracts by Warburton, and a Warburtonian, not admitted into the Collection of their respective Works." After an able and "fond, though not undistinguishing," consideration of Warburton's character, he says, "In two immortal works, Johnson has stood

It seems strange, that two such men as Johnson and Warburton, who lived in the same age and country, should not only not have been in any degree of intimacy, but been almost personally unacquainted. But such instances, though we must wonder at them, are not rare. If I am rightly informed, after a careful inquiry, they never met but once, which was at the house of Mrs. French, in London, well known for her elegant assemblies, and bringing eminent characters together. The interview proved to be mutually agreeable.

I am well informed, that Warburton said of Johnson,

forth in the foremost rank of his admirers. By the testimony of such a man, impertinence must be abashed, and malignity itself must be softened. Of literary merit, Johnson, as we all know, was a sagacious, but a most severe judge. Such was his discernment, that he pierced into the most secret springs of human actions; and such was his integrity, that he always weighed the moral characters of his fellow-creatures in 'the balance of the sanctuary.' He was too courageous to propitiate a rival, and too proud to truckle to a superior. Warburton he knew, as I know him, and as every man of sense and virtue would wish to be known,—I mean, both from his own writings, and from the writings of those who dissented from his principles, or who envied his reputation. But, as to favours, he had never received or asked any from the Bishop of Gloucester: and if my memory fails me not, he had seen him only once, when they met almost without design, conversed without much effort, and parted without any lasting impression of hatred or affection. Yet, with all the ardour of sympathetic genius, Johnson had done that spontaneously and ably, which, by some writers, had been before attempted injudiciously, and which, by others, from whom more successful attempts might have been expected, has not *hitherto* been done at all. He spoke well of Warburton, without insulting those whom Warburton despised. He suppressed not the imperfections of this extraordinary man, while he endeavoured to do justice to his numerous and transcendental excellencies. He defended him when living, amidst the clamours of his enemies; and praised him when dead, amidst the *silence of his friends.*"

Having availed myself of this editor's eulogy on my departed friend, for which I warmly thank him, let me not suffer the lustre of his reputation, honestly acquired by profound learning and vigorous eloquence, to be tarnished by a charge of illiberality. He has been accused of invidiously dragging again into light certain writings of a person respectable by his talents, his learning, his station, and his age, which were published a great many years ago, and have since, it is said, been silently given up by their author. But when it is considered that these writings were not *sins of youth,* but deliberate works of one well-advanced in life, overflowing at once with flattery to a great man of great interest in the Church, and with unjust and acrimonious abuse of two men of eminent merit; and that, though it would have been unreasonable to expect an humiliating recantation, no apology whatever has been made in the cool of the evening, for the oppressive fervour of the heat of the day; no slight relenting indication has appeared in any note, or any corner of later publications; is it not fair to understand him as superciliously persevering? When he allows the shafts to remain in the wounds, and will not stretch forth a lenient hand, is it wrong, is it not generous to become an indignant avenger?—BOSWELL.

I admire him, but I cannot bear his style;" and that Johnson being told of this, said, "That is exactly my case as to him." The manner in which he expressed his admiration of the fertility of Warburton's genius and of the variety of his materials, was, "The table is always full, Sir. He brings things from the north, and the south, and from every quarter. In his 'Divine Legation,' you are always entertained. He carries you round and round, without carrying you forward to the point; but then you have no wish to be carried forward." He said to the Rev. Mr. Strahan, "Warburton is perhaps the last man who has written with a mind full of reading and reflection."

It is remarkable, that in the Life of Broome, Johnson takes notice of Dr. Warburton using a mode of expression which he himself used, and that not seldom, to the great offence of those who did not know him. Having occasion to mention a note, stating the different parts which were executed by the associated translators of "The Odyssey," he says, "Dr. Warburton told me, in his warm language, that he thought the relation given in the note *a lie*. The language is *warm* indeed; and, I must own, cannot be justified in consistency with a decent regard to the established forms of speech." Johnson had accustomed himself to use the word *lie*, to express a mistake or an error in relation; in short, when the *thing was not so as told*, though the relator did not *mean* to deceive. When he thought there was intentional falsehood in the relator, his expression was, "He *lies*, and he *knows* he *lies*."

Speaking of Pope's not having been known to excel in conversation, Johnson observes, that "traditional memory retains no sallies of raillery, or sentences of observation; nothing either pointed or solid, wise or merry; and that one apophthegm only is recorded." In this respect, Pope differed widely from Johnson, whose conversation was, perhaps, more admirable than even his writings, however excellent. Mr. Wilkes has, however, favoured me with one repartee of Pope, of which Johnson was not informed. Johnson, after justly censuring him for having "nursed in his mind a foolish disesteem of kings," tells us, "yet a little regard shown him by the Prince of Wales melted his obduracy; and he had not much to say when he was asked by his Royal Highness, *how he could love a Prince, while he disliked Kings?*" The answer which Pope made was, "The young lion is harmless, and even playful; but when his claws are full grown he becomes cruel, dreadful, and mischievous."

But although we have no collection of Pope's sayings, it is not therefore to be concluded, that he was not agreeable in social intercourse; for Johnson has been heard to say, that "the happiest conversation is that of which nothing is distinctly remembered, but a general effect of pleasing impression." The late Lord Somerville,[1] who saw much of great and brilliant life, told me, that he had dined in company with Pope, and that after dinner the *little man*, as he called him, drank his bottle of Burgundy, and was exceedingly gay and entertaining.

I cannot withhold from my great friend a censure of at least culpable inattention to a nobleman, who, it has been shown, behaved to him with uncommon politeness. He says, "Except Lord Bathurst, none of Pope's noble friends were such as that a good man would wish to have his intimacy with them known to posterity." This will not apply to Lord Mansfield, who was not ennobled in Pope's lifetime; but Johnson should have recollected, that Lord Marchmont was one of those noble friends. He includes his lordship along with Lord Bolingbroke, in a charge of neglect of the papers which Pope left by his will; when, in truth, as I myself pointed out to him, before he wrote that Poet's life, the papers were "committed to *the sole care and judgment* of Lord Bolingbroke, unless he (Lord Bolingbroke) shall not survive me;" so that Lord Marchmont had no concern whatever with them. After the first edition of the Lives, Mr. Malone, whose love of justice is equal to his accuracy, made, in my hearing, the same remark to Johnson; yet he omitted to correct the erroneous statement.[2] These particulars I mention, in the belief that there was only forgetfulness in my friend; but I owe this much to the Earl of Marchmont's reputation, who, were

[1] James Lord Somerville, who died in 1766.—MALONE.
Let me here express my grateful remembrance of Lord Somerville's kindness to me, at a very early period. He was the first person of high rank that took particular notice of me in the way most flattering to a young man fondly ambitious of being distinguished for his literary talents; and by the honour of his encouragement made me think well of myself, and aspire to deserve it better. He had a happy art of communicating his varied knowledge of the world, in short remarks and anecdotes, with a quiet pleasant gravity that was exceedingly engaging. Never shall I forget the hours which I enjoyed with him at his apartments in the royal palace of Holyrood-house, and at his seat near Edinburgh, which he himself had formed with an elegant taste.—BOSWELL.

[2] This neglect, however, assuredly did not arise from any ill-will towards Lord Marchmont, but from inattention; just as he neglected to correct the statement concerning the family of Thomson, the poet, after it had been shown to be erroneous.—MALONE.

there no other memorials, will be immortalized by that line of Pope, in the verses on his Grotto:

"And the bright flame was shot through Marchmont's soul."

Various Readings in the Life of POPE.

"[Somewhat free] *sufficiently bold* in his criticism.
"All the gay [niceties] *varieties* of diction.
"Strikes the imagination with far [more] *greater* force.
"It is [probably] *certainly* the noblest version of poetry which the world has ever seen.
"Every sheet enabled him to write the next with [less trouble] *more facility.*
"No man sympathises with [vanity depressed] *the sorrows of vanity.*
"It had been [criminal] *less easily excused.*
"When he [threatened to lay down] *talked of laying down* his pen.
"Society [is so named emphatically in opposition to] *politically regulated, is a state contra-distinguished from* a state of nature.
"A fictitious life of an [absurd] *infatuated* scholar.
"A foolish [contempt, disregard] *disesteem* of kings.
"His hopes and fears, his joys and sorrows [were like those of other mortals] *acted strongly upon his mind.*
"Eager to pursue knowledge, and attentive to [accumulate] *retain it.*
"A mind [excursive] *active,* ambitious, and adventurous.
"In its [noblest] *widest* searches still longing to go forward.
"He wrote in such a manner as might expose him to few [neglects] *hazards.*
"The [reasonableness] *justice* of my determination.
"A [favourite] *delicious* employment of the poets.
"More terrific and more powerful [beings] *phantoms* perform on the stormy ocean.
"The inventor of [those] *this* petty [beings] *nation.*
"The [mind] *heart* naturally loves truth."

In the Life of Addison we find an unpleasing account of his having lent Steele a hundred pounds, and "reclaimed his loan by an execution." In the new edition of the *Biographia Britannica,* the authenticity of this anecdote is denied. But Mr. Malone has obliged me with the following note concerning it:—

"March 15, 1782.

"Many persons having doubts concerning this fact, I applied to Dr. Johnson to learn on what authority he asserted it. He told me he had it from Savage, who lived in intimacy with Steele, and who mentioned that Steele told him the story with tears in his eyes. Ben Victor, Dr. Johnson said, likewise informed him of this remarkable transaction, from the relation of Mr. Wilkes, the comedian, who was also an intimate of Steele's.[1] Some, in defence of Addison, have said that 'the act was done with the good-natured view of rousing Steele, and correcting that profusion which always made him necessitous.' 'If that were the case,' said Johnson, 'and that he only wanted to alarm Steele, he would afterwards have *returned* the money to his friend, which it is not pretended he did. This, too,' he added, 'might be retorted by an advocate for Steele, who might allege, that he did not repay the loan *intentionally*, merely to see whether Addison would be mean and ungenerous enough to make use of legal process to recover it. But of such speculations there is no end: we cannot dive into the hearts of men; but their actions are open to observation.'

"I then mentioned to him that some people thought that Mr. Addison's character was so pure, that the fact, *though true*, ought to have been suppressed. He saw no reason for this. 'If nothing but the bright side of characters should be shown, we should sit down in despondency, and think it utterly impossible to imitate them in *anything*. The sacred writers,' he observed, 'related the vicious as well as the virtuous actions of men; which had this moral effect, that it kept mankind from *despair*, into which otherwise they would naturally fall, were they not supported by the recollection that others had offended like themselves, and by penitence and amendment of life had been restored to the favour of Heaven.'

"E. M."

The last paragraph of this note is of great importance; and I request that my readers may consider it with particular attention. It will be afterwards referred to in this work.

Various Readings in the Life of ADDISON.

"[But he was our first example] *He was, however, one of our earliest examples* of correctness.

"And [overlook] *despise* their masters.

"His instructions were such as the [state] *character* of his [own time] *readers* made [necessary] *proper*.

"His purpose was to [diffuse] *infuse* literary curiosity by gentle and unsuspected conveyance [among] *into* the gay, the idle, and the wealthy.

"Framed rather for those that [wish] *are learning* to write.

"Domestic [manners] *scenes*."

In his Life of Parnell, I wonder that Johnson omitted to insert an Epitaph which he had long before composed for that amiable man without ever writing it down, but

---

[1] The late Mr. Burke informed me, in 1792, that Lady Dorothea Primrose (who died at a great age, I think in 1768, and had been well acquainted with Steele) told him the same story.—MALONE.

which he was so good as, at my request, to dictate to me, by which means it has been preserved.

> " *Hic requiescit* THOMAS PARNELL, *S. T. P.*
>
> "Qui sacerdos pariter et poeta,
> Utrasque partes ita implevit,
> Ut neque sacredoti suavitas poetæ,
> Nec poetæ sacerdotis sanctitas, deesset."

Various Readings in the Life of PARNELL.

"About three years [after] *afterwards*.

"[Did not much want] *was in no great need of* improvement.

"But his prosperity *did not last long* [was clouded with that which took away all his powers of enjoying either profit or pleasure, the death of his wife, whom he is said to have lamented with such sorrow, as hastened his end.][1] His end, whatever was the cause, was now approaching.

"In the Hermit, the [composition] *narrative*, as it is less airy, is less pleasing."

In the Life of Blackmore, we find that writer's reputation generously cleared by Johnson from the cloud of prejudice which the malignity of contemporary wits had raised around it. In this spirited exertion of justice he has been imitated by Sir Joshua Reynolds, in his praise of the architecture of Vanbrugh.

We trace Johnson's own character in his observations on Blackmore's "magnanimity as an author." "The incessant attacks of his enemies, whether serious or merry, are never discovered to have disturbed his quiet, or to have lessened his confidence in himself." Johnson, I recollect, once told me, laughing heartily, that he understood it had been said of him, "He *appears* not to feel; but when he is *alone*, depend upon it, he *suffers sadly*." I am as certain as I can be of any man's real sentiments, that he *enjoyed* the perpetual shower of little hostile arrows as evidences of his fame.

Various Readings in the Life of BLACKMORE.

"To [set] *engage* poetry [on the side] *in the cause* of virtue.
"He likewise [established] *enforced* the truth of Revelation.

---

[1] I should have thought that Johnson, who had felt the severe affliction from which Parnell never recovered, would have preserved this passage.—BOSWELL.

He omitted it, doubtless, because he afterwards learnt that, however he might have lamented his wife, his end was hastened by other means.—MALONE.

"[Kindness] *benevolence* was ashamed to favour.

"His practice, which was once [very extensive] *invidiously great.*

"There is scarcely any distemper of dreadful name [of] which he has not [shown] *taught his reader* how [it is to be opposed] *to oppose.*

"Of this [contemptuous] *indecent* arrogance.

"[He wrote] *but produced* likewise a work of a different kind.

"At least [written] *compiled* with integrity.

"Faults which many tongues [were desirous] *would have made haste* to publish.

"But though he [had not] *could not boast of* much critical knowledge.

"He [used] *waited for* no felicities of fancy.

"He had ever elated his [mind] *views* born to that ideal perfection which every [mind] *genius* born to excel is condemned always to pursue and never overtake.

"The [first great] *fundamental* principle of wisdom and of virtue."

Various Readings in the Life of PHILIPS.

"His dreadful [rival] *antagonist* Pope.

"They [have not often much] *are not loaded with* thought.

"In his translation from Pindar, he [will not be denied to have reached] *found the art of reaching* all the obscurity of the Theban bard."

Various Readings in the Life of CONGREVE.

"Congreve's conversation must surely have been *at least* equally pleasing with his writings.

"It apparently [requires] *pre-supposes* a familiar knowledge of many characters.

"Reciprocation of [similes] *conceits.*

"The dialogue is quick and [various] *sparkling.*

"Love for love; a comedy [more drawn from life] *of nearer alliance to life.*

"The general character of his miscellanies is, that they show little wit and [no] *little* virtue.

"[Perhaps] *certainly* he had not the fire requisite for the higher species of lyric poetry."

Various Readings in the Life of TICKELL.

"[Longed] *long wished* to peruse it.

"At the [accession] *arrival* of King George.

"Fiction [unnaturally] *unskilfully* compounded of Grecian deities and Gothic fairies."

Various Readings in the Life of AKENSIDE.

"For [another] *a different* purpose.

"[A furious] *an unnecessary* and outrageous zeal.

"[Something which] *what* he called and thought liberty.

"[A favourer of innovation] *lover of contradiction*.
"Warburton's [censure] *objections*.
"His rage [for liberty] *of patriotism*.
"Mr. Dyson with [a zeal] *an ardour* of friendship."

In the Life of Lyttelton, Johnson seems to have been not favourably disposed towards that nobleman. Mrs. Thrale suggests that he was offended by *Molly Aston's* preference of his lordship to him.[1] I can by no means join

---

[1] Let not my readers smile to think of Johnson's being a candidate for female favour. Mr. Peter Garrick assured me, that he was told by a lady, that in her opinion Johnson was "a very *seducing man*." Disadvantages of person and manner may be forgotten, where intellectual pleasure is communicated to a susceptible mind; and that Johnson was capable of feeling the most delicate and disinterested attachment, appears from the following letter which is published by Mrs. Thrale, with some others to the same person, of which the excellence is not so apparent:—

"TO MISS BOOTHBY.

"DEAREST MADAM,   January, 1775.
"Though I am afraid your illness leaves you little leisure for the reception of airy civilities, yet I cannot forbear to pay you my congratulations on the new year; and to declare my wishes that your years to come may be many and happy. In this wish, indeed, I include myself, who have none but you on whom my heart reposes; yet surely I wish your good, even though your situation were such as should permit you to communicate no gratifications to, dearest, dearest Madam, your, &c.
"SAM. JOHNSON."
There is still a slight mistake in the text. It was not Molly Aston, but Hill Boothby for whose affections Johnson and Lord Lyttelton were rival candidates. See Mrs. Piozzi's "Anecdotes," p. 160. After mentioning the death of Mrs. Fitzherbert (who was a daughter of Mr. Meynel, of Bradley, in Derbyshire), and Johnson's high admiration of her, she adds, "The friend of this lady, Miss Boothby, succeeded her in the management of Mr. Fitzherbert's family, and in the esteem of Dr. Johnson; though he told me, she pushed her piety to bigotry, her devotion to enthusiasm: that she somewhat disqualified herself for the duties of *this* life, by her perpetual aspirations after the *next:* such was, however, the purity of her mind, he said, and such the graces of her manner, that Lord Lyttelton and he used to strive for her preference with an emulation that occasioned hourly disgust, and ended in lasting animosity. 'You may see,' said he to me, when the Poets' Lives were printed, 'that dear Boothby is at my heart still.'"
Miss Hill Boothby, who was the only daughter of Brook Boothby, Esq., and his wife, Elizabeth Fitzherbert, was somewhat older than Johnson. She was born October 27, 1708, and died January 16, 1756. Six letters addressed to her by Johnson in the year 1755, are printed in Mrs. Piozzi's Collection; and a Prayer composed by him on her death may be found in his "Prayers and Meditations." His affection for her induced him to preserve and bind up in a volume thirty-three of her letters, which were purchased from the widow of his servant, Francis Barber, and published by R. Phillips, in 1805.
But highly as he valued this lady, his attachment to Miss *Molly* Aston (afterwards Mrs. Brodie), appears to have been still more ardent. He burned (says Mrs. Piozzi) many letters in the last week [of his life], I am told, and those written by his mother drew from him a flood of tears, when the paper they were written on was all consumed. Mr. Sastres

in the censure bestowed by Johnson on his lordship, whom he calls "poor Lyttelton," for returning thanks to the Critical Reviewers, for having "kindly commended" his "Dialogues of the Dead." Such "acknowledgments," says my friend, "never can be proper, since they must be paid either for flattery or for justice." In my opinion the most upright man, who has been tried on a false accusation, may, when he is acquitted, make a bow to his jury. And when those who are so much the arbiters of literary merit, as in a considerable degree to influence the public opinion, review an author's work *placido lumine*, when I am afraid mankind in general are better pleased with severity, he may surely express a grateful sense of their civility.

Various Readings in the Life of LYTTELTON.

"He solaced [himself] *his grief* by writing a long poem to her memory.

"The production rather [of a mind that means well than thinks vigorously] *as it seems of leisure than of study, rather effusions than compositions.*

"His last literary [work] *production.*

"[Found the way] *undertook* to persuade."

As the introduction to his critical examination of the genius and writings of Young, he did Mr. Herbert Croft, then a barrister of Lincoln's-inn, now a clergyman, the honour to adopt a Life of Young written by that gentleman, who was the friend of Dr. Young's son, and wished to vindicate him from some very erroneous remarks to his prejudice. Mr. Croft's performance was subjected to the revision of Dr. Johnson, as appears from the following note to Mr. John Nichols:[1]

"This Life of Dr. Young was written by a friend of his son. What is crossed with black is expunged by the author; what is crossed with red is expunged by me. If you find anything more that can be well omitted, I shall not be sorry to see it yet shorter."

saw him cast a melancholy look upon their ashes which he took up and examined, to see if a word was still legible. Nobody has ever mentioned what became of Miss Aston's letters, though he once told me himself, they should be the last papers he would destroy, and added these lines with a very faltering voice:

"Then from his closing eyes thy form shall part,
And the last pang shall tear thee from his heart;
Life's idle business at one gasp be o'er,
The Muse forgot, and thou beloved no more."

Additions to Mrs. Piozzi's Collection of Dr. Johnson's Letters.—MALONE.

[1] "Gentleman's Magazine," vol. iv. p. 10.—BOSWELL.

It has always appeared to me to have a considerable share of merit, and to display a pretty successful imitation of Johnson's style. When I mentioned this to a very eminent literary character,[1] he opposed me vehemently, exclaiming, "No, no, it is *not* a good imitation of Johnson; it has all his pomp without his force; it has all the nodosities of the oak without its strength." This was an image so happy, that one might have thought he would have been satisfied with it; but he was not. And setting his mind again to work, he added, with exquisite felicity, "It has all the contortions of the sibyl, without the inspiration."

Mr. Croft very properly guards us against supposing that Young was a gloomy man; and mentions, that "his parish was indebted to the good-humour of the author of 'The Night Thoughts' for an assembly and a bowling-green." A letter from a noble foreigner is quoted, in which he is said to have been "very pleasant in conversation."

Mr. Langton, who frequently visited him, informs me, that there was an air of benevolence in his manner, but that he could obtain from him less information than he had hoped to receive from one who had lived so much in intercourse with the brightest men of what has been called the Augustan age of England; and that he showed a degree of eager curiosity concerning the common occurrences that were then passing, which appeared somewhat remarkable in a man of such intellectual stores, of such an advanced age, and who had retired from life with declared disappointment in his expectations.

An instance at once of his pensive turn of mind, and his cheerfulness of temper, appeared in a little story which he himself told to Mr. Langton, when they were walking in his garden: "Here," said he, "I had put a handsome sundial, with this inscription, *Eheu fugaces!* which (speaking with a smile) was sadly verified, for by the next morning my dial had been carried off!"

It gives me much pleasure to observe, that however Johnson may have casually talked, yet when he sits, as "an ardent judge zealous to his trust, giving sentence" upon the excellent works of Young, he allows them the

---

[1] The late Mr. Burke.—MALONE.

[2] The late Mr. James Ralph told Lord Macartney, that he passed an evening with Dr. Young, at Lord Melcombe's (then Mr. Doddington's), at Hammersmith. The Doctor happening to go out into the garden, Mr. Doddington observed to him, on his return, that it was a dreadful night, as in truth it was, there being a violent storm of rain and wind. "No, Sir," replied the Doctor, "it is a very fine night. THE LORD is abroad." —BOSWELL.

high praise to which they are justly entitled. "The 'Universal Passion' (says he) is indeed a very great performance,—his distichs have the weight of solid sentiment, and his points the sharpness of resistless truth."

But I was most anxious concerning Johnson's decision upon "Night Thoughts," which I esteem as a mass of the grandest and richest poetry that human genius has ever produced; and was delighted to find this character of that work: "In his 'Night Thoughts,' he has exhibited a very wide display of original poetry, variegated with deep reflection and striking allusions: a wilderness of thought, in which the fertility of fancy scatters flowers of every hue and of every odour. This is one of the few poems in which blank verse could not be changed for rhyme but with disadvantage." And afterwards, "Particular lines are not to be regarded; the power is in the whole; and in the whole there is a magnificence like that ascribed to Chinese plantation, the magnificence of vast extent and endless diversity."

But there is in this poem not only all that Johnson so well brings in view, but a power of the *pathetic* beyond almost any example that I have seen. He who does not feel his nerves shaken and his heart pierced by many passages in this extraordinary work, particularly by that most affecting one which describes the gradual torment suffered by the contemplation of an objection of affectionate attachment visibly and certainly decaying into dissolution, must be of a hard and obstinate frame.

To all the other excellencies of "Night Thoughts" let me add the great and peculiar one, that they contain not only the noblest sentiments of virtue, and contemplations on immortality, but the *Christian Sacrifice*, the *Divine Propitiation*, with all its interesting circumstances, and consolations to "a wounded spirit," solemnly and poetically displayed in such imagery and language, as cannot fail to exalt, animate, and soothe the truly pious. No book whatever can be recommended to young persons, with better hopes of seasoning their minds with *vital religion*, than "Young's Night Thoughts."

In the Life of Swift, it appears to me that Johnson had a certain degree of prejudice against that extraordinary man, of which I have elsewhere had occasion to speak. Mr. Thomas Sheridan imputed it to a supposed apprehension in Johnson, that Swift had not been sufficiently active in obtaining for him an Irish degree when it was solicited;[1]

[1] See vol. i. p. 104.—BOSWELL.

but of this there was not sufficient evidence; and let me not
presume to charge Johnson with injustice, because he did
not think so highly of the writings of this author, as I have
done from my youth upwards. Yet that he had an unfavourable bias is evident, were it only from that passage in
which he speaks of Swift's practice of saving, as, "first
ridiculous and at last detestable:" and yet after some
examination of circumstances, finds himself obliged to own,
that "it will perhaps appear that he only liked one mode of
expense better than another, and saved merely that he
might have something to give."

One observation which Johnson makes in Swift's Life
should be often inculcated: "It may be justly supposed,
that there was in his conversation, what appears so frequently in his letters, an affectation of familiarity with the
great, an ambition of momentary equality, sought and
enjoyed by the neglect of those ceremonies which custom
has established as the barriers between one order of society
and another. This transgression of regularity was by himself and his admirers termed greatness of soul; but a great
mind disdains to hold anything by courtesy, and therefore
never usurps what a lawful claimant may take away. He
that encroaches on another's dignity, puts himself in his
power; he is either repelled with helpless indignity, or
endured by clemency and condescension."

Various Readings in the Life of SWIFT.

"Charity may be persuaded to think that it might be written
by a man of a peculiar [opinions] *character*, without ill intention.

"He did not [disown] *deny* it.

"[To] *by* whose kindness it is not unlikely that he was [indebted
for] *advanced to* his benefices.

"[With] *for* this purpose he had recourse to Mr. Harley.

"Sharpe, whom he [represents] *describes* as 'the harmless tool
of others' hate.'

"Harley was slow because he was [irresolute] *doubtful*.

"When [readers were not many] *we were not yet a nation of
readers*.

"[Every man who] *he that could say he* knew him.

"Every man of known influence has so many [more] petitions
[than] *which* he [can] *cannot* grant, that he must necessarily offend
more than he [can gratify] *gratifies*.

"Ecclesiastical [preferments] *benefices*.

"Swift [procured] *contrived* an interview.

"[As a writer] *In his works* he has given very different specimens.

"On all common occasions he habitually [assumes] *affects* a style
of [superiority] *arrogance*.

"By the [omission] *neglect* of those ceremonies.

"That their merits filled the world [and] *or that* there was no [room for] *hope of* more."

I have not confined myself to the order of the "Lives,' in making my few remarks. Indeed a different order is observed in the original publication, and in the collection of Johnson's Works. And should it be objected, that many of my various readings are inconsiderable, those who make an objection will be pleased to consider, that such small particulars are intended for those who are nicely critical in composition, to whom they will be an acceptable selection.

"Spence's Anecdotes," which are frequently quoted and referred to in Johnson's "Lives of the Poets," are in a manuscript collection, made by the Rev. Mr. Joseph Spence, containing a number of particulars concerning eminent men. To each anecdote is marked the name of the person on whose authority it is mentioned. This valuable collection is the property of the Duke of Newcastle, who, upon the application of Sir Lucas Pepys, was pleased to permit it to be put into the hands of Dr. Johnson, who I am sorry to think made but an awkward return. "Great assistance," says he, "has been given me by Mr. Spence's Collection, of which I consider the communication as a favour worthy of public acknowledgment:" but he has not owned to whom he was obliged; so that the acknowledgment is unappropriated to his Grace.

While the world in general was filled with admiration of Johnson's "Lives of the Poets," there were narrow circles in which prejudice and resentment were fostered, and from which attacks of different sorts issued against him.[2] By some violent Whigs he was arraigned of injustice to Milton; by some Cambridge men of depreciating Gray; and his expressing with a dignified freedom what he really thought of George Lord Lyttelton, gave offence to some of the friends of that nobleman, and particularly produced a declaration of war against him from Mrs. Montagu, the ingenious essayist on Shakespeare, between whom and his

[1] The Reverend Joseph Spence, A.M., rector of Great Harwood, in Buckinghamshire, and Prebendary of Durham, died at Byfleet, in Surrey, August 20, 1768. He was a Fellow of New College, in Oxford, and held the office of Professor of Poetry in that University from 1728 to 1738.—MALONE.

[2] From this disreputable class, I except an ingenious though not satisfactory defence of Hammond, which I did not see till lately, by the favour of its author, my amiable friend, the Rev. Mr. Bevill, who published it without his name. It is a juvenile performance, but elegantly written, with classical enthusiasm of sentiment, and yet with a becoming modesty and great respect for Dr. Johnson.—BOSWELL.

lordship a commerce of reciprocal compliments had long been carried on. In this war the smallest powers in alliance with him were of course led to engage, at least on the defensive, and thus I for one was excluded from the enjoyment of "A Feast for Reason," such as Mr. Cumberland has described, with a keen, yet just and delicate pen, in his "Observer." These minute inconveniences gave not the least disturbance to Johnson. He nobly said, when I talked to him of the feeble though shrill outcry which had been raised, "Sir, I considered myself as entrusted with a certain portion of truth. I have given my opinion sincerely; let them show where they think me wrong."

CHAPTER XIX.—1781

*Johnson's Correspondence with Warren Hastings—Mr.
Chambers—Mr. Hoole—Liberty and Necessity—Doctors
Marlay, Heath, and Moss—Picture of a Man, by Shake-
speare and Milton—Registration of Deeds—Duty of
an M.P.—Deportment of Bishops—"Merriment of
Parsons"—Rev. Zachariah Mudge—Dr. Harte—
Mahogany Liquor—On Dancing—Sir P. J. Clerk and
Mr. Perkins—American War—Dudley Long—Talking
—Death of Mr. Thrale—Queen's Arms Club—Mr.
Hoole—Mrs. Lucy Porter—Mr. Berenger—Robin Hood
Society—Apparitions—Dinner at Mrs. Garrick's—Mr.
T. Hollis—Printer's Devil—Whigs and Tories—Death
of Mr. W. Strahan*

WHILE my friend is thus contemplated in the splendour
derived from his last and perhaps most admirable work, I
introduce him with peculiar propriety as the correspondent
of Warren Hastings! a man whose regard reflects dignity
even upon Johnson; a man, the extent of whose abilities
was equal to that of his power; and who, by those who are
fortunate enough to know him in private life, is admired
for his literature and taste, and beloved for the candour,
moderation, and mildness of his character. Were I
capable of paying a suitable tribute of admiration to him,
I should certainly not withhold it at a moment when it is
not possible that I should be suspected of being an interested
flatterer.[1] But how weak would be my voice after that of
the millions whom he governed. His condescending and
obliging compliance with my solicitation, I with humble
gratitude acknowledge; and while by publishing his letter
to me, accompanying the valuable communication, I do
eminent honour to my great friend, I shall entirely disregard any invidious suggestions, that as I in some degree
participate in the honour, I have, at the same time, the
gratification of my own vanity in view.

[1] January, 1791.—BOSWELL.

"TO JAMES BOSWELL, ESQ.

"SIR,   Park-lane, Dec. 2, 1790.

"I have been fortunately spared the troublesome suspense of a long search, to which, in performance of my promise, I had devoted this morning, by lighting upon the objects of it among the first papers that I laid my hands on. My veneration for your great and good friend, Dr. Johnson, and the pride, or I hope something of a better sentiment, which I indulge in possessing such memorials of his good will towards me, having induced me to bind them in a parcel containing other select papers, and labelled with the titles appertaining to them. They consist but of three letters which I believe were all that I ever received from Dr. Johnson. Of these, one, which was written in quadruplicate, under the different dates of its respective dispatches, has already been made public, but not from any communication of mine. This, however, I have joined to the rest, and have now the pleasure of sending them to you for the use to which you informed me it was your desire to destine them.

"My promise was pledged with the condition, that if the letters were found to contain anything which should render them improper for the public eye, you would dispense with the performance of it. You will have the goodness, I am sure, to pardon my recalling this stipulation to your recollection, as I shall be loath to appear negligent of that obligation which is always implied in an epistolary confidence. In the reservation of that right I have read them over with the most scrupulous attention, but I have not seen in them the slightest cause on that ground to withhold them from you. But, though not on that, yet on another ground, I own I feel a little, yet but a little, reluctance to part with them—I mean on that of my own credit, which I fear will suffer by the information conveyed by them, that I was early in the possession of such valuable instructions for the beneficial employment of the influence of my late station, and (as it may seem) have so little availed myself of them. Whether I could, if it were necessary, defend myself against such an imputation, it little concerns the world to know. I look only to the effect which these relics may produce, considered as evidences of the virtues of their author; and believing that they will be found to display an uncommon warmth of private friendship, and a mind ever attentive to the improvement and extension of useful knowledge, and solicitous for the interests of mankind, I can cheerfully submit to the little sacrifice of my own fame, and contribute to the illustration of so great and venerable a character. They cannot be better applied for that end than by being entrusted to your hands. Allow me, with this offering, to infer from it a proof of the very great esteem with which I have the honour to profess myself, Sir,

"Your most obedient and most humble servant,

"WARREN HASTINGS."

"P.S. At some future time, and when you have no further occasion for these papers, I shall be obliged to you if you will return them.

The last of the three letters thus graciously put into my hands, and which has already appeared in public, belongs to this year; but I shall previously insert the first two in the order of their dates. They altogether form a grand group in my biographical picture.

"TO THE HONOURABLE WARREN HASTINGS, ESQ.

"Sir,   March 30, 1774.

"Though I have had but little personal knowledge of you, I have had enough to make me wish for more; and though it be now a long time since I was honoured by your visit, I had too much pleasure from it to forget it. By those whom we delight to remember, we are unwilling to be forgotten; and therefore I cannot omit this opportunity of reviving myself in your memory by a letter which you will receive from the hands of my friend Mr. Chambers,[1] a man whose purity of manners and vigour of mind are sufficient to make every thing welcome that he brings.

"That this is my only reason for writing will be too apparent by the uselessness of my letter to any other purpose. I have no questions to ask; not that I want curiosity after either the ancient or present state of regions, in which have been seen all the power and splendour of wide-extended empire; and which, as by some grant of natural superiority, supply the rest of the world with almost all that pride desires, and luxury enjoys. But my knowledge of them is too scanty to furnish me with proper topics of inquiry; I can only wish for information: and hope that a mind comprehensive like yours will find leisure amidst the cares of your important station, to inquire into many subjects of which the European world either thinks not at all, or thinks with deficient intelligence and uncertain conjecture. I shall hope, that he who once intended to increase the learning of his country by the introduction of the Persian language, will examine nicely the traditions and histories of the East; that he will survey the wonders of its ancient edifices, and trace the vestiges of its ruined cities; and that, at his return, we shall know the arts and opinions of a race of men from whom very little has been hitherto derived.

"You, Sir, have no need of being told by me how much may be added by your attention and patronage to experimental knowledge and natural history. There are arts of manufacture practised in the countries in which you preside, which are yet very imperfectly known here, either to artificers or philosophers. Of the natural productions, animate and inanimate, we yet have so little intelligence that our books are filled, I fear, with conjectures about things which an Indian peasant knows by his senses.

"Many of those things my first wish is to see, my second to know, by such accounts as a man like you will be able to give.

"As I have not skill to ask proper questions, I have likewise no such access to great men as can enable me to send you any political

---

[1] Afterwards Sir Robert Chambers, one of his Majesty's Judges in India.—BOSWELL.

information. Of the agitations of an unsettled government, and the struggles of a feeble ministry, care is doubtless taken to give you more exact accounts than I can obtain. If inclined to interest yourself much in public transactions, it is no misfortune to you to be distant from them.

"That literature is not totally forsaking us, and that your favourite language is not neglected, will appear from the book,[1] which I should have pleased myself more with sending, if I could have presented it bound; but time was wanting. I beg, however, Sir, that you will accept it from a man very desirous of your regard; and that if you think me able to gratify you by anything more important you will employ me.

"I am now going to take leave, perhaps a very long leave, of my dear Mr. Chambers. That he is going to live where you govern, may justly alleviate the regret of parting; and the hope of seeing both him and you again, which I am not willing to mingle with doubt, must at present comfort as it can, Sir,

" Your most humble servant,
"Sam Johnson."

TO THE SAME.

"Sir,   London, Dec. 20, 1774.

"Being informed that, by the departure of a ship, there is now an opportunity of writing to Bengal, I am unwilling to slip out of your memory by my own negligence, and therefore take the liberty of reminding you of my existence, by sending you a book which is not yet made public.

"I have lately visited a region less remote and less illustrious than India, which afforded some occasions for speculation; what has occurred to me I have put into the volume,[2] of which I beg your acceptance.

"Men in your station seldom have presents totally disinterested; my book is received—let me now make my request.

"There is, Sir, somewhere within your government a young adventurer, one Chauncey Lawrence, whose father is one of my oldest friends. Be pleased to show the young man what countenance is fit, whether he wants to be restrained by your authority, or encouraged by your favour. His father is now President of the College of Physicians, a man venerable for his knowledge, and more venerable for his virtue.

"I wish you a prosperous government, a safe return, and a long enjoyment of plenty and tranquillity.

"I am, Sir, your most obedient and most humble servant,
"Sam. Johnson."

TO THE SAME.

"Sir,   Jan. 9, 1781.

"Amidst the importance and multiplicity of affairs in which your great office engages you, I take the liberty of recalling your

---

[1] Jones's "Persian Grammar."—Boswell.
[2] "Journey to the Western Islands of Scotland."—Boswell.

attention for a moment to literature, and will not prolong the interruption by an apology which your character makes needless.

"Mr. Hoole, a gentleman long known and long esteemed in the India House, after having translated 'Tasso,' has undertaken 'Ariosto.' How well he is qualified for his undertaking he has already shown. He is desirous, Sir, of your favour in promoting his proposals, and flatters me by supposing that my testimony may advance his interest.

"It is a new thing for a clerk of the India House to translate poets; it is new for a Governor of Bengal to patronise learning. That he may find his ingenuity rewarded, and that learning may flourish under your protection, is the wish of, Sir, your most humble servant,

"SAM. JOHNSON."

I wrote to him in February, complaining of having been troubled by a recurrence of the perplexing question of Liberty and Necessity; and mentioning that I hoped soon to meet him again in London.

"TO JAMES BOSWELL, ESQ.

"DEAR SIR,   March 14, 1781.

"I hoped you had got rid of all this hypocrisy of misery. What have you to do with Liberty and Necessity? Or what more than to hold your tongue about it? Do not doubt but I shall be most heartily glad to see you here again, for I love every part about you but your affectation of distress.

"I have at last finished my Lives, and have laid up for you a load of copy, all out of order, so that it will amuse you a long time to set it right. Come to me, my dear Bozzy, and let us be as happy as we can. We will go again to the Mitre, and talk old times over. I am, dear Sir, yours affectionately,

"SAM. JOHNSON."

On Monday, March 19, I arrived in London, and on Tuesday, the 20th, met him in Fleet-street, walking, or rather indeed moving along; for his peculiar march is thus described in a very just and picturesque manner, in a short Life[1] of him published very soon after his death:—"When he walked the streets, what with the constant roll of his head, and the concomitant motion of his body, he appeared

---

[1] Published by Kearsley, with this well-chosen motto of Shakespeare's:—
"——————— From his cradle
He was a scholar, and a ripe and good one;
And to add greater honours to his age
Than man could give him, he died fearing Heaven."—BOSWELL.

to make his way by that motion, independent of his feet."
That he was often much stared at while he advanced in
this manner, may easily be believed; but it was not safe
to make sport of one so robust as he was.   Mr. Langton
saw him one day, in a fit of absence, by a sudden start,
drive the load off a porter's back, and walk forward briskly,
without being conscious of what he had done.   The porter
was very angry, but stood still, and eyed the huge figure
with much earnestness, till he was satisfied that his wisest
course was to be quiet, and take up his burden again.

Our accidental meeting in the street, after a long separation, was a pleasing surprise to us both.   He stepped aside
with me into Falcon-court, and made kind inquiries about
my family, and as we were in a hurry going different ways,
I promised to call on him next day; he said he was engaged
to go out in the morning.   "Early, Sir?" said I.   JOHNSON:
"Why, Sir, a London morning does not go with the sun."

I waited on him next evening, and he gave me great
portion of his original manuscript of his "Lives of the
Poets," which he had preserved for me.

I found on visiting his friend, Mr. Thrale, that he was
now very ill, and had removed, I suppose by the solicitation
of Mrs. Thrale, to a house in Grosvenor-square.   I was
sorry to see him sadly changed in his appearance.

He told me I might now have the pleasure to see Dr.
Johnson drink wine again, for he had lately returned to it.
When I mentioned this to Johnson, he said, "I drink it
now sometimes, but not socially."   The first evening that
I was with him at Thrale's, I observed he poured a large
quantity of it into a glass, and swallowed it greedily.
Every thing about his character and manners was forcible
and violent; there never was any moderation; many a day
did he fast, many a year did he refrain from wine; but when
he did eat, it was voraciously; when he did drink wine, it
was copiously.   He could practise abstinence, but not
temperance.

Mrs. Thrale and I had a dispute, whether Shakespeare
or Milton had drawn the most admirable picture of a man.[1]

---

[1] Shakespeare makes Hamlet thus describe his father:—

   "See what a grace was seated on this brow,
    Hyperion's curls, the front of Jove himself,
    An eye like Mars, to threaten and command:
    A station like the herald, Mercury,
    New-lighted on a heaven-kissing hill;
    A combination, and a form, indeed,
    Where every God did seem to set his seal,
    To give the world assurance of a man."

I was for Shakespeare; Mrs. Thrale for Milton; and after a fair hearing, Johnson decided for my opinion.[1]

I told him of one of Mr. Burke's playful sallies upon Dean Marlay:[2] "I don't like the Deanery of *Ferns*, it sounds so like a *barren* title."—"Dr. *Heath* should have it," said I.   Johnson laughed, and condescending to trifle in the same mode of conceit, suggested Dr. *Moss*.

He said, "Mrs. Montagu has dropped me.   Now, Sir, there are people whom one should like very well to drop, but would not wish to be dropped by."   He certainly was vain of the society of ladies, and could make himself very agreeable to them, when he chose it; Sir Joshua Reynolds agreed with me that he could.   Mr. Gibbon, with his usual sneer, controverted it, perhaps in resentment of Johnson's having talked with some disgust of his ugliness, which one would think a *philosopher* would not mind. Dean Marlay wittily observed, "A lady may be vain, when she can turn a wolf-dog into a lap-dog."

The election for Ayrshire, my own county, was this spring tried upon a petition, before a committee of the House of Commons.   I was one of the counsel for the sitting member, and took the liberty of previously stating different points to Johnson, who never failed to see them clearly, and to supply me with some good hints.   He dictated to me the following note upon the registration of deeds:—

"All laws are made for the convenience of the community; what is legally done should be legally recorded, that the state of things may be known, and that wherever evidence is requisite, evidence may be had.   For this reason, the obligation to frame and establish a legal register is enforced by a legal penalty, which penalty is the want of that perfection and plenitude of right which a register would give.   Thence it follows that this is not an objection merely legal, for the reason on which the law stands being equitable, makes it an equitable objection.

Milton thus portrays our first parent, Adam:—
    "His fair large front and eye sublime declared
     Absolute rule; and hyacinthine locks
     Round from his parted forelock manly hung
     Clust'ring, but not beneath his shoulders broad."—Boswell.

[1] It is strange that the picture drawn by the unlearned Shakespeare should be full of classical images, and that by the learned Milton void of them.   Milton's description appears to me more picturesque.—Kearney.

[2] Dr. Richard Marlay, afterwards Lord Bishop of Waterford, a very amiable, benevolent, and ingenious man.   He was chosen a member of the Literary Club in 1777, and died in Dublin, July 2, 1802, in his 75th year.—Malone.

"This," said he, "you must enlarge on, when speaking to the committee. You must not argue there, as if you were arguing in the schools; close reasoning will not fix their attention—you must say the same thing over and over again, in different words. If you say it but once, they miss it in a moment of inattention. It is unjust, Sir, to censure lawyers for multiplying words when they argue; it is often *necessary* for them to multiply words."

His notion of the duty of a Member of Parliament sitting upon an election-committee was very high; and when he was told of a gentleman upon one of those committees, who read the newspapers part of the time, and slept the rest, while the merits of a vote were examined by the counsel; and, as an excuse, when challenged by the chairman for such behaviour, bluntly answered, "I had made up my mind upon that case;"—Johnson, with an indignant contempt, said, "If he was such a rogue as to make up his mind upon a case without hearing it, he should not have been such a fool as to tell it." "I think," said Mr. Dudley Long, now North, "the Doctor has pretty plainly made him out to be both rogue and fool."

Johnson's profound reverence for the Hierarchy made him expect from bishops the highest degree of decorum; he was offended even at their going to taverns: "A bishop," said he, "has nothing to do at a tippling-house. It is not indeed immoral in him to go to a tavern; neither would it be immoral in him to whip a top in Grosvenor-square; but, if he did, I hope the boys would fall upon him, and apply the whip to *him*. There are gradations in conduct; there is morality—decency—propriety. None of these should be violated by a bishop. A bishop should not go to a house where he may meet a young fellow leading out a wench." BOSWELL: "But, Sir, every tavern does not admit women." JOHNSON: "Depend upon it, Sir, any tavern will admit a well-dressed man and a well-dressed woman; they will not perhaps admit a woman whom they see every night walking by their door, in the street. But a well-dressed man may lead in a well-dressed woman to any tavern in London. Taverns sell meat and drink, and will sell them to any body who can eat and can drink. You may as well say, that a mercer will not sell silks to a woman of the town."

He also disapproved of bishops going to routs, at least of their staying at them longer than their presence commanded respect. He mentioned a particular bishop. "Poh!" said Mrs. Thrale, "the Bishop of ——— is never minded at a rout." BOSWELL: "When a bishop places himself in a situation where he has no distinct character, and is of no consequence, he degrades the dignity of his order." JOHNSON: "Mr. Boswell, Madam, has said it as correctly as it could be."

Nor was it only in the dignitaries of the Church that Johnson required a particular decorum and delicacy of behaviour; he justly considered that the clergy, as persons set apart for the sacred office of serving at the altar, and impressing the minds of men with the awful concerns of a future state, should be somewhat more serious than the generality of mankind, and have a suitable composure of manners. A due sense of the dignity of their profession, independent of higher motives, will ever prevent them from losing their distinction in an indiscriminate sociality; and did such as affect this, know how much it lessens them in the eyes of those whom they think to please by it, they would feel themselves much mortified.

Johnson, and his friend, Beauclerk, were once together in company with several clergymen, who thought that they should appear to advantage, by assuming the lax jollity of *men of the world;* which, as it may be observed in similar cases, they carried to noisy excess. Johnson, who they expected would be *entertained*, sat grave and silent for some time; at last, turning to Beauclerk, he said, by no means in a whisper, "This merriment of parsons is mighty offensive."

Even the dress of a clergyman should be in character, and nothing can be more despicable than conceited attempts at avoiding the appearance of the clerical order; attempts which are as ineffectual as they are pitiful. Dr. Porteus, now Bishop of London, in his excellent charge when presiding over the diocese of Chester, justly animadverts upon this subject; and observes, of a reverend fop, that he "can be but *half a beau.*"

Addison, in "The Spectator," has given us a fine portrait of a clergyman who is supposed to be a member of his *Club;* and Johnson has exhibited a model, in the character of Mr. Mudge,[1] which has escaped the collectors of his works, but which he owned to me, and which indeed he showed to Sir Joshua Reynolds at the time when it was written. It bears the genuine marks of Johnson's best manner, and is as follows:—

"The Reverend Mr. *Zachariah Mudge*, Prebendary of Exeter, and Vicar of St. Andrew's in Plymouth, a man equally eminent for his virtues and abilities, and at once beloved as a companion and

---

[1] See vol. i. p. 264.—BOSWELL.

reverenced as a pastor. He had the general curiosity to which no kind of knowledge is indifferent or superfluous; and that general benevolence by which no order of men is hated or despised.

"His principles both of thought and action were great and comprehensive. By a solicitous examination of objections, and judicious comparison of opposite arguments, he attained what inquiry never gives but to industry and perspicuity, a firm and unshaken settlement of conviction. But his firmness was without asperity; for, knowing with how much difficulty truth was sometimes found, he did not wonder that many missed it.

"The general course of his life was determined by his profession; he studied the sacred volumes in the original languages; with what diligence and success his 'Notes upon the Psalms' give sufficient evidence. He once endeavoured to add the knowledge of Arabic to that of Hebrew; but finding his thoughts too much diverted from other studies, after some time desisted from his purpose.

"His discharge of parochial duties was exemplary. How his 'Sermons' were composed may be learned from the excellent volume which he has given to the public; but how they were delivered, can be known only to those that heard them; for as he appeared in the pulpit, words will not easily describe him. His delivery, though unconstrained, was not negligent; and though forcible, was not turbulent: disdaining anxious nicety of emphasis, and laboured artifice of action, it captivated the hearer by its natural dignity, it roused the sluggish, and fixed the volatile, and detained the mind upon the subject, without directing it to the speaker.

"The grandeur and solemnity of the preacher did not intrude upon his general behaviour. At the table of his friends he was a companion communicative and attentive, of unaffected manners, of manly cheerfulness, willing to please, and easy to be pleased. His acquaintance was universally solicited, and his presence obstructed no enjoyment which religion did not forbid. Though studious he was popular; though argumentative he was modest; though inflexible he was candid; and though metaphysical, yet orthodox." [1]

On Friday, March 30, I dined with him at Sir Joshua Reynolds's, with the Earl of Charlemont, Sir Annesley Stewart, Mr. Eliot, of Port-Eliot, Mr. Burke, Dean Marlay, Mr. Langton: a most agreeable day, of which I regret that every circumstance is not preserved; but it is unreasonable to require such a multiplication of felicity.

Mr. Eliot, with whom Dr. Walter Harte had travelled, talked to us of his "History of Gustavus Adolphus," which he said was a very good book in the German translation. JOHNSON: "Harte was excessively vain. He put copies of his book in manuscript into the hands of Lord Chesterfield and Lord Granville, that they might revise it.

---

[1] "London Chronicle," May 2, 1769. This respectable man is there mentioned to have died on the 3rd of April, that year, at Cofflect, the seat of Thomas Veale, Esq., in his way to London.—BOSWELL.

Now how absurd was it to suppose that two such noblemen would revise so big a manuscript. Poor man! he left London the day of the publication of his book, that he might be out of the way of the great praise he was to receive; and he was ashamed to return, when he found how ill his book had succeeded. It was unlucky in coming out on the same day with Robertson's 'History of Scotland.' His husbandry, however, is good." Boswell: "So he was fitter for that than for heroic history: he did well, when he turned his sword into a ploughshare."

Mr. Eliot mentioned a curious liquor peculiar to his country, which the Cornish fishermen drink. They call it *Mahogany*; and it is made of two parts gin, and one part treacle, well beaten together. I begged to have some of it made, which was done with proper skill by Mr. Eliot. I thought it very good liquor; and said it was a counterpart of what is called *Athol Porridge* in the Highlands of Scotland, which is a mixture of whiskey and honey. Johnson said, "That must be a better liquor than the Cornish, for both its component parts are better." He also observed, "*Mahogany* must be a modern name; for it is not long since the wood called mahogany was known in this country." I mentioned his scale of liquors:— claret for boys,—port for men,—brandy for heroes. "Then," said Mr. Burke, "let me have claret: I love to be a boy; to have the careless gaiety of boyish days." Johnson: "I should drink claret, too, if it would give me that; but it does not; it neither makes boys men, nor men boys. You'll be drowned by it, before it has any effect upon you."

I ventured to mention a ludicrous paragraph in the newspapers, that Dr. Johnson was learning to dance of Vestris.[1] Lord Charlemont, wishing to excite him to talk, proposed in a whisper, that he should be asked whether it was true. "Shall I ask him?" said his lordship. We were, by a great majority, clear for the experiment. Upon which his lordship very gravely, and with a courteous air, said, "Pray, Sir, is it true that you are taking lessons of Vestris?" This was risking a good deal, and required the boldness of a general of Irish Volunteers to make the attempt. Johnson was at first startled, and in some heat answered, "How can your lordship ask so simple a question?" But immediately recovering himself, whether

---

[1] This was Gaetano Apoline Balthazar Vestris, at that time a celebrated professor of the art of dancing. He was born at Florence in 1729, and was for many years at the head of his profession in the great capital of French gaiety. He died in 1808.—Ed.

from unwillingness to be deceived, or to appear deceived, or whether from real good humour, he kept up the joke: "Nay, but if anybody were to answer the paragraph, and contradict it, I'd have a reply, and would say, that he who contradicted it was no friend either to Vestris or me. For why should not Dr. Johnson add to his other powers a little corporeal agility? Socrates learned to dance at an advanced age, and Cato learned Greek at an advanced age. Then it might proceed to say, that this Johnson, not content with dancing on the ground, might dance on the rope; and they might introduce the elephant dancing on the rope. A nobleman[1] wrote a play, called 'Love in a Hollow Tree.' He found out that it was a bad one, and therefore wished to buy up all the copies, and burn them. The Duchess of Marlborough had kept one; and when he was against her at an election, she had a new edition of it printed, and prefixed to it, as a frontispiece, an elephant dancing on a rope; to show, that his lordship's writing comedy was as awkward as an elephant dancing on a rope."

On Sunday, April 1, I dined with him at Mr. Thrale's, with Sir Philip Jenning Clerk and Mr. Perkins,[2] who had the superintendence of Mr. Thrale's brewery, with a salary of five hundred pounds a year. Sir Philip had the appearance of a gentleman of ancient family, well advanced in life. He wore his own white hair in a bag of goodly size, a black velvet coat, with an embroidered waistcoat, and very rich laced ruffles; which Mrs. Thrale said were old fashioned, but which, for that reason, I thought the more respectable, more like a Tory; yet Sir Philip was then in Opposition in Parliament. "Ah, Sir," said Johnson, "ancient ruffles and modern principles do not agree." Sir Philip defended the Opposition to the American war ably and with temper, and I joined him. He said, the majority of the nation was against the ministry. JOHNSON: "I, Sir, am against the ministry; but it is for having too little of that, of which Opposition thinks they have too much. Were I minister, if any man wagged his finger against me, he should be turned out; for that which it is in the power of Government to give at pleasure to one or to another, should be given to the supporters of Government. If you will not oppose at the expense of losing your place, your opposition will not be honest, you will feel no serious grievance; and the present Opposition is only a contest to get what others have. Sir Robert

William, the first Viscount Grimston.—BOSWELL.
[2] See vol. i. p. 538, n.—BOSWELL.

Walpole acted as I would do. As to the American war, the *sense* of the nation is *with* the ministry. The majority of those who can *understand* is with it; the majority of those who can only *hear*, is against it; and as those who can only hear are more numerous than those who can understand, and Opposition is always loudest, a majority of the rabble will be for Opposition."

This boisterous vivacity entertained us; but the truth in my opinion was, that those who could understand the best were against the American war, as almost every man now is, when the question has been coolly considered.

Mrs. Thrale gave high praise to Mr. Dudley Long (now North). JOHNSON: "Nay, my dear lady, don't talk so. Mr. Long's character is very *short*. It is nothing. He fills a chair. He is a man of genteel appearance, and that is all.[1] I know nobody who blasts by praise as you do: for whenever there is exaggerated praise, everybody is set against a character. They are provoked to attack it. Now there is Pepys;[2] you praised that man with such disproportion, that I was incited to lessen him, perhaps more than he deserves. His blood is upon your head. By the same principle, your malice defeats itself; for your censure is too violent. And yet," looking to her with a leering smile, "she is the first woman in the world, could she but restrain that wicked tongue of hers; she would be the only woman, could she but command that little whirligig."

Upon the subject of exaggerated praise I took the liberty to say, that I thought there might be very high praise given to a known character which deserved it, and therefore it would not be exaggerated. Thus, one might say of Mr. Edmund Burke, he is a very wonderful man. JOHNSON: "No, Sir, you would not be safe, if another man had a mind perversely to contradict. He might

[1] Here Johnson condescended to play upon the words *long* and *short*. But little did he know that, owing to Mr. Long's reserve in his presence, he was talking thus of a gentleman distinguished amongst his acquaintance for acuteness of wit,—one to whom, I think, the French expression "*Il petille d'esprit*," is particularly suited. He has gratified me by mentioning that he heard Dr. Johnson say, "Sir, if I were to lose Boswell, it would be a limb amputated."—BOSWELL.

[2] William Weller Pepys, Esq., one of the Masters in the High Court of Chancery, and well known in polite circles. My acquaintance with him is not sufficient to enable me to speak of him from my own judgment. But I know that both at Eton and Oxford he was the intimate friend of the late Sir James Macdonald, the *Marcellus* of Scotland, whose extraordinary talents, learning, and virtues, will ever be remembered with admiration and regret.—BOSWELL.

answer, 'Where is all the wonder? Burke is, to be sure, a man of uncommon abilities, with a great quantity of matter in his mind, and a great fluency of language in his mouth. But we are not to be stunned and astonished by him.' So you see, Sir, even Burke would suffer, not from any fault of his own, but from your folly."

Mrs. Thrale mentioned a gentleman who had acquired a fortune of £4000 a year in trade, but was absolutely miserable, because he could not talk in company; so miserable, that he was impelled to lament his situation in the street to ――, whom he hates, and who he knows despises him. "I am a most unhappy man," said he. "I am invited to conversations. I go to conversations; but, alas! I have no conversation." JOHNSON: "Man commonly cannot be successful in different ways. This gentleman has spent, in getting £4000 a year, the time in which he might have learned to talk; and now he cannot talk." Mr. Perkins made a shrewd and droll remark: "If he had got his £4000 a year as a mountebank, he might have learnt to talk at the same time that he was getting his fortune."

Some other gentlemen came in. The conversation concerning the person whose character Dr. Johnson had treated so slightingly, as he did not know his merit, was resumed. Mrs. Thrale said, "You think so of him, Sir, because he is quiet, and does not exert himself with force. You'll be saying the same thing of Mr. ―― there, who sits as quiet――." This was not well bred; and Johnson did not let it pass without correction. "Nay, Madam, what right have you to talk thus? Both Mr. ―― and I have reason to take it ill. *You* may talk so of Mr. ――; but why do you make *me* do it? Have I said anything against Mr. ――? You have *set* him, that I might shoot him; but I have not shot him."

One of the gentlemen said, he had seen three folio volumes of Dr. Johnson's sayings collected by me. "I must put you right, Sir," said I; "for I am very exact in authenticity. You could not see folio volumes, for I have none: you might have seen some in quarto and octavo. This is an inattention which one should guard against." JOHNSON: "Sir, it is a want of concern about veracity. He does not know that he saw *any* volumes. If he had seen them he could have remembered their size."

Mr. Thrale appeared very lethargic to-day. I saw him again on Monday evening, at which time he was not thought to be in immediate danger; but early on the morning of Wednesday the 4th he expired. Johnson was in the house, and thus mentions the event:—"I felt almost the last flutter of his pulse, and looked for the last time upon the face that for fifteen years had never been turned upon me but with respect and benignity."[1] Upon that day there was a *call* of the Literary Club; but Johnson apologised for his absence by the following note:—

"Wednesday.

"Mr. Johnson knows that Sir Joshua Reynolds and the other gentlemen will excuse his incompliance with the call, when they are told that Mr. Thrale died this morning."

Mr. Thrale's death was a very essential loss to Johnson, who, although he did not foresee all that afterwards happened, was sufficiently convinced that the comforts which Mr. Thrale's family afforded him, would now in a great measure cease. He, however, continued to show a kind attention to his widow and children as long as it was acceptable: and he took upon him, with a very earnest concern, the office of one of his executors, the importance of which seemed greater than usual to him, from his circumstances having been always such, that he had scarcely any share in the real business of life. His friends of the Club were in hopes that Mr. Thrale might have made a liberal provision for him for his life, which, as Mr. Thrale left no son and a very large fortune, it would have been highly to his honour to have done; and, considering Dr. Johnson's age, could not have been of long duration; but he bequeathed him only two hundred pounds, which was the legacy given to each of his executors. I could not but be somewhat diverted by hearing Johnson talk in a pompous manner of his new office, and particularly of the concerns of the brewery, which it was at last resolved should be sold. Lord Lucan tells a very good story, which, if not precisely exact, is certainly characteristical: that when the sale of Thrale's brewery was going forward, Johnson appeared bustling about, with an inkhorn and pen in his button-hole, like an exciseman; and on being asked what he really considered to be the value of the property which was to be disposed of, answered, "We are not here to sell a parcel of boilers and vats, but the potentiality of growing rich beyond the dreams of avarice."

[1] "Prayers and Meditations," p. 191.—Boswell.
Johnson's expressions on this occasion remind us of Isaac Walton's eulogy on Whitgift, in his "Life of Hooker." "He lived to be present at the expiration of her [Q. Elizabeth's] last breath, and to behold the closing of those eyes that had long looked upon him with reverence and affection."—Kearney.

On Friday, April 6, he carried me to dine at a club, which, at his desire, had been lately formed at the Queen's Arms, in St. Paul's Churchyard. He told Mr. Hoole, that he wished to have a *City Club*, and asked him to collect one; "but," said he, "don't let them be *patriots*." The company were to-day very sensible, well-behaved meil. I have preserved only two particulars of his conversation. He said he was glad Lord George Gordon had escaped, rather than that a precedent should be established for hanging a man for *constructive treason ;* which, in consistency with his true, manly, constitutional Toryism, he considered would be a dangerous engine of arbitrary power. And upon its being mentioned that an opulent and very indolent Scotch nobleman, who totally resigned the management of his affairs to a man of knowledge and abilities, had claimed some merit by saying, "The next best thing to managing a man's own affairs well, is being sensible of incapacity, and not attempting it, but having full confidence in one who can do it." JOHNSON: "Nay, Sir, this is paltry. There is a middle course. Let a man give application, and depend upon it he will soon get above a despicable state of helplessness, and attain the power of acting for himself."

On Saturday, April 7, I dined with him at Mr. Hoole's, with Governor Bouchier and Captain Orme, both of whom had been long in the East Indies; and being men of good sense and observation, were very entertaining. Johnson defended the oriental regulation of different *casts* of men, which was objected to as totally destructive of the hopes of rising in society by personal merit. He showed that there was a *principle* in it sufficiently plausible by analogy. "We see," said he, "in metals that there are different species; and so likewise in animals, though one species may not differ very widely from another, as in the species of dogs,—the cur, the spaniel, and the mastiff. The Brahmins are the mastiffs of mankind."

On Thursday, April 12, I dined with him at a Bishop's, where were Sir Joshua Reynolds, Mr. Berenger, and some more company. He had dined the day before at another Bishop's. I have unfortunately recorded none of his conversation at the Bishop's where we dined together: but I have preserved his ingenious defence of his dining twice abroad in Passion-week; a laxity, in which I am convinced he would not have indulged himself at the time when he wrote his solemn paper in "The Rambler," upon that awful season. It appeared to me, that by being much more in company, and enjoying more luxurious living, he had contracted a keener relish for pleasure, and was consequently less rigorous in his religious rites. This he would not acknowledge; but he reasoned with admirable sophistry, as follows: "Why, Sir, a Bishop's calling company together in this week, is, to use the vulgar phrase, not *the thing.* But you must consider laxity is a bad thing: but preciseness is also a bad thing; and your general character may be more hurt by preciseness than by dining with a Bishop in Passion-week. There might be a handle for reflection. It might be said, 'He refuses to dine with a Bishop in Passion-week, but was three Sundays absent from church.'" BOSWELL: "Very true, Sir. But suppose a man to be uniformly of good conduct, would it not be better that he should refuse to dine with a Bishop in this week, and so not encourage a bad practice by his example?" JOHNSON: "Why, Sir, you are to consider whether you might not do more harm by lessening the influence of a Bishop's character by your disapprobation in refusing him, than by going to him."

"TO MRS. LUCY PORTER, IN LICHFIELD.

"DEAR MADAM,   London, April 12, 1781.

"Life is full of troubles. I have just lost my dear friend Thrale. I hope he is happy; but I have had a great loss. I am otherwise pretty well. I require some care of myself, but that care is not ineffectual; and when I am out of order, I think it often my own fault.

"The spring is now making quick advances. As it is the season in which the whole world is enlivened and invigorated, I hope that both you and I shall partake of its benefits. My desire is to see Lichfield; but being left executor to my friend, I know not whether I can be spared; but I will try, for it is now long since we saw one another, and how little we can promise ourselves many more interviews, we are taught by hourly examples of mortality. Let us try to live so as that mortality may not be an evil. Write to me soon, my dearest; your letters will give me great pleasure.

"I am sorry that Mr. Porter has not had his box; but by sending it to Mr. Mathias, who very readily undertook its conveyance, I did the best I could, and perhaps before now he has it.

"Be so kind as to make my compliments to my friends; I have a great value for their kindness, and hope to enjoy it before summer is past. Do write to me.

"I am, dearest love, your most humble servant,
                                   "SAM. JOHNSON."

On Friday, April 13, being Good Friday, I went to St. Clement's church with him as usual. There I saw again his old fellow-collegian, Edwards, to whom I said,

"I think, Sir, Dr. Johnson and you meet only at church." "Sir," said he, "it is the best place we can meet in, except Heaven, and I hope we shall meet there too." Dr. Johnson told me, that there was very little communication between Edwards and him, after their unexpected renewal of acquaintance. "But," said he smiling, "he met me once, and said, 'I am told you have written a very pretty book called *The Rambler*.' I was unwilling that he should leave the world in total darkness, and sent him a set."

Mr. Berenger visited him to-day, and was very pleasing. We talked of an evening society for conversation at a house in town, of which we were all members, but of which Johnson said, "It will never do, Sir. There is nothing served about there, neither tea, nor coffee, nor lemonade, nor anything whatever; and depend upon it, Sir, a man does not love to go to a place from whence he comes out exactly as he went in." I endeavoured, for argument's sake, to maintain that men of learning and talents might have very good intellectual society, without the aid of any little gratifications of the senses. Berenger joined with Johnson, and said, that without these any meeting would be dull and insipid. He would therefore have all the slight refreshments; nay, it would not be amiss to have some cold meat, and a bottle of wine upon a sideboard. "Sir," said Johnson to me with an air of triumph, "Mr. Berenger knows the world. Everybody loves to have good things furnished to them without any trouble. I told Mrs. Thrale once, that as she did not choose to have card-tables, she should have a profusion of the best sweet-meats, and she would be sure to have company enough come to her." I agreed with my illustrious friend upon this subject; for it has pleased GOD to make man a composite animal, and where there is nothing to refresh the body, the mind will languish.

On Sunday, April 15, being Easter-day, after solemn worship in St. Paul's church, I found him alone; Dr. Scott, of the Commons, came in. He talked of its having been said, that Addison wrote some of his best papers in "The Spectator," when warm with wine. Dr. Johnson did not seem willing to admit this. Dr. Scott, as a confirmation of it, related that Blackstone, a sober man, composed his Commentaries with a bottle of port before him; and found his mind invigorated and supported, in the fatigue of his great work, by a temperate use of it.

I told him, that in a company where I had lately been, a desire was expressed to know his authority for the shocking story of Addison's sending an execution into

Steele's house.[1] "Sir," said he, "it is generally known; it is known to all who are acquainted with the literary history of that period; it is as well known as that he wrote 'Cato.'" Mr. Thomas Sheridan once defended Addison to me by alleging that he did it in order to cover Steele's goods from other creditors, who were going to seize them.

We talked of the difference between the mode of education at Oxford, and that in those colleges where instruction is chiefly conveyed by lectures. JOHNSON: "Lectures were once useful; but now, when all can read, and books are so numerous, lectures are unnecessary. If your attention fails, and you miss a part of the lecture, it is lost; you cannot go back as you do upon a book." Dr. Scott agreed with him. "But yet," said I, "Dr. Scott, you yourself gave lectures at Oxford." He smiled. "You laughed," then said I, "at those who came to you."

Dr. Scott left us, and soon afterwards we went to dinner. Our company consisted of Mrs. Williams, Mrs. Desmoulins, Mr. Levett, Mr. Allen the printer, [Mr. Macbean,] and Mrs. Hall, sister of the Reverend Mr. John Wesley, and resembling him, as I thought, both in figure and manner. Johnson produced now, for the first time, some handsome silver salvers, which he told me he had bought fourteen years ago; so it was a great day. I was not a little amused by observing Allen perpetually struggling to talk in the manner of Johnson, like the little frog in the fable blowing himself up to resemble the stately ox.

I mentioned a kind of religious Robin Hood Society, which met every Sunday evening at Coachmakers'-hall, for free debate; and that the subject for this night was, the text which relates, with other miracles which happened at our Saviour's death, "And the graves were opened, and many bodies of the saints which slept arose, and came out of the graves after his resurrection, and went into the holy city, and appeared unto many." Mrs. Hall said it was a very curious subject, and she should like to hear it discussed. JOHNSON (somewhat warmly): "One would not go to such a place to hear it,—one would not be seen in such a place—to give countenance to such a meeting." I, however, resolved that I would go. "But, Sir," said she to Johnson, "I should like to hear *you* discuss it." He seemed reluctant to engage in it. She talked of the resurrection of the human race in general, and maintained that we shall be raised with the same bodies. JOHNSON:

---

[1] See this explained in p. 380 of this volume.—BOSWELL.

"Nay, Madam, we see that it is not to be the same body; for the Scripture uses the illustration of grain sown, and we know that the grain which grows is not the same with what is sown. You cannot suppose that we shall rise with a diseased body; it is enough if there be such a sameness as to distinguish identity of person." She seemed desirous of knowing more, but he left the question in obscurity.

Of apparitions,[1] he observed, "A total disbelief of them is adverse to the opinion of the existence of the soul between death and the last day; the question simply is, whether departed spirits ever have the power of making themselves perceptible to us. A man who thinks he has seen an apparition, can only be convinced himself; his authority will not convince another; and his conviction, if rational, must be founded on being told something which cannot be known but by supernatural means."

He mentioned a thing as not unfrequent, of which I had never heard before,—being *called*, that is, hearing one's name pronounced by the voice of a known person at a great distance, far beyond the possibility of being reached by any sound uttered by human organs. An acquaintance, on whose veracity I can depend, told me, that walking home one evening to Kilmarnock, he heard himself called from a wood, by the voice of a brother who had gone to America; and the next packet brought accounts of that brother's death. Macbean asserted that this inexplicable calling was a thing very well known. Dr. Johnson said, that one day at Oxford, as he was turning the key of his chamber, he heard his mother distinctly call—*Sam*. She was then at Lichfield; but nothing ensued. This phenomenon is, I think, as wonderful as any other mysterious fact, which many people are very slow to believe, or rather, indeed, reject with an obstinate contempt.

Some time after this, upon his making a remark which escaped my attention, Mrs. Williams and Mrs. Hall were

[1] As this subject frequently recurs in these volumes, the reader may be led erroneously to suppose that Dr. Johnson was so fond of such discussions, as frequently to introduce them. But the truth is, that the author himself delighted in talking concerning ghosts, and what he has frequently denominated *the mysterious;* and therefore took every opportunity of *leading* Johnson to converse on such subjects.—MALONE.

The author of this work was most undoubtedly fond of the *mysterious,* and perhaps upon some occasions may have directed the conversation to those topics, when they would not spontaneously have suggested themselves to Johnson's mind; but that *he* also had a love for speculations of that nature, may be gathered from his writings throughout.—J. BOSWELL, JUN.

both together striving to answer him. He grew angry, and called out loudly, "Nay, when you both speak at once it is intolerable." But checking himself, and softening, he said, "This one may say, though you *are* ladies." Then he brightened into gay humour, and addressed them in the words of one of the songs in "The Beggar's Opera:"—

"But two at a time there's no mortal can bear."

"What, Sir," said I, "are you going to turn Captain Macheath?" There was something as pleasantly ludicrous in this scene as can be imagined. The contrast between Macheath, Polly, and Lucy—and Dr. Samuel Johnson; blind, peevish Mrs. Williams; and lean, lank, preaching Mrs. Hall, was exquisite.

I stole away to Coachmakers'-hall, and heard the difficult text of which we had talked, discussed with great decency, and some intelligence, by several speakers. There was a difference of opinion as to the appearance of ghosts in modern times, though the arguments for it, supported by Mr. Addison's authority, preponderated. The immediate subject of debate was embarrassed by the *bodies* of the saints having been said to rise, and by the question what became of them afterwards: did they return again to their graves, or were they translated to heaven? Only one evangelist mentions the fact (St. Matthew, xxvii. 52, 53), and the commentators whom I have looked at do not make the passage clear. There is, however, no occasion for our understanding it farther than to know that it was one of the extraordinary manifestations of divine power, which accompanied the most important event that ever happened.

On Friday, April 20, I spent with him one of the happiest days that I remember to have enjoyed in the whole course of my life. Mrs. Garrick, whose grief for the loss of her husband was, I believe, as sincere as wounded affection and admiration could produce, had this day, for the first time since his death, a select party of his friends to dine with her.[1] The company was, Miss Hannah More, who lived with her, and whom she called her chaplain; Mrs. Boscawen,

[1] Mrs. Garrick was born at Vienna, in 1725. Her maiden name was Viegel, which she changed to Violette, at the command of the Empress Maria-Theresa, whose patronage she had attracted by her consummate skill as an opera dancer. She arrived in England in 1744, and was married to David Garrick in 1749, when the Earl of Burlington gave the bride a marriage portion of £6,000. She remained a widow and survived her husband for forty years. She died in 1822, aged 97.—ED.

Mrs. Elizabeth Carter, Sir Joshua Reynolds, Dr. Burney, Dr. Johnson, and myself. We found ourselves very elegantly entertained at her house in the Adelphi, where I have passed many a pleasing hour with him "who gladdened life." She looked well, talked of her husband with complacency, and while she cast her eyes on his portrait, which hung over the chimney-piece, said, that "death was now the most agreeable object to her." The very semblance of David Garrick was cheering. Mr. Beauclerk, with happy propriety, inscribed under that fine portrait of him, which by Lady Diana's kindness is now the property of my friend Mr. Langton, the following passage from his beloved Shakespeare:—

> "———————— A merrier man,
> Within the limit of becoming mirth,
> I never spent an hour's talk withal.
> His eye begets occasion for his wit;
> For every object that the one doth catch,
> The other turns to a mirth-moving jest;
> Which his fair tongue (Conceit's expositor)
> Delivers in such apt and gracious words,
> That aged years play truant at his tales,
> And younger hearings are quite ravished:
> So sweet and voluble is his discourse."

We were all in fine spirits; and I whispered to Mrs. Boscawen, "I believe this is as much as can be made of life." In addition to a splendid entertainment, we were regaled with Lichfield ale, which had a peculiar appropriate value. Sir Joshua, and Dr. Burney, and I, drank cordially of it to Dr. Johnson's health; and though he would not join us, he as cordially answered, "Gentlemen, I wish you all as well as you do me."

The general effect of this day dwells upon my mind in fond remembrance; but I do not find much conversation recorded. What I have preserved shall be faithfully given.

One of the company mentioned Mr. Thomas Hollis, the strenuous Whig, who used to send over Europe presents of democratical books, with their boards stamped with daggers and caps of liberty. Mrs. Carter said, "he was a bad man: he used to talk uncharitably." JOHNSON: "Poh! poh! Madam; who is the worse for being talked of uncharitably? Besides, he was a dull poor creature as ever lived: and I believe he would not have done harm to a man whom he knew to be of very opposite principles to his own. I remember once at the Society of Arts, when

an advertisement was to be drawn up, he pointed me out
as the man who could do it best. This, you will observe,
was kindness to me. I, however, slipped away, and escaped
it."

Mrs. Carter having said of the same person, "I doubt
he was an atheist." JOHNSON: "I don't know that. He
might perhaps have become one, if he had had time
to ripen (smiling). He might have *exuberated* into an
atheist."

Sir Joshua Reynolds praised "Mudge's[1] Sermons."
JOHNSON: "Mudge's Sermons are good but not practical.
He grasps more sense than he can hold; he takes more
corn than he can make into meal; he opens a wide prospect,
but it is so distant, it is indistinct. I love 'Blair's Sermons.'
Though the dog is a Scotchman, and a Presbyterian, and
everything he should not be, I was the first to praise them.
Such was my candour" (smiling). MRS. BOSCAWEN:
"Such his great merit, to get the better of all your
prejudices." JOHNSON: "Why, Madam, let us compound
the matter; let us ascribe it to my candour and his
merit."

In the evening we had a large company in the drawing-
room; several ladies, the Bishop of Killaloe, Dr. Percy,
Mr. Chamberlayne of the Treasury, &c. &c. Somebody
said, the life of a mere literary man could not be very
entertaining. JOHNSON: "But it certainly may. This is
a remark which has been made, and repeated, without
justice; why should the life of a literary man be less entertaining than the life of any other man? Are there not as
interesting varieties in such a life? As *a literary life* it
may be very entertaining." BOSWELL: "But it must be
better surely, when it is diversified with a little active
variety—such as his having gone to Jamaica; or—his
having gone to the Hebrides." Johnson was not displeased
at this.

Talking of a very respectable author, he told us a curious
circumstance in his life, which was, that he had married a
printer's devil. REYNOLDS: "A printer's devil, Sir! Why,
I thought a printer's devil was a creature with a black face
and in rags." JOHNSON: "Yes, Sir. But I suppose he
had her face washed, and put clean clothes on her. (Then
looking very serious and very earnest). And she did not
disgrace him;—the woman had a bottom of good sense."
The word *bottom*, thus introduced, was so ludicrous, when
contrasted with his gravity, that most of us could not

---

[1] See p. 399 of this volume.—BOSWELL.

forbear tittering and laughing; though I recollect that the Bishop of Killaloe kept his countenance with perfect steadiness, while Miss Hannah More slily hid her face behind a lady's back who sat on the same settee with her. His pride could not bear that any expression of his should excite ridicule, when he did not intend it; he therefore resolved to assume and exercise despotic power, glanced sternly around, and called out, in a strong tone, "Where's the merriment?" Then collecting himself, and looking awful, to make us feel how he could impose restraint, and as it were searching his mind for a still more ludicrous word, he slowly pronounced, "I say the *woman* was *fundamentally* sensible;" as if he had said, hear this now, and laugh if you dare. We all sat composed as at a funeral.

He and I walked away together; we stopped a little while by the rails of the Adelphi, looking on the Thames, and I said to him, with some emotion, that I was now thinking of two friends we had lost, who once lived in the buildings behind us, Beauclerk and Garrick. "Ay, Sir," said he tenderly, "and two such friends as cannot be supplied."

For some time after this day I did not see him very often, and of the conversation which I did enjoy, I am sorry to find I have preserved but little. I was at this time engaged in a variety of other matters, which required exertion and assiduity, and necessarily occupied almost all my time.

One day having spoken very freely of those who were then in power, he said to me, "Between ourselves, Sir, I do not like to give opposition the satisfaction of knowing how much I disapprove of the ministry." And when I mentioned that Mr. Burke had boasted how quiet the nation was in George the Second's reign, when Whigs were in power, compared with the present reign, when Tories governed;—"Why, Sir," said he, "you are to consider that Tories, having more reverence for government, will not oppose with the same violence as Whigs, who being unrestrained by that principle, will oppose by any means."

This month he lost not only Mr. Thrale, but another friend, Mr. William Strahan, junior, printer, the eldest son of his old and constant friend, printer to his Majesty.

"TO MRS. STRAHAN.

"DEAR MADAM,   April 23, 1781.

"The grief which I feel for the loss of a very kind friend is sufficient to make me know how much you suffer by the death of an amiable son: a man, of whom I think it may be truly said, that no one knew him who does not lament him. I look upon myself as having a friend, another friend, taken from me.

"Comfort, dear Madam, I would give you, if I could; but I know how little the forms of consolation can avail. Let me, however, counsel you not to waste your health in unprofitable sorrow, but go to Bath, and endeavour to prolong your own life; but when we have all done all that we can, one friend must in time lose the other. I am, dear Madam,

"Your most humble servant,
"SAM. JOHNSON."

CHAPTER XX.—1781

Johnson dines with Wilkes and Dr. Beattie—Letter-writing — Bet Flint — Oratory — Beauclerk's Library — Blue-stocking Clubs—Stillingfleet—The Countess of Cork— Johnson's "List of Subscribers"—"Talking for Victory" —A "cui bono" Man—"Heroic Epistle to Sir W. Chambers"—Johnson's Commendation of Lord Carlisle's Poems—Dr. Barnard—"Of Tory and Whig"—Boswell's Departure for Scotland—Visit to Welwyn—Dr. Young —On Original Sin—Rev. Mr. Palmer and the Unitarians —Ancient Egyptians—Wealth—Rev. Mr. Smith—Luton Hoe, Seat of Lord Bute—Society of Procurators, in Scotland—Mr. Robertson, of "The Caledonian Mercury"

On Tuesday, May 8, I had the pleasure of again dining with Johnson and Mr. Wilkes, at Mr. Dilly's. No *negociation* was now required to bring them together; for Johnson was so well satisfied with the former interview, that he was very glad to meet Wilkes again, who was this day seated between Dr. Beattie and Dr. Johnson (between *Truth* and *Reason*, as General Paoli said, when I told him of it). Wilkes: " I have been thinking, Dr. Johnson, that there should be a bill brought into Parliament that the controverted elections for Scotland should be tried in that country at their own Abbey of Holyrood-house, and not here, for the consequence of trying them here is, that we have an inundation of Scotchmen, who come up and never go back again. Now here is Boswell, who is come upon the election for his own county, which will not last a fortnight." Johnson: "Nay, Sir, I see no reason why they should be tried at all; for, you know, one Scotchman is as good as another." Wilkes: "Pray, Boswell, how much may be got in a year by an Advocate at the Scotch bar?" Boswell: "I believe, two thousand pounds." Wilkes: "How can it be possible to spend that money in Scotland?" Johnson: "Why, Sir, the money may be spent in England; but there is a harder question. If one man in Scotland gets possession of two thousand pounds, what remains for all the rest of the nation?" Wilkes: "You know, in the last war, the immense booty which Thurot carried off by the complete plunder of seven Scotch isles; he re-embarked with *three* and *sixpence*." Here again Johnson and Wilkes joined in extravagant sportive raillery upon the supposed poverty of Scotland, which Dr. Beattie and I did not think it worth our while to dispute.

The subject of quotation being introduced, Mr. Wilkes censured it as pedantry. JOHNSON: "No, Sir, it is a good thing; there is a community of mind in it. Classical quotation is the *parole* of literary men all over the world." WILKES: "Upon the continent they all quote the Vulgate Bible. Shakespeare is chiefly quoted here; and we quote also Pope, Prior, Butler, Waller, and sometimes Cowley."

We talked of letter-writing. JOHNSON: "It is now become so much the fashion to publish letters, that, in order to avoid it, I put as little into mine as I can." BOSWELL: "Do what you will, Sir, you cannot avoid it. Should you even write as ill as you can, your letters would be published as curiosities:

'Behold a miracle! instead of wit,
    See two dull lines with Stanhope's pencil writ.'"

He gave us an entertaining account of *Bet Flint*, a woman of the town, who, with some eccentric talents and much effrontery, forced herself upon his acquaintance. "Bet," said he, "wrote her own life in verse,[1] which she brought to me, wishing that I would furnish her with a preface to it (laughing). I used to say of her, that she was generally slut and drunkard;—occasionally, whore and thief. She had, however, genteel lodgings, a spinnet on which she played, and a boy that walked before her chair. Poor Bet was taken up on a charge of stealing a counterpane, and tried at the Old Bailey. Chief Justice ———, who loved a wench, summed up favourably, and she was acquitted.[2] After which, Bet said, with a gay and satisfied

---

[1] Johnson, whose memory was wonderfully retentive, remembered the first four lines of this curious production, which have been communicated to me by a young lady of his acquaintance:—
    "When first I drew my vital breath,
    A little minikin I came upon earth;
    And then I came from a dark abode,
    Into this gay and gaudy world."—BOSWELL.

[2] The account which Johnson had received on this occasion was not quite accurate. Bet was tried at the Old Bailey in September, 1758, not by the Chief Justice here alluded to (who, however, tried another cause on the same day), but before Sir William Moreton, Recorder; and she was acquitted, not in consequence of any *favourable summing up*

air, 'Now that the counterpane is *my own*, I shall make a petticoat of it.'"

Talking of oratory, Mr. Wilkes described it as accompanied with all the charms of poetical expression. JOHNSON: "No, Sir; oratory is the power of beating down your adversary's arguments, and putting better in their place." WILKES: "But this does not move the passions." JOHNSON: "He must be a weak man, who is to be so moved." WILKES (naming a celebrated orator): "Amidst all the brilliancy of ———'s imagination, and the exuberance of his wit, there is a strange want of *taste*. It was observed of Apelles's Venus, that her flesh seemed as if she had been nourished by roses: his oratory would sometimes make one suspect that he eats potatoes and drinks whiskey."

Mr. Wilkes observed, how tenacious we are of forms in this country; and gave, as an instance, the vote of the House of Commons for remitting money to pay the army in America *in Portugal pieces*, when, in reality, the remittance is made not in Portugal money, but in our specie. JOHNSON: "Is there not a law, Sir, against exporting the current coin of the realm?" WILKES: "Yes, Sir, but might not the House of Commons, in case of real evident necessity, order our own current coin to be sent into our own colonies?"—Here Johnson, with that quickness of recollection which distinguished him so eminently, gave the *Middlesex Patriot* an admirable retort upon his own ground. "Sure, Sir, *you* don't think a *resolution of the House of Commons* equal to *the law of the land.*" WILKES (at once perceiving the application): "GOD forbid, Sir."— To hear what had been treated with such violence in "The False Alarm," now turned into pleasant repartee, was extremely agreeable. Johnson went on:—"Locke observes well, that a prohibition to export the current coin is impolitic; for when the balance of trade happens to be against a state, the current coin *must* be exported."

Mr. Beauclerk's great library was this season sold in London by auction. Mr. Wilkes said, he wondered to

of the judge, but because the prosecutrix, Mary Walthow, could not prove that the goods charged to have been stolen (a counterpane, a silver spoon, two napkins, &c.) were her property. Bet does not appear to have lived at that time in a very *genteel* style; for she paid for her ready-furnished *room* in Meard's-court, Dean-street, Soho, from which these articles were alleged to be stolen, only *five shillings* a week. Mr. James Boswell took the trouble to examine the Sessions Paper, to ascertain these particulars.—MALONE.

[1] Mr. Wilkes mistook the objection of Euphranor to the Theseus of Parrhasius for a description of the Venus of Apelles. Vide Plutarch, "Bellone an pace clariores Athenienses,"—KEARNEY.

find in it such a numerous collection of sermons: seeming to think it strange that a gentleman of Mr. Beauclerk's character in the gay world should have chosen to have many compositions of that kind. Johnson: "Why, Sir, you are to consider, that sermons make a considerable branch of English literature; so that a library must be very imperfect if it has not a numerous collection of sermons:[1] and in all collections, Sir, the desire of augmenting

[1] Mr. Wilkes probably did not know that there is in an English sermon the most comprehensive and lively account of that entertaining faculty, for which he himself was so much admired.   It is in Dr. Barrow's first volume, and fourteenth sermon, "Against Foolish Talking and Jesting."   My old acquaintance, the late Corbyn Morris, in his ingenious "Essay on Wit, Humour, and Ridicule," calls it "a *profuse* description of wit;" but I do not see how it could be curtailed, without leaving out some good circumstance of discrimination.   As it is not generally known, and may perhaps dispose some to read sermons, from which they may receive real advantage, while looking only for entertainment, I shall here subjoin it.

"But first," says the learned preacher, "it may be demanded, what the thing we speak of is?   Or what this facetiousness (or *wit*, as he calls it before) doth import?   To which questions I might reply, as Democritus did to him that asked the definition of a man, ''Tis that which we all see and know.'   Any one better apprehends what it is by acquaintance, than I can inform him by description.   It is, indeed, a thing so versatile and multiform, appearing in so many shapes, so many postures, so many garbs, so variously apprehended by several eyes and judgments, that it seemed no less hard to settle a clear and certain notion thereof, than to make a portrait of Proteus, or to define the figure of the fleeting air.   Sometimes it lieth in pat allusion to a known story, or in seasonable application of a trivial saying, or in forging an apposite tale; sometimes it playeth in words and phrases, taking advantage from the ambiguity of their sense, or the affinity of their sound; sometimes it is wrapped in a dress of humorous expression; sometimes it lurketh under an odd similitude; sometimes it is lodged in a sly question, in a smart answer, in a quirkish reason, in a shrewd intimation, in cunningly diverting or cleverly retorting an objection; sometimes it is couched in a bold scheme of speech, in a tart irony, in a lusty hyperbole, in a startling metaphor, in a plausible reconciling of contradictions, or in acute nonsense; sometimes a scenical representation of persons or things, a counterfeit speech, a mimical look or gesture, passeth for it; sometimes an affected simplicity, sometimes a presumptuous bluntness, giveth it being; sometimes it riseth only from a lucky hitting upon what is strange; sometimes from a crafty wresting obvious matter to the purpose. Often it consisteth in one knows not what, and springeth up one can hardly tell how.   Its ways are unaccountable and inexplicable; being answerable to the numberless rovings of fancy, and windings of language. It is, in short, a manner of speaking out of the simple and plain way (such as reason teacheth and proveth things by), which by a pretty surprising uncouthness in conceit or expression, doth affect and amuse the fancy, stirring in it some wonder, and breeding some delight thereto. It raiseth admiration, as signifying a nimble sagacity of apprehension, a special felicity of invention, a vivacity of spirit, and reach of wit more than vulgar; it seeming to argue a rare quickness of parts, that one can fetch in remote conceits applicable; a notable skill, that he can dexterously accommodate them to the purpose before him; together with

them grows stronger in proportion to the advance in acquisition; as motion is accelerated by the continuance of the *impetus*. Besides, Sir," looking at Mr. Wilkes with a placid but significant smile, "a man may collect sermons with intention of making himself better by them. I hope Mr. Beauclerk intended, that some time or other that should be the case with him."

Mr. Wilkes said to me, loud enough for Dr. Johnson to hear, "Dr. Johnson should make me a present of his 'Lives of the Poets,' as I am a poor patriot who cannot afford to buy them." Johnson seemed to take no notice of this hint; but in a little while he called to Mr. Dilly, "Pray, Sir, be so good as to send a set of my Lives to Mr. Wilkes, with my compliments." This was accordingly done; and Mr. Wilkes paid Dr. Johnson a visit, was courteously received, and sat with him a long time.

The company gradually dropped away. Mr. Dilly himself was called down stairs upon business; I left the room for some time; when I returned, I was struck with observing Dr. Samuel Johnson and John Wilkes, Esq., literally *tête-à-tête;* for they were reclined upon their chairs, with their heads leaning almost close to each other, and talking earnestly, in a kind of confidential whisper, of the personal quarrel between George the Second and the King of Prussia. Such a scene of perfectly easy sociality between two such opponents in the war of political controversy, as that which I now beheld, would have been an excellent subject for a picture. It presented to my mind the happy days which are foretold in Scripture, when the lion shall lie down with the kid.[1]

After this day there was another pretty long interval, during which Dr. Johnson and I did not meet. When I

a lively briskness of humour, not apt to damp those sportful flashes of imagination. (Whence, in Aristotle, such persons are termed ἐπιδέξιοι, dexterous men, and εὔστροφοι, men of facile or versatile manners, who can easily turn themselves to all things, or turn all things to themselves.) It also procureth delight, by gratifying curiosity with its rareness, as semblance of difficulty (as monsters, not for their beauty, but their rarity; as juggling tricks, not for their use, but their abstruseness, are beheld with pleasure); by diverting the mind from its road of serious thoughts; by instilling gaiety and airiness of spirit; by provoking to such dispositions of spirit in way of emulation or complaisance; and by seasoning matters, otherwise distasteful or insipid, with an unusual and thence grateful tang."—BOSWELL.

[1] When I mentioned this to the Bishop of Killaloe, "With the *goat*," said his lordship. Such, however, was the engaging politeness and pleasantry of Mr. Wilkes, and, such the social good humour of the bishop, that when they dined together at Mr. Dilly's, where I also was, they were mutually agreeable.—BOSWELL.

mentioned it to him with regret, he was pleased to say, "Then, Sir, let us live double."

About this time it was much the fashion for several ladies to have evening assemblies, where the fair sex might participate in conversation with literary and ingenious men, animated by a desire to please. These societies were denominated *Blue-stocking Clubs*, the origin of which title being little known, it may be worth while to relate it. One of the most eminent members of those societies, when they first commenced, was Mr. Stillingfleet,[1] whose dress was remarkably grave, and in particular it was observed that he wore blue stockings. Such was the excellence of his conversation, that his absence was felt as so great a loss, that it used to be said, "We can do nothing without the *blue stockings;*" and thus by degrees the title was established. Miss Hannah More has admirably described a *Blue-stocking Club*, in her "*Bas Bleu*," a poem in which many of the persons who were most conspicuous there are mentioned.

Johnson was prevailed with to come sometimes into these circles, and did not think himself too grave even for the lively Miss Monckton (now Countess of Cork), who used to have the finest *bit of blue* at the house of her mother, Lady Galway. Her vivacity enchanted the sage, and they used to talk together with all imaginable ease.[2] A singular instance happened one evening, when she insisted that some of Sterne's writings were very pathetic. Johnson bluntly denied it. "I am sure," said she, "they have affected *me*."—"Why," said Johnson smiling, and rolling himself about, "that is, because, dearest, you're a dunce." When she some time afterwards mentioned this to him, he said, with equal truth and politeness, "Madam, if I had thought so, I certainly should not have said it."

Another evening Johnson's kind indulgence towards me had a pretty difficult trial. I had dined at the Duke of Montrose's with a very agreeable party, and his Grace, according to his usual custom, had circulated the bottle very freely. Lord Graham and I went together to Miss

---

[1] Mr. Benjamin Stillingfleet, author of tracts relating to natural history, &c.—BOSWELL.

Benjamin Stillingfleet was the grandson of the learned Bishop Stillingfleet, and besides his works on natural history, he was known as the author of "A Treatise on the Principles and the Powers of Harmony." He held the situation of barrack-master at Kensington, and died in 1771, at the age of 69.—ED.

[2] This lady survived to upwards of ninety years of age, and died at her residence in New Burlington-street, in 1840.—ED.

Monckton's, where I certainly was in extraordinary spirits, and above all fear or awe. In the midst of a great number of persons of the first rank, amongst whom I recollect, with confusion, a noble lady of the most stately decorum, I placed myself next to Johnson, and thinking myself now fully his match, talked to him in a loud and boisterous manner, desirous to let the company know how I could contend with *Ajax*. I particularly remember pressing him upon the value of the pleasures of the imagination, and as an illustration of my argument, asking him, "What, Sir, supposing I were to fancy that the —— (naming the most charming Duchess in his Majesty's dominions) were in love with me, should I not be very happy?" My friend with much address evaded my interrogatories, and kept me as quiet as possible; but it may easily be conceived how he must have felt.[1] However, when a few days afterwards I waited upon him and made an apology, he behaved with the most friendly gentleness.

While I remained in London this year, Johnson and I dined together at several places. I recollect a placid day

---

[1] Next day I endeavoured to give what had happened the most ingenious turn I could, by the following verses:—

TO THE HONOURABLE MISS MONCKTON.

Not that with th' excellent Montrose
    I had the happiness to dine;
Not that I late from table rose,
    From Graham's wit, from generous wine.

It was not these alone which led
    On sacred manners to encroach;
And made me feel what most I dread,
    Johnson's just frown, and self-reproach.

But when I enter'd, not abash'd,
    From your bright eyes were shot such rays,
At once intoxication flash'd,
    And all my frame was in a blaze!

But not a brilliant blaze, I own
    Of the dull smoke I'm yet asham'd;
I was a dreary ruin grown,
    And not enlighten'd though inflam'd.

Victim at once to wine and love,
    I hope, Maria, you'll forgive;
While I invoke the powers above,
    That henceforth I may wiser live.

The lady was generously forgiving, returned me an obliging answer, and I thus obtained an *Act of Oblivion*, and took care never to offend again.—BOSWELL.

at Dr. Butter's, who had now removed from Derby to Lower Grosvenor-street, London; but of his conversation on that and other occasions, during this period, I neglected to keep any regular record, and shall therefore insert here some miscellaneous articles which I find in my Johnsonian notes.

His disorderly habits, when "making provision for the day that was passing over him," appear from the following anecdote, communicated to me by Mr. John Nichols:— "In the year 1763, a young bookseller, who was an apprentice to Mr. Whiston, waited on him with a subscription to his 'Shakespeare;' and observing that the Doctor made no entry in any book of the subscriber's name, ventured diffidently to ask whether he would please to have the gentleman's address, that it might be properly inserted in the printed list of subscribers.—'*I shall print no List of Subscribers*,' said Johnson, with great abruptness: but almost immediately recollecting himself, added, very complacently, 'Sir, I have two very cogent reasons for not printing any list of subscribers:—one, that I have lost all the names,—the other, that I have spent all the money.'"

Johnson could not brook appearing to be worsted in argument, even when he had taken the wrong side, to show the force and dexterity of his talents. When, therefore, he perceived that his opponent gained ground, he had recourse to some sudden mode of robust sophistry. Once, when I was pressing upon him with visible advantage, he stopped me thus:—"My dear Boswell, let's have no more of this; you'll make nothing of it. I'd rather have you whistle a Scotch tune."

Care, however, must be taken to distinguish between Johnson when he "talked for victory," and Johnson when he had no desire but to inform and illustrate.—"One of Johnson's principal talents," says an eminent friend of his,[1] "was shown in maintaining the wrong side of an argument, and in a splendid perversion of the truth. If you could contrive to have his fair opinion on a subject, and without any bias from personal prejudice, or from a wish to be victorious in argument, it was wisdom itself, not only convincing, but overpowering."

He had, however, all his life habituated himself to consider conversation as a trial of intellectual vigour and skill; and to this, I think, we may venture to ascribe that unexampled richness and brilliancy which appeared in his own. As a proof at once of his eagerness for colloquial

---

[1] The late Right Hon. William Gerrard Hamilton.—MALONE.

distinction, and his high notion of this eminent friend, he once addressed him thus:—"——, we now have been several hours together; and you have said but one thing for which I envied you."

He disliked much all speculative desponding considerations, which tended to discourage men from diligence and exertion. He was in this like Dr. Shaw,[1] the great traveller, who, Mr. Daines Barrington told me, used to say, "I hate a *cui bono* man." Upon being asked by a friend what he should think of a man who was apt to say *non est tanti;* —"That he's a stupid fellow, Sir," answered Johnson. "What would these *tanti* men be doing the while?" When I, in a low-spirited fit, was talking to him with indifference of the pursuits which generally engage us in a course of action, and inquiring a *reason* for taking so much trouble; "Sir," said he, in an animated tone, "it is driving on the system of life."

He told me that he was glad that I had, by General Oglethorpe's means, become acquainted with Dr. Shebbeare. Indeed that gentleman, whatever objections were made to him, had knowledge and abilities much above the class of ordinary writers, and deserves to be remembered as a respectable name in literature, were it only for his admirable "Letters on the English Nation," under the name of "Battista Angeloni, a Jesuit."

Johnson and Shebbeare[2] were frequently named together, as having in former reigns had no predilection for the family of Hanover. The author of the celebrated "Heroic Epistle to Sir William Chambers," introduces them in one line, in a list of those "who tasted the sweets of his present Majesty's reign." Such was Johnson's candid relish of the merit of that satire, that he allowed Dr. Goldsmith, as he told me, to read it to him from beginning to end, and did not refuse his praise to its execution.

Goldsmith could sometimes take adventurous liberties with him, and escaped unpunished. Beauclerk told me that when Goldsmith talked of a project for having a third theatre in London solely for the exhibition of new plays,

[1] Known by his "Travels, or Observations relating to several parts of Barbary and the Levant." He was born in 1692, and died in 1751.—Ed.

[2] I recollect a ludicrous paragraph in the newspapers, that the King had pensioned both a *He*-bear and a *She*-bear.—Boswell.

Dr. Shebbeare was a physician and political writer of some repute. For his violence he was once pilloried, and twice imprisoned. Afterwards, under the administration of Lord Bute, he supported the government, and obtained a pension. He published "Letters to the People of England," "The History of the Sumatrans," and many other political tracts. He was born at Bideford, co. Devon, and died in 1788.—Ed.

in order to deliver authors from the supposed tyranny of managers, Johnson treated it slightingly, upon which Goldsmith said, "Ay, ay, this may be nothing to you, who can now shelter yourself behind the corner of a pension;" and Johnson bore this with good-humour.

Johnson praised the Earl of Carlisle's poems,[1] which his lordship had published with his name, as not disdaining to be a candidate for literary fame. My friend was of opinion, that when a man of rank appeared in that character, he deserved to have his merit handsomely allowed.[2] In this I think he was more liberal than Mr. William Whitehead, in his "Elegy to Lord Villiers," in which, under the pretext of "superior toils demanding all their care, he discovers a jealousy of the great paying their court to the Muses:

> "——— ——— to the chosen few
> Who dare excel, thy fost'ring aid afford;
> Their arts, their magic powers, with honours due
> Exalt;—but be thyself what they record."

[1] Frederick Howard, fifth Earl of Carlisle, the uncle and guardian of Lord Byron; to whom the noble poet dedicated his "Hours of Idleness," although he afterwards satirized him in his "English Bards." Some of Lord Carlisle's literary works bear the stamp of poetic genius. The tragedies of "A Father's Vengeance," and "The Step-mother," have been published with a collection of his lordship's poems. He was born in 1748, and died in 1825.—ED.

[2] Men of rank and fortune, however, should be pretty well assured of having a real claim to the approbation of the public as writers, before they venture to stand forth. Dryden, in his preface to "All for Love," thus expresses himself:—

"Men of pleasant conversation, at least esteemed so, and endued with a trifling kind of fancy, perhaps helped out by a smattering of Latin, are ambitious to distinguish themselves from the herd of gentlemen by their poetry:

'Rarus enim fermè sensus communis in illa
Fortuna.'—*Juv.* Sat. viii. 73.

And is not this a wretched affectation, not to be contented with what fortune has done for them, and sit down quietly with their estates, but they must call their wits in question, and needlessly expose their nakedness to public view? Not considering that they are not to expect the same approbation from sober men, which they have found from their flatterers after the third bottle. If a little glittering in discourse has passed them on us for witty men, where was the necessity of undeceiving the world? Would a man, who has an ill title to an estate, but yet is in possession of it, would he bring it out of his own accord to be tried at Westminster? We who write, if we want the talents, yet have the excuse that we do it for a poor subsistence; but what can be urged in their defence who, not having the vocation of poverty to scribble, out of mere wantonness take pains to make themselves ridiculous? Horace was certainly in the right where he said, 'That no man is satisfied with his own condition.' A poet is not pleased, because he is not rich; and the rich are discontented because the poets will not admit them of their number."—BOSWELL.

Johnson had called twice on the Bishop of Killaloe before his lordship set out for Ireland, having missed him the first time. He said, "It would have hung heavy on my heart if I had not seen him. No man ever paid more attention to another than he has done to me;[1] and I have neglected him, not wilfully, but from being otherwise occupied. Always, Sir, set a high value on spontaneous kindness. He whose inclination prompts him to cultivate your friendship of his own accord, will love you more than one whom you have been at pains to attach to you."

Johnson told me that he was once much pleased to find that a carpenter, who lived near him, was very ready to show him some things in his business which he wished to see: "It was paying," said he, "respect to literature."

I asked him, if he was not dissatisfied with having so small a share of wealth, and none of those distinctions in the state which are the objects of ambition. He had only a pension of three hundred a year. Why was he not in such circumstances as to keep his coach? Why had he not some considerable office? JOHNSON: "Sir, I have never complained of the world; nor do I think that I have reason to complain. It is rather to be wondered at that I have so much. My pension is more out of the usual course of things than any instance that I have known. Here, Sir, was a man avowedly no friend to Government at the time, who got a pension without asking for it. I never courted the great: they sent for me; but I think they now give me up. They are satisfied: they have seen enough of me." Upon my observing that I could not believe this, for they must certainly be highly pleased by his conversation; conscious of his own superiority, he answered, "No, Sir; great lords and great ladies don't love to have their mouths stopped." This was very expressive of the effect which the

---

[1] This gave me very great pleasure; for there had been once a pretty smart altercation between Dr. Barnard and him, upon a question whether a man could improve himself after the age of 45; when Johnson, in a hasty humour, expressed himself in a manner not quite civil. Dr. Barnard made it the subject of a copy of pleasant verses, in which he supposed himself to learn different perfections from different men. They concluded with delicate irony:—

> "Johnson shall teach me how to place
> In fairest light each borrow'd grace;
> From him I'll learn to write,—
> Copy his clear familiar style,
> And, by the roughness of his file,
> Grow, like *himself, polite* !"

I know not whether Johnson ever saw the poem, but I had occasion to find that as Dr. Barnard and he knew each other better, their mutual regard increased.—BOSWELL.

force of his understanding and brilliancy of his fancy could not but produce; and, to be sure, they must have found themselves strangely diminished in his company. When I warmly declared how happy I was at all times to hear him;—"Yes, Sir," said he; "but if you were Lord Chancellor, it would not be so; you would then consider your own dignity."

There was much truth and knowledge of human nature in this remark. But certainly one should think, that in whatever elevated state of life a man who *knew* the value of the conversation of Johnson might be placed, though he might prudently avoid a situation in which he might appear lessened by comparison, yet he would frequently gratify himself in private with the participation of the rich intellectual entertainment which Johnson could furnish. Strange, however, is it, to consider how few of the great sought his society; so that if one were disposed to take occasion for satire on that account, very conspicuous objects present themselves. His noble friend, Lord Elibank, well observed, that if a great man procured an interview with Johnson, and did not wish to see him more, it showed a mere idle curiosity, and a wretched want of relish for extraordinary powers of mind. Mrs. Thrale justly and wittily accounted for such conduct by saying, that Johnson's conversation was by much too strong for a person accustomed to obsequiousness and flattery; it was *mustard in a young child's mouth !*

One day, when I told him that I was a zealous Tory, but not enough "according to knowledge," and should be obliged to him for "a reason," he was so candid, and expressed himself so well, that I begged of him to repeat what he had said, and I wrote down as follows:—

"OF TORY AND WHIG.

"A wise Tory and a wise Whig, I believe, will agree. Their principles are the same, though their modes of thinking are different. A high Tory makes government unintelligible: it is lost in the clouds. A violent Whig makes it impracticable: he is for allowing so much liberty to every man, that there is not power enough to govern any man. The prejudice of the Tory is for establishment; the prejudice of the Whig is for innovation. A Tory does not wish to give more real power to Government, but that Government should have more reverence. Then they differ as to the Church. The Tory is not for giving more legal power to the Clergy, but wishes they should have a considerable influence, founded on the opinion of mankind: the Whig is for limiting and watching them with a narrow jealousy."

"TO MR. PERKINS.

"SIR,   June 2, 1781.

"However often I have seen you, I have hitherto forgotten the
note, but I have now sent it; with my good wishes for the prosperity
of you and your partner,[1] of whom, from our short conversation,
I could not judge otherwise than favourably.

"I am, Sir, your most humble servant,

"SAM. JOHNSON."

On Saturday, June 2, I set out for Scotland, and had
promised to pay a visit in my way, as I sometimes did, at
Southill, in Bedfordshire, at the hospitable mansion of
Squire Dilly, the elder brother of my worthy friends, the
booksellers, in the Poultry. Dr. Johnson agreed to be of
the party this year, with Mr. Charles Dilly and me, and to
go and see Lord Bute's seat at Luton Hoe. He talked
little to us in the carriage, being chiefly occupied in reading
Dr. Watson's[2] second volume of "Chemical Essays,"
which he liked very well, and his own "Prince of Abyssinia," on which he seemed to be intensely fixed; having
told us that he had not looked at it since it was first published. I happened to take it out of my pocket this day,
and he seized upon it with avidity. He pointed out to me
the following remarkable passage: "By what means,"
said the prince, "are the Europeans thus powerful; or why,
since they can so easily visit Asia and Africa for trade or
conquest, cannot the Asiatics and Africans invade their
coasts, plant colonies[3] in their ports, and give laws to
their natural princes? The same wind that carried them
back would bring us thither." "They are more powerful,
Sir, than we," answered Imlac, "because they are wiser.
Knowledge will always predominate over ignorance, as
man governs the other animals. But why their knowledge
is more than ours, I know not what reason can be given,
but the unsearchable will of the Supreme Being." He
said, "This, Sir, no man can explain otherwise."

[1] Mr. Barclay, a descendant of Robert Barclay, of Ury, the celebrated
apologist of the people called Quakers, and remarkable for maintaining
the principles of his venerable progenitor, with as much of the elegance
of modern manners as is consistent with primitive simplicity.—BOSWELL.

[2] Now Bishop of Llandaff, one of the poorest bishoprics in this kingdom.
His lordship has written with much zeal to show the propriety of
equalising the revenues of bishops. He has informed us that he has
burnt all his chemical papers. The friends of our excellent constitution,
now assailed on every side by innovators and levellers, would have less
regretted the suppression of some of his lordship's other writings.—
BOSWELL.

[3] The Phœnicians and Carthaginians did plant colonies in Europe.—
KEARNEY.

We stopped at Welwyn, where I wished much to see, in company with Johnson, the residence of the author of "Night Thoughts," which was then possessed by his son, Mr. Young. Here some address was requisite, for I was not acquainted with Mr. Young, and had I proposed to Dr. Johnson that we should send to him, he would have checked my wish, and perhaps been offended. I therefore concerted with Mr. Dilly, that I should steal away from Dr. Johnson and him, and try what reception I could procure from Mr. Young; if unfavourable, nothing was to be said; but if agreeable, I should return and notify it to them. I hastened to Mr. Young's, found he was at home, sent in word that a gentleman desired to wait upon him, and was shown into a parlour, where he and a young lady, his daughter, were sitting. He appeared to be a plain, civil, country gentleman; and when I begged pardon for presuming to trouble him, but that I wished much to see his place, if he would give me leave; he behaved very courteously, and answered, "By all means, Sir; we are just going to drink tea; will you sit down?" I thanked him, but said that Dr. Johnson had come with me from London, and I must return to the inn to drink tea with him; that my name was Boswell; I had travelled with him in the Hebrides. "Sir," said he, "I should think it a great honour to see Dr. Johnson here. Will you allow me to send for him?" Availing myself of this opening, I said that "I would go myself and bring him, when he had drunk tea; he knew nothing of my calling here." Having been thus successful, I hastened back to the inn, and informed Dr. Johnson that "Mr. Young, son of Dr. Young, the author of 'Night Thoughts,' whom I had just left, desired to have the honour of seeing him at the house where his father lived." Dr. Johnson luckily made no inquiry how this invitation had arisen, but agreed to go; and when we entered Mr. Young's parlour he addressed him with a very polite bow, "Sir, I had a curiosity to come and see this place. I had the honour to know that great man, your father." We went into the garden, where we found a gravel walk, on each side of which was a row of trees, planted by Dr. Young, which formed a handsome Gothic arch; Dr. Johnson called it a fine grove. I beheld it with reverence.

We sat some time in the summer-house, on the outside wall of which was inscribed, "*Ambulantes in horto audiebant vocem Dei ;*" and, in reference to a brook by which it is situated, "*Vivendi rectè qui prorogat horam,*" &c. I said to Mr. Young, that I had been told his father was cheerful.

"Sir," said he, "he was too well-bred a man not to be cheerful in company; but he was gloomy when alone. He never was cheerful after my mother's death, and he had met with many disappointments." Dr. Johnson observed to me afterward, "That this was no favourable account of Dr. Young; for it is not becoming in a man to have so little acquiescence in the ways of Providence, as to be gloomy because he has not obtained as much preferment as he expected; nor to continue gloomy for the loss of his wife. Grief has its time." The last part of this censure was theoretically made. Practically, we know that grief for the loss of a wife may be continued very long, in proportion as affection has been sincere. No man knew this better than Dr. Johnson.

We went into the church, and looked at the monument erected by Mr. Young to his father. Mr. Young mentioned an anecdote, that his father had received several thousand pounds of subscription-money for his "Universal Passion," but had lost it in the South-sea.[1] Dr. Johnson thought this must be a mistake, for he had never seen a subscription-book.

Upon the road we talked of the uncertainty of profit with which authors and booksellers engage in the publication of literary works. JOHNSON: "My judgment, I have found, is no certain rule as to the sale of a book." BOSWELL: "Pray, Sir, have you been much plagued with authors sending you their works to revise?" JOHNSON: "No, Sir; I have been thought a sour surly fellow." BOSWELL: "Very lucky for you, Sir, in that respect." I must, however, observe, that notwithstanding what he now said, which he no doubt imagined at the time to be the fact, there was, perhaps, no man who more frequently yielded to the solicitations even of very obscure authors, to read their manuscripts, or more liberally assisted them with advice and correction.

He found himself very happy at Squire Dilly's, where there is always abundance of excellent fare, and a hearty welcome.

On Sunday, June 3, we all went to Southill church, which is very near to Mr. Dilly's house. It being the first Sunday of the month, the holy sacrament was administered, and I stayed to partake of it. When I came afterwards into Dr. Johnson's room, he said, "You did right

---

[1] This assertion is disproved by a comparison of dates. The first four satires of Young were published in 1725. The South-sea scheme (which appears to be meant), was in 1720.—MALONE.

to stay and receive the communion; I had not thought of it." This seemed to imply that he did not choose to approach the altar without a previous preparation, as to which good men entertain different opinions, some holding that it is irreverent to partake of that ordinance without considerable premeditation; others, that whoever is a sincere Christian, and in a proper frame of mind to discharge any other ritual duty of our religion, may, without scruple, discharge this most solemn one. A middle notion I believe to be the just one, which is, that communicants need not think a long train of preparatory forms indispensably necessary; but neither should they rashly and lightly venture upon so awful and mysterious an institution. Christians must judge each for himself, what degree of retirement and self-examination is necessary upon each occasion.

Being in a frame of mind which I hope, for the felicity of human nature, many experience, in fine weather, at the country-house of a friend, consoled and elevated by pious exercises, I expressed myself with an unrestrained fervour to my "Guide, Philosopher, and Friend:" "My dear Sir, I would fain be a good man; and I am very good now. I fear God, and honour the King; I wish to do no ill, and to be benevolent to all mankind." He looked at me with a benignant indulgence; but took occasion to give me wise and salutary caution. "Do not, Sir, accustom yourself to trust to *impressions*. There is a middle state of mind between conviction and hypocrisy. of which many are conscious. By trusting to impressions, a man may gradually come to yield to them, and at length be subject to them, so as not to be a free agent, or, what is the same thing in effect, to *suppose* that he is not a free agent. A man who is in that state should not be suffered to live; if he declares he cannot help acting in a particular way, and is irresistibly impelled, there can be no confidence in him, no more than in a tiger. But, Sir, no man believes himself to be impelled irresistibly; we know that he who says he believes it, lies. Favourable impressions at particular moments, as to the state of our souls, may be deceitful and dangerous. In general, no man can be sure of his acceptance with God; some, indeed, may have had it revealed to them. St. Paul, who wrought miracles, may have had a miracle wrought on himself, and may have obtained supernatural assurance of pardon, and mercy, and beatitude; yet St. Paul, though he expresses strong hope, also expresses fear, lest, having preached to others, he himself should be a cast-away."

The opinion of a learned Bishop of our acquaintance, as to there being merit in religious faith, being mentioned; —JOHNSON: "Why, yes, Sir, the most licentious man, were hell open before him, would not take the most beautiful strumpet to his arms. We must, as the Apostle says, live by faith, not by sight."

I talked to him of original sin,[1] in consequence of the fall of man, and of the atonement made by our SAVIOUR. After some conversation, which he desired me to remember, he, at my request, dictated to me as follows:—

"With respect to original sin, the inquiry is not necessary; for whatever is the cause of human corruption, men are evidently and confessedly so corrupt, that all the laws of heaven and earth are insufficient to restrain them from crimes.

"Whatever difficulty there may be in the conception of vicarious punishments, it is an opinion which has had possession of mankind in all ages. There is no nation that has not used the practice of sacrifices. Whoever, therefore, denies the propriety of vicarious punishments, holds an opinion which the sentiments and practice of mankind have contradicted, from the beginning of the world. The great sacrifice for the sins of mankind was offered at the death of the Messiah, who is called in Scripture, 'The Lamb of God, that taketh away the sins of the world.' To judge of the reasonableness of the scheme of redemption, it must be considered as necessary to the government of the universe, that God should make known his perpetual and irreconcileable detestation of moral evil. He might indeed punish, and punish only the offenders; but as the end of punishment is not revenge of crimes, but propagation of virtue, it was more becoming the Divine clemency to find another manner of proceeding, less destructive to man, and at least equally powerful to promote goodness. The end of punishment is to reclaim and warn. *That* punishment will both reclaim and warn, which shows evidently such abhorrence of sin in God, as may deter us from it, or strike us with dread of vengeance when we have committed it. This is effected by vicarious punishment. Nothing could more testify the opposition between the nature of God and moral evil, or more amply display his justice, to men and angels, to all orders and successions of beings, than that it was necessary for the highest and purest nature, even for Divinity itself, to pacify the demands of

[1] Dr. Ogden, in his second sermon "On the Articles of the Christian Faith," with admirable acuteness thus addresses the opposers of that doctrine, which accounts for the confusion, sin, and misery, which we find in this life: "It would be severe in God, you think, to *degrade* us to such a sad state as this, for the offence of our first parents: but you can allow him to *place* us in it without any inducement. Are our calamities lessened for not being ascribed to Adam? If your condition be unhappy, is it not still unhappy, whatever was the occasion? with the aggravation of this reflection, that if it was as good as it was at first designed, there seems to be somewhat the less reason to look for its amendment."— BOSWELL.

vengeance by a painful death; of which the natural effect will be, that when justice is appeased, there is a proper place for the exercise of mercy, and that such propitiation shall supply, in some degree, the imperfections of our obedience, and the inefficacy of our repentance; for obedience and repentance, such as we can perform, are still necessary. Our Saviour has told us that he did not come to destroy the law, but to fulfil: to fulfil the typical law by the performance of what those types had foreshown; and the moral law, by precepts of greater purity and higher exaltation."

Here he said, " GOD bless you with it." I acknowledged myself much obliged to him; but I begged that he would go on as to the propitiation being the chief object of our most holy faith. He then dictated this one other paragraph:

"The peculiar doctrine of Christianity is that of an universal sacrifice, and perpetual propitiation. Other prophets only proclaimed the will and the threatenings of God. Christ satisfied his justice."

The Reverend Mr. Palmer,[1] Fellow of Queen's College, Cambridge, dined with us. He expressed a wish that a better provision were made for parish clerks. JOHNSON: " Yes, Sir, a parish-clerk should be a man who is able to make a will, or write a letter for any body in the parish."

I mentioned Lord Monboddo's notion[2] that the ancient Egyptians, with all their learning and all their arts, were not only black, but woolly-haired. Mr. Palmer asked how did it appear upon examining the mummies? Dr. Johnson approved of this test.

---

[1] This unfortunate person, whose full name was Thomas Fysche Palmer, afterwards went to Dundee, in Scotland, where he officiated as minister to a congregation of the sect who call themselves *Unitarians,* from a notion that they distinctively worship ONE GOD, because they *deny* the mysterious doctrine of the TRINITY. They do not advert that the great body of the Christian Church in maintaining that mystery maintain also the *Unity* of the GODHEAD: the "TRINITY in UNITY!—three persons and one GOD." The Church humbly adores the DIVINITY as exhibited in the holy scriptures. The Unitarian sect vainly presumes to comprehend and define the ALMIGHTY. Mr. Palmer having heated his mind with political speculations, became so much dissatisfied with our excellent Constitution, as to compose, publish, and circulate writings, which were found to be so seditious and dangerous, that, upon being found guilty by a Jury, the Court of Justiciary in Scotland sentenced him to transportation for fourteen years. A loud clamour against this sentence was made by some members of both Houses of Parliament; but both Houses approved of it by a great majority; and he was conveyed to the settlement for convicts in New South Wales.—BOSWELL.

Mr. T. F. Palmer was of Queen's College, in Cambridge, where he took the degree of Master of Arts in 1772, and that of S. T. B. in 1781. He died on his return from Botany Bay, in the year 1803.—MALONE.

[2] Taken from Herodotus.—BOSWELL.

Although upon most occasions I never heard a more strenuous advocate for the advantages of wealth than Dr. Johnson, he this day, I know not from what caprice, took the other side. "I have not observed," said he, "that men of very large fortunes enjoy anything extraordinary that makes happiness. What has the Duke of Bedford? What has the Duke of Devonshire? The only great instance that I have ever known of the enjoyment of wealth was, that of Jamaica Dawkins, who going to visit Palmyra, and hearing that the way was infested by robbers, hired a troop of Turkish horse to guard him."

Dr. Gibbons, the dissenting minister, being mentioned, he said, "I took to Dr. Gibbons." And addressing himself to Mr. Charles Dilly, added, "I shall be glad to see him. Tell him, if he'll call on me, and dawdle over a dish of tea in an afternoon, I shall take it kind."

The Rev. Mr. Smith, Vicar of Southill, a very respectable man, with a very agreeable family, sent an invitation to us to drink tea. I remarked Dr. Johnson's very respectful politeness. Though always fond of changing the scene, he said, "We must have Mr. Dilly's leave. We cannot go from your house, Sir, without your permission." We all went, and were well satisfied with our visit. I however remember nothing particular, except a nice distinction which Dr. Johnson made with respect to the power of memory, maintaining that forgetfulness was a man's own fault. "To remember and to recollect," said he, "are different things. A man has not the power to recollect what is not in his mind; but when a thing is in his mind he may remember it."

The remark was occasioned by my leaning back on a chair, which a little before I had perceived to be broken, and pleading forgetfulness as an excuse. "Sir," said he, "its being broken was certainly in your mind."

When I observed that a housebreaker was in general very timorous;—JOHNSON: "No wonder, Sir; he is afraid of being shot getting *into* a house, or hanged when he has got *out* of it."

He told us, that he had in one day written six sheets of a translation from the French; adding, "I should be glad to see it now. I wish that I had copies of all the pamphlets written against me, as it is said Pope had. Had I known that I should make so much noise in the world, I should have been at pains to collect them. I believe there is hardly a day in which there is not something about me in the newspapers."

On Monday, June 4, we all went to Luton Hoe, to see Lord Bute's magnificent seat,[1] for which I had obtained a ticket. As we entered the park, I talked in a high style of my old friendship with Lord Mountstuart, and said, "I shall probably be much at this place." The sage, aware of human vicissitudes, gently checked me: "Don't you be too sure of that." He made two or three peculiar observations; as when shown the botanical garden, "is not *every* garden a botanical garden?" When told that there was a shubbery to the extent of several miles: "That is making a very foolish use of the ground; a little of it is very well." When it was proposed that we should walk on the pleasure-ground; "Don't let us fatigue ourselves. Why should we walk there? Here's a fine tree, let's get to the top of it." But, upon the whole, he was very much pleased. He said, "This is one of the places I do not regret having come to see. It is a very stately place, indeed; in the house magnificence is not sacrificed to convenience, nor convenience to magnificence. The library is very splendid; the dignity of the rooms is very great; and the quantity of pictures is beyond expectation—beyond hope."

It happened, without any previous concert, that we visited the seat of Lord Bute upon the King's birthday; we dined and drank his Majesty's health at an inn, in the village of Luton.

In the evening I put him in mind of his promise to favour me with a copy of his celebrated letter to the Earl of Chesterfield, and he was at last pleased to comply with this earnest request, by dictating it to me from his memory; for he believed that he himself had no copy. There was an animated glow in his countenance while he thus recalled his high-minded indignation.

He laughed heartily at a ludicrous action in the Court of Session, in which I was counsel. The Society of *Procurators*, or Attorneys, entitled to practise in the inferior courts at Edinburgh, had obtained a royal charter, in which they had taken care to have their ancient designation of *Procurators* changed into that of *Solicitors*, from a notion, as they supposed, that it was more *genteel* : and this new title they displayed by a public advertisement for a *General Meeting* at their Hall.

It has been said, that the Scottish nation is not distinguished for humour; and indeed, what happened on this occasion may in some degree justify the remark; for although this society had contrived to make themselves

[1] Luton Hoe was entirely destroyed by fire in November, 1843.—Ed.

a very prominent object for the ridicule of such as might stoop to it, the only joke to which it gave rise was the following paragraph, sent to the newspaper called *The Caledonian Mercury*.

"A correspondent informs us that the Worshipful Society of Chaldeans, Cadies, or Running-Stationers of this city, are resolved, in imitation, and encouraged by the singular success of their brethren, of an *equally respectable* Society, to apply for a Charter of their Privileges, particularly of the sole privilege of PROCURING, in the most extensive sense of the word, exclusive of chairmen, porters, penny-post men, and other *inferior* ranks, their brethren, the R—y—l S—l—rs, *alias* P—c—rs, *before the* INFERIOR courts of this city, always excepted.

"Should the Worshipful Society be successful, they are farther resolved not to be *puffed up* thereby, but to demean themselves with more equanimity and decency than their *R-y-l, learned*, and *very modest* brethren above mentioned have done, upon their late dignification and exaltation."

A majority of the members of the society prosecuted Mr. Robertson, the publisher of the paper, for damages; and the first judgment of the whole court very wisely dismissed the action: *Solventur risu tabulæ, tu missus abibis*. But a new trial or review was granted upon a petition, according to the forms in Scotland. This petition I was engaged to answer, and Dr. Johnson, with great alacrity, furnished me this evening with what follows:—

"All injury is either of the person, the fortune, or the fame. Now it is a certain thing, it is proverbially known that *a jest breaks no bones*. They never have gained half-a-crown less in the whole profession since this mischievous paragraph has appeared; and as to their reputation, what is their reputation but an instrument of getting money? If, therefore, they have lost no money, the question upon reputation may be answered by a very old position,— *De minimis non curat Prætor*.

"Whether there was, or was not, an *animus injuriandi*, is not worth inquiring, if no *injuria* can be proved. But the truth is, there was no *animus injuriandi*. It was only an *animus irritandi*,[1] which happening to be exercised upon a *genus irritabile*, produced unexpected violence of resentment. Their irritability arose only from an opinion of their own importance, and their delight in their new exaltation. What might have been borne by a *Procurator* could not be borne by a *Solicitor*. Your lordships well know that *honores mutant mores*. Titles and dignities play strongly on the fancy. As a madman is apt to think himself grown suddenly great, so he that grows suddenly great is apt to borrow a little from the

---

[1] Mr. Robertson altered this word to *Jocandi*, he having found in Blackstone that to *irritate* is actionable.—BOSWELL.

madman.   To co-operate with their resentment would be to promote their phrenzy; nor is it possible to guess to what they might proceed, if to the new title of Solicitor should be added the elation of victory and triumph.

"We consider your lordships as the protectors of our rights, and the guardians of our virtues; but believe it not included in your high office, that you should flatter our vices, or solace our vanity; and as vanity only dictates this prosecution, it is humbly hoped your lordships will dismiss it.

"If every attempt, however light or ludicrous, to lessen another's reputation, is to be punished by a judicial sentence, what punishment can be sufficiently severe for him who attempts to diminish the reputation of the Supreme Court of Justice, by reclaiming upon a cause already determined, without any change in the state of the question?   Does it not imply hopes that the Judges will change their opinion?   Is not uncertainty and inconstancy in the highest degree disreputable to a Court?   Does it not suppose that the former judgment was temerarious or negligent?   Does it not lessen the confidence of the public?   Will it not be said, that *jus est aut in-cognitum, aut vagum?* and will not the consequence be drawn, *misera est servitus?*   Will not the rules of action be obscure?   Will not he who knows himself wrong to-day, hope that the Courts of Justice will think him right to-morrow?   Surely, my lords, these are attempts of dangerous tendency, which the solicitors, as men versed in the law, should have foreseen and avoided.   It was natural for an ignorant printer to appeal from the Lord Ordinary; but from lawyers, the descendants of lawyers, who have practised for three hundred years, and have now raised themselves to a higher de-nomination, it might be expected, that they should know the reverence due to a judicial determination; and having been once dismissed, should sit down in silence."

I am ashamed to mention, that the court, by a plurality of voices, without having a single additional circumstance before them, reversed their own judgment, made a serious matter of this dull and foolish joke, and adjudged Mr. Robertson to pay to the society five pounds (sterling money) and costs of suit.   The decision will seem strange to English lawyers.

*Marrying a pretty Woman—Johnson's Charity to the Poor
—Mr. Bewley's Enthusiasm for Johnson—Sir J.
Sinclair—Mr. Hector—Death of Mr. Levett—Johnson's
Satisfaction at the Dissolution of the Ministry—General
Correspondence—Mr. Malone—Johnson's Despondency
—Dr. Lawrence—Johnson's Lamentations for the Loss
of Friends—Mrs. Careless—Passage from " The Beauties
of Johnson" — Evils of Poverty — Mr. Perkins —
Sanitary Rules—Reprinting of " The Lives of the Poets."*

ON Tuesday, June 5, Johnson was to return to London.
He was very pleasant at breakfast. I mentioned a friend
of mine having resolved never to marry a pretty woman.
JOHNSON: "Sir, it is a very foolish resolution to resolve
not to marry a pretty woman. Beauty is of itself very
estimable. No, Sir, I would prefer a pretty woman, unless
there are objections to her. A pretty woman may be
foolish; a pretty woman may be wicked; a pretty woman
may not like me. But there is no such danger in marrying
a pretty woman as is apprehended; she will not be perse-
cuted if she does not invite persecution. A pretty woman,
if she has a mind to be wicked, can find a readier way than
another; and that is all."

I accompanied him in Mr. Dilly's chaise to Shefford,
where, talking of Lord Bute's never going to Scotland, he
said, "As an Englishman, I should wish all the Scotch
gentlemen should be educated in England, and Scotland
would become a province; they would spend all their rents
in England." This is a subject of much consequence, and
much delicacy. The advantage of an English education
is unquestionably very great to Scotch gentlemen of
talents and ambition; and regular visits to Scotland, and
perhaps other means, might be effectually used to prevent
them from being totally estranged from their native
country, any more than a Cumberland or Northumberland
gentleman, who has been educated in the south of England.
I own, indeed, that it is no small misfortune for Scotch
gentlemen, who have neither talents nor ambition, to be

educated in England, where they may be perhaps distinguished only by a nickname, lavish their fortune in giving expensive entertainments to those who laugh at them, and saunter about as mere idle insignificant hangers-on even upon the foolish great; when, if they had been judiciously brought up at home, they might have been comfortable and creditable members of society.

At Shefford I had another affectionate parting from my revered friend, who was taken up by the Bedford coach, and carried to the metropolis. I went with Messrs. Dilly, to see some friends at Bedford; dined with the officers of the militia of the county, and next day proceeded on my journey.

"TO BENNET LANGTON, ESQ.

"DEAR SIR,   Bolt-court, June 16, 1781.
"How welcome your account of yourself and your invitation to your new house was to me I need not tell you, who consider our friendship not only as formed by choice, but as matured by time. We have been now long enough acquainted to have many images in common, and therefore to have a source of conversation which neither the learning nor the wit of a new companion can supply.

"My Lives are now published; and if you will tell me whither I shall send them, that they may come to you, I will take care that you shall not be without them.

"You will, perhaps, be glad to hear that Mrs. Thrale is disencumbered of her brewhouse; and that it seemed to the purchaser so far from an evil, that he was content to give for it a hundred and thirty-five thousand pounds. Is the nation ruined?

"Please to make my respectful compliments to Lady Rothes, and keep me in the memory of all the little dear family, particularly Mrs. Jane.   I am, Sir,
                    "Your affectionate humble servant,
                                        "SAM. JOHNSON."

Johnson's charity to the poor was uniform and extensive, both from inclination and principle. He not only bestowed liberally out of his own purse, but, what is more difficult as well as rare, would beg from others, when he had proper objects in view. This he did judiciously as well as humanely. Mr. Philip Metcalfe tells me, that when he has asked him for some money for persons in distress, and Mr. Metcalfe has offered what Johnson thought too much, he insisted on taking less, saying, "No, no, Sir; we must not *pamper* them."

I am indebted to Mr. Malone, one of Sir Joshua Reynolds's executors, for the following note, which was found among his papers after his death, and which, we may presume, his unaffected modesty prevented him from communicating to me with the other letters from Dr. Johnson with which he was pleased to furnish me. However slight in itself, as it does honour to that illustrious painter, and most amiable man, I am happy to introduce it.

"TO SIR JOSHUA REYNOLDS.

"DEAR SIR,   June 23, 1781.

"It was not before yesterday that I received your splendid benefaction. To a hand so liberal in distributing I hope nobody will envy the power of acquiring.

"I am, dear Sir, your obliged and most humble servant,

"SAM. JOHNSON."

"TO THOMAS ASTLE, ESQ.

"SIR,   July 17, 1781.

"I am ashamed that you have been forced to call so often for your books; but it has been by no fault on either side. They have never been out of my hands, nor have I ever been at home without seeing you; for to see a man so skilful in the antiquities of my country, is an opportunity of improvement not willingly to be missed.

"Your notes on Alfred[1] appear to me very judicious and accurate; but they are too few. Many things familiar to you are unknown to me, and to most others; and you must not think too favourably of your readers. By supposing them knowing, you will leave them ignorant. Measure of land, and value of money, it is of great importance to state with care. Had the Saxons any gold coin?

"I have much curiosity after the manners and transactions of the middle ages, but have wanted either diligence or opportunity, or both. You, Sir, have great opportunities, and I wish you both diligence and success.

"I am, Sir, &c.,

"SAM. JOHNSON."

The following curious anecdote I insert in Dr. Burney's own words:

"Dr. Burney related to Dr. Johnson the partiality which his writings had excited in a friend of Dr. Burney's, the late Mr. Bewley, well known in Norfolk by the name of the *Philosopher of Massingham:* who, from the Ramblers and Plan of his Dictionary, and long before the author's fame was established by the Dictionary itself, or any other work, had conceived such a reverence for him, that he earnestly begged Dr. Burney to give him the cover of his

---

[1] The will of King Alfred, alluded to in this letter, from the original Saxon, in the library of Mr. Astle, has been printed at the expense of the University of Oxford.—BOSWELL.

first letter he had received from him, as a relic of so estimable a writer. This was in 1755. In 1760, when Dr. Burney visited Dr. Johnson at the Temple in London, where he had then chambers, he happened to arrive there before he was up; and being shown into the room where he was to breakfast, finding himself alone, he examined the contents of the apartment, to try whether he could undiscovered steal anything to send to his friend Bewley, as another relic of the admirable Dr. Johnson. But finding nothing better to his purpose, he cut some bristles off his hearth-broom, and enclosed them in a letter to his country enthusiast, who received them with due reverence.   The doctor was so sensible of the honour done him by a man of genius and science, to whom he was an utter stranger, that he said to Dr. Burney, 'Sir, there is no man possessed of the smallest portion of modesty, but must be flattered with the admiration of such a man. I will give him a set of my Lives, if he will do me the honour to accept of them.' In this he kept his word; and Dr. Burney had not only the pleasure of gratifying his friend with a present more worthy of his acceptance than the segment from the hearth-broom, but soon after introducing him to Dr. Johnson himself in Bolt-court, with whom he had the satisfaction of conversing a considerable time, not a fortnight before his death; which happened in St. Martin's-street, during his visit to Dr. Burney, in the house where the great Sir Isaac Newton had lived and died before."

In one of his little memorandum-books is the following minute:—

"August 9, 3 P.M. ætat 72, in the summer-house at Streatham.

"After innumerable resolutions formed and neglected, I have retired hither, to plan a life of great diligence, in hope that I may yet be useful, and be daily better prepared to appear before my Creator and my Judge, from whose infinite mercy I humbly call for assistance and support.

"My purpose is,

"To pass eight hours every day in some serious employment.

"Having prayed, I purpose to employ the next six weeks upon the Italian language, for my settled study."

How venerably pious does he appear in these moments of solitude, and how spirited are his resolutions for the improvement of his mind, even in elegant literature, at a very advanced period of life, and when afflicted with many complaints.

In autumn he went to Oxford, Birmingham, Lichfield, and Ashbourne, for which very good reasons might be given in the conjectural yet positive manner of writers, who are proud to account for every event which they relate. He himself, however, says, "The motives of my journey I hardly know; I omitted it last year, and am not willing to miss it again."[1] But some good considerations arise, amongst which is the kindly recollection of Mr. Hector, surgeon, of Birmingham. "Hector is likewise an old friend, the only companion of my childhood that passed through the school with me. We have always loved one another; perhaps we may be made better by some serious conversation, of which, however, I have no distinct hope."

He says too, "At Lichfield, my native place, I hope to show a good example by frequent attendance on public worship."

My correspondence with him during the rest of this year was, I know not why, very scanty, and all on my side. I wrote him one letter to introduce Mr. Sinclair (now Sir John) the member for Caithness, to his acquaintance; and informed him in another, that my wife had again been affected with alarming symptoms of illness.

In 1782, his complaints increased, and the history of his life this year is little more than a mournful recital of the variations of his illness, in the midst of which, however, it will appear from his letters, that the powers of his mind were in no degree impaired.

"TO JAMES BOSWELL, ESQ.

"DEAR SIR,   January 5, 1782.
"I sit down to answer your letter on the same day in which I received it, and am pleased that my first letter of the year is to you. No man ought to be at ease while he knows himself in the wrong: and I have not satisfied myself with my long silence. The letter relating to Mr. Sinclair, however, was, I believe, never brought.

"My health has been tottering this last year: and I can give no very laudable account of my time. I am always hoping to do better than I have ever hitherto done.

"My journey to Ashbourne and Staffordshire was not pleasant; for what enjoyment has a sick man visiting the sick. Shall we ever have another frolic like our journey to the Hebrides?

"I hope that dear Mrs. Boswell will surmount her complaints. In losing her you will lose your anchor, and be tost, without stability, by the waves of life.[2] I wish both her and you very many years, and very happy.

------

[1] "Prayers and Meditations," p. 201.
[2] The truth of this has been proved by sad experience.—BOSWELL. Mrs. Boswell died June 4, 1789.—MALONE.

"For some months past I have been so withdrawn from the world, that I can send you nothing particular. All your friends, however, are well, and will be glad of your return to London.

"I am, dear Sir, yours most affectionately,
            "SAM. JOHNSON."

At a time when he was less able than he had once been to sustain a shock, he was suddenly deprived of Mr. Levett,[1] which event he thus communicated to Dr. Lawrence.

"SIR,   January 17, 1782.

"Our old friend Mr. Levett, who was last night eminently cheerful, died this morning. The man who lay in the same room, hearing an uncommon noise, got up and tried to make him speak but without effect. He then called Mr. Holder, the apothecary, who, though when he came he thought him dead, opened a vein, but could draw no blood. So has ended the long life of a very useful and very blameless man.

"I am, Sir, your most humble servant,
            "SAM. JOHNSON."

In one of his memorandum-books, in my possession, is the following entry:—"January 20, Sunday. Robert Levett was buried in the churchyard of Bridewell, between one and two in the afternoon. He died on Thursday 17, about seven in the morning, by an instantaneous death. He was an old and faithful friend; I have known him from about 46. *Commendavi.* May God have mercy on him. May he have mercy on me."

Such was Johnson's affectionate regard for Levett, that he honoured his memory with the following pathetic verses:—

"Condemn'd to Hope's delusive mine,
    As on we toil from day to day,
By sudden blast or slow decline
    Our social comforts drop away.

Well try'd through many a varying year,
    See LEVETT to the grave descend;
Officious, innocent, sincere,
    Of every friendless name the friend.

Yet still he fills affection's eye,
    Obscurely wise, and coarsely kind,
Nor, letter'd arrogance,[2] deny
    Thy praise to merit unrefined.

---

[1] See an account of him in "The Gentleman's Magazine," Feb. 1785.—BOSWELL.

[2] In both editions of Sir John Hawkins's Life of Dr. Johnson, "lettered *Ignorance*" is printed.—BOSWELL.

When fainting nature call'd for aid,
   And hov'ring Death prepared the blow,
His vigorous remedy display'd
   The power of art without the show.

In Misery's darkest caverns known,
   His ready help was ever nigh,
Where hopeless Anguish pour'd his groan,
   And lonely Want retired to die.[1]

No summons mock'd by chill delay.
   No petty gains disdain'd by pride;
The modest wants of every day
   The toil of every day supplied.

His virtues walk'd their narrow round,
   Nor made a pause, nor left a void;
And sure the eternal Master found
   His single talent well employ'd.

The busy day, the peaceful night,
   Unfelt, uncounted, glided by;
His frame was firm, his powers were bright,
   Though now his eightieth year was nigh.

Then, with no throbs of fiery pain,
   No cold gradations of decay,
Death broke at once the vital chain,
   And freed his soul the nearest way."

In one of Johnson's registers of this year, there occurs the following curious passage: "Jan. 20. The ministry is dissolved. I prayed with Francis, and gave thanks."[2] It has been the subject of discussion, whether there are two distinct particulars mentioned here? Or that we are to understand the giving of thanks to be in consequence of the dissolution of the ministry? In support of the last of these conjectures may be urged his mean opinion of that ministry, which has frequently appeared in the course of this work; and it is strongly confirmed by what he said on the subject to Mr. Seward:—"I am glad the ministry is removed. Such a bunch of imbecility never disgraced a country. If they sent a messenger into the City to take up a printer, the messenger was taken up instead of the printer, and committed by the sitting alderman. If they sent one army to the relief of another, the first army was

---

[1] Johnson repeated this line to me thus:—
    "And Labour steals an hour to die."
But he afterwards altered it to the present reading.—BOSWELL.
[2] "Prayers and Meditations," p. 209.

defeated and taken before the second arrived. I will not say that what they did was always wrong; but it was always done at a wrong time."

"TO MRS. STRAHAN.

"Dear Madam,   February 4, 1782.

"Mrs. Williams showed me your kind letter. This little habitation is now but a melancholy place, clouded with the gloom of disease and death. Of the four inmates, one has been suddenly snatched away; two are oppressed by very afflictive and dangerous illness: and I tried yesterday to gain some relief by a third bleeding, from a disorder which has for some time distressed me, and I think myself to-day much better.

"I am glad, dear Madam, to hear that you are so far recovered as to go to Bath. Let me once more entreat you to stay till your health is not only obtained but confirmed. Your fortune is such as that no moderate expense deserves your care; and you have a husband, who, I believe, does not regard it. Stay, therefore, till you are quite well. I am, for my part, very much deserted; but complaint is useless. I hope God will bless you, and I desire you to form the same wish for me.

"I am, dear Madam,
"Your most humble servant,
"Sam. Johnson."

"TO EDMOND MALONE, ESQ.

"Sir,   Feb. 27, 1782.

"I have for many weeks been so much out of order, that I have gone out only in a coach to Mrs. Thrale's, where I can use all the freedom that sickness requires. Do not, therefore, take it amiss, that I am not with you and Dr. Farmer. I hope hereafter to see you often. I am Sir,
"Your most humble servant,
"Sam. Johnson."

TO THE SAME.

"Dear Sir,   March 2, 1782.

"I hope I grow better, and shall soon be able to enjoy the kindness of my friends. I think this wild adherence to Chatterton [1] more unaccountable than the obstinate defence of Ossian. In

[1] This Note was in answer to one which accompanied one of the earliest pamphlets on the subject of Chatterton's forgery, entitled "Cursory Observations on the Poems attributed to Thomas Rowley," &c. Mr. Thomas Warton's very able "Inquiry" appeared about three months afterwards; and Mr. Tyrwhitt's admirable "Vindication of his Appendix," in the summer of the same year, left the believers in his daring imposture nothing but "the resolution to say again what had been said before." Daring, however, as this fiction was, and wild as was the adherence to Chatterton, both were greatly exceeded in 1795 and the following year, by a still more audacious imposture, and the pertinacity of one of

Ossian there is a national pride, which may be forgiven, though it cannot be applauded. In Chatterton there is nothing but the resolution to say again what has once been said. I am, Sir,

" Your humble servant,

"SAM. JOHNSON."

These short letters show the regard which Dr. Johnson entertained for Mr. Malone, who the more he is known is the more highly valued. It is much to be regretted that Johnson was prevented from sharing the elegant hospitality of that gentleman's table, at which he would, in every respect, have been fully gratified. Mr. Malone, who has so ably succeeded him as an editor of Shakespeare, has, in his preface, done great and just honour to Johnson's memory.

"TO MRS. LUCY PORTER, IN LICHFIELD.

"DEAR MADAM,   London, March 2, 1782.

" I went away from Lichfield ill, and have had a troublesome time with my breath; for some weeks I have been disordered by a cold, of which I could not get the violence abated, till I had been let blood three times. I have not, however, been so bad but that I could have written, and am sorry that I neglected it.

"My dwelling is but melancholy; both Williams, and Desmoulins, and myself are very sickly: Frank is not well; and poor Levett died in his bed the other day, by a sudden stroke; I suppose not one minute passed between health and death; so uncertain are human things.

"Such is the appearance of the world about me; I hope your scenes are more cheerful. But whatever befalls us, though it is wise to be serious, it is useless and foolish, and perhaps sinful, to be gloomy. Let us, therefore, keep ourselves as easy as we can; though the loss of friends will be felt, and poor Levett had been a faithful adherent for thirty years.

"Forgive me, my dear love, the omission of writing; I hope to mend that and my other faults. Let me have your prayers.

"Make my compliments to Mrs. Cobb, and Miss Adey, and Mr. Pearson, and the whole company of my friends. I am, my dear, your most humble servant,

"SAM. JOHNSON."

TO THE SAME.

Bolt-court, Fleet-street,

March 19, 1782.

"DEAR MADAM,

" My last was but a dull letter, and I know not that this will be much more cheerful; I am, however, willing to write, because you are desirous to hear from me.

its adherents, who has immortalised his name by publishing a bulky volume, of which the direct and manifest object was, to prove the authenticity of certain papers attributed to Shakespeare, after the fabricator of the spurious trash had publicly acknowledged the imposture!
—MALONE.

"My disorder has now begun its ninth week, for it is not yet over. I was last Thursday blooded for the fourth time, and have since found myself much relieved, but I am very tender, and easily hurt; so that since we parted I have had but little comfort, but I hope that the spring will recover me, and that in the summer I shall see Lichfield again; for I will not delay my visit another year to the end of autumn.

"I have, by advertising, found poor Mr. Levett's brothers in Yorkshire, who will take the little he has left: it is but little, yet it will be welcome, for I believe they are of very low condition.

"To be sick, and see nothing but sickness and death, is but a gloomy state; but I hope better times, even in this world, will come, and whatever this world may withhold or give, we shall be happy in a better state. Pray for me, my dear Lucy.

"Make my compliments to Mrs. Cobb, and Miss Adey, and my old friend Hetty Bailey, and to all the Lichfield ladies. I am, dear Madam,

" Yours affectionately,
"SAM. JOHNSON."

On the day on which this letter was written, he thus feelingly mentions his respected friend and physician, Dr. Lawrence:—"Poor Lawrence has almost lost the sense of hearing; and I have lost the conversation of a learned, intelligent, and communicative companion, and a friend whom long familiarity has much endeared. Lawrence is one of the best men whom I have known. '*Nostrum omnium, miserere Deus.*'" [1]

It was Dr. Johnson's custom, when he wrote to Dr. Lawrence concerning his own health, to use the Latin language. I have been favoured by Miss Lawrence with one of these letters as a specimen:

"T. LAWRENCIO, Medico, S.

"Maiis Calendis, 1782.

"Novum frigus, nova tussis, nova spirandi difficultas, novam sanguinis missionem suadent, quam tamen te inconsulto nolim fieri. Ad te venire vix possum, nec est cur ad me venias. Licere vel non licere uno verbo dicendum est: cætera mihi et Holdero [2] reliqueris. Si per te licet, imperatur nuncio Holderum ad me deducere.

"Postquam tu discesseris, quo me vertam?" [3]

[1] "Prayers and Meditations," p. 207.

[2] Mr. Holder, in the Strand, Dr. Johnson's apothecary.—BOSWELL.

[3] Soon after the above letter, Dr. Lawrence left London, but not before the palsy had made so great a progress as to render him unable to write for himself. The following are extracts from letters addressed by Dr. Johnson to one of his daughters:—

"You will easily believe with what gladness I read that you had heard once again that voice to which we have all so often delighted to

"TO CAPTAIN LANGTON,[1] IN ROCHESTER.

Bolt-court, Fleet-street,

"DEAR SIR,   March 20, 1782.

" It is now long since we saw one another; and, whatever has been the reason, neither you have written to me, nor I to you. To let friendship die away by negligence and silence, is certainly not wise. It is voluntarily to throw away one of the greatest comforts of this weary pilgrimage, of which when it is, as it must be taken finally away, he that travels on alone, will wonder how his esteem could be so little. Do not forget me; you see that I do not forget you. It is pleasing, in the silence of solitude, to think that there is one at least, however distant, of whose benevolence there is little doubt, and whom there is yet hope of seeing again.

"Of my life, from the time we parted, the history is mournful. The spring of last year deprived me of Thrale, a man whose eye for fifteen years had scarcely been turned upon me but with respect or tenderness; for such another friend the general course of human things will not suffer man to hope. I passed the summer at Streatham, but there was no Thrale; and having idled away the summer with a weakly body and neglected mind, I made a journey to Staffordshire on the edge of winter. The season was dreary; I was sickly, and found the friends sickly whom I went to see. After a sorrowful sojourn, I returned to a habitation possessed for the present by two sick women, where my dear old friend, Mr. Levett, to whom, as he used to tell me, I owe your acquaintance, died a few weeks ago, suddenly in his bed. There passed not, I believe, a minute between health and death. At night, as at Mrs. Thrale's, I was musing in

---

attend. May you often hear it. If we had his mind, and his tongue, we could spare the rest.

"I am not vigorous, but much better than when dear Dr. Lawrence held my pulse the last time. Be so kind as to let me know, from one little interval to another, the state of his body. I am pleased that he remembers me, and hope that it never can be possible for me to forget him. July 22, 1782."

"I am much delighted even with the small advances which dear Dr. Lawrence makes towards recovery. If we could have again but his mind, and his tongue in his mind, and his right hand, we should not much lament the rest. I should not despair of helping the swelled hand by electricity, if it were frequently and diligently supplied.

"Let me know from time to time whatever happens; and I hope I need not tell you how much I am interested in every change. Aug. 26, 1782."

"Though the account with which you favoured me in your last letter could not give me the pleasure that I wished, yet I was glad to receive it; for my affection to my dear friend makes me desirous of knowing his state, whatever it be. I beg, therefore, that you continue to let me know, from time to time, all that you observe.

"Many fits of severe illness have, for about three months past, forced my kind physician often upon my mind. I am now better; and hope gratitude, as well as distress, can be a motive to remembrance. Bolt-court, Fleet-street, Feb. 4, 1783."—BOSWELL.

[1] Mr. Langton being at this time on duty at Rochester, he is addressed by his military title.—BOSWELL.

my chamber, I thought with uncommon earnestness, that however I might alter my code of life, or whithersoever I might remove, I would endeavour to retain Levett about me. In the morning my servant brought me word that Levett was called to another state, a state for which, I think, he was not unprepared, for he was very useful to the poor. How much soever I valued him, I now wish that I had valued him more.[1]

"I have myself been ill more than eight weeks of a disorder, from which, at the expense of about fifty ounces of blood, I hope I am now recovering.

"You, dear Sir, have, I hope, a more cheerful scene; you see George fond of his book, and the pretty misses airy and lively, with my own little Jenny equal to the best; and in whatever can contribute to your quiet or pleasure, you have Lady Rothes ready to concur. May whatever you enjoy of good be increased, and whatever you suffer of evil be diminished. I am, dear Sir,

"Your humble servant,

"SAM. JOHNSON."

"TO MR. HECTOR, IN BIRMINGHAM.[2]

"DEAR SIR,   London, March 21, 1782.

" I hope I do not very grossly flatter myself to imagine that you and dear Mrs. Careless [3] will be glad to hear some account of me. I performed the journey to London with very little inconvenience, and came safe to my habitation, where I found nothing but ill health, and of consequence, very little cheerfulness. I then went to visit a little way into the country, where I got a complaint by a cold which has hung eight weeks upon me, and from which I am, at the expense of fifty ounces of blood, not yet free. I am afraid I must once more owe my recovery to warm weather, which seems to make no advances towards us.

"Such is my health, which will, I hope, soon grow better. In other respects I have no reason to complain. I know not that I have written anything more generally commended than the Lives of the Poets; and have found the world willing enough to caress me, if my health had invited me to be in much company; but this season I have been almost wholly employed in nursing myself.

"When summer comes I hope to see you again, and will not put off my visit to the end of the year. I have lived so long in London, that I did not remember the difference of seasons.

---

[1] Johnson has here expressed a sentiment similar to that contained in one of Shenstone's stanzas, to which, in his life of that poet, he has given high praise:—
  "I prized every hour that went by,
    Beyond all that had pleased me before:
  But now they are gone, and I sigh,
    And I grieve that I prized them no more."—J. BOSWELL, JUN.

[2] A part of this letter having been torn off, I have, from the evident meaning, supplied a few words and half words at the ends and beginning of lines.—BOSWELL.

[3] See vol. i. pp. 656; 657.—BOSWELL.

"Your health, when I saw you, was much improved. You will be prudent enough not to put it in danger. I hope, when we meet again, we shall congratulate each other upon fair prospects of longer life: though what are the pleasures of the longest life, when placed in comparison with a happy death?

"I am, dear Sir, yours most affectionately,
"SAM. JOHNSON."

TO THE SAME.

[*Without a date, but supposed to be about this time.*]

"DEAR SIR,

"That you and dear Mrs. Careless should have care or curiosity about my health, gives me that pleasure which every man feels from finding himself not forgotten. In age we feel again that love of our native place and our early friends, which, in the bustle or amusements of middle life, were overborne and suspended. You and I should now naturally cling to one another. We have outlived most of those who could pretend to rival us in each other's kindness. In our walk through life we have dropped our companions, and are now to pick up such as chance may offer us, or to travel on alone. You, indeed, have a sister, with whom you can divide the day; I have no natural friend left; but Providence has been pleased to preserve me from neglect; I have not wanted such alleviations of life as friendship could supply. My health has been, from my twentieth year, such as has seldom afforded me a single day of ease; but it is at least not worse: and I sometimes make myself believe it is better. My disorders are, however, still sufficiently oppressive.

"I think of seeing Staffordshire again this autumn, and intend to find my way through Birmingham, where I hope to see you and dear Mrs. Careless well.

"I am, Sir, your affectionate friend,
"SAM. JOHNSON."

I wrote to him at different dates; regretted that I could not come to London this spring, but hoped we should meet somewhere in the summer; mentioned the state of my affairs, and suggested hopes of some preferment; informed him, that as "The Beauties of Johnson" had been published in London, some obscure scribbler had published, at Edinburgh, what he called "The Deformities of Johnson."

"TO JAMES BOSWELL, ESQ.

"DEAR SIR,   London, March 28, 1782.

"The pleasure which we used to receive from each other on Good Friday and Easter-day, we must be this year content to miss. Let us, however, pray for each other, and hope to see one another yet from time to time with mutual delight. My disorder has been a cold, which impeded the organs of respiration and kept me many weeks in a state of great uneasiness; but by repeated phlebotomy it is now relieved; and, next to the recovery of Mrs. Boswell, I flatter myself that you will rejoice at mine.

"What we shall do in the summer, it is yet too early to consider. You want to know what you shall do now; I do not think this time of bustle and confusion, like to produce any advantage to you.[1] Every man has those to reward and gratify who have contributed to his advancement. To come hither with such expectations at the expense of borrowed money, which, I find, you know not where to borrow, can hardly be considered prudent. I am sorry to find, what your solicitations seem to imply, that you have already gone the whole length of your credit. This is to set the quiet of your whole life at hazard. If you anticipate your inheritance, you can at last inherit nothing; all that you receive must pay for the past. You must get a place or pine in penury, with the empty name of a great estate. Poverty, my dear friend, is so great an evil, and pregnant with so much temptation, and so much misery, that I cannot but earnestly enjoin you to avoid it. Live on what you have; live if you can on less; do not borrow either for vanity or pleasure; the vanity will end in shame, and the pleasure in regret: stay therefore at home, till you have saved money for your journey hither.

"'The Beauties of Johnson' are said to have got money to the collector; if 'The Deformities' have the same success, I shall be a still more extensive benefactor.

"Make my compliments to Mrs. Boswell, who is, I hope, reconciled to me: and to the young people, whom I have never offended.

"You never told me the success of your plea against the solicitors.

"I am, dear Sir, your most affectionate,
"SAM. JOHNSON."

Notwithstanding his afflicted state of body and mind this year, the following correspondence affords a proof, not only of his benevolence and conscientious readiness to relieve a good man from error, but by his clothing one of the sentiments in his "Rambler" in different language, not inferior to that of the original, shows his extraordinary command of clear and forcible expression.

A clergyman at Bath wrote to him, that in "The Morning Chronicle," a passage in "The Beauties of Johnson," article Death, had been pointed out as supposed by some readers to recommend suicide, the words being, "To die is the fate of man; but to die with lingering anguish is generally his folly;" and respectfully suggesting to him, that such an erroneous notion of any sentence in the writings of an acknowledged friend of religion and virtue, should not pass uncontradicted.

Johnson thus answered the clergyman's letter:

[1] On the preceding day the Ministry had been changed.—MALONE.

"TO THE REVEREND MR. ———, AT BATH.

"Sir,   May 15, 1782.
"Being now in the country in a state of recovery, as I hope, from a very oppressive disorder, I cannot neglect the acknowledgment of your Christian letter. The book called 'The Beauties of Johnson,' is the production of I know not whom: I never saw it but by casual inspection, and considered myself as utterly disengaged from its consequences. Of the passage you mention, I remember some notice in some paper, but knowing that it must be misrepresented, I thought of it no more, nor do I know where to find it in my own books. I am accustomed to think little of newspapers; but an opinion so weighty and serious as yours has determined me to do, what I should, without your seasonable admonition, have omitted; and I will direct my thought to be shown in its true state.[1] If I could find the passage I would direct you to it. I suppose the tenor is this:—
'Acute diseases are the immediate and inevitable strokes of Heaven; but of them the pain is short, and the conclusion speedy; chronical disorders, by which we are suspended in tedious torture between life and death, are commonly the effect of our own misconduct and intemperance. To die, &c.' This, Sir, you see, is all true and all blameless. I hope some time in the next week to have all rectified. My health has been lately much shaken; if you favour me with any answer, it will be a comfort to me to know that I have your prayers. I am, &c.,
                                    "Sam. Johnson."

This letter, as might be expected, had its full effect, and the clergyman acknowledged it in grateful and pious terms.[2]
The following letters require no extracts from mine to introduce them.

"TO JAMES BOSWELL, ESQ.

"Dear Sir,   London, June 3, 1782.
"The earnestness and tenderness of your letter is such, that I cannot think myself showing it more respect than it claims by sitting down to answer it on the day on which I received it.

[1] What follows, appeared in "The Morning Chronicle" of May 29, 1782.—A correspondent having mentioned, in "The Morning Chronicle" of December 12, the last clause of the following paragraph, as seeming to favour suicide, we are requested to print the whole passage, that its true meaning may appear, which is not to recommend suicide but exercise:—
"Exercise cannot secure us from that dissolution to which we are decreed; but while the soul and body continue united, it can make the association pleasing, and give probable hopes that they shall be disjoined by an easy separation. It was a principle among the ancients, that acute diseases are from Heaven, and chronical from ourselves; the dart of death, indeed, falls from Heaven, but we poison it by our own misconduct: to die is the fate of man; but to die with lingering anguish is generally his folly."—Boswell.
[2] The Correspondence may be seen at length in "The Gentleman's Magazine," Feb., 1786.—Boswell.

This year has afflicted me with a very irksome and severe disorder. My respiration has been much impeded, and much blood has been taken away. I am now harassed by a catarrhous cough, from which my purpose is to seek relief by change of air; and I am therefore preparing to go to Oxford.

"Whether I did right in dissuading you from coming to London this spring, I will not determine. You have not lost much by missing my company; I have scarcely been well for a single week. I might have received comfort from your kindness; but you would have seen me afflicted, and, perhaps, found me peevish. Whatever might have been your pleasure or mine, I know not how I could have honestly advised you to come hither with borrowed money. Do not accustom yourself to consider debt only as an inconvenience—you will find it a calamity. Poverty takes away so many means of doing good, and produces so much inability to resist evil, both natural and moral, that it is by all virtuous means to be avoided. Consider a man whose fortune is very narrow, whatever be his rank by birth, or whatever his reputation by intellectual excellence, what can he do, or what evil can he prevent? That he cannot help the needy is evident; he has nothing to spare. But, perhaps, his advice or admonition may be useful. His poverty will destroy his influence; many more can find that he is poor, than that he is wise; and few will reverence the understanding that is of so little advantage to its owner. I say nothing of the personal wretchedness of a debtor, which, however, has passed into a proverb. Of riches it is not necessary to write the praise. Let it, however, be remembered, that he who has money to spare has it always in his power to benefit others; and of such power a good man must always be desirous.

"I am pleased with your account of Easter.[1] We shall meet, I hope, in autumn, both well and both cheerful; and part each the better for the other's company.

"Make my compliments to Mrs. Boswell, and to the young charmers.

"I am, &c.,

"SAM. JOHNSON."

"TO MR. PERKINS.

"DEAR SIR,   July 28, 1782.

" I am much pleased that you are going a very long journey, which may, by proper conduct, restore your health and prolong your life.

"Observe these rules:—

"1. Turn all care out of your head as soon as you mount the chaise.

"2. Do not think about frugality; your health is worth more than it can cost.

"3. Do not continue any day's journey to fatigue.

"4. Take now and then a day's rest.

---

[1] Which I celebrated in the Church-of-England chapel at Edinburgh, founded by Lord Chief Baron Smith, of respectable and pious memory.— BOSWELL.

"5. Get a smart sea-sickness if you can.

"6. Cast away all anxiety, and keep your mind easy.

"7. This last direction is the principal; with an unquiet mind, neither exercise, nor diet, nor physic, can be of much use.

"I wish you, dear Sir, a prosperous journey, and a happy recovery.

"I am, dear Sir,
"Your most affectionate humble servant,
"SAM. JOHNSON."

"TO JAMES BOSWELL, ESQ.

"DEAR SIR,   August 24, 1782.

"Being uncertain whether I should have any call this autumn into the country, I did not immediately answer your kind letter. I have no call; but if you desire to meet me at Ashbourne, I believe I can come thither; if you had rather come to London, I can stay at Streatham: take your choice.

"This year has been very heavy. From the middle of January to the middle of June I was battered by one disorder after another! I am now very much recovered, and hope still to be better. What happiness it is that Mrs. Boswell has escaped.

"My 'Lives' are reprinting, and I have forgotten the author of Gray's character.[1] Write immediately, and it may be perhaps yet inserted.

"Of London or Ashbourne you have your free choice; at any place I shall be glad to see you. I am, dear Sir, yours, &c.,
"SAM. JOHNSON."

[1] The Rev. Mr. Temple, Vicar of St. Gluvias, Cornwall.—BOSWELL.

CHAPTER XXII.—1782—1783

*Death of Boswell's Father—Johnson's Advice—His Corres-
pondence with Boswell and his Lady—Poverty an Enemy
to Human Happiness—Mrs. Thrale's Coolness to
Johnson—His parting Prayer on leaving Streatham
—Mr. Metcalfe—Visit to Cowdray—John Nichols—
—Wilson's "Archæological Dictionary"—Dr. Patten
—Boswell's Arrival in London—The Royal Family—
Conversation—Lies of Vanity—Johnson's Antipathy to
the Scotch—General Oglethorpe—Opium—Neglect of
Merit—Use of Riches—Goldsmith and Lord Shelburne
—Crabbe's "Village"*

ON the 30th of August I informed him that my honoured
father had died that morning; a complaint, under which he
had long laboured, having suddenly come to a crisis, while
I was upon a visit at the seat of Sir Charles Preston, from
whence I had hastened the day before, upon receiving a
letter by express.

"TO JAMES BOSWELL, ESQ.

"DEAR SIR,   London, Sept. 7, 1782.

"I have struggled through this year with so much infirmity of
body, and such strong impressions of the fragility of life, that
death, whenever it appears, fills me with melancholy; and I cannot
hear without emotion of the removal of any one, whom I have known,
into another state.

"Your father's death had every circumstance that could enable
you to bear it; it was at a mature age, and it was expected; and
as his general life had been pious, his thoughts had doubtless for
many years past been turned upon eternity. That you did not
find him sensible must doubtless grieve you; his disposition towards
you was undoubtedly that of a kind, though not of a fond father.
Kindness, at least actual, is in our power, but fondness is not; and
if by negligence or imprudence you had extinguished his fondness,
he could not at will rekindle it. Nothing then remained between
you but mutual forgiveness of each other's faults, and mutual
desire of each other's happiness.

"I shall long to know his final disposition of his fortune.

"You, dear Sir, have now a new station, and have therefore
new cares and new employments. Life, as Cowley seems to say,
ought to resemble a well-ordered poem; of which one rule generally

455

received is, that the exordium should be simple, and should promise little. Begin your new course of life with the least show, and the least expense possible; you may at pleasure increase both, but you cannot easily diminish them. Do not think your estate your own, while any man can call upon you for money which you cannot pay; therefore begin with timorous parsimony. Let it be your first care not to be in any man's debt.

"When the thoughts are extended to a future state, the present life seems hardly worthy of all those principles of conduct, and maxims of prudence, which one generation of men has transmitted to another; but upon a closer view, when it is perceived how much evil is produced, and how much good is impeded by embarrassment and distress, and how little room the expedients of poverty leave for the exercise of virtue, it grows manifest that the boundless importance of the next life enforces some attention to the interest of this.

"Be kind to the old servants, and secure the kindness of the agents and factors; do not disgust them by asperity, or unwelcome gaiety, or apparent suspicion. From them you must learn the real state of your affairs, the characters of your tenants, and the value of your lands.

"Make my compliments to Mrs. Boswell; I think her expectations from air and exercise are the best that she can form. I hope she will live long and happily.

"I forgot whether I told you that Rasay has been here; we dined cheerfully together. I entertained lately a young gentleman from Corrichatachin.

"I received your letters only this morning.

"I am, dear Sir, yours, &c.,
"SAM. JOHNSON."

In answer to my next letter, I received one from him, dissuading me from hastening to him as I had proposed; what is proper for publication is the following paragraph, equally just and tender:—

"One expense, however, I would not have you spare; let nothing be omitted that can preserve Mrs. Boswell, though it should be necessary to transplant her for a time into a softer climate. She is the prop and stay of your life. How much must your children suffer by losing her."

My wife was now so much convinced of his sincere friendship for me, and regard for her, that, without any suggestion on my part, she wrote him a very polite and grateful letter.

"DR. JOHNSON TO MRS. BOSWELL.

"DEAR LADY,   London, Sep. 7, 1782.

"I have not often received so much pleasure as from your invitation to Auchinleck. The journey thither and back is, indeed, too great for the latter part of the year; but if my health were fully recovered, I would suffer no little heat and cold, nor a wet or a rough road to keep me from you. I am, indeed, not without hope of seeing Auchinleck again; but to make it a pleasant place I must see its lady well, and brisk, and airy. For my sake, therefore, among many greater reasons, take care, dear Madam, of your health, spare no expense, and want no attendance that can procure ease, or preserve it. Be very careful to keep your mind quiet; and do not think it too much to give an account of your recovery to, Madam, yours, &c.,

"SAM. JOHNSON."

"TO JAMES BOSWELL, ESQ.

"DEAR SIR, London, Dec. 7, 1782.

"Having passed almost this whole year in a succession of disorders, I went in October to Brighthelmstone, whither I came in a state of so much weakness, that I rested four times in walking between the inn and the lodging. By physic and abstinence I grew better, and am now reasonably easy, though at a great distance from health. I am afraid, however, that health begins, after seventy, and long before, to have a meaning different from that which it had at thirty. But it is culpable to murmur at the established order of the creation, as it is vain to oppose it; he that lives, must grow old; and he that would rather grow old than die, has GOD to thank for the infirmities of old age.

"At your long silence I am rather angry. You do not, since now you are the head of your house, think it worth your while to try whether you or your friend can live longer without writing, nor suspect that, after so many years of friendship, when I do not write to you, I forget you. Put all such useless jealousies out of your head, and disdain to regulate your own practice by the practice of another, or by any other principle than the desire of doing right.

"Your economy, I suppose, begins now to be settled; your expenses are adjusted to your revenue, and all your people in their proper places. Resolve not to be poor: whatever you have, spend less. Poverty is a great enemy to human happiness; it certainly destroys liberty, and it makes some virtues impracticable, and others extremely difficult.

"Let me know the history of your life since your accession to your estate;—how many houses, how many cows, how much land in your own hand, and what bargains you make with your tenants.

*   *   *   *   *

"Of my 'Lives of the Poets,' they have printed a new edition in octavo, I hear, of three thousand. Did I give a set to Lord Hailes? If I did not, I will do it out of these. What did you make of all your copy?

"Mrs. Thrale and the three Misses are now, for the winter, in Argyle-street. Sir Joshua Reynolds has been out of order, but is well again; and I am, dear Sir, your affectionate humble servant,

"SAM. JOHNSON."

"TO DR. SAMUEL JOHNSON.

"DEAR SIR,   Edinburgh, Dec. 20, 1782.

"I was made happy by your kind letter, which gave us the agreeable hopes of seeing you in Scotland again.

"I am much flattered by the concern you are pleased to take in my recovery. I am better, and hope to have it in my power to convince you by my attention, of how much consequence I esteem your health to the world and to myself.

"I remain, Sir, with grateful respect,
"Your obliged and obedient servant,
"MARGARET BOSWELL."

The death of Mr. Thrale had made a very material alteration with respect to Johnson's reception in that family. The manly authority of the husband no longer curbed the lively exuberance of the lady; and as her vanity had been fully gratified, by having the Colossus of Literature attached to her for many years, she gradually became less assiduous to please him. Whether her attachment to him was already divided by another object, I am unable to ascertain; but it is plain that Johnson's penetration was alive to her neglect or forced attention; for on the 6th of October this year we find him making a "parting use of the library" at Streatham, and pronouncing a prayer, which he composed on leaving Mr. Thrale's family.[1]

"Almighty God, Father of all mercy, help me by thy grace, that I may, with humble and sincere thankfulness, remember the comforts and conveniences which I have enjoyed at this place; and that I may resign them with holy submission, equally trusting in thy protection when Thou givest, and when Thou takest away. Have mercy upon me, O Lord, have mercy upon me.

"To thy fatherly protection, O Lord, I commend this family. Bless, guide, and defend them, that they may so pass through this world, as finally to enjoy in thy presence everlasting happiness, for Jesus Christ's sake. Amen."

One cannot read this prayer, without some emotions not very favourable to the lady whose conduct occasioned it.

In one of his memorandum-books I find, "Sunday, went to church at Streatham. *Templo valedixi cum osculo.*"

He met Mr. Philip Metcalfe often at Sir Joshua Reynolds's, and other places, and was a good deal with him at Brighthelmstone this autumn, being pleased at once with his excellent table and animated conversation. Mr. Metcalfe showed him great respect, and sent him a note that he might have the use of his carriage whenever he pleased.

'"Prayers and Meditations," p. 214.

Johnson (3rd October, 1782) returned this polite answer:—
"Mr. Johnson is very much obliged by the kind offer of
the carriage, but he has no desire of using Mr. Metcalfe's
carriage, except when he can have the pleasure of Mr.
Metcalfe's company." Mr. Metcalfe could not but be
highly pleased that his company was thus valued by
Johnson, and he frequently attended him in airings.   They
also went together to Chichester, and they visited Petworth,
and Cowdray, the venerable seat of the Lords Montacute.[1]
"Sir," said Johnson, "I should like to stay here four-and-
twenty hours.   We see here how our ancestors lived."

That his curiosity was still unabated, appears from two
letters to Mr. John Nichols, of the 10th and 20th of October
this year.   In one he says, "I have looked into your
'Anecdotes,' and you will hardly thank a lover of literary
history for telling you, that he has been much informed and
gratified.   I wish you would add your own discoveries
and intelligence to those of Dr. Rawlinson, and undertake
the Supplement to Wood.   Think of it."   In the other,
"I wish, Sir, you could obtain some fuller information of
Jortin, Markland, and Thirlby.   They were three contemporaries of great eminence."

"TO SIR JOSHUA REYNOLDS.

"DEAR SIR,   Brighthelmstone, Nov. 14, 1782.
"I heard yesterday of your late disorder, and should think ill
of myself if I had heard of it without alarm.   I heard likewise of
your recovery, which I sincerely wish to be complete and permanent.
Your country has been in danger of losing one of its brightest
ornaments, and I of losing one of my oldest and kindest friends;
but I hope you will still live long, for the honour of the nation: and
that more enjoyment of your elegance, your intelligence, and your
benevolence is still reserved for, dear Sir, your most affectionate, &c.,
                                        "SAM. JOHNSON."

The Reverend Mr. Wilson, having dedicated to him his
"Archæological Dictionary," that mark of respect was thus
acknowledged:

"TO THE REVEREND MR. WILSON, CLITHEROE,
LANCASHIRE.

"REVEREND SIR,   December 31, 1782.
"That I have long omitted to return you thanks for the honour
conferred upon me by your dedication, I entreat you with great
earnestness not to consider as more faulty than it is.   A very

---

[1] This venerable mansion has since been totally destroyed by fire.—
MALONE.

importunate and oppressive disorder has for some time debarred
me from the pleasures, and obstructed me in the duties, of life.
The esteem and kindness of wise and good men is one of the last
pleasures which I can be content to lose; and gratitude to those
from whom this pleasure is received, is a duty of which I hope
never to be reproached with the final neglect.   I therefore now
return you thanks for the notice which I have received from you,
and which I consider as giving to my name not only more bulk, but
more weight; not only as extending its superficies, but as increasing
its value.   Your book was evidently wanted, and will, I hope, find
its way into the school; to which, however, I do not mean to confine
it; for no man has so much skill in ancient rites and practices as
not to want it.   As I suppose myself to owe part of your kindness
to my excellent friend, Dr. Patten, he has likewise a just claim to
my acknowledgment, which I hope you, Sir, will transmit.   There
will soon appear a new edition of my Poetical Biography; if you will
accept of a copy to keep me in your mind, be pleased to let me know
how it may be conveniently conveyed to you.   This present is
small, but it is given with good will by, Reverend Sir, your most, &c.,
                                                    "SAM. JOHNSON."

In 1783, he was more severely afflicted than ever, as
will appear in the course of his correspondence; but still
the same ardour for literature, the same constant piety,
the same kindness for his friends, and the same vivacity,
both in conversation and writing, distinguished him.

Having given Dr. Johnson a full account of what I was
doing at Auchinleck, and particularly mentioned what I
knew would please him,—my having brought an old man
of eighty-eight from a lonely cottage to a comfortable
habitation within my enclosures, where he had good
neighbours near to him,—I received an answer in February,
of which I extract what follows:—

" I am delighted with your account of your activity at Auchinleck, and wish the old gentleman, whom you have so kindly removed,
may live long to promote your prosperity by his prayers.   You have
now a new character and new duties; think on them, and practise
them.

" Make an impartial estimate of your revenue; and, whatever it is,
live upon less.   Resolve never to be poor.   Frugality is not only the
basis of quiet, but of beneficence.   No man can help others that
wants help himself; we must have enough before we have to spare.

" I am glad to find that Mrs. Boswell grows well; and hope that,
to keep her well, no care nor caution will be omitted.   May you long
live happily together.

" When you come hither, pray bring with you Baxter's Anacreon.
I cannot get that edition in London." [1]

---

[1] Dr. Johnson should seem not to have sought diligently for Baxter's
Anacreon, for there are two editions of that book, and they are frequently
found in the London Sale Catalogues.—MALONE.

On Friday, March 21, having arrived in London the night before, I was glad to find him at Mrs. Thrale's house, in Argyle-street; appearances of friendship between them being still kept up. I was shown into his room, and after the first salutation he said, "I am glad you are come: I am very ill." He looked pale, and was distressed with a difficulty of breathing: but after the common inquiries he assumed his usual strong animated style of conversation. Seeing me now, for the first time, as a *Laird*, or proprietor of land, he began thus:—"Sir, the superiority of a country-gentleman over the people upon his estate is very agreeable: and he who says he does not feel it to be agreeable, lies; for it must be agreeable to have a casual superiority over those who are by nature equal to us." Boswell: "Yet, Sir, we see great proprietors of land who prefer living in London." Johnson: "Why, Sir, the pleasure of living in London, the intellectual superiority that is enjoyed there, may counter-balance the other. Besides, Sir, a man may prefer the state of the country-gentleman upon the whole, and yet there may never be a moment when he is willing to make the change to quit London for it." He said, "It is better to have five per cent. out of land than out of money, because it is more secure; but the readiness of transfer, and promptness of interest, make many people rather choose the funds. Nay, there is another disadvantage belonging to land, compared with money. A man is not so much afraid of being a hard creditor, as of being a hard landlord." Boswell: "Because there is a sort of kindly connexion between a landlord and his tenants." Johnson: "No, Sir, many landlords with us never see their tenants. It is because if a landlord drives away his tenants, he may not get others; whereas the demand for money is so great, it may always be lent."

He talked with regret and indignation of the factious opposition to Government at this time, and imputed it in a great measure to the revolution. "Sir," said he, in a low voice, having come nearer to me, while his old prejudices seemed to be fomenting in his mind, "this Hanoverian family is *isolée* here. They have no friends. Now the Stuarts had friends who stuck by them so late as 1745. When the right of the King is not reverenced, there will not be reverence for those appointed by the King."

His observation, that the present royal family has no friends, has been too much justified by the very ungrateful behaviour of many who were under great obligations to his Majesty; at the same time there are honourable exceptions: and the very next year after this conversation, and ever since, the King has had as extensive and generous support as ever was given to any monarch, and has had the satisfaction of knowing that he was more and more endeared to his people.

He repeated to me his verses on Mr. Levett, with an emotion which gave them full effect; and then he was pleased to say, " You must be as much with me as you can. You have done me good. You cannot think how much better I am since you came in."

He sent a message to acquaint Mrs. Thrale that I was arrived. I had not seen her since her husband's death. She soon appeared, and favoured me with an invitation to stay to dinner, which I accepted. There was no other company but herself and three of her daughters, Dr. Johnson, and I. She too said she was very glad I was come, for she was going to Bath, and should have been sorry to leave Dr. Johnson before I came. This seemed to be attentive and kind; and I who had not been informed of any change, imagined all to be as well as formerly. He was little inclined to talk at dinner, and went to sleep after it; but when he joined us in the drawing-room, he seemed revived, and was again himself.

Talking of conversation, he said, "There must, in the first place, be knowledge; there must be materials;—in the second place, there must be a command of words;—in the third place, there must be imagination, to place things in such views as they are not commonly seen in:—and in the fourth place, there must be presence of mind, and a resolution that it is not to be overcome by failures; this last is an essential requisite; for want of it many people do not excel in conversation. Now I want it; I throw up the game upon losing a trick." I wondered to hear him talk thus of himself, and said, " I don't know, Sir, how this may be; but I am sure you beat other people's cards out of their hands." I doubt whether he heard this remark. While he went on talking triumphantly, I was fixed in admiration, and said to Mrs. Thrale, "Oh, for short-hand to take this down."— "You'll carry it all in your head," said she; "a long head is as good as short-hand."

It has been observed, and wondered at, that Mr. Charles Fox never talked with any freedom in the presence of Dr. Johnson; though it is well known, and I myself can witness, that his conversation is various, fluent, and exceedingly agreeable. Johnson's own experience, however, of that gentleman's reserve, was a sufficient reason for his going on thus:—"Fox never talks in private company; not from any determination not to talk, but because he had not the first

motion. A man who is used to the applause of the House
of Commons, has no wish for that of a private company.
A man accustomed to throw for a thousand pounds, if set
down to throw for sixpence, would not be at the pains to
count his dice. Burke's talk is the ebullition of his mind;
he does not talk from a desire of distinction, but because his
mind is full."

He thus curiously characterized one of our old acquaintance:— "——— is a good man, Sir; but he is a vain man
and a liar. He, however, only tells lies of vanity; of
victories, for instance, in conversation, which never
happened." This alluded to a story which I had repeated
from that gentleman, to entertain Johnson with its wild
bravado: "This Johnson, Sir," said he, "whom you are all
afraid of, will shrink, if you come close to him in argument,
and roar as loud as he. He once maintained the paradox,
that there is no beauty but in utility." "Sir," said I,
"what say you to the peacock's tail, which is one of the
most beautiful objects in nature, but would have as much
utility if its feathers were all of one colour." He *felt*
what I thus produced, and had recourse to his usual
expedient, ridicule; exclaiming, 'A peacock has a tail, and
a fox has a tail;' and then he burst out into a laugh.—'Well,
Sir,' said I, with a strong voice, looking him full in the face,
'you have unkennelled your fox; pursue him if you dare.'
He had not a word to say, Sir."—Johnson told me, that
this was fiction from beginning to end.[1]

After musing for some time, he said, "I wonder how I
should have any enemies; for I do harm to nobody."[2]
BOSWELL: "In the first place, Sir, you will be pleased to
recollect, that you set out with attacking the Scotch; so
you got a whole nation for your enemies." JOHNSON:

[1] Were I to insert all the stories which have been told of contests
boldly maintained with him, imaginary victories obtained over him, of
reducing him to silence, and of making him own that his antagonist had
the better of him in argument, my volumes would swell to an immoderate
size. One instance, I find, has circulated both in conversation and in
print; that when he would not allow the Scotch writers to have merit,
the late Dr. Rose, of Chiswick, asserted, that he could name one Scotch
writer, whom Dr. Johnson himself would allow to have written better
than any man of the age; and upon Johnson's asking who it was, answered,
"Lord Bute, when he signed the warrant for your pension." Upon which
Johnson, struck with the repartee, acknowledged that this *was* true.
When I mentioned it to Johnson, "Sir," said he, "if Rose said this, I
never heard it."—BOSWELL.
[2] This reflection was very natural in a man of a good heart, who was
not conscious of any ill-will to mankind, though the sharp sayings which
were sometimes produced by his discrimination and vivacity, which he
perhaps did not recollect, were, I am afraid, too often remembered with
resentment.—BOSWELL.

"Why, I own, that by my definition of *oats* I meant to vex them." BOSWELL: "Pray, Sir, can you trace the cause of your antipathy to the Scotch?" JOHNSON: "I cannot, Sir." BOSWELL: "Old Mr. Sheridan says, it was because they sold Charles the First." JOHNSON: "Then, Sir, old Mr. Sheridan has found out a very good reason."

Surely the most obstinate and sulky nationality, the most determined aversion to this great and good man, must be cured, when he is seen thus playing with one of his prejudices, of which he candidly admitted that he could not tell the reason. It was, however, probably owing to his having had in his view the worst part of the Scottish nation, the needy adventurers, many of whom he thought were advanced above their merits, by means which he did not approve. Had he in his early life been in Scotland, and seen the worthy, sensible, independent gentlemen, who live rationally and hospitably at home, he never could have entertained such unfavourable and unjust notions of his fellow-subjects. And accordingly we find, that when he did visit Scotland, in the latter period of his life, he was fully sensible of all that it deserved, as I have already pointed out, when speaking of his "Journey to the Western Islands."

Next day, Saturday, March 22, I found him still at Mrs. Thrale's; but he told me that he was to go to his own house in the afternoon. He was better, but I perceived he was an unruly patient, for Sir Lucas Pepys, who visited him, while I was with him, said, "If you were *tractable*, Sir, I should prescribe for you."

I related to him a remark which a respectable friend had made to me, upon the then state of Government, when those who had been long in opposition had attained to power, as it was supposed, against the inclination of the Sovereign. "You need not be uneasy," said this gentleman, "about the King. He laughs at them all; he plays them one against another." JOHNSON: "Don't think so, Sir. The King is as much oppressed as a man can be. If he plays them one against another, he *wins* nothing."

I had paid a visit to General Oglethorpe in the morning, and was told by him that Dr. Johnson saw company on Saturday evenings, and he would meet me at Johnson's that night. When I mentioned this to Johnson, not doubting that it would please him, as he had a great value for Oglethorpe, the fretfulness of his disease unexpectedly showed itself; his anger suddenly kindled, and he said, with vehemence, "Did not you tell him not to come? Am I to be *hunted* in this manner?" I satisfied him that I could not divine that the visit would not be convenient, and that I certainly could not take it upon me of my own accord to forbid the General.

I found Dr. Johnson in the evening in Mrs. Williams's room, at tea and coffee with her and Mrs. Desmoulins, who were also both ill; it was a sad scene, and he was not in a very good humour. He said of a performance that had lately come out, "Sir, if you should search all the mad-houses in England, you would not find ten men who would write so, and think it sense."

I was glad when General Oglethorpe's arrival was announced, and we left the ladies. Dr. Johnson attended him in the parlour, and was as courteous as ever. The General said, he was busy reading the writers of the middle age. Johnson said they were very curious. OGLETHORPE: "The House of Commons has usurped the power of the nation's money, and used it tyrannically. Government is now carried on by corrupt influence, instead of the inherent right in the King." JOHNSON: "Sir, the want of inherent right in the King occasions all this disturbance. What we did at the Revolution was necessary; but it broke our constitution."[1] OGLETHORPE: "My father did not think it necessary."

On Sunday, March 23, I breakfasted with Dr. Johnson, who seemed much relieved, having taken opium the night before. He, however, protested against it, as a remedy that should be given with the utmost reluctance, and only in extreme necessity. I mentioned how commonly it was used in Turkey, and that therefore it could not be so per-nicious as he apprehended. He grew warm, and said, "Turks take opium, and Christians take opium; but Russel, in his account of Aleppo, tells us, that it is as disgraceful in Turkey to take too much opium, as it is with us to get drunk. Sir, it is amazing how things are exaggerated. A gentle-man was lately telling, in a company where I was present, that in France, as soon as a man of fashion marries, he takes an opera girl into keeping; and this he mentioned as a general custom. 'Pray, Sir,' said I, 'how many opera girls may there be?' He answered, 'About four-score.'

[1] I have, in my "Journal of a Tour to the Hebrides," fully expressed my sentiments upon this subject. The Revolution was *necessary*, but not a subject for *glory;* because it for a long time blasted the generous feelings of *loyalty*. And now, when by the benignant effect of time the present Royal Family are established in our *affections,* how unwise is it to revive by celebrations the memory of a shock, which it would surely have been better that our constitution had not required.— BOSWELL.

'Well then, Sir,' said I, 'you see there can be no more than fourscore men of fashion who can do this.'"

Mrs. Desmoulins made tea, and she and I talked before him upon a topic which he had once borne patiently from me when we were by ourselves,—his not complaining of the world, because he was not called to some great office, nor had attained to great wealth. He flew into a violent passion, I confess with some justice, and commanded us to have done. "Nobody," said he, "has a right to talk in this manner, to bring before a man his own character, and the events of his life, when he does not choose it should be done. I never have sought the world: the world was not to seek me. It is rather wonderful that so much has been done for me. All the complaints which are made of the world are unjust. I never knew a man of merit neglected: it was generally by his own fault that he failed of success. A man may hide his head in a hole: he may go into the country, and publish a book now and then, which nobody reads, and then complains he is neglected. There is no reason why any person should exert himself for a man who has written a good book: he has not written it for any individual. I may as well make a present to a postman who brings me a letter. When patronage was limited, an author expected to find a Mæcenas, and complained if he did not find one. Why should he complain? This Mæcenas has others as good as he, or others who have got the start of him." Boswell: "But surely, Sir, you will allow that there are men of merit at the bar who never get practice." Johnson: "Sir, you are sure that practice is got from an opinion that the person employed deserves it best; so that if a man of merit at the bar does not get practice, it is from error, not from injustice. He is not neglected. A horse that is brought to market may not be bought, though he is a very good horse: but that is from ignorance, not from intention."

There was in this discourse much novelty, ingenuity, and discrimination, such as is seldom to be found. Yet I cannot help thinking that men of merit, who have no success in life, may be forgiven for *lamenting*, if they are not allowed to *complain*. They may consider it as *hard* that their merit should not have its suitable distinction. Though there is no intentional injustice towards them on the part of the world, their merit not having been perceived, they may yet repine against *fortune* or *fate*, or by whatever name they choose to call the supposed mythological power of *Destiny*. It has, however, occurred to me, as a consolatory thought, that men of merit should consider thus:—How much harder would it be, if the same persons had both all the merit and all the prosperity. Would not this be a miserable distribution for the poor dunces? Would men of merit exchange their intellectual superiority, and the enjoyments arising from it, for external distinction and the pleasures of wealth? If they would not, let them not envy others, who are poor where they are rich, a compensation which is made to them. Let them look inwards and be satisfied; recollecting, with conscious pride, what Virgil finely says of *Corycius Senex*, and which I have, in another place,[1] with truth and sincerity applied to Mr. Burke:—

> "Regum æquabat opes animis."

On the subject of the right employment of wealth, Johnson observed, "A man cannot make a bad use of his money, so far as regards society, if he do not hoard it; for if he either spends it or lends it out, society has the benefit. It is in general better to spend money than to give it away; for industry is more promoted by spending money than by giving it away. A man who spends his money is sure he is doing good with it: he is not sure when he gives it away. A man who spends ten thousand a year will do more good than a man who spends two thousand, and gives away eight."

In the evening I came to him again. He was somewhat fretful from his illness. A gentleman asked him whether he had been abroad to-day. "Don't talk so childishly," said he. "You may as well ask if I hanged myself to-day." I mentioned politics. Johnson: "Sir, I'd as soon have a man to break my bones as talk to me of public affairs, internal or external. I have lived to see things all as bad as they can be."

Having mentioned his friend, the second Lord Southwell, he said: "Lord Southwell was the highest bred man, without insolence, that I ever was in company with; the most *qualitied* I ever saw. Lord Orrery was not dignified; Lord Chesterfield was, but he was insolent. Lord ———— is a man of coarse manners, but a man of abilities and information. I don't say he is a man I would set at the head of a nation, though perhaps he may be as good as the next Prime Minister that comes; but he is a man to be at the head of a Club;—I don't say *our* Club;—for there is no such Club." Boswell: "But, Sir, was he not once a factious

---

[1] Letter to the People of Scotland against the Attempt to diminish the Number of the Lords of Session, 1785.—Boswell.

man?" JOHNSON: "O yes, Sir; as factious a fellow as could be found; one who was for sinking us all into the mob." BOSWELL: "How then, Sir, did he get into favour with the King?" JOHNSON: "Because, Sir, I suppose he promised the King to do whatever the King pleased."

He said, "Goldsmith's blundering speech to Lord Shelburne, which has been so often mentioned, and which he really did make to him, was only a blunder in emphasis:— 'I wonder they should call your Lordship *Malagrida*, for Malagrida was a very good man;'—meant, I wonder they should use *Malagrida* as a term of reproach."

Soon after this time I had an opportunity of seeing, by means of one of his friends, a proof that his talents, as well as his obliging service to authors, were ready as ever. He had revised "The Village," an admirable poem, by the Reverend Mr. Crabbe. Its sentiments, as to the false notions of rustic happiness and rustic virtue, were quite congenial with his own; and he had taken the trouble, not only to suggest slight corrections and variations, but to furnish some lines, when he thought he could give the writer's meaning better than in the words of the manuscript.[1]

[1] I shall give an instance, marking the original by Roman, and Johnson's substitution in Italic characters:—

> "In fairer scenes, where peaceful pleasures spring,
> Tityrus, the pride of Mantuan swains, might sing;
> But charmed by him, or smitten with his views,
> Shall modern poets court the Mantuan Muse ?
> From Truth and Nature shall we widely stray,
> Where Fancy leads, or Virgil led the way ?"

> "*On Mincio's banks, in Cæsar's bounteous reign,*
> *If Tityrus found the golden age again,*
> *Must sleepy bards the flattering dream prolong,*
> *Mechanic echoes of the Mantuan song ?*
> From Truth and Nature shall we widely stray,
> *Where Virgil, not where Fancy, leads the way ?*"

Here we find Johnson's poetical and critical powers undiminished. I must, however, observe, that the aids he gave to this poem, as to "The Traveller," and "Deserted Village," of Goldsmith, were so small as by no means to impair the distinguishing merit of the author.—BOSWELL

CHAPTER XXIII.—1783

Penuriousness of Wealth—Lord Mansfield—Harrington's "Nugæ Antiquæ"—Motto on Johnson's Portrait—"Quod Deus vult perdere," &c.—On Happiness—Johnson's Powers of Conversation—Mr. Welch—Dr. Buchanan—Grub Street—Sir Wm. Chambers—Bishop Hurd — Reserve of Englishmen — Morice Morgann, Derrick, and Smart —"The Great Twalmley"— A Charade—Mr. Cambridge—Johnson's Love of Children and Animals—Abp. Stuart—"The Turkish Spy"— Mr. Windham—Mr. Lowe on Hospitality—Walled Gardens—Mr. Walker on the Origin of Language— Moorfields—A singular Character.

On Sunday, March 30, I found him at home in the evening, and had the pleasure to meet with Dr. Brocklesby, whose reading, and knowledge of life, and good spirits, supply him with a never-failing source of conversation. He mentioned a respectable gentleman, who became extremely penurious near the close of his life. Johnson said there must have been a degree of madness about him. "Not at all, Sir," said Dr. Brocklesby, "his judgment was entire." Unluckily, however, he mentioned that, although he had a fortune of twenty-seven thousand pounds, he denied himself many comforts, from an apprehension that he could not afford them. "Nay, Sir," cried Johnson, "when the judgment is so disturbed that a man cannot count, that is pretty well."

I shall here insert a few of Johnson's sayings, without the formality of dates, as they have no reference to any particular time or place.

"The more a man extends and varies his acquaintance the better," This, however, was meant with a just restriction; for he, on another occasion, said to me, "Sir, a man may be so much of everything, that he is nothing of anything."

"Raising the wages of day-labourers is wrong; for it does not make them live better, but only makes them idler; and idleness is a very bad thing for human nature."

469

"It is a very good custom to keep a journal for a man's own use; he may write upon a card a day all that is necessary to be written, after he has had experience of life. At first there is a great deal to be written, because there is a great deal of novelty; but when once a man has settled his opinions, there is seldom much to be set down."

"There is nothing wonderful in the Journal[1] which we see Swift kept in London; for it contains slight topics, and it might soon be written."

I praised the accuracy of an account-book of a lady whom I mentioned. JOHNSON: "Keeping accounts, Sir, is of no use when a man is spending his own money, and has nobody to whom he is to account. You won't eat less beef to-day, because you have written down what it cost yesterday." I mentioned another lady who thought as he did, so that her husband could not get her to keep an account of the expense of the family, as she thought it enough that she never exceeded the sum allowed her. JOHNSON: "Sir, it is fit she should keep an account because her husband wishes it; but I do not see its use." I maintained that keeping an account had this advantage, that it satisfies a man that his money has not been lost or stolen, which he might sometimes be apt to imagine, were there no written state of his expense; and besides, a calculation of economy, so as not to exceed one's income, cannot be made without a view of the different articles in figures, that one may see how to retrench in some particulars less necessary than others. This he did not attempt to answer.

Talking of an acquaintance of ours, whose narratives, which abounded in curious and interesting topics, were unhappily found to be very fabulous, I mentioned Lord Mansfield's having said to me, "Suppose we believe one *half* of what he tells." JOHNSON: "Ay; but we don't know *which* half to believe. By his lying we lose not only our

---

[1] In his Life of Swift, he thus speaks of this Journal:—

"In the midst of his power and his politics, he kept a journal of his visits, his walks, his interviews with ministers, and quarrels with his servant, and transmitted it to Mrs. Johnson and Mrs. Dingley, to whom he knew that whatever befel him was interesting, and no account could be too minute. Whether these diurnal trifles were properly exposed to eyes which had never received any pleasure from the Dean, may be reasonably doubted: they have, however, some odd attractions: the reader finding frequent mention of names which he has been used to consider as important, goes on in hope of information; and as there is nothing to fatigue attention if he is disappointed, he can hardly complain."

It may be added, that the reader not only hopes to find, but does find, in this very entertaining Journal, much curious information, respecting persons and things, which he will in vain seek for in other books of the same period.—MALONE.

reverence for him, but all comfort in his conversation."
BOSWELL: "May we not take it as amusing fiction?"
JOHNSON: "Sir, the misfortune is, that you will insensibly
believe as much of it as you incline to believe."

It is remarkable, that notwithstanding their congeniality
in politics, he never was acquainted with a late eminent
noble judge [Mansfield], whom I have heard speak of him,
as a writer, with great respect.   Johnson, I know not upon
what degree of investigation, entertained no exalted opinion
of his lordship's intellectual character.   Talking of him to
me one day, he said, "It is wonderful, Sir, with how little
real superiority of mind men can make an eminent figure
in public life."   He expressed himself to the same purpose
concerning another law-lord, who, it seems, once took a
fancy to associate with the wits of London; but with so little
success, that Foote said, "What can he mean by coming
among us? He is not only dull himself, but the cause of
dulness in others."   Trying him by the test of his colloquial
powers, Johnson had found him very defective.   He once
said to Sir Joshua Reynolds, "This man now has been ten
years about town, and has made nothing of it;" meaning
as a companion.   He said to me, "I never heard anything
from him in company that was at all striking; and depend
upon it, Sir, it is when you come close to a man in conversation, that you discover what his real abilities are: to make
a speech in a public assembly is a knack.   Now I honour
Thurlow, Sir; Thurlow is a fine fellow; he fairly puts his
mind to yours."

After repeating to him some of his pointed, lively sayings,
I said, "It is a pity, Sir, you don't always remember your
own good things, that you may have a laugh when you will."
JOHNSON: "Nay, Sir, it is better that I forget them, that
I may be reminded of them, and have a laugh on their
being brought to my recollection."

When I recalled to him his having said as we sailed up
Locklomond, "That if he wore anything fine, it should be
very fine;" I observed that all his thoughts were upon a
great scale.   JOHNSON: "Depend upon it, Sir, every man
will have as fine a thing as he can get; as large a diamond
for his ring."   BOSWELL: "Pardon me, Sir; a man of a

---

[1] Knowing as well as I do what precision and elegance of oratory his
Lordship can display, I cannot but suspect that his unfavourable appearance in a social circle, which drew such animadversions upon him, must
be owing to a cold affectation of consequence, from being reserved and
stiff.   If it be so, and he might be an agreeable man if he would, we
cannot be sorry that he misses his aim.—BOSWELL.

narrow mind will not think of it; a slight trinket will satisfy him:

> 'Nec sufferre queat majoris pondera gemmæ.'"

I told him I should send him some "Essays" that I had written,[1] which I hoped he would be so good as to read, and pick out the good ones.   JOHNSON: "Nay, Sir, send me only the good ones; don't make *me* pick them."

I heard him once say, "Though the proverb '*Nullum numen abest, si sit prudentia,*' does not always prove true, we may be certain of the converse of it, '*Nullum numen adest, si sit imprudentia.*'"

Once, when Mr. Seward was going to Bath, and asked his commands, he said, "Tell Dr. Harrington that I wish he would publish another volume of the '*Nugæ Antiquæ*;'[2] it is a very pretty book."[3]   Mr. Seward seconded this wish, and recommended to Dr. Harrington to dedicate it to Johnson, and take for his motto what Catullus says to Cornelius Nepos:

> "————namque tu solebas,
>   Meas esse aliquid putare NUGAS."

As a small proof of his kindliness and delicacy of feeling, the following circumstance may be mentioned:—One evening, when we were in the street together, and I told him I was going to sup at Mr. Beauclerk's, he said, "I'll go with you." After having walked part of the way, seeming to recollect something, he suddenly stopped, and said, "I cannot go,—but *I do not love Beauclerk the less.*"

On the frame of his portrait, Mr. Beauclerk had inscribed,

> "———— Ingenium ingens
>   Inculto latet hoc sub corpore."

After Mr. Beauclerk's death, when it became Mr. Langton's property, he made the inscription be defaced.   Johnson said complacently, "It was kind in you to take it off;" and then, after a short pause, added, "and not unkind in him to put it on."

---

[1] Under the title of "The Hypochondriac."—MALONE.

[2] It has since appeared.—BOSWELL.

[3] A new and greatly improved edition of this very curious collection was published by Mr. Park in 1804, in 2 vols. 8vo.   In this edition the letters are chronologically arranged, and the account of the Bishops, which was formerly printed from a very corrupt copy, is taken from Sir John Harrington's original manuscript which he presented to Henry, Prince of Wales, and is now in the Royal Library in the Museum.— MALONE.

He said, "How few of his friends' houses would a man choose to be at, when he is sick!" He mentioned one or two. I recollect only Thrale's.

He observed, "There is a wicked inclination in most people to suppose an old man decayed in his intellects. If a young or middle-aged man, when leaving a company, does not recollect where he laid his hat, it is nothing; but if the same inattention is discovered in an old man, people will shrug up their shoulders, and say, 'his memory is going.'"

When I once talked to him of some of the sayings which every body repeats, but nobody knows where to find; such as, *Quos* DEUS *vult perdere, prius dementat ;* he told me that he was once offered ten guineas to point out from whence *Semel insanivimus omnes* was taken. He could not do it; but many years afterwards met with it by chance in *Johannes Baptista Mantuanus.*[1]

I am very sorry that I did not take a note of an eloquent argument in which he maintained that the situation of

---

[1] The words occur (as Mr. Bindley observes to me), in the First Eclogue of Mantuanus, *De honesto Amore,* &c.

"Id commune malum; semel insanivimus omnes."

With the following elucidation of the other saying—*Quos Deus* (it should rather be *Quem Jupiter) vult perdere, prius dementat*—Mr. Boswell was furnished by Mr. Richard How, of Apsley, in Bedfordshire, as communicated to that gentleman by his friend Mr. John Pitts, late Rector of Great Brickhill, in Buckinghamshire:

"Perhaps no scrap of Latin whatever has been more quoted than this. It occasionally falls even from those who are scrupulous even to pedantry in their Latinity, and will not admit a word into their compositions which has not the sanction of the first age. The word *demento* is of no authority, either as a verb active or neuter.—After a long search, for the purpose of deciding a bet, some gentlemen of Cambridge found it among the fragments of Euripides, in what edition I do not recollect, where it is given as a translation of a Greek Iambic:—

Ον Θεὸς θέλει ολπάέσαι, πρῶτ' ἀποφρενοῖ.

The above scrap was found in the hand-writing of a suicide of fashion, Sir D. O., some years ago, lying on the table of the room where he had destroyed himself. The suicide was a man of classical acquirements: he left no other paper behind him."

Another of these proverbial sayings—

"*Incidit in Scyllam, cupiens vitare Charybdim;*"

I some years ago, in a note on a passage in "The Merchant of Venice," traced to its source. It occurs (with a slight variation) in "The Alexandreis," of Philip Gaultier (a poet of the thirteenth century), which was printed at Lyons in 1558. Darius is the person addressed:—

"———————— Quo tendis inertem,
Rex periture, fugam? nescis, heu! perdite, nescis
Quem fugias: hostes incurris, dum fugis hostem;
Incidis in Scyllam, cupiens vitare Charybdim."

The author of this line was first ascertained by Galleottus Martius,

Prince of Wales was the happiest of any person's in the kingdom, even beyond that of the Sovereign. I recollect only—the enjoyment of hope,—the high superiority of rank, without the anxious cares of government,—and a great degree of power, both from natural influence wisely used, and from the sanguine expectations of those who look forward to the chance of future favour.

Sir Joshua Reynolds communicated to me the following particulars:—

Johnson thought the poems, published as translations from Ossian, had so little merit, that he said, "Sir, a man might write such stuff for ever, if he would *abandon* his mind to it."

He said, "A man should pass a part of his time with *the laughers*, by which means anything ridiculous or particular about him might be presented to his view, and corrected." I observed, he must have been a bold laugher who would have ventured to tell Dr. Johnson of any of his particularities.

Having observed the vain ostentatious importance of many people in quoting the authority of Dukes and Lords, as having been in their company, he said, he went to the other extreme, and did not mention his authority when he should have done it, had it not been that of a Duke or a Lord.

Dr. Goldsmith said once to Dr. Johnson, that he wished for some additional members to the LITERARY CLUB, to give it an agreeable variety; for, said he, there can now be nothing new among us: we have travelled over one another's minds. Johnson seemed a little angry, and said, "Sir, you have not travelled over *my* mind, I promise you." Sir Joshua, however, thought Goldsmith right; observing, that "when people have lived a great deal together, they know

who died in 1476; as is observed in "Menagiana," vol. iii., p. 130, edit. 1762.—For an account of Philip Gaultier, see "Vossius de Poet. Latin." p. 254, fol. 1697.

A line not less frequently quoted than any of the preceding, was suggested for inquiry, several years ago, in a note on "The Rape of Lucrece:"—

"Solamen miseris socios habuisse doloris:"

But the author of this verse has not, I believe, been discovered.— MALONE.

[1] I am happy, however, to mention a pleasing instance of his enduring with great gentleness to hear one of his most striking particularities pointed out:—Miss Hunter, a niece of his friend Christopher Smart, when a very young girl, struck by his extraordinary motions, said to him, "Pray, Dr. Johnson, why do you make such strange gestures?"— "From bad habit," he replied. "Do you, my dear, take care to guard against bad habits." This I was told by the young lady's brother at Margate.—BOSWELL.

what each of them will say on every subject.   A new understanding, therefore, is desirable; because though it may
only furnish the same sense upon a question which would
have been furnished by those with whom we are accustomed to live, yet this sense will have a different colouring; and colouring is of much effect in everything else as
well as in painting."

Johnson used to say that he made it a constant rule
to talk as well as he could both as to sentiment and expression, by which means, what had been originally effort
became familiar and easy.   The consequence of this, Sir
Joshua observed, was, that his common conversation in
all companies was such as to secure him universal attention,
as something above the usual colloquial style was expected.

Yet, though Johnson had this habit in company, when
another mode was necessary, in order to investigate truth,
he could descend to a language intelligible to the meanest
capacity.   An instance of this was witnessed by Sir Joshua
Reynolds, when they were present at an examination of a
little blackguard boy, by Mr. Saunders Welch, the late
Westminster Justice.   Welch, who imagined that he was
exalting himself in Dr. Johnson's eyes by using big words,
spoke in a manner that was utterly unintelligible to the
boy; Dr. Johnson perceiving it, addressed himself to the
boy, and changed the pompous phraseology into colloquial
language.   Sir Joshua Reynolds, who was much amused
by this procedure, which seemed a kind of reversing of
what might have been expected from the two men, took
notice of it to Dr. Johnson, as they walked away by themselves.   Johnson said, that it was continually the case;
and that he was always obliged to *translate* the justice's
swelling diction (smiling), so as that his meaning might
be understood by the vulgar, from whom information was
to be obtained.

Sir Joshua once observed to him, that he had talked
above the capacity of some people with whom they had
been in company together.   "No matter, Sir," said Johnson;
"they consider it as a compliment to be talked to, as if
they were wiser than they are.   So true is this, Sir, that
Baxter made it a rule, in every sermon that he preached,
to say something that was above the capacity of his
audience."[1]

[1] The justness of this remark is confirmed by the following story,
for which I am indebted to Lord Elliot:—A country parson, who was
remarkable for quoting scraps of Latin in his sermons, having died, one
of the parishioners was asked how he liked his successor? "He is a
very good preacher," was his answer, "but no *latiner.*"—BOSWELL.

Johnson's dexterity in retort, when he seemed to be driven to an extremity by his adversary, was very remarkable. Of his power in this respect, our common friend, Mr. Windham, of Norfolk, has been pleased to furnish me with an eminent instance. However unfavourable to Scotland, he uniformly gave liberal praise to George Buchanan, as a writer. In a conversation concerning the literary merits of the two countries, in which Buchanan was introduced, a Scotchman, imagining that on this ground he should have an undoubted triumph over him, exclaimed, "Ah, Dr. Johnson, what would you have said of Buchanan, had he been an Englishman"?—"Why, Sir," said Johnson after a little pause, "I should *not* have said of Buchanan, had he been an *Englishman*, what I will now say of him as a *Scotchman*,—that he was the only man of genius his country ever produced."

And this brings to my recollection another instance of the same nature. I once reminded him, that when Dr. Adam Smith was expatiating on the beauties of Glasgow, he had cut him short by saying, "Pray, Sir, have you ever seen Brentford?" and I took the liberty to add, "My dear Sir, surely that was *shocking*."—"Why, then, Sir," he replied, "YOU have never seen Brentford."

Though his usual phrase for conversation was *talk*, yet he made a distinction; for when he once told me that he dined the day before at a friend's house, with "a very pretty company;" and I asked him if there was good conversation, he answered, "No, Sir; we had *talk* enough, but no *conversation;* there was nothing *discussed*."

Talking of the success of the Scotch in London, he imputed it, in a considerable degree, to their spirit of nationality. "You know, Sir," said he, "that no Scotchman publishes a book, or has a play brought upon the stage, but there are five hundred people ready to applaud him."

He gave much praise to his friend Dr. Burney's elegant and entertaining travels, and told Mr. Seward that he had them in his eye, when writing his "Journey to the Western Islands of Scotland."

Such was his sensibility, and so much was he affected by pathetic poetry, that, when he was reading Dr. Beattie's "Hermit," in my presence, it brought tears into his eyes.[1]

He disapproved much of mingling real facts with fiction.

---

[1] The particular passage which excited this strong emotion was, as I have heard from my father, the third stanza, "'Tis night," &c.—J. BOSWELL, JUN.

On this account he censured a book entitled "Love and Madness."

Mr. Hoole told him he was born in Moorfields, and had received part of his early instruction in *Grub-street*. "Sir," said Johnson, smiling, "you have been *regularly* educated." Having asked who was his instructor, and Mr. Hoole having answered, "My uncle, Sir, who was a tailor;" Johnson, recollecting himself, said, "Sir, I knew him; we called him the *metaphysical tailor*. He was of a club in Old-street, with me and George Psalmanazar, and some others: but pray, Sir, was he a good tailor?" Mr. Hoole having answered that he believed he was too mathematical, and used to draw squares and triangles on his shopboard, so that he did not excel in the cut of a coat;—"I am sorry for it," said Johnson; "for I would have every man to be master of his own business."

In pleasant reference to himself and Mr. Hoole, as brother authors, he often said, "Let you and I, Sir, go together, and eat a beefsteak in Grub-street."

Sir William Chambers, the great architect[1] whose works show a sublimity of genius, and who is esteemed by all who know him, for his social, hospitable, and generous qualities, submitted the manuscript of his "Chinese Architecture," to Dr. Johnson's perusal. Johnson was much pleased with it, and said, "It wants no addition nor correction, but a few lines of introduction;" which he furnished, and Sir William adopted.[2]

He said to Sir William Scott, "The age is running mad after innovation; and all the business of the world is to be done in a new way; men are to be hanged in a new way; Tyburn itself is not safe from the fury of innovation."

---

[1] The Honourable Horace Walpole, late Earl of Orford, thus bears testimony to this gentleman's merit as a writer:—Mr. Chambers' "Treatise on Civil Architecture," is the most sensible book, and the most exempt from prejudices, that ever was written on that science.—Preface to "Anecdotes of Painting in England."—Boswell.

[2] The introductory lines are these: "It is difficult to avoid praising too little or too much. The boundless panegyrics which have been lavished upon the Chinese learning, policy, and arts, show with what power novelty attracts regard, and how naturally esteem swells into admiration.

"I am far from desiring to be numbered among the exaggerators of Chinese excellence. I consider them as great, or wise, only in comparison with the nations that surround them; and have no intention to place them in competition either with the ancients or with the moderns of this part of the world; yet they must be allowed to claim our notice as a distinct and very singular race of men: as the inhabitants of a region divided by its situation from all civilised countries, who have formed their own manners, and invented their own arts, without the assistance of example."—Boswell.

It having been argued that this was an improvement—
"No, Sir," said he, "eagerly, it is *not* an improvement;
they object, that the old method drew together a number
of spectators. Sir, executions are intended to draw
spectators. If they do not draw spectators, they don't
answer their purpose. The old method was most satisfactory to all parties; the public was gratified by a procession; the criminal was supported by it. Why is all this
to be swept away?" I perfectly agree with Dr. Johnson
upon this head, and am persuaded that executions now,
the solemn procession being discontinued, have not nearly
the effect which they formerly had. Magistrates, both in
London and elsewhere, have, I am afraid, in this had too
much regard to their own ease.

Of Dr. Hurd, Bishop of Worcester, Johnson said to
a friend—"Hurd, Sir, is one of a set of men who account
for everything systematically; for instance, it has been
a fashion to wear scarlet breeches; these men who would
tell you that, according to causes and effects, no other
wear could at that time have been chosen." He, however,
said of him at another time to the same gentleman, "Hurd,
Sir, is a man whose acquaintance is a valuable acquisition."

That learned and ingenious Prelate, it is well known,
published at one period of his life "Moral and Political
Dialogues," with a wofully whiggish cast. Afterwards,
his Lordship having thought better, came to see his error,
and republished the work with a more constitutional
spirit. Johnson, however, was unwilling to allow him
full credit for his political conversion. I remember when
his Lordship declined the honour of being Archbishop
of Canterbury, Johnson said, "I am glad he did not
go to Lambeth; for, after all, I fear he is a Whig in his
heart."

Johnson's attention to precision and clearness in expression was very remarkable. He disapproved of a paren-
thesis; and I believe, in all his voluminous writings, not
half a dozen of them will be found. He never used the
phrases *the former* and *the latter*, having observed that
they often occasioned obscurity; he therefore contrived to
construct his sentences so as not to have occasion for
them, and would even rather repeat the same words, in
order to avoid them. Nothing is more common than to
mistake surnames, when we hear them carelessly uttered
for the first time. To prevent this, he used not only to
pronounce them slowly and distinctly, but to take the
trouble of spelling them—a practice which I have often
followed, and which I wish were general.

Such was the heat and irritability of his blood, that not only did he pare his nails to the quick, but scraped the joints of his fingers with a penknife, till they seemed quite red and raw.

The heterogeneous composition of human nature was remarkably exemplified in Johnson. His liberality in giving his money to persons in distress was extraordinary. Yet there lurked about him a propensity to paltry saving. One day I owned to him that " I was occasionally troubled with a fit of *narrowness.*" "Why, Sir," said he, "so am I. *But I do not tell it.*" He has now and then borrowed a shilling of me, and when I asked him for it again, seemed to be rather out of humour. A droll little circumstance once occurred:—As if he meant to reprimand my minute exactness as a creditor, he thus addressed me: "Boswell, *lend* me sixpence—*not to be repaid.*"

This great man's attention to small things was very remarkable. As an instance of it, he one day said to me, "Sir, when you get silver in change for a guinea, look carefully at it; you may find some curious piece of coin."

Though a stern *true-born Englishman*, and fully prejudiced against all other nations, he had discernment enough to see, and candour enough to censure, the cold reserve too common among Englishmen towards strangers: "Sir," said he, "two men of any other nation who are shown into a room together, at a house where they are both visitors, will immediately find some conversation. But two Englishmen will probably go each to a different window, and remain in obstinate silence. Sir, we as yet do not enough understand the common rights of humanity."

Johnson was, at a certain period of his life, a good deal with the Earl of Shelburne, now Marquis of Lansdowne, as he doubtless could not but have a due value for that nobleman's activity of mind, and uncommon acquisitions of important knowledge, however much he might disapprove of other parts of his lordship's character, which were widely different from his own.

Morice Morgann, Esq., author of the very ingenious "Essay on the Character of Falstaff,"[1] being a particular friend of his lordship, had once an opportunity of entertaining Johnson for a day or two at Wycombe, when this lord was absent, and by him I have been favoured with two anecdotes.

[1] Johnson being asked his opinion of this Essay, answered, "Why, Sir, we shall have the man come forth again; and as he has proved Falstaff to be no coward, he may prove Iago to be a very good character." —Boswell.

One is not a little to the credit of Johnson's candour. Mr. Morgann and he had a dispute pretty late at night, in which Johnson would not give up, though he had the wrong side, and, in short, both kept the field. Next morning, when they met in the breakfast-room, Dr. Johnson accosted Mr. Morgann thus: "Sir, I have been thinking on our dispute last night—*you were in the right.*"

The other was as follows:—Johnson, for sport perhaps, or from the spirit of contradiction, eagerly maintained that Derrick had merit as a writer. Mr. Morgann argued with him directly in vain. At length he had recourse to this device. "Pray, Sir," said he, "whether do you reckon Derrick or Smart the best poet?" Johnson at once felt himself roused, and answered, "Sir, there is no settling the point of precedency between a louse and a flea."

Once when checking my boasting too frequently of myself in company, he said to me, "Boswell, you often vaunt so much as to provoke ridicule. You put me in mind of a man who was standing in the kitchen of an inn with his back to the fire, and thus accosted the person next him, 'Do you know, Sir, who I am?' 'No, Sir,' said the other, 'I have not that advantage.' 'Sir,' said he, 'I am the *great* TWALMLEY, who invented the New Floodgate Iron.'"[1] The Bishop of Killaloe, on my repeating the story to him, defended TWALMLEY, by observing that he was entitled to the epithet of *great;* for Virgil, in his group of worthies in the Elysian fields—

"Hic manus, ob patriam pugnando vulnera passi,"[2] &c.

mentions

"Inventas aut qui vitam excoluere per artes."

He was pleased to say to me one morning, when we were left alone in his study, "Boswell, I think I am easier with you than with almost anybody."

He would not allow Mr. David Hume any credit for his political principles, though similar to his own; saying of him, "Sir, he was a Tory by chance."

His acute observation of human life made him remark, "Sir, there is nothing by which a man exasperates most people more, than by displaying a superior ability of

---

[1] What the *great* TWALMLEY was so proud of having invented, was neither more nor less than a kind of box-iron for smoothing linen.—BOSWELL.

[2] Æn. vi. 660.

brilliancy in conversation. They seem pleased at the time; but their envy makes them curse him at their hearts."

My readers will probably be surprised to hear that the great Dr. Johnson could amuse himself with so slight and playful a species of composition as a *Charade*. I have recovered one which he made on Dr. *Barnard*, now Lord Bishop of Killaloe;[1] who has been pleased for many years to treat me with so much intimacy and social ease, that I may presume to call him not only my right reverend, but my very dear friend. I therefore, with peculiar pleasure, give to the world a just and elegant compliment thus paid to his lordship by Johnson.

CHARADE.

"My *first*[2] shuts out thieves from your house or your room,
My *second*[3] expresses a Syrian perfume.
My *whole*[4] is a man in whose converse is shared,
The strength of a Bar and the sweetness of Nard."

Johnson asked Richard Owen Cambridge, Esq., if he had read the Spanish translation of Sallust, said to be written by a Prince of Spain, with the assistance of his tutor, who is professedly the author of a treatise annexed, on the Phœnician language.

Mr. Cambridge commended the work, particularly as he thought the translator understood his author better than is commonly the case with translators; but said, he was disappointed in the purpose for which he borrowed the book; to see whether a Spaniard could be better furnished with inscriptions from monuments, coins, or other antiquities, which he might more probably find on a coast, so immediately opposite to Carthage, than the antiquaries of any other countries.   JOHNSON: "I am very sorry you were not gratified in your expectations."   CAMBRIDGE: "The language would have been of little use, as there is no history existing in that tongue to balance the partial accounts which the Roman writers have left us."   JOHNSON: "No, Sir; they have not been *partial;* they have told their own story, without shame or regard to equitable treatment of their injured enemy; they had no compunction, no feeling for a Carthaginian. Why, Sir, they would never have borne Virgil's description of Æneas's treatment of Dido, if she had not been a Carthaginian."

I gratefully acknowledge this and other communications

[1] Afterwards translated to the see of Limerick.—MALONE.
[2] Bar.   [3] Nard.   [4] Barnard.—BOSWELL.

from Mr. Cambridge, whom, if a beautiful villa on the banks of the Thames, a few miles distant from London, a numerous and excellent library, which he accurately knows and reads, a choice collection of pictures, which he understands and relishes, an easy fortune, an amiable family, an extensive circle of friends and acquaintance, distinguished by rank, fashion, and genius, a literary fame, various elegant and still increasing colloquial talents rarely to be found, and, with all these means of happiness, enjoying, when well advanced in years, health and vigour of body, serenity and animation of mind—do not entitle to be addressed *fortunate senex!* I know not to whom, in any age, that expression could with propriety have been used. Long may he live to hear and to feel it![1]

Johnson's love of little children, which he discovered upon all occasions, calling them "pretty dears," and giving them sweetmeats, was an undoubted proof of the real humanity and gentleness of his disposition.

His uncommon kindness to his servants, and serious concern, not only for their comfort in this world, but their happiness in the next, was another unquestionable evidence of what all who were intimately acquainted with him, knew to be true.

Nor would it be just under this head, to omit the fondness which he showed for animals which he had taken under his protection. I never shall forget the indulgence with which he treated Hodge his cat: for whom he himself used to go out and buy oysters, lest the servants having that trouble should take a dislike to the poor creature. I am, unluckily, one of those who have an antipathy to a cat, so that I am uneasy when in the room with one; and I own, I frequently suffered a good deal from the presence of the same Hodge. I recollect him one day scrambling up Dr. Johnson's breast, apparently with much satisfaction, while my friend, smiling, and half-whistling, rubbed down his back, and pulled him by the tail; and, when I observed he was a fine cat, saying: "Why, yes, Sir; but I have had cats whom I liked better than this;" and then, as if perceiving Hodge to be out of countenance, adding, "but he is a very fine cat, a very fine cat indeed."

This reminds me of the ludicrous account which he gave Mr. Langton, of the despicable state of a young gentleman of good family. "Sir, when I heard of him last,

---

[1] Mr. Cambridge enjoyed all the blessings here enumerated for many years after this passage was written. He died at his seat near Twickenham, Sept. 17, 1802, in his eighty-sixth year.—MALONE.

he was running about town shooting cats." And then, in a sort of kindly reverie, he bethought himself of his own favourite cat, and said, "But Hodge shan't be shot: no, no, Hodge shall not be shot."

He thought Mr. Beauclerk made a shrewd and judicious remark to Mr. Langton, who, after having been for the first time in company with a well known wit about town, was warmly admiring and praising him,—"See him again," said Beauclerk.

His respect for the Hierarchy, and particularly the dignitaries of the Church, has been more than once exhibited in the course of this work. Mr. Seward saw him presented to the Archbishop of York, and described his *bow to an Archbishop*, as such a studied elaboration of homage, such an extension of limb, such a flexion of body, as have seldom or ever been equalled.

I cannot help mentioning, with much regret, that by my own negligence I lost an opportunity of having the history of my family from its founder, Thomas Boswell, in 1504, recorded and illustrated by Johnson's pen. Such was his goodness to me, that when I presumed to solicit him for so great a favour, he was pleased to say, "Let me have all the materials you can collect, and I will do it both in Latin and English; then let it be printed, and copies of it be deposited in various places for security and preservation." I can now only do the best I can to make up for this loss, keeping my great master steadily in view. Family histories, like the *imagines majorum* of the ancients, excite to virtue; and I wish that they who really have blood would be more careful to trace and ascertain its course. Some have affected to laugh at the history of the house of Yvery:[1] it would be well if many others would transmit their pedigrees to posterity, with the same accuracy and generous zeal, with which the noble lord, who compiled that work, has honoured and perpetuated his ancestry.

On Thursday, April 10, I introduced to him, at his house in Bolt-court, the Honourable and Reverend William Stuart,[2] son of the Earl of Bute; a gentleman truly worthy of being known to Johnson; being, with all the advantages of high birth, learning, travel, and elegant manners, an exemplary parish priest in every respect.

---

[1] Written by John, Earl of Egmont.—MALONE.

[2] At that time Vicar of Luton, in Bedfordshire, where he lived for some years, and fully merited the character given of him in the text; now [1806] Lord Archbishop of Armagh, and Primate of Ireland.—MALONE.

After some compliments on both sides, the tour which Johnson and I had made to the Hebrides was mentioned. —JOHNSON: "I got an acquisition of more ideas by it than by anything that I remember. I saw quite a different system of life." BOSWELL: "You would not like to make the same journey again?" JOHNSON: "Why no, Sir; not the same: it is a tale told. Gravina, an Italian critic, observes, that every man desires to see that of which he has read; but no man desires to read an account of what he has seen: so much does description fall short of reality. Description only excites curiosity: seeing satisfies it. Other people may go and see the Hebrides." BOSWELL: "I should wish to go and see some country totally different from what I have been used to; such as Turkey, where religion and everything else are different." JOHNSON: "Yes, Sir; there are two subjects of curiosity,—the Christian world and the Mahometan world. All the rest may be considered as barbarous." BOSWELL: "Pray, Sir, is 'The Turkish Spy' a genuine book?" JOHNSON: "No, Sir. Mrs. Manley, in her Life, says that her father wrote the first two volumes: and in another book, 'Dunton's Life and Errors,' we find that the rest was written by one Sault, at two guineas a sheet, under the direction of Dr. Midgeley."[1]

BOSWELL: "This has been a very factious reign, owing to the too great indulgence of government." JOHNSON: "I think so, Sir. What at first was lenity, grew timidity. Yet this is reasoning _à posteriori_, and may not be just. Supposing a few had at first been punished, I believe faction would have been crushed; but it might have been said, that it was a sanguinary reign. A man cannot tell _à priori_ what will be best for government to do. This reign has been very unfortunate. We have had an unsuccessful war; but that does not prove that we have been ill governed. One side or other must prevail in war, as one or other must win at play. When we beat Louis, we were not better governed; nor were the French better governed when Louis beat us."

On Saturday, April 12, I visited him, in company with

---

[1] "The Turkish Spy" was pretended to have been written originally in Arabic; from Arabic translated into Italian, and thence into English. The real author of the work, which was, in fact, originally written in Italian, was I. P. Marana, a Genoese, who died at Paris in 1693.—BOSWELL.

John Dunton, in his life, says, that "Mr. _William Bradshaw_ received from Mr. Midgeley forty shillings a sheet for writing part of 'The Turkish Spy:'" but I do not find that he any where mentions _Sault_ as engaged in that work.—MALONE.

Mr. Windham, of Norfolk, whom, though a Whig, he highly valued. One of the best things he ever said was to this gentleman; who, before he set out for Ireland as secretary to Lord Northington, when Lord Lieutenant, expressed to the sage some modest and virtuous doubts, whether he could bring himself to practise those arts which it is supposed a person in that situation has occasion to employ. "Don't be afraid, Sir," said Johnson, with a pleasant smile, "you will soon make a very pretty rascal."

He talked to-day a good deal of the wonderful extent and variety of London, and observed that men of curious inquiry might see in it such modes of life as very few could even imagine. He in particular recommended to us to *explore Wapping*, which we resolved to do.[1]

Mr. Lowe, the painter, who was with him, was very much distressed that a large picture which he had painted was refused to be received into the Exhibition of the Royal Academy. Mrs. Thrale knew Johnson's character so superficially as to represent him as unwilling to do small acts of benevolence, and mentions, in particular, that he would hardly take the trouble to write a letter in favour of his friends. The truth, however, is, that he was remarkable, in an extraordinary degree, for what she denies to him; and, above all, for this very sort of kindness, writing letters for those to whom his solicitations might be of service. He now gave Mr. Lowe the following, of which I was diligent enough, with his permission, to take copies at the next coffee-house, while Mr. Windham was so good as to stay by me.

"TO SIR JOSHUA REYNOLDS.

"Sir,   April 12, 1783.

"Mr. Lowe considers himself as cut off from all credit and all hope, by the rejection of his picture from the exhibition. Upon this work he has exhausted all his powers, and suspended all his expectations; and certainly, to be refused an opportunity of taking the opinion of the public, is in itself a very great hardship. It is to be condemned without a trial.

"If you could procure the revocation of this incapacitating edict, you would deliver an unhappy man from great affliction. The council has sometimes reversed its own determination; and I hope that, by your interposition, this luckless picture may be got admitted.

"I am, &c.,
"Sam. Johnson."

---

[1] We accordingly carried our scheme into execution in October 1792; but whether from that uniformity which has in modern times, in a great degree, spread through every part of the metropolis, or from our want of sufficient exertion, we were disappointed.—Boswell.

"TO MR. BARRY.

"SIR,   April 12, 1783.
"Mr. Lowe's exclusion from the exhibition gives him more trouble than you and the other gentlemen of the council could imagine or intend.   He considers disgrace and ruin as the inevitable consequence of your determination.

"He says that some pictures have been received after rejection; and if there be any such precedent, I earnestly entreat that you will use your interest in his favour.   Of his work I can say nothing; I pretend not to judge of painting; and this picture I never saw: but I conceive it extremely hard to shut out any man from the possibility of success; and therefore I repeat my request that you will propose the re-consideration of Mr. Lowe's case; and if there be any among the council with whom my name can have any weight, be pleased to communicate to them the desire of, Sir,

" Your most humble servant,
"SAM. JOHNSON."

Such intercession was too powerful to be resisted; and Mr. Lowe's performance was admitted at Somerset Place. The subject, as I recollect, was the Deluge, at that point of time when the water was verging to the top of the last uncovered mountain.   Near to the spot was seen the last of the antediluvian race, exclusive of those who were saved n the ark of Noah.   This was one of those giants, then the inhabitants of the earth, who had still strength to swim, and with one of his hands held aloft his infant child.   Upon the small remaining dry spot appeared a famished lion, ready to spring at the child and devour it.   Mr. Lowe told me that Johnson said to him, "Sir, your picture is noble and probable."   "A compliment indeed," said Mr. Lowe, "from a man who cannot lie, and cannot be mistaken."

About this time he wrote to Mrs. Lucy Porter, mentioning his bad health, and that he intended a visit to Lichfield.   "It is," says he, "with no great expectation of amendment that I make every year a journey into the country; but it is pleasant to visit those whose kindness has been often experienced."

On April 18 (being Good Friday) I found him at breakfast, in his usual manner upon that day, drinking tea without milk, and eating a cross-bun to prevent faintness.   We went to St. Clement's church, as formerly.   When we came home from church, he placed himself on one of the stone seats at his garden door, and I took the other, and thus in the open air, and in a placid frame of mind, he talked away very easily.   JOHNSON: "Were I a country gentleman, I should not be very hospitable; I should not have crowds in my house."   BOSWELL: "Sir Alexander Dick tells me, that he remembers having a thousand people in a year to dine at his house; that is, reckoning each person as one, each time that he dined there." JOHNSON: "That, Sir, is about three a day," BOSWELL: "How your statement lessens the idea." JOHNSON: "That, Sir, is the good of counting. It brings everything to a certainty, which before floated in the mind indefinitely." BOSWELL: "But *Omne ignotum pro magnifico est*: one is sorry to have this diminished." JOHNSON: "Sir, you should not allow yourself to be delighted with error." BOSWELL: "Three a-day seem but few." JOHNSON: "Nay, Sir, he who entertains three a-day does very liberally. And if there is a large family, the poor entertain those three; for they eat what the poor would get: there must be superfluous meat; it must be given to the poor, or thrown out." BOSWELL: "I observe in London, that the poor go about and gather bones, which I understand are manufactured." JOHNSON: "Yes, Sir; they boil them, and extract a grease from them for greasing wheels and other purposes. Of the best pieces they make a mock ivory, which is used for hafts to knives, and various other things; the coarser pieces they burn and pound, and sell the ashes." BOSWELL: "For what purpose, Sir?" JOHNSON: "Why, Sir, for making a furnace for the chemists for melting iron. A paste made of burnt bones will stand a stronger heat than anything else. Consider, Sir, if you are to melt iron, you cannot line your pot with brass, because it is softer than iron, and would melt sooner; nor with iron, for though malleable iron is harder than cast iron, yet it would not do; but a paste of burnt bones will not melt." BOSWELL: "Do you know, Sir, I have discovered a manufacture to a great extent, of what you only piddle at,—scraping and drying the peel of oranges.[1] At a place in Newgate-street, there is a prodigious quantity prepared, which they sell to the distillers." JOHNSON: "Sir, I believe they make a higher thing out of them than a spirit; they make what is called orange-butter, the oil of the orange inspissated, which they mix perhaps with common pomatum, and make it fragrant. The oil does not fly off in the drying."

BOSWELL: "I wish to have a good walled garden." JOHNSON: "I don't think it would be worth the expense to you. We compute in England, a park-wall at a thou-

---

[1] It is suggested to me, by an anonymous annotator on my work, that the reason why Dr. Johnson collected the peels of squeezed oranges may be found in the 358th Letter in Mrs. Piozzi's Collection, where it appears that he recommended "dried orange-peel, finely powdered," as a medicine.—BOSWELL.

sand pounds a mile; now a garden-wall must cost at least as much. You intend your trees should grow higher than a deer will leap. Now let us see;—for a hundred pounds you could only have forty-four square yards, which is very little; for two hundred pounds, you may have eighty-four square yards, which is very well. But when will you get the value of two hundred pounds of walls, in fruit, in your climate? No, Sir, such contention with Nature is not worth while. I would plant an orchard, and have plenty of such fruit as ripens well in your country. My friend, Dr. Madden, of Ireland, said, that, 'in an orchard there should be enough to eat, enough to lay up, enough to be stolen, and enough to rot upon the ground.' Cherries are an early fruit; you may have them, and you may have the early apples and pears." BOSWELL: "We cannot have nonpareils." JOHNSON: "Sir, you can no more have nonpareils than you can have grapes." BOSWELL: "We have them, Sir; but they are very bad." JOHNSON: "Nay, Sir, never try to have a thing merely to show that you *cannot* have it. From ground that would let for forty shillings you may have a large orchard; and you see it costs you only forty shillings. Nay, you may graze the ground when the trees are grown up; you cannot, while they are young." BOSWELL: "Is not a good garden a very common thing in England, Sir?" JOHNSON: "Not so common, Sir, as you imagine. In Lincolnshire there is hardly an orchard; in Staffordshire very little fruit." BOSWELL: "Has Langton no orchard?" JOHNSON: "No, Sir." BOSWELL: "How so, Sir?" JOHNSON: "Why, Sir, from the general negligence of the country. He has it not, because nobody else has it." BOSWELL: "A hot-house is a certain thing; I may have that." JOHNSON: "A hot-house is pretty certain; but you must first build it, then you must keep fires in it, and you must have a gardener to take care of it." BOSWELL: "But if I have a gardener at any rate—" JOHNSON: "Why, yes." BOSWELL: "I'd have it near my house; there is no need to have it in the orchard." JOHNSON: "Yes, I'd have it near my house. I would plant a great many currants; the fruit is good, and they make a pretty sweetmeat."

I record this minute detail, which some may think trifling, in order to show clearly how this great man, whose mind could grasp such large and extensive subjects, as he has shown in his literary labours, was yet well informed in the common affairs of life, and loved to illustrate them.

Mr. Walker, the celebrated master of elocution, came

in, and then we went up stairs into the study. I asked him if he had taught many clergymen. JOHNSON: "I hope not." WALKER: "I have taught only one, and he is the best reader I ever heard, not by my teaching, but by his own natural talents." JOHNSON: "Were he the best reader in the world, I would not have it told that he was taught." Here was one of his peculiar prejudices. Could it be any disadvantage to the clergyman to have it known that he was taught an easy and graceful delivery? BOSWELL: "Will you not allow, Sir, that a man may be taught to read well?" JOHNSON: "Why, Sir, so far as to read better than he might do without being taught, yes. Formerly it was supposed that there was no difference in reading, but that one read as well as another." BOSWELL: "It is wonderful to see old Sheridan as enthusiastic about oratory as ever." WALKER: "His enthusiasm, as to what oratory will do, may be too great: but he reads well." JOHNSON: "He reads well, but he reads low; and you know it is much easier to read low than to read high; for when you read high, you are much more limited, your loudest note can be but one, and so the variety is less in proportion to the loudness. Now some people have occasion to speak to an extensive audience, and must speak loud to be heard." WALKER: "The art is to read strong, though low."

Talking of the origin of language;—JOHNSON: "It must have come by inspiration. A thousand, nay, a million of children could not invent a language. While the organs are pliable, there is not understanding enough to form a language; by the time that there is understanding enough, the organs are become stiff. We know that after a certain age we cannot learn to pronounce a new language. No foreigner, who comes to England when advanced in life, ever pronounces English tolerably well; at least such instances are very rare. When I maintain that language must have come by inspiration, I do not mean that inspiration is required for rhetoric, and all the beauties of language; for when once man has language, we can conceive that he may gradually form modifications of it. I mean only that inspiration seems to me to be necessary to give man the faculty of speech; to inform him that he may have speech; which I think he could no more find out without inspiration than cows or hogs would think of such a faculty." WALKER: "Do you think, Sir, that there are any perfect synonymes in any language?" JOHNSON: "Originally there were not; but by using words negligently, or in poetry, one word comes to be confounded with another."

He talked of Dr. Dodd. "A friend of mine," said he, "came to me, and told me, that a lady wished to have Dr. Dodd's picture in a bracelet, and asked me for a motto. I said, I could think of no better than *Currat Lex*. I was very willing to have him pardoned; that is, to have the sentence changed to transportation; but, when he was once hanged, I did not wish he should be made a saint."

Mrs. Burney, wife of his friend Dr. Burney, came in, and he seemed to be entertained with her conversation.

Garrick's funeral was talked of as extravagantly expensive. Johnson, from his dislike to exaggeration, would not allow that it was distinguished by any extraordinary pomp. "Were there not six horses to each coach?" said Mrs. Burney. JOHNSON: "Madam, there were no more six horses than six phœnixes."

Mrs. Burney wondered that some very beautiful new buildings should be erected in Moorfields, in so shocking a situation as between Bedlam and St. Luke's Hospital; and said she could not live there. JOHNSON: "Nay, Madam, you see nothing there to hurt you. You no more think of madness by having windows that look to Bedlam, than you think of death by having windows that look to a churchyard." MRS. BURNEY: "We may look to a churchyard, Sir; for it is right that we should be kept in mind of death." JOHNSON: "Nay, Madam, if you go to that, it is right that we should be kept in mind of madness, which is occasioned by too much indulgence of imagination. I think a very moral use may be made of these new buildings; I would have those who have heated imaginations live there, and take warning." MRS. BURNEY: "But, Sir, many of the poor people that are mad, have become so from disease, or from distressing events. It is, therefore, not their fault, but their misfortune; and therefore to think of them is a melancholy consideration."

Time passed on in conversation till it was too late for the service of the church at three o'clock. I took a walk, and left him alone for some time; then returned, and we had coffee and conversation again by ourselves.

I stated the character of a noble friend of mine, as a curious case for his opinion:—"He is the most inexplicable man to me that I ever knew. Can you explain him, Sir? He is, I really believe, noble-minded, generous, and princely. But his most intimate friends may be separated from him for years, without his ever asking a question concerning them. He will meet them with a formality, a coldness, a stately indifference; but when they come close to him, and fairly engage him in conversation, they find him as easy, pleasant, and kind as they could wish. One then supposes that what is so agreeable will soon be renewed; but stay away from him for half a year, and he will neither call on you, nor send to inquire about you." JOHNSON: "Why, Sir, I cannot ascertain his character exactly, as I do not know him; but I should not like to have such a man for my friend. He may love study, and wish not to be interrupted by his friends; *Amici fures temporis.* He may be a frivolous man, and be so much occupied with petty pursuits, that he may not want friends. Or he may have a notion that there is a dignity in appearing indifferent, while he in fact may not be more indifferent at his heart than another."

We went to evening prayers at St. Clement's, at seven, and then parted.

CHAPTER XXIV.—1783

Increase of London, and its Population—Natural Affections —Duel between Riddell and Cunningham—On Corpulency—Government of India—Dr. Shebbeare—Payment for Reviewing—Religious Disbelief—Liberty of Conscience—Mallet's first Essay—On Reading—Virgil and Homer—Cant—Hospitality—Sheridan—Friendship— Barry's Pictures—Christian Devotion—Richard Baxter —Miss Philips—Correspondence—Johnson attacked by Paralysis—Mr. Davies—Johnson's Recovery—Visits Rochester and Heale—Death of Mrs. Williams—Miscellaneous Conversation

ON Sunday, April 20, being Easter-day, after attending solemn service at St. Paul's, I came to Dr. Johnson, and found Mr. Lowe, the painter, sitting with him. Mr. Lowe mentioned the great number of new buildings of late in London, yet that Dr. Johnson had observed, that the number of inhabitants was not increased. JOHNSON: "Why, Sir, the bills of mortality prove that no more people die now than formerly; so it is plain no more live. The register of births proves nothing; for not one-tenth of the people of London are born there." BOSWELL: "I believe, Sir, a great many of the children born in London die early." JOHNSON: "Why, yes, Sir." BOSWELL: "But those who do live, are as stout and strong people as any: Dr. Price says, they must be naturally strong to get through." JOHNSON: "That is system, Sir. A great traveller observes, that it is said there are no weak or deformed people among the Indians; but he with much sagacity assigns the reason of this, which is, that the hardship of their life, as hunters, and fishers, does not allow weak or diseased children to grow up. Now had I been an Indian I must have died early; my eyes would not have served me to get food. I indeed now could fish, give me English tackle; but had I been an Indian I must have starved, or they would have knocked me on the head, when they saw I could do nothing.

Boswell: "Perhaps they would have taken care of you; we are told they are fond of oratory; you would have talked to them." Johnson: "Nay, Sir, I should not have lived long enough to be fit to talk; I should have been dead before I was ten years old. Depend upon it, Sir, a savage, when he is hungry, will not carry about with him a looby of nine years old, who cannot help himself. They have no affection, Sir." Boswell: "I believe natural affection, of which we hear so much, is very small." Johnson: "Sir, natural affection is nothing: but affection from principle and established duty, is sometimes wonderfully strong." Lowe: "A hen, Sir, will feed her chickens in preference to herself." Johnson: "But we don't know that the hen is hungry; let the hen be fairly hungry, and I'll warrant she'll peck the corn herself. A cock, I believe, will feed hens instead of himself; but we don't know that the cock is hungry." Boswell: "And that, Sir, is not from affection but gallantry. But some of the Indians have affection." Johnson: "Sir, that they help some of their children is plain; for some of them live, which they could not do without being helped."

I dined with him. The company were, Mrs. Williams, Mrs. Desmoulins, and Mr. Lowe. He seemed not to be well, talked little, grew drowsy soon after dinner, and retired, upon which I went away.

Having next day gone to Mr. Burke's seat in the country, from whence I was recalled by an express, that a near relation of mine had killed his antagonist in a duel, and was himself dangerously wounded, I saw little of Dr. Johnson till Monday, April 28, when I spent a considerable part of the day with him, and introduced the subject, which then chiefly occupied my mind. Johnson: "I do not see, Sir, that fighting is absolutely forbidden in scripture; I see revenge forbidden, but not self defence." Boswell: "The Quakers say it is; 'Unto him that smiteth thee on one cheek, offer him also the other.'" Johnson: "But stay, Sir; the text is meant only to have the effect of moderating passion; it is plain that we are not to take it in a literal sense. We see this from the context, where there are other recommendations, which I warrant you the Quaker will not take literally; as, for instance, 'From him that would borrow of thee, turn thou not away.' Let a man whose credit is bad, come to a Quaker, and say, 'Well, Sir, lend me a hundred pounds;' he will find him as unwilling as any other man. No, Sir, a man may shoot the man who invades his character, as he may shoot him who attempts

to break into his house.[1]   So in 1745, my friend Tom
Cumming the Quaker, said he would not fight, but
he would drive an ammunition cart; and we know that
the Quakers have sent flannel waistcoats to our soldiers,
to enable them to fight better."   BOSWELL: "When a man
is the aggressor, and by ill-usage forces on a duel in which
he is killed, have we not little ground to hope that he is
gone to a state of happiness?"   JOHNSON: "Sir, we are not
to judge determinately of the state in which a man leaves
this life.   He may in a moment have repented effectually,
and it is possible may have been accepted of God.   There
is, in 'Camden's Remains,' an epitaph upon a very wicked
man, who was killed by a fall from his horse, in which he
is supposed to say,

> 'Between the stirrup and the ground,
> I mercy asked, I mercy found.' "[2]

BOSWELL: "Is not the expression in the Burial-service,
'in the *sure* and *certain* hope of a blessed resurrection,'
too strong to be used indiscriminately, and, indeed, sometimes when those over whose bodies it is said, have been
notoriously profane?"   JOHNSON: "It is sure and certain
hope, Sir; not *belief*."   I did not insist farther; but cannot
help thinking that less positive words would be more
proper.[3]

---

[1] I think it necessary to caution my readers against concluding that
in this or any other conversation of Dr. Johnson, they have his serious
and deliberate opinion on the subject of duelling.   In my "Journal of
a Tour to the Hebrides," 3 edit. p. 386, it appears that he made this
frank confession; "Nobody at times talks more laxly than I do;" and
ibid. p. 231, "he fairly owned he could not explain the rationality of
duelling."   We may, therefore, infer that he could not think that
justifiable, which seems so inconsistent with the spirit of the Gospel.
At the same time, it must be confessed that from the prevalent notions
of honour, a gentleman who receives a challenge is reduced to a dreadful
alternative.   A remarkable instance of this is furnished by a clause in
the will of the late Colonel Thomas, of the Guards, written the night
before he fell in a duel, September 3, 1783: "In the first place, I commit
my soul to Almighty GOD, in hopes of his mercy and pardon for the
irreligious step I now (in compliance with the unwarrantable customs
of this wicked world) put myself under the necessity of taking."—
BOSWELL.

[2] In repeating this epitaph Johnson improved it.   The original runs
thus:—

> "*Betwixt* the stirrup and the ground,
> Mercy I asked, mercy I found."—MALONE.

[3] Upon this objection the Reverend Mr. Ralph Churton, Fellow of
Brazenose College, Oxford, has favoured me with the following satisfactory observation.   "The passage in the Burial-service does not mean
the resurrection of the person interred, but the general resurrection;
it is in sure and certain hope of *the* resurrection—not *his* resurrection.

Talking of a man who was grown very fat, so as to be incommoded with corpulency; he said, "He eats too much, Sir." BOSWELL: "I don't know, Sir; you will see one man fat who eats moderately, and another lean who eats a great deal." JOHNSON: "Nay, Sir, whatever may be the quantity that a man eats, it is plain that if he is too fat, he has eaten more than he should have done. One man may have a digestion that consumes food better than common; but it is certain that solidity is increased by putting something to it." BOSWELL: "But may not solids swell and be distended? JOHNSON: "Yes, Sir, they may swell and be distended; but that is not fat."

We talked of the accusation against a gentleman for supposed delinquencies in India. JOHNSON: "What foundation there is for accusation I know not; but they will not get at him. Where bad actions are committed at so great a distance, a delinquent can obscure the evidence till the scent becomes cold: there is a cloud between which cannot be penetrated: therefore all distant power is bad. I am clear that the best plan for the government of India is a despotic governor; for if he be a good man, it is evidently the best government: and supposing him to be a bad man, it is better to have one plunderer than many. A governor, whose power is checked, lets others plunder, that he himself may be allowed to plunder; but if despotic, he sees that the more he lets others plunder, the less there will be for himself, so he restrains them; and though he himself plunders, the country is a gainer, compared with being plundered by numbers."

I mentioned the very liberal payment which had been received for reviewing; and, as evidence of this, that it had been proved in a trial, that Dr. Shebbeare had received six guineas a sheet for that kind of literary labour. JOHNSON: "Sir, he might get six guineas for a particular sheet, but not *communibus sheetibus*." BOSWELL: "Pray, Sir, by a sheet of review is it meant that it shall be all of the writer's own composition? or are extracts, made from

Where the deceased is really spoken of, the expression is very different, 'as our hope is this our brother doth' [rest in Christ], a mode of speech consistent with everything but absolute certainty that the person departed doth *not* rest in Christ, which no one can be assured of without immediate revelation from Heaven. In the first of these places, also, 'eternal life' does not necessarily mean eternity of bliss, but merely the eternity of the state, whether in happiness or in misery, to ensue upon the resurrection; which is probably the sense of 'the life everlasting,' in the Apostles' Creed. See Wheatly and Bennet on the Common Prayer."—BOSWELL.

the book reviewed, deducted?" JOHNSON: "No, Sir; it
is a sheet, no matter of what." BOSWELL: "I think that
it is not reasonable." JOHNSON: "Yes, Sir, it is. A
man will more easily write a sheet all his own, than read
an octavo volume to get extracts." To one of Johnson's
wonderful fertility of mind, I believe writing was really
easier than reading and extracting; but with ordinary men
the case is very different. A great deal, indeed, will depend
upon the care and judgment with which extracts are made.
I can suppose the operation to be tedious and difficult;
but in many instances we must observe crude morsels
cut out of books as if at random; and when a large extract
is made from one place, it surely may be done with very
little trouble. One, however, I must acknowledge, might
be led, from the practice of reviewers, to suppose that
they take a pleasure in original writing; for we often
find, that instead of giving an accurate account of what
has been done by the author whose work they are
reviewing, which is surely the proper business of a
literary journal, they produce some plausible and
ingenious conceits of their own, upon the topics which
have been discussed.

Upon being told that old Mr. Sheridan, indignant at
the neglect of his oratorical plans, had threatened to go
to America—JOHNSON: "I hope he will go to America."
BOSWELL: "The Americans don't want oratory." JOHN-
SON: "But we can want Sheridan."

On Monday, April 28, I found him at home in the fore-
noon, and Mr. Seward with him. Horace having been
mentioned—BOSWELL: "There is a great deal of thinking in his works. One finds there almost everything but
religion." SEWARD: "He speaks of his returning to it,
in his Ode *Parcus Deorum cultor et infrequens.*" JOHNSON:
"Sir, he was not in earnest; this was merely poetical."
BOSWELL: "There are, I am afraid, many people who have
no religion at all." SEWARD: "And sensible people too."
JOHNSON: "Why, Sir, not sensible in that respect. There
must be either a natural or a moral stupidity, if one lives
in a total neglect of so very important a concern." SEWARD:
"I wonder that there should be people without religion."
JOHNSON: "Sir, you need not wonder at this, when you
consider how large a proportion of almost every man's
life is passed without thinking of it. I myself was for
some years totally regardless of religion. It had dropped
out of my mind. It was at an early part of my life.
Sickness brought it back, and I hope I have never lost it
since." BOSWELL: "My dear Sir, what a man must you

have been without religion! Why you must have gone on drinking, and swearing, and—" Johnson (with a smile): "I drank enough and swore enough to be sure." Seward: "One should think that sickness, and the view of death, would make more men religious." Johnson: "Sir, they do not know how to go about it; they have not the first notion. A man who has never had religion before, no more grows religious, when he is sick, than a man who has never learned figures can count when he has need of calculation."

I mentioned a worthy friend of ours whom we valued much, but observed that he was too ready to introduce religious discourse upon all occasions. Johnson: "Why yes, Sir, he will introduce religious discourse without seeing whether it will end in instruction and improvement, or produce some profane jest. He would introduce it in the company of Wilkes, and twenty more such."

I mentioned Dr. Johnson's excellent distinction between liberty of conscience and liberty of teaching. Johnson: "Consider, Sir; if you have children whom you wish to educate in the principles of the Church of England, and there comes a Quaker who tries to pervert them to his principles, you would drive away the Quaker. You would not trust to the predomination of right, which you believe is in your opinions; you will keep wrong out of their heads. Now the vulgar are the children of the State. If any one attempts to teach them doctrines contrary to what the State approves, the magistrate may and ought to restrain him." Seward: "Would you restrain private conversation, Sir?" Johnson: "Why, Sir, it is difficult to say where private conversation begins and where it ends. If we three should discuss even the great question concerning the existence of a Supreme Being by ourselves, we should not be restrained; for that would be to put an end to all improvement. But if we should discuss it in the presence of ten boarding-school girls and as many boys, I think the magistrate would do well to put us in the stocks, to finish the debate there."

Lord Hailes had sent him a present of a curious little printed poem, on repairing the University of Aberdeen, by David *Malloch*, which he thought would please Johnson, as affording clear evidence that Mallet had appeared even as a literary character by the name of *Malloch*, his changing which to one of softer sound, had given Johnson occasion to introduce him into his Dictionary, under the article *Alias*.[1] This piece was, I suppose, one of Mallet's first essays. It is preserved in his works, with several variations. Johnson having read aloud, from the beginning of it, where there were some common-place assertions, as to the superiority of ancient times:—"How false," said he, "is all this, to say that in ancient times learning was not a disgrace to a peer as it is now. In ancient times a peer was as ignorant as any one else. He would have been angry to have it thought he could write his name. Men in ancient times dared to stand forth with a degree of ignorance with which nobody would dare now to stand forth. I am always angry, when I hear ancient times praised at the expense of modern times. There is now a great deal more learning in the world than there was formerly, for it is universally diffused. You have, perhaps, no man who knows as much Greek and Latin as Bentley; no man who knows as much mathematics as Newton; but you have many more men who know Greek and Latin, and who know mathematics."

On Thursday, May 1, I visited him in the evening along with young Mr. Burke. He said, "It is strange that there should be so little reading in the world, and so much writing. People in general do not willingly read, if they can have anything else to amuse them. There must be an external impulse; emulation, or vanity, or avarice. The progress which the understanding makes through a book, has more pain than pleasure in it. Language is scanty, and inadequate to express the nice gradations and mixtures of our feelings. No man reads a book of science from pure inclination. The books that we do read with pleasure are light compositions, which contain a quick succession of events. However, I have this year read all Virgil through. I read a book of the Æneid every night; so it was done in twelve nights, and I had a great delight in it. The Georgics did not give me so much pleasure, except the fourth book.

[1] Malloch, as Mr. Bindley observes to me, "continued to write his name thus, *after he came to London*. His verses prefixed to the second edition of Thomson's 'Winter' are so subscribed, and so are his Letters written in London, and published a few years ago in 'The European Magazine;' but he soon afterwards adopted the alteration to Mallet, for he is so called in the list of subscribers to 'Savage's Miscellanies,' printed in 1726; and thenceforward uniformly *Mallet*, in all his writings." —MALONE.

A notion has been entertained that no such exemplification of *Alias* is to be found in "Johnson's Dictionary," and that the whole story was waggishly fabricated by Wilkes in "The North Briton." The real fact is, that it is not to be found in the folio or quarto editions, but was added by Johnson in his own *octavo* abridgment, in 1756.— J. BOSWELL, JUN.

The Eclogues I have almost all by heart. I do not think the story of the Æneid interesting. I like the story of the Odyssey much better; and this, not on account of the wonderful things which it contains; for there are wonderful things enough in the Æneid—the ships of the Trojans turned to sea-nymphs,—the tree at Polydorus's tomb dropping blood. The story of the Odyssey is interesting, as a great part of it is domestic. It has been said there is pleasure in writing, particularly in writing verses. I allow you may have pleasure from writing, after it is over, if you have written well;[1] but you don't go willingly to it again. I know, when I have been writing verses, I have run my finger down the margin, to see how many I had made, and how few I had to make."

He seemed to be in a very placid humour, and although I have no note of the particulars of young Mr. Burke's conversation, it is but justice to mention in general, that it was such that Dr. Johnson said to me afterwards, "He did very well indeed; I have a mind to tell his father."

"TO SIR JOSHUA REYNOLDS.

"Dear Sir,   May 2, 1783.

"The gentleman who waits on you with this, is Mr. Cruikshanks, who wishes to succeed his friend Dr. Hunter, as Professor of Anatomy in the Royal Academy. His qualifications are very generally known, and it adds dignity to the institution that such men[2] are candidates.

"I am, Sir, your most humble servant,

"Sam. Johnson."

I have no minute of any interview with Johnson till Thursday, May 15th, when I find what follows:—Boswell: "I wish much to be in Parliament, Sir." Johnson: "Why, Sir, unless you come resolved to support any administration, you would be the worse for being in Parliament, because you would be obliged to live more expensively." Boswell: "Perhaps, Sir, I should be the less happy for being in Parliament. I never would sell my vote, and I should be vexed if things went wrong." Johnson: "That's cant, Sir. It would not vex you more in the house than in the gallery; public affairs vex no man." Boswell: "Have not they vexed yourself a little, Sir? Have not you been vexed by all the turbulence of this reign, and by

---

[1] "Dum pingit, fruitur arte; postquam pinxerit, fruitur fructu artis." (*Seneca*.)—Kearney.

[2] Let it be remembered, by those who accuse Dr. Johnson of illiberality, that both were *Scotchmen*."—Boswell.

that absurd vote of the House of Commons, 'That the influence of the Crown has increased, is increasing, and ought to be diminished?'" JOHNSON: "Sir, I have never slept an hour less, nor eat an ounce less meat. I would have knocked the factious dogs on the head, to be sure; but I was not *vexed*." BOSWELL: "I declare, Sir, upon my honour, I did imagine I was vexed, and took a pride in it; but it *was*, perhaps, cant; for I own I neither eat less, nor slept less." JOHNSON: "My dear friend, clear your *mind* of cant. You may *talk* as other people do: you may say to a man, 'Sir I am your most humble servant.' You are *not* his most humble servant. You may say, 'These are bad times; it is a melancholy thing to be reserved to such times.' You don't mind the times. You tell a man, 'I am sorry you had such bad weather the last day of your journey, and were so much wet.' You don't care sixpence whether he is wet or dry. You may *talk* in this manner; it is a mode of talking in society: but don't *think* foolishly."

I talked of living in the country. JOHNSON: "Don't set up for what is called hospitality: it is a waste of time, and a waste of money; you are eaten up, and not the more respected for your liberality. If your house be like an inn, nobody cares for you. A man who stays a week with another, makes him a slave for a week." BOSWELL: "But there are people, Sir, who make their houses a home to their guests, and are themselves quite easy." JOHNSON: "Then, Sir, home must be the same to the guests, and they need not come."

Here he discovered a notion common enough in persons not much accustomed to entertain company, that there must be a degree of elaborate attention, otherwise company will think themselves neglected; and such attention is no doubt very fatiguing. He proceeded: "I would not, however, be a stranger in my own country; I would visit my neighbours, and receive their visits; but I would not be in haste to return visits. If a gentleman comes to see me, I tell him he does me a great deal of honour. I do not go to see him perhaps for ten weeks; then we are very complaisant to each other. No, Sir, you will have much more influence by giving or lending money where it is wanted, than by hospitality."

On Saturday, May 17, I saw him for a short time. Having mentioned that I had that morning been with old Mr. Sheridan, he remembered their former intimacy with a cordial warmth, and said to me, "Tell Mr. Sheridan, I shall be glad to see him, and shake hands with him." BOSWELL: "It is to me very wonderful that resentment

should be kept up so long." JOHNSON: "Why, Sir, it is
not altogether resentment that he does not visit me; it
is partly falling out of the habit,—partly disgust, as one
has at a drug that has made him sick. Besides, he knows
that I laugh at his oratory."

Another day I spoke of one of our friends, of whom he,
as well as I, had a very high opinion. He expatiated in his
praise; but added, "Sir, he is a cursed Whig, a *bottomless*
Whig, as they all are now."

I mentioned my expectations from the interest of an
eminent person then in power; adding, "but I have no
claim but the claim of friendship; however, some people
will go a great way for that motive." JOHNSON: "Sir,
they will go all the way from that motive." A gentleman
talked of retiring. "Never think of that," said Johnson.
The gentleman urged, "I should then do no ill." JOHN-
SON: "Nor no good either. Sir, it would be a civil suicide."

On Monday, May 26, I found him at tea, and the
celebrated Miss Burney, the author of "Evelina" and
"Cecilia," with him. I asked, if there would be any speakers
in Parliament, if there were no places to be obtained.
JOHNSON: "Yes, Sir. Why do you speak here? Either
to instruct and entertain, which is a benevolent motive;
or for distinction, which is a selfish motive." I mentioned
"Cecilia." JOHNSON (with an air of animated satisfaction): "Sir, if you talk of 'Cecilia,' talk on."

We talked of Mr. Barry's exhibition of his pictures.
JOHNSON: "Whatever the hand may have done, the mind
has done its part. There is a grasp of mind there, which
you find no where else." [1]

I asked, whether a man naturally virtuous, or one who
has overcome wicked inclinations, is the best. JOHNSON:
"Sir, to *you* the man who has overcome wicked inclinations
is not the best. He has more merit to *himself*. I would
rather trust my money to a man who has no hands, and
so a physical impossibility to steal, than to a man of the
most honest principles. There is a witty satirical story of
Foote. He had a small bust of Garrick placed upon his
bureau. 'You may be surprised,' said he, 'that I allow
him to be so near my gold; but, you will observe, he has
no hands.'"

On Friday, May 29, being to set out for Scotland next
morning, I passed a part of the day with him in more
than usual earnestness; as his health was in a more pre-

[1] In Mr. Barry's printed analysis, or description of these pictures,
he speaks of Johnson's character in the highest terms.—BOSWELL.

carious state than at any time when I had parted from him.
He, however, was quick and lively, and critical, as usual.
I mentioned one who was a very learned man.   JOHNSON:
"Yes, Sir, he has a great deal of learning; but it never
lies straight.   There is never one idea by the side of
another; 'tis all entangled: and then he drives it so awk-
wardly upon conversation!"

I stated to him an anxious thought, by which a sincere
Christian might be disturbed, even when conscious of having
lived a good life, so far as is consistent with human infirmity; he might fear that he should afterwards fall away,
and be guilty of such crimes as would render all his former
religion vain.   Could there be, upon this awful subject,
such a thing as balancing of accounts; suppose a man who
has led a good life for seven years, commits an act of wickedness, and instantly dies, will his former good life have
any effect in his favour?   JOHNSON: "Sir, if a man has
led a good life for seven years, and then is hurried by passion
to do what is wrong, and is suddenly carried off, depend
upon it he will have the reward of his seven years' good
life: GOD will not take a catch of him.   Upon this principle
Richard Baxter believes that a suicide may be saved.   'If,'
says he, 'it should be objected that what I maintain may
encourage suicide, I answer, I am not to tell a lie to prevent
it.'"   BOSWELL: "But does not the text say, 'As the tree
falls, so it must lie'?"   JOHNSON: "Yes, Sir; as the tree
falls: but," after a little pause, "that is meant as to the
general state of the tree, not what is the effect of a
sudden blast."   In short, he interpreted the expression as
referring to condition, not to position.   The common notion,
therefore, seems to be erroneous; and Shenstone's witty
remark on divines trying to give the tree a jerk
upon a death-bed, to make it lie favourably, is not well
founded.

I asked him what works of Richard Baxter's I should
read.   He said, "Read any of them; they are all good."

He said, "Get as much force of mind as you can.   Live
within your income.   Always have something saved at
the end of the year.   Let your imports be more than your
exports, and you'll never go far wrong."

I assured him, that in the extensive and various range
of his acquaintance there never had been any one who had
a more sincere respect and affection for him than I had.
He said, "I believe it, Sir.   Were I in distress, there is
no man to whom I should sooner come than to you.   I
should like to come and have a cottage in your park,
toddle about, live mostly on milk, and be taken care of

by Mrs. Boswell.   She and I are good friends now—are we not?"

Talking of devotion, he said, "Though it be true that 'God dwelleth not in temples made with hands,' yet in this state of being, our minds are more piously affected in places appropriated to divine worship, than in others. Some people have a particular room in their houses, where they say their prayers; of which I do not disapprove, as it may animate their devotion."

He embraced me, and gave me his blessing, as usual when I was leaving him for any length of time.   I walked from his door to-day, with a fearful apprehension of what might happen before I returned.

"TO THE RIGHT HONOURABLE WILLIAM WINDHAM.

"Sir,   London, May 31, 1783.

"The bringer of this letter is the father of Miss Philips,[1] a singer, who comes to try her voice on the stage at Dublin.

"Mr. Philips is one of my old friends; and as I am of opinion that neither he nor his daughter will do anything that can disgrace their benefactors, I take the liberty of entreating you to countenance and protect them so far as may be suitable to your station and character; [2] and shall consider myself as obliged by any favourable notice which they shall have the honour of receiving from you.

"I am, Sir, your most humble servant,
"Sam. Johnson."

The following is another instance of his active benevolence:—

"TO SIR JOSHUA REYNOLDS.

"Dear Sir,   June 2, 1783.

"I have sent you some of my godson's [3] performances, of which I do not pretend to form any opinion.   When I took the liberty of mentioning him to you, I did not know what I have since been told, that Mr. Moser had admitted him among the students of the Academy.   What more can be done for him, I earnestly entreat you to consider; for I am very desirous that he should derive some advantage from my connection with him.   If you are inclined to see him, I will bring him to wait on you at any time that you shall be pleased to appoint.

"I am, Sir, your most humble servant,
"Sam. Johnson."

[1] Now the celebrated Mrs. Crouch.—Boswell.

[2] Mr. Windham was at this time in Dublin, Secretary to the Earl of Northington, then Lord Lieutenant of Ireland.—Boswell.

[3] Son of Mr. Samuel Paterson.—Boswell.

My anxious apprehensions at parting with him this year proved to be but too well founded; for not long afterwards he had a dreadful stroke of the palsy, of which there are very full and accurate accounts in letters written by himself, to show with what composure of mind, and resignation to the Divine Will, his steady piety enabled him to behave.

"TO MR. EDMUND ALLEN.

"DEAR SIR,   June 17, 1783.

" It has pleased God, this morning, to deprive me of the powers of speech; and as I do not know but that it may be his farther good pleasure to deprive me soon of my senses, I request you will, on the receipt of this note, come to me, and act for me, as the exigencies of my case may require.

" I am, sincerely yours,
"SAM. JOHNSON."

"TO THE REVEREND DR. JOHN TAYLOR.

"DEAR SIR,   June 17, 1783.

" It has pleased God, by a paralytic stroke in the night, to deprive me of speech.

" I am very desirous of Dr. Heberden's assistance, as I think my case is not past remedy.   Let me see you as soon as it is possible. Bring Dr. Heberden with you, if you can; but come yourself at all events.   I am glad you are so well, when I am so dreadfully attacked.

" I think that by a speedy application of stimulants much may be done.   I question if a vomit, vigorous and rough, would not rouse the organs of speech to action.   As it is too early to send, I will try to recollect what I can, that can be suspected to have brought on this dreadful distress.

" I have been accustomed to bleed frequently for an asthmatic complaint, but have forborne for some time by Dr. Pepys's persuasion, who perceived my legs beginning to swell.   I sometimes alleviate a painful, or, more properly, an oppressive, constriction of my chest, by opiates; and have lately taken opium frequently, but the last, or two last times, in smaller quantities.   My largest dose is three grains, and last night I took but two.   You will suggest these things (and they are all that I can call to mind) to Dr. Heberden.   I am, &c.,

"SAM. JOHNSON."

Two days after he wrote thus to Mrs. Thrale:[1]

" On Monday, the 16th, I sat for my picture [to Miss Reynolds], and walked a considerable way with little inconvenience.   In the afternoon and evening I felt myself light and easy, and began to plan schemes of life. Thus I went to bed, and in a short time waked and sat up, as has been long my custom, when I felt a confusion and indistinctness in my head, which lasted I suppose about half a minute. I was alarmed, and prayed God, that however he might afflict my body, he would spare my understanding. This prayer, that I might try the integrity of my faculties, I made in Latin verse. The lines were not very good, but I knew them not to be very good: I made them easily, and concluded myself to be unimpaired in my faculties.

"Soon after I perceived that I had suffered a paralytic stroke, and that my speech was taken from me. I had no pain, and so little dejection in this dreadful state, that I wondered at my own apathy, and considered that perhaps death itself, when it should come, would excite less horror than seems now to attend it.

"In order to rouse the vocal organs, I took two drams. Wine has been celebrated for the production of eloquence. I put myself into violent motion and I think repeated it; but all was vain. I then went to bed, and, strange as it may seem, I think slept. When I saw light, it was time to contrive what I should do. Though God stopped my speech, he left me my hand; I enjoyed a mercy which was not granted to my dear friend Lawrence, who now perhaps overlooks me as I am writing, and rejoices that I have what he wanted. My first note was necessarily to my servant, who came in talking, and could not immediately comprehend why he should read what I put into his hands.

"I then wrote a card to Mr. Allen, that I might have a discreet friend at hand, to act as occasion should require. In penning this note, I had some difficulty; my hand, I knew not how nor why, made wrong letters. I then wrote to Dr. Taylor to come to me, and bring Dr. Heberden: and I sent to Dr. Brocklesby, who is my neighbour. My physicians are very friendly, and give me great hopes; but you may imagine my situation. I have so far recovered my vocal powers as to repeat the Lord's Prayer with no very imperfect articulation. My memory, I hope, yet remains as it was; but such an attack produces solicitude for the safety of every faculty."

"TO MR. THOMAS DAVIES.

"DEAR SIR, June 18, 1783.

"I have had, indeed, a very heavy blow; but God, who yet spares my life, I humbly hope will spare my understanding, and restore my speech. As I am not at all helpless, I want no particular assistance, but am strongly affected by Mrs. Davies's tenderness; and when I think she can do me good, shall be very glad to call upon her. I had ordered friends to be shut out, but one or two have found the way in; and if you come you shall be admitted, for I know not whom I can see that will bring more amusement on his tongue, or more kindness in his heart.

"I am, &c.
"SAM. JOHNSON."

It gives me great pleasure to preserve such a memorial of Johnson's regard for Mr. Davies, to whom I was indebted for my introduction to him.[1] He indeed loved Davies cordially, of which I shall give the following little evidence. One day, when he had treated him with too much asperity, Tom, who was not without pride and spirit, went off in a passion; but he had hardly reached home, when Frank, who had been sent after him, delivered this note: "Come, come, dear Davies, I am always sorry when we quarrel; send me word that we are friends."

"TO JAMES BOSWELL, ESQ.

"DEAR SIR,   London, July 3, 1783.
"Your anxiety about my health is very friendly, and very agreeable with your general kindness. I have, indeed, had a very frightful blow. On the 17th of last month, about three in the morning, as near as I can guess, I perceived myself almost totally deprived of speech. I had no pain. My organs were so obstructed that I could say *no*, but could scarcely say *yes*. I wrote the necessary directions, for it pleased God to spare my hand, and sent for Dr. Heberden and Dr. Brocklesby. Between the time in which I discovered my own disorder, and that in which I sent for the doctors, I had, I believe, in spite of my surprise and solicitude, a little sleep, and nature began to renew its operations. They came and gave the directions which the disease required, and from that time I have been continually improving in articulation. I can now speak; but the nerves are weak, and I cannot continue discourse long; but strength, I hope, will return. The physicians consider me as cured. I was last Sunday at church. On Tuesday I took an airing to Hampstead, and dined with the Club, where Lord Palmerston was proposed, and, against my opinion, was rejected.[2] I designed to go next week with Mr. Langton, to Rochester, where I purpose to stay about ten days, and then try some other air. I have many kind invitations. Your brother has very frequently inquired after me. Most of my friends have, indeed, been very attentive. Thank dear Lord Hailes for his present.

"I hope you found at your return everything gay and prosperous, and your lady in particular, quite recovered and confirmed. Pay her my respects.

"I am, dear Sir, your most humble servant,
"SAM. JOHNSON."

"TO MRS. LUCY PORTER, IN LICHFIELD

"DEAR MADAM,   London, July 5, 1783.
"The account which you give of your health is but melancholy.

---

[1] Poor Derrick, however, though he did not himself introduce me to Dr. Johnson as he promised, had the merit of introducing me to Davies, the immediate introductor.—BOSWELL.
[2] His lordship was soon after chosen, and is now a member of the Club.—BOSWELL.

May it please GOD to restore you. My disease affected my speech, and still continues, in some degree, to obstruct my utterance; my voice is distinct enough for a while; but the organs being still weak are quickly weary; but in other respects I am, I think, rather better than I have lately been; and can let you know my state without the help of any other hand.

"In the opinion of my friends, and in my own, I am gradually mending. The physicians consider me as cured, and I had leave four days ago, to wash the cantharides from my head. Last Tuesday I dined at the Club.

"I am going next week into Kent, and purpose to change the air frequently this summer; whether I shall wander so far as Staffordshire I cannot tell. I should be glad to come. Return my thanks to Mrs. Cobb, and Mr. Pearson, and all that have shown attention to me.

"Let us, my dear, pray for one another, and consider our sufferings as notices mercifully given us to prepare ourselves for another state.

"I live now but in a melancholy way. My old friend Mr. Levett is dead, who lived with me in the house, and was useful and companionable; Mrs. Desmoulins is gone away; and Mrs. Williams is so much decayed, that she can add little to another's gratifications. The world passes away, and we are passing with it; but there is, doubtless, another world, which will endure for ever. Let us all fit ourselves for it.

> "I am, &c.,
> "SAM. JOHNSON."

Such was the general vigour of his constitution, that he recovered from this alarming and severe attack with wonderful quickness; so that in July he was able to make a visit to Mr. Langton at Rochester, where he passed about a fortnight, and made little excursions as easily as at any time of his life. In August he went as far as the neighbourhood of Salisbury, to Heale, the seat of William Bowles, Esq., a gentleman whom I have heard him praise for exemplary religious order in his family. In his diary I find a short but honourable mention of this visit:— "August 28, I came to Heale without fatigue. 30, I am entertained quite to my mind."[1]

---

[1] In his letter to Mrs. Thrale, written on the 13th of August, we find the following melancholy paragraph:—

"I am now broken with disease, without the alleviation of familiar friendship or domestic society: I have no middle state between clamour and silence, between general conversation and self-tormenting solitude. Levett is dead, and poor Williams is making haste to die: I know not if she will ever more come out of her chamber."

In a subsequent letter, August 26, he adds, "Mrs. Williams fancies now and then that she grows better; but her vital powers appear to be slowly burning out. Nobody thinks, however, that she will very soon be quite wasted, and as she suffers me to be of very little use to her I

"TO DR. BROCKLESBY.

"DEAR SIR,   Heale, near Salisbury, Aug. 29, 1783.

"Without appearing to want a just sense of your kind attention, I cannot omit to give an account of the day which seemed to appear in some sort perilous. I rose at five, and went out at six; and having reached Salisbury about nine, went forward a few miles in my friend's chariot. I was no more wearied with the journey, though it was a high-hung, rough coach, than I should have been forty years ago. We shall now see what air will do. The country is all a plain, and the house in which I am, so far as I can judge from my window, for I write before I have left my chamber, is sufficiently pleasant.

"Be so kind as to continue your attention to Mrs. Williams; it is a great consolation to the well, and still greater to the sick, that they find themselves not neglected; and I know that you will be desirous of giving comfort, even where you have no great hope of giving help.

"Since I wrote the former part of the letter, I find that by the course of the post I cannot send it before the thirty-first.

"I am, &c.,
"SAM. JOHNSON."

While he was here, he had a letter from Dr. Brocklesby, acquainting him of the death of Mrs. Williams,[1] which affected him a good deal. Though for several years her

---

have determined to pass some time with Mr. Bowles, near Salisbury, and have taken a place for Thursday.

"Some benefit may be perhaps received from change of air, some from change of company, and some from mere change of place. It is not easy to grow well in a chamber where one has long been sick, and where everything seen, and every person speaking revives and impresses images of pain. Though it be true that no man can run away from himself, yet he may escape from many causes of useless uneasiness. That *the mind is its own place*, is the boast of a fallen angel that had learned to lie. External locality has great effects, at least upon all embodied beings. I hope this little journey will afford me at least some suspense of melancholy."—MALONE.

[1] In his letter to Miss Susanna Thrale, Sept. 9, 1783, he thus writes: "Pray show Mamma this passage of a letter from Dr. Brocklesby. 'Mrs. Williams, from mere inanition, has at length paid the great debt to nature about three o'clock this morning. (Sept. 6.) She died without a struggle, retaining her faculties to the very last, and, as she expressed it, having set her house in order, was prepared to leave it, at the last summons of nature.'"

In his letter to Mrs. Thrale, Sept. 22, he adds, "Poor Williams has, I hope, seen the end of her afflictions. She acted with prudence, and she bore with fortitude. She has left me.

'Thou thy weary task hast done,
Home art gone, and ta'en thy wages.'

Had she had good humour and prompt elocution, her universal curiosity and comprehensive knowledge would have made her the delight of all that knew her. She has left her little to your charity school."—MALONE.

temper had not been complacent, she had valuable qualities, and her departure left a blank in his house. Upon this occasion he, according to his habitual course of piety, composed a prayer.[1]

I shall here insert a few particulars concerning him, with which I have been favoured by one of his friends.

"He had once conceived the design of writing the Life of Oliver Cromwell, saying, that he thought it must be highly curious to trace his extraordinary rise to the supreme power, from so obscure a beginning. He at length laid aside his scheme, on discovering that all that can be told of him is already in print; and that it is impracticable to procure any authentic information in addition to what the world is already possessed of."[2]

"He had likewise projected, but at what part of his life is not known, a work to show how small a quantity of REAL FICTION there is in the world; and that the same images, with very little variation, have served all the authors who have ever written."

"His thoughts, in the latter part of his life, were frequently employed on his deceased friends. He often muttered these, or such like sentences: 'Poor man! and then he died.'"

"Speaking of a certain literary friend, 'He is a very pompous puzzling fellow,' said he; 'he lent me a letter once that somebody had written to him, no matter what it was about; but he wanted to have the letter back, and expressed a mighty value for it; he hoped it was to be met with again, he would not lose it for a thousand pounds. I laid my hand upon it soon afterwards, and gave it him. I believe I said I was very glad to have met with it. Oh, then he did not know that it signified anything.

[1] "Prayers and Meditations," p. 226.

[2] Mr. Malone observes, "This, however, was entirely a mistake, as appears from the Memoirs published by Mr. Noble. Had Johnson been furnished with the materials which the industry of that gentleman has procured, and with others which, it is believed, are yet preserved in manuscript, he would, without doubt, have produced a most valuable and curious history of Cromwell's life."

I may add, that, had Johnson given us a Life of Cromwell, we should not have been disgusted in numberless instances with—"My Lord Protector" and "My Lady Protectress;" and certainly the brutal ruffian who presided in the bloody assembly that murdered their sovereign would have been characterised by very different epithets than those which are applied to him in this work, where we find him described as "the bold and determined Bradshaw."—MALONE.

So you see, when the letter was lost it was worth a thousand pounds, and when it was found it was not worth a farthing."

"The style and character of his conversation is pretty generally known; it was certainly conducted in conformity with a precept of Lord Bacon, but it is not clear, I apprehend, that this conformity was either perceived or intended by Johnson. The precept alluded to is as follows:—'In all kinds of speech, either pleasant, grave, severe, or ordinary, it is convenient to speak leisurely, and rather drawlingly than hastily; because hasty speech confounds the memory, and oftentimes, besides the unseemliness, drives a man either to stammering, a nonplus, or harping on that which should follow; whereas a slow speech confirmeth the memory, addeth a conceit of wisdom to the hearers, besides a seemliness of speech and countenance.'[1] Dr. Johnson's method of conversation was certainly calculated to excite attention, and to amuse and instruct (as it happened), without wearying or confusing his company. He was always most perfectly clear and perspicuous; and his language was so accurate, and his sentences so neatly constructed, that his conversation might have been all printed without any correction. At the same time, it was easy and natural; the accuracy of it had no appearance of labour, constraint, or stiffness; he seemed more correct than others, by the force of habit, and the customary exercises of his powerful mind."

"He spoke often in praise of French literature. 'The French are excellent in this,' he would say; 'they have a book on every subject.' From what he had seen of them he denied them the praise of superior politeness, and mentioned, with very visible disgust, the custom they have of spitting on the floors of their apartments. 'This,' said the Doctor, 'is as gross a thing as can well be done; and one wonders how any man, or set of men, can persist in so offensive a practice for a whole day together; one should expect that the first effort towards civilization would remove it even among savages.'"

"'Baxter's Reasons of the Christian Religion,' he thought contained the best collection of the evidences of the divinity of the Christian system."

"Chemistry was always an interesting pursuit with Dr. Johnson. Whilst he was in Wiltshire he attended some experiments that were made by a physician at Salisbury,

[1] Hints for Civil Conversation.—Bacon's Works, 4to., vol. i., p. 571.—MALONE.

on the new kinds of air.   In the course of the experiments, frequent mention being made of Dr. Priestley, Dr. Johnson knit his brows, and in a stern manner inquired, 'Why do we hear so much of Dr. Priestley!'[1]   He was very properly answered, 'Sir, because we are indebted to him for these important discoveries.'   On this Dr. Johnson appeared well content, and replied, 'Well, well, I believe we are; and let every man have the honour he has merited.'"

"A friend was one day, about two years before his death, struck with some instance of Dr. Johnson's great candour.   'Well, Sir,' said he, 'I will always say that you are a very candid man.'—'Will you?' replied the Doctor; 'I doubt then you will be very singular.   But indeed, Sir,'

---

[1] I do not wonder at Johnson's displeasure when the name of Dr. Priestley was mentioned; for I know no writer who has been suffered to publish more pernicious doctrines. I shall instance only three. First, *Materialism;* by which *mind* is denied to human nature, which, if believed, must deprive us of every elevated principle. Secondly, *Necessity ;* or the doctrine that every action, whether good or bad, is included in an unchangeable and unavoidable system; a notion utterly subversive of moral government. Thirdly, that we have no reason to think that the *future* world (which, as he is pleased to *inform* us, will be adapted to our *merely improved* nature), will be materially different from *this ;* which, if believed, would sink wretched mortals into despair, as they could no longer hope for the "rest that remaineth for the people of GOD," or for that happiness which is revealed to us as something beyond our present conceptions; but would feel themselves doomed to a continuation of the uneasy state under which they now groan.   I say nothing of the petulant intemperance with which he dares to insult the venerable establishments of his country.

As a specimen of his writings, I shall quote the following passage, which appears to me equally absurd and impious, and which might have been retorted upon him by the men who were prosecuted for burning his house.   "I cannot," says he, "as a *necessarian* (meaning *necessitarian*), hate *any man;* because I consider him as *being*, in all respects, just what GOD has *made him to be;* and also as *doing, with respect to me,* nothing but what he was *expressly designed* and *appointed* to do; GOD being the *only cause,* and men nothing more than the *instruments* in his hands to execute *all his pleasure.*"—Illustrations of Philosophical Necessity, p. 111.

The Rev. Dr. Parr, in a late tract, appears to suppose that *Dr. Johnson not only endured, but almost solicited, an interview with Dr. Priestley.* In justice to Dr. Johnson, I declare my firm belief that he never did. My illustrious friend was particularly resolute in not giving countenance to men whose writings he considered as pernicious to society.   I was present at Oxford when Dr. Price, even before he had rendered himself so generally obnoxious by his zeal for the French revolution, came into a company where Johnson was, who instantly left the room.   Much more would he have reprobated Dr. Priestley.

Whoever wishes to see a perfect delineation of this *literary Jack of all trades,* may find it in an ingenious tract, entitled, "A small Whole-length of Dr. Priestley," printed for Rivingtons, in St. Paul's-church-yard.—BOSWELL.

continued he, 'I look upon myself to be a man very much misunderstood. I am not an uncandid, nor am I a severe man. I sometimes say more than I mean, in jest; and people are apt to believe me serious: however, I am more candid than I was when I was younger. As I know more of mankind, I expect less of them, and am ready now to call a man *a good man*, upon easier terms than I was formerly.'"

CHAPTER XXV.—1783

Johnson's Return from Heale—His Ill-health—Mrs. Williams's
Benefactions—Mrs. Siddons—Kemble—Death of Mr.
Porter—Gerard Hamilton—Lord Carlisle and Mrs.
Chapone—Johnson's Critique on Lord Carlisle's Tragedy
—Unconstitutional Influence Exercised by Scotch Peers
—Mickle, and his Translation of the Lusiad—Authen-
ticity of Ossian, and Johnson's Refutation of the Essex-
street Club, and its Rules

ON his return from Heale he wrote to Dr. Burney:—

"I came home on the 18th of September, at noon, to a very dis-
consolate house. You and I have lost our friends; but you have
more friends at home. My domestic companion is taken from me. She
is much missed, for her acquisitions were many, and her curiosity
universal; so that she partook of every conversation. I am not
well enough to go much out; and to sit, and eat, or fast alone, is very
wearisome. I always mean to send my compliments to all the
ladies."

His fortitude and patience met with severe trials during
this year. The stroke of the palsy has been related circumstantially; but he was also afflicted with the gout,
and was, besides, troubled with a complaint which not only
was attended with immediate inconvenience, but threatened
him with a chirurgical operation, from which most men
would shrink. The complaint was a *sarcocele*, which
Johnson bore with uncommon firmness, and was not at
all frightened while he looked forward to amputation.
He was attended by Mr. Pott and Mr. Cruikshank. I have
before me a letter of the 30th of July this year, to Mr.
Cruikshank, in which he says: "I am going to put myself
into your hands:" and another accompanying a set of
his "Lives of the Poets," in which he says, "I beg your
acceptance of these volumes, as an acknowledgment of the
great favours which you have bestowed on, Sir, your
most obliged and most humble servant." I have in my
possession several more letters from him to Mr. Cruikshank,
and also to Dr. Mudge, at Plymouth, which it would be

improper to insert, as they are filled with unpleasing technical details. I shall, however, extract from his letters to Dr. Mudge such passages as show either a felicity of expression or the undaunted state of his mind.

"My conviction of your skill, and my belief of your friendship, determine me to entreat your opinion and advice."

"In this state I with great earnestness desire you to tell me what is to be done. Excision is doubtless necessary to the cure, and I know not any means of palliation. The operation is doubtless painful; but is it dangerous? The pain I hope to endure with decency; but I am loath to put life into much hazard."

"By representing the gout as an antagonist to the palsy, you have said enough to make it welcome. This is not strictly the first fit; but I hope it is as good as the first; for it is the second that ever confined me; and the first was ten years ago, much less fierce and fiery than this."

"Write, dear Sir, what you can to inform or encourage me. The operation is not delayed by any fears or objections of mine."

"TO BENNET LANGTON, ESQ.

"Dear Sir,   London, Sept. 29, 1783.

"You may very reasonably charge me with insensibility of your kindness and that of Lady Rothes, since I have suffered so much time to pass without paying any acknowledgment. I now, at last, return my thanks; and why I did it not sooner I ought to tell you. I went into Wiltshire as soon as I well could, and was there much employed in palliating my own malady. Disease produces much selfishness. A man in pain is looking after ease; and lets most other things go as chance shall dispose of them. In the meantime I have lost a companion,[1] to whom I have had recourse for domestic amusement for thirty years, and whose variety of knowledge never was exhausted; and now return to a habitation vacant and desolate. I carry about a very troublesome and dangerous complaint which admits no cure but by the chirurgical knife. Let me have your prayers.

                                        "I am, &c.
                                        "Sam Johnson."

Happily the complaint abated without his being put to the torture of amputation. But we must surely admire the manly resolution which he discovered, while it hung over him.

In a letter to the same gentleman he writes. "The gout has, within these four days, come upon me with a violence which I never experienced before. It made me helpless as an infant." And in another, having mentioned Mrs.

[1] Mrs. Anna Williams.—Boswell.

Williams, he says,—"whose death following that of Levett, has now made my house a solitude. She left her little substance to a charity-school. She is, I hope, where there is neither darkness, nor want, nor sorrow."

I wrote to him, begging to know the state of his health, and mentioned that "Baxter's Anacreon, which is in the library at Auchinleck, was, I find, collated by my father in 1727, with the MS. belonging to the University of Leyden, and he has made a number of notes upon it. Would you advise me to publish a new edition of it?"

His answer was dated September 30.—"You should not make your letters such rarities, when you know, or might know, the uniform state of my health. It is very long since I heard from you; and that I have not answered is a very insufficient reason for the silence of a friend. Your Anacreon is a very uncommon book; neither London nor Cambridge can supply a copy of that edition. Whether it should be reprinted, you cannot do better than consult Lord Hailes. Besides my constant and radical disease, I have been for these ten days much harassed with the gout; but that has now remitted. I hope GOD will yet grant me a little longer life, and make me less unfit to appear before him."

He this autumn received a visit from the celebrated Mrs. Siddons. He gives this account of it in one of his letters to Mrs. Thrale, October 27:—

"Mrs. Siddons, in her visit to me, behaved with great modesty and propriety, and left nothing behind her to be censured or despised. Neither praise nor money, the two powerful corruptors of mankind, seemed to have depraved her. I shall be glad to see her again. Her brother Kemble calls on me, and pleases me very well. Mrs. Siddons and I talked of plays; and she told me her intention of exhibiting this winter the characters of Constance, Catherine, and Isabella, in Shakespeare."

Mr. Kemble has favoured me with the following minute of what passed at this visit:—

"When Mrs. Siddons came into the room, there happened to be no chair ready for her, which he observing, said with a smile, 'Madam, you who so often occasion a want of seats to other people, will the more easily excuse the want of one yourself.'

"Having placed himself by her, he with great good humour entered upon a consideration of the English drama; and, among other inquiries, particularly asked her which of Shakespeare's characters she was most pleased with. Upon her answering that she thought the character of Queen Catherine in Henry the Eighth the most natural:—'I think so, too, Madam,' said he; 'and whenever

you perform it, I will once more hobble out to the theatre myself.'
Mrs. Siddons promised she would do herself the honour of acting his
favourite part for him; but many circumstances happened to prevent the representation of King Henry the Eighth during the Doctor's
life.

"In the course of the evening he thus gave his opinion upon the
merits of some of the principal performers whom he remembered
to have seen upon the stage. 'Mrs. Porter in the vehemence of
rage, and Mrs. Clive in the sprightliness of humour, I have never
seen equalled. What Clive did best, she did better than Garrick;
but could not do half so many things well; she was a better romp
than any I ever saw in nature.—Pritchard, in common life, was a
vulgar idiot; she would talk of her *gownd;* but, when she appeared
upon the stage, seemed to be inspired by gentility and understanding.
—I once talked with Colley Cibber, and thought him ignorant of the
principles of his art.—Garrick, Madam, was no declaimer; there was
not one of his own scene-shifters who could not have spoken *To be,
or not to be,* better than he did; yet he was the only actor I ever
saw, whom I could call a master both in tragedy and comedy;
though I liked him best in comedy. A true conception of character,
and natural expression of it, were his distinguished excellencies.'
Having expatiated, with his usual force and eloquence, on Mr.
Garrick's extraordinary eminence as an actor, he concluded with
this compliment to his social talents: 'And after all, Madam, I
thought him less to be envied on the stage than at the head of a table.'"

Johnson, indeed, had thought more upon the subject
of acting than might be generally supposed. Talking of
it one day to Mr. Kemble, he said, "Are you, Sir, one of
those enthusiasts who believe yourself transformed into
the very character you represent?" Upon Mr. Kemble's
answering that he had never felt so strong a persuasion
himself: "To be sure not, Sir," said Johnson, "the thing
is impossible. And if Garrick really believed himself
to be that monster Richard the Third, he deserved to be
hanged every time he performed it."[1]

---

[1] My worthy friend, Mr. John Nichols, was present when Mr. Henderson, the actor, paid a visit to Dr. Johnson, and was received in a very
courteous manner.—See "Gentleman's Magazine," June, 1791.

I found, among Dr. Johnson's papers, the following letter to him,
from the celebrated Mrs. Bellamy:—

"TO DR. JOHNSON.

"No. 10, Duke-street, St. James's, May 11, 1783.

"SIR,—The flattering remembrance of the partiality you honoured
me with, some years ago, as well as the humanity you are known to
possess, has encouraged me to solicit your patronage at my benefit.

"By a long Chancery suit, and a complicated train of unfortunate
events, I am reduced to the greatest distress, which obliges me once
more to request the indulgence of the public.

"Give me leave to solicit the honour of your company, and to assure
you, if you grant my request, the gratification I shall feel, from being

"TO MRS. LUCY PORTER, IN LICHFIELD.

"DEAR MADAM,   Bolt-court, Fleet-street, Nov. 10, 1783.

"The death of poor Mr. Porter, of which your maid has sent an account, must have very much surprised you. The death of a friend is almost always unexpected: we do not love to think of it, and therefore are not prepared for its coming. He was, I think, a religious man, and therefore that his end was happy.

"Death has likewise visited my mournful habitation. Last month died Mrs. Williams, who had been to me for thirty years in the place of a sister: her knowledge was great, and her conversation pleasing. I now live in cheerless solitude.

"My two last years have passed under the pressure of successive diseases. I have lately had the gout with some severity. But I wonderfully escaped the operation which I mentioned, and am upon the whole restored to health beyond my own expectation.

"As we daily see our friends die round us, we that are left must cling closer, and, if we can do nothing more, at least pray for one another; and remember, that as others die we must die too, and prepare ourselves diligently for the last great trial.

"I am, Madam, yours affectionately,
"SAM. JOHNSON."

A pleasing instance of the generous attention of one of his friends has been discovered by the publication of Mrs. Thrale's collection of Letters. In a letter to one of the Miss Thrales, he writes, "A friend, whose name I will tell, when your mamma has tried to guess it, sent to my physician to inquire whether this long train of illness had brought me into difficulties for want of money, with an invitation to send to him for what occasion required. I shall write this night to thank him, having no need to borrow." And afterwards, in a letter to Mrs. Thrale, "Since you cannot guess, I will tell you, that the generous man was Gerard Hamilton. I returned him a very thankful and respectful letter."

I applied to Mr. Hamilton, by a common friend, and he has been so obliging as to let me have Johnson's letter to him upon this occasion, to adorn my collection.

"TO THE RIGHT HONOURABLE WILLIAM GERARD HAMILTON.

"DEAR SIR,   November 19, 1783.

"Your kind inquiries after my affairs, and your generous offers, have been communicated to me by Dr. Brocklesby. I return thanks

patronised by Dr. Johnson, will be infinitely superior to any advantage that may arise from the benefit; as I am, with the profoundest respect, Sir, your most obedient humble servant, G. A. BELLAMY."

I am happy in recording these particulars, which prove that my illustrious friend lived to think much more favourably of players than he appears to have done in the early part of his life.—BOSWELL.

with great sincerity, having lived long enough to know what gratitude is due to your friendship; and entreat that my refusal may not be imputed to sullenness or pride.   I am, indeed, in no want.   Sickness is, by the generosity of my physicians, of little expense to me. But if any unexpected exigence should press me, you shall see, dear Sir, how cheerfully I can be obliged to so much liberality.   I am, Sir,
"Your most obedient and most humble servant,
"SAM. JOHNSON."

I find in this, as in former years, notices of his kind attention to Mrs. Gardiner, who, though in the humble station of a tallow-chandler upon Snow Hill, was a woman of excellent good sense, pious and charitable.[1]   She told me, she had been introduced to him by Mrs. Masters, the poetess, whose volumes he revised, and, it is said, illuminated here and there with a ray of his own genius.   Mrs. Gardiner was very zealous for the support of the Ladies' Charity-school, in the parish of St. Sepulchre.   It is confined to females; and, I am told, it afforded a hint for the story of *Betty Broom*, in "The Idler."   Johnson this year, I find, obtained for it a sermon from the late Bishop of St. Asaph, Dr. Shipley, whom he, in one of his letters to Mrs. Thrale, characterises as "knowing and conversable;" and whom all who knew his Lordship, even those who differed from him in politics, remember with much respect.

The Earl of Carlisle having written a tragedy, entitled "THE FATHER'S REVENGE," some of his Lordship's friends applied to Mrs. Chapone, to prevail on Dr. Johnson to read and give his opinion of it, which he accordingly did, in a letter to that lady.   Sir Joshua Reynolds 'having informed me that this letter was in Lord Carlisle's possession, though I was not fortunate enough to have the honour of being known to his Lordship, trusting to the general courtesy of literature, I wrote to him, requesting the favour of a copy of it, and to be permitted to insert it in my life of Dr. Johnson.   His Lordship was so good as to comply with my request, and has thus enabled me to enrich my work with a very fine piece of writing, which displays both the critical skill and politeness of my illustrious friend; and perhaps the curiosity which it will excite may induce the noble and elegant author to gratify the world by the publication[2] of a performance, of which Dr. Johnson has spoken in such terms.

---

[1] In his will, Dr. Johnson left her a book "at her election, to keep as a token of remembrance."—MALONE.

[2] A few copies only of this tragedy have been printed, and given to the author's friends.—BOSWELL.

"TO MRS. CHAPONE.

"MADAM,   Nov. 28, 1783.

"By sending the tragedy to me a second time,[1] I think that a very honourable distinction has been shown me, and I did not delay the perusal, of which I am now to tell the effect.

"The construction of the play is not completely regular; the stage is too often vacant, and the scenes are not sufficiently connected. This, however, would be called by Dryden only a mechanical defect; which takes away little from the power of the poem, and which is seen rather than felt.

"A rigid examiner of the diction might, perhaps, wish some words changed, and some lines more vigorously terminated. But from such petty imperfections what writer was ever free?

"The general form and force of the dialogue is of more importance. It seems to want that quickness of reciprocation which characterises the English drama, and is not always sufficiently fervid or animated.

"Of the sentiments, I remember not one that I wish omitted. In the imagery I cannot forbear to distinguish the comparison of joy succeeding grief to light rushing on the eye accustomed to darkness. It seems to have all that can be desired to make it please. It is new, just, and delightful.[2]

"With the characters, either as conceived or preserved, I have no fault to find; but was much inclined to congratulate a writer, who, in defiance of prejudice and fashion, made the Archbishop a good man, and scorned all thoughtless applause, which a vicious churchman would have brought him.

"The catastrophe is affecting. The Father and Daughter, both culpable, both wretched, and both penitent, divide between them our pity and our sorrow.

"Thus, Madam, I have performed what I did not willingly undertake, and could not decently refuse. The noble writer will be pleased to remember that sincere criticism ought to raise no resentment, because judgment is not under the control of will; but involuntary criticism, as it has still less of choice, ought to be more remote from possibility of offence.

                                        "I am, &c.,
                                          "SAM. JOHNSON."

I consulted him on two questions of a very different nature: one, Whether the unconstitutional influence exercised by the Peers of Scotland in the election of the representatives of the Commons, by means of fictitious

---

[1] Dr. Johnson having been very ill when the tragedy was first sent to him, had declined the consideration of it.—BOSWELL.

[2] "I could have borne my woes; that stranger Joy
     Wounds while it smiles:—The long imprison'd wretch,
     Emerging from the night of his damp cell,
     Shrinks from the sun's bright beams; and that which flings
     Gladness o'er all, to him is agony."—BOSWELL.

qualifications, ought not to be resisted;—the other, What in propriety and humanity, should be done with old horses unable to labour. I gave him some account of my life at Auchinleck; and expressed my satisfaction that the gentlemen of the county had, at two public meetings, elected me their *Præses*, or Chairman.

"TO JAMES BOSWELL, ESQ.

"DEAR SIR,   London, Dec. 24, 1783.

"Like all other men who have great friends, you begin to feel the pangs of neglected merit; and all the comfort that I can give you is, by telling you that you have probably more pangs to feel, and more neglect to suffer. You have, indeed, begun to complain too soon; and I hope I am the only confidant of your discontent. Your friends have not yet had leisure to gratify personal kindness; they have hitherto been busy in strengthening their ministerial interest. If a vacancy happens in Scotland, give them early intelligence; and as you can serve Government as powerfully as any of your probable competitors, you may make in some sort a warrantable claim.

"Of the exaltations and depressions of your mind you delight to talk, and I hate to hear. Drive all such fancies from you.

"On the day when I received your letter, I think, the foregoing page was written, to which one disease or another has hindered me from making any additions. I am now a little better. But sickness and solitude press me very heavily. I could bear sickness better, if I were relieved from solitude.

"The present dreadful confusion of the public ought to make you wrap yourself up in your hereditary possessions, which, though less than you may wish, are more than you can want; and in an hour of religious retirement, return thanks to GOD, who has exempted you from any strong temptation to faction, treachery, plunder, and disloyalty.

"As your neighbours distinguish you by such honours as they can bestow, content yourself with your station, without neglecting your profession. Your estate and the courts will find you full employment, and your mind well occupied will be quiet.

"The usurpation of the nobility, for they apparently usurp all the influence they gain by fraud and misrepresentation, I think it certainly lawful, perhaps your duty, to resist. What is not their own, they have only by robbery.

"Your question about the horses gives me more perplexity. I know not well what advice to give you. I can only recommend a rule which you do not want;—give as little pain as you can. I suppose that we have a right to their service while their strength lasts; what we can do with them afterwards, I cannot so easily determine. But let us consider. Nobody denies, that man has a right first to milk the cow, and to shear the sheep, and then to kill them for his table. May he not, by parity of reason, first work a horse, and then kill him the easiest way, that he may have the

means of another horse, or food for cows and sheep? Man is influenced in both cases by different motives of self-interest. He that
rejects the one must reject the other.

> "I am, &c.,
> "Sam. Johnson."

"A happy and pious Christmas, and many happy years to you,
your lady, and children."

The late ingenious, Mr. Mickle, some time before his
death, wrote me a letter concerning Dr. Johnson, in which
he mentions, "I was upwards of twelve years acquainted
with him, was frequently in his company, always talked
with ease to him, and can truly say, that I never received
from him one rough word."

In this letter he relates his having, while engaged in
translating the Lusiad, had a dispute of considerable
length with Johnson, who, as usual, declaimed upon the
misery and corruption of a sea life, and used this expression:—"It had been happy for the world, Sir, if your hero
Gama, Prince Henry of Portugal, and Columbus, had never
been born, or that their schemes had never gone farther
than their own imaginations."—"This sentiment," says
Mr. Mickle, "which is to be found in his 'Introduction to
the World Displayed,' I, in my Dissertation prefixed to
the Lusiad, have controverted; and though authors are
said to be bad judges of their own works, I am not ashamed
to own to a friend, that that Dissertation is my favourite
above all that I ever attempted in prose. Next year,
when the Lusiad was published, I waited on Dr. Johnson,
who addressed me with one of his good-humoured smiles:—
'Well, you have remembered our dispute about Prince
Henry, and have cited me too. You have done your part
very well indeed: you have made the best of your argument;
but I am not convinced yet.'

"Before publishing the Lusiad, I sent Mr. Hoole a proof
of that part of the introduction, in which I make mention
of Dr. Johnson, yourself, and other well-wishers to the work,
begging it might be shown to Dr. Johnson. This was
accordingly done; and in place of the simple mention of
him which I had made, he dictated to Mr. Hoole the sentence
as it now stands.

"Dr. Johnson told me, in 1772, that, about twenty years
before that time, he himself had a design to translate the
Lusiad, of the merit of which he spoke highly, but had
been prevented by a number of other engagements."

Mr. Mickle reminds me, in this letter, of a conversation
at dinner one day at Mr. Hoole's with Dr. Johnson, when

Mr. Nicol, the King's bookseller, and I, attempted to controvert the maxim, "better that ten guilty should escape, than one innocent person suffer;" and were answered by Dr. Johnson with great power of reasoning and eloquence. I am very sorry that I have no record of that day; but I well recollect my illustrious friend's having ably shown that, unless civil institutions ensure protection to the innocent, all the confidence which mankind should have in them would be lost.

I shall here mention what, in strict chronological arrangement, should have appeared in my account of last year; but may more properly be introduced here, the controversy having not been closed till this. The Rev. Mr. Shaw, a native of one of the Hebrides, having entertained doubts of the authenticity of the poems ascribed to Ossian, divested himself of national bigotry; and having travelled in the Highlands and Islands of Scotland, and also in Ireland, in order to furnish himself with materials for a Gaelic Dictionary, which he afterwards compiled, was so fully satisfied that Dr. Johnson was in the right upon the question, that he candidly published a pamphlet, stating his conviction, and the proofs and reasons on which it was founded. A person at Edinburgh, of the name of Clark, answered this pamphlet with much zeal, and much abuse of its author. Johnson took Mr. Shaw under his protection, and gave him his assistance in writing a reply, which has been admired by the best judges, and by many been considered as conclusive. A few paragraphs, which sufficiently mark their great author, shall be selected.

"My assertions are, for the most part, purely negative: I deny the existence of Fingal, because in a long and curious peregrination through the Gaelic regions I have never been able to find it. What I could not see myself I suspect to be equally invisible to others; and I suspect with the more reason, as among all those who have seen it no man can show it.

"Mr. Clark compares the obstinacy of those who disbelieve the genuineness of Ossian to a blind man, who should dispute the reality of colours, and deny that the British troops are clothed in red. The blind man's doubt would be rational, if he did not know by experience that others have a power which he himself wants; but what perspicacity has Mr. Clark which Nature has withheld from me or the rest of mankind?

"The true state of the parallel must be this. Suppose a man, with eyes like his neighbours, was told by a boasting corporal, that the troops, indeed, wore red clothes for their ordinary dress, but that every soldier had likewise a suit of black velvet, which he put on when the King reviews them. This he thinks strange, and desires to see the fine clothes, but finds nobody in forty thousand men that can produce either coat or waistcoat.   One, indeed, has left them in his chest at Port Mahon; another has always heard that he ought to have velvet clothes somewhere; and a third has heard somebody say, that soldiers ought to wear velvet.   Can the inquirer be blamed if he goes away believing that a soldier's red coat is all that he has?

"But the most obdurate incredulity may be shamed or silenced by facts.   To overpower contradictions, let the soldier show his velvet coat, and the Fingalist the original of Ossian.

"The difference between us and the blind man is this: the blind man is unconvinced, because he cannot see; and we, because, though we can see, we find that nothing can be shown."

Notwithstanding the complication of disorders under which Johnson now laboured, he did not resign himself to despondency and discontent, but with wisdom and spirit endeavoured to console and amuse his mind with as many innocent enjoyments as he could procure.   Sir John Hawkins has mentioned the cordiality with which he insisted that such of the members of the old club in Ivy-lane as survived, should meet again and dine together, which they did, twice at a tavern, and once at his house; and in order to ensure himself society in the evening for three days in the week, he instituted a club at the Essex Head, in Essex-street, then kept by Samuel Greaves, an old servant of Mr. Thrale's.

"TO SIR JOSHUA REYNOLDS.

"Dear Sir,   Dec. 4, 1783.

"It is inconvenient to me to come out; I should else have waited on you with an account of a little evening Club which we are establishing in Essex-street, in the Strand, and of which you are desired to be one.   It will be held at the Essex Head, now kept by an old servant of Thrale's.   The company is numerous, and, as you will see by the list, miscellaneous.   The terms are lax, and the expenses light.   Mr. Barry was adopted by Dr. Brocklesby, who joined with me in forming the plan.   We meet thrice a week, and he who misses forfeits twopence.

"If you are willing to become a member, draw a line under your name.   Return the list.   We meet for the first time on Monday at eight.

"I am, &c.,
"Sam. Johnson."

It did not suit Sir Joshua to be one of this club.   But when I mention only Mr. Daines Barrington, Dr. Brocklesby, Mr. Murphy, Mr. John Nichols, Mr. Cooke, Mr. Joddrel, Mr. Paradise, Dr. Horsley, Mr. Windham,[1] I shall suffi-

---

[1] I was in Scotland when this Club was founded, and during all the winter.   Johnson, however, declared I should be a member, and

ciently obviate the misrepresentation of it by Sir John Hawkins, as if it had been a low ale-house association, by which Johnson was degraded. Johnson himself, like his namesake Old Ben, composed the Rules of his Club.[1]

In the end of this year he was seized with a spasmodic asthma of such violence, that he was confined to the house in great pain, being sometimes obliged to sit all night in his chair, a recumbent posture being so hurtful to his respiration, that he could not endure lying in bed; and there came upon him, at the same time, that oppressive and fatal disease, a dropsy. It was a very severe winter, which probably aggravated his complaints; and

invented a word upon the occasion; "Boswell," said he, "is a very *club-able* man." When I came to town, I was proposed by Mr. Barrington, and chosen. I believe there are few societies where there is better conversation or more decorum. Several of us resolved to continue it after our great founder was removed by death. Other members were added; and now, above eight years since that loss, we go on happily.— BOSWELL.

1   RULES.
        "To-day deep thoughts with me resolve to drench
        In mirth, which after no repenting draws."—MILTON.
    "The Club shall consist of four-and-twenty.
    "The meetings shall be on the Monday, Thursday, and Saturday of every week; but in the week before Easter there shall be no meeting.
    "Every member is at liberty to introduce a friend once a week, but not oftener.
    "Two members shall oblige themselves to attend in their turn every night from eight to ten, or to procure two to attend in their room.
    "Every member present at the Club shall spend at least sixpence; and every member who stays away shall forfeit threepence.
    "The master of the house shall keep an account of the absent members: and deliver to the President of the night a list of the forfeits incurred.
    "When any member returns after absence, he shall immediately lay down his forfeits; which, if he omits to do, the President shall require.
    "There shall be no general reckoning, but every man shall adjust his own expenses.
    "The night of indispensable attendance will come to every member once a month. Whoever shall for three months together omit to attend himself, or by substitution, nor shall make any apology in the fourth month, shall be considered as having abdicated the Club.
    "When a vacancy is to be filled, the name of the candidate, and of the member recommending him, shall stand in the Club-room three nights. On the fourth he may be chosen by ballot; six members at least being present, and two-thirds of the ballot being in his favour; or the majority, should the numbers not be divisible by three.
    "The master of the house shall give notice, six days before, to each of those members whose turn of necessary attendance is come.
    "The notice may be in these words:—'Sir, On ———, the ——— of ———, will be your turn of presiding at the Essex Head. Your company is therefore earnestly requested.'
    "One penny shall be left by each member for the waiter."
    Johnson's definition of a Club in this sense, in his Dictionary, is "An assembly of good fellows, meeting under certain conditions. — BOSWELL.

the solitude in which Mr. Levett and Mrs. Williams had left him, rendered his life very gloomy. Mrs. Desmoulins, who still lived, was herself so very ill, that she could contribute very little to his relief. He, however, had none of that unsocial shyness which we commonly see in people afflicted with sickness. He did not hide his head from the world, in solitary abstraction; he did not deny himself to the visits of his friends and acquaintances; but at all times, when he was not overcome by sleep, was ready for conversation as in his best days.

"TO MRS. LUCY PORTER, IN LICHFIELD.

"Dear Madam,   London, Nov. 29, 1783.

"You may, perhaps, think me negligent that I have not written to you again upon the loss of your brother; but condolences and consolations are such common and such useless things, that the omission of them is no great crime: and my own diseases occupy my mind, and engage my care. My nights are miserably restless, and my days, therefore, are heavy. I try, however, to hold up my head as high as I can.

"I am sorry that your health is impaired; perhaps the spring and the summer may, in some degree, restore it; but if not, we must submit to the inconveniences of time, as to the other dispensations of Eternal Goodness. Pray for me, and write to me, or let Mr. Pearson write for you.

"I am, &c.,
"Sam. Johnson."

CHAPTER XXVI.—1784

The last year of Johnson's Life—"Burton's Books"—The Essex Head—Correspondence—Johnson's continued ill-health—Drs. Gillespie, Heberden, Cullen, Hope, and Munro—Johnson's advice to Boswell—Lord Portmore —Mr. Ozias Humphry—Johnson's Melancholy Thoughts at the Approach of Death—His Advice to Miss Langton —Boswell's Arrival in London—Colonel Vallancy— Johnson on earnest Disputation—Dines at the Essex Head Club with a Constellation of Ladies—Mrs. Montagu—Foote—Mrs. Thrale's altered Conduct— Bishop Douglas—Capel Lofft—Thomas à Kempis—Miss Helen Maria Williams

AND now I am arrived at the last year of the life of SAMUEL JOHNSON; a year in which, although passed in severe indisposition, he nevertheless gave many evidences of the continuance of those wondrous powers of mind, which raised him so high in the intellectual world. His conversation and his letters of this year were in no respect inferior to those of former years.

The following is a remarkable proof of his being alive to the most minute curiosities of literature.

"TO MR. DILLY, BOOKSELLER, IN THE POULTRY.

"Sir,   Jan. 6, 1784.

"There is in the world a set of books which used to be sold by the booksellers on the bridge, and which I must entreat you to procure me. They are called 'Burton's Books;'[1] the title of one is

[1] The following list comprises several of these books; but probably is incomplete:—

1. Historical Remarks on London and Westminster	- -	1681
2. Wars in England, Scotland, and Ireland -	- - -	1681
3. Wonderful Prodigies	- - - -	1681
4. English Empire in America	- - - - -	1685
5. Surprising Miracles of Nature and Art	- - -	1685
6. History of Scotland and Ireland	- - - -	1685
7. Nine Worthies of the World	- - - -	1687
8. The English Hero, or Sir Francis Drake -	- -	1687
9. Memorable Accidents, and unheard-of Transactions	- -	1693
10. History of Oliver Cromwell	- - - -	1698
11. Unparalleled Varieties -	- - - -	1699

MALONE.

'Admirable Curiosities,' 'Rarities,' and 'Wonders in England.'   I believe there are about five or six of them; they seem very proper to allure backward readers: be so kind as to get them for me, and send me them with the best printed edition of 'Baxter's Call to the Unconverted.'

"I am, &c.,
"Sam. Johnson."

"TO MR PERKINS.

"Dear Sir,   Jan. 21, 1784.

"I was very sorry not to see you when you were so kind as to call on me; but to disappoint friends, and if they are not very good-natured, to disoblige them, is one of the evils of sickness.   If you will please to let me know which of the afternoons in this week I shall be favoured with another visit by you and Mrs. Perkins, and the young people, I will take all the measures that I can to be pretty well at that time.   I am, dear Sir,

"Your most humble servant,
"Sam. Johnson."

His attention to the Essex Head Club appears from the following letter to Mr. Alderman Clark, a gentleman for whom he deservedly entertained a great regard.

"TO RICHARD CLARK, ESQ.

"Dear Sir,   Jan. 27, 1784.

"You will receive a requisition, according to the rules of the Club, to be at the house as president of the night.   This turn comes once a month, and the member is obliged to attend, or send another in his place.   You were enrolled in the Club by my invitation, and I ought to introduce you; but as I am hindered by sickness, Mr. Hoole will very properly supply my place as introductor, or yours as president.   I hope in milder weather to be a very constant attendant.

"I am, Sir, &c.,
"Sam. Johnson."

"You ought to be informed that the forfeits began with the year, and that every night of non-attendance incurs the mulct of threepence; that is, ninepence a week."

On the 8th of January I wrote to him, anxiously inquiring as to his health, and enclosing my "Letter to the People of Scotland on the present State of the Nation."

"I trust," said I, "that you will be liberal enough to make allowance for my differing from you on two points (the Middlesex election and the American War), when my general principles of government are according to your own heart, and when, at a crisis of doubtful event, I stand forth with honest zeal as an ancient and faithful Briton. My reason for introducing those two points was, that as my opinions with regard to them had been declared at the periods when they were least favourable, I might have the credit of a man who is not a worshipper of ministerial power."

"TO JAMES BOSWELL, ESQ.

"DEAR SIR,   Feb. 11, 1784.

"I hear of many inquiries which your kindness has disposed you to make after me. I have long intended you a long letter, which perhaps the imagination of its length hindered me from beginning. I will, therefore, content myself with a shorter.

"Having promoted the institution of a new Club in the neighbourhood, at the house of an old servant of Thrale's, I went thither to meet the company, and was seized with a spasmodic asthma, so violent, that with difficulty I got to my own house, in which I have been confined eight or nine weeks, and from which I know not when I shall be able to go even to church. The asthma, however, is not the worst. A dropsy gains ground upon me; my legs and thighs are very much swollen with water, which I should be content if I could keep there, but I am afraid that it will soon be higher. My nights are very sleepless and very tedious. And yet I am extremely afraid of dying.

"My physicians try to make me hope, that much of my malady is the effect of cold, and that some degree at least of recovery is to be expected from vernal breezes and summer suns. If my life is prolonged to autumn, I should be glad to try a warmer climate; though how to travel with a diseased body, without a companion to conduct me, and with very little money, I do not well see. Ramsay has recovered his limbs in Italy; and Fielding was sent to Lisbon, where, indeed, he died; but he was, I believe, past hope when he went. Think for me what I can do.

"I received your pamphlet, and when I write again may perhaps tell you some opinion about it; but you will forgive a man struggling with disease his neglect of disputes, politics, and pamphlets. Let me have your prayers. My compliments to your lady, and young ones. Ask your physicians about my case: and desire Sir Alexander Dick to write me his opinion.

"I am, dear Sir, &c.,
"SAM. JOHNSON."

"TO MRS. LUCY PORTER, IN LICHFIELD.

"MY DEAREST LOVE,   Feb. 23, 1784.

"I have been extremely ill of an asthma and dropsy, but received, by the mercy of GOD, sudden and unexpected relief last Thursday, by the discharge of twenty pints of water. Whether I shall continue free, or shall fill again, cannot be told. Pray for me.

"Death, my dear, is very dreadful; let us think nothing worth our care but how to prepare for it; what we know amiss in ourselves let us make haste to amend, and put our trust in the mercy of GOD, and the intercession of our SAVIOUR.

"I am, dear Madam, your most humble servant,
"SAM. JOHNSON."

"TO JAMES BOSWELL, ESQ.

"DEAR SIR,   London, Feb. 27, 1784.

"I have just advanced so far towards recovery as to read a pamphlet; and you may reasonably suppose that the first pamphlet which I read was yours. I am very much of your opinion, and, like you, feel great indignation at the indecency with which the King is every day treated. Your paper contains very considerable knowledge of history and of the constitution, very properly produced and applied. It will certainly raise your character,[1] though perhaps it may not make you a Minister of State.

*   *   *   *   *   *

"I desire you to see Mrs. Stewart once again, and tell her, that in the letter-case was a letter relating to me, for which I will give her, if she is willing to give it me, another guinea. The letter is of consequence only to me.

"I am, dear Sir, &c.,
"SAM. JOHNSON."

In consequence of Johnson's request that I should ask our physicians about his case, and desire Sir Alexander Dick to send his opinion, I transmitted him a letter from that very amiable baronet, then in his eighty-first year, with his faculties as entire as ever; and mentioned his expressions to me in the note accompanying it,—"With my most affectionate wishes for Dr. Johnson's recovery, in which his friends, his country, and all mankind have so deep a stake;" and at the same time a full opinion upon his case by Dr. Gillespie, who, like Dr. Cullen, had the advantage of having passed through the gradations of surgery and pharmacy, and by study and practice had attained to such skill, that my father settled on him two hundred pounds a year for five years, and fifty pounds a year during his life, as an *honorarium* to secure his particular attendance.

---

[1] I sent it to Mr. Pitt, with a letter, in which I thus expressed myself: "My principles may appear to you too monarchical: but I know and am persuaded, they are not inconsistent with the true principles of liberty. Be this as it may, you, Sir, are now the Prime Minister, called by the Sovereign to maintain the rights of the crown, as well as those of the people, against a violent faction. As such, you are entitled to the warmest support of every good subject in every department." He answered, "I am extremely obliged to you for the sentiments you do me the honour to express, and have observed with great pleasure the *zealous and able support* given to the cause of the public in the work you were so good to transmit me."—BOSWELL.

The opinion was conveyed in a letter to me, beginning, " I am sincerely sorry for the bad state of health your very learned and illustrious friend, Dr. Johnson, labours under at present."

"TO JAMES BOSWELL, ESQ.

"DEAR SIR,   London, March 2, 1784.
"Presently after I had sent away my last letter, I received your kind medical packet.   I am very much obliged both to you and to your physicians for your kind attention to my disease.   Dr. Gillespie has sent me an excellent *consilium medicum*, all solid practical experimental knowledge.   I am at present, in the opinion of my physicians (Dr. Heberden and Dr. Brocklesby), as well as my own, going on very hopefully.   I have just begun to take vinegar of squills.   The powder hurt my stomach so much, that it could not be continued.

"Return Sir Alexander Dick my sincere thanks for his kind letter; and bring with you the rhubarb [1] which he so tenderly offers me.

"I hope dear Mrs. Boswell is now quite well, and that no evil, either real or imaginary, now disturbs you.
                                  "I am, &c.,
                                       "SAM. JOHNSON."

I also applied to three of the eminent physicians who had chairs in our celebrated school of medicine at Edinburgh, Doctors Cullen, Hope, and Munro, to each of whom I sent the following letter:—

"DEAR SIR,   March 7, 1784.
"Dr. Johnson has been very ill for some time; and in a letter of anxious apprehension he writes to me, 'Ask your physicians about my case.'

"This you see, is not authority for a regular consultation: but I have no doubt of your readiness to give your advice to a man so eminent, and who, in his Life of Garth, has paid your profession a just and elegant compliment: 'I believe every man has found in physicians great liberality and dignity of sentiment, very prompt effusions of beneficence, and willingness to exert a lucrative art, where there is no hope of lucre.'

"Dr. Johnson is aged seventy-four.   Last summer he had a stroke of the palsy, from which he recovered almost entirely.   He had, before that, been troubled with a catarrhous cough.   This winter he was seized with a spasmodic asthma, by which he has been confined to his house for about three months.   Dr. Brocklesby writes to me, that upon the least admission of cold, there is such a constriction upon his breast, that he cannot lie down in his bed,

[1] From his garden at Prestonfield, where he cultivated that plant with such success, that he was presented with a gold medal by the Society of London for the encouragement of Arts, Manufactures, and Commerce.—BOSWELL.

but is obliged to sit up all night, and gets rest and sometimes sleep, only by means of laudanum and syrup of poppies; and that there are œdematous tumours in his legs and thighs. Dr. Brocklesby trusts a good deal to the return of mild weather. Dr. Johnson says, that a dropsy gains ground upon him; and he seems to think that a warmer climate would do him good. I understand he is now rather better, and is using vinegar of squills.

"I am, with great esteem, dear Sir,

"Your most obedient humble servant,

"JAMES BOSWELL."

All of them paid the most polite attention to my letter, and its venerable object. Dr. Cullen's words concerning him were, "It would give me the greatest pleasure to be of any service to a man whom the public properly esteem, and whom I esteem and respect as much as I do Dr. Johnson." Dr. Hope's, "Few people have a better claim on me than your friend, as hardly a day passes that I do not ask his opinion about this or that word." Dr. Munro's, "I most sincerely join you in sympathizing with that very worthy and ingenious character, from whom his country has derived much instruction and entertainment."

Dr. Hope corresponded with his friend Dr. Brocklesby. Doctors Cullen and Munro wrote their opinions and prescriptions to me, which I afterwards carried with me to London, and, so far as they were encouraging, communicated to Johnson. The liberality on the one hand, and grateful sense of it on the other, I have great satisfaction in recording.

"TO JAMES BOSWELL, ESQ.

"DEAR SIR,   London, March 18, 1784.

"I am too much pleased with the attention which you and your dear lady [1] show to my welfare, not to be diligent in letting you know the progress which I make towards health. The dropsy, by GOD's blessing, has now run almost totally away by natural evacuation: and the asthma, if not irritated by cold, gives me little trouble. While I am writing this, I have not any sensation of debility or disease. But I do not yet venture out, having been confined to the house, from the 13th of December, now a quarter of a year.

"When it will be fit for me to travel as far as Auchinleck, I am not able to guess; but such a letter as Mrs. Boswell's might draw any man, not wholly motionless, a great way. Pray tell the dear lady how much her civility and kindness have touched and gratified me.

"Our parliamentary tumults have now begun to subside, and the king's authority is in some measure re-established. Mr. Pitt

---

[1] Who had written him a very kind letter.—BOSWELL.

will have great power; but you must remember, that what he has to give, must, at least for some time, be given to those who gave, and those who preserve, his power. A new minister can sacrifice little to esteem or friendship; he must, till he is settled, think only of extending his interest.

* * * * * *

"If you come hither through Edinburgh, send for Mrs. Stewart, and give for me another guinea for the letter in the old case, to which I shall not be satisfied with my claim, till she gives it me.

"Please to bring with you Baxter's Anacreon; and if you procure heads of Hector Boëce, the historian, and Arthur Johnston, the poet, I will put them in my room; or any other of the fathers of Scottish literature.

"I wish you an easy and happy journey, and hope I need not tell you that you will be welcome to, dear Sir,

"Your most affectionate humble servant,

"SAM JOHNSON."

I wrote to him, March 28, from York, informing him that I had a high gratification in the triumph of monarchical principles over aristocratical influence, in that great county, in an address to the King; that I was thus far on my way to him, but that news of the dissolution of Parliament having arrived, I was to hasten back to my own country, where I had carried an Address to his Majesty by a great majority, and had some intention of being a candidate to represent the county in Parliament.

"TO JAMES BOSWELL, ESQ.

"DEAR SIR,   London, March 30, 1784.

"You could do nothing so proper as to hasten back when you found the Parliament dissolved. With the influence which your address must have gained you, it may reasonably be expected that your presence will be of importance, and your activity of effect.

"Your solicitude for me gives me that pleasure which every man feels from the kindness of such a friend; and it is with delight I relieve it by telling, that Dr. Brocklesby's account is true, and that I am, by the blessing of GOD, wonderfully relieved.

"You are entering upon a transaction which requires much prudence. You must endeavour to oppose without exasperating; to practise temporary hostility, without producing enemies for life. This is, perhaps, hard to be done; yet it has been done by many, and seems most likely to be effected by opposing merely upon general principles, without descending to personal or particular censures or objections. One thing I must enjoin you, which is seldom observed in the conduct of elections;—I must entreat you to be scrupulous in the use of strong liquors. One night's drunkenness may defeat the labours of forty days well employed. Be firm, but not clamorous; be active, but not malicious; and you may form such an interest, as may not only exalt yourself, but dignify your family.

"We are, as you may suppose, all busy here.   Mr. Fox resolutely stands for Westminster, and his friends say will carry the election. However that be, he will certainly have a seat.   Mr. Hoole has just told me, that the city leans towards the king.

"Let me hear, from time to time, how you are employed, and what progress you make.

"Make dear Mrs. Boswell, and all the young Boswells, the sincere compliments of, Sir,

"Your affectionate humble servant,

"SAM. JOHNSON."

To Mr. Langton he wrote with the cordiality which was suitable to the long friendship which had subsisted between him and that gentleman.

"March 27.

"Since you left me, I have continued, in my own opinion and in Dr. Brocklesby's, to grow better with respect to all my formidable and dangerous distempers; though to a body battered and shaken as mine has lately been, it is to be feared that weak attacks may be sometimes mischievous.   I have, indeed, by standing carelessly at an open window, got a very troublesome cough, which it has been necessary to appease by opium, in larger quantities than I like to take, and I have not found it give way so readily as I expected; its obstinacy, however, seems at last disposed to submit to the remedy, and I know not whether I should then have a right to complain of any morbid sensation.   My asthma is, I am afraid, constitutional and incurable; but it is only occasional, and unless it be excited by labour or by cold, gives me no molestation, nor does it lay very close siege to life; for Sir John Floyer, whom the physical race consider as author of one of the best books upon it, panted on to ninety, as was supposed; and why were we content with supposing a fact so interesting, of a man so conspicuous? because he corrupted, at perhaps seventy or eighty, the register, that he might pass for younger than he was.   He was not much less than eighty when to a man of rank who modestly asked his age, he answered, 'Go look;' though he was in general a man of civility and elegance.

"The ladies, I find, are at your house all well, except Miss Langton, who will probably soon recover her health by light suppers. Let her eat at dinner as she will, but not take a full stomach to bed. —Pay my sincere respects to dear Miss Langton in Lincolnshire; let her know that I mean not to break our league of friendship, and that I have a set of Lives for her, when I have the means of sending it."

"April 8.

"I am still disturbed by my cough; but what thanks have I not to pay, when my cough is the most painful sensation that I feel? and from that I expect hardly to be released, while winter continues to gripe us with so much pertinacity.   The year has now advanced eighteen days beyond the equinox, and still there is very little remission of the cold.   When warm weather comes, which surely must come at last, I hope it will help both me and your young lady.

"The man so busy about addresses is neither more nor less than our own Boswell, who had come as far as York towards London, but turned back on the dissolution, and is said now to stand for some place. Whether to wish him success, his best friends hesitate.

"Let me have your prayers for the completion of my recovery: I am now better than I ever expected to have been. May GOD add to his mercies the grace that may enable me to use them according to his will. My compliments to all."

                                              "April 13.

"I had this evening a note from Lord Portmore,[1] desiring that I would give you an account of my health. You might have had it with less circumduction. I am, by God's blessing, I believe, free from all morbid sensations, except a cough, which is only troublesome. But I am still weak, and can have no great hope of strength till the weather shall be softer. The summer, if it be kindly, will, I hope, enable me to support the winter. GOD, who has so wonderfully restored me, can preserve me in all seasons.

"Let me inquire in my turn after the state of your family, great and little. I hope Lady Rothes and Miss Langton are both well. That is a good basis of content. Then how goes George on with his studies? How does Miss Mary? And how does my own Jenny? I think I owe Jenny a letter, which I will take care to pay. In the mean time tell her that I acknowledge the debt.

"Be pleased to make my compliments to the ladies. If Mrs. Langton comes to London, she will favour me with a visit, for I am not well enough to go out."

"TO OZIAS HUMPHRY,[2] ESQ.

"SIR,   April 5, 1784.

"Mr. Hoole has told me with what benevolence you listened to a request which I was almost afraid to make, of leave to a young

---

[1] To which Johnson returned this answer:—
    "TO THE RIGHT HONOURABLE EARL OF PORTMORE.
                        "Bolt-court, Fleet-street, April 13, 1784.

"DR. JOHNSON acknowledges with great respect the honour of Lord Portmore's notice. He is better than he was; and will, as his Lordship directs, write to Mr. Langton."—BOSWELL.

[2] The eminent painter, representative of the ancient family of Homfrey (now Humphry) in the West of England; who, as appears from their arms which they have invariably used, have been (as I have seen authenticated by the best authority) one of those among the knights and esquires of honour who are represented by Hollingshed as having issued from the Tower of London on coursers apparelled for the *justes*, accompanied by ladies of honour, leading every one a knight with a chain of gold, passing through the streets of London into Smithfield, on Sunday, at three o'clock in the afternoon, being the first Sunday after Michaelmas, in the fourteenth year of King Richard II. This family once enjoyed large possessions; but, like others, have lost them in the progress of ages. Their blood, however, remains to them well

painter[1] to attend you from time to time in your painting-room, to see your operations, and receive your instructions.

"The young man has perhaps good parts, but has been without a regular education. He is my godson, and therefore I interest myself in his progress and success, and shall think myself much favoured if I receive from you a permission to send him.

"My health is, by GOD's blessing, much restored, but I am not yet allowed by my physicians to go abroad; nor, indeed, do I think myself yet able to endure the weather.   I am, Sir,
                    "Your most humble servant,
                              "SAM. JOHNSON."

TO THE SAME.

"SIR,   April 10, 1784.

"The bearer is my godson, whom I take the liberty of recommending to your kindness; which I hope he will deserve by his respect to your excellence, and his gratitude for your favours.
            "I am, Sir,
                  "Your most humble servant,
                              "SAM. JOHNSON."

TO THE SAME.

"SIR,   May 31, 1784.

"I am very much obliged by your civilities to my godson, but must beg of you to add to them the favour of permitting him to see you paint, that he may know how a picture is begun, advanced, and completed.

"If he may attend you in a few of your operations, I hope he will show that the benefit has been properly conferred, both by his proficiency and his gratitude.   At least I shall consider you as enlarging your kindness to, Sir,
                  "Your humble servant,
                              "SAM. JOHNSON."

"TO THE REV. DR. TAYLOR, ASHBOURNE, DERBYSHIRE.

"DEAR SIR,   London, Easter-Monday, April 12, 1784.

"What can be the reason that I hear nothing from you?   I hope nothing disables you from writing.   What I have seen, and what I have felt, gives me reason to fear everything.   Do not omit giving me the comfort of knowing, that after all my losses I have yet a friend left.

"I want every comfort.   My life is very solitary and very cheerless.   Though it has pleased GOD wonderfully to deliver me from the dropsy, I am yet very weak, and have not passed the door since the 13th of December.   I hope for some help from warm weather, which will surely come in time.

ascertained; and they may hope, in the revolution of events, to recover that rank in society for which, in modern times, fortune seems to be an indispensable requisite.—BOSWELL.

[1] Son of Mr. Samuel Paterson, eminent for his knowledge of books.—BOSWELL.

"I could not have the consent of the physicians to go to church yesterday: I therefore received the holy sacrament at home, in the room where I communicated with dear Mrs. Williams, a little before her death. O my friend, the approach of death is very dreadful. I am afraid to think on that which I know I cannot avoid. It is vain to look round and round for that help which cannot be had. Yet we hope and hope, and fancy that he who has lived to-day may live to-morrow. But let us learn to derive our hope only from GOD.

"In the mean time, let us be kind to one another. I have no friend now living but you [1] and Mr. Hector, that was the friend of my youth. Do not neglect, dear Sir, yours affectionately,

"SAM. JOHNSON."

"TO MRS. LUCY PORTER, IN LICHFIELD.

"MY DEAR,   London, April 26, 1784.

"I write to you now, to tell you that I am so far recovered, that on the 21st I went to church, to return thanks, after a confinement of more than four long months.

"My recovery is such as neither myself nor the physicians at all expected, and is such as that very few examples have been known of the like. Join with me, my dear love, in returning thanks to GOD.

"Dr. Vyse has been with [me] this evening: he tells me that you likewise have been much disordered, but that you are now better. I hope that we shall some time have a cheerful interview. In the mean time let us pray for one another.

"I am, Madam, your humble servant,

"SAM. JOHNSON."

What follows is a beautiful specimen of his gentleness and complacency to a young lady his godchild, one of the daughters of his friend Mr. Langton, then I think in her seventh year. He took the trouble to write it in a large round hand, nearly resembling printed characters, that she might have the satisfaction of reading it herself. The original lies before me, but shall be faithfully restored to her; and I dare say will be preserved by her as a jewel, as long as she lives.

"TO MISS JANE LANGTON, IN ROCHESTER, KENT.

"MY DEAREST MISS JENNY,   May 10, 1784.

"I am sorry that your pretty letter has been so long without being answered; but, when I am not pretty well, I do not always write plain enough for young ladies. I am glad, my dear, to see that you write so well, and hope that you mind your pen, your book,

---

[1] This friend of Johnson's youth survived him somewhat more than three years, having died Feb. 19, 1788.—MALONE.

and your needle; for they are all necessary. Your books will give you knowledge, and make you respected; and your needle will find you useful employment when you do not care to read. When you are a little older, I hope you will be diligent in learning arithmetic; and, above all, that through your whole life you will carefully say your prayers, and read your Bible.

"I am, my dear, your most humble servant,
"SAM. JOHNSON."

On Wednesday, May 5, I arrived in London, and next morning had the pleasure to find Dr. Johnson greatly recovered. I but just saw him; for a coach was waiting to carry him to Islington, to the house of his friend the Rev. Mr. Strahan, where he went sometimes for the benefit of good air, which, notwithstanding his having formerly laughed at the general opinion upon the subject, he now acknowledged was conducive to health.

One morning afterwards, when I found him alone, he communicated to me with solemn earnestness, a very remarkable circumstance which had happened in the course of his illness, when he was much distressed by the dropsy. He had shut himself up, and employed a day in particular exercises of religion,—fasting, humiliation, and prayer. On a sudden he obtained extraordinary relief, for which he looked up to Heaven with grateful devotion. He made no direct inference from this fact; but from his manner of telling it, I could perceive that it appeared to him as something more than an incident in the common course of events. For my own part, I have no difficulty to avow that cast of thinking, which by many modern pretenders to wisdom is called *superstitious*. But here I think even men of dry rationality may believe, that there was an intermediate interposition of Divine Providence, and that "the fervent prayer of this righteous man"[1] availed.

[1] Upon this subject there is a very fair and judicious remark in the Life of Dr. Abernethy, in the first edition of "The Biographia Britannica," which I should have been glad to see in his Life, which has been written for the second edition of that valuable work. "To deny the exercise of a particular Providence in the Deity's government of the world, is certainly impious, yet nothing serves the cause of the scorner more than incautious forward zeal in determining the particular instances of it."

In confirmation of my sentiments, I am also happy to quote that sensible and elegant writer, Mr. Melmoth, in Letter VIII. of his collection, published under the name of *Fitzosborne*. "We may safely assert, that the belief of a particular Providence is founded upon such probable reasons as may well justify our assent. It would scarce, therefore, be wise to renounce an opinion which affords so firm a support to the soul, in those seasons wherein she stands in most need of assistance, merely because it is not possible, in questions of this kind, to solve every difficulty which attends them."—BOSWELL.

On Sunday, May 9, I found Colonel Vallancy, the cele-brated antiquary and engineer of Ireland, with him. On Monday, the 10th, I dined with him at Mr. Paradise's, where was a large company; Mr. Bryant, Mr. Joddrel, Mr. Hawkins Browne, &c. On Thursday, the 13th, I dined with him at Mr. Joddrel's, with another large company; the Bishop of Exeter, Lord Monboddo,[1] Mr. Murphy, &c.

On Saturday, May 15, I dined with him at Dr. Brock-lesby's, where were Colonel Vallancy, Mr. Murphy, and that ever-cheerful companion, Mr. Devaynes, apothecary to his Majesty. Of these days, and others on which I saw him, I have no memorials, except the general recollection of his being able and animated in conversation, and appear-ing to relish society as much as the youngest man. I find only these three small particulars:—When a person was mentioned, who said, "I have lived fifty-one years in this world, without having had ten minutes of uneasiness," he exclaimed, "The man who says so, lies: he attempts to impose on human credulity." The Bishop of Exeter[2] in vain observed, that men were very different. His Lord-ship's manner was not impressive; and I learnt afterwards, that Johnson did not find out that the person who talked to him was a prelate; if he had, I doubt not that he would have treated him with more respect; for once talking of George Psalmanazar, whom he reverenced for his piety, he said, "I should as soon think of contradicting a BISHOP." One of the company provoked him greatly by doing what he could least of all bear, which was quoting something of his own writing, against what he then maintained. "What, Sir," cried the gentleman, "do you say to

'The busy day, the peaceful night,
Unfelt, uncounted, glided by'?"[3]

Johnson finding himself thus presented as giving an instance of a man who had lived without uneasiness, was much offended; for he looked upon such a quotation as unfair.

[1] I was sorry to observe Lord Monboddo avoid any communication with Dr. Johnson. I flattered myself that I had made them very good friends (see "Journal of a Tour to the Hebrides," third edition, p. 67), but unhappily his lordship had resumed and cherished a violent pre-judice against my illustrious friend, to whom I must do the justice to say, there was on his part not the least anger, but a good-humoured sportiveness. Nay, though he knew of his Lordship's indisposition towards him, he was even kindly; as appeared from his inquiring of me after him, by an abbreviation of his name, "Well, how does *Monny?*"—BOSWELL.

[2] Dr. John Ross.—MALONE.

[3] Verses on the death of Mr. Levett; *vide* p. 444 *ante*.—BOSWELL.

His anger burst out in an unjustifiable retort, insinuating that the gentleman's remark was a sally of ebriety; "Sir, there is one passion I would advise you to command; when you have drunk out that glass, don't drink another." Here was exemplified what Goldsmith said of him, with the aid of a very witty image from one of Cibber's comedies: "There is no arguing with Johnson: for if his pistol misses fire, he knocks you down with the butt-end of it."

Another was this: when a gentleman of eminence in the literary world was violently censured for attacking people by anonymous paragraphs in newspapers, he, from the spirit of contradiction as I thought, took up his defence, and said, "Come, come, this is not so terrible a crime; he means only to vex them a little. I do not say that I should do it; but there is a great difference between him and me; what is fit for Hephæstion is not fit for Alexander."— Another, when I told him that a young and handsome countess had said to me, " I should think that to be praised by Dr. Johnson would make one a fool all one's life;" and that I answered, "Madam, I shall make him a fool to-day, by repeating this to him;" he said, " I am too old to be made a fool; but if you say I am made a fool, I shall not deny it. I am much pleased with a compliment, especially from a pretty woman."

On the evening of Saturday, May 15, he was in fine spirits at our Essex Head Club. He told us, "I dined yesterday at Mrs. Garrick's with Mrs. Carter, Miss Hannah More, and Miss Fanny Burney. Three such women are not to be found: I know not where I could find a fourth, except Mrs. Lennox, who is superior to them all." BOSWELL: "What! had you them all to yourself, Sir?"   JOHNSON: " I had them all, as much as they were had; but it might have been better had there been more company there." BOSWELL: "Might not Mrs. Montagu have been a fourth?" JOHNSON: "Sir, Mrs. Montagu does not make a trade of her wit; but Mrs. Montagu is a very extraordinary woman; she has a constant stream of conversation, and it is always impregnated; it has always meaning." BOSWELL: "Mr. Burke has a constant stream of conversation." JOHNSON: " Yes, Sir; if a man were to go by chance at the same time with Burke under a shed, to shun a shower, he would say—'This is an extraordinary man.' If Burke should go into a stable to see his horse dressed, the ostler would say—'We have had an extraordinary man here.'" BOSWELL: "Foote was a man who never failed in conversation. If he had gone into a stable—" JOHNSON: "Sir, if he had gone into the stable, the ostler would have said, here has been a comical fellow; but he would not have respected him." BOSWELL: "And, Sir, the ostler would have answered him, would have given him as good as he brought, as the common saying is." JOHNSON: "Yes, Sir; and Foote would have answered the ostler.—When Burke does not descend to be merry, his conversation is very superior indeed. There is no proportion between the powers which he shows in serious talk and in jocularity. When he lets himself down to that, he is in the kennel." I have in another place[1] opposed, and I hope with success, Dr. Johnson's very singular and erroneous notion as to Mr. Burke's pleasantry. Mr. Windham now said low to me, that he differed from our great friend in this observation; for that Mr. Burke was often very happy in his merriment. It would not have been right for either of us to have contradicted Johnson at this time, in a society all of whom did not know and value Mr. Burke as much as we did. It might have occasioned something more rough, and at any rate would probably have checked the flow of Johnson's good humour. He called to us with a sudden air of exultation, as the thought started into his mind, "Oh! gentlemen, I must tell you a very great thing. The Empress of Russia has ordered 'The Rambler' to be translated into the Russian language:[2] so I shall be read on the banks of the Wolga. Horace boasts that his fame would extend as far as the banks of the Rhone; now the Wolga is farther from me than the Rhone was from Horace." BOSWELL: "You must certainly be pleased with this, Sir." JOHNSON: "I am pleased, Sir, to be sure. A man is pleased to find he has succeeded in that which he has endeavoured to do."

One of the company mentioned his having seen a noble person driving in his carriage, and looking exceedingly well, notwithstanding his great age. JOHNSON: "Ah, Sir, that is nothing. Bacon observes, that a stout healthy old man is like a tower undermined."

On Sunday, May 16, I found him alone; he talked of Mrs. Thrale with much concern, saying, "Sir, she has done everything wrong, since Thrale's bridle was off her neck;" and was proceeding to mention some circumstances which have since been the subject of public discussion, when he was interrupted by the arrival of Dr. Douglas, now Bishop of Salisbury.

---

[1] "Journal of a Tour to the Hebrides," third edition, p. 20.—BOSWELL.

[2] I have since heard that the report was not well founded; but the elation discovered by Johnson, in the belief that it was true, showed a noble ardour for literary fame.—BOSWELL.

Dr. Douglas, upon this occasion, refuted a mistaken notion which is very common in Scotland, that the ecclesiastical discipline of the Church of England, though duly enforced, is insufficient to preserve the morals of the clergy, inasmuch as all delinquents may be screened by appealing to the Convocation, which being never authorised by the king to sit for the dispatch of business, the appeal never can be heard. Dr. Douglas observed, that this was founded upon ignorance; for that the bishops have sufficient power to maintain discipline, and that the sitting of the Convocation was wholly immaterial in this respect, it being not a court of judicature, but, like a parliament, to make canons and regulations as times may require.

Johnson, talking of the fear of death, said, "Some people are not afraid, because they look upon salvation as the effect of an absolute decree, and think they feel in themselves the marks of sanctification. Others, and those the most rational in my opinion, look upon salvation as conditional; and, as they never can be sure that they have complied with the conditions, they are afraid."

In one of his little manuscript diaries, about this time, I find a short notice, which marks his amiable disposition more certainly than a thousand studied declarations.— "Afternoon spent cheerfully and elegantly, I hope without offence to God or man; though in no holy duty, yet in the general exercise and cultivation of benevolence."

On Monday, May 17, I dined with him at Mr. Dilly's, where were Colonel Vallancy, the Reverend Dr. Gibbons, and Mr. Capel Lofft, who, though a most zealous Whig, has a mind so full of learning and knowledge, and so much exercised in various departments, and withal so much liberality, that the stupendous powers of the literary Goliath, though they did not frighten this little David of popular spirit, could not but excite his admiration. There was also Mr. Braithwaite of the Post-office, that amiable and friendly man, who, with modest and unassuming manners, has associated with many of the wits of the age. Johnson was very quiescent to-day. Perhaps too I was indolent. I find nothing more of him in my notes, but that, when I mentioned that I had seen in the King's library sixty-three editions of my favourite Thomas à Kempis,—amongst which it was in eight languages, Latin, German, French, Italian, Spanish, English, Arabic, and Armenian,—he said, he thought it unnecessary to collect many editions of a book, which were all the same, except as to the paper and print; he would have the original, and all the translations, and all the editions which had any variations in the text.

He approved of the famous collection of editions of Horace by Douglas, mentioned by Pope, who is said to have had a closet filled with them; and he added, "every man should try to collect one book in that manner, and present it to a public library."

On Tuesday, May 18, I saw him for a short time in the morning. I told him that the mob had called out, as the King passed, "No Fox—No Fox," which I did not like. He said, "They were right, Sir." I said, I thought not; for it seemed to be making Mr. Fox the King's competitor. There being no audience, so that there could be no triumph in a victory, he fairly agreed with me. I said it might do very well, if explained thus: "Let us have no Fox;" understanding it as a prayer to his Majesty not to appoint that gentleman minister.

On Wednesday, May 19, I sat a part of the evening with him, by ourselves. I observed, that the death of our friends might be a consolation against the fear of our own dissolution, because we might have more friends in the other world than in this. He perhaps felt this as a reflection upon his apprehension as to death; and said, with heat, "How can a man know *where* his departed friends are, or whether they will be his friends in the other world. How many friendships have you known formed upon principles of virtue? Most friendships are formed by caprice or by chance, mere confederacies in vice or leagues in folly."

We talked of our worthy friend Mr. Langton. He said, "I know not who will go to Heaven if Langton does not. Sir, I could almost say, *Sit anima mea cum Langtono.*" I mentioned a very eminent friend as a virtuous man. JOHNSON: "Yes, Sir, but ———— has not the evangelical virtue of Langton. ————, I am afraid, would not scruple to pick up a wench."

He however charged Mr. Langton with what he thought want of judgment upon an interesting occasion. "When I was ill," said he, "I desired he would tell me sincerely in what he thought my life was faulty. Sir, he brought me a sheet of paper, on which he had written down several texts of Scripture, recommending Christian charity. And when I questioned him what occasion I had given for such an animadversion, all that he could say amounted to this,— that I sometimes contradicted people in conversation. Now what harm does it do to any man to be contradicted?" BOSWELL: "I suppose he meant the *manner* of doing it; roughly and harshly." JOHNSON: "And who is the worse for that?" BOSWELL: "It hurts people of weaker nerves." JOHNSON: "I know no such weak-nerved people." Mr.

Burke, to whom I related this conference, said, "It is well if, when a man comes to die, he has nothing heavier upon his conscience than having been a little rough in conversation."

Johnson, at the time when the paper was presented to him, though at first pleased with the attention of his friend, whom he thanked in an earnest manner, soon exclaimed, in a loud and angry tone, "What is your drift, Sir?" Sir Joshua Reynolds pleasantly observed, that it was a scene for a comedy, to see a penitent get into a violent passion, and belabour his confessor.[1]

I have preserved no more of his conversation at the times when I saw him during the rest of this month, till Sunday, the 30th of May, when I met him in the evening at Mr. Hoole's, where there was a large company both of ladies and gentlemen. Sir James Johnston happened to say, that he paid no regard to the arguments of counsel at the bar of the House of Commons, because they were paid for speaking. JOHNSON: "Nay, Sir, argument is argument. You cannot help paying regard to their arguments, if they are good. If it were testimony, you might disregard it, if you knew that it were purchased. There is a beautiful image in Bacon[2] upon this subject: testimony is like an arrow shot from a long bow; the force of it depends on the strength of the hand that draws it. Argument is like an arrow from a cross-bow, which has equal force though shot by a child."

[1] After all, I cannot but be of opinion, that as Mr. Langton was seriously requested by Dr. Johnson to mention what appeared to him erroneous in the character of his friend he was bound, as an honest man, to intimate what he really thought, which he certainly did in the most delicate manner: so that Johnson himself, when in a quiet frame of mind, was pleased with it. The texts suggested are now before me, and I shall quote a few of them:—"Blessed are the meek, for they shall inherit the earth." *Mat.* v. 5.—"I therefore, the prisoner of the LORD, beseech you that ye walk worthy of the vocation wherewith ye are called, with all lowliness and meekness, with long-suffering, forbearing one another in love." *Ephes.* v. 1, 2.—"And above all these things put on charity, which is the bond of perfectness." *Col.* iii. 14.—"Charity suffereth long, and is kind: charity envieth not: charity vaunteth not itself, is not puffed up: doth not behave itself unseemly, is not easily provoked." 1 *Cor.* xiii. 4, 5.—BOSWELL.

[1] Dr. Johnson's memory deceived him. The passage referred to is not Bacon's, but Boyle's: and may be found, with a slight variation, in Johnson's Dictionary, under the word *Crossbow.*—So happily selected are the greater part of the examples in that incomparable work, that if the most striking passages found in it were collected by one of our modern book-makers, under the title of "The Beauties of Johnson's Dictionary," they would form a very pleasing and popular volume.—MALONE.

He had dined that day at Mr. Hoole's, and Miss Helen Maria Williams being expected in the evening, Mr. Hoole put into his hands her beautiful "Ode on the Peace:"[1] Johnson read it over, and when this elegant and accomplished young lady[2] was presented to him, he took her by the hand in the most courteous manner, and repeated the finest stanza of her poem; this was the most delicate and pleasing compliment he could pay. Her respectable friend, Dr. Kippis, from whom I had this anecdote, was standing by, and was not a little gratified.

Miss Williams told me, that the only other time she was fortunate enough to be in Dr. Johnson's company, he asked her to sit down by him, which she did, and upon her inquiring how he was, he answered, " I am very ill, indeed, Madam. I am very ill even when you are near me; what should I be were you at a distance?"

He had now a great desire to go to Oxford, as his first jaunt after his illness. We talked of it for some days, and I had promised to accompany him. He was impatient and fretful to-night, because I did not at once agree to go with him on Thursday. When I considered how ill he had been, and what allowance should be made for the influence of sickness upon his temper, I resolved to indulge him, though with some inconvenience to myself, as I wished to attend the musical meeting in honour of Handel, in Westminster Abbey, on the following Saturday.

In the midst of his own diseases and pains, he was ever compassionate to the distresses of others, and actively earnest in procuring them aid, as appears from a note to Sir Joshua Reynolds, of June, in these words:—" I am ashamed to ask for some relief for a poor man, to whom, I hope, I have given what I can be expected to spare. The man importunes me, and the blow goes round.   I am going to try another air on Thursday."

---

[1] The peace made by that very able statesman, the Earl of Shelburne, now Marquis of Lansdowne, which may fairly be considered as the foundation of all the prosperity of Great Britain since that time.— BOSWELL.

[2] In the first edition of my work, the epithet *amiable* was given. I was sorry to be obliged to strike it out; but I could not in justice suffer it to remain, after this young lady had not only written in favour of the savage anarchy with which France has been visited, but had (as I have been informed by good authority), walked without horror over the ground at the Tuileries when it was strewed with the naked bodies of the faithful Swiss guards, who were barbarously massacred for having bravely defended, against a crew of ruffians, the Monarch whom they had taken an oath to defend. From Dr. Johnson she could now expect not endearment but repulsion.—BOSWELL.

CHAPTER XXVII.—1784

*Johnson's Departure for Oxford—Mrs. Beresford—Knotting
—Arrival at Oxford—Dr. Adams—Bishop Newton—
Archibald Campbell—Nonjurors—Mrs. Kennicot—In-
fidel Writers—Roman Catholic Religion—Bishop Hurd's
Sermons—Whig and Tory—Miss Adams—Dr. Wall—
Dr. Radcliffe's Fellowships—Forms of Prayer—Jeremy
Taylor—Dr. Nowell—Rev. H. Bate—John Henderson
—The Rev. Sir Herbert Croft—Lord Lyttelton's Vision—
Johnson's Horror of Death—Balance of Misery—The
Rev. R. Churton's Remarks on Boswell's Johnson—On
Truth—Junius—Pope's "Dunciad"—Mr. Lewis—
Mickle—The English Bar—Chief Justice Hale*

ON Thursday, June 3, the Oxford post-coach took us up
in the morning at Bolt-court. The other two passengers
were Mrs. Beresford and her daughter, two very agreeable
ladies from America; they were going to Worcestershire,
where they then resided. Frank had been sent by his master
the day before to take places for us; and I found from the
way-bill that Dr. Johnson had made our names be put down.
Mrs. Beresford, who had read it, whispered me," Is this the
great Dr. Johnson?" I told her it was; so she was then
prepared to listen. As she soon happened to mention in a
voice so low that Johnson did not hear it, that her husband
had been a member of the American Congress, I cautioned
her to beware of introducing that subject, as she must
know how very violent Johnson was against the people of
that country. He talked a great deal. But I am sorry I
have preserved little of the conversation. Miss Beresford
was so much charmed, that she said to me aside, "How he
does talk! Every sentence is an essay." She amused
herself in the coach with knotting; he would scarcely allow
this species of employment any merit. "Next to mere
idleness," said he, "I think knotting is to be reckoned in
the scale of insignificance; though I once attempted to
learn knotting. Dempster's sister," looking to me,
"endeavoured to teach me it; but I made no progress."

I was surprised at his talking without reserve in the
public post-coach of the state of his affairs: "I have," said

545

he, "about the world, I think, above a thousand pounds, which I intend shall afford Frank an annuity of seventy pounds a year." Indeed his openness with people at a first interview was remarkable. He said once to Mr. Langton, "I think I am like Squire Richard in ' The Journey to London,' *I'm never strange in a strange place.*" He was truly *social*. He strongly censured what is much too common in England among persons of condition,—maintaining an absolute silence, when unknown to each other; as, for instance, when occasionally brought together in a room before the master or mistress of the house has appeared. "Sir, that is being so uncivilized as not to understand the common rights of humanity."

At the inn where we stopped he was exceedingly dissatisfied with some roast mutton which he had for dinner. The ladies, I saw, wondered to see the great philosopher, whose wisdom and wit they had been admiring all the way, get into ill-humour from such a cause. He scolded the waiter, saying, "It is as bad as bad can be; it is ill-fed, ill-killed, ill-kept, and ill-drest."

He bore the journey very well, and seemed to feel himself elevated as he approached Oxford, that magnificent and venerable seat of Learning, Orthodoxy, and Toryism. Frank came in the heavy coach, in readiness to attend him; and we were received with the most polite hospitality at the house of his old friend Dr. Adams, Master of Pembroke College, who had given us a kind invitation. Before we were set down, I communicated to Johnson my having engaged to return to London directly, for the reason I have mentioned, but that I would hasten back to him again. He was pleased that I had made this journey merely to keep him company. He was easy and placid with Dr. Adams, Mrs. and Miss Adams, and Mrs. Kennicot, widow of the learned Hebræan, who was here on a visit. He soon dispatched the inquiries which were made about his illness and recovery, by a short and distinct narrative; and then assuming a gay air, repeated from Swift,—

"Nor think on our approaching ills,
And talk of spectacles and pills."

Dr. Newton,[1] the Bishop of Bristol, having been men-

[1] Dr. Newton, in his account of his own Life, after animadverting upon Mr. Gibbon's History, says—"Dr. Johnson's 'Lives of the Poets' afforded more amusement; but candour was much hurt and offended at the malevolence that predominates in every part. Some passages, it must be allowed, are judicious and well written, but make not sufficient compensation for so much spleen and ill-humour. Never was any

tioned, Johnson, recollecting the manner in which he had
been censured by that Prelate, thus retaliated:—"Tom
knew he should be dead before what he has said of me
would appear. He durst not have printed it while he was
alive." DR. ADAMS: "I believe his 'Dissertations on the
Prophecies' is his great work." JOHNSON: "Why Sir, it
is *Tom's* great work; but how far it is great, or how much
of it is Tom's, are other questions. I fancy a considerable
part of it was borrowed." DR. ADAMS: "He was a very
successful man." JOHNSON: "I don't think so, Sir. He
did not get very high. He was late in getting what he did
get; and he did not get it by the best means. I believe he
was a gross flatterer."

I fulfilled my intention of going to London, and returned
to Oxford on Wednesday the 9th of June, when I was happy
to find myself again in the same agreeable circle at Pembroke College, with the comfortable prospect of making some
stay. Johnson welcomed my return with more than
ordinary glee.

He talked with great regard of the Honourable Archibald Campbell, whose character he had given at the Duke
of Argyle's table, when we were at Inverary;[1] and at this
time wrote out for me, in his own hand, a fuller account
of that learned and venerable writer, which I have published in its proper place. Johnson made a remark this
evening which struck me a good deal. "I never," said he,
"knew a nonjuror who could reason."[2] Surely he did not

biographer more sparing of his praise, or more abundant in his censures.
He seemingly delights more in exposing blemishes, than in recommending beauties; slightly passes over excellencies, enlarges upon imperfections, and, not content with his own severe reflections, revives old
scandal, and produces large quotations from the forgotten works of
former critics. His reputation was so high in the republic of letters,
that it wanted not to be raised upon the ruins of others. But these
Essays, instead of raising a higher idea than was before entertained of
his understanding, have certainly given the world a worse opinion of his
temper."—The Bishop was therefore the more surprised and concerned
for his townsman, for "*he respected him not only for his genius and learning,
but valued him much for the more amiable part of his character, his humanity
and charity, his morality and religion.*" The last sentence we may consider
as the general and permanent opinion of Bishop Newton. The remarks
which precede it must, by all who have read Johnson's admirable work,
be imputed to the disgust and peevishness of old age. I wish they had
not appeared, and that Dr. Johnson had not been provoked by them to
express himself not in respectful terms of a Prelate whose labours were
certainly of considerable advantage both to literature and religion.—
BOSWELL.

[1] Journal of a Tour to the Hebrides," third edit. p. 371.—BOSWELL.

[2] The Rev. Mr. Agutter has favoured me with a note of a dialogue
between Mr. John Henderson and Dr. Johnson on this topic, as related
by Mr. Henderson, and it is evidently so authentic that I shall here

mean to deny that faculty to many of their writers; to Hickes, Brett, and other eminent divines of that persuasion; and did not recollect that the seven Bishops, so justly celebrated for their magnanimous resistance of arbitrary power, were yet nonjurors to the new Government. The nonjuring clergy of Scotland, indeed, who, excepting a few, have lately, by a sudden stroke, cut off all ties of allegiance to the house of Stuart, and resolved to pray for our present lawful Sovereign by name, may be thought to have confirmed this remark; as it may be said, that the divine indefeasible hereditary right which they professed to believe, if ever true, must be equally true still. Many of my readers will be surprised, when I mention that Johnson assured me he had never in his life been in a nonjuring meeting-house.

Next morning, at breakfast, he pointed out a passage in Savage's "Wanderer," saying, "These are fine verses."— "If," said he, "I had written with hostility of Warburton in my Shakespeare, I should have quoted this couplet:

> 'Here Learning, blinded first, and then beguiled,
> Looks dark as Ignorance, as Frenzy wild.'

You see they'd have fitted him to a _T_" (smiling). DR. ADAMS: "But you did not write against Warburton." JOHNSON: "No, Sir, I treated him with great respect both in my preface and in my notes."

Mrs. Kennicot spoke of her brother, the Rev. Mr. Chamberlayne, who had given up great prospects in the Church of England on his conversion to the Roman Catholic faith. Johnson, who warmly admired every man who acted from a conscientious regard to principle, erroneous or not, exclaimed fervently, "GOD bless him."

Mrs. Kennicot, in confirmation of Dr. Johnson's opinion, that the present was not worse than former ages, mentioned that her brother assured her, there was now less infidelity on the Continent than there had been; Voltaire and Rousseau were less read. I asserted, from good authority, that Hume's infidelity was certainly less read. JOHNSON: "All infidel writers drop into oblivion, when

---

insert it:—Henderson: "What do you think, Sir, of William Law?" Johnson: "William Law, Sir, wrote the best piece of Parenetic Divinity; but William Law was no reasoner." Henderson: "Jeremy Collier, Sir?" Johnson: "Jeremy Collier fought without a rival, and therefore could not claim the victory." Mr. Henderson mentioned Kenn and Kettlewell; but some objections were made; at last he said, "But, Sir, what do you think of Lesley?" Johnson: "Charles Lesley I had forgotten. Lesley _was_ a reasoner, and _a reasoner who was not to be reasoned against._" —BOSWELL.

personal connexions and the floridness of novelty are gone;
though now and then a foolish fellow, who thinks he can
be witty upon them, may bring them again into notice.
There will sometimes start up a college joker, who does
not consider that what is a joke in a college will not do in
the world. To such defenders of religion I would apply a
stanza of a poem which I remember to have seen in some
old collection:

> "'Henceforth be quiet and agree,
> Each kiss his empty brother;
> Religion scorns a foe like thee,
> But dreads a friend like t'other.'

The point is well, though the expression is not correct;
one, and not *thee*, should be opposed to *t'other*." [1]

On the Roman Catholic religion he said, "If you join
the Papists externally, they will not interrogate you
strictly as to your belief in their tenets. No reasoning
Papist believes every article of their faith. There is one
side on which a good man might be persuaded to embrace
it. A good man of a timorous disposition, in great doubt of
his acceptance with God, and pretty credulous, may be glad
to be of a church where there are so many helps to get to
heaven. I would be a Papist if I could. I have fear enough;
but an obstinate rationality prevents me. I shall never be
a Papist, unless on the near approach of death, of which
I have great terror. I wonder that women are not all
Papists." Boswell: "They are not more afraid of death
than men are." Johnson: "Because they are less wicked."
Dr. Adams: "They are more pious." Johnson: "No,
hang 'em, they are not more pious. A wicked fellow is
the most pious when he takes to it. He'll beat you all at
piety."

He argued in defence of some of the peculiar tenets of
the Church of Rome. As to the giving the bread only to
the laity he said, "They may think, that in what is merely

---

[1] I have inserted the stanza as Johnson repeated it from memory;
but I have since found the poem itself, in "The Foundling Hospital for
Wit," printed at London, 1749. It is as follows:—

> "Epigram, *occasioned by a religious dispute at Bath.*
>
> "On Reason, Faith, and Mystery high,
> Two wits harangue the table;
> B——y believes he knows not why,
> N——h swears 'tis all a fable.
>
> "Peace, coxcombs, peace, and both agree;
> N——h, kiss thy empty brother;
> Religion laughs at foes like thee,
> And dreads a friend like t'other."—Boswell.

ritual, deviations from the primitive mode may be admitted on the ground of convenience; and I think they are as well warranted to make this alteration, as we are to substitute sprinkling in the room of the ancient baptism." As to the invocation of saints, he said, "Though I do not think it authorized, it appears to me, that the communion of saints in the Creed means the communion with the saints in Heaven, as connected with 'the holy Catholic church.'"[1] He admitted the influence of evil spirits upon our minds, and said, "Nobody who believes the New Testament can deny it."

I brought a volume of Dr. Hurd, the Bishop of Worcester's Sermons, and read to the company some passages from one of them, upon this text, "*Resist the Devil, and he will fly from you.*" James iv. 7. I was happy to produce so judicious and elegant a supporter[2] of a doctrine, which, I know not why, should, in this world of imperfect knowledge, and therefore of wonder and mystery in a thousand instances, be contested by some with an unthinking assurance and flippancy.

After dinner, when one of us talked of there being a great enmity between Whig and Tory:—JOHNSON: "Why, not so much, I think, unless when they come into competition with each other. There is none when they are only

---

[1] Walker, in his "Divine Poesie," Canto first, has the same thought finely expressed:—

> "The Church triumphant, and the Church below,
> In songs of praise their present union show;
> Their joys are full; our expectation long,
> In life we differ, but we join in song;
> Angels and we, assisted by this art,
> May sing together, though we dwell apart."—BOSWELL.

[2] The Sermon thus opens:—"That there are angels and spirits, good and bad; that at the head of these last there is ONE more considerable and malignant than the rest who, in the form, or under the name of a *serpent*, was deeply concerned in the fall of man, and whose *head*, as the prophetic language is, the son of man was one day to *bruise;* that this evil spirit, though that prophecy be in part completed, has not yet received his death's wound, but is still permitted, for ends unsearchable to us, and in ways which we cannot particularly explain, to have a certain degree of power in this world hostile to its virtue and happiness, and sometimes exerted with too much success; all this is so clear from Scripture, that no believer, unless he be first of all *spoiled by philosophy and vain deceit* can possibly entertain a doubt of it."

Having treated of *possessions*, his lordship says, "As I have no authority to affirm that there *are* now any such, so neither may I presume to say with confidence, that there are *not* any."

"But then with regard to the influence of evil spirits at this day upon the SOULS of men, I shall take leave to be a great deal more peremptory." Then, having stated the various proofs, he adds, "All this, I say, is so manifest to every one who reads the Scriptures, that,

common acquaintance, none when they are of different
sexes. A Tory will marry into a Whig family, and a Whig
into a Tory family, without any reluctance. But indeed,
in a matter of much more concern than political tenets,
and that is religion, men and women do not concern themselves much about difference of opinion; and ladies set no
value on the moral character of men who pay their addresses
to them; the greatest profligate will be as well received as
the man of the greatest virtue, and this by a very good
woman, by a woman who says her prayers three times a
day." Our ladies endeavoured to defend their sex from
this charge; but he roared them down! "No, no! a lady
will take Jonathan Wild as readily as St. Austin, if he has
threepence more; and, what is worse, her parents will give
her to him. Women have a perpetual envy of our vices;
they are less vicious than we, not from choice, but because
we restrict them; they are the slaves of order and fashion;
their virtue is of more consequence to us than our own,
so far as concerns this world."

Miss Adams mentioned a gentleman of licentious character, and said, "Suppose I had a mind to marry that gentleman, would my parents consent?" Johnson: "Yes, they'd
consent, and you'd go. You'd go, though they did not
consent." Miss Adams: "Perhaps their opposing might
make me go." Johnson: "Oh, very well; you'd take one
whom you think a bad man, to have the pleasure of vexing
your parents. You put me in mind of Dr. Barrowby, the
physician, who was very fond of swine's flesh. One day,
when he was eating it, he said, ' I wish I was a Jew.'—'Why
so?' said somebody; 'the Jews are not allowed to eat your
favourite meat.'—'Because,' said he, ' I should then have
the gust of eating it, with the pleasure of sinning.'"
Johnson then proceeded in his declamation.

Miss Adams soon afterwards made an observation that
I do not recollect, which pleased him much; he said, with

---

if we respect their authority, the question concerning the reality of the
demoniac influence upon the minds of men is clearly determined."

Let it be remembered, that these are not the words of an anti-
quated or obscure enthusiast, but of a learned and polite prelate now
alive, and were spoken, not to a vulgar congregation, but to the Honourable
Society of Lincoln's Inn. His lordship in this Sermon explains the
words, "Deliver us from evil," in the Lord's Prayer, as signifying a
request to be protected from "the evil one," that is, the Devil. This
is well illustrated in a short but excellent Commentary by my late
worthy friend, the Rev. Dr. Lort, of whom it may be truly said, "Multis
ille bonis flebilis occidit." It is remarkable that Waller, in his "Reflections on the several Petitions in that sacred form of devotion," has
understood this in the same sense:—

"Guard us from all temptations of the Foe."—Boswell.

a good-humoured smile, "That there should be so much excellence united with so much *depravity* is strange."

Indeed, this lady's good qualities, merit, and accomplishments, and her constant attention to Dr. Johnson, were not lost upon him. She happened to tell him that a little coffee-pot, in which she had made him coffee, was the only thing she could call her own. He turned to her with a complacent gallantry, "Don't say so, my dear; I hope you don't reckon my heart as nothing."

I asked him if it was true, as reported, that he had said lately, "I am for the King against Fox; but I am for Fox against Pitt." JOHNSON: "Yes, Sir; the King is my master; but I do not know Pitt; and Fox is my friend."

"Fox," added he, "is a most extraordinary man. Here is a man," describing him in strong terms of objection in some respects, according as he apprehended, but which exalted his abilities the more, "who has divided the kingdom with Cæsar; so that it was a doubt whether the nation should be ruled by the sceptre of George III., or the tongue of Fox."

Dr. Wall, physician at Oxford, drank tea with us. Johnson had in general a peculiar pleasure in the company of physicians, which was certainly not abated by the conversation of this learned, ingenious, and pleasing gentleman. Johnson said, "It is wonderful how little good Radcliffe's travelling fellowships have done. I know nothing that has been imported by them; yet many additions to our medical knowledge might be got in foreign countries. Inoculation, for instance, has saved more lives than war destroyed; and the cures performed by the Peruvian bark are innumerable. But it is in vain to send our travelling physicians to France, and Italy, and Germany; for all that is known there is known here: I'd send them out of Christendom; I'd send them among barbarous nations."

On Friday, June 11, we talked at breakfast of forms of prayer. JOHNSON: "I know of no good prayers but those in the 'Book of Common Prayer.'" DR. ADAMS (in a very earnest manner): "I wish, Sir, you would compose some family prayers." JOHNSON: "I will not compose prayers for you, Sir, because you can do it for yourself. But I have thought of getting together all the books of prayers which I could, selecting those which should appear to me the best, putting out some, inserting others, adding some prayers of my own, and prefixing a discourse on prayer." We all now gathered about him, and two or three of us at a time joined in pressing him to execute this plan. He seemed to be a little displeased at the manner of our importunity, and in great agitation called out, "Do not talk thus of what is so awful. I know not what time God will allow me in this world. There are many things which I wish to do." Some of us persisted, and Dr. Adams said, "I never was more serious about anything in my life." Johnson: "Let me alone, let me alone; I am overpowered." And then he put his hands before his face, and reclined for some time upon the table.

I mentioned Jeremy Taylor's using, in his forms of prayer, "I am the chief of sinners," and other such self-condemning expressions. "Now," said I, "this cannot be said with truth by every man, and therefore is improper for a general printed form. I myself cannot say that I am the worst of men; I *will* not say so." Johnson: "A man may know, that physically, that is, in the real state of things, he is not the worst man; but that morally he may be so. Law observes, that 'every man knows something worse of himself, than he is sure of in others.' You may not have committed such crimes as some men have done, but you do not know against what degree of light they have sinned. Besides, Sir, 'the chief of sinners' is a mode of expression for 'I am a great sinner.' So St. Paul, speaking of our Saviour's having died to save sinners, says, 'of whom I am the chief:' yet he certainly did not think himself so bad as Judas Iscariot." Boswell: "But, Sir, Taylor means it literally, for he founds a conceit upon it. When praying for the conversion of sinners, and of himself in particular, he says, 'Lord, thou wilt not leave thy *chief* work undone.'" Johnson: "I do not approve of figurative expressions in addressing the Supreme Being; and I never use them. Taylor gives a very good advice: 'Never lie in your prayers: never confess more than you really believe; never promise more than you mean to perform.'" I recollected this precept in his "Golden Grove;" but his *example* for prayer contradicts his *precept*.

Dr. Johnson and I went in Dr. Adams's coach to dine with Dr. Nowell, Principal of St. Mary Hall, at his beautiful villa at Iffley, on the banks of the Isis, about two miles from Oxford. While we were upon the road, I had the resolution to ask Johnson whether he thought that the roughness of his manner had been an advantage or not, and if he would not have done more good, if he had been more gentle. I proceeded to answer myself thus: "Perhaps it has been of advantage, as it has given weight to what you said: you could not, perhaps, have talked with such authority without it." Johnson: "No, Sir; I have done more good as I am. Obscenity and impiety have always been repressed in my company." BOSWELL: "True, Sir; and that is more than can be said of every Bishop. Greater liberties have been taken in the presence of a Bishop, though a very good man, from his being milder, and therefore not commanding such awe. Yet, Sir, many people who might have been benefited by your conversation, have been frightened away. A worthy friend of ours has told me, that he has often been afraid to talk to you." JOHNSON: "Sir, he need not have been afraid, if he had anything rational to say.[1] If he had not, it was better he did not talk."

Dr. Nowell is celebrated for having preached a sermon before the House of Commons, on the 30th of January, 1772, full of high Tory sentiments, for which he was thanked as usual, and printed it at their request; but, in the midst of that turbulence and faction which disgraced a part of the present reign, the thanks were afterwards ordered to be expunged. This strange conduct sufficiently exposes itself; and Dr. Nowell will ever have the honour which is due to a lofty friend of our monarchical constitution. Dr. Johnson said to me, "Sir, the Court will be very much to blame if he is not promoted." I told this to Dr. Nowell; and asserting my humbler, though not less zealous, exertions in the same cause, I suggested, that whatever return we might receive, we should still have the consolation of being like Butler's steady and generous Royalist,

> "True as the dial to the sun,
> Although it be not shone upon."

We were well entertained, and very happy at Dr. Nowell's, where was a very agreeable company; and we drank "Church and King" after dinner, with true Tory cordiality.

We talked of a certain clergyman of extraordinary character, who, by exerting his talents in writing on temporary topics, and displaying uncommon intrepidity. had raised himself to affluence. I maintained that we ought not to be indignant at his success; for merit of every sort was entitled to reward. JOHNSON: "Sir, I will not allow this man to have merit. No, Sir; what he has is rather the contrary; I will, indeed, allow him courage, and on this account we so far give him credit. We have more respect for a man who robs boldly on the highway, than for

---

[1] The words of Erasmus, as my learned friend Dr. Kearney observes to me, may be applied to Johnson:—"Qui ingenium, sensum, dictionem hominis noverant, multis non offenduntur, quibus graviter erant offendendi, qui hæc ignorarunt."—MALONE.

a fellow who jumps out of a ditch, and knocks you down behind your back. Courage is a quality so necessary for maintaining virtue, that it is always respected, even when it is associated with vice."

I censured the coarse invectives which were become fashionable in the House of Commons, and said, that if members of Parliament must attack each other personally in the heat of debate, it should be done more genteelly. JOHNSON: "No, Sir; that would be much worse. Abuse is not so dangerous when there is no vehicle of wit or delicacy, no subtle conveyance. The difference between coarse and refined abuse is as the difference between being bruised by a club, and wounded by a poisoned arrow." I have since observed his position eloquently expressed by Dr. Young:—

> "As the soft plume gives swiftness to the dart,
>   Good breeding sends the satire to the heart."

On Saturday, June 12, there drank tea with us, at Dr. Adams's, Mr. John Henderson, student of Pembroke College, celebrated for his wonderful acquirements in alchemy, judicial astrology, and other abstruse and curious learning:[1] and the Reverend Herbert Croft, who, I am afraid, was somewhat mortified by Dr. Johnson's not being highly pleased with some "Family Discourses," which he had printed; they were in too familiar a style to be approved of by so manly a mind. I have no note of this evening's conversation, except a single fragment. When I mentioned Thomas Lord Lyttelton's vision, the prediction of the time of his death and its exact fulfilment;—JOHNSON: "It is the most extraordinary thing that has happened in my day. I heard it with my own ears, from his uncle, Lord Westcote.[2] I am so glad to have every evidence of the spiritual world, that I am willing to believe it." DR. ADAMS: "You have evidence enough; good evidence, which needs not such support." JOHNSON: "I like to have more."

Mr. Henderson, with whom I had sauntered in the venerable walks of Merton College, and found him a very learned and pious man, supped with us. Dr. Johnson surprised him not a little, by acknowledging, with a look of horror, that he was much oppressed by the fear of death. The amiable Dr. Adams suggested that GOD was infinitely

---

[1] See an account of him in a sermon by the Rev. Mr. Agutter.— BOSWELL.

[2] A correct account of Lord Lyttelton's supposed vision may be found in Nash's "History of Worcestershire—Additions and Corrections," p. 36.—MALONE.

good. JOHNSON: "That he is infinitely good, as far as the perfection of his nature will allow, I certainly believe; but it is necessary for good upon the whole, that individuals should be punished. As to an *individual*, therefore, he is not infinitely good; and as I cannot be *sure* that I have fulfilled the conditions on which salvation is granted, I am afraid I may be one of those who shall be damned." (Looking dismally.) DR. ADAMS: "What do you mean by damned?" JOHNSON (passionately and loudly): "Sent to hell, Sir, and punished everlastingly." DR. ADAMS: "I don't believe that doctrine." JOHNSON: "Hold, Sir; do you believe that some will be punished at all?" DR. ADAMS: "Being excluded from heaven will be a punishment; yet there may be no great positive suffering." JOHNSON: "Well, Sir, but if you admit any degree of punishment, there is an end of your argument for infinite goodness simply considered; for infinite goodness would inflict no punishment whatever. There is no infinite goodness physically considered; morally there is." BOSWELL: "But may not a man attain to such a degree of hope as not to be uneasy from the fear of death?" JOHNSON: "A man may have such a degree of hope as to keep him quiet. You see I am not quiet, from the vehemence with which I talk; but I do not despair." MRS. ADAMS: "You seem, Sir, to forget the merits of our Redeemer." JOHNSON: "Madam, I do not forget the merits of my Redeemer; but my Redeemer has said that he will set some on his right hand and some on his left."—He was in gloomy agitation, and said, "I'll have no more on't."—If what has now been stated should be urged by the enemies of Christianity, as if its influence on the mind were not benignant, let it be remembered, that Johnson's temperament was melancholy, of which such direful apprehensions of futurity are often a common effect. We shall presently see, that when he approached nearer to his awful change, his mind became tranquil, and he exhibited as much fortitude as becomes a thinking man in that situation.

From the subject of death we passed to discourse of life, whether it was upon the whole more happy or miserable. Johnson was decidedly for the balance of misery:[1] in

[1] The Rev. Mr. Ralph Churton, fellow of Brazenose College, Oxford, has favoured me with the following remarks on my work, which, he is pleased to say, "I have hitherto extolled and cordially approve."

"The chief part of what I have to observe is contained in the following transcript, from a letter to a friend, which, with his concurrence, I copied for this purpose; and, whatever may be the merit or justness of the remarks, you may be sure that, being written to a most intimate

confirmation of which I maintained, that no man would choose to lead over again the life which he had experienced.

friend, without any intention that they ever should go farther, they are the genuine and undisguised sentiments of the writer:—

'Jan. 6, 1792.

'Last week I was reading the second volume of Boswell's Johnson, with increasing esteem for the worthy author, and increasing veneration of the wonderful and excellent man who is the subject of it. The writer throws in, now and then, very properly, some serious religious reflections; but there is one remark, in my mind an obvious and just one, which I think he has not made, that Johnson's "morbid melancholy," and constitutional infirmities, were intended by Providence, like St. Paul's thorn in the flesh, to check intellectual conceit and arrogance; which the consciousness of his extraordinary talents, awake as he was to the voice of praise, might otherwise have generated in a very culpable degree. Another observation strikes me, that in consequence of the same natural indisposition, and habitual sickliness, (for he says he scarcely passed one day without pain after his twentieth year,) he considered and represented human life, as a scene of much greater misery than is generally experienced. There may be persons bowed down with affliction all their days, and there are those, no doubt, whose iniquities rob them of rest; but neither calamities nor crimes, I hope and believe, do so much and so generally abound, as to justify the dark picture of life which Johnson's imagination designed, and his strong pencil delineated. This I am sure, the colouring is far too gloomy for what I have experienced, though, as far as I can remember, I have had more sickness (I do not say more severe, but only more in quantity), than falls to the lot of most people. But then daily debility and occasional sickness were far overbalanced by intervenient days, and, perhaps, weeks void of pain, and overflowing with comfort. So that, in short, to return to the subject, human life, as far as I can perceive from experience or observation, is not that state of constant wretchedness which Johnson always insisted it was, which misrepresentation (for such it surely is) his biographer has not corrected, I suppose, because, unhappily, he has himself a large portion of melancholy in his constitution, and fancied the portrait a faithful copy of life.'"

The learned writer then proceeds thus in his letter to me:—

"I have conversed with some sensible men on this subject, who all seem to entertain the same sentiments respecting life with those which are expressed or implied in the foregoing paragraph. It might be added, that as the representation here spoken of, appears not consistent with fact and experience, so neither does it seem to be countenanced by Scripture. There is, perhaps, no part of the sacred volume which at first sight promises so much to lend its sanction to these dark and desponding notions as the book of Ecclesiastes, which so often, and so emphatically, proclaims the vanity of things sublunary. But 'the design of this whole book (as it has been justly observed) is not to put us out of conceit with life, but to cure our vain expectations of a complete and perfect happiness in this world—to convince us that there is no such thing to be found in mere external enjoyments, and to teach us to seek for happiness in the practice of virtue, in the knowledge and love of GOD, and in the hopes of a better life. For this is the application of all, Let us hear, &c., xii. 13. Not only his duty, but his happiness, too, For GOD, &c., v. 14.'—See 'Sherlock on Providence,' p. 299.

"The New Testament tells us, indeed, and most truly, that 'sufficient unto the day is the evil thereof;' and, therefore, wisely forbids us to increase our burden by forebodings of sorrows; but I think it nowhere says that even our ordinary afflictions are not consistent with a very considerable degree of positive comfort and satisfaction. And, ac-

Johnson acceded to that opinion in the strongest terms. This is an inquiry often made; and its being a subject of

cordingly, one whose sufferings as well as merits were conspicuous, assures us, that in proportion 'as the sufferings of CHRIST abounded in them, so their consolation also abounded by CHRIST,' 2 Cor. i. 5. It is needless to cite, as indeed it would be endless even to refer to, the multitude of passages, in both Testaments, holding out, in the strongest language, promises of blessings, even in this world, to the faithful servant of GOD. I will only refer to St. Luke xviii. 29, 30, and 1 Tim. iv. 8.

"Upon the whole, setting aside instances of great and lasting bodily pain, of minds peculiarly oppressed by melancholy, and of severe temporal calamities, from which extraordinary cases we surely should not form our estimate of the general tenor and complexion of life; excluding these from the account, I am convinced that as well the gracious constitution of things which Providence has ordained, as the declarations of Scripture and the actual experience of individuals, authorize the sincere Christian to hope that his humble and constant endeavours to perform his duty, chequered as the best life is with many failings, will be crowned with a greater degree of present peace, serenity, and comfort, than he could reasonably permit himself to expect, if he measured his views and judged of life from the opinion of Dr. Johnson, often and energetically expressed in the Memoirs of him, without any animadversion or censure by his ingenious biographer. If he himself, upon reviewing the subject, shall see the matter in this light, he will, in an octavo edition, which is eagerly expected, make such additional marks or corrections as he shall judge fit, lest the impressions which these discouraging passages may leave on the reader's mind, should in any degree hinder what otherwise the whole spirit and energy of the work tends, and, I hope, successfully, to promote,—pure morality and true religion."

Though I have, in some degree, obviated any reflections against my illustrious friend's dark views of life, when considering, in the course of this work, his "Rambler" and his "Rasselas," I am obliged to Mr. Churton for complying with my request of his permission to insert his remarks, being conscious of the weight of what he judiciously suggests as to the melancholy in my own constitution. His more pleasing views of life, I hope are just,—"Valeant, quantum valere possunt."

Mr. Churton concludes his letter to me in these words:—"Once, and only once, I had the satisfaction of seeing your illustrious friend; and as I feel a particular regard for all whom he distinguished with his esteem and friendship, so I derive much pleasure from reflecting that I once beheld, though but transiently, near our college gate, one whose works will for ever delight and improve the world, who was a sincere and zealous son of the Church of England, an honour to his country, and an ornament to human nature."

His letter was accompanied with a present from himself of his "Sermons at the Bampton Lecture," and from his friend, Dr. Townson, the venerable Rector of Malpas, in Cheshire, of his "Discourses on the Gospels," together with the following extract of a letter from that excellent person, who is now gone to receive the reward of his labours:— "Mr. Boswell is not only very entertaining in his works, but they are so replete with moral and religious sentiments, without an instance, as far as I know, of a contrary tendency, that I cannot help having a great esteem for him; and if you think such a trifle as a copy of the Discourses, ex dono authoris, would be acceptable to him, I should be happy to give him this small testimony of my regard."

Such spontaneous testimonies of approbation from such men, without any personal acquaintance with me, are truly valuable and encouraging. —BOSWELL.

disquisition is a proof that much misery presses upon human feelings; for those who are conscious of a felicity of existence, would never hesitate to accept of a repetition of it. I have met with very few who would.   I have heard Mr. Burke make use of a very ingenious and plausible argument on this subject: "Every man," said he, "would lead his life over again: for every man is willing to go on and take an addition to his life, which, as he grows older, he has no reason to think will be better, or even so good, as what has preceded."   I imagine, however, the truth is, that there is a deceitful hope that the next part of life will be free from the pains, and anxieties, and sorrows, which we have already felt.   We are, for wise purposes, "condemned to hope's delusive mine," as Johnson finely says; and I may also quote the celebrated lines of Dryden, equally philosophical and poetical:—

> "When I consider life, 'tis all a cheat,
> Yet fool'd with hope, men favour the deceit;
> Trust on, and think to-morrow will repay;
> To-morrow's falser than the former day;
> Lies worse; and while it says we shall be blest
> With some new joys, cuts off what we possest.
> Strange cozenage! none would live past years again;
> Yet all hope pleasure in what yet remain;
> And from the dregs of life think to receive
> What the first sprightly running could not give."[1]

It was observed to Dr. Johnson, that it seemed strange that he, who has so often delighted his company by his lively and brilliant conversation, should say he was miserable.   JOHNSON: "Alas! it is all outside; I may be cracking my joke, and cursing the sun: *Sun, how I hate thy beams!*" I knew not well what to think of this declaration; whether to hold it as a genuine picture of his mind,[2] or as the effect of his persuading himself contrary to the fact, that the position which he had assumed as to human unhappiness was true.   We may apply to him a sentence in Mr. Greville's "Maxims, Characters, and Reflections;" a book which is entitled to much more praise than it has received: "ARISTARCHUS is charming; how full of knowledge, of sense, of sentiment.   You get him with difficulty to your supper; and after having delighted everybody and himself for a few

[1] "Aurengzebe," Act iv. Sc. 1.—BOSWELL.

[2] Yet there is no doubt that a man may appear very gay in company who is sad at heart.   His merriment is like the sound of drums and trumpets in a battle, to drown the groans of the wounded and dying.—BOSWELL.

hours, he is obliged to return home;—he is finishing his
treatise, to prove that unhappiness is the portion of man."

On Sunday, June 13, our philosopher was calm at
breakfast. There was something exceedingly pleasing in
our leading a College life, without restraint, and with
superior elegance, in consequence of our living in the
Master's house, and having the company of ladies. Mrs.
Kennicot related, in his presence, a lively saying of Dr.
Johnson to Miss Hannah More, who had expressed a wonder
that the poet, who had written "Paradise Lost," should
write such poor Sonnets:—"Milton, Madam, was a genius
that could cut a colossus from a rock, but could not carve
heads upon cherry stones."

We talked of the casuistical question, whether it was
allowable at any time to depart from *Truth?* JOHNSON:
"The general rule is, that truth should never be violated,
because it is of the utmost importance to the comfort of
life, that we should have a full security by mutual faith; and
occasional inconveniences should be willingly suffered, that
we may preserve it. There must, however, be some
exceptions. If, for instance, a murderer should ask you
which way a man is gone, you may tell him what is not
true, because you are under a previous obligation not to
betray a man to a murderer." BOSWELL: "Supposing the
person who wrote *Junius* were asked whether he was the
author, might he deny it?" JOHNSON: "I don't know
what to say to this. If you were *sure* that he wrote *Junius*,
would you, if he denied it, think as well of him afterwards?
Yet it may be urged, that what a man has no right to ask,
you may refuse to communicate; and there is no other
effectual mode of preserving a secret and an important
secret, the discovery of which may be very hurtful to you,
but a flat denial; for if you are silent, or hesitate, or evade,
it will be held equivalent to a confession. But stay, Sir,
here is another case. Supposing the author had told me
confidentially that he had written *Junius*, and I were
asked if he had, I should hold myself at liberty to deny it,
as being under a previous promise, express or implied, to
conceal it. Now what I ought to do for the author, may I
not do for myself? But I deny the lawfulness of telling a
lie to a sick man, for fear of alarming him. You have no
business with consequences; you are to tell the truth.
Besides, you are not sure what effect your telling him that
he is in danger may have. It may bring his distemper
to a crisis, and that may cure him. Of all lying, I have
the greatest abhorrence of this, because I believe it has
been frequently practised on myself."

I cannot help thinking that there is much weight in the opinion of those who have held, that truth, as an eternal and immutable principle, ought, upon no account whatever, to be violated, from supposed previous or superior obligations, of which every man being to judge for himself, there is great danger that we too often, from partial motives, persuade ourselves that they exist; and probably, whatever extraordinary instances may sometimes occur, where some evil may be prevented by violating this noble principle, it would be found that human happiness would, upon the whole, be more perfect, were truth universally preserved.

In the notes to "The Dunciad," we find the following verses, addressed to Pope: [1]

> "While malice, Pope, denies thy page
>   Its own celestial fire;
> While critics, and while bards in rage,
>   Admiring, wont admire:
>
> While wayward pens thy worth assail,
>   And envious tongues decry;
> These times, though many a friend bewail,
>   These times bewail not I.
>
> But when the world's loud praise is thine,
>   And spleen no more shall blame:
> When with thy Homer thou shalt shine
>   In one establish'd fame!
>
> When none shall rail, and every lay
>   Devote a wreath to thee;
> That day (for come it will) that day
>   Shall I lament to see."

It is surely not a little remarkable, that they should appear without a name. Miss Seward, knowing Dr. Johnson's almost universal and minute literary information, signified a desire that I should ask him who was the author. He was prompt with his answer:—"Why, Sir, they were written by one Lewis, who was either under-master or an usher of Westminster school, and published a Miscellany, in which 'Grongar Hill' first came out." [2]

---

[1] The annotator calls them "amiable verses."—Boswell.

[2] Lewis's Verses addressed to Pope (as Mr. Bindley suggests to me), were first published in a collection of pieces in verse and prose on occasion of "The Dunciad," 8vo. 1732. They are there called an Epigram. "Grongar Hill," the same gentleman observes, was first printed in Savage's Miscellanies, as an *Ode* (it is singular that Johnson should not have recollected this), and was *re-printed* in the same year (1726), in Lewis's Miscellany, in the form it now bears.

In that Miscellany, as the Rev. Mr. Blakeway observes to me, "the

Johnson praised them highly, and repeated them with a noble animation. In the twelfth line, instead of "one establish'd fame," he repeated "one unclouded flame," which he thought was the reading in former editions: but I believe was a flash of his own genius. It is much more poetical than the other.

On Monday, June 14, and Tuesday, 15th, Dr. Johnson and I dined (on one of them, I forget which) with Mr. Mickle, translator of "The Lusiad," at Wheatley,—a very pretty country place a few miles from Oxford; and on the other with Dr. Wetherell, Master of University College. From Dr. Wetherell's he went to visit Mr. Sackville Parker, the bookseller; and when he returned to us he gave the following account of his visit, saying, "I have been to see my old friend, Sack Parker; I find he has married his maid; he has done right. She had lived with him many years in great confidence, and they had mingled minds; I do not think he could have found any wife that would have made him so happy. The woman was very attentive and civil to me; she pressed me to fix a day for dining with them, and to say what I liked, and she would be sure to get it for me. Poor Sack! he is very ill indeed.[1] We parted as never to

beautiful poem, 'Away, let nought to love displeasing,' &c. (re-printed in 'Percy's Reliques,' vol. i. b. iii. No. 14), first appeared."

Lewis was author of "Philip of Macedon," a tragedy, published in 1727, and dedicated to Pope; and in 1730 he published a second volume of miscellaneous poems.

As Dr. Johnson settled in London not long after the verses addressed to Pope first appeared, he probably then obtained some information concerning their author, David Lewis, whom he has described as an usher of Westminster school; yet the Dean of Westminster, who has been pleased at my request to make some inquiry on this subject, has not found any vestige of his having ever been employed in this situation. A late writer ("Environs of London," iv. 171), supposed that the following inscription in the churchyard of the church of Low Leyton, in Essex, was intended to commemorate this poet:—

"Sacred to the memory of David Lewis, Esq., who died the 8th day of April, 1760, aged 77 years; a great favourite of the Muses, as his many excellent pieces in poetry sufficiently testify.

'Inspired verse may on this marble live,
But can no honour to thy ashes give.'

Also Mary, the wife of the above-named David Lewis, fourth daughter of Newdigate Owsley, Esq., who departed this life the 10th of October, 1774, aged 90 years."

But it appears to me improbable that this monument was erected for the author of the Verses to Pope, and of the tragedy already mentioned; the language both of the dedication prefixed to that piece, and of the dedication addressed to the Earl of Shaftesbury, and prefixed to the Miscellanies, 1730, denoting a person who moved in a lower sphere than this Essex squire seems to have done.—MALONE.

[1] He died at Oxford in his 89th year, Dec. 10, 1796.—MALONE.

meet again. It has quite broken me down." This pathetic narrative was strangely diversified with the grave and earnest defence of a man's having married his maid. I could not but feel it as in some degree ludicrous.

In the morning of Tuesday, June 15, while we sat at Dr. Adams's, we talked of a printed letter from the Rev. Herbert Croft, to a young gentleman who had been his pupil, in which he advised him to read to the end of whatever books he should begin to read. JOHNSON: "This is surely a strange advice; you may as well resolve that whatever men you happen to get acquainted with, you are to keep to them for life. A book may be good for nothing; or there may be only one thing in it worth knowing: are we to read it all through? These voyages (pointing to the three large volumes of 'Voyages to the South Sea,' which were just come out), *who* will read them through? A man had better work his way before the mast, than read them through; they will be eaten by rats and mice, before they are read through. There can be little entertainment in such books; one set of savages is like another." BOSWELL: "I do not think the people of Otaheité can be reckoned savages." JOHNSON: "Don't cant in defence of savages." BOSWELL: "They have the art of navigation." JOHNSON: "A dog or a cat can swim." BOSWELL: "They carve very ingeniously." JOHNSON: "A cat can scratch, and a child with a nail can scratch." I perceived this was none of the *mollia tempora fandi ;* so desisted.

Upon his mentioning that when he came to college he wrote his first exercises twice over, but never did so afterwards;—MISS ADAMS: "I suppose, Sir, you could not make them better?" JOHNSON: "Yes, Madam, to be sure, I could make them better. Thought is better than no thought." MISS ADAMS: "Do you think, Sir, you could make your Ramblers better?" JOHNSON: "Certainly I could." BOSWELL: "I'll lay a bet, Sir, you cannot." JOHNSON: "But I will, Sir, if I choose. I shall make the best of them you shall pick out better."—BOSWELL: "But you may add to them. I will not allow of that." JOHNSON: "Nay, Sir, there are three ways of making them better;— putting out, adding, or correcting."

During our visit at Oxford, the following conversation passed between him and me on the subject of my trying my fortune at the English bar. Having asked, whether a very extensive acquaintance in London, which was very valuable, and of great advantage to a man at large, might not be prejudicial to a lawyer, by preventing him from giving sufficient attention to his business?—JOHNSON: "Sir, you will attend to business as business lays hold of you. When not actually employed, you may see your friends as much as you do now. You may dine at a club every day, and sup with one of the members every night; and you may be as much at public places as one who has seen them all would wish to be. But you must take care to attend constantly in Westminster Hall; both to mind your business, as it is almost all learnt there (for nobody reads now), and to show that you want to have business. And you must not be too often seen at public places, that competitors may not have it to say, 'He is always at the playhouse or at Ranelagh, and never to be found at his chambers.' And, Sir, there must be a kind of solemnity in the manner of a professional man. I have nothing particular to say to you on the subject. All this I should say to any one; I should have said it to Lord Thurlow twenty years ago."

The PROFESSION may probably think this representation of what is required in a barrister who would hope for success, to be much too indulgent; but certain it is, that as

"The wits of Charles found easier ways to fame,"

some of the lawyers of this age, who have risen high, have by no means thought it absolutely necessary to submit to that long and painful course of study which a Plowden, a Coke, and a Hale considered as requisite. My respected friend, Mr. Langton, has shown me, in the hand-writing of his grandfather, a curious account of a conversation which he had with Lord Chief Justice Hale, in which that great man tells him, "That for two years after he came to the inn of the court, he studied sixteen hours a day; however (his Lordship added), that by this intense application he almost brought himself to his grave, though he were of a very strong constitution, and after reduced himself to eight hours; but that he would not advise anybody to so much; that he thought six hours a day, with attention and constancy, was sufficient; that man must use his body as he would his horse and his stomach: not tire him at once, but rise with an appetite."

CHAPTER XXVIII.—1784

Johnson's Return to London—Rev. Mr. Astle—Mr. Cator—
Horace Walpole—" Ever-memorable" John Hales—" No,
Sir"—Lord Chatham—Burke's Defence of Johnson—
" Tommy Townshend"—Trained Bands of London—
Johnson's Apology to the Compositor—Attitudenizing—
Johnson's Warmth in Argument—His Visit to Maryle-
bone Gardens—His Attention to Dress—His Last
Dinner at " The Literary Club"—Intended Journey to
Italy—Public Criminals—Mr. Vilette—Dr. Knox—
Mr. Pinkerton—Jamaica—Lord Chesterfield—Lord Eliot
—Lord Thurlow's Letter in favour of Johnson—His
Sensibility—Italy—Mrs. Thrale's intended Marriage,
and her Anecdotes of Johnson

ON Wednesday, June 19th, Dr. Johnson and I returned to
London; he was not well to-day, and said very little, employing himself chiefly in reading Euripides. He expressed
some displeasure at me, for not observing sufficiently the
various objects on the road. " If I had your eyes, Sir,"
said he, " I should count the passengers." It was wonderful how accurate his observation of visual objects was,
notwithstanding his imperfect eyesight, owing to a habit
of attention. That he was much satisfied with the respect
paid to him at Dr. Adams's is thus attested by himself:
" I returned last night from Oxford, after a fortnight's
abode with Dr. Adams, who treated me as well as I could
expect or wish; and he that contents a sick man, a man
whom it is impossible to please, has surely done his part
well." [1]

After his return to London from this excursion, I saw
him frequently, but have few memorandums; I shall therefore here insert some particulars which I have collected
at various times.

The Rev. Mr. Astle, of Ashbourne, in Derbyshire, brother
to the learned and ingenious Thomas Astle, Esq., was from
his early years known to Dr. Johnson, who obligingly
advised him as to his studies, and recommended to him the

"Letters to Mrs. Thrale," vol. ii. p. 372.—BOSWELL.

following books, of which a list, which he has been pleased to communicate, lies before me, in Johnson's own hand-writing:—

"Universal History (ancient)—Rollin's Ancient History—Puffendorf's Introduction to History—Vertot's History of Knights of Malta—Vertot's Revolution of Portugal—Vertot's Revolution of Sweden—Carte's History of England—Present State of England—Geographical Grammar—Prideaux's Connexion—Nelson's Feasts and Fasts—Duty of Man—Gentleman's Religion—Clarendon's History—Watt's Improvement of the Mind—Watt's Logic—Nature Displayed—Louth's English Grammar—Blackwell on the Classics—Sherlock's Sermons—Burnett's Life of Hale—Dupin's History of the Church—Shuckford's Connexions—Law's Serious Call—Walton's Complete Angler—Sandys's Travels—Sprat's History of the Royal Society—England's Gazetteer—Goldsmith's Roman History—Some Commentaries on the Bible."

It having been mentioned to Dr. Johnson, that a gentleman who had a son whom he imagined to have an extreme degree of timidity, resolved to send him to a public school, that he might acquire confidence;—"Sir," said Johnson, "this is a preposterous expedient for removing his infirmity; such a disposition should be cultivated in the shade. Placing him at a public school is forcing an owl upon day."

Speaking of a gentleman whose house was much frequented by low company: "Rags, Sir," said he, "will always make their appearance, where they have a right to do it."

Of the same gentleman's mode of living, he said, "Sir, the servants, instead of doing what they are bid, stand round the table in idle clusters, gaping upon the guests; and seem as unfit to attend a company as to steer a man of war."

A dull country magistrate gave Johnson a long tedious account of his exercising his criminal jurisdiction, the result of which was having sentenced four convicts to transportation. Johnson, in an agony of impatience to get rid of such a companion, exclaimed, "I heartily wish, Sir, that I were a fifth."

Johnson was present when a tragedy was read, in which there occurred this line:—

"Who rules o'er freemen should himself be free."

The company having admired it much—"I cannot agree with you," said Johnson; "it might as well be said,

'Who drives fat oxen should himself be fat.'"

He was pleased with the kindness of Mr. Cator, who was joined with him in Mr. Thrale's important trust, and thus describes him:[1] "There is much good in his character, and much usefulness in his knowledge." He found a cordial solace at that gentleman's seat at Beckenham, in Kent, which is indeed one of the finest places at which I ever was a guest; and where I find more and more a hospitable welcome.

Johnson seldom encouraged general censure of any profession; but he was willing to allow a due share of merit to the various departments necessary in civilized life. In a splenetic, sarcastical. or jocular frame of mind, however, he would sometimes utter a pointed saying of that nature. One instance has been mentioned, where he gave a sudden satirical stroke to the character of an attorney. The too indiscriminate admission to that employment, which requires both abilities and integrity, has given rise to injurious reflections, which are totally inapplicable to many very respectable men who exercise it with reputation and honour.

Johnson having argued for some time with a pertinacious gentleman: his opponent, who had talked in a very puzzling manner, happened to say, "I don't understand you, Sir;" upon which Johnson observed, "Sir, I have found you an argument; but I am not obliged to find you an understanding."

Talking to me of *Horry Walpole* (as Horace late Earl of Orford was often called), Johnson allowed that he got together a great many curious little things, and told them in an elegant manner. Mr. Walpole thought Johnson a more amiable character after reading his Letters to Mrs. Thrale: but never was one of the true admirers of that great man.[2] We may suppose a prejudice conceived, if he ever heard Johnson's account to Sir George Staunton, that when he made the speeches in Parliament for the Gentleman's Magazine, "he always took care to put Sir Robert Walpole in the wrong, and to say everything he could against the electorate of Hanover." The celebrated Heroic Epistle, in which Johnson is satirically introduced, has been ascribed both to Mr. Walpole and Mr. Mason. One day at Mr. Courtenay's, when a gentleman expressed his opinion that there was more energy in that poem than could be expected from Mr. Walpole, Mr. Warton, the late

---

[1] "Letters to Mrs. Thrale," vol. ii. p. 284.—Boswell.

[2] In his Posthumous Works, he has spoken of Johnson in the most contemptuous manner.—Malone.

Laureat, observed, " It may have been written by Walpole, and *buckram'd* by Mason."[1]

He disapproved of Lord Hailes, for having modernised the language of the ever-memorable John Hales of Eton, in an edition which his lordship published of that writer's works. "An author's language, Sir," said he, "is a characteristical part of his composition, and is also characteristical of the age in which he writes. Besides, Sir, when the language is changed we are not sure that the sense is the same. No, Sir: I am sorry Lord Hailes has done this."

Here it may be observed, that his frequent use of the expression, *No, Sir*, was not always to intimate contradiction; for he would say so when he was about to enforce an affirmative proposition which had not been denied, as in the instance last mentioned. I used to consider it as a kind of flag of defiance: as if he had said, "Any argument you may offer against this, is not just. No, Sir, it is not." It was like Falstaff's "I deny your Major."

Sir Joshua Reynolds having said that he took the altitude of a man's taste by his stories and his wit, and of his understanding by the remarks which he repeated; being always sure that he must be a weak man, who quotes common things with an emphasis as if they were oracles; —Johnson agreed with him; and Sir Joshua having also observed that the real character of a man was found out by his amusements—Johnson added, "Yes, Sir; no man is a hypocrite in his pleasures."

I have mentioned Johnson's general aversion to pun. He once, however, endured one of mine.—When we were talking of a numerous company in which he had distinguished himself highly, I said, "Sir, you were a cod surrounded by smelts. Is not this enough for you? at a time too when you were not *fishing* for a compliment?" He laughed at this with a complacent approbation. Old Mr. Sheridan observed, upon my mentioning it to him, "He liked your compliment so well, he was willing to take it with *pun sauce*." For my own part, I think no innocent species of wit or pleasantry should be suppressed: and that a good pun may be admitted among the smaller excellencies of lively conversation.

Had Johnson treated at large *De Claris Oratoribus*, he might have given us an admirable work. When the Duke of Bedford attacked the ministry as vehemently as he could,

[1] It is now (1804) *known* that the "Heroic Epistle" was written by Mason.—MALONE.

for having taken upon them to extend the time for the importation of corn, Lord Chatham, in his first speech in the House of Lords, boldly avowed himself to be an adviser of that measure. "My colleagues," said he, "as I was confined by indisposition, did me the signal honour of coming to the bed-side of a sick man, to ask his opinion. But, had they not thus condescended, I should have *taken up my bed and walked*, in order to have delivered that opinion at the Council-board." Mr. Langton, who was present, mentioned this to Johnson, who observed, "Now, Sir, we see that he took these words as he found them; without considering, that though the expression in Scripture, *take up thy bed and walk*, strictly suited the instance of the sick man restored to health and strength, who would of course be supposed to carry his bed with him, it could not be proper in the case of a man who was lying in a state of feebleness, and who certainly would not add to the difficulty of moving at all, that of carrying his bed."

When I pointed out to him in the newspaper one of Mr. Grattan's animated and glowing speeches, in favour of the freedom of Ireland, in which this expression occurred (I know not if accurately taken):—"We will persevere till there is not one link of the English chain left to clank upon the rags of the meanest beggar in Ireland;"—"Nay, Sir," said Johnson, "don't you perceive that *one* link cannot clank?"

Mrs. Thrale has published,[1] as Johnson's, a kind of parody or counterpart of a fine poetical passage in one of Mr. Burke's speeches on American Taxation. It is vigorously but somewhat coarsely executed; and, I am inclined to suppose, is not quite correctly exhibited. I hope he did not use the words *"vile agents"* for the Americans in the House of Parliament: and if he did so, in an extempore effusion, I wish the lady had not committed it to writing.

Mr. Burke uniformly showed Johnson the greatest respect; and when Mr. Townshend, now Lord Sydney, at a period when he was conspicuous in opposition, threw out some reflection in Parliament upon the grant of a pension to a man of such political principles as Johnson, Mr. Burke, though then of the same party with Mr. Townshend, stood warmly forth in defence of his friend, to whom, he justly observed, the pension was granted solely on account of his eminent literary merit. I am well assured, that Mr. Townshend's attack upon Johnson was the occasion of his

[1] "Anecdotes," p. 43.—BOSWELL.

"hitching in a rhyme;" for that in the original copy of Goldsmith's character of Mr. Burke, in his "Retaliation," another person's name stood in the couplet where Mr. Townshend is now introduced:—

"Though fraught with all learning kept straining his throat,
  To persuade *Tommy Townshend* to lend him a vote."

It may be worth remarking, among the *minutiæ* of my collection, that Johnson was once drawn to serve in the militia, the Trained Bands of the City of London, and that Mr. Rackstrow, of the Museum in Fleet-street, was his colonel. It may be believed he did not serve in person; but the idea, with all its circumstances, is certainly laughable. He upon that occasion provided himself with a musket, and with a sword and belt, which I have seen hanging in his closet.

He was very constant to those whom he once employed, if they gave him no reason to be displeased.—When somebody talked of being imposed on in the purchase of tea and sugar, and such articles: "That will not be the case," said he, "if you go to a *stately shop*, as I always do. In such a shop it is not worth their while to take a petty advantage."

An author of most anxious and restless vanity being mentioned,—"Sir," said he, "there is not a young sapling upon Parnassus more severely blown about by every wind of criticism than that poor fellow."

The difference, he observed, between a well-bred and an ill-bred man is this: "One immediately attracts your liking, the other your aversion. You love the one till you find reason to hate him; you hate the other till you find reason to love him."

The wife of one of his acquaintance had fraudulently made a purse for herself out of her husband's fortune. Feeling a proper compunction in her last moments, she confessed how much she had secreted; but, before she could tell where it was placed, she was seized with a convulsive fit and expired. Her husband said, he was more hurt by her want of confidence in him, than by the loss of his money. "I told him," said Johnson, "that he should console himself: for *perhaps* the money might be *found*, and he was *sure* that his wife was *gone*."

A foppish physician once reminded Johnson of his having been in company with him on a former occasion:—"I do not remember it, Sir." The physician still insisted; adding that he that day wore so fine a coat that it must have attracted his notice.   "Sir," said Johnson, "had you been dipped in Pactolus, I should not have noticed you."

He seemed to take a pleasure in speaking in his own style; for when he had carelessly missed it, he would repeat the thought translated into it.   Talking of the comedy of "The Rehearsal," he said, "It has not wit enough to keep it sweet."   This was easy;—he therefore caught himself, and pronounced a more round sentence: "It has not vitality enough to preserve it from putrefaction."

He censured a writer of entertaining travels for assuming a feigned character, saying (in his sense of the word), "he carries out one lie; we know not how many be brings back."   At another time, talking of the same person, he observed, "Sir, your assent to a man whom you have never known to falsify, is a debt: but after you have known a man to falsify, your assent to him then is a favour."

Though he had no taste for painting, he admired much the manner in which Sir Joshua Reynolds treated of his art, in his "Discourses to the Royal Academy."   He observed one day of a passage in them, "I think I might as well have said this myself:" and once, when Mr. Langton was sitting by him, he read one of them very eagerly, and expressed himself thus:—"Very well, Master Reynolds; very well, indeed.   But it will not be understood."

When I observed to him that painting was so far inferior to poetry, that the story or even emblem which it communicates must be previously known, and mentioned, as a natural and laughable instance of this, that a little Miss, on seeing a picture of Justice with the scales, had exclaimed to me, "See, there's a woman selling sweetmeats"; he said, "Painting, Sir, can illustrate, but cannot inform."

No man was more ready to make an apology, when he had censured unjustly, than Johnson.   When a proof-sheet of one of his works was brought to him, he found fault with the mode in which a part of it was arranged, refused to read it, and in a passion desired that the compositor[1] might be sent to him.   The compositor was Mr. Manning, a decent sensible man, who had composed about one-half of his "Dictionary," when in Mr. Strahan's printing-house; and a great part of his "Lives of the Poets," when in that of Mr. Nichols; and who (in his seventy-seventh year) when in Mr. Baldwin's printing-house, composed a part of the first edition of this work concerning him.   By producing

---

[1] Compositor in the printing-house means the person who adjusts the types in the order in which they are to stand for printing; and arranges what is called the *form*, from which an impression is taken.—BOSWELL.

the manuscript he at once satisfied Dr. Johnson that he was not to blame. Upon which Johnson candidly and earnestly said to him, "Mr. Compositor, I ask your pardon; Mr. Compositor, I ask your pardon again and again."

His generous humanity to the miserable was almost beyond example. The following instance is well attested. Coming home late one night, he found a poor woman lying in the street so much exhausted that she could not walk. He took her upon his back, and carried her to his house, where he discovered that she was one of those wretched females who had fallen into the lowest state of vice, poverty, and disease. Instead of harshly upbraiding her, he had her taken care of with all tenderness for a long time, at a considerable expense, till she was restored to health, and endeavoured to put her into a virtuous way of living.[1]

He thought Mr. Caleb Whitefoord singularly happy in hitting on the signature of *Papyrius Cursor*, to his ingenious and diverting cross-readings of the newspapers; it being a real name of an ancient Roman, and clearly expressive of the thing done in this lively conceit.

He once in his life was known to have uttered what is called a *bull*. Sir Joshua Reynolds, when they were riding together in Devonshire, complained that he had a very bad horse, for that even when going downhill he moved slowly step by step. "Ay," said Johnson, "and when he *goes* uphill, he *stands still*."

He had a great aversion to gesticulating in company. He called once to a gentleman who offended him in that point, "Don't *attitudenize*." And when another gentleman thought he was giving additional force to what he uttered, by expressive movements of his hands, Johnson fairly seized them, and held them down.

An author of considerable eminence having engrossed a good share of the conversation in the company of Johnson, and having said nothing but what was trifling and insignificant; Johnson, when he was gone, observed to us, "It is wonderful what a difference there sometimes is between a man's powers of writing and of talking. ——— writes with great spirit, but is a poor talker; had he held his tongue, we might have supposed him to have been restrained by modesty; but he has spoken a great deal to-day; and have you heard what stuff it was?"

[1] The circumstance therefore alluded to, in Mr. Courtenay's "Poetical Character" of him, is strictly true. My informer was Mrs. Desmoulins, who lived many years in Dr. Johnson's house.—BOSWELL.

A gentleman having said that a *congé d'elire* has not, perhaps, the force of a command, but may be considered only as a strong recommendation;—"Sir," replied Johnson, who overheard him, "it is such a recommendation, as if I should throw you out of a two pair of stairs window, and recommend you to fall soft." [1]

Mr. Steevens, who passed many a social hour with him during their long acquaintance, which commenced when they both lived in the Temple, has preserved a good number of particulars concerning him, most of which are to be found in the department of Apophthegms, &c. in the Collection of "Johnson's Works." But he has been pleased to favour me with the following, which are original:—

"One evening, previous to the trial of Baretti, a consultation of his friends was held at the house of Mr. Cox, the solicitor, in Southampton-buildings, Chancery-lane. Among others present were, Mr. Burke and Dr. Johnson, who differed in sentiments concerning the tendency of some part of the defence the prisoner was to make. When the meeting was over, Mr. Steevens observed, that the question between him and his friend had been agitated with rather too much warmth. 'It may be so, Sir (replied the Doctor), for Burke and I should have been of one opinion, if we had had no audience.'"

"Dr. Johnson once assumed a character in which perhaps even Mr. Boswell never saw him. His curiosity having been excited by the praises bestowed on the celebrated Torré's fireworks at Marylebone Gardens, he desired Mr. Steevens to accompany him thither. The evening had proved showery; and soon after the few people present were assembled, public notice was given, that the conductors to the wheels, suns, stars, &c., were so thoroughly water-soaked, that it was impossible any part of the exhibition should be made. 'This is a mere excuse,' says the Doctor, 'to save their crackers for a more profitable company. Let us both hold up our sticks, and threaten to break those coloured lamps that surround the orchestra, and we shall soon have our wishes gratified. The core of the fire-works cannot be injured; let the different pieces be touched in their respective centres, and they will do their offices as well as ever.'—Some young men who

---

[1] This has been printed in other publications, "fall *to the ground*." But Johnson himself gave me the true expression which he had used as above, meaning that the recommendation left as little choice in the one case as the other.—Boswell.

overheard him, immediately began the violence he had recommended, and an attempt was speedily made to fire some of the wheels which appeared to have received the smallest damage; but to little purpose were they lighted, for most of them completely failed.—The author of 'The Rambler,' however, may be considered, on this occasion, as the ringleader of a successful riot, though not as a skilful pyrotechnist.''

"It has been supposed that Dr. Johnson, so far as fashion was concerned, was careless of his appearance in public. But this is not altogether true, as the following slight instance may show:—Goldsmith's last comedy was to be represented during some court-mourning; and Mr. Steevens appointed to call on Dr. Johnson, and carry him to the tavern where he was to dine with others of the Poet's friends. The Doctor was ready dressed, but in coloured clothes; yet being told that he would find every one else in black, received the intelligence with a profusion of thanks, hastened to change his attire, all the while repeating his gratitude for the information that had saved him from an appearance so improper in the front row of a front box. 'I would not,' added he, 'for ten pounds, have seemed so retrograde to any general observance.'''

"He would sometimes found his dislikes on very slender circumstances. Happening one day to mention Mr. Flaxman, a Dissenting Minister, with some compliment to his exact memory in chronological matters, the Doctor replied, 'Let me hear no more of him, Sir. That is the fellow who made the Index to my Ramblers, and set down the name of Milton thus:—Milton, *Mr*. John.'''

Mr. Steevens adds this testimony: "It is unfortunate, however. for Johnson, that his particularities and frailties can be more distinctly traced than his good and amiable exertions. Could the many bounties he studiously concealed, the many acts of humanity he performed in private, be displayed with equal circumstantiality, his defects would be so far lost in the blaze of his virtues, that the latter only would be regarded."

Though, from my very high admiration of Johnson, I have wondered that he was not courted by all the great and all the eminent persons of his time, it ought fairly to be considered, that no man of humble birth, who lived entirely by literature, in short, no author by profession, ever rose in this country into that personal notice which he did. In the course of this work a numerous variety of names has been mentioned, to which many might be added. I cannot omit Lord and Lady Lucan, at whose house he often enjoyed all that an elegant table and the best company can contribute to happiness; he found hospitality united with extraordinary accomplishments, and embellished with charms of which no man could be insensible.

On Tuesday, June 22, I dined with him at the Literary Club, the last time of his being in that respectable society. The other members present were the Bishop of St. Asaph, Lord Eliot, Lord Palmerston, Dr. Fordyce, and Mr. Malone. He looked ill; but had such a manly fortitude, that he did not trouble the company with melancholy complaints. They all showed evident marks of kind concern about him, with which he was much pleased, and he exerted himself to be as entertaining as his indisposition allowed him.

The anxiety of his friends to preserve so estimable a life, as long as human means might be supposed to have influence, made them plan for him a retreat from the severity of a British winter, to the mild climate of Italy. This scheme was at last brought to a serious resolution at General Paoli's, where I had often talked of it. One essential matter, however, I understood was necessary to be previously settled, which was obtaining such an addition to his income as would be sufficient to enable him to defray the expense in a manner becoming the first literary character of a great nation, and, independent of all his other merits, the author of the Dictionary of the English Language. The person to whom I above all others thought I should apply to negociate this business, was the Lord Chancellor,[1] because I knew that he highly valued Johnson, and that Johnson highly valued his Lordship; so that it was no degradation of my illustrious friend to solicit for him the favour of such a man. I have mentioned what Johnson said of him to me when he was at the bar; and after his Lordship was advanced to the seals he said of him, "I would prepare myself for no man in England but Lord Thurlow. When I am to meet with him I should wish to know a day before." How he would have prepared himself, I cannot conjecture. Would he have selected certain topics, and considered them in every view, so as to be in readiness to argue them at all points? and what may we suppose those topics to have been? I once started the curious inquiry to the great man who was the subject of this compliment; he smiled, but did not pursue it.

I first consulted with Sir Joshua Reynolds, who perfectly coincided in opinion with me; and I therefore, though

[1] Edward Lord Thurlow, who died September 11, 1806.—MALONE.

personally very little known to his Lordship, wrote to him,[1] stating the case, and requesting his good offices for Dr. Johnson. I mentioned that I was obliged to set out for Scotland early in the following week; so that, if his lordship should have any commands for me as to this pious negociation, he would be pleased to send them before that time; otherwise Sir Joshua Reynolds would give all attention to it.

This application was made, not only without any suggestion on the part of Johnson himself, but was utterly unknown to him; nor had he the smallest suspicion of it. Any insinuations, therefore, which since his death have been thrown out, as if he had stopped to ask what was superfluous, are without any foundation. But, had he asked it, it would not have been superfluous; for though the money he had saved proved to be more than his friends imagined, or than I believe he himself, in his carelessness concerning worldly matters, knew it to be, had he travelled upon the Continent, an augmentation of his income would by no means have been unnecessary.

On Wednesday, June 23, I visited him in the morning, after having been present at the shocking sight of fifteen men executed before Newgate. I said to him, I was sure that human life was not machinery, that is to say, a chain of fatality planned and directed by the Supreme Being, as it had in it so much wickedness and misery, so many instances of both, as that by which my mind was now clouded.

Were it machinery, it would be better than it is in these respects, though less noble, as not being a system of moral government. He agreed with me now, as he always did, upon the great question of the liberty of the human will, which has been in all ages perplexed with so much sophistry: "But, Sir, as to the doctrine of necessity, no man believes it. If a man should give me arguments that I do not see, though I could not answer them, should I believe that I do not see?" It will be observed, that Johnson at all times made the just distinction between doctrines *contrary* to reason, and doctrines *above* reason.

Talking of the religious discipline proper for unhappy convicts, he said, "Sir, one of our regular clergy will probably not impress their minds sufficiently: they should

---

[1] It is strange that Sir John Hawkins should have related that the application was made by Sir Joshua Reynolds, when he could so easily have been informed of the truth by inquiring of Sir Joshua. Sir John's carelessness to ascertain facts is very remarkable.—BOSWELL.

be attended by a Methodist preacher;[1] or a Popish priest."
Let me however observe, in justice to the Rev. Mr. Vilette,
who has been Ordinary of Newgate for no less than eighteen
years, in the course of which he has attended many hun-
dreds of wretched criminals, that his earnest and humane
exhortations have been very effectual.   His extraordinary
diligence is highly praiseworthy, and merits a distinguished
reward."[2]

On Thursday, June 24, I dined with him at Mr. Dilly's,
where were the Rev. Mr. (now Dr.) Knox, master of Tun-
bridge-school, Mr. Smith, vicar of Southill, Dr. Beattie,
Mr. Pinkerton, author of various literary performances,
and the Rev. Dr. Mayo.   At my desire old Mr. Sheridan
was invited, as I was earnest to have Johnson and him
brought together again by chance, that a reconciliation
might be effected.   Mr. Sheridan happened to come early,
and, having learnt that Dr. Johnson was to be there, went
away; so I found, with sincere regret, that my friendly
intentions were hopeless.   I recollect nothing that passed
this day, except Johnson's quickness, who, when Dr.
Beattie observed, as something remarkable which had
happened to him, that he had chanced to see both No. 1,
and No. 1000, of the hackney-coaches, the first and the
last:—"Why, Sir," said Johnson, "there is an equal chance
for one's seeing those two numbers as any other two."
He was clearly right: yet the seeing of the two extremes,
each of which is in some degree more conspicuous than the
rest, could not but strike one in a stronger manner than
the sight of any other two numbers.   Though I have
neglected to preserve his conversation, it was perhaps at
this interview that Dr. Knox formed the notion of it,
which he has exhibited in his "Winter Evenings."

On Friday, June 25, I dined with him at General Paoli's,
where he says, in one of his letters to Mrs. Thrale, "I love
to dine."   There was a variety of dishes much to his taste,
of all which he seemed to me to eat so much, that I was
afraid he might be hurt by it; and I whispered to the
General my fear, and begged he might not press him.
"Alas!" said the General, "see how very ill he looks; he
can live but a very short time.   Would you refuse any

[1] A friend of mine happened to be passing by a *field congregation* in
the environs of London, when a Methodist preacher quoted this passage
with triumph.—Boswell.

[2] I trust that the City of London, now happily in unison with the
Court, will have the justice and generosity to obtain preferment for this
reverend gentleman, now a worthy old servant of that magnificent
corporation.—Boswell.

slight gratifications to a man under sentence of death? There is a humane custom in Italy, by which persons in that melancholy situation are indulged with having whatever they like best to eat and drink, even with expensive delicacies."

I showed him some verses on Lichfield by Miss Seward, which I had that day received from her, and had the pleasure to hear him approve of them. He confirmed to me the truth of a high compliment which I had been told he had paid to that lady, when she mentioned to him "The Colombiade," an epic poem, by Madame Du Boccage: —"Madam, there is not anything equal to your description of the sea round the North Pole, in your Ode on the death of Captain Cooke."

On Sunday, June 27th, I found him rather better. I mentioned to him a young man who was going to Jamaica with his wife and children, in expectation of being provided for by two of her brothers settled in that island, one a clergyman, and the other a physician. JOHNSON: "It is a wild scheme, Sir, unless he has a positive and deliberate invitation. There was a poor girl, who used to come about me, who had a cousin in Barbadoes, that, in a letter to her, expressed a wish she should come out to that island, and expatiated on the comforts and happiness of her situation. The poor girl went out: her cousin was much surprised, and asked her how she could think of coming. 'Because,' said she, 'you invited me.'—'Not I,' answered the cousin. The letter was then produced. 'I see it is true,' said she, 'that I did invite you: but I did not think you would come.' They lodged her in an out-house, where she passed her time miserably: and as soon as she had an opportunity she returned to England. Always tell this, when you hear of people going abroad to relations, upon a notion of being well received. In the case which you mention it is probable the clergyman spends all he gets, and the physician does not know how much he is to get."

We this day dined at Sir Joshua Reynolds's with General Paoli, Lord Eliot (formerly Mr. Eliot, of Port Eliot), Dr. Beattie, and some other company. Talking of Lord Chesterfield:—JOHNSON: "His manner was exquisitely elegant, and he had more knowledge than I expected." BOSWELL: "Did you find, Sir, his conversation to be of a superior style?" JOHNSON: "Sir, in the conversation which I had with him I had the best right to superiority, for it was upon philology and literature." Lord Eliot, who had travelled at the same time with Mr. Stanhope, Lord Chesterfield's natural son, justly observed, that it was strange that a man who showed he had so much affection for his son as Lord Chesterfield did, by writing so many long and anxious letters to him, almost all of them when he was Secretary of State, which certainly was a proof of great goodness of disposition, should endeavour to make his son a rascal.   His Lordship told us, that Foote had intended to bring on the stage a father who had thus tutored his son, and to show the son an honest man to every one else, but practising his father's maxims upon him, and cheating him.   JOHNSON: "I am much pleased with this design; but I think there was no occasion to make the son honest at all.   No; he should be a consummate rogue: the contrast between honesty and knavery would be the stronger.   It should be contrived so that the father should be the only sufferer by the son's villany, and thus there would be poetical justice."

He put Lord Eliot in mind of Dr. Walter Harte.   "I know," said he, "Harte was your Lordship's tutor, and he was also tutor to the Peterborough family.   Pray, my Lord, do you recollect any particulars that he told you of Lord Peterborough?   He is a favourite of mine, and is not enough known; his character has been only ventilated in party pamphlets."   Lord Eliot said, if Dr. Johnson would be so good as to ask him any questions, he would tell what he could recollect.   Accordingly some things were mentioned.   "But," said his Lordship, "the best account of Lord Peterborough that I have happened to meet with, is in 'Captain Carleton's Memoirs.'   Carleton was descended of an ancestor who had distinguished himself at the siege of Derry.   He was an officer; and what was rare at that time, had some knowledge of engineering."   Johnson said, he had never heard of the book.   Lord Eliot had it at Port Eliot; but after a good deal of inquiry, procured a copy in London, and sent it to Johnson, who told Sir Joshua Reynolds that he was going to bed when it came; but was so much pleased with it, that he sat up till he had read it through, and found in it such an air of truth, that he could not doubt of its authenticity; adding, with a smile (in allusion to Lord Eliot's having recently been raised to the peerage), "I did not think *a young Lord* could have mentioned to me a book in the English history that was not known to me."

An addition to our company came after we went up to the drawing-room: Dr. Johnson seemed to rise in spirits as his audience increased.   He said, "He wished Lord Orford's pictures, and Sir Ashton Lever's Museum, might be purchased by the public, because both the money, and the pictures, and the curiosities would remain in the country; whereas if they were sold into another kingdom, the nation would indeed get some money, but would lose the pictures and the curiosities, which it would be desirable we should have, for improvement in taste and natural history. The only question was, as the nation was much in want of money, whether it would not be better to take a large price from a foreign State?"

He entered upon a curious discussion of the difference between intuition and sagacity; one being immediate in its effect, the other requiring a circuitous process; one, he observed, was the *eye* of the mind, the other the *nose* of the mind.

A young gentleman present took up the argument against him, and maintained that no man ever thinks of the *nose of the mind*, not adverting that though that figurative sense seems strange to us, as very unusual, it is truly not more forced than Hamlet's " In my *mind's eye*, Horatio." He persisted much too long, and appeared to Johnson as putting himself forward as his antagonist with too much presumption: upon which he called to him, in a loud tone, "What is it you are contending for, if you *be* contending?"—And afterwards imagining that the gentleman retorted upon him with a kind of smart drollery, he said, "Mr. ———, it does not become you to talk so to me. Besides, ridicule is not your talent; you have *there* neither intuition nor sagacity."—The gentleman protested that he had intended no improper freedom, but had the greatest respect for Dr. Johnson. After a short pause, during which we were somewhat uneasy;—JOHNSON: "Give me your hand, Sir. You were too tedious, and I was too short." MR. ———: "Sir, I am honoured by your attention in any way." JOHNSON: "Come, Sir, let's have no more of it. We offended one another by our contention; let us not offend the company by our compliments."

He now said, "He wished much to go to Italy, and that he dreaded passing the winter in England." I said nothing; but enjoyed a secret satisfaction in thinking that I had taken the most effectual measures to make such a scheme practicable.

On Monday, June 28, I had the honour to receive from the Lord Chancellor the following letter:—

"TO JAMES BOSWELL, ESQ.

"SIR,

"I should have answered your letter immediately, if (being much engaged when I received it) I had not put it in my pocket, and forgot to open it till this morning.

"I am much obliged to you for the suggestion; and I will adopt and press it as far as I can. The best argument, I am sure, and I hope it is not likely to fail, is Dr. Johnson's merit.—But it will be necessary, if I should be so unfortunate as to miss seeing you, to converse with Sir Joshua on the sum it will be proper to ask,—in short, upon the means of setting him out. It would be a reflection on us all, if such a man should perish for want of the means to take care of his health.   Yours, &c.

"Thurlow."

This letter gave me very high satisfaction. I next day went and showed it to Sir Joshua Reynolds, who was exceedingly pleased with it. He thought that I should now communicate the negociation to Dr. Johnson, who might afterwards complain, if the attention with which he had been honoured should be too long concealed from him. I intended to set out for Scotland next morning; but Sir Joshua cordially insisted that I should stay another day, that Johnson and I might dine with him, that we three might talk of his Italian tour, and, as Sir Joshua expressed himself, "have it all out." I hastened to Johnson, and was told by him that he was rather better to-day. Boswell: "I am very anxious about you, Sir, and particularly that you should go to Italy for the winter, which I believe is your own wish." Johnson: "It is, Sir." Boswell: "You have no objection, I presume, but the money it would require." Johnson: "Why no, Sir."—Upon which I gave him a particular account of what had been done, and read to him the Lord Chancellor's letter. He listened with much attention; then warmly said, "This is taking prodigious pains about a man."—"Oh, Sir," said I, with most sincere affection, "your friends would do every thing for you." He paused,—grew more and more agitated,—till tears started into his eyes, and he exclaimed, with fervent emotion, "God bless you all." I was so affected that I also shed tears.—After a short silence, he renewed and extended his grateful benediction, "God bless you all, for Jesus Christ's sake." We both remained for some time unable to speak.—He rose suddenly and quitted the room, quite melted in tenderness. He stayed but a short time, till he had recovered his firmness. Soon after he returned I left him, having first engaged him to dine at Sir Joshua Reynolds's next day.—I never was again under that roof which I had so long reverenced.

On Wednesday, June 30, the friendly confidential dinner with Sir Joshua Reynolds took place,—no other company being present. Had I known that this was the last time that I should enjoy, in this world, the conversation of a friend whom I so much respected, and from whom I derived so much instruction and entertainment, I should have been deeply affected. When I now look back to it, I am vexed that a single word should have been forgotten.

Both Sir Joshua and I were so sanguine in our expectations, that we expatiated with confidence on the liberal provision which we were sure would be made for him, conjecturing whether munificence would be displayed in one large donation, or in an ample increase of his pension. He himself caught so much of our enthusiasm, as to allow himself to suppose it not impossible that our hopes might in one way or other be realised. He said that he would rather have his pension doubled than a grant of a thousand pounds; "For," said he, "though probably I may not live to receive as much as a thousand pounds, a man would have the consciousness that he should pass the remainder of his life in splendour, how long soever it might be." Considering what a moderate proportion an income of six hundred pounds a year bears to innumerable fortunes in this country, it is worthy of remark, that a man so truly great should think it splendour.

As an instance of extraordinary liberality of friendship, he told us, that Dr. Brocklesby had upon this occasion offered him a hundred a year for his life. A grateful tear started into his eye, as he spoke this in a faltering tone.

Sir Joshua and I endeavoured to flatter his imagination with agreeable prospects of happiness in Italy. "Nay," said he, "I must not expect much of that. When a man goes to Italy merely to feel how he breathes the air, he can enjoy very little."

Our conversation turned upon living in the country, which Johnson, whose melancholy mind required the dissipation of quick successive variety, had habituated himself to consider as a kind of mental imprisonment. "Yet, Sir," said I, "there are many people who are content to live in the country." JOHNSON: "Sir, it is in the intellectual world as in the physical world: we are told by natural philosophers that a body is at rest in the place that is fit for it; they who are content to live in the country, are *fit* for the country."

Talking of various enjoyments, I argued that a refinement of taste was a disadvantage, as they who have attained to it must be seldomer pleased than those who have no nice discrimination, and are therefore satisfied with everything that comes in their way. JOHNSON: "Nay, Sir; that is a paltry notion. Endeavour to be as perfect as you can in every respect."

I accompanied him, in Sir Joshua Reynolds's coach, to the entry of Bolt-court.   He asked me whether I would not go with him to his house: I declined it, from an apprehension that my spirits would sink.   We bade adieu to each other affectionately in the carriage.   When he had got down upon the foot-pavement, he called out, "Fare you well;" and without looking back, sprung away with a kind of pathetic briskness, if I may use that expression, which seemed to indicate a struggle to conceal uneasiness, and impressed me with a foreboding of our long, long separation.

I remained one day more in town, to have the chance of talking over my negociation with the Lord Chancellor; but the multiplicity of his Lordship's important engagements did not allow of it; so I left the management of the business in the hands of Sir Joshua Reynolds.

*Incorrectness of Mrs. Piozzi's Anecdotes—Lord Chancellor
Thurlow's Benevolence—Johnson's Letter of Thanks to
Him—His Affection for the Memory of his Wife—He
sets out for Derbyshire and Staffordshire—Revisits
Lichfield and Ashbourne—His Letters to his Friends—
His State of Health—Mr. Windham—Johnson visits
Chatsworth—Air Balloons—Johnson's Opinion of their
Utility—Mr. Hoole—Mr. Nichols—The Literary Club
—Dr. Burney—Mr. Langton—General Correspondence
—Johnson affected with Asthma and Dropsy—His
Charity, and Letter to Mr. Heely*

SOON after this time Dr. Johnson had the mortification
of being informed by Mrs. Thrale, that "what she supposed
he never believed"[1] was true; namely, that she was actually
going to marry Signor Piozzi, an Italian music master.
He endeavoured to prevent it; but in vain. If she would
publish the whole of the correspondence that passed between Dr. Johnson and her on the subject, we should have
a full view of his real sentiments. As it is, our judgment
must be biassed by that characteristic specimen which
Sir John Hawkins has given us:—"Poor Thrale, I thought
that either her virtue or her vice would have restrained
her from such a marriage. She is now become a subject
for her enemies to exult over; and for her friends, if she
has any left, to forget, or pity."[2]

It must be admitted that Johnson derived a considerable portion of happiness from the comforts and elegancies
which he enjoyed in Mr. Thrale's family; but Mrs. Thrale
assures us he was indebted for these to her husband
alone, who certainly respected him sincerely. Her words
are—

"Veneration for his virtue, reverence for his talents, delight in his
conversation, and habitual endurance of a yoke my husband first

[1] "Letters to Mrs. Thrale," vol. ii. p. 375.—BOSWELL.
[2] Dr. Johnson's Letter to Sir John Hawkins, "Life," p. 570.—BOSWELL.

put upon me, and of which he contentedly bore his share for sixteen or seventeen years, made me go on so long with Mr. Johnson; but the perpetual confinement I will own to have been terrifying in the first years of our friendship, and irksome in the last; nor could I pretend to support it without help, when my coadjutor was no more." [1]

Alas! how different is this from the declarations which I have heard Mrs. Thrale make in his lifetime, without a single murmur against any peculiarities, or against any one circumstance which attended their intimacy.

As a sincere friend of the great man whose life I am writing, I think it necessary to guard my readers against the mistaken notion of Dr. Johnson's character, which this lady's "Anecdotes" of him suggest; for, from the very nature and form of her book, "it lends deception lighter wings to fly."

"Let it be remembered," says an eminent critic,[2] "that she has comprised in a small volume all that she could recollect of Dr. Johnson in *twenty years*, during which period, doubtless, some severe things were said by him; and they who read the book in *two hours*, naturally enough suppose that his whole conversation was of this complexion. But the fact is, I have been often in his company, and never *once* heard him say a severe thing to any one: and many others can attest the same. When he did say a severe thing, it was generally extorted by ignorance pretending to knowledge, or by extreme vanity or affectation.

"Two instances of inaccuracy," added he, "are peculiarly worthy of notice.

"It is said,[3] 'That natural roughness of his manner, so often mentioned, would, notwithstanding the regularity of his notions, burst through them all from time to time; and he once bade a very celebrated lady, who praised him with too much zeal perhaps, or perhaps too strong an emphasis (which always offended him) to consider what her flattery was worth, before she choked him with it.'

"Now let the genuine anecdote be contrasted with this.—The person thus represented as being harshly treated, though a very celebrated lady, was *then* just come to London from an obscure situation in the country. At Sir Joshua Reynolds's one evening she met Dr. Johnson. She very soon began to pay her court to him in the most fulsome strain. 'Spare me, I beseech you, dear Madam,' was his reply. She still *laid it on.* 'Pray, Madam, let us have no more of this,' he rejoined. Not paying any attention to these warnings, she continued still her eulogy. At length, provoked by this indelicate and *vain* obtrusion of compliment, he exclaimed, 'Dearest lady, consider with yourself what your flattery is worth, before you bestow it so freely.'

[1] "Anecdotes," p. 293.—Boswell.
[2] Who has been pleased to furnish me with his remarks.—Boswell.
[3] "Anecdotes," p. 183.—Boswell.

"How different does this story appear, when accompanied with all these circumstances which really belong to it, but which Mrs. Thrale either did not know, or has suppressed.

"She says, in another place,[1] 'One gentleman, however, who dined at a nobleman's house in his company, and that of Mr. Thrale, to whom I was obliged for the anecdote, was willing to enter the lists in defence of King William's character; and having opposed and contradicted Johnson two or three times, petulantly enough, the master of the house began to feel uneasy, and expect disagreeable consequences; to avoid which he said, loud enough for the Doctor to hear,—Our friend here has no meaning now in all this, except just to relate at club to-morrow how he teased Johnson at dinner to-day; this is all to do himself honour.—No, upon my word (replied the other), I see no honour in it, whatever you may do.—Well, Sir (returned Dr. Johnson sternly), if you do not see the honour, I am sure I feel the disgrace.'

"This is all sophisticated.   Mr. Thrale was *not* in the company, though he might have related the story to Mrs. Thrale.   A friend, from whom I had the story, was present; and it was *not* at the house of a nobleman.   On the observation being made by the master of the house on a gentleman's contradicting Johnson, that he had talked for the honour, &c., the gentleman muttered, in a low voice, 'I see no honour in it;' and Dr. Johnson said nothing; so all the rest (though *bien trouvée*) is mere garnish."

I have had occasion several times, in the course of this work, to point out the incorrectness of Mrs. Thale, as to particulars which consisted with my own knowledge. But indeed she has, in flippant terms enough, expressed her disapprobation of that anxious desire of authenticity which prompts a person, who is to record conversations, to write them down *at the moment*.[2]   Unquestionably, if they are to be recorded at all, the sooner it is done the better.   This lady herself says [3]—

"To recollect, however, and to repeat the sayings of Dr. Johnson, is almost all that can be done by the writers of his Life; as his life, at least since my acquaintance with him, consisted in little else than talking, when he was not employed in some serious piece of work."

She boasts of her having kept a common-place book; and we find she noted, at one time or other, in a very lively manner, specimens of the conversation of Dr. Johnson, and of those who talked with him; but had she done it recently, they probably would have been less erroneous; and we should have been relieved from those disagreeable

[1] "Anecdotes," p. 242.—BOSWELL.
[2] Ibid. p. 44.—BOSWELL.
[3] Ibid. p. 23.—BOSWELL.

doubts of their authenticity, with which we must now peruse them.

She says of him [1]—

"He was the most charitable of mortals, without being what we call an active friend. Admirable at giving counsel; no man saw his way so clearly; but he would not stir a finger for the assistance of those to whom he was willing enough to give advice."

And again, on the same page,—

"If you want a slight favour, you must apply to people of other dispositions; for not a step would Johnson move to obtain a man a vote in a society, to repay a compliment which might be useful or pleasing, to write a letter of request, &c., or to obtain a hundred pounds a year more for a friend who perhaps had already two or three. No force could urge him to diligence, no importunity could conquer his resolution to stand still."

It is amazing that one who had such opportunities of knowing Dr. Johnson, should appear so little acquainted with his real character. I am sorry this lady does not advert, that she herself contradicts the assertion of his being obstinately defective in the *petites morales*, in the little endearing charities of social life, in conferring smaller favours; for she says [2]—

"Dr. Johnson was liberal enough in granting literary assistance to others, I think; and innumerable are the Prefaces, Sermons, Lectures, and Dedications which he used to make for people who begged of him."

I am certain that *a more active friend* has rarely been found in any age. This work, which I fondly hope will rescue his memory from obloquy, contains a thousand instances of his benevolent exertions in almost every way that can be conceived; and particularly in employing his pen with a generous readiness for those to whom its aid could be useful. Indeed, his obliging activity in doing little offices of kindness, both by letters and personal application, was one of the most remarkable features in his character; and for the truth of this I can appeal to a number of his respectable friends,—Sir Joshua Reynolds, Mr. Langton, Mr. Hamilton, Mr. Burke, Mr. Windham, Mr. Malone, the Bishop of Dromore, Sir William Scott, Sir Robert Chambers.—And can Mrs. Thrale forget the

[1] "Anecdotes," p. 51.—Boswell.
[2] Ibid. p. 193.—Boswell.

advertisements which he wrote for her husband at the time of his election contest; the epitaphs on him and her mother; the playful and even trifling verses, for the amusement of her and her daughters; his corresponding with her children, and entering into their minute concerns, which shows him in the most amiable light?

She relates that[1]—

"Mr. Ch—lm—ley unexpectedly rode up to Mr. Thrale's carriage, in which Mr. Thrale, and she, and Dr. Johnson were travelling; that he paid them all his proper compliments, but observing that Dr. Johnson, who was reading, did not see him, tapt him gently on the shoulder. 'Tis Mr. Ch—lm—ley,' says my husband. 'Well, Sir—and what if it is Mr. Ch—lm—ley?' says the other, sternly, just lifting his eyes a moment from his book, and returning to it again with renewed avidity."

This surely conveys a notion of Johnson, as if he had been grossly rude to Mr. Cholmondeley,[2] a gentleman whom he always loved and esteemed. If, therefore, there was an absolute necessity for mentioning the story at all, it might have been thought that her tenderness for Dr. Johnson's character would have disposed her to state anything that could soften it. Why then is there a total silence as to what Mr. Cholmondeley told her?—that Johnson, who had known him from his earliest years, having been made sensible of what had doubtless a strange appearance, took occasion, when he afterwards met him, to make a very courteous and kind apology. There is another little circumstance which I cannot but remark. Her book was published in 1785. She had then in her possession a letter from Dr. Johnson, dated in 1777,[3] which begins thus: "Cholmondeley's story shocks me, if it be true, which I can hardly think, for I am utterly unconscious of it: I am very sorry, and very much ashamed." Why then publish the anecdote? Or if she did, why not add the circumstances, with which she was well acquainted?

In his social intercourse she thus describes him:[4]—

"Ever musing till he was called out to converse, and conversing till the fatigue of his friends, or the promptitude of his own temper to take offence, consigned him back again to silent meditation."

[1] "Anecdotes," p. 258.—BOSWELL.

[2] George James Cholmondeley, Esq., grandson of George, third Earl of Cholmondeley, and one of the Commissioners of Excise—a gentleman respected for his abilities and elegance of manners.—BOSWELL.

[3] "Letters to Mrs. Thrale," vol. ii. p. 12.—BOSWELL.

[4] "Anecdotes," p. 23.—BOSWELL.

Yet, in the same book,[1] she tells us:—

"He was, however, seldom inclined to be silent, when any moral or literary question was started; and it was on such occasions that, like the sage in 'Rasselas,' he spoke, and attention watched his lips, he reasoned, and conviction closed his periods."

His conversation, indeed, was so far from ever fatiguing his friends, that they regretted when it was interrupted or ceased, and could exclaim, in Milton's language,—

"With thee conversing, I forgot all time."

I certainly, then, do not claim too much in behalf of my illustrious friend in saying, that however smart and entertaining Mrs. Thrale's "Anecdotes" are, they must not be held as good evidence against him; for wherever an instance of harshness and severity is told, I beg leave to doubt its perfect authenticity; for though there may have been *some* foundation for it, yet, like that of his re-proof to the "very celebrated lady," it may be so exhibited in the narration as to be very unlike the real fact.

The evident tendency of the following anecdote[2] is to represent Dr. Johnson as extremely deficient in affection, tenderness, or even common civility:—

"When I one day lamented the loss of a first cousin killed in America,—'Prithee, my dear,' said he, 'have done with canting; how would the world be worse for it, I may ask, if all your relations were at once spitted like larks and roasted for Presto's supper?' (Presto was the dog that lay under the table while we talked)."

I suspect this too of exaggeration and distortion. I allow that he made her an angry speech; but let the circumstances fairly appear, as told by Mr. Baretti, who was present:—

"Mrs. Thrale, while supping very heartily upon larks, laid down her knife and fork, and abruptly exclaimed, 'Oh, my dear Johnson, do you know what has happened? The last letters from abroad have brought us an account that our poor cousin's head was taken off by a cannon-ball.' Johnson, who was shocked both at the fact and her light unfeeling manner of mentioning it, replied, 'Madam, it would give *you* very little concern if all your relations were spitted like those larks, and drest for Presto's supper.'"[3]

[1] "Anecdotes," p. 302.—Boswell.

[2] Ibid. p. 63.—Boswell.

[3] Upon mentioning this to my friend, Mr. Wilkes, he, with his usual readiness, pleasantly matched it with the following *sentimental anecdote*. He was invited by a young man of fashion at Paris to sup with him and a lady who had been for some time his mistress, but with whom he was

It is with concern that I find myself obliged to animadvert on the inaccuracies of Mrs. Piozzi's "Anecdotes," and perhaps I may be thought to have dwelt too long upon her little collection. But as from Johnson's long residence under Mr. Thrale's roof, and his intimacy with her, the account which she has given of him may have made an unfavourable and unjust impression, my duty, as a faithful biographer, has obliged me reluctantly to perform this unpleasing task.

Having left the *pious negociation*, as I called it, in the best hands, I shall here insert what relates to it. Johnson wrote to Sir Joshua Reynolds, on July 6, as follows:— "I am going, I hope, in a few days, to try the air of Derbyshire, but hope to see you before I go. Let me, however, mention to you what I have much at heart.—If the Chancellor should continue his attention to Mr. Boswell's request, and confer with you on the means of relieving my languid state, I am very desirous to avoid the appearance of asking money upon false pretences. I desire you to represent to his lordship, what, as soon as it is suggested, he will perceive to be reasonable.—That, if I grow much worse, I shall be afraid to leave my physicians, to suffer the inconveniences of travel, and pine in the solitude of a foreign country;—that, if I grow much better, of which indeed there is now little appearance, I shall not wish to leave my friends and my domestic comforts; for I do not travel for pleasure or curiosity; yet if I should recover, curiosity would revive.—In my present state, I am desirous to make a struggle for a little longer life, and hope to obtain some help from a softer climate. Do for me what you can." He wrote to me July 26:—"I wish your affairs could have permitted a longer and continued exertion of your zeal and kindness. They that have your kindness may want your ardour. In the mean time I am very feeble, and very dejected."

By a letter from Sir Joshua Reynolds I was informed, that the Lord Chancellor had called on him, and acquainted him that the application had not been successful; but that his lordship, after speaking highly in praise of Johnson,

going to part. He said to Mr. Wilkes that he really felt very much for her, she was in such distress, and that he meant to make her a present of two hundred louis-d'ors. Mr. Wilkes observed the behaviour of mademoiselle, who sighed indeed very piteously, and assumed every pathetic air of grief, but eat no less than three French pigeons, which are as large as English partridges, besides other things. Mr. Wilkes whispered the gentleman, "We often say in England, *Excessive sorrow is exceeding dry*, but I never heard *Excessive sorrow is exceeding hungry*. Perhaps one hundred will do." The gentleman took the hint.—BOSWELL.

as a man who was an honour to his country, desired Sir Joshua to let him know, that on granting a mortgage of his pension, he should draw on his lordship to the amount of five or six hundred pounds; and that his lordship explained the meaning of the mortgage to be, that he wished the business to be conducted in such a manner, that Dr. Johnson should appear to be under the least possible obligation. Sir Joshua mentioned, that he had by the same post communicated all this to Dr. Johnson.

How Johnson was affected upon the occasion will appear from what he wrote to Sir Joshua Reynolds:—

"Ashbourne, Sept. 9.

"Many words I hope are not necessary between you and me, to convince you what gratitude is excited in my heart by the Chancellor's liberality, and your kind offices.   *   *   *   *   *

I have enclosed a letter to the Chancellor, which, when you have read it, you will be pleased to seal with a head, or any other general seal, and convey it to him.   Had I sent it directly to him, I should have seemed to overlook the favour of your intervention."

"TO THE LORD HIGH CHANCELLOR.[1]

"My Lord,   September, 1784.

"After a long and not inattentive observation of mankind, the generosity of your lordship's offer raises in me not less wonder than gratitude.   Bounty so liberally bestowed, I should gladly receive, if my condition made it necessary; for to such a mind, who would not be proud to own his obligations?   But it has pleased God to restore me to so great a measure of health, that if I should now appropriate so much of a fortune destined to do good, I could not escape from myself the charge of advancing a false claim.   My journey to the continent, though I once thought it necessary, was never much encouraged by my physicians; and I was very desirous that your Lordship should be told of it by Sir Joshua Reynolds, as an event very uncertain; for if I grew much better, I should not be willing; if much worse, not able, to migrate.   Your Lordship was first solicited without my knowledge; but when I was told that you were pleased to honour me with your patronage, I did not expect to hear of a refusal; yet as I have had no long time to brood hope, and have not rioted in imaginary opulence, this cold reception has been scarce a disappointment; and, from your Lordship's kindness, I have re-

[1] Sir Joshua Reynolds, on account of the excellence both of the sentiment and expression of this letter, took a copy of it, which he showed to some of his friends; one of whom, who admired it, being allowed to peruse it leisurely at home, a copy was made, and found its way into the newspapers and magazines.   It was transcribed with some inaccuracies.   I print it from the original draft in Johnson's own handwriting.—Boswell.

ceived a benefit, which only men like you are able to bestow.   I shall
now live *mihi carior*, with a higher opinion of my own merit.

"I am, my Lord, your Lordship's most obliged,
"Most grateful, and most humble servant,
"SAM. JOHNSON."

Upon this unexpected failure I abstain from presuming
to make any remarks, or to offer any conjectures.

Having, after repeated reasonings, brought Dr. Johnson
to agree to my removing to London, and even to furnish
me with arguments in favour of what he had opposed, I
wrote to him requesting he would write them for me; he
was so good as to comply, and I shall extract that part
of his letter to me of June 11, as a proof how well he could
exhibit a cautious yet encouraging view of it:

"I remember, and entreat you to remember, that *virtus est
vitium fugere ;* the first approach to riches is security from poverty.
The condition upon which you have my consent to settle in London
is, that your expense never exceeds your annual income.   Fixing
this basis of security, you cannot be hurt, and you may be very much
advanced.   The loss of your Scottish business, which is all that you
can lose, is not to be reckoned as any equivalent to the hopes and
possibilities that open here upon you.   If you succeed, the question
of prudence is at an end; everybody will think that done right which
ends happily; and though your expectations, of which I would not
advise you to talk too much, should not be totally answered, you
can hardly fail to get friends who will do for you all that your
present situation allows you to hope; and if, after a few years,
you should return to Scotland, you will return with a mind supplied
by various conversation, and many opportunities of inquiry, with
much knowledge, and materials for reflection and instruction."

Let us now contemplate Johnson thirty years after the
death of his wife still retaining for her all the tenderness
of affection.

"TO THE REVEREND MR. BAGSHAW, AT BROMLEY.[1]

"SIR,   July 12, 1784.
"Perhaps you may remember, that in the year 1753 you committed to the ground my dear wife.   I now entreat your permission
to lay a stone upon her; and have sent the inscription, that, if you
find it proper, you may signify your allowance.

"You will do me a great favour by showing the place where she
lies, that the stone may protect her remains.

"Mr. Ryland will wait on you for the inscription,[2] and procure
it to be engraved.   You will easily believe that I shrink from this

[1] See vol. i. p. 518.—BOSWELL.
[2] Printed in his works.—BOSWELL.

mournful office.   When it is done, if I have any strength remaining,
I will visit Bromley once again, and pay you part of the respect to
which you have a right from, Reverend Sir,

"Your most humble servant,

"SAM. JOHNSON."

On the same day he wrote to Mr. Langton:—

"I cannot but think that in my languid and anxious state I
have some reason to complain that I receive from you neither
inquiry nor consolation.   You know how much I value your friendship, and with what confidence I expect your kindness, if I wanted
any act of tenderness that you could perform; at least, if you do not
know it, I think your ignorance is your own fault.   Yet how
long is it that I have lived almost in your neighbourhood without
the least notice.—I do not, however, consider this neglect as particularly shown to me; I hear two of your most valuable friends
make the same complaint.   But why are all thus overlooked?   You
are not oppressed by sickness; you are not distracted by business;
if you are sick, you are sick of leisure:—And allow yourself to be
told, that no disease is more to be dreaded or avoided.   Rather to
do nothing than to do good, is the lowest state of a degraded mind.
Boileau says to his pupil,

'Que les vers ne soient pas votre éternel emploi,
Cultivez vos amis.'————

That voluntary debility, which modern language is content to term
indolence, will, if it is not counteracted by resolution, render in time
the strongest faculties lifeless, and turn the flame to the smoke of
virtue.—I do not expect nor desire to see you, because I am much
pleased to find that your mother stays so long with you, and I
should think you neither elegant nor grateful, if you did not study
her gratification.—You will pay my respects to both the ladies, and
to all the young people.—I am going northward for a while, to try
what help the country can give me; but if you will write, the letter
will come after me."

Next day he set out on a jaunt to Staffordshire and
Derbyshire, flattering himself that he might be in some
degree relieved.

During his absence from London he kept up a correspondence with several of his friends, from which I shall
select what appears to me proper for publication, without
attending nicely to chronological order.

To Dr. Brocklesby he writes:—

"Ashbourne, July 20.

"The kind attention which you have so long shown to my health
and happiness makes it as much a debt of gratitude as a call of
interest, to give you an account of what befalls me, when accident

recovers [1] me from your immediate care.—The journey of the first day was performed with very little sense of fatigue; the second day brought me to Lichfield, without much lassitude; but I am afraid that I could not have bore such violent agitation for many days together.   Tell Dr. Heberden, that in the coach I read 'Ciceronianus,' which I concluded as I entered Lichfield.   My affection and understanding went along with Erasmus, except that once or twice he somewhat unskilfully entangles Cicero's civil or moral, with his rhetorical character.—I stayed five days at Lichfield, but, being unable to walk, had no great pleasure, and yesterday (19th) I came hither, where I am to try what air and attention can perform.— Of any improvement in my health I cannot yet please myself with the perception.   *   *   *   *   *   *   * —The asthma has no abatement.   Opiates stop the fit, so as that I can sit and sometimes lie easy, but they do not now procure me the power of motion; and I am afraid that my general strength of body does not increase.   The weather indeed is not benign; but how low is he sunk whose strength depends upon the weather! —I am now looking into Floyer, who lived with his asthma to almost his ninetieth year.   His book by want of order is obscure; and his asthma, I think, not of the same kind with mine.   Something however I may perhaps learn.—My appetite still continues keen enough; and, what I consider as a symptom of radical health, I have a voracious delight in raw summer fruit, of which I was less eager a few years ago.—You will be pleased to communicate this account to Dr. Heberden, and if anything is to be done, let me have your joint opinion.—Now—*abile, curæ!* let me inquire after the Club." [2]

"July 31.   Not recollecting that Dr. Heberden might be at Windsor, I thought your letter long in coming.   But, you know, *nocitura petuntur*, the letter which I so much desired tells me that I have lost one of my best and tenderest friends. [3]   My comfort is, that he appeared to live like a man that had always before his eyes the fragility of our present existence, and was therefore, I hope, not unprepared to meet his Judge.—Your attention, dear Sir, and that of Dr. Heberden, to my health, is extremely kind.   I am loth to think that I grow worse; and cannot fairly prove, even to my own partiality, that I grow much better."

"August 5.   I return you thanks, dear Sir, for your unwearied attention, both medicinal and friendly, and hope to prove the effect of your care by living to acknowledge it."

"August 12.   Pray be so kind as to have me in your thoughts, and mention my case to others as you have opportunity.   I seem to myself neither to gain nor lose strength.   I have lately tried milk, but have yet found no advantage, and I am afraid of it merely as a liquid.   My appetite is still good, which I know is dear Dr. Heberden's criterion of the *vis vitæ*.—As we cannot now see each other, do

---

[1] This is probably an error either of the transcript or the press. *Removes* seems to be the word intended.—MALONE.

[2] At the Essex Head, Essex-street.—BOSWELL.

[3] Mr. Allen, the printer.—BOSWELL.

not omit to write; for you cannot think with what warmth of expectation I reckon the hours of a post-day."

"August 14.   I have hitherto sent you only melancholy letters;
you will be glad to hear some better account.   Yesterday the
asthma remitted, perceptibly remitted, and I moved with more ease
than I have enjoyed for many weeks.   May GOD continue his
mercy.—This account I would not delay, because I am not a lover
of complaints, or complainers, and yet I have, since we parted,
uttered nothing till now but terror and sorrow.   Write to me,
dear Sir."

"August 16.   Better, I hope, and better.   My respiration gets
more and more ease and liberty.   I went to church yesterday, after
a very liberal dinner, without any inconvenience; it is indeed no long
walk, but I never walked it without difficulty, since I came, before.
*   *   *   *   *   * The intention was only to overpower the seeming *vis inertiæ* of the pectoral and pulmonary muscles.
I am favoured with a degree of ease that very much delights me, and
do not despair of another race upon the stairs of the Academy.—
If I were, however, of a humour to see, or to show the state of my
body, on the dark side, I might say,

'Quid te exempta juvat spinis de pluribus una?' [1]

The nights are still sleepless, and the water rises, though it does not
rise very fast.   Let us, however, rejoice in all the good that we have.
The remission of one disease will enable nature to combat the rest.—
The squills I have not neglected; for I have taken more than a
hundred drops a day, and one day took two hundred and fifty,
which, according to the popular equivalent of a drop to a grain, is
more than half an ounce.—I thank you, dear Sir, for your attention
in ordering the medicines; your attention to me has never failed.
If the virtue of medicines could be enforced by the benevolence of
the prescriber, how soon should I be well!"

"August 19.   The relaxation of the asthma still continues, yet
I do not trust it wholly to itself, but soothe it now and then with an
opiate.   I not only perform the perpetual act of respiration with
less labour, but I can walk with fewer intervals of rest and with
greater freedom of motion.   I never thought well of Dr. James's
compounded medicines; his ingredients appear to me sometimes in-
efficacious and trifling, and sometimes heterogeneous and destructive
of each other.   This prescription exhibits a composition of about
three hundred and thirty grains, in which there are four grains of
emetic tartar, and six drops [of] thebaic tincture.   He that writes
thus, surely writes for show.   The basis of his medicine is the gum
ammoniacum, which dear Dr. Lawrence used to give, but of which I
never saw any effect.   We will, if you please, let this medicine alone.
The squills have every suffrage, and in the squills we will rest for
the present."

"August 21.   The kindness which you show, by having me in
your thoughts upon all occasions, will, I hope, always fill my heart

---

[1] Horat. epist. ii. 212.—BOSWELL.

with gratitude. Be pleased to return my thanks to Sir George Baker, for the consideration which he has bestowed upon me.—Is this the balloon that has been so long expected, this balloon to which I subscribed, but without payment? It is a pity that philosophers have been disappointed, and shame that they have been cheated; but I know not well how to prevent either. Of this experiment I have read nothing. Where was it exhibited? and who was the man that ran away with so much money? Continue, dear Sir, to write often and more at a time, for none of your prescriptions operate to their proper uses more certainly than your letters operate as cordials."

"August 26. I suffered you to escape last post without a letter: but you are not to expect such indulgence very often; for I write not so much because I have anything to say, as because I hope for an answer; and the vacancy of my life here makes a letter of great value.—I have here little company and little amusement, and thus abandoned to the contemplation of my own miseries, I am something gloomy and depressed; this too I resist as I can, and find opium, I think, useful; but I seldom take more than one grain.—Is not this strange weather? Winter absorbed the spring, and now autumn is come before we have had summer. But let not our kindness for each other imitate the inconstancy of the seasons."

"Sept. 2. Mr. Windham has been here to see me; he came, I think, forty miles out of his way, and stayed about a day and a half; perhaps I make the time shorter than it was. Such conversation I shall not have again till I come back to the regions of literature; and there Windham is, *inter stellas*[1] *Luna minores.*" He then mentions the effects of certain medicines, as taken; that "Nature is recovering its original powers, and the functions returning to their proper state. God continue his mercies, and grant me to use them rightly."

"Sept. 9. Do you know the Duke and Duchess of Devonshire? And have you ever seen Chatsworth? I was at Chatsworth on Monday; I had seen it before, but never when its owners were at home: I was very kindly received, and honestly pressed to stay; but I told them that a sick man is not a fit inmate of a great house. But I hope to go again some time."

"Sept. 11. I think nothing grows worse, but all rather better, except sleep, and that of late has been at its old pranks. Last evening I felt, what I had not known for a long time, an inclination to walk for amusement; I took a short walk, and came back again neither breathless nor fatigued. This has been a gloomy, frigid, ungenial summer; but of late it seems to mend. I hear the heat sometimes mentioned, but I do not feel it:

'Præterea minimus gelido jam in corpore sanguis
Febre calet sola.'[2]

[1] It is remarkable that so good a Latin scholar as Johnson should have been so inattentive to the metre, as by mistake to have written *stellas* instead of *ignes.*—BOSWELL.

[2] Juvenal, Sat. x. 217.—BOSWELL.

I hope, however, with good help, to find means of supporting a winter at home, and to hear and tell at the Club what is doing, and what ought to be doing in the world.   I have no company here, and shall naturally come home hungry for conversation.   To wish you, dear Sir, more leisure, would not be kind; but what leisure you have, you must bestow upon me."

"Sept. 16.   I have now let you alone for a long time, having indeed little to say.   You charge me somewhat unjustly with luxury.   At Chatsworth, you should remember that I have eaten but once; and the doctor, with whom I live, follows a milk diet. I grow no fatter, though my stomach, if it be not disturbed by physic, never fails me.   I now grow weary of solitude, and think of removing next week to Lichfield—a place of more society, but otherwise of less convenience.   When I am settled, I shall write again.   Of the hot weather that you mentioned, we have [not] had in Derbyshire very much, and for myself I seldom feel heat, and suppose that my frigidity is the effect of my distemper; a supposition which naturally leads me to hope that a hotter climate may be useful.   But I hope to stand another English winter."

"Lichfield, Sept. 29.   On one day I had three letters about the air balloon: yours was far the best, and has enabled me to impart to my friends in the country an idea of this species of amusement. In amusement, mere amusement, I am afraid it must end; for I do not find that its course can be directed so as that it should serve any purposes of communication: and it can give no new intelligence of the state of the air at different heights, till they have ascended above the height of mountains, which they seem never likely to do.   I came hither on the 27th.   How long I shall stay, I have not determined.   My dropsy is gone, and my asthma much remitted; but I have felt myself a little declining these two days, or at least to-day; but such vicissitudes must be expected.   One day may be worse than another; but this last month is far better than the former: if the next should be as much better than this, I shall run about the town on my own legs."

"October 6.   The fate of the balloon I do not much lament; to make new balloons, is to repeat the jest again.   We now know a method of mounting into the air, and, I think, are not likely to know more.   The vehicles can serve no use till we can guide them; and they can gratify no curiosity till we mount with them to greater heights than we can reach without; till we rise above the tops of the highest mountains, which we have yet not done.   We know the state of the air in all its regions, to the top of Teneriffe, and therefore, learn nothing from those who navigate a balloon below the clouds.   The first experiment, however, was bold, and deserved applause and reward.   But since it has been performed, and its event is known, I had rather now find a medicine that can ease an asthma."

"October 25.   You write to me with a zeal that animates, and a tenderness that melts me.   I am not afraid either of a journey to London, or a residence in it.   I came down with little fatigue, and am now not weaker.   In the smoky atmosphere I was delivered from the dropsy, which I consider as the original and radical disease.

The town is my element; [1] there are my friends, there are my books, to which I have not yet bid farewell, and there are my amusements. Sir Joshua told me long ago, that my vocation was to public life, and I hope still to keep my station, till GOD shall bid me *Go in peace.*"

"TO MR. HOOLE.

"Ashbourne, Aug. 7.

"Since I was here, I have two little letters from you, and have not had the gratitude to write.   But every man is most free with his best friends, because he does not suppose that they can suspect him of intentional incivility.   One reason for my omission is, that being in a place to which you are wholly a stranger, I have no topics of correspondence.   If you had any knowledge of Ashbourne, I could tell you of two Ashbourne men, who being last week condemned at Derby to be hanged for a robbery, went and hanged themselves in their cell.   But this, however it may supply us with talk, is nothing to you.   Your kindness, I know, would make you glad to hear some good of me, but I have not much good to tell; if I grow not worse, it is all that I can say.   I hope Mrs. Hoole receives more help from her migration.   Make her my compliments, and write again to, Sir, your affectionate servant."

"Aug. 13.   I thank you for your affectionate letter.   I hope we shall both be the better for each other's friendship, and I hope we shall not very quickly be parted.   Tell Mr. Nichols that I shall be glad of his correspondence, when his business allows him a little remission; though to wish him less business, that I may have more pleasure, would be too selfish.   To pay for seats at the balloon is not very necessary, because in less than a minute, they who gaze at a mile's distance will see all that can be seen.   About the wings I am of your mind; they cannot at all assist it, nor I think regulate its motion. I am now grown somewhat easier in my body, but my mind is sometimes depressed.   About the Club I am in no great pain.   The forfeitures go on, and the house, I hear, is improved for our future meetings.   I hope we shall meet often and sit long."

"Sept. 4.   Your letter was, indeed, long in coming, but it was very welcome.   Our acquaintance has now subsisted long, and our recollection of each other involves a great space, and many little occurrences, which melt the thoughts to tenderness.   Write to me, therefore, as frequently as you can.   I hear from Dr. Brocklesby

---

[1] His love of London continually appears.   In a letter from him to Mrs. Smart, wife of his friend the poet, which is published in a well written life of him, prefixed to an edition of his Poems, in 1791, there is the following sentence:—"To one that has passed so many years in the pleasures and opulence of London, there are few places that can give much delight."

Once, upon reading that line in the curious epitaph quoted in "The Spectator,"

"Born in New England, did in London die,"

he laughed, and said, "I do not wonder at this.   It would have been strange, if born in London, he had died in New England."—BOSWELL.

and Mr. Ryland, that the Club is not crowded.   I hope we shall enliven it when winter brings us together."

"TO DR. BURNEY.

"August 2.

"The weather, you know, has not been balmy; I am now reduced to think, and am at last content to talk of the weather. Pride must have a fall.[1]   I have lost dear Mr. Allen; and wherever I turn, the dead or the dying meet my notice, and force my attention upon misery and mortality.   Mrs. Burney's escape from so much danger, and her ease after so much pain, throws, however, some radiance of hope upon the gloomy prospect.   May her recovery be perfect, and her continuance long.   I struggle hard for life.   I take physic, and take air; my friend's chariot is always ready.   We have run this morning twenty-four miles, and could run forty-eight more.   *But who can run the race with death?*"

"Sept. 4.   [Concerning a private transaction, in which his opinion was asked, and after giving it he makes the following reflections, which are applicable on other occasions.]   Nothing deserves more compassion than wrong conduct with good meaning; than loss or obloquy suffered by one, who, as he is conscious only of good intentions, wonders why he loses that kindness which he wishes to preserve; and not knowing his own fault, if, as may sometimes happen, nobody will tell him, goes on to offend by his endeavours to please.   I am delighted by finding that our opinions are the same.   You will do me a real kindness by continuing to write. A post-day has now been long a day of recreation."

"Nov. 1.   Our correspondence paused for want of topics.   I had said what I had to say on the matter proposed to my consideration; and nothing remained but to tell you, that I waked or slept; that I was more or less sick.   I drew my thoughts in upon myself, and supposed yours employed upon your book.   That your book has been delayed I am glad, since you have gained an opportunity of being more exact.   Of the caution necessary in adjusting narratives there is no end.   Some tell what they do not know, that they may not seem ignorant, and others from mere indifference about truth.   All truth is not, indeed, of equal importance; but, if little violations are allowed, every violation will in time be thought little; and a writer should keep himself vigilantly on his guard against the first temptations to negligence or supineness.   I had ceased to write, because respecting you I had no more to say, and respecting myself could say little good.   I cannot boast of advance-

---

[1] There was no information for which Dr. Johnson was less grateful than for that which concerned the weather.   It was in allusion to his impatience with those who were reduced to keep conversation alive by observations on the weather, that he applied the old proverb to himself.   If any one of his intimate acquaintance told him it was hot or cold, wet or dry, windy or calm, he would stop them, by saying "Poh! poh! you are telling us that of which none but men in a mine or a dungeon can be ignorant.   Let us bear with patience, or enjoy in quiet, elementary changes, whether for the better or the worse, as they are never secrets."   —Burney.

ment, and in case of convalescence it may be said, with few exceptions, *non progredi est regredi.* I hope I may be excepted. My great difficulty was with my sweet Fanny,[1] who, by her artifice of inserting her letter in yours, had given me a precept of frugality which I was not at liberty to neglect; and I know not who were in town under whose cover I could send my letter. I rejoice to hear that you are so well, and have a delight particularly sympathetic in the recovery of Mrs. Burney.''

"TO MR. LANGTON.

"August 25.

"The kindness of your last letter, and my omission to answer it, begins to give you, even in my opinion, a right to recriminate, and to charge me with forgetfulness for the absent. I will, therefore, delay no longer to give an account of myself, and wish I could relate what would please either myself or my friend.—On July 13, I left London, partly in hope of help from new air and change of place, and partly excited by the sick man's impatience of the present. I got to Lichfield in a stage vehicle, with very little fatigue, in two days, and had the consolation[2] to find, that since my last visit my three old acquaintances are all dead.—July 20, I went to Ashbourne, where I have been till now; the house in which we live is repairing. I live in too much solitude, and am often deeply dejected. I wish we were nearer, and rejoice in your removal to London. A friend, at once cheerful and serious, is a great acquisition. Let us not neglect one another for the little time which Providence allows us to hope.—Of my health I cannot tell you, what my wishes persuaded me to expect, that it is much improved by the season or by remedies. I am sleepless; my legs grow weary with a very few steps, and the water breaks its boundaries in some degree. The asthma, however, has remitted; my breath is still much obstructed, but is more free than it was. Nights of watchfulness produce torpid days; I read very little, though I am alone; for I am tempted to supply in the day what I lost in bed. This is my history; like all other histories a narrative of misery. Yet am I so much better than in the beginning of the year, that I ought to be ashamed of complaining. I now sit and write with very little sensibility of pain or weakness; but when I rise I shall find my legs betraying me. Of the money which you mentioned, I have no immediate need. Keep it, however, for me, unless some exigence requires it. Your papers I will show you certainly, when you would see them; but I am a little angry at you for not keeping minutes of your own *acceptum et expensum*, and think a little time might be spared from Aristophanes, for the *res familiares.* Forgive me, for I mean well. I hope, dear Sir, that you and Lady Rothes, and all the young people, too many to enumerate, are well and happy. GOD bless you all.''

[1] The celebrated Miss Fanny Burney.—BOSWELL.

[2] Probably some word has been here omitted before *consolation;* perhaps *sad,* or *miserable;* or the word *consolation* has been printed by mistake, instead of *mortification;* but the original letter not being now (1798) in Mr. Langton's hands, the error (if it be one), cannot be corrected.—MALONE.

"TO MR. WINDHAM.

"August.

"The tenderness with which you have been pleased to treat me, through my long illness, neither health nor sickness can, I hope, make me forget; and you are not to suppose, that after we parted you were no longer in my mind. But what can a sick man say, but that he is sick? His thoughts are necessarily concentred in himself: he neither receives nor can give delight; his inquiries are after alleviations of pain, and his efforts are to catch some momentary comfort.—Though I am now in the neighbourhood of the Peak, you must expect no account of its wonders, of its hills, its waters, its caverns, or its mines; but I will tell you, dear Sir, what I hope you will not hear with less satisfaction, that for about a week past my asthma has been less afflictive."

"Lichfield, October 2.

"I believe you had been long enough acquainted with the *phænomena* of sickness, not to be surprised that a sick man wishes to be where he is not, and where it appears to everybody but himself that he might easily be, without having the resolution to remove. I thought Ashbourne a solitary place, but did not come hither till last Monday.—I have here more company, but my health has for this last week not advanced; and in the languor of disease how little can be done? Whither or when I shall make my next remove, I cannot tell; but I entreat you, dear Sir, to let me know, from time to time, where you may be found, for your residence is a very powerful attractive to, Sir, your most humble servant."

"TO MR. PERKINS.

"Dear Sir,   Lichfield, Oct. 4,1784.

"I cannot but flatter myself that your kindness for me will make you glad to know where I am, and in what state.

"I have been struggling very hard with my diseases. My breath has been very much obstructed, and the water has attempted to encroach upon me again. I past the first part of the summer at Oxford, afterwards I went to Lichfield, thence to Ashbourne, in Derbyshire, and a week ago I returned to Lichfield.

"My breath is now much easier, and the water is in a great measure run away, so that I hope to see you again before winter.

"Please make my compliments to Mrs. Perkins, and to Mr. and Mrs. Barclay.

"I am, dear Sir, your most humble servant,

"Sam. Johnson."

"TO THE RIGHT HON. WILLIAM GERARD HAMILTON.

"Dear Sir,   Lichfield, Oct. 20, 1784.

"Considering what reason you gave me in the spring to conclude that you took part in whatever good or evil might befal me, I ought not to have omitted so long the account which I am now about to give you.—My diseases are an asthma and a dropsy, and, what is less curable, seventy-five. Of the dropsy, in the beginning

B.L.J.: II—T

of the summer, or in the spring, I recovered to a degree which struck with wonder both me and my physicians: the asthma now is likewise, for a time, very much relieved. I went to Oxford, where the asthma was very tyrannical, and the dropsy began again to threaten me; but seasonable physic stopped the inundation: I then returned to London, and in July took a resolution to visit Staffordshire and Derbyshire, where I am yet struggling with my disease. The dropsy made another attack, and was not easily ejected, but at last gave way. The asthma suddenly remitted in bed, on the 13th of August, and, though now very oppressive, is, I think, still something gentler than it was before the remission. My limbs are miserably debilitated, and my nights are sleepless and tedious.— When you read this, dear Sir, you are not sorry that I wrote no sooner. I will not prolong my complaints. I hope still to see you *in a happier hour*, to talk over what we have often talked, and perhaps to find new topics of merriment, or new incitements to curiosity.

"I am, dear Sir, &c.

"SAM. JOHNSON."

"TO JOHN PARADISE, ESQ.[1]

"DEAR SIR,   Lichfield, Oct. 27, 1784.

"Though in all my summer's excursion I have given you no account of myself, I hope you think better of me than to imagine it impossible for me to forget you, whose kindness to me has been too great and too constant not to have made its impression on a harder breast than mine. Silence is not very culpable, when nothing pleasing is suppressed. It would have alleviated none of your complaints to have read my vicissitudes of evil. I have struggled hard with very formidable and obstinate maladies; and though I cannot talk of health, think all praise due to my Creator and Preserver for the continuance of my life. The dropsy has made two attacks, and has given way to medicine; the asthma is very oppressive, but that has likewise once remitted. I am very weak, and very sleepless; but it is time to conclude the tale of misery. I hope, dear Sir, that you grow better, for you have likewise your share of human evil, and that your lady and the young charmers are well.

"I am, dear Sir, &c.,

"SAM. JOHNSON."

"TO MR. GEORGE NICOL.[2]

"DEAR SIR,   Ashbourne, Aug. 19, 1784.

"Since we parted, I have been much oppressed by my asthma, but it has lately been less laborious. When I sit I am almost at

---

[1] Son of the late Peter Paradise, Esq., his Britannic Majesty's Consul at Salonica, in Macedonia, by his lady, a native of that country. He studied at Oxford, and has been honoured by that University with the degree of LL.D. He is distinguished not only by his learning and talents, but by an amiable disposition, gentleness of manners, and a very general acquaintance with well-informed and accomplished persons of almost all nations.—BOSWELL.

Mr. Paradise died, December 12, 1795.—MALONE.

[2] Bookseller to his Majesty.—BOSWELL.

ease, and I can walk, though yet very little, with less difficulty for this week past, than before.   I hope I shall again enjoy my friends, and that you and I shall have a little more literary conversation. Where I now am, everything is very liberally provided for me but conversation.   My friend is sick himself, and the reciprocation of complaints and groans afford not much of either pleasure or instruction.   What we have not at home this town does not supply, and I shall be glad of a little imported intelligence, and hope that you will bestow now and then, a little time on the relief, and entertainment of, Sir, yours, &c.

"Sam. Johnson."

"TO MR. CRUIKSHANK.

"Dear Sir,   Ashbourne, Aug. 19, 1784.

"Do not suppose that I forget you; I hope I shall never be accused of forgetting my benefactors.   I had, till lately, nothing to write but complaints upon complaints, of miseries upon miseries; but within this fortnight I have received great relief.   Have your lecturers any vacation?   If you are released from the necessity of daily study, you may find time for a letter to me.   [In this letter he states the particulars of his case.]   In return for this account of my health let me have a good account of yours, and of your prosperity in all your undertakings.

"I am, dear Sir, yours, &c.,
"Sam. Johnson."

"TO MR. THOMAS DAVIES.

"August 14.

"The tenderness with which you always treat me, makes me culpable in my own eyes for having omitted to write in so long a separation; I had, indeed, nothing to say that you could wish to hear.   All has been hitherto misery accumulated upon misery, disease corroborating disease, till yesterday my asthma was perceptibly and unexpectedly mitigated.   I am much comforted with this short relief, and am willing to flatter myself that it may continue and improve.   I have at present such a degree of ease, as not only may admit the comforts, but the duties of life.   Make my compliments to Mrs. Davies.   Poor dear Allen, he was a good man."

"TO SIR JOSHUA REYNOLDS.

"Ashbourne, July 21.

"The tenderness with which I am treated by my friends, make it reasonable to suppose that they are desirous to know the state of my health, and a desire so benevolent ought to be gratified.   I came to Lichfield in two days without any painful fatigue, and on Monday came hither, where I purpose to stay and try what air and regularity will effect.   I cannot yet persuade myself that I have made much progress in recovery.   My sleep is little, my breath is very much encumbered, and my legs are very weak.   The water has increased a little, but has again run off. The most distressing symptom is want of sleep."

"August 19. Having had since our separation little to say that could please you or myself by saying, I have not been lavish of useless letters; but I flatter myself that you will partake of the pleasure with which I can now tell you, that about a week ago I felt suddenly a sensible remission of my asthma, and consequently a greater lightness of action and motion. Of this grateful alleviation I know not the cause, nor dare depend upon its continuance, but while it lasts I endeavour to enjoy it, and am desirous of communicating, while it lasts, my pleasure to my friends. Hitherto, dear Sir, I had written, before the post, which stays in this town but a little while, brought me your letter. Mr. Davies seems to have represented my little tendency to recover in terms too splendid. I am still restless, still weak, still watery, but the asthma is less oppressive. Poor Ramsay![1] On which side soever I turn, mortality presents its formidable frown. I left three old friends at Lichfield, when I was last there, and now found them all dead. I no sooner lost sight of dear Allan, than I am told that I shall see him no more. That we must all die, we always knew; I wish I had sooner remembered it. Do not think me intrusive or importunate, if I now call, dear Sir, upon you to remember it."

"Sept. 2. I am glad that a little favour from the court has intercepted your furious purposes. I could not in any case have approved such public violence of resentment, and should have considered any who encouraged it, as rather seeking sport for themselves, than honour for you. Resentment gratifies him who intended an injury, and pains him unjustly who did not intend it. But all this is now superfluous. I still continue by GOD's mercy to mend. My breath is easier, my nights are quieter, and my legs are less in bulk, and stronger in use. I have, however, yet a great deal to overcome before I can yet attain even an old man's health. Write, do write to me now and then; we are now old acquaintance, and perhaps few people have lived so much and so long together, with less cause of complaint on either side. The retrospection of this is very pleasant, and I hope we shall never think on each other with less kindness."

"Sept. 9. I could not answer your letter before this day, because I went on the sixth to Chatsworth, and did not come back till the post was gone. Many words, I hope, are not necessary between you and me, to convince you what gratitude is excited in my heart, by the Chancellor's liberality and your kind offices. I did not indeed expect that what was asked by the Chancellor would have been refused; but since it has, we will not tell that anything has been asked. I have enclosed a letter to the Chancellor, which, when you have read it, you will be pleased to seal with a head, or other general seal, and convey it to him; had I sent it directly to him, I should have seemed to overlook the favour of your intervention. My last letter told you of my advance in health, which, I

[1] Allan Ramsay, Esq., painter to his Majesty, who died August 10, 1784, in the 71st year of his age, much regretted by his friends.—BOSWELL.

think, in the whole, still continues. Of the hydropic tumour, there is now very little appearance; the asthma is much less troublesome, and seems to remit something day after day. I do not despair of supporting an English winter. At Chatsworth, I met young Mr. Burke, who led me very commodiously into conversation with the duke and duchess. We had a very good morning. The dinner was public."

"Sept. 18. I flattered myself that this week would have given me a letter from you, but none has come. Write to me now and then, but direct your next to Lichfield.—I think, and I hope am sure, that I still grow better: I have sometimes good nights; but am still in my legs weak, but so much mended, that I go to Lichfield in hope of being able to pay my visits on foot, for there are no coaches.—I have three letters this day, all about the balloon; I could have been content with one. Do not write about the balloon, whatever else you may think proper to say."

"October 2. I am always proud of your approbation, and therefore was much pleased that you liked my letter. When you copied it, you invaded the Chancellor's right rather than mine.— The refusal I did not expect, but I had never thought much about it, for I doubted whether the Chancellor had so much tenderness for me as to ask. He, being keeper of the King's conscience, ought not to be supposed capable of an improper petition.—All is not gold that glitters, as we have often been told; and the adage is verified in your place and my favour; but if what happens does not make us richer, we must bid it welcome, if it makes us wiser.—I do not at present grow better, nor much worse: my hopes, however, are somewhat abated, and a very great loss is the loss of hope, but I struggle on as I can."

"TO MR. JOHN NICHOLS.

"Lichfield, October 20.

"When you were here, you were pleased, as I am told, to think my absence an inconvenience. I should certainly have been very glad to give so skilful a lover of antiquities any information about my native place, of which, however, I know not much, and have reason to believe that not much is known.—Though I have not given you any amusement, I have received amusement from you. At Ashbourne, where I had very little company, I had the luck to borrow 'Mr. Bowyer's Life'; a book so full of contemporary history, that a literary man must find some of his old friends. I thought that I could now and then have told you some hints worth your notice; and perhaps we may talk a life over. I hope we shall be much together; you must now be to me what you were before, and what dear Mr. Allen was, besides. He was taken unexpectedly away, but I think he was a very good man.—I have made little progress in recovery. I am very weak, and very sleepless: but I live on and hope."

This various mass of correspondence, which I have thus brought together, is valuable, both as an addition

to the store which the public already has of Johnson's
writings, and as exhibiting a genuine and noble specimen
of vigour and vivacity of mind, which neither age nor sickness could impair or diminish.

It may be observed, that his writings in every way,
whether for the public, or privately to his friends, was by
fits and starts; for we see frequently, that many letters
are written on the same day.   When he had once overcome
his aversion to begin, he was, I suppose, desirous to go on,
in order to relieve his mind from the uneasy reflection of
delaying what he ought to do.

While in the country, notwithstanding the accumula-
tion of illness which he endured, his mind did not lose its
powers.   He translated an Ode of Horace, which is printed
in his works, and composed several prayers.   I shall insert
one of them, which is so wise and energetic, so philosophical
and so pious, that I doubt not of its affording consolation
to many a sincere Christian, when in a state of mind to
which I believe the best are sometimes liable.[1]

And here I am enabled fully to refute a very unjust
reflection, by Sir John Hawkins, both against Dr. Johnson
and his faithful servant, Mr. Francis Barber; as if both
of them had been guilty of culpable neglect towards a
person of the name of Heely, whom Sir John chooses to
call a *relation* of Dr. Johnson's.   The fact is, that Mr.
Heely was not his relation; he had indeed been married
to one of his cousins, but she had died without having
children, and he had married another woman; so that
even the slight connexion which there once had been by
alliance was dissolved.   Dr. Johnson, who had shown very
great liberality to this man while his first wife was alive,
as has appeared in a former part of this work,[2] was humane

---

[1] *Against inquisitive and perplexing thoughts.*   "O Lord, my maker
and protector, who hast graciously sent me into this world to work out
my salvation, enable me to drive from me all such unquiet and perplexing thoughts as may mislead or hinder me in the practice of those
duties which Thou has required.   When I behold the works of thy hands,
and consider the course of thy providence, give me grace always to
remember that thy thoughts are not my thoughts, nor thy ways my
ways.   And while it shall please Thee to continue me in this world,
where much is to be done, and little to be known, teach me by thy
Holy Spirit, to withdraw my mind from unprofitable and dangerous
inquiries, from difficulties vainly curious, and doubts impossible to be
solved.   Let me rejoice in the light which Thou hast imparted; let me
serve Thee with active zeal and humble confidence, and wait with
patient expectation for the time in which the soul which Thou receivest
shall be satisfied with knowledge.   Grant this, O Lord, for JESUS
CHRIST'S sake.   Amen."—BOSWELL.

[2] Vol. i. p. 364.

and charitable enough to continue his bounty to him occasionally; but surely there was no strong call of duty upon
him or upon his legatee, to do more.   The following letter,
obligingly communicated to me by Mr. Andrew Strahan,
will confirm what I have stated:—

"TO MR. HEELY, NO. 5, IN PYE-STREET, WESTMINSTER.

"SIR,   Ashbourne, August 12, 1784.
"As necessity obliges you to call so soon again upon me, you
should at least have told the smallest sum that will supply your
present want: you cannot suppose that I have much to spare.   Two
guineas is as much as you ought to be behind with your creditor.—
If you wait on Mr. Strahan, in New-street, Fetter-lane, or in his
absence, on Mr. Andrew Strahan, show this, by which they are
entreated to advance you two guineas, and to keep this as a voucher.
                              "I am, Sir, your humble servant,
                                        "SAM. JOHNSON."

Indeed it is very necessary to keep in mind that Sir
John Hawkins has unaccountably viewed Johnson's character and conduct in almost every particular, with an
unhappy prejudice.[1]

---

[1] I shall add one instance only to those which I have thought it incumbent on me to point out.   Talking of Mr. Garrick's having signified
his willingness to let Johnson have the loan of any of his books to assist
him in his edition of Shakespeare, Sir John says (p. 444), "Mr. Garrick
knew not what risk he ran by this offer.   Johnson had so strange a
forgetfulness of obligations of this sort, that few who lent him books
ever saw them again."   This surely conveys a most unfavourable insinuation, and has been so understood.   Sir John mentions the single
case of a curious edition of Politian, which, he tells us, appeared to
belong to Pembroke College, which probably had been considered by
Johnson as his own, for upwards of fifty years.   Would it not be fairer
to consider this as an inadvertence, and draw no general inference?
The truth is, that Johnson was so attentive that in one of his manuscripts
in my possession, he has marked in two columns books borrowed and
books lent.
   In Sir John Hawkins's compilation, there are, however, some passages concerning Johnson which have unquestionable merit.   One of
them I shall transcribe, in justice to a writer whom I have had too much
occasion to censure, and to show my fairness as the biographer of my
illustrious friend:—"There was wanting in his conduct and behaviour
that dignity which results from a regular and ordinary course of action,
and by an irresistible power commands esteem.   He could not be said
to be a staid man, nor so to have adjusted in his mind the balance of
reason and passion, as to give occasion to say what may be observed of
some men, that all they do is just, fit, and right."   Yet a judicious friend
well suggests, "It might, however, have been added, that such men are
often merely just, and rigidly correct, while their hearts are cold and
unfeeling; and that Johnson's virtues were of a much higher tone than
those of the *staid, orderly man* here described."—BOSWELL.

CHAPTER XXX.—1784

*Johnson's Last Visit to Lichfield—Uttoxeter—The Learned
Pig—Johnson's Visit to Oxford—Dr. Adams—Corres-
pondence—Johnson's increasing Indisposition—His Re-
turn to the Metropolis—Various Works Contemplated
by him—List of the Authors of Universal History—
Rev. John Swinton—Johnson's Knowledge of Greek—
Imitations of his Style—Mr. Burrowes—George Colman
—Dr. Robertson—Mr. Gibbon—Miss Burney—Arch-
deacon Nares—"The Mirror"—Rev. Dr. Knox—
Johnson's Affection for his departed Relations—His
approaching Dissolution—His Fears of Death—His
Prayers*

WE now behold Johnson for the last time in his native
city, for which he ever retained a warm affection, and which,
by a sudden apostrophe, under the word *Lich.* he introduces with reverence, into his immortal work, the English
Dictionary:—"*Salve magna parens!*"[1] While here, he felt
a revival of all the tenderness of filial affection, an instance
of which appeared in his ordering the grave-stone and inscription over Elizabeth Blaney[2] to be substantially and
carefully renewed.

To Mr. Henry White, a young clergyman, with whom
he now formed an intimacy, so as to talk to him with great

---

[1] The following circumstance, mutually to the honour of Johnson and
the corporation of his native city, has been communicated to me by the
Rev. Dr. Vyse, from the town clerk:—"Mr. Simpson has now before
him a record of the respect and veneration which the corporation of
Lichfield, in the year 1767, had for the merits and learning of Dr. Johnson.
His father built the corner house in the Market-place, the two fronts of
which, towards Market and Broad Market-street, stood upon waste land
of the corporation, under a forty years' lease, which was then expired. On
the 15th of August, 1767, at a common hall of the bailiffs and citizens, it
was ordered (and that without any solicitation), that a lease should be
granted to Samuel Johnson, Doctor of Laws, of the encroachments at
his house, for the term of ninety-nine years, at the old rent, which was
five shillings. Of which, as town-clerk, Mr. Simpson had the honour
and pleasure of informing him, and that he was desired to accept it,
without paying any fine on the occasion, which lease was afterwards
granted, and the doctor died possessed of this property."—BOSWELL.

[2] See vol. i. p. 40.—ED.

freedom, he mentioned that he could not in general accuse himself of having been an undutiful son.

"Once, indeed," said he, "I was disobedient; I refused to attend my father to Uttoxeter market.   Pride was the source of that refusal, and the remembrance of it was painful.   A few years ago I desired to atone for this fault; I went to Uttoxeter in very bad weather, and stood for a considerable time bareheaded in the rain, on the spot where my father's stall used to stand.   In contrition I stood, and I hope the penance was expiatory."

"I told him," says Miss Seward, "in one of my latest visits to him, of a wonderful learned pig, which I had seen at Nottingham; and which did all that we have observed exhibited by dogs and horses.   The subject amused him. 'Then,' said he, 'the pigs are a race unjustly calumniated. *Pig* has, it seems, not been wanting to *man*, but *man* to *pig*.   We do not allow *time* for his education; we kill him at a year old.'   Mr. Henry White, who was present, observed that if this instance had happened in or before Pope's time, he would not have been justified in instancing the swine as the lowest degree of grovelling instinct.   Dr. Johnson seemed pleased with the observation, while the person who made it proceeded to remark, that great torture must have been employed, ere the indocility of the animal could have been subdued.—'Certainly,' said the Doctor; 'but (turning to me), how old is your pig?'   I told him, three years old.   'Then,' said he, 'the pig has no cause to complain; he would have been killed the first year if he had not been *educated*, and protracted existence is a good recompense for very considerable degrees of torture.'"

As Johnson had now very faint hopes of recovery, and as Mrs. Thrale was no longer devoted to him, it might have been supposed that he would naturally have chosen to remain in the comfortable house of his beloved wife's daughter, and end his life where he began it.   But there was in him an animated and lofty spirit,[1] and however complicated diseases might depress ordinary mortals, all who saw him beheld and acknowledged the *invictum animum Catonis*.[2]   Such was his intellectual ardour even

---

[1] Burke suggested to me as applicable to Johnson, what Cicero, in his "Cato Major," says of Appius:—"Intentum enim animum, tanquam arcum, habebat, nec languescens succumbebat senectuti;" repeating, at the same time, the following noble words in the same passage:—"Ita enim senectus honesta est, si se ipsa defendit, si jus suum retinet, si nemini emancipata est, si usque ad extremum vitæ spiritum vindicat jus suum." —Boswell.

[2] *Atrocem* animum Catonis, are Horace's words, and it may be doubted

at this time, that he said to one friend, "Sir, I look upon every day to be lost, in which I do not make a new acquaintance;" and to another when talking of his illness, "I will be conquered; I will not capitulate."

And such was his love of London, so high a relish had he of its magnificent extent, and variety of intellectual entertainment, that he languished when absent from it, his mind having become quite luxurious from the long habit of enjoying the metropolis; and therefore, although at Lichfield, surrounded with friends who loved and revered him, and for whom he had a very sincere affection, he still found that such conversation as London affords, could be found no where else. These feelings joined, probably to some flattering hopes of aid from the eminent physicians and surgeons in London, who kindly and generously attended him without accepting fees, made him resolve to return to the capital.

From Lichfield he came to Birmingham, where he passed a few days with his worthy old schoolfellow, Mr. Hector, who thus writes to me: "He was very solicitous with me to recollect some of our most early transactions, and transmit them to him, for I perceived nothing gave him greater pleasure than calling to mind those days of our innocence. I complied with his request, and he only received them a few days before his death. I have transcribed for your inspection, exactly the minutes I wrote to him." This paper having been found in his repositories after his death, Sir John Hawkins has inserted it entire, and I have made occasional use of it and other communications from Mr. Hector,[1] in the course of this work. I have both visited and corresponded with him since Dr. Johnson's death, and by my inquiries concerning a great variety of particulars have obtained additional information. I followed the same mode with the Reverend Dr. Taylor, in whose presence I wrote down a good deal of what he could tell; and he, at my request, signed his name to give it authenticity. It is very rare to find any person who is able to give a distinct account of the life even of one whom he has known inti-

whether *atrox* is used by any other original writer in the same sense. *Stubborn* is perhaps the most correct translation of this epithet.—MALONE.

[1] It is a most agreeable circumstance attending the publication of this work, that Mr. Hector has survived his illustrious schoolfellow so many years; that he still retains his health and spirits; and has gratified me with the following acknowledgment:—"I thank you, most sincerely thank you, for the great and long-continued entertainment your Life of Dr. Johnson has afforded me, and others of my particular friends." Mr. Hector, besides setting me right as to the verse on a Sprig of

mately, without questions being put to them.   My friend
Dr. Kippis has told me, that on this account it is a practice
with him to draw out a biographical catechism.

Johnson then proceeded to Oxford, where he was again
kindly received by Dr. Adams,[1] who was pleased to give
the following account in one of his letters (Feb. 17th,
1785):—

"His last visit was, I believe, to my house, which he left, after
a stay of four or five days.   We had much serious talk together,
for which I ought to be the better as long as I live.   You will remember some discourse which we had in the summer on the subject
of prayer, and the difficulty of this sort of composition.   He reminded me of this, and of my having wished him to try his hand,
and to give us a specimen of the style and manner that he approved.
He added, that he was now in a right frame of mind, and as he could
not possibly employ his time better, he would in earnest set about
it.   But I find upon inquiry, that no papers of this sort were left
behind him, except a few short ejaculatory forms suitable to his
present situation."

Myrtle (see vol. i. p. 76, n.) has favoured me with two English odes,
written by Dr. Johnson, at an early period of his life, which will appear
in my edition of his Poems.—BOSWELL.
    This early and worthy friend of Johnson died at Birmingham,
September 2, 1794.—MALONE.
    [1] This amiable and excellent man survived Dr. Johnson about four
years, having died in January, 1789, at Gloucester, where a monument
is erected to his memory, with the following inscription:—

Sacred to the Memory of
W I L L I A M   A D A M S, D. D.,
Master of Pembroke College, Oxford,
Prebendary of this Cathedral, and
Archdeacon of Llandaff.
Ingenious, Learned, Eloquent,
He ably defended the truth of Christianity;
Pious, Benevolent, and Charitable,
He successfully inculcated its sacred Precepts.
Pure, and undeviating in his own Conduct,
He was tender and compassionate to the Failings of others.
Ever anxious for the welfare and happiness of Mankind,
He was on all occasions forward to encourage
Works of public Utility, and extensive Beneficence.
In the Government of the College over which he presided,
His vigilant Attention was uniformly exerted
To promote the important Objects of the institution;
Whilst the mild Dignity of his Deportment,
His gentleness of Disposition, and urbanity of Manners,
Inspired Esteem, Gratitude, and Affection.
Full of Days, and matured in Virtue,
He died Jan. 13th, 1789, aged 82.

    A very just character of Dr. Adams may also be found in "The
Gentleman's Magazine" for 1789, vol. lix. p. 214.   His only daughter
(see p. 551) was married in July, 1788, to B. Hyatt, Esq., of Painswick
in Gloucestershire.—MALONE.

Dr. Adams had not then received accurate information on this subject; for it has since appeared that various prayers had been composed by him at different periods, which intermingled with pious resolutions, and some short notes of his life, were entitled by him "Prayers and Meditations," and have, in pursuance of his earnest requisition, in the hopes of doing good, been published, with a judicious well-written preface, by the Rev. Mr. Strahan, to whom he delivered them. This admirable collection, to which I have frequently referred in the course of this work, evinces, beyond all his compositions for the public, and all the eulogies of his friends and admirers, the sincere virtue and piety of Johnson. It proves with unquestionable authenticity, that amidst all his constitutional infirmities, his earnestness to conform his practice to the precepts of Christianity was unceasing, and that he habitually endeavoured to refer every transaction of his life to the will of the Supreme Being.

He arrived in London on the 16th of November, and next day sent to Dr. Burney the following note, which I insert as the last token of his remembrance of that ingenious and amiable man, and as another of the many proofs of the tenderness and benignity of his heart:—

"Mr. Johnson, who came home last night, sends his respects to dear Dr. Burney, and all the dear Burneys, little and great."

"TO MR. HECTOR, IN BIRMINGHAM.

"DEAR SIR,   London, Nov. 17, 1784.
" I did not reach Oxford until Friday morning, and then I sent Francis to see the balloon fly, but could not go myself. I stayed at Oxford till Tuesday, and then came in the common vehicle easily to London. I am as I was, and having seen Dr. Brocklesby, am to ply the squills; but, whatever be their efficacy, this world must soon pass away. Let us think seriously on our duty.—I send my kindest respects to dear Mrs. Careless: let me have the prayers of both. We have all lived long, and must soon part. GOD have mercy on us, for the sake of our Lord Jesus Christ. Amen.
                                        "I am, &c.,
                                        "SAM. JOHNSON."

His correspondence with me, after his letter on the subject of my settling in London, shall now, as far as is proper, be produced in one series.

July 26, he wrote to me from Ashbourne:—

"On the 14th I came to Lichfield, and found everybody glad

enough to see me. On the 20th, I came hither, and found a house half-built, of very uncomfortable appearance; but my own room has not been altered. That a man worn with diseases, in his seventy-second or third year, should condemn part of his remaining life to pass among ruins and rubbish, and that no inconsiderable part, appears to me very strange.—I know that your kindness makes you impatient to know the state of my health, in which I cannot boast of much improvement. I came through the journey without much inconvenience, but when I attempt self-motion I find my legs weak, and my breath very short; this day I have been much disordered. I have no company; the Doctor[1] is busy in his fields, and goes to bed at nine, and his whole system is so different from mine, that we seem formed for different elements; I have, therefore, all my amusements to seek within myself."

Having written to him in bad spirits, a letter filled with dejection and fretfulness, and at the same time expressing anxious apprehensions concerning him, on account of a dream which had disturbed me; his answer was chiefly in terms of reproach, for a supposed charge of "affecting discontent, and indulging the vanity of complaint." It, however, proceeded:—

"Write to me often, and write like a man. I consider your fidelity and tenderness as a great part of the comforts which are yet left me, and sincerely wish we could be nearer to each other.— * * * * * * * *. My dear friend, life is very short and very uncertain; let us spend it as well as we can. My worthy neighbour, Allen, is dead. Love me as well as you can. Pay my respects to dear Mrs. Boswell. Nothing ailed me at that time; let your superstition at last have an end."

Feeling very soon, that the manner in which he had written might hurt me, he two days afterwards, July 28, wrote to me again, giving me an account of his sufferings; after which, he thus proceeds:—

"Before this letter, you will have had one which I hope you will not take amiss; for it contains only truth, and that truth kindly intended. *Spartam quam nactus es orna ;* make the most and best of your lot, and compare yourself not with the few that are above you, but with the multitudes which are below you. * * * * * *. Go steadily forward with lawful business or honest diversions. 'Be (as Temple says of the Dutchman) *well when you are not ill, and pleased when you are not angry.'* This may seem but an ill return for your tenderness; but I mean it well, for I love you with great ardour and sincerity. Pay my respects to dear Mrs. Boswell, and teach the young ones to love me."

The Rev. Dr. Taylor.—Boswell.

I unfortunately was so much indisposed during a considerable part of the year, that it was not, or at least I thought it was not, in my power to write to my illustrious friend as formerly, or without expressing such complaints as offended him. Having conjured him not to do me the injustice of charging me with affectation, I was with much regret long silent. His last letter to me then came, and affected me very tenderly.

"TO JAMES BOSWELL, ESQ.

"DEAR SIR,   Lichfield, Nov. 5, 1784.

"I have this summer sometimes amended, and sometimes relapsed, but upon the whole, have lost ground very much. My legs are extremely weak, and my breath very short, and the water is now increasing upon me. In this uncomfortable state your letters used to relieve; what is the reason that I have them no longer? Are you sick, or are you sullen? Whatever be the reason, if it be less than necessity, drive it away; and of the short life that we have, make the best use for yourself and for your friends. * * * * * * I am sometimes afraid that your omission to write has some real cause, and shall be glad to know that you are not sick, and that nothing ill has befallen dear Mrs. Boswell, or any of your family.

"I am, Sir, yours, &c.,
"SAM. JOHNSON."

Yet it was not a little painful to me to find, that in a paragraph of this letter, which I have omitted, he still persevered in arraigning me as before, which was strange in him who had so much experience of what I suffered. I, however, wrote to him two as kind letters as I could; the last of which came too late to be read by him, for his illness increased more rapidly upon him than I had apprehended; but I had the consolation of being informed that he spoke of me on his death-bed with affection, and I look forward with humble hope of renewing our friendship in a better world.

I now relieve the readers of this work from any farther personal notice of its author; who, if he should be thought to have obtruded himself too much upon their attention, requests them to consider the peculiar plan of his biographical undertaking.

Soon after Johnson's return to the metropolis, both the asthma and dropsy became more violent and distressful. He had for some time kept a journal in Latin of the state of his illness, and the remedies which he used, under the title of *Ægri Ephemeris*, which he began on the 6th of July, but continued it no longer than the 8th of November;

finding, I suppose, that it was a mournful and unavailing register. It is in my possession; and is written with great care and accuracy.

Still his love of literature did not fail.[1] A very few days

[1] It is truly wonderful to consider the extent and constancy of Johnson's literary ardour, notwithstanding the melancholy which clouded and embittered his existence. Besides the numerous and various works which he executed, he had, at different times, formed schemes of a great many more, of which the following catalogue was given by him to Mr. Langton, and by that gentleman presented to his Majesty:

"DIVINITY.

"A small book of precepts and directions for piety: the hint taken from the directions in Morton's exercise.

"PHILOSOPHY, HISTORY, AND LITERATURE IN GENERAL.

"History of Criticism, as it relates to judging of authors, from Aristotle to the present age. An account of the rise and improvements of that art; of the different opinions of authors, ancient and modern.

"Translation of the History of Herodian.

"New edition of Fairfax's Translation of Tasso, with notes, glossary, &c.

"Chaucer, a new edition of him, from manuscripts and old editions, with various readings, conjectures, remarks on his language, and the changes it had undergone from the earliest times to his age, and from his to the present; with notes explanatory of customs, &c., and reference to Boccace, and other authors from whom he has borrowed, with an account of the liberties he has taken in telling the stories; his life, and an exact etymological glossary.

"Aristotle's Rhetoric, a translation of it into English.

"A collection of Letters, translated from the modern writers, with some account of the several authors.

"Oldham's Poems, with notes, historical and critical.

"Roscommon's Poems, with notes.

"Lives of the Philosophers, written with a polite air, in such a manner as may divert, as well as instruct.

"History of the Heathen Mythology, with an explication of the fables, both allegorical and historical; with references to the poets.

"History of the State of Venice, in a compendious manner.

"Aristotle's Ethics, an English translation of them, with notes.

"Geographical Dictionary, from the French.

"Hierocles upon Pythagoras, translated into English, perhaps with notes. This is done by Norris.

"A book of Letters, upon all kind of subjects.

"Claudian, a new edition of his works, *cum notis variorum*, in the manner of Burman.

"Tully's Tusculan Questions, a translation of them.

"Tully's De Naturá Deorum, a translation of those books.

"Benzo's New History of the New World, to be translated.

"Machiavel's History of Florence, to be translated.

"History of the Revival of Learning in Europe, containing an account of whatever contributed to the restoration of literature; such as controversies, printing, the destruction of the Greek empire, the encouragement of great men, with the lives of the most eminent patrons, and most eminent early professors of all kinds of learning in different countries.

"A body of Chronology, in verse, with historical notes.

before his death he transmitted to his friend Mr. John Nichols, a list of the authors of the Universal History,

"A table of the Spectators, Tatlers, and Guardians, distinguished by figures into six degrees of value, with notes, giving the reasons of preference or degradation.

"A Collection of Letters from English authors, with a preface giving some account of the writers; with reasons for selection, and criticism upon styles; remarks on each letter, if needful.

"A Collection of Proverbs from various languages. Jan. 6.—53.

"A Dictionary to the Common Prayer, in imitation of Calmet's Dictionary of the Bible.   March.—52.

"A Collection of Stories and Examples, like those of Valerius Maximus.   Jan. 10,—53.

"From Ælian, a volume of select Stories, perhaps from others. Jan. 28,—53.

"Collection of Travels, Voyages, Adventures, and Descriptions of Countries.

"Dictionary of Ancient History and Mythology.

"Treatise on the Study of Polite Literature, containing the history of learning, directions for editions, commentaries, &c.

"Maxims, Characters, and Sentiments, after the manner of Bruyere, collected out of ancient authors, particularly the Greek with Apophthegms.

"Classical Miscellanies, Select Translations from ancient Greek and Latin authors.

"Lives of Illustrious Persons, as well of the active as the learned, in imitation of Plutarch.

"Judgment of the learned upon English authors.

"Poetical Dictionary of the English tongue.

"Considerations upon the present state of London.

"Collection of Epigrams, with notes and observations.

"Observations on the English language, relating to words, phrases, and modes of speech.

"Minutiæ Literariæ, Miscellaneous reflections, criticisms, emendations, notes.

"History of the Constitution.

"Comparison of Philosophical and Christian Morality, by sentences collected from the moralists and fathers.

"Plutarch's Lives, in English, with notes.

"POETRY AND WORKS OF IMAGINATION.

"Hymn to Ignorance.

"The Palace of Sloth—a vision.

"Coluthus, to be translated.

"Prejudice—a poetical essay.

"The Palace of Nonsense—a vision."

Johnson's extraordinary facility of composition, when he shook off his constitutional indolence, and resolutely sat down to write, is admirably described by Mr. Courtenay, in his "Poetical Review," which I have several times quoted:—

"While through life's maze he sent a piercing view,
His mind expansive to the object grew.
With various stores of erudition fraught,
The lively image, the deep-searching thought,
Slept in repose;—but when the moment press'd,
The bright ideas stood at once confess'd;

mentioning their several shares in that work. It has, according to his direction, been deposited in the British

> Instant his genius sped its vigorous rays,
> And o'er the letter'd world diffused a blaze:
> As womb'd with fire the cloud electric flies,
> And calmly o'er th' horizon seems to rise.
> Touch'd by the pointed steel, the lightning flows,
> And all th' expanse with rich effulgence glows."

We shall in vain endeavour to know with exact precision every production of Johnson's pen. He owned to me that he had written about forty sermons; but as I understood that he had given or sold them to different persons, who were to preach them as their own, he did not consider himself at liberty to acknowledge them. Would those who were thus aided by him, who are still alive, and the friends of those who are dead, fairly inform the world, it would be obligingly gratifying a reasonable curiosity, to which there should, I think, now be no objection. Two volumes of them, published since his death, are sufficiently ascertained; see p. 154. I have before me, in his hand-writing, a fragment of twenty quarto leaves, of a translation into English of Sallust, *De Bello Catilinario.* When it was done I have no notion; but it seems to have no very superior merit to mark it as his. Besides the publications heretofore mentioned, I am satisfied, from internal evidence, to admit also as genuine the following, which, notwithstanding all my chronological care, escaped me in the course of this work:—

"Considerations on the Case of Dr. Trapp's Sermons," published in 1739, in "The Gentleman's Magazine." It is a very ingenious defence of the right of *abridging* an author's work, without being held as infringing his property. This is one of the nicest questions in the *Law of Literature;* and I cannot help thinking that the indulgence of abridging is often exceedingly injurious to authors and booksellers, and should in very few cases be permitted. At any rate, to prevent difficult and uncertain discussion, and give an absolute security to authors in the property of their labours, no abridgment whatever should be permitted, till after the expiration of such a number of years as the Legislature may be pleased to fix.

But, though it has been confidently ascribed to him, I cannot allow that he wrote a Dedication to both Houses of Parliament of a book entitled "The Evangelical History Harmonized." He was no *croaker;* no declaimer against *the times.* He would not have written, "That we are fallen upon an age in which corruption is not barely universal, is universally confessed." Nor, "Rapine preys on the public without opposition, and perjury betrays it without inquiry." Nor would he, to excite a speedy reformation, have conjured up such phantoms of terror as these:—"A few years longer, and perhaps all endeavours will be in vain. We may be swallowed by an earthquake; we may be delivered to our enemies." This is not Johnsonian.

There are, indeed, in this Dedication several sentences constructed upon the model of those of Johnson. But the imitation of the form, without the spirit of his style, has been so general, that this of itself is not sufficient evidence. Even our newspaper writers aspire to it. In an account of the funeral of Edwin, the comedian, in "The Diary" of Nov. 9, 1790, that son of drollery is thus described: "A man who had so often cheered the sullenness of vacancy, and suspended the approaches of sorrow." And in "The Dublin Evening Post," August 16, 1791, there is the following paragraph: "It is a singular circumstance, that in a city like this, containing 200,000 people, there are three months in the year during which no place of public amusement is open. Long vacation

Museum, and is printed in "The Gentleman's Magazine" for December, 1784.[1]

During his sleepless nights he amused himself by translating into Latin verse, from the Greek, many of the epigrams in *The Anthologia*. These translations, with some other poems by him in Latin, he gave to his friend Mr. Langton, who, having added a few notes, sold them to the booksellers for a small sum to be given to some of

is here a vacation from pleasure, as well as business; nor is there any mode of passing the listless evenings of declining summer, but in the riots of a tavern, or the stupidity of a coffee house."

I have not thought it necessary to specify every copy of verses written by Johnson, it being my intention to publish an authentic edition of all his poetry, with notes.—BOSWELL.

[1] As the letter accompanying this list (which fully supports the observation in the text) was written but a week before Dr. Johnson's death, the reader may not be displeased to find it here preserved:

"TO MR. NICHOLS.

Dec. 6, 1784.

"The late learned Mr. Swinton, having one day remarked that one man, meaning, I suppose, no man but himself, could assign all the parts of the Ancient Universal History to their proper authors, at the request of Sir Robert Chambers or of myself, gave the account which I now transmit to you in his own hand; being willing that of so great a work the history should be known, and that each writer should receive his due proportion of praise from posterity.

"I recommend to you to preserve this scrap of literary intelligence in Mr. Swinton's own hand, or to deposit it in the Museum, that the veracity of this account may never be doubted.

"I am, Sir, your most humble servant,

"SAM. JOHNSON."

Mr. S————n.

The History of the Carthaginians.
,,   Numidians.
,,   Mauritanians.
,,   Gætulians.
,   Garamanthes.
,,   Melano Gætulians.
,,   Nigritæ.
,,   Cyrenaica.
,,   Marmarica.
,,   Regio Syrtica.
,,   Turks, Tartars, and Moguls.
,,   Indians.
,,   Chinese.
Dissertation on the peopling of America.
,,   independency of the Arabs.

The Cosmogony, and a small part of the History immediately following; by Mr. Sale.

To the birth of Abraham; chiefly by Mr. Shelvock.

History of the Jews, Gauls, and Spaniards; by Mr. Psalmanaazar.

Xenophon's Retreat; by the same.

History of the Persians and the Constantinopolitan Empire; by Dr. Campbell.

History of the Romans; by Mr. Bower.—BOSWELL.

Johnson's relations, which was accordingly done; and they
are printed in the collection of his works.

A very erroneous notion has circulated as to Johnson's
deficiency in the knowledge of the Greek language, partly
owing to the modesty with which, from knowing how much
there was to be learnt, he used to mention his own comparative acquisitions.   When Mr. Cumberland[1] talked to
him of the Greek fragments which are so well illustrated
in "The Observer," and of the Greek dramatists in general,
he candidly acknowledged his insufficiency in that particular
branch of Greek literature.   Yet it may be said, that though
not a great, he was a good Greek scholar.   Dr. Charles
Burney, the younger, who is universally acknowledged by
the best judges, to be one of the few men of this age who
are very eminent for their skill in that noble language,
has assured me, that Johnson could give a Greek word for
almost every English one; and that although not sufficiently
conversant in the niceties of the language, he, upon some
occasions discovered, even in these, a considerable degree
of critical acumen.   Mr. Dalzel, professor of Greek at
Edinburgh, whose skill in it is unquestionable, mentioned
to me, in very liberal terms, the impression which was made
upon him by Johnson, in a conversation which they had
in London concerning that language.   As Johnson, therefore, was undoubtedly one of the first Latin scholars in
modern times, let us not deny to his fame some additional
splendour from Greek.

I shall now fulfil my promise of exhibiting specimens
of various sorts of imitation of Johnson's style.

In "The Transactions of the Royal Irish Academy,
1787," there is an "Essay on the Style of Dr. Samuel
Johnson," by the Rev. Robert Burrowes, whose respect for
the great object of his criticism[2] is thus evinced in the
concluding paragraph:—

"I have singled him out from the great body of the English
writers, because his universally acknowledged beauties would be

[1] Mr. Cumberland assures me, that he was always treated with great
courtesy by Dr. Johnson, who, in his "Letters to Mrs. Thrale," vol. ii.
p. 68, thus speaks of that learned, ingenious, and accomplished gentleman: "The want of company is an inconvenience, but Mr. Cumberland
is a million."—BOSWELL.

[2] We must smile at a little inaccuracy of metaphor in the Preface to
the Transactions, which is written by Mr. Burrowes.   The *critic of the
style* of Johnson having, with a just zeal for literature, observed, that
the whole nation are called on to exert themselves, afterwards says:
"They are *called on* by every *tie* which can have a laudable influence
on the heart of man."—BOSWELL.

most apt to induce imitation; and I have treated rather on his faults than his perfections, because an essay might comprise all the observations I could make upon his faults while volumes would not be sufficient for a treatise on his perfections."

Mr. Burrowes has analyzed the composition of Johnson, and pointed out its peculiarities with much acuteness; and I would recommend a careful perusal of his Essay to those, who being captivated by the union of perspicuity and splendour which the writings of Johnson contain, without having a sufficient portion of his vigour of mind, may be in danger of becoming bad copyists of his manner. I, however, cannot but observe, and I observe it to his credit, that this learned gentleman has himself caught no mean degree of the expansion and harmony, which, independent of all other circumstances, characterize the sentences of Johnson. Thus, in the preface to the volume in which the Essay appears, we find—

"If it be said that in societies of this sort, too much attention is frequently bestowed on subjects barren and speculative, it may be answered, that no one science is so little connected with the rest, as not to afford many principles whose use may extend considerably beyond the science to which they primarily belong; and that no proposition is so purely theoretical as to be totally incapable of being applied to practical purposes. There is no apparent connexion between duration and the cycloidal arch, the properties of which duly attended to, have furnished us with our best regulated methods of measuring time; and he who has made himself master of the nature and affections of the logarithmic curve, is not aware that he has advanced considerably towards ascertaining the proportionable density of the air at its various distances from the surface of the earth."

The ludicrous imitators of Johnson's style are innumerable. Their general method is to accumulate hard words, without considering that, although he was fond of introducing them occasionally, there is not a single sentence in all his writings where they are crowded together, as in the first verse of the following imaginary ode by him to Mrs. Thrale,[1] which appeared in the newspapers:—

[1] Johnson's wishing to unite himself with this rich widow was much talked of, but I believe without foundation. The report, however, gave occasion to a poem, not without characteristical merit, entitled, "Ode to Mrs. Thrale, by Samuel Johnson, LL.D., on their supposed approaching Nuptials:" printed for Mr. Faulder, in Bond-street. I shall quote as a specimen, the first three stanzas.

"If e'er my fingers touch'd the lyre,
In satire fierce, in pleasure gay;

> "*Cervisial coctor's viduate* dame,
> *Opins't* thou his gigantic fame,
>   *Procumbing* at that shrine;
> Shall, *catenated* by thy charms,
> A captive in thy *ambient* arms,
>   *Perennially* be thine?"

This, and a thousand other such attempts, are totally unlike the original, which the writers imagined they were turning into ridicule. There is not similarity enough for burlesque, or even for caricature.

Mr. Colman, in his "Prose on several Occasions," has "A Letter from Lexiphanes; containing Proposals for a *Glossary* or *Vocabulary* of the *Vulgar Tongue:* intended as a supplement to a larger Dictionary." It is evidently meant as a sportive sally of ridicule on Johnson, whose style is thus imitated, without being grossly overcharged:—

"It is easy to foresee that the idle and illiterate will complain that I have increased their labours by endeavouring to diminish them; and that I have explained what is more easy by what is more difficult—*ignotum per ignotius.* I expect, on the other hand, the liberal acknowledgments of the learned. He who is buried in scholastic retirement, secluded from the assemblies of the gay, and remote from the circles of the polite, will at once comprehend the definitions, and be grateful for such a seasonable and necessary elucidation of his mother-tongue."

Annexed to this letter is a short specimen of the work, thrown together in a vague and desultory manner, not even adhering to alphabetical concatenation.[1]

> Shall not my Thralia's smiles inspire?
> Shall Sam refuse the sportive lay?

> "My dearest lady! view your slave,
>   Behold him as your very *Scrub;*
> Eager to write as author grave,
>   Or govern well the brewing-tub.

> To rich felicity thus raised,
>   My bosom glows with amorous fire,
> Porter no longer shall be praised,
>   'Tis I myself am *Thrale's Entire.*"—Boswell.

[1] "*Higgledy-piggledy,*—Conglomeration and confusion.

"*Hodge-podge,*—A culinary mixture of heterogeneous ingredients; applied metaphorically to all discordant combinations.

"*Tit for Tat,*—Adequate retaliation.

"*Shilly Shally,*—Hesitation and irresolution.

"*Feel fa! fum!*—Gigantic intonations.

"*Rigmarole,*—Discourse, incoherent and rhapsodical.

"*Crincum-crancum,*—Lines of irregularity and involution.

"*Ding dong,*—Tintinabulary chimes, used metaphorically to signify dispatch and vehemence."—Boswell.

The serious imitators of Johnson's style, whether intentionally or by the imperceptible effect of its strength and animation, are, as I have had already occasion to observe, so many, that I might introduce quotations from a numerous body of writers in our language, since he appeared in the literary world. I shall point out the following:—

WILLIAM ROBERTSON, D.D.

"In other parts of the globe, man, in his rudest state, appears as Lord of the creation, giving law to various tribes of animals which he has tamed and reduced to subjection. The Tartar follows his prey on the horse which he has reared, or tends his numerous herds which furnish him both with food and clothing; the Arab has rendered the camel docile, and avails himself of its persevering strength; the Laplander has formed the reindeer to be subservient to his will; and even the people of Kamschatka have trained their dogs to labour. This command over the inferior creatures is one of the noblest prerogatives of man, and among the greatest efforts of his wisdom and power. Without this, his dominion is incomplete. He is a monarch who has no subjects; a master without servants; and must perform every operation by the strength of his own arm." [1]

EDWARD GIBBON, ESQ.

"Of all our passions and appetites, the love of power is of the most imperious and unsociable nature, since the pride of one man requires the submission of the multitude. In the tumult of civil discord the laws of society lose their force, and their place is seldom supplied by those of humanity. The ardour of contention, the pride of victory, the despair of success, the memory of past injuries, and the fear of future dangers, all contribute to inflame the mind, and to silence the voice of pity." [2]

MISS BURNEY.

"My family, mistaking ambition for honour, and rank for dignity, have long planned a splendid connection for me, to which, though my invariable repugnance has stopped any advances, their wishes and their views immovably adhere. I am but too certain they will now listen to no other. I dread, therefore, to make a trial where I despair of success; I know not how to risk a prayer with those who may silence me by a command." [3]

[1] "History of America," vol. i. quarto, p. 332.—BOSWELL.
[2] "Decline and fall of the Roman Empire," vol. i. chap. iv.—BOSWELL.
[3] "Cecilia," book vii. chap. i.—BOSWELL.

REVEREND MR. NARES.[1]

" In an enlightened and improving age, much perhaps is not to be apprehended from the inroads of mere caprice; at such a period it will generally be perceived, that needless irregularity is the worst of all deformities, and that nothing is so truly elegant in language as the simplicity of unviolated analogy.—Rules will, therefore, be observed, so far as they are known and acknowledged: but, at the same time, the desire of improvement having been once excited will not remain inactive; and its efforts, unless assisted by knowledge, as much as they are prompted by zeal, will not unfrequently be found pernicious; so that the very persons whose intention it is to perfect the instrument of reason, will deprave and disorder it unknowingly. At such a time, then, it becomes peculiarly necessary that the analogy of language should be fully examined and understood; that its rules should be carefully laid down; and that it should be clearly known how much it contains, which being already right should be defended from change and violation; how much it has that demands amendment; and how much that, for fear of greater inconveniences, must, perhaps, be left unaltered though irregular."

A distinguished author in "The Mirror,"[2] a periodical paper, published at Edinburgh, has imitated Johnson very closely. Thus, in No. 16,—

"The effects of the return of spring have been frequently remarked as well in relation to the human mind as to the animal and vegetable world. The reviving power of this season has been traced from the fields to the herds that inhabit them, and from the lower class of beings up to man. Gladness and joy are described as prevailing through universal Nature, animating the low of the cattle, the carol of the birds, and the pipe of the shepherd."

The Rev. Dr. Knox, master of Tunbridge school, appears to have the *imitari aveo* of Johnson's style perpetually in his mind; and to his assiduous, though not servile, study of it, we may partly ascribe the extensive popularity of his writings.[3]

---

[1] The passage which I quote is taken from that gentleman's " Elements of Orthoepy; containing a distinct View of the whole Analogy of the English Language, so far as relates to Pronunciation, Accent, and Quantity," London, 1784.   I beg leave to offer my particular acknowledgments to the author of a work of uncommon merit and great utility. I know no book which contains, in the same compass, more learning, polite literature, sound sense, accuracy of arrangement, and perspicuity of expression.—BOSWELL.

[2] That collection was presented to Dr. Johnson, I believe, by its authors; and I heard him speak very well of it.—BOSWELL.

[3] It were to be wished, that he had imitated that great man in every respect, and had not followed the example of Dr. Adam Smith, in ungraciously attacking his venerable *Alma Mater,* Oxford.   It must, however, be observed, that he is much less to blame than Smith: he only

In his "Essays, Moral and Literary," No. 3, we find the following passage:—

"The polish of external grace may indeed be deferred till the approach of manhood. When solidity is obtained by pursuing the modes prescribed by our forefathers, then may the file be used. The firm substance will bear attrition, and the lustre then acquired will be durable."

There is, however, one in No. 11, which is blown up into such tumidity, as to be truly ludicrous. The writer means to tell us, that members of Parliament, who have run in debt by extravagance, will sell their votes to avoid an arrest,[1] which he thus expresses:—

"They who build houses and collect costly pictures and furnitures, with the money of an honest artizan or mechanic, will be very glad of emancipation from the hands of a bailiff, by a sale of their senatorial suffrage."

But I think the most perfect imitation of Johnson is a professed one, entitled "A Criticism on Gray's Elegy in a Country Churchyard," said to be written by Mr. Young, professor of Greek at Glasgow, and of which let him have the credit, unless a better title can be shown. It has not only the particularities of Johnson's style, but that very species of literary discussion and illustration for which he was eminent.—Having already quoted so much from others, I shall refer the curious to this performance, with an assurance of much entertainment.

Yet whatever merit there may be in any imitations of Johnson's style, every good judge must see that they are

objects to certain particulars; Smith to the whole institution, though indebted for much of his learning to an exhibition which he enjoyed for many years at Baliol College. Neither of them, however, will do any hurt to the noblest university in the world. While I animadvert on what appears to me exceptionable in some of the works of Dr. Knox, I cannot refuse due praise to others of his productions; particularly his sermons, and to the spirit with which he maintains, against presumptuous heretics, the consolatory doctrines peculiar to the Christian Revelation. This he has done in a manner equally strenuous and conciliating. Neither ought I to omit mentioning a remarkable instance of his candour. Notwithstanding the wide difference of our opinions, upon the important subject of University education, in a letter to me concerning this work, he thus expresses himself: "I thank you for the very great entertainment your Life of Johnson gives me. It is a most valuable work. Yours is a new species of biography. Happy for Johnson that he had so able a recorder of his wit and wisdom."—BOSWELL.

[1] Dr. Knox, in his "Moral and Literary" abstraction, may be excused for not knowing the political regulations of his country. No senator can be in the hands of a bailiff.—BOSWELL.

obviously different from the original; for all of them are either deficient in its force, or overloaded with its peculiarities; and the powerful sentiment to which it is suited is not to be found.

Johnson's affection for his departed relations seemed to grow warmer as he approached nearer to the time when he might hope to see them again. It probably appeared to him that he should upbraid himself with unkind inattention, were he to leave the world without having paid a tribute of respect to their memory.

"TO MR. GREEN, APOTHECARY, AT LICHFIELD.

"DEAR SIR,   Dec. 2, 1784.
"I have enclosed the Epitaph for my father, mother, and brother, to be all engraved on the large size, and laid in the middle aisle in St. Michael's church, which I request the clergyman and churchwardens to permit.

"The first care must be to find the exact place of interment, that the stone may protect the bodies. Then let the stone be deep, massy, and hard; and do not let the difference of ten pounds, or more, defeat our purpose.

"I have enclosed ten pounds, and Mrs. Porter will pay you ten more, which I gave her for the same purpose. What more is wanted shall be sent; and I beg that all possible haste may be made, for I wish to have it done while I am yet alive. Let me know, dear Sir, that you receive this. I am, Sir,
                    "Your most humble servant,
                              "SAM. JOHNSON."

"TO MRS. LUCY PORTER, IN LICHFIELD.[1]

"DEAR MADAM,   Dec. 2, 1784.
"I am very ill, and desire your prayers. I have sent Mr. Green the Epitaph, and a power to call on you for ten pounds.

"I laid this summer a stone over Tetty, in the chapel of Bromley, in Kent. The inscription is in Latin, of which this is the English. [Here a translation.]

"That this is done, I thought it fit that you should know. What care will be taken of us, who can tell? May GOD pardon and bless us, for JESUS CHRIST's sake.
                    "I am, &c.,
                              "SAM. JOHNSON."

My readers are now, at last, to behold SAMUEL JOHNSON preparing himself for that doom, from which the most exalted powers afford no exemption to man. Death had

[1] This lady, whose name so frequently occurs in the course of this work, survived Dr. Johnson just thirteen months. She died at Lichfield, in her 71st year, January 13, 1786, and bequeathed the principal part of her fortune to the Rev. Mr. Pearson, of Lichfield.—MALONE.

always been to him an object of terror; so that, though by no means happy, he still clung to life with an eagerness at which many have wondered. At any time when he was ill, he was very much pleased to be told that he looked better. An ingenious member of the *Eumelian Club*[1] informs me, that upon one occasion, when he said to him that he saw health returning to his cheek, Johnson seized him by the hand and exclaimed, "Sir, you are one of the kindest friends I ever had."

His own state of his views of futurity will appear truly rational; and may, perhaps, impress the unthinking with seriousness.

"You know," says he,[2] " I never thought confidence with respect to futurity, any part of the character of a brave, a wise, or a good man. Bravery has no place where it can avail nothing; wisdom impresses strongly the consciousness of those faults, of which it is, perhaps, itself, an aggravation; and goodness, always wishing to be better, and imputing every deficiency to criminal negligence, and every fault to voluntary corruption, never dares to suppose the condition of forgiveness fulfilled, nor what is wanting in the crime supplied by penitence.

"This is the state of the best; but what must be the condition of him whose heart will not suffer him to rank himself among the best, or among the good?—Such must be his dread of the approaching trial, as will leave him little attention to the opinion of those whom he is leaving for ever; and the serenity that is not felt, it can be no virtue to feign."

His great fear of death, and the strange dark manner in which Sir John Hawkins imparts the uneasiness which he expressed on account of offences with which he charged himself, may give occasion to injurious suspicions, as if there had been something of more than ordinary criminality weighing upon his conscience. On that account, therefore, as well as from the regard to truth which he inculcated,[3] I am to mention (with all possible respect and delicacy, however,) that his conduct, after he came to London, and had associated with Savage and others, was not so strictly virtuous, in one respect, as when he was a younger man. It was well known that his amorous inclinations were

---

[1] A Club in London, founded by the learned and ingenious physician, Dr. Ash, in honour of whose name it was called *Eumelian*, from the Greek Εὐμελίας : though it was warmly contended, and even put to a vote, that it should have the more obvious appellation of *Fraxinean,* from the Latin.—BOSWELL.

[2] Mrs. Thrale's collection, March 10, 1784. Vol. ii. p. 3.—BOSWELL.

[3] See what he said to Mr. Malone, p. 381 of this volume.—BOSWELL.

uncommonly strong and impetuous. He owned to many of his friends, that he used to take women of the town to taverns, and hear them relate their history. In short, it must not be concealed, that, like many other good and pious men, among whom we may place the apostle Paul upon his own authority, Johnson was not free from propensities which were ever "warring against the law of his mind,"—and that in his combats with them, he was sometimes overcome.

Here let the profane and licentious pause; let them not thoughtlessly say that Johnson was an *hypocrite*, or that his *principles* were not firm, because his *practice* was not uniformly conformable to what he professed.

Let the question be considered independent of moral and religious associations; and no man will deny that thousands, in many instances, act against conviction. Is a prodigal, for example, an *hypocrite*, when he owns he is satisfied that his extravagance will bring him to ruin and misery? We are *sure* he *believes* it; but immediate inclination, strengthened by indulgence, prevails over that belief in influencing his conduct. Why then shall credit be refused to the *sincerity* of those who acknowledge their persuasion of moral and religious duty, yet sometimes fail of living as it requires? I heard Dr. Johnson once observe, "There is something noble in publishing truth, though it condemns one's self." [1] And one who said in his presence. "he had no notion of people being in earnest in their good professions, whose practice was not suitable to them," was thus reprimanded by him:—"Sir, are you so grossly ignorant of human nature as not to know that a man may be very sincere in good principles without having good practice?" [2]

But let no man encourage or soothe himself in "presumptuous sin," from knowing that Johnson was sometimes hurried into indulgences which he thought criminal. I have exhibited this circumstance as a shade in so great a character, both from my sacred love of truth, and to show that he was not so weakly scrupulous as he had been represented by those who imagine that the sins, of which

---

[1] "Journal of a Tour to the Hebrides," 3rd edit. p. 209. On the same subject, in his letter to Mrs. Thrale, dated Nov. 29, 1783, he makes the following just observations: "Life to be worthy of a rational being, must be always in progression; we must always purpose to do more or better than in time past. The mind is enlarged and elevated by mere purposes, though they end as they began, by airy contemplation. We compare and judge, though we do not practise."—BOSWELL.

[2] "Journal of a Tour to the Hebrides," p. 374.—BOSWELL.

a deep sense was upon his mind, were merely such little
venial trifles as pouring milk into his tea on Good Friday.
His understanding will be defended by my statement, if
his consistency of conduct be in some degree impaired.
But what wise man would, for momentary gratifications,
deliberately subject himself to suffer such uneasiness as
we find was experienced by Johnson in reviewing his conduct
as compared with his notion of the ethics of the gospel?
Let the following passages be kept in remembrance:—

"O GOD, giver and preserver of all life, by whose power I was
created, and by whose providence I am sustained, look down upon
me with tenderness and mercy; grant that I may not have been
created to be finally destroyed; that I may not be preserved to add
wickedness to wickedness."—(Prayers and Med. p. 47.)

"O LORD, let me not sink into total depravity; look down upon
me, and rescue me at last from the captivity of sin," (p. 68.)

"Almighty and most merciful Father, who has continued my
life from year to year, grant that by longer life I may become less
desirous of sinful pleasures, and more careful of eternal happiness,"
(p. 84.)

"Let not my years be multiplied to increase my guilt; but as
my age advances, let me become more pure in my thoughts, more
regular in my desires, and more obedient to thy laws," (p. 120.)

"Forgive, O merciful LORD, whatever I have done contrary
to thy laws.   Give me such a sense of my wickedness as may produce
true contrition and effectual repentance; so that when I shall be
called into another state, I may be received among the sinners to
whom sorrow and reformation have obtained pardon, for JESUS
CHRIST's sake.   Amen," (p. 130.)

Such was the distress of mind, such the penitence of
Johnson, in his hours of privacy, and in his devout
approaches to his Maker.   His *sincerity*, therefore, must
appear to every candid mind unquestionable.

It is of essential consequence to keep in view, that
there was in this excellent man's conduct no false principle
of *commutation*, no *deliberate* indulgence in sin, in consideration of a counterbalance of duty.   His offending, and his
repenting, were distinct and separate,[1] and when we consider
his almost unexampled attention to truth, his inflexible
integrity, his constant piety, who will dare to "cast a stone
at him?"   Besides, let it never be forgotten, that he
cannot be charged with any offence indicating badness of

---

[1] Dr. Johnson related, with very earnest approbation, a story of a
gentleman, who, in an impulse of passion, overcame the virtue of a
young woman.   When she said to him, "I am afraid we have done
wrong!" he answered, "Yes, we have done wrong; for I would not
debauch her mind."—BOSWELL.

heart, anything dishonest, base, or malignant; but that, on the contrary, he was charitable in an extraordinary degree; so that even in one of his own rigid judgments of himself (Easter-eve, 1781), while he says, " I have corrected no external habits," he is obliged to own, "I hope that since my last communion I have advanced by pious reflections, in my submission to GOD, and my benevolence to man." [1]

I am conscious that this is the most difficult and dangerous part of my biographical work, and I cannot but be very anxious concerning it.   I trust that I have got through it, preserving at once my regard to truth,— to my friend,—and to the interests of virtue and religion. Nor can I apprehend that more harm can ensue from the knowledge of the irregularities of Johnson, guarded as I have stated it, than from knowing that Addison and Parnell were intemperate in the use of wine; which he himself, in his Lives of those celebrated writers and pious men, has not forborne to record.

[1] "Prayers and Meditations," p. 192.—BOSWELL.

*Johnson's last Illness—His Liberality to his Black Servant
—His Will and Codicil—The kind Attachment of his
Friends—Extracts from his Miscellaneous Conversation
—Rev. Mr. Budworth—Samuel Boyse—"Thuanus"—
The Death-bed—Death of Johnson—His Funeral—His
Various Busts and Portraits—His Monument and
Inscription—Concluding Reflections*

IT is not my intention to give a very minute detail of the
particulars of Johnson's remaining days, of whom it was
now evident, that the crisis was fast approaching, when
he must *"die like men, and fall like one of the princes."*
Yet it will be instructive, as well as gratifying to the
curiosity of my readers, to record a few circumstances, on
the authenticity of which they may perfectly rely, as I
have been at the utmost pains to obtain an accurate
account of his last illness, from the best authority.

Dr. Heberden, Dr. Brocklesby, Dr. Warren, and Dr.
Butter, physicians, generously attended him, without
accepting any fees, as did Mr. Cruikshank, surgeon; and all
that could be done from professional skill and ability was
tried, to prolong a life so truly valuable. He himself,
indeed, having, on account of his very bad constitution,
been perpetually applying himself to medical inquiries,
united his own efforts with those of the gentlemen who
attended him; and imagining that the dropsical collection
of water which oppressed him might be drawn off by making
incisions in his body, he, with his usual resolute defiance
of pain, cut deep when he thought that his surgeon had
done it too tenderly.[1]

About eight or ten days before his death, when Dr.
Brocklesby paid him his morning visit, he seemed very
low and desponding, and said, "I have been as a dying

[1] This bold experiment Sir John Hawkins has related in such a manner
as to suggest a charge against Johnson of intentionally hastening his end;
a charge so very inconsistent with his character in every respect, that
it is injurious even to refute it, as Sir John has thought it necessary to
do. It is evident that what Johnson did in hopes of relief, indicated an
extraordinary eagerness to retard his dissolution.—BOSWELL.

man all night." He then emphatically broke out in the words of Shakespeare,—

> "Canst thou not minister to a mind diseased;
> Pluck from the memory a rooted sorrow;
> Raze out the written troubles of the brain;
> And, with some sweet oblivious antidote,
> Cleanse the stuff'd bosom of that perilous stuff,
> Which weighs upon the heart?"

To which Dr. Brocklesby readily answered, from the same great poet:

> ———therein the patient
> Must minister to himself."

Johnson expressed himself much satisfied with the application.

On another day, after this, when talking on the subject of prayer, Dr. Brocklesby repeated from Juvenal,

> "Orandum est, ut sit mens sana in corpore sano,"

and so on to the end of the tenth satire; but in running it quickly over, he happened, in the line,

> "Qui spatium vitæ extremum inter munera ponat,"

to pronounce *supremum* for *extremum ;* at which Johnson's critical ear instantly took offence, and discoursing vehemently on the unmetrical effect of such a lapse, he showed himself as full as ever of the spirit of the grammarian.

Having no other relations,[1] it had been for some time

---

[1] The author in a former page has shown the injustice of Sir John Hawkins's charge against Johnson, with respect to a person of the name of Heely, whom he has inaccurately represented as a relation of Johnson's. See p. 606.—That Johnson was anxious to discover whether any of his relations were living, is evinced by the following letter, written not long before he made his will:—

"TO THE REV. DR. VYSE, IN LAMBETH.
   "Sir,   Bolt-court, Fleet-street, Nov. 29, 1784.
   "I am desirous to know whether Charles Scrimshaw, of Woodsease (I think), in your father's neighbourhood, be now living; what is his condition, and where he may be found.   If you can conveniently make an inquiry about him, and can do it without delay, it will be an act of great kindness to me, he being very nearly related to me.   I beg you to pardon this trouble.   I am, Sir, your most humble servant,
                                             "Sam. Johnson."
   In conformity to the wish expressed in the preceding leter, an inquiry was made, but no descendants of Charles Scrimshaw or of his sisters were discovered to be living.   Dr. Vyse informs me that Dr. Johnson told him, "he was disappointed in the inquiries he had made after his relations."   There is therefore no ground whatsoever for supposing that he was unmindful of them, or neglected them.—Malone.

Johnson's intention to make a liberal provision for his faithful servant, Mr. Francis Barber, whom he looked upon as particularly under his protection, and whom he had all along treated truly as an humble friend. Having asked Dr. Brocklesby what would be a proper annuity to a favourite servant, and being answered that it must depend on the circumstances of the master; and, that in the case of a nobleman, fifty pounds a year was considered as an adequate reward for many years' faithful service:—"Then," said Johnson, "shall I be *nobilissimus*, for I mean to leave Frank seventy pounds a year, and I desire you to tell him so." It is strange, however, to think, that Johnson was not free from that general weakness of being averse to execute a will, so that he delayed it from time to time; and had it not been for Sir John Hawkins's repeatedly urging it I think it is probable that his kind resolution would not have been fulfilled. After making one, which, as Sir John Hawkins informs me, extended no farther than the promised annuity, Johnson's final disposition of his property was established by a Will and Codicil, of which copies are subjoined.[1]

---

[1] "IN THE NAME OF GOD. AMEN. I, SAMUEL JOHNSON, being in full possession of my faculties, but fearing this night may put an end to my life, do ordain this my last Will and Testament. I bequeath to God a soul polluted by many sins, but I hope purified by Jesus Christ. I leave seven hundred and fifty pounds in the hands of Bennet Langton, Esq.; three hundred pounds in the hands of Mr. Barclay and Mr. Perkins, brewers; one hundred and fifty pounds in the hands of Dr. Percy, Bishop of Dromore; one thousand pounds, Three per cent. Annuities in the public funds; and one hundred pounds now lying by me in ready money: all these before-mentioned sums and property I leave, I say, to Sir Joshua Reynolds, Sir John Hawkins, and Dr. William Scott, of Doctors' Commons, in trust, for the following uses:—That is to say, to pay to the representatives of the late William Innys, bookseller, in St. Paul's Churchyard, the sum of two hundred pounds; to Mrs. White, my female servant, one hundred pounds stock in the Three per cent. Annuities aforesaid. The rest of the aforesaid sums of money and property, together with my books, plate, and household furniture, I leave to the before-mentioned Sir Joshua Reynolds, Sir John Hawkins, and Dr. William Scott, also in trust, to be applied, after paying my debts, to the use of Francis Barber, my man-servant, a negro, in such manner as they shall judge most fit and available to his benefit. And I appoint the aforesaid Sir Joshua Reynolds, Sir John Hawkins, and Dr. William Scott, sole executors of this my last will and testament, hereby revoking all former wills and testaments whatever. In witness whereof, I hereunto subscribe my name, and affix my seal, this eighth day of December, 1784.

"SAM. JOHNSON (L.S.)

"Signed, sealed, published, declared and delivered, by the said testator, as his last will and testament, in the presence of us, the word *two* being first inserted in the opposite page.

"GEORGE STRAHAN.
"JOHN DESMOULINS."

The considerations of numerous papers of which he was possessed, seems to have struck Johnson's mind with a sudden anxiety, and as they were in great confusion, it is much to be lamented that he had not entrusted some

* By way of Codicil to my last will and testament, I, SAMUEL JOHNSON, give, devise, and bequeath my messuage or tenement situate at Lichfield, in the county of Stafford, with the appurtenances in the tenure and occupation of Mrs. Bond, of Lichfield aforesaid, or of Mr. Hinchman, her under-tenant, to my executors in trust, to sell and dispose of the same; and the money arising from such sale I give and bequeath as follows—viz., to Thomas and Benjamin, the sons of Fisher Johnson, late of Leicester, and ———— Whiting, daughter of Thomas Johnson, late of Coventry, and the grand-daughter of the said Thomas Johnson, one full and equal fourth part each; but in case there shall be more grand-daughters than one of the said Thomas Johnson, living at the time of my decease, I give and bequeath the part or share of that one to and equally between such grand-daughters. I give and bequeath to the Rev. Mr. Rogers, of Berkley, near Froom, in the county of Somerset, the sum of one hundred pounds, requesting him to apply the same towards the maintenance of Elizabeth Herne, a lunatic. I also give and bequeath to my god-children, the son and daughter of Mauritius Lowe, painter, each of them one hundred pounds of my stock in the Three per cent. Consolidated Annuities, to be applied and disposed of by and at the discretion of my executors, in the education or settlement in the world of them my said legatees. Also I give and bequeath to Sir John Hawkins, one of my executors, the Annales Ecclesiastici of Baronius, and Holinshed's and Stowe's Chronicles, and also an octavo Common Prayer Book. To Bennet Langton, Esq., I give and bequeath my Polyglot Bible. To Sir Joshua Reynolds, my great French Dictionary, by Martiniere, and my own copy of my folio English Dictionary of the last revision. To Dr. William Scott, one of my executors, the Dictionnaire de Commerce, and Lectius's edition of the Greek Poets. To Mr. Windham, Poetæ Græci Heroici per Henricum Stephanum. To the Rev. Mr. Strahan, Vicar of Islington, in Middlesex, Mill's Greek Testament, Beza's Greek Testament, by Stephens, all my Latin Bibles, and my Greek Bible, by Wechelius. To Dr. Heberden, Dr. Brocklesby, Dr. Butter, and Mr. Cruikshank, the surgeon who attended me, Mr. Holder, my apothecary, Gerard Hamilton, Esq., Mrs. Gardiner, of Snow-hill, Mrs. Frances Reynolds, Mr. Hoole, and the Reverend Mr. Hoole, his son, each a book at their election, to keep as a token of remembrance. I also give and bequeath to Mr. John Desmoulins, two hundred pounds Consolidated Three per cent. Annuities; and to Mr. Sastres, the Italian master, the sum of five pounds, to be laid out in books of piety for his own use. And whereas the said Bennet Langton hath agreed, in consideration of the sum of seven hundred and fifty pounds mentioned in my will to be in his hands, to grant and secure an annuity of seventy pounds, payable during the life of me and my servant, Francis Barber, and the life of the survivor of us, to Mr. George Stubbs, in trust for us; my mind and will is, that in case of my decease before the said agreement shall be perfected, the said sum of seven hundred and fifty pounds, and the bond for securing the said sum, shall go to the said Francis Barber; and I hereby give and bequeath to him the same, in lieu of the bequest in his favour, contained in my said will. And I hereby empower my executors to deduct and retain all expenses that shall or may be incurred in the execution of my said will, or of this codicil thereto, out of such estate and effects as I shall die possessed of. All the rest, residue, and remainder of my estate and effects I give and bequeath to my said executors, in trust for the said Francis Barber, his

faithful and discreet person with the care and selection of them: instead of which, he, in a precipitate manner, burnt large masses of them with little regard, as I apprehend, to discrimination.   Not that I suppose we have thus been

executors and administrators.   Witness my hand and seal, this ninth day of December, 1784.

"SAM. JOHNSON (L.S.)

"Signed, sealed, published, declared, and delivered by the said Samuel Johnson, as and for a codicil to his last will and testament, in the presence of us, who, in his presence, and at his request, and also in the presence of each other, have hereto subscribed our names as witnesses.

"JOHN COPELY,
"WILLIAM GIBSON,
"HENRY COLE."

Upon these testamentary deeds it is proper to make a few observa-tions.

His express declaration with his dying breath as a Christian, as it had been often practised in such solemn writings, was of real consequence from this great man, for the conviction of a mind equally acute and strong, might well overbalance the doubts of others, who were his contemporaries.   The expression *polluted* may, to some, convey an impression of more than ordinary contamination; but that is not warranted by its genuine meaning, as appears from "The Rambler," No. 42.   The same word is used in the will of Dr. Sanderson, Bishop of Lincoln, who was piety itself.

His legacy of two hundred pounds to the representatives of Mr. Innys, bookseller, in St. Paul's Churchyard, proceeded from a very worthy motive.   He told Sir John Hawkins that, his father having become a bankrupt, Mr. Innys had assisted him with money or credit to continue his business.   "This," said he, "I consider as an obligation on me to be grateful to his descendants."

The amount of his property proved to be considerably more than he had supposed it to be.   Sir John Hawkins estimates the bequest to Francis Barber at a sum little short of fifteen hundred pounds, including an annuity of seventy pounds to be paid to him by Mr. Langton, in consideration of seven hundred and fifty pounds, which Johnson had lent to that gentleman.   Sir John seems not a little angry at this bequest, and mutters "a caveat against ostentatious bounty and favour to negroes." But surely when a man has money entirely of his own acquisition, especially when he has no near relations, he may, without blame, dispose of it as he pleases, and with great propriety to a faithful servant. Mr. Barber, by the recommendation of his master, retired to Lichfield, where he might pass the rest of his days in comfort.

It has been objected that Johnson has omitted many of his best friends, when leaving books to several as tokens of his last remembrance.   The names of Dr. Adams, Dr. Taylor, Dr. Burney, Mr. Hector, Mr. Murphy, the author of this work, and others who were intimate with him, are not to be found in his will.   This may be accounted for by considering, that as he was very near his dissolution at the time, he probably mentioned such as happened to occur to him; and that he may have recollected that he had formerly shown others such proofs of his regard, that it was not necessary to crowd his will with their names.   Mrs. Lucy Porter was much displeased that nothing was left to her; but besides what I have now stated, she should have considered that she had left nothing to Johnson by her will, which was made during his lifetime, as appeared at her decease.

deprived of any compositions which he had ever intended for the public eye; but from what escaped the flames, I judge that many curious circumstances relating both to himself, and other literary characters, have perished.

Two very valuable articles, I am sure, we have lost, which were two quarto volumes, containing a full, fair, and most particular account of his own life, from his earliest recollection. I owned to him, that having accidentally seen them, I had read a great deal in them; and apologizing for the liberty I had taken, asked him if I could help it. He placidly answered, "Why, Sir, I do not think you could have helped it." I said that I had, for once in my life, felt half an inclination to commit theft. It had come into my mind to carry off those two volumes, and never see him more. Upon my inquiring how this would have affected him, "Sir," said he, "I believe I should have gone mad."[1]

His enumerating several persons in one group, and leaving them "each a book at their election," might possibly have given occasion to a curious question as to the order of choice, had they not luckily fixed on different books. His library, though by no means handsome in its appearance, was sold by Mr. Christie for two hundred and forty-seven pounds nine shillings; many people being desirous to have a book which had belonged to Johnson. In many of them he had written little notes; sometimes tender memorials of his departed wife: as, "This was dear Tetty's book;" sometimes occasional remarks of different sorts. Mrs. Lyons, of Clifford's-inn, has favoured me with the two following:—

In "Holy Rules and Helps to Devotions, by Bryan Duppa, Lord Bishop of Winton," *"Preces quidam videtur diligenter tractasse; spero non inauditus."*

In "The Rosicrucian infallible Axiomata, by John Heydon, Gent.," prefixed to which are some verses addressed to the author, signed Ambr. Waters, A.M. Coll. Ex. Oxon, *"These Latin verses were written to Hobbes by Bathurst, upon his Treatise on Human Nature, and have no relation to the book.———An odd fraud."*—Boswell.

Francis Barber, Dr. Johnson's principal legatee, died in the infirmary at Stafford, after undergoing a painful operation, Feb. 13, 1801.—Malone.

[1] One of these volumes, Sir John Hawkins informs us, he put into his pocket; for which the excuse he states is, that he meant to preserve it from falling into the hands of a person whom he describes so as to make it sufficiently clear who is meant; "having strong reasons," said he, "to suspect that this man might find and make an ill use of the book." Why Sir John should suppose that the gentleman alluded to would act in this manner, he has not thought fit to explain. But what he did was not approved of by Johnson; who, upon being acquainted of it without delay by a friend, expressed great indignation, and warmly insisted on the book being delivered up; and, afterwards, in the supposition of his missing it, without knowing by whom it had been taken, he said, "Sir, I should have gone out of the world distrusting half mankind." Sir John next day wrote a letter to Johnson, assigning reasons for his conduct; upon which Johnson observed to Mr. Langton, "Bishop Sanderson could not have dictated a better letter. I could almost say *Melius est sic pœnituisse quam non errasse."* The agitation into which Johnson was thrown by this incident, probably made him hastily burn those precious records which must ever be regretted.—Boswell.

During his last illness, Johnson experienced the steady
and kind attachment of his numerous friends. Mr. Hoole
has drawn up a narrative of what passed in the visits
which he paid him during that time, from the 10th of
November to the 13th of December, the day of his death,
inclusive, and has favoured me with a perusal of it, with
permission to make extracts, which I have done. Nobody
was more attentive to him than Mr. Langton,[1] to whom
he tenderly said, *Te teneam moriens deficiente manu.* And
I think it highly to the honour of Mr. Windham, that his
important occupations as an active statesman did not
prevent him from paying assiduous respect to the dying
sage whom he revered. Mr. Langton informs me, that one
day he found Mr. Burke and four or five more friends
sitting with Johnson. Mr. Burke said to him, ' I am afraid,
Sir, such a number of us may be oppressive to you.'—' No,
Sir,' said Johnson, ' it is not so; and I must be in a wretched
state, indeed, when your company would not be a delight
to me.' Mr. Burke, in a tremulous voice, expressive of
being very tenderly affected, replied, ' My dear Sir, you have
always been too good to me.' Immediately afterwards
he went away. This was the last circumstance in the
acquaintance of these two eminent men."

The following particulars of his conversation within a
few days of his death, I give on the authority of Mr. John
Nichols: [2]—

---

[1] Mr. Langton, whose name so often occurs in these volumes, survived Johnson several years. He died at Southampton, Dec. 18, 1801.—
MALONE.

[2] On the same undoubted authority I give a few articles, which should
have been inserted in chronological order; but which, now that they are
before me, I should be sorry to omit:—

"In 1736, Dr. Johnson had a particular inclination to have been
engaged as an assistant to the Reverend Mr. Budworth, then head master
of the Grammar-school at Brewood, in Staffordshire, 'an excellent person, who possessed every talent of a perfect instructor of youth, in a
degree which (to use the words of one of the brightest ornaments of
literature, the Reverend Dr. Hurd, Bishop of Worcester) has been
rarely found in any of that profession since the days of Quintilian.'
Mr. Budworth, 'who was less known in his lifetime, from that obscure
situation to which the caprice of fortune oft condemns the most accomplished characters, than his highest merit deserved,' had been bred
under Mr. Blackwell, at Market Bosworth, where Johnson was some time
an usher; which might naturally lead to the application. Mr. Budworth
was certainly no stranger to the learning or abilities of Johnson, as he
more than once lamented his having been under the necessity of declining the engagement, from an apprehension that the paralytic affection, under which our great Philologist laboured through life, might
become the object of imitation or of ridicule, among his pupils." Captain
Budworth, his grandson, has confirmed to me this anecdote.

"He said that the Parliamentary Debates were the only part of his writings which then gave him any compunction; but that at the time he wrote them, he had no conception he was imposing upon the world, though they were frequently written from very slender materials, and often from none at all—the mere coinage of his own imagination. He never wrote any part of his works with equal velocity. Three columns of the Magazine in an hour was no uncommon effort, which was faster than most persons could have transcribed that quantity.

"Of his friend Cave, he always spoke with great affection. 'Yet,' said he, 'Cave (who never looked out of his window but with a view to the Gentleman's Magazine) was a penurious paymaster; he would contract for lines by the hundred, and expect the long hundred; but he was a good man, and always delighted to have his friends at his table.'

"When talking of a regular edition of his own works, he said, that he had power (from the booksellers) to print such an edition, if his health admitted it; but had no power to assign over any edition, unless he could add notes, and so alter them as to make them new works, which his state of health forbade him to think of. 'I may possibly live,'

"Among the early associates of Johnson, at St. John's Gate, was Samuel Boyse, well known by his ingenious productions; and not less noted for his imprudence. It was not unusual for Boyse to be a customer to the pawnbroker. On one of these occasions, Dr. Johnson collected a sum of money to redeem his friend's clothes, which in two days after were pawned again. 'The sum,' said Johnson, 'was collected by sixpences, at a time when to me sixpence was a serious consideration.'

"Speaking one day of a person for whom he had a real friendship, but in whom vanity was somewhat too predominant, he observed, that 'Kelly was so fond of displaying on his sideboard the plate which he possessed, that he added to it his spurs. For my part,' said he, 'I never was master of a pair of spurs but once, and they are now at the bottom of the ocean. By the carelessness of Boswell's servant, they were dropped from the end of the boat, on our return from the Isle of Sky.'"

The late Reverend Mr. Samuel Badcock, having been introduced to Dr. Johnson by Mr. Nichols, some years before his death, thus expressed himself in a letter to that gentleman:—

"How much I am obliged to you for the favour you did me in introducing me to Dr. Johnson! *Tantum vidi Virgilium.* But to have seen him, and to have received a testimony of respect from him was enough. I recollect all the conversation, and shall never forget one of his expressions. Speaking of Dr. P—— (whose writings, I saw, he estimated at a low rate, he said, 'You have proved him as deficient in *probity* as he is in learning.' I called him an *'Index-scholar;'* but he was not willing to allow him a claim even to that merit. He said, 'that he borrowed from those who had been borrowers themselves, and did not know that the mistakes he adopted had been answered by others.' I often think of our short, but precious, visit to this great man. I shall consider it as a kind of an *era* in my life."—BOSWELL.

said he, 'or rather breathe, three days, or perhaps three weeks; but find myself daily and gradually weaker.'

"He said at another time, three or four days only before his death, speaking of the little fear he had of undergoing a chirurgical operation, 'I would give one of these legs for a year more of life—I mean of comfortable life, not such as that which I now suffer;' and lamented much his inability to read during his hours of restlessness. 'I used formerly,' he added, 'when sleepless in bed, *to read like a Turk*.'

"Whilst confined by his last illness, it was his regular practice to have the church-service read to him by some attentive and friendly divine. The Rev. Mr. Hoole performed this kind office in my presence for the last time, when, by his own desire, no more than the litany was read; in which his responses were in the deep and sonorous voice which Mr. Boswell has occasionally noticed, and with the most profound devotion that can be imagined. His hearing not being quite perfect, he more than once interrupted Mr. Hoole, with 'Louder, my dear Sir, louder, I entreat you, or you pray in vain!'—and when the service was ended, he, with great earnestness, turned round to an excellent lady who was present, saying, 'I thank you, Madam, very heartily, for your kindness in joining me in this solemn exercise. Live well, I conjure you; and you will not feel the compunction at the last, which I now feel.' So truly humble were the thoughts which this great and good man entertained of his own approaches to religious perfection.

"He was earnestly invited to publish a volume of 'Devotional Exercises;' but this (though he listened to the proposal with much complacency, and a large sum of money was offered for it) he declined, from motives of the sincerest modesty.

"He seriously entertained the thought of translating 'Thuanus.' He often talked to me on the subject, and once in particular, when I was rather wishing that he would favour the world, and gratify his sovereign, by a Life of Spenser (which he said that he would readily have done, had he been able to obtain any new materials for the purpose), he added, 'I have been thinking again, Sir, of "Thuanus;" it would not be the laborious task which you have supposed it. I should have no trouble but that of dictation, which would be performed as speedily as an amanuensis could write.'"

It is to the mutual credit of Johnson and divines of different communions, that although he was a steady Church of England man, there was, nevertheless, much

agreeable intercourse between him and them. Let me
particularly name the late Mr. La Trobe, and Mr. Hutton,
of the Moravian profession. His intimacy with the English
Benedictines at Paris, has been mentioned; and as an
additional proof of the charity in which he lived with good
men of the Romish Church, I am happy in this opportunity
of recording his friendship with the Rev. Thomas Hussey,
D.D., his Catholic Majesty's Chaplain of Embassy at the
Court of London, that very respectable man, eminent not
only for his powerful eloquence as a preacher, but for his
various abilities and acquisitions. Nay, though Johnson
loved a Presbyterian the least of all, this did not prevent
his having a long and uninterrupted social connexion with
the Rev. Dr. James Fordyce, who, since his death, hath
gratefully celebrated him in a warm strain of devotional
composition.

Amidst the melancholy clouds which hung over the
dying Johnson, his characteristical manner showed itself
on different occasions.

When Dr. Warren, in the usual style, hoped that he was
better, his answer was, "No, Sir; you cannot conceive
with what acceleration I advance towards death."

A man whom he had never seen before was employed
one night to sit up with him. Being asked next morning
how he liked his attendant, his answer was, "Not at all,
Sir; the fellow's an idiot; he is as awkward as a turnspit
when first put into the wheel, and as sleepy as a dormouse."

Mr. Windham having placed a pillow conveniently to
support him, he thanked him for his kindness, and said,
"That will do—all that a pillow can do."

He repeated with great spirit a poem, consisting of
several stanzas, in four lines, in alternate rhyme, which
he said he had composed some years before,[1] on occasion
of a rich, extravagant young gentleman's coming of age,
saying, he had never repeated it but once since he composed
it, and had given but one copy of it. That copy was given
to Mrs. Thrale, now Piozzi, who has published it in a book
which she entitles "British Synonimy," but which is truly
a collection of entertaining remarks and stories, no matter
whether accurate or not. Being a piece of exquisite

---

[1] In 1780. See his letter to Mrs. Thrale, dated August 8, 1780:—
"You have heard in the papers how —— is come to age. I have enclosed
a short song of congratulation, which you must not show to anybody.
It is odd that it should come into anybody's head. I hope you will read
it with candour; it is, I believe, one of the author's first essays in that
way of writing, and a beginner is always to be treated with tenderness."
—Malone.

satire, conveyed in a strain of pointed vivacity and humour, and in a manner of which no other instance is to be found in Johnson's writings, I shall here insert it.

> Long-expected one-and-twenty,
>   Ling'ring year, at length is flown;
> Pride and pleasure, pomp and plenty,
>   Great *******, are now your own.
>
> Loosen'd from the minor's tether,
>   Free to mortgage or to sell,
> Wild as wind, and light as feather,
>   Bid the sons of thrift farewell.
>
> Call the Betseys, Kates, and Jennies,
>   All the names that banish care;
> Lavish of your grandsire's guineas,
>   Show the spirit of an heir.
>
> All that prey on vice and folly
>   Joy to see their quarry fly;
> There the gamester, light and jolly,
>   There the lender grave and sly.
>
> Wealth, my lad, was made to wander,
>   Let it wander as it will;
> Call the jockey, call the pander,
>   Bid them come and take their fill.
>
> When the bonny blade carouses,
>   Pockets full, and spirits high—
> What are acres? what are houses?
>   Only dirt, or wet or dry.
>
> Should the guardian friend or mother
>   Tell the woes of wilful waste;
> Scorn their counsel, scorn their pother,
>   You can hang or drown at last.

As he opened a note which his servant brought to him, he said, "An odd thought strikes me—we shall receive no letters in the grave."

He requested three things of Sir Joshua Reynolds:— To forgive him thirty pounds which he had borrowed of him; to read the Bible; and never to use his pencil on a Sunday. Sir Joshua readily acquiesced.

Indeed he showed the greatest anxiety for the religious improvement of his friends, to whom he discoursed of its infinite consequence. He begged of Mr. Hoole to think of what he had said, and to commit it to writing; and upon being afterwards assured that this was done, pressed his hands, and in an earnest tone thanked him.   Dr. Brocklesby having attended him with the utmost assiduity and kindness as his physician and friend, he was peculiarly desirous that this gentleman should not entertain any loose speculative notions, but be confirmed in the truths of Christianity, and insisted on his writing down in his presence, as nearly as he could collect it, the import of what passed on the subject; and Dr. Brocklesby having complied with the request, he made him sign the paper, and urged him to keep it in his own custody as long as he lived.

Johnson, with that native fortitude, which, amidst all his bodily distress and mental sufferings, never forsook him, asked Dr. Brocklesby, as a man in whom he had confidence, to tell him plainly whether he could recover. "Give me," said he, "a direct answer."   The doctor having first asked him if he could bear the whole truth, which way soever it might lead, and being answered that he could, declared that, in his opinion, he could not recover without a miracle.   "Then," said Johnson, "I will take no more physic, not even my opiates; for I have prayed that I may render up my soul to God unclouded."   In this resolution he persevered, and, at the same time, used only the weakest kinds of sustenance.   Being pressed by Mr. Windham to take somewhat more generous nourishment, lest too low a diet should have the very effect which he dreaded, by debilitating his mind, he said, "I will take anything but inebriating sustenance."

The Rev. Mr. Strahan, who was the son of his friend, and had been always one of his great favourites, had, during his last illness, the satisfaction of contributing to soothe and comfort him. That gentleman's house at Islington, of which he is vicar, afforded Johnson, occasionally and easily, an agreeable change of place and fresh air, and he attended also upon him in town in the discharge of the sacred offices of his profession.

Mr. Strahan has given me the agreeable assurance, that after being in much agitation, Johnson became quite composed, and continued so till his death.

Dr. Brocklesby, who will not be suspected of fanaticism, obliged me with the following accounts:—

"For some time before his death, all his fears were calmed and absorbed by the prevalence of his faith, and his trust in the merits and *propitiation* of Jesus Christ.

"He talked often to me about the necessity of faith in the *sacrifice* of Jesus, as necessary beyond all good works whatever, for the salvation of mankind.

"He pressed me to study Dr. Clarke, and to read his

Sermons. I asked him why he pressed Dr. Clarke, an Arian.[1] 'Because,' said he, 'he is fullest on the *propitiatory sacrifice.*'"

Johnson having thus in his mind the true Christian scheme, at once rational and consolatory, uniting justice and mercy in the DIVINITY, with the improvement of human nature, previous to his receiving the Holy Sacrament in his apartment, composed and fervently uttered this prayer.[2]

"Almighty and most merciful Father, I am now, as to human eyes it seems, about to commemorate, for the last time, the death of thy Son JESUS CHRIST, our Saviour and Redeemer. Grant, O LORD, that my whole hope and confidence may be in his merits, and thy mercy; enforce and accept my imperfect repentance; make this commemoration available to the confirmation of my faith, the establishment of my hope, and the enlargement of my charity; and make the death of thy Son JESUS CHRIST effectual to my redemption. Have mercy upon me, and pardon the multitude of my offences. Bless my friends; have mercy upon all men. Support me by thy Holy Spirit, in the days of weakness, and at the hour of death; and receive me, at my death, to everlasting happiness, for the sake of JESUS CHRIST. Amen."

Having, as has been already mentioned, made his will on the 8th and 9th of December, and settled all his worldly affairs, he languished till Monday, the 13th of that month, when he expired about seven o'clock in the evening, with so little apparent pain that his attendants hardly perceived when his dissolution took place.

Of his last moments, my brother, Thomas David, has furnished me with the following particulars:—

"The Doctor, from the time that he was certain his death was near, appeared to be perfectly resigned, was seldom or never fretful or out of temper, and often said to his faithful servant, who gave me this account, 'Attend,

---

[1] The change of his sentiments with regard to Dr. Clarke is thus mentioned to me in a letter from the late Dr. Adams, Master of Pembroke College, Oxford:—"The doctor's prejudices were the strongest, and certainly in another sense the weakest, that ever possessed a sensible man. You know his extreme zeal for orthodoxy. But did you ever hear what he told me himself? That he had made it a rule not to admit Dr. Clarke's name in his Dictionary. This, however, wore off. At some distance of time he advised with me what books he should read in defence of the Christian religion. I recommended 'Clarke's Evidences of Natural and Revealed Religion,' as the best of the kind; and I find in what is called his 'Prayers and Meditations,' that he was frequently employed in the latter part of his time in reading Clarke's Sermons."—BOSWELL.

[2] The Rev. Mr. Strahan took care to have it preserved, and has inserted it in "Prayers and Meditations," p. 216.—BOSWELL.

Francis, to the salvation of your soul, which is the object of greatest importance;' he also explained to him passages in the scripture, and seemed to have pleasure in talking upon religious subjects.

"On Monday, the 13th of December, the day on which he died, a Miss Morris, daughter to a particular friend of his, called, and said to Francis that she begged to be permitted to see the Doctor, that she might earnestly request him to give her his blessing. Francis went into his room, followed by the young lady, and delivered the message. The Doctor turned himself in the bed, and said, 'GOD bless you, my dear!' These were the last words he spoke. His difficulty of breathing increased till about seven o'clock in the evening, when Mr. Barber and Mrs. Desmoulins, who were sitting in the room, observing that the noise he made in breathing had ceased, went to the bed, and found he was dead."

About two days after his death, the following very agreeable account was communicated to Mr. Malone, in a letter by the Honourable John Byng, to whom I am much obliged for granting me permission to introduce it in my work.

"DEAR SIR,

"Since I saw you, I have had a long conversation with Cawston,[1] who sat up with Dr. Johnson, from nine o'clock on Sunday evening, till ten o'clock on Monday morning. And from what I can gather from him, it should seem, that Dr. Johnson was perfectly composed, steady in hope, and resigned to death. At the interval of each hour, they assisted him to sit up in his bed, and move his legs, which were in much pain; when he regularly addressed himself to fervent prayers; and though, sometimes, his voice failed him, his sense never did, during that time. The only sustenance he received was cider and water. He said his mind was prepared, and the time to his dissolution seemed long. At six in the morning, he inquired the hour, and, on being informed, said that all went on regularly, and he felt he had but a few hours to live.

"At ten o'clock in the morning, he parted from Cawston, saying, 'You should not detain Mr. Windham's servant:—I thank you; bear my remembrance to your master.' Cawston says, that no man could appear more collected, more devout, or less terrified at the thoughts of the approaching minute.

"This account, which is so much more agreeable than, and somewhat different from, yours, have given us the satisfaction of thinking that that great man died as he lived, full of resignation, strengthened in faith, and joyful in hope."

A few days before his death, he had asked Sir John Hawkins, as one of his executors, where he should be buried; and on being answered, "Doubtless in Westminster Abbey,"

[1] Servant to the Right Hon. William Windham.—BOSWELL.

seemed to feel a satisfaction very natural to a poet; and indeed, in my opinion, very natural to every man of any imagination, who has no family sepulchre in which he can be laid with his fathers. Accordingly, upon Monday, December 20, his remains were deposited in that noble and renowned edifice; and over his grave was placed a large blue flag-stone, with this inscription:—

SAMUEL JOHNSON LL.D
Obiit XIII die Decembris
Anno Domini
MDCCLXXXIV.
Ætatis suæ LXXV.

JOHNSON'S TOMB, WESTMINSTER ABBEY

His funeral was attended by a respectable number of his friends, particularly some of the members of the Literary Club as were then in town; and was also honoured with the presence of several of the Reverend Chapter of Westminster.   Mr. Burke, Sir Joseph Banks, Mr. Windham, Mr. Langton, Sir Charles Bunbury, and Mr. Colman, bore his pall.   His schoolfellow, Dr. Taylor, performed the mournful office of reading the burial-service.

I trust I shall not be accused of affectation when I declare, that I find myself unable to express all that I felt upon the loss of such a "guide, philosopher, and friend."[1]   I shall,

---

[1] On the subject of Johnson I may adopt the words of Sir John Harrington, concerning his venerable tutor and diocesan, Dr. John Still, Bishop of Bath and Wells:—"Who hath given me some helps, more hopes, all encouragements in my best studies; to whom I never came but I grew more religious; from whom I never went, but I parted better instructed.   Of him, therefore, my acquaintance, my friend, my instructor, if I speak much it were not to be marvelled; if I speak frankly, it is not to be blamed; and though I speak partially, it were to be pardoned." *Nugæ Antiquæ*, vol. i. p. 136.   There is one circumstance in Sir John's character of Bishop Still, which is peculiarly applicable to Johnson:— "He became so famous a disputer that the learnedest were even afraid to dispute with him; and he finding his own strength, could not stick to warn them in their arguments to take heed to their answers, like a perfect fencer that will tell aforehand in which button he will give the venew, or like a cunning chess-player that will appoint aforehand with which pawn and in what place he will give the mate."—BOSWELL.

therefore, not say one word of my own, but adopt those of an eminent friend,[1] which he uttered with an abrupt felicity superior to all studied compositions:—"He has made a chasm, which not only nothing can fill up, but which nothing has a tendency to fill up. Johnson is dead. Let us go to the next best—there is nobody; no man can be said to put you in mind of Johnson."

As Johnson had abundant homage paid to him during his life,[2] so no writer in this nation ever had such an accumu-

[1] The late Right Hon. William Gerard Hamilton, who had been intimately acquainted with Dr. Johnson near thirty years.   He died in London, July 16, 1796, in his 69th or 70th year.—MALONE.

[2] Beside the Dedications to him by Dr. Goldsmith, the Rev. Dr. Franklin, and the Rev. Mr. Wilson, which I have mentioned according to their dates, there was one by a lady, of a versification of "Aningait and Ajut," and one by the ingenious Mr. Walker, of his "Rhetorical Grammar." I have introduced into this work several compliments paid to him in the writings of his contemporaries; but the number of them is so great, that we may fairly say that there was almost a general tribute.

Let me not be forgetful of the honour done to him by Colonel Myddleton, of Gwaynynog, near Denbigh; who, on the banks of a rivulet in his park, where Johnson delighted to stand and repeat verses, erected an urn with the following inscription:—
"This spot was often dignified by the presence of
SAMUEL JOHNSON, LL.D.
Whose moral writings, exactly conformable to the precepts of Christianity
Gave ardour to Virtue and confidence to Truth."

As no inconsiderable circumstance of his fame, we must reckon the extraordinary zeal of the artists to extend and perpetuate his image. I can enumerate a bust by Mr. Nollekens, and the many casts which are made from it; several pictures by Sir Joshua Reynolds, from one of which, in the possession of the Duke of Dorset, Mr. Humphry executed a beautiful miniature in enamel: one by Mrs. Frances Reynolds, Sir Joshua's sister; one by Mr. Zoffanij; and one by Mr. Opie; and the following engravings of his portrait: 1. One by Cooke, from Sir Joshua, for the Proprietors' edition of his folio Dictionary.—2. One from ditto, by ditto, for their quarto edition.—3. One from Opie, by Heath, for Harrison's edition of his Dictionary.—4. One from Nollekens' bust of him, by Bartolozzi, for Fielding's quarto edition of his Dictionary.— 5. One small, from Harding, by Trotter, for his "Beauties."—6. One small, from Sir Joshua, by Trotter, for his "Lives of the Poets."—7. One small, from Sir Joshua, by Hall, for "The Rambler."—8. One small, from an original drawing, in the possession of Mr. John Simco, etched by Trotter, for another edition of his "Lives of the Poets."—9. One small, no painter's name, etched by Taylor, for his Johnsoniana.—10. One folio whole-length, with his oak-stick, as described in Boswell's "Tour," drawn and etched by Trotter.—11. One large mezzotinto, from Sir Joshua, by Doughty.—12. One large Roman head, from Sir Joshua, by Marchi.—13. One octavo, holding a book to his eye, from Sir Joshua, by Hall, for his works.—14. One small, from a drawing from the life, and engraved by Trotter, for his Life, published by Kearsley.—15. One large, from Opie, by Mr. Townley (brother of Mr. Townley, of the Commons), an ingenious artist, who resided some time at Berlin, and has the honour of being engraver to his Majesty the King of Prussia.   This is one of the finest mezzotintos that ever was executed; and what renders

lation of literary honours after his death. A sermon upon
that event was preached in St. Mary's Church, Oxford,
before the University, by the Rev. Mr. Agutter, of Magdalen
College.[1] The Lives, the Memoirs, the Essays, both in
prose and verse, which have been published concerning him,
would make many volumes. The numerous attacks too
upon him, I consider as part of his consequence, upon the
principle which he himself so well knew and asserted. Many
who trembled at his presence, were forward in assault,
when they no longer apprehended danger. When one of
his little pragmatical foes was invidiously snarling at his
fame, at Sir Joshua Reynolds's table, the Rev. Dr. Parr
exclaimed, with his usual bold animation, "Ay, now that
the old lion is dead, every ass thinks he may kick at him."

A monument for him, in Westminster Abbey, was
resolved upon soon after his death, and was supported by
a most respectable contribution; but the Dean and Chapter
of St. Paul's having come to a resolution of admitting
monuments there, upon a liberal and magnificent plan,
that cathedral was afterwards fixed on, as the place in
which a cenotaph should be erected to his memory; and
in the cathedral of his native city of Lichfield, a smaller
one is to be erected.[2] To compose his epitaph could not

it of extraordinary value, the plate was destroyed after four or five impressions only were taken off. One of them is in the possession of Sir
William Scott. Mr. Townley has lately been prevailed with to execute
and publish another of the same, that it may be more generally circulated
among the admirers of Dr. Johnson.—16. One large, from Sir Joshua's
first picture of him, by Heath, for this work, in quarto.—17. One octavo,
by Baker, for the octavo edition.—18. And one for "Lavater's Essays
on Physiognomy," in which Johnson's countenance is analyzed upon the
principles of that fanciful writer.—There are also several seals with his
head cut on them, particularly a very fine one by that eminent artist,
Edward Burch, Esq. R.A., in the possession of the younger Dr. Charles
Burney.

Let me add, as a proof of the popularity of his character, that there
are copper pieces struck at Birmingham, with his head impressed on
them, which pass current as halfpence there, and in the neighbouring
parts of the country.—BOSWELL.

[1] It is not yet published.—In a letter to me, Mr. Agutter says, "My
sermon before the University was more engaged with Dr. Johnson's
moral than his *intellectual* character. It particularly examined his fear
of death, and suggested several reasons for the apprehensions of the
good, and the indifference of the infidel in their last hours; this was
illustrated by contrasting the death of Dr. Johnson and Mr. Hume; the
text was Job. xxi. 22—26."—BOSWELL.

[2] This monument has been since erected. It consists of a medallion,
with a tablet beneath, on which is this inscription:
"The friends of SAMUEL JOHNSON, LL.D.
A native of Lichfield,
Erected this monument,
As a tribute of respect

but excite the warmest competition of genius.[1] If *laudari a laudato viro* be praise, which is highly estimable, I should not forgive myself were I to omit the following sepulchral verses on the author of "The English Dictionary," written by the right Hon. Henry Flood:[2]

> To the memory of a man of extensive learning,
> A distinguished moral writer, and a sincere Christian.
> He died Dec. 13, 1784, aged 75."—Malone.

[1] The Rev. Dr. Parr, on being requested to undertake it, thus expressed himself in a letter to William Seward, Esq.

"I leave this mighty task to some hardier and some abler writer. The variety and splendour of Johnson's attainments, the peculiarities of his character, his private virtues, and his literary publications, fill me with confusion and dismay, when I reflect upon the confined and difficult species of composition, in which alone they can be expressed, with propriety, upon his monument."

But I understand that this great scholar, and warm admirer of Johnson, has yielded to repeated solicitations, and executed the very difficult undertaking.—Boswell.

Dr. Johnson's monument, consisting of a Colossal Figure leaning against a column (but not very strongly resembling him), has since the death of our author been placed in St. Paul's Cathedral, having been first opened to public view, Feb. 23, 1796. The Epitaph was written by the Rev. Dr. Parr, and is as follows:—

$$A \quad \overset{P}{X} \quad \Omega$$

SAMVELI · IOHNSON
GRAMMATICO · ET · CRITICO
SCRIPTORVM · ANGLICORVM · LITTERATE · PERITO
POETAE · EVMINIBVS · SENTENTIARVM
ET · PONDERIBVS · VERBORVM · ADMIRABILI
MAGISTRO · VIRTVTIS · GRAVISSIMO
HOMINI · OPTIMO · ET · SINGVLARIS · EXEMPLI
QVI · VIXIT · ANN · Lxxv · MENS · iI. · DIEB · xiiiI
DECESSIT · IDIB · DECEMBR · ANN · CHRIST · cIɔ · Iɔcc · LXXXIIII
SEPVLT · IN · AED · SANCT · PETR · WESTMONASTERIENS.
xiiI · KAL . IANVAR · ANN · CHRIST · cIɔ · Iɔcc · LXXXV
AMICI · ET · SODALES · LITTERARII
PECVNIA · CONLATA
H · M · FACIVND · CVRAVER.

On a scroll in his hand are the following words:
ΕΝΜΑΚΑΡΕΣΣΙΠΟΝΩΝΑΝΤΞΑΙΟΣΙΕΗΑΜΟΙΒΗ

On one side of the monument—Faciebat Johannes Bacon Scvlptor, Ann. Christ. m.dcc.lxxxxv.

The Subscription for this monument, which cost eleven hundred guineas, was begun by the Literary Club, and completed by the aid of Dr. Johnson's other friends and admirers.—Malone.

[2] To prevent any misconception on this subject, Mr. Malone, by whom these lines were obligingly communicated, requests me to add the following remark:—

"In justice to the late Mr. Flood, now himself wanting, and highly meriting, an epitaph from his country, to which his transcendent talents did the highest honour, as well as the most important service; it should be observed, that these lines were by no means intended as a regular monumental inscription for Dr. Johnson. Had he undertaken to write

"No need of Latin or of Greek to grace
    Our Johnson's memory, or inscribe his grave;
His native language claims this mournful space,
    To pay the immortality he gave."

The character of Samuel Johnson has, I trust, been so developed in the course of this work, that they who have honoured it with a perusal, may be considered as well acquainted with him. As, however, it may be expected that I should collect into one view the capital and distinguishing features of this extraordinary man, I shall endeavour to acquit myself of that part of my biographical undertaking,[1] however difficult it may be to do that which many of my readers will do better for themselves.

His figure was large and well formed, and his countenance of the cast of an ancient statue; yet his appearance was rendered strange and somewhat uncouth by convulsive cramps, by the scars of that distemper which it was once imagined the royal touch could cure, and by a slovenly mode of dress. He had the use only of one eye; yet so much does mind govern and even supply the deficiency of organs, that his visual perceptions, as far as they extended, were uncommonly quick and accurate. So morbid was his temperament that he never knew the natural joy of a free and vigorous use of his limbs; when he walked, it was like the struggling gait of one in fetters: when he rode, he had no command or direction of his horse, but was carried as if in a balloon. That with his constitution and habits of life he should have lived seventy-five years, is a proof that an inherent *vivida vis* is a powerful preservative of the human frame.

Man is, in general, made up of contradictory qualities; and these will ever show themselves in strange succession

an appropriate and discriminative epitaph for that excellent and extraordinary man, those who knew Mr. Flood's vigour of mind, will have no doubt that he would have produced one worthy of his illustrious subject. But the fact was merely this: In Dec. 1789, after a large subscription had been made for Dr. Johnson's monument, to which Mr. Flood liberally contributed, Mr. Malone happened to call on him at his house, in Berners-street, and the conversation turning on the proposed monument, Mr. Malone maintained that the epitaph, by whomsoever it should be written, ought to be in Latin. Mr. Flood thought differently. The next morning, in the postscript to a note on another subject, he mentioned that he continued of the same opinion as on the preceding day, and subjoined the lines at the head of this page.—BOSWELL.

[1] As I do not see any reason to give a different character of my illustrious friend now, from what I formerly gave, the greatest part of the sketch of him in my "Journal of a Tour to the Hebrides" is here adopted.—BOSWELL.

where a consistency, in appearance at least, if not reality, has not been attained by long habits of philosophical discipline. In proportion to the native vigour of the mind, the contradictory qualities will be the more prominent, and more difficult to be adjusted; and, therefore, we are not to wonder that Johnson exhibited an eminent example of this remark which I have made upon human nature. At different times he seemed a different man, in some respects: not, however, in any great or essential article, upon which he had fully employed his mind, and settled certain principles of duty, but only in his manners, and in the display of argument and fancy in his talk. He was prone to superstition, but not to credulity. Though his imagination might incline him to a belief of the marvellous and the mysterious, his vigorous reason examined the evidence with jealousy. He was a sincere and zealous Christian, of high Church of England and monarchical principles, which he would not tamely suffer to be questioned; and had, perhaps, at an early period, narrowed his mind somewhat too much, both as to religion and politics. His being impressed with the danger of extreme latitude in either, though he was of a very independent spirit, occasioned his appearing somewhat unfavourable to the prevalence of that noble freedom of sentiment which is the best possession of man. Nor can it be denied that he had many prejudices, which, however, frequently suggested many of his pointed sayings, that rather show a playfulness of fancy than any settled malignity. He was steady and inflexible in maintaining the obligations of religion and morality; both from a regard for the order of society, and from a veneration for the Great Source of all order; correct, nay, stern in his taste; hard to please, and easily offended; impetuous and irritable in his temper, but of a most humane and benevolent heart,[1] which showed itself not only in a most liberal charity, as far as his circumstances would allow, but in a thousand instances of active benevolence. He was afflicted with a bodily disease, which made him often restless and fretful; and with a constitutional melancholy, the clouds of which darkened the brightness of his fancy, and gave a gloomy cast to his whole course of thinking; we, therefore, ought

---

[1] In the *Olla Podrida*, a collection of Essays published at Oxford, there is an admirable paper upon the character of Johnson, written by the Rev. Dr. Horne, the last excellent Bishop of Norwich. The following passage is eminently happy:—"To reject wisdom, because the person of him who communicates it is uncouth, and his manners are inelegant;—what is it, but to throw away a pine-apple, and assign for a reason the roughness of its coat?"—BOSWELL.

not to wonder at his sallies of impatience and passion at any time, especially when provoked by obtrusive ignorance, or presuming petulance; and allowance must be made for his uttering hasty and satirical sallies even against his best friends. And, surely, when it is considered that "amidst sickness and sorrow" he exerted his faculties in so many works for the benefit of mankind, and particularly that he achieved the great and admirable Dictionary of our language, we must be astonished at his resolution. The solemn text, "Of him to whom much is given, much will be required," seems to have been ever present to his mind, in a rigorous sense, and to have made him dissatisfied with his labours and acts of goodness, however comparatively great; so that the unavoidable consciousness of his superiority was, in that respect, a cause of disquiet. He suffered so much from this, and from the gloom which perpetually haunted him, and made solitude frightful, that it may be said of him, "If in this life only he had hope, he was of all men most miserable." He loved praise, when it was brought to him; but was too proud to seek for it. He was somewhat susceptible of flattery. As he was general and unconfined in his studies, he cannot be considered as master of any one particular science; but he had accumulated a vast and various collection of learning and knowledge, which was so arranged in his mind as to be ever in readiness to be brought forth. But his superiority over other learned men consisted chiefly in what may be called the art of thinking, the art of using his mind—a certain continual power of seizing the useful substance of all that he knew, and exhibiting it in a clear and forcible manner; so that knowledge, which we often see to be no better than lumber in men of dull understanding, was in him true, evident, and actual wisdom. His moral precepts are practical; for they are drawn from an intimate acquaintance with human nature. His maxims carry conviction; for they are founded on the basis of common sense, and a very attentive and minute survey of real life. His mind was so full of imagery, that he might have been perpetually a poet; yet it is remarkable, that however rich his prose is in this respect, his poetical pieces, in general, have not much of that splendour, but are rather distinguished by strong sentiment, and acute observation, conveyed in harmonious and energetic verse, particularly in heroic couplets. Though usually grave, and even awful in his deportment, he possessed uncommon and peculiar powers of wit and humour; he frequently indulged himself in colloquial pleasantry; and the heartiest merriment was often enjoyed in his company; with this great advantage,

that it was entirely free from any poisonous tincture of
vice or impiety—it was salutary to those who shared in it.
He had accustomed himself to such accuracy in his common
conversation,[1] that he at all times expressed his thoughts
with great force, and an elegant choice of language, the
effect of which was aided by his having a loud voice, and
a slow deliberate utterance. In him were united a most
logical head with a most fertile imagination, which gave
him an extraordinary advantage in arguing; for he could
reason close or wide, as he saw best for the moment.
Exulting in his intellectual strength and dexterity, he could,
when he pleased, be the greatest sophist that ever contended
in the lists of declamation; and, from a spirit of contradiction and a delight in showing his powers, he would often

---

[1] Though a perfect resemblance of Johnson is not to be found in any
age, parts of his character are admirably expressed by Clarendon, in
drawing that of Lord Falkland, whom the noble and masterly historian
describes at his seat near Oxford:—"Such an immenseness of wit, such
a solidity of judgment, so infinite a fancy bound in by a most logical
ratiocination. His acquaintance was cultivated by the most polite
and accurate men, so that his house was an university in less volume,
whither they came, not so much for repose as study, and to examine
and refine those grosser propositions, which laziness and consent made
current in conversation."
  Bayle's account of *Menage* may also be quoted as exceedingly applicable to the great subject of this work:—"His illustrious friends erected
a very glorious monument to him in the collection entitled *Menagiana*.
Those who judge of things aright will confess that this collection is
very proper to show the extent of genius and learning which was the
character of Menage. And I may be bold to say that *the excellent works
he published will not distinguish him from other learned men so advantage-
ously as this*. To publish books of great learning, to make Greek and
Latin verses exceedingly well turned, is not a common talent, I own;
neither is it extremely rare. It is incomparably more difficult to find
men who can furnish discourse about an infinite number of things, and
who can diversify them a hundred ways. How many authors are there
who are admired for their works, on account of the vast learning that
is displayed in them, who are not able to sustain a conversation. Those
who know Menage only by his books might think he resembled those
learned men; but if you show the *Menagiana*, you distinguish him from
them, and make him known by a talent which is given to a very few
learned men. There it appears that he was a man who spoke off-hand
a thousand good things. His memory extended to what was ancient and
modern; to the court and to the city; to the dead and to the living languages; to things serious and things jocose; in a word, to a thousand sorts
of subjects. That which appeared a trifle to some readers of the *Menagiana*, who did not consider circumstances, caused admiration in other
readers, who minded the difference between what a man speaks without
preparation, and that which he prepares for the press; and, therefore,
we cannot sufficiently commend the care which his illustrious friends
took to erect a monument so capable of giving him immortal glory.
They were not obliged to rectify what they had heard him say; for,
in so doing, they had not been faithful historians of his conversation."—
BOSWELL.

maintain the wrong side with equal warmth and ingenuity; so that when there was an audience, his real opinions could seldom be gathered from his talk; though when he was in company with a single friend, he would discuss a subject with genuine fairness; but he was too conscientious to make error permanent and pernicious, by deliberately writing it; and in all his numerous works, he earnestly inculcated what appeared to him to be the truth; his piety being constant, and the ruling principle of all his conduct.

Such was Samuel Johnson, a man whose talents, acquirements, and virtues, were so extraordinary, that the more his character is considered, the more he will be regarded by the present age, and by posterity, with admiration and reverence.

CHRONOLOGICAL LIST OF DR. JOHNSON'S WORKS

The works to which an *asterisk* (*) is affixed are those of which Dr. Johnson acknowledged the authorship to his friends, while those marked by a *dagger* (†) are ascertained to be his by internal evidence. In this list, drawn up by the biographer, the poetical works are not included. These consist of a Latin translation of Pope's "Messiah," "London," and "The Vanity of Human Wishes," imitated from Juvenal; a Prologue on the Opening of Drury-lane Theatre by Mr. Garrick; and "Irene," a Tragedy, besides some minor pieces.

1735. Abridgment and Translation of Lobo's Voyage to Abyssinia.*
1738. Part of a translation of Father Paul Sarpi's History of the Council of Trent.*
    [N. B. As this work, after some sheets were printed, suddenly stopped, I know not whether any part of it is now to be found.]

FOR THE GENTLEMAN'S MAGAZINE.

Preface.†
Life of Father Paul.*
1739. A complete Vindication of the Licenser of the Stage from the malicious and scandalous aspersions of Mr. Brooke, author of Gustavus Vasa.*
    Marmor Norfolciense: or, an Essay on an ancient prophetical inscription in monkish rhyme, lately discovered near Lynne in Norfolk: by Probus Britannicus.*

FOR THE GENTLEMAN'S MAGAZINE.

Life of Boerhaave.
Address to the Reader.†
Appeal to the Public in behalf of the Editor.†
Considerations on the case of Dr. Trapp's Sermons; a plausible attempt to prove that an Author's work may be abridged without injuring his property.*

1740.   FOR THE GENTLEMAN'S MAGAZINE.

Preface.†
Life of Admiral Drake.*
Life of Admiral Blake.*
Life of Philip Barretier.*
Essay on Epitaphs.*

1741.   FOR THE GENTLEMAN'S MAGAZINE.

Preface.
A free translation of the Jests of Hicrocles, with an intro-
    duction.†
Debate on the Humble Petition and Advice of the Rump
    Parliament to Cromwell in 1657, to assume the Title of
    King: abridged, methodized, and digested.†
Translation of Abbé Guyon's Dissertation on the Amazons.†
Translation of Fontenelle's Panegyric on Dr. Morin.†

1742.   FOR THE GENTLEMAN'S MAGAZINE.

Preface.†
Essay on the Account of the Conduct of the Duchess of
    Marlborough.*
An Account of the Life of Peter Burman.*
The Life of Sydenham, afterwards prefixed to Dr. Swan's
    Edition of his Works.*
Proposals for printing Bibliotheca Harleiana, or a Catalogue
    of the Library of the Earl of Oxford, afterwards prefixed
    to the first volume of that Catalogue, in which the Latin
    Accounts of the Books were written by him.*
Abridgment, entitled Foreign History.†
Essay on the Description of China, from the French of Du
    Halde.†
1743. Dedication to Dr. Mead of Dr. James's Medicinal Dictionary.†

             FOR THE GENTLEMAN'S MAGAZINE.

Preface.*
Parliamentary Debates under the name of Debates in the
    Senate of Lilliput, from Nov. 19, 1740, to Feb. 23, 1742–3,
    inclusive.*
Considerations on the Dispute between Crousaz and Warburton
    on Pope's Essay on Man.†
A Letter, announcing that the Life of Mr. Savage was speedily
    to be published by a person who was favoured with his
    confidence.†
Advertisement   for   Osborne   concerning   the   Harleian
    Catalogue.†
1744. Life of Richard Savage.*
Preface to the Harleian Miscellany.*

FOR THE GENTLEMAN'S MAGAZINE.

Preface.†
1745. Miscellaneous observations on the Tragedy of Macbeth, with remarks on Sir T. H.'s (Sir Thomas Hanmer's) Edition of Shakespeare, and proposals for a new Edition of that Poet.*
1747. Plan for a Dictionary of the English Language, addressed to Philip Dormer, Earl of Chesterfield.*

FOR THE GENTLEMAN'S MAGAZINE.

1748. Life of Roscommon.*
Foreign History, November.†

FOR MR. DODSLEY'S PRECEPTOR.

Preface.†
Vision of Theodore the Hermit.*
1750. "The Rambler," the first Paper of which was published 20th of March this year, and the last 17th of March, 1752, the day on which Mrs. Johnson died.*[1]
Letter in "The General Advertiser" to excite the attention of the Public to the performance of "Comus," which was next day to be acted at Drury-lane Playhouse for the benefit of Milton's Grand-daughter.*
Preface and Postscript to Lauder's Pamphlet, entitled, "An Essay on Milton's Use and Imitation of the Moderns in his Paradise Lost."*
1751. Life of Cheynel, in the Miscellany called "The Student."*
Letter for Lauder, addressed to the Rev. Dr. John Douglas, acknowledging his Fraud concerning Milton, in terms of suitable Contrition.*
Dedication to the Earl of Middlesex, of Mrs. Charlotte Lennox's "Female Quixote."†
1753. Dedication to John, Earl of Orrery, of Shakespeare Illustrated, by Mrs. Charlotte Lennox.*
During this and the following year he wrote and gave to his much-loved friend Dr. Bathurst, the Papers in "The Adventurer," signed T.*
1754. Life of Edward Cave in "The Gentleman's Magazine."*
1755. A Dictionary, with a Grammar and History of the English Language.*
An Account of an Attempt to ascertain the Longitude at Sea, by an exact Theory of the Variations of the Magnetical Needle, with a Table of the Variations at the most remarkable Cities in Europe, from the year 1660 to 1860.* This he wrote for Mr. Zachariah Williams, an ingenious ancient

[1] This is a mistake. The last number of "The Rambler" appeared on the *fourteenth* of March, three days before Mrs. Johnson died.— MALONE.

Welsh Gentleman, father of Mrs. Ann Williams, whom he for many years kindly lodged in his house. It was published with a Translation into Italian by Signor Baretti. In a Copy of it, which he presented to the Bodleian Library at Oxford, is pasted a character of the late Mr. Zachariah Williams, plainly written by Johnson.†

1756. An Abridgment of his Dictionary.*

Several Essays in "The Universal Visitor," which there is some difficulty in ascertaining. All that are marked with two asterisks have been ascribed to him, although I am confident, from internal evidence, that we should except from these "The Life of Chaucer," "Reflections on the State of Portugal," and "An Essay on Architecture:" and from the same evidence I am confident that he wrote "Further Thoughts on Agriculture," and "A Dissertation on the State of Literature and Authors." The Dissertation on the Epitaphs written by Pope he afterwards acknowledged, and added to his "Idler."

Life of Sir T. Browne, prefixed to a new edition of his Christian Morals.*

IN THE LITERARY MAGAZINE, OR UNIVERSAL REVIEW,

Which began in January, 1756, his *Original Essays* are,

The Preliminary Address.†
An Introduction to the Political State of Great Britain.†
Remarks on the Militia Bill.†
Observations on his Britannic Majesty's Treaties with the Empress of Russia and the Landgrave of Hesse Cassel.†
Observations on the Present State of Affairs.†
Memoirs of Frederick III. King of Prussia.†
In the same Magazine his Reviews are of the following books:—"Birch's History of the Royal Society."— "Browne's Christian Morals."—"Warton's Essay on the Writings and Genius of Pope, vol. i."—"Hampton's Translation of Polybius."—"Sir Isaac Newton's Arguments in proof of a Deity."—"Borlase's History of the Isles of Scilly." — "Home's Experiments on Bleaching." — "Browne's History of Jamaica."—"Hales on Distilling Sea Waters, Ventilators in Ships, and curing an ill Taste in Milk."—"Lucas's Essay on Waters."—"Keith's Catalogue of the Scottish Bishops."—"Philosophical Transactions, vol. xlix."—"Miscellanies, by Elizabeth Harrison." —"Evans's Map, and Account of the Middle Colonies in America."—"The Cadet, a Military Treatise."—"The Conduct of the Ministry relating to the present War impartially examined."†

Mrs. Lennox's "Translation of Sully's Memoirs."—"Letter on the Case of Admiral Byng."—"Appeal to the People concerning Admiral Byng."—"Hanway's Eight Days' Journey, and Essay on Tea."—"Some further Particulars in Relation to the Case of Admiral Byng, by a gentleman of Oxford."*

Mr. Jonas Hanway having written an angry Answer to the Review of his Essay on Tea, Johnson, in the same Collection, made a reply to it.* This is the only instance, it is believed, when he condescended to take notice of anything that had been written against him; and here his chief intention seems to have been to make sport.

Dedication to the Earl of Rochford of, and Preface to Mr. Payne's Introduction to the Game of Draughts.*

Introduction to "The London Chronicle," an evening paper which still subsists with deserved credit.*

1757. Speech on the subject of an Address to the Throne after the Expedition to Rochefort, delivered by one of his friends in some public meeting. It is printed in "The Gentleman's Magazine" for October, 1785.†

The first two paragraphs of the Preface to Sir William Chambers's Designs of Chinese Buildings, &c.*

1758. "The Idler," which began April 5, in this year, and was continued till April 5, 1760.*

An Essay on the Bravery of the English Common Soldiers was added to it when published in volumes.*

1759. Rasselas, Prince of Abyssinia, a Tale.*

Advertisement for the Proprietors of "The Idler" against certain persons who pirated those Papers as they came out singly, in a Newspaper called "The Universal Chronicle, or Weekly Gazette."†

For Mrs. Charlotte Lennox's English Version of Brumoy,— "A Dissertation on the Greek Comedy," and the General Conclusion of the Book.†

Introduction to "The World Displayed," a collection of Voyages and Travels.*

Three letters in "The Gazetteer," concerning the best plan for Blackfriars Bridge.*

1760. Address of the Painters to George III. on his Accession to the Throne.†

Dedication of Baretti's Italian and English Dictionary to the Marq. of Abreu, then Envoy-Extraordinary from Spain at the Court of Great Britain.†

Review in "The Gentleman's Magazine," of M. Tytler's acute and able Vindication of Mary Queen of Scots.*

Introduction to the proceedings of the Committee for Clothing the French Prisoners.*

1761. Preface to "Rolt's Dictionary of Trade and Commerce."*

Corrections and Improvements for Mr. Gwyn, the Architect's Pamphlet, entitled, "Thoughts on the Coronation of George III."*

1762. Dedication to the King, of the Rev. Dr. Kennedy's "Complete System of Astronomical Chronology, unfolding the Scriptures," 4to. edition.*

Preface to the Catalogue of the Artists' Exhibition.†

1763. Character of Collins in "The Poetical Calendar," published by Fawkes and Woty.*

Dedication to the Earl of Shaftesbury of the edition of Roger Ascham's English Works, published by the Rev. Mr. Bennet.*

The Life of Ascham, also prefixed to that edition.*

Review of "Telemachus," a Masque, by the Rev. George Graham, of Eton College, in "The Critical Review."*

Dedication to the Queen, of Mr. "Hoole's Translation of Tasso."*

Account of the Detection of the Imposture of the Cock-lane Ghost, published in the Newspapers and "Gentleman's Magazine."*

1764. Part of a Review of Grainger's "Sugar Cane, a Poem," in "The London Chronicle."*

Review of Goldsmith's "Traveller, a Poem," in "The Critical Review."*

1765. The Plays of William Shakespeare, in eight volumes, 8vo., with Notes.*

1766. "The Fountains, a Fairy Tale," in Mrs. Williams's Miscellanies.*

1767. Dedication to the King, of Mr. Adams's "Treatise on the Globes."*

1769. Character of the Rev. Mr. Zach. Mudge, in "The London Chronicle."*

1770. The False Alarm.*

1771. Thoughts on the late Transactions respecting Falkland's Islands.*

1772. Defence of a Schoolmaster; dictated to me for the House of Lords.*

Argument in support of the Law of *Vicious Intromission*; dictated to me for the Court of Session in Scotland.*

1773. Preface to Macbean's "Dictionary of Ancient Geography."

Argument in Favour of the Rights of Lay Patrons; dictated to me for the General Assembly of the Church of Scotland.*

1774. The Patriot.*

1775. A Journey to the Western Islands of Scotland.*

Proposals for publishing the Works of Mrs. Charlotte Lennox, in three volumes quarto.*

Preface to Baretti's Easy Lessons in Italian and English.†

Taxation no Tyranny; an answer to the Resolutions and Address of the American Congress.*

Argument on the Case of Dr. Memis; dictated to me for the Court of Session in Scotland.*

Argument to prove that the Corporation of Stirling was corrupt; dictated to me for the House of Lords.*

1776. Argument in Support of the Right of immediate and personal Reprehension from the Pulpit; dictated to me.*

Proposals for publishing an Analysis of the Scotch Celtic Language, by the Reverend William Shaw.*

1777. Dedication to the King of the Posthumous Works of Dr. Pearce, Bishop of Rochester.*

Additions to the Life and Character of that Prelate; prefixed to those Works.*

Various Papers and Letters in Favour of the Reverend Dr. Dodd.

1780. Advertisement for his friend Mr. Thrale to the Worthy Electors of the Borough of Southwark.*

The first Paragraph of Mr. Thomas Davies's Life of Garrick.*

1781. Prefaces, Biographical and Critical, to the Works of the most eminent English Poets; afterwards published with the Title of the Lives of the English Poets.*

Argument on the Importance of the Registration of Deeds; dictated to me for an Election Committee of the House of Commons.*

On the Distinction between Tory and Whig; dictated to me.*

On Vicarious Punishments, and the great Propitiation for the Sins of the World, by Jesus Christ; dictated to me.*

Argument in favour of Joseph Knight, an African Negro, who claimed his Liberty in the Court of Session in Scotland, and obtained it; dictated to me.*

Defence of Mr. Robertson, Printer of "The Caledonian Mercury," against the Society of Procurators in Edinburgh, for having inserted in his paper a ludicrous Paragraph against them; demonstrating that it was not an injurious Libel; dictated to me.*

1782. The greatest part, if not the whole, of a Reply, by the Reverend Mr. Shaw, to a person at Edinburgh, of the name of Clarke, refuting his arguments for the authenticity of the Poems published by Mr. James Macpherson as Translations from Ossian.†

1784. List of the Authors of the Universal History, deposited in the British Museum, and printed in "The Gentleman's Magazine" for December, this year.*

VARIOUS YEARS.

Letters to Mrs. Thrale.*

Prayers and Meditations, which he delivered to the Rev. Mr. Strahan, enjoining him to publish them.*

Sermons, left for publication by John Taylor, LL.D., Prebendary of Westminster, and given to the World by the Rev. Samuel Hayes, A.M.†[1]

---

[1] To this List of the Writings of Dr. Johnson, Mr. Alexander Chalmers, with considerable probability, suggests to me that we may add the following:—

IN THE GENTLEMAN'S MAGAZINE.

1747. Lauder's Proposals for printing "The Adamus Exul" of Grotius, vol xx. p. 404.

1750. Address to the Public, concerning Miss Williams's Miscellanies, vol. xx. p. 428.

Such was the number and variety of the prose works of this extraordinary man, which I have been able to discover, and am at liberty to mention; but we ought to keep in mind, that there must undoubtedly have been many more which are yet concealed; and we may add to the account the numerous Letters which he wrote, of which a considerable part are yet unpublished. It is hoped that those persons in whose possession they are will favour the world with them.

JAMES BOSWELL.

1753. Preface.
   Notice of Mr. Edward Cave's death, inserted in the last page of the Index.

IN THE LITERARY MAGAZINE.

1756. "Observations on the foregoing Letter;" i.e., A Letter on the American Colonies, vol. i. p. 66.—MALONE.

30

GOOD BOOKS ARE